THE PRINCIPLES OF DEDUCTIVE LOGIC

THE PRINCIPLES
OF DEDUCTIVE
LOGIC

John T. Kearns

STATE UNIVERSITY OF NEW YORK PRESS

Published by
State University of New York Press, Albany

For information, address State University of New York
Press, State University Plaza, Albany, N.Y., 12246

Library of Congress Cataloging in Publication Data

Kearns, John T., 1936–
　　The Principles of deductive logic.

　　Includes index.
　　1. Logic. 2. Language and logic.　I. Title.
BC71.K33 1987　　　　162　　　　　86-23035
ISBN 0-88706-478-7
ISBN 0-88706-479-5 (pbk.)

10　9　8　7　6　5　4　3　2　1

Contents

Preface

This book is intended for a course that serves general educational purposes. Such a course is of value to every undergraduate. The book also serves as an introduction for students who will specialize in logic or philosophy.

The present book covers the same material as other texts in deductive logic. It also includes material not commonly found in other texts. Considerable attention is given to incompatibility and to the details involved in applying formal logic to ordinary English. The concern with the application of logic to ordinary language is perhaps the most distinctive feature of this book. It gives this text a utility for general education.

The course which uses this text is intended to help students use language more carefully, more precisely, and more effectively, in speaking and writing, and in understanding what they read and hear. I feel that standard logic courses sometimes teach skills which are useful only for passing tests in logic courses. I would like this book to advance a new understanding of logic and its relevance to our ordinary practice. A course in deductive logic is a suitable component of any undergraduate education.

In this book I have borrowed ideas from my former colleague William T. Parry. He has helped me understand the importance of syllogistic logic. My treatment of distribution in categorical sentences is derived from him. So are many details in my presentation of symbolic logic. In the deductive systems I employ, I have borrowed conditional subproofs from my teacher Frederic B. Fitch. I have made use of the substitution notation of Alonzo Church. I also follow Church in accepting C. S. Peirce's suggestion that we use the spelling 'premiss' for the premisses that figure in logic.

I owe a debt to the students in classes where I used earlier versions of this book. Also to the reviewers, even the nasty ones, who noted various shortcomings in the earlier versions. The present text has gained a lot from their comments and suggestions. Many colleagues have helped me understand logic and what it is good for. These include, but aren't limited to, William T. Parry, John Corcoran, and Charles Lambros.

Chapter **1**

Applied Logic: What We Hope to Accomplish

1-0 SUMMARY

At the beginning of each chapter, section 0 provides a brief summary of the material found in the chapter.

Chapter 1 describes the material to be covered in this book, and the goals that our study of logic should accomplish. It explains terminology for some fundamental concepts of logical interest. These include the concepts of syntax, semantics, analytic truth, entailment, and incompatibility.

1-1 THE NATURE OF LOGIC

Most introductory logic courses and logic texts cover pretty much the same material, but different logicians hold different views about what logic is the study of. Many such views are possible; in this section, we will look at three important and historically influential views.

The first view is that logic studies the most general features of reality. A science like physics deals with specific portions and aspects of reality (with, say, material objects, their ultimate constituents, and laws governing their interaction). But logic is concerned with absolutely everything, whether it is merely possible or actually exists. Logical laws are highly general and abstract, having little specific content—such as the version of the Law of Contradiction which claims that a thing can't both exist and not exist at the same time. In contrast with the laws of physics, the laws of logic cannot even be imagined as not holding. Some pioneers of modern logic, including Gottlob Frege and Bertrand Russell, conceived logic in this way.

The second view is that logic is a study of reasoning, or the norms which govern reasoning. On this view, logic provides criteria for distinguishing correct from incorrect reasoning. This view of logic seems to have been held (most of the time) by Aristotle, who founded logic as a subject for study.

The third view is that logic is a study of language. Certain aspects and features of language are of logical interest. It is difficult to describe these now in an enlightening way, but we will learn what they are as we learn logic. The logician tries to understand and explain these features of language. For example, one logical task is giving a linguistic char-acterization of correct reasoning. Another is finding features which mark the sentences expressing logical laws.

No matter which view a logician holds, he will carry out his studies in pretty much the same way. The different views of logic lead to different emphases in the study of logic rather than to different problems or results. In the present text, the third view has been adopted. I believe this conception of logic makes the best sense of the history of logic, and of research currently being carried out in logic.

1-2 TALKING ABOUT WORDS

Since we will be concerned with language, we must develop techniques for talking about words. In sentence (1):

(1) Red is Bill's favorite color.

the word 'red' is used normally, but in sentence (2):

(2) Red is an adjective.

it is not. Sentence (2) says something about the word, not the color. (If we didn't notice the difference between (1) and (2), we might conclude that Bill's favorite color is an adjective—which would be silly.) To distinguish these two uses, we shall (in writing) put single quotes around a word when we use it to talk about itself. We will write sentence (2) like this:

(2) 'Red' is an adjective.

This use of single quotes takes the fun out of many children's riddles, as you can see in this example:

Railroad crossing, see all the cars. Can you spell 'that' without any 'r's?

The word enclosed in single quotes has been used, but not in its normal manner. We have *mentioned* the word. We can also mention a word without using it:

The first word defined in the *American Heritage Dictionary* begins with an 'a.'

Using single quotes is only one of many techniques for indicating that a word is being mentioned.

Single words aren't the only expressions we can mention. We can talk about longer expressions too:

The expression 'tall, blue-eyed man' is a noun phrase.

The relative clause 'that came to dinner' didn't come to dinner.

We can mention sentences or groups of them. Our use of single quotes doesn't interfere with the familiar use of double quotes to enclose what someone has said. We sometimes combine both sorts of quotes as in:

Bill said, "'Red' is my favorite adjective."

*Exercise: Section 2

(Exercises marked with an asterisk have the answers given at the back of this book. Their main function is to enable you to know whether you have understood the material they deal with. It is helpful if you actually write down answers to questions. Doing this makes you commit yourself more fully to the answers you select, and should help you to remember any errors.)

For 1–3, determine which of the following are true.

1. If a word is mentioned, it is not being used.

2. An expression is enclosed in single quotes to indicate that it is being mentioned instead of being used normally.

3. A word that is mentioned will always be enclosed in single quotes.

For 4–5, rewrite the following, using single quotes.

4. To be or not to be is a line in *Hamlet*.

5. Short is longer than long.

1-3 SPEECH ACTS

A language isn't just a collection of words which stand for objects and express ideas and feelings. I find it most helpful to regard the expressions in a language as instruments that can be used to perform various tasks. When someone uses an expression to say (or write) something, that person has performed a *speech act*. The study of speech acts has recently become very important in philosophy and linguistics, largely due to the work of the philosophers J. L. Austin and John Searle.

Some expressions are used to identify, or refer to, a single individual. Proper names and other singular terms, like 'the capital of Montana' can be used to refer. Some expressions are used to identify or pick out a kind of thing. A common noun like 'dog,' or a noun phrase like 'dog with rabies' can be used in this way. Predicates such as 'jogs' or 'is a jogger' are used to represent what things are or may be; they are used to characterize things. Sentences are typically used to represent either specific things or things of a kind as characterized in a certain way. In addition, an act of using a sentence may have a certain force which indicates whether what is represented actually exists, or the speaker merely wants it to exist, or the speaker is asking whether it exists, etc. In the study of speech acts, this is called *illocutionary force*. If an act of using a sentence has illocutionary force, this is an *illocutionary act*.

Although people use expressions to perform speech acts, we often talk as if it were the expressions that performed the actions. We say that 'George Washington' refers to the first president of the United States, or that the sentence 'George Washington was a military leader' represents George Washington as being a military leader. This practice is harmless once we understand that what we say about expressions really applies to acts of using expressions. In conceiving logic as a study of language, I really have in mind that logic is concerned with properties and relations of speech acts. But we carry out the study of logic by focussing on the expressions used to perform the speech acts.

A person who uses a sentence to say something that can be evaluated in terms of truth and falsity has performed a *propositional act*. Someone who uses a sentence to ask a question has performed an illocutionary act that isn't a propositional act. But if he uses a sentence to make an assertion, his speech act is propositional. Propositional acts will be the center of attention in our study of logic. We characterize propositional acts in terms of what the speaker uses the sentence to represent—what the speaker says with the sentence. If different people use the same sentence to say the same thing, they have performed different propositional acts. But they have performed the same specific kind of propositional act. It is also possible to use one sentence on different occasions to say different things. If Megan says, "Today is Thursday" on a particular Thursday, and then uses the same sentence a week later, she has made different claims. Her two propositional acts are specifically different, because she has used the same words to talk about different days.

Although strictly speaking it is propositional acts that are true or false, we will often—even usually—speak of sentences as being true or false. A sentence used to perform a propositional act is *used propositionally*. If a sentence is used to perform a certain specific kind of propositional act, it has been given a certain propositional use. A sentence is only true or false with respect to a propositional use. But when we consider a given sentence, it is usually clear what propositional use is intended. This justifies our practice of speaking of sentences as being true or false.

Instead of talking about propositional uses, many philosophers and logicians consider *propositions*. These propositions are not expressions—they don't contain words, and can't be written or spoken. Propositions are not mental either. They are abstract objects *expressed by* sentences (when used propositionally). Propositions are true or false. Instead of saying that one sentence can have different propositional uses, these philosophers say that one sentence can be used to express different propositions. (Propositions are often claimed to be the objects of belief and knowledge.) My own view is that there are no such abstract propositions. Philosophers who describe propositions are simply describing sentences with some features omitted. But the account in this text is neutral with respect to the issue of whether there are such things as propositions. However, we will have no need to deal with propositions in discussing the logical features of sentences.

*Exercise: Section 3

Determine which of the following are true.

1. If a sentence is used propositionally, then that sentence must be true.

2. One and the same sentence might be true with respect to one propositional use and false with respect to a different propositional use.

3. A sentence cannot be both true and false with respect to the same (specific) propositional use.

4. The next sentence, sentence 5, is true.

5. The preceding sentence, sentence 4, is false.

1-4 A LANGUAGE IS A COMPLEX SYSTEM

Different speech acts are related to one another in many different ways. For example, using and accepting one sentence can commit a person to accepting another. The person who asserts that today is Sunday is committed to accepting the sentence 'Tomorrow is Monday.' If we consider expressions with respect to the speech acts they can be used to perform, we find that they form a complex and intricate system. Many of the linguistic features which go to make up the system of language belong to two important classes. These are associated with different studies of language. *Syntax* is a study which classifies expressions into various categories (such as *nouns, verbs*, etc.), and states principles according to which expressions of various categories can be combined. (For example, an adjective can modify a noun, so adjectives and nouns have a certain *syntactic* relation. Adjectives are not related to prepositions in the same way, for an adjective doesn't modify a preposition.) *Semantics* is a study of the meanings of expressions and the truth conditions of sentences. Semantic relations between expressions are based on their meanings. The words 'scarlet' and 'red' are related in such a way that whatever is scarlet is red. It is a consequence of the meanings of these two words that whatever is scarlet must be red. The relation of the word 'cow' to 'mammal' is similar to the relation of 'scarlet' to 'red'; whatever is a cow must be a mammal. This is sometimes called a relation of *inclusion*. A relation of inclusion which can be traced to the meanings of words must be distinguished from the relation between such expressions as 'asbestos' and 'cause of cancer.' It may be true that whatever is asbestos or contains asbestos is a cause of cancer (in suitable circumstances), but this relation is not a consequence of the meanings of the two expressions. The relation between 'asbestos' and 'cause of cancer' is due to the relation between objects denoted by the expressions. It is not a semantic relation.

Another important relation between expressions is illustrated by the two words 'red' and 'green.' Whatever is red (all over) isn't green; 'red' is *incompatible* with 'green.' And this incompatibility is tied to the meanings of the two expressions.

The expressions in a language are not only related to one another, but also to nonlinguistic objects. The word 'car' is related to 'automobile' and to 'vehicle.' It is also related to cars. The word 'car' *denotes* cars. (People *use* the word to denote cars.) To talk about the world we live in, we must be able to connect words to objects in the world. Many words denote objects we don't experience directly, but the words which do denote objects of experience are needed for fastening language to the world. The word 'red' is one of these. A person would not be said to understand the word 'red' unless he could recognize red objects. (A blind or color-blind person can have a partial understanding of the word, but not the full understanding possible for a person with normal vision.) The connection between the word 'car' and cars seems less close than that between 'red' and red objects. But it is much closer than that between 'electron' and electrons. Electrons cannot be directly experienced. (But we can explain how electrons are related to the objects we do experience.)

*Exercise: Section 4

Which of the following pairs of expressions are related, as a consequence of their meanings, by inclusion? Which are related by incompatibility? (Some pairs are not linked by either relation.)

1. bachelor; unmarried male human

2. bird; mammal

3. human being; object found in North America

4. cousin; uncle

5. logician; human being

1-5 LOGICALLY IMPORTANT SEMANTIC FEATURES

In logic, our chief focus is on semantic features of sentences. In this course, it will be on semantic features of sentences that can be used to perform propositional acts. We are interested in features of expressions other than sentences primarily because of their connection to features of sentences.

One important semantic feature is *analytic truth*, or *analyticity*. An *analytic* sentence is a sentence suited to be used propositionally, which represents things in a redundant fashion and which makes no commitment to the existence of nonlinguistic objects. The sentence 'Any dog is a dog' represents things in a redundant fashion. The subject denotes a dog and the predicate simply repeats the subject. The sentence itself does not indicate that dogs exist—though we know they do—so the sentence is analytically true. The sentence 'Ten dogs are dogs' also represents things in a redundant fashion. But it indicates a commitment to there being (at least) ten dogs. This sentence isn't analytic.

The sentence 'Any dog is an animal' is another analytic sentence. The subject picks out a dog. But as a matter of language—it is part of the meaning of 'dog'—one of the criteria for something's being a dog is that it be an animal. This criterion is merely spelled out by the predicate.

The above definition of 'analytic' seeks to capture the "basic idea" of analyticity. This definition does not furnish much guidance for determining difficult cases. I will provide a different, epistemic, definition of 'analytic.' ('Epistemic' is related to 'epistemology' which is a name for the study of knowledge.) The other definition is this: A sentence is analytic if it is true, and can be determined to be true simply on the basis of understanding it. This does not mean that an analytic sentence must be obviously true, or self-evident. It may be necessary to think about the matter, to engage in reasoning, to determine that an analytic sentence is true. But if a sentence is analytic, we can determine that it is true without obtaining any information other than information about the meanings of words.

Analytic truth is a *property* of some sentences. *Entailment* is a semantic *relation* between sentences that has some similarity to the relation of inclusion linking words. Sentence (1):

(1) Bill's car is scarlet.

entails sentence (2):

(2) Bill's car is red.

An epistemic definition of 'entail' goes like this: One or more sentences entail a further sentence if it can be determined simply on the basis of understanding them that it isn't possible for the first sentence(s) to be true when the further sentence isn't; it isn't possible for the first sentences to be true without the further sentence being true.

Incompatibility is another logically important semantic relation between sentences. Two or more sentences are incompatible if we can determine simply on the basis of understanding them that it isn't possible for them to be true together. Sentence (2) is incompatible with:

(3) Bill's car is green.

and also with (4):

(4) Bill's car is not red.

*Exercise: Section 5

Which of the following are true?

1. If a sentence isn't analytic, then it isn't true.

2. If one sentence entails a second sentence, and the second is true, then so is the first.

3. Three true sentences can't be incompatible with one another.

1-6 APPLIED LOGIC

In this book and the course for which it is the text, our principal efforts will be directed toward detecting those English sentences and groups of sentences that have logically important semantic features. Analytic truth, entailment, and incompatibility are three of the features we will look for. The purpose of this study is to understand our language better and to use it more effectively. Even though we are concerned with English sentences, we will make use of artificial languages. We construct and investigate artificial logical languages, then we apply them as instruments to gain an increased understanding of ordinary English. In investigating the artificial languages, we use various techniques. One of the most important is that of proofs; we prove results in the artificial languages. In applying the artificial languages as instruments, we translate ordinary sentences into the artificial languages, we determine how close the translations come to the originals, and we determine what are the logical features of the translations.

The procedure just described indicates that the present book is a text for applied logic. We are concerned to use logical techniques to gain understanding of English sentences and arguments. Applied logic can be contrasted with logical theory, which concentrates on investigating artificial languages and deductive systems. The main goal of logical theory is establishing results about the languages and systems.

It is intended that the present book, as a text in applied logic, will give students a better understanding of the meanings of various English sentences, and a greater understanding and awareness of semantic features exemplified in ordinary English. The understanding of the meanings of English sentences is the ability to grasp exactly what a person is saying when he uses a given sentence. What are its truth conditions? What is a person who accepts it committed to? This understanding is enhanced by our translating ordinary sentences into logical languages, and by our study of evaluation procedures. The understanding and awareness of semantic features is improved by learning how to evaluate sentences and arguments in artificial languages. A student who gains a better understanding of entailment should be better able to tell when some sentences entail another. He should be better able to reason correctly. But he should be able to do these things without going through the processes that we employ in this book. One goal of this book and its course is to give students a better understanding of ordinary language, so that they can use it more skillfully, more effectively, and more precisely.

There is a second goal related to the first—it is, in part, included under the first goal. This is to give a better understanding of what is involved in backing up, or justifying, a claim, and to improve the ability to do this. In the present book, the proofs constructed in investigating artificial languages will be the most important tools for improving the ability to justify. But we will also learn other techniques for justifying. Students aren't expected to remember and use the specific techniques of justification we employ. But studying this book should help in coming up with whatever justification is appropriate in a given situation.

Part of what is needed to give a justification is the ability to recognize cases of semantic features and the ability to come up with sentences entailed by a given group of sentences. In addition to possessing these abilities, a person must be able to put together various justifying elements to make a case. To provide justification a person must be able to organize. He must organize his thinking. He must organize his verbal presentation. The organizing skills that go into constructing proofs can also be used for solving problems and providing justifications in other circumstances.

1-7 PHILOSOPHY OF LOGIC

Logic is usually associated with philosophy. Logic courses are commonly offered by philosophy departments, though mathematics departments also give logic courses. The connection between logic and such other areas of philosophy as epistemology or metaphysics isn't clear. There seems to be no more connection between logic and other areas of philosophy than there is between logic and physics or logic and mathematics. Every subject is formulated in language and requires deductive inferences. Knowledge of logic is useful to workers in every field.

Though someone might argue that logic has as much to do with linguistics as it does with philosophy, there is an explanation for logic being included in philosophy. At the beginning of the modern period (in the fifteenth and sixteenth centuries), philosophy was understood differently than it is today. All systematic knowledge of the world that doesn't depend on divine revelation was considered to belong to philosophy. Theology was excluded. So was mathematics, since it wasn't thought to be knowledge of the world. The natural and social sciences were considered part of philosophy—though they didn't exist in anything like their present forms. The word 'science' was also used then, but science and philosophy were pretty much the same thing.

The natural sciences were first considered to be natural philosophy. As various bodies of knowledge developed, they came to require specialized techniques, and became regarded as separate disciplines. Originally philosophy included almost all knowledge. Now it includes only what is left after various branches separated themselves from philosophy. There is no reason why the different areas of philosophy should have much in common with one another. The different areas do agree in not requiring data acquired by specialized techniques or instruments. Each area of philosophy deals with phenomena that are accessible, and familiar, to the ordinary person.

The last part of the nineteenth century and the twentieth century have seen enormous progress in logic. I think that if some of the developments of the twentieth century had taken place in the nineteenth, there would have been a move to regard logic as a separate subject matter. There would now be departments of logic; logic courses would no longer be given by departments of philosophy. But there is not now and will not be a move to create a new subject matter. The modern university has considerable inertia. It is more difficult to create new departments now than it was in the nineteenth century. It no longer seems important to do so.

As an area of philosophy, logic may not seem very philosophical (whatever that means). But we can ask philosophical questions about logic, and develop philosophical views of logic. (It is possible to do this with any subject.) The attention to a philosophical view of logic is one of the distinctive features of the present book. For example, I have taken the position—and made it explicit—that logic is a study of language rather than a study of thought or reasoning, or of principles governing correct reasoning. Throughout the book I will not only present the subject matter of logic, but I will also try to understand logic and logical techniques. This is the philosophy of logic, for it belongs to the philosophy of a subject to determine what the subject amounts to, and what is the significance of its techniques and procedures.

Chapter 2

Some Preliminary Matters

2-0 SUMMARY

This chapter discusses inferences and arguments, and the difference between deductive and inductive criteria for evaluating them. Two auxiliary topics are covered in optional sections: definitions and informal fallacies. These topics are related to the main concerns of the course, but can be omitted without affecting the study of more central topics.

2-1 DEFINITIONS (OPT)

One goal of this course is that students will use language more effectively. This goal will be achieved primarily by studying logically important semantic features of sentences. But there are some auxiliary topics we will cover that also contribute to our goal. Two of these are covered in the present chapter: definitions and informal fallacies. A definition explains the meaning of an expression. Being able to define an expression is an important linguistic skill. A helpful definition produced at the appropriate time often makes what a person says much more effective.

To understand an expression, we must know its place in the system of expressions that constitutes a language. This place is determined by its relations to other expressions and, for certain expressions, by its relations to objects it denotes. To understand the word 'although,' we must know how to use it to form longer expressions, and how expressions containing it are related. This word does not denote objects. But to understand 'sweet,' it is not sufficient to relate 'sweet' to other words. We must also be able to recognize sweet things.

To define an expression, we must locate the expression in the system of language. In defining an expression, we perform a speech act. Although the sentence we use to perform this act is a definition, a sentence that can be used as a definition can often be used in performing other kinds of speech acts. This sentence:

(1) Water is the substance whose molecules consist of two atoms of hydrogen combined with one atom of oxygen.

might once have been used to make a conjecture, and can now be used to define 'water.' We can tell by looking at a sentence that it is suitable for use as a definition; we cannot say that it must be used as a definition. In (1), the expression being defined is used normally. But it can also be mentioned:

(2) 'Water' denotes the substance whose molecules consist of two atoms of hydrogen combined with one atom of oxygen.

To define an expression, we must have some appreciation of the status of the expression being defined. We can either explain the meaning of an expression that already belongs to the language. Or we can use a definition to *stipulate* the meaning of an expression. A *stipulative* definition either introduces an expression into the language or amends the meaning of an expression already in the language.

A sentence used to explain an expression that belongs to the language is used propositionally. Such a definition is true or false. Since it is false that a rectangle is a four-sided plane figure with four right angles and adjacent sides unequal, it would be incorrect to define 'rectangle' this way. A more satisfactory definition is:

(3) A rectangle is a four-sided plane figure with four right angles.

(Remember, we could also use the following for a definition:

(4) 'Rectangle' means a four-sided plane figure with four right angles.)

A sentence used as a stipulative definition is not evaluated as true or false. We may criticize such a definition for various reasons, but not for assigning the wrong meaning to the defined expression. There are several kinds of stipulative definition. One kind introduces an entirely new expression into the language. A second kind of stipulative definition involves *vague* expressions. In the present context, 'vague' is a technical term, and does not have its ordinary meaning. A denoting expression is vague if cases arise where it is not possible to determine whether the expression denotes these cases. A denoting expression has certain criteria associated with it by the language to which it belongs. An object which satisfies these criteria is denoted by the expression. An object which doesn't satisfy the criteria isn't denoted. Consider the word 'chair.' To be a chair, an object must be a piece of furniture, with a back, designed for one person to sit on. The properties (1) *being a piece of furniture,* (2) *having a back,* (3) *designed for one person to sit on* are the criteria for the word 'chair.' Chairs satisfy these criteria (chairs are denoted by the word 'chair'). Automobiles don't satisfy these criteria; automobiles are certainly not chairs.

Most words which denote objects we experience have criteria which are not sufficient for deciding, for every object, whether or not the object is denoted by the word. There are clear cases of objects which are denoted, and there are clear cases of objects which aren't denoted. But there are also *borderline cases*—where the criteria prove insufficient for determining whether the objects are denoted. The word 'chair' is vague, because I find it impossible to determine whether a bucket seat in a car is a chair. Bucket seats are borderline cases for 'chair.' (We can expect to find disagreement from one person to the next over which are and are not borderline cases for a given expression.)

A borderline case for a vague term is not just a case which proves difficult to evaluate. Suppose someone asked us if some yellowish metal is gold. It might be hard to tell whether that metal is gold, but this difficulty does not make the metal a borderline case for the word 'gold.' There are established procedures for determining if some metal is gold, even if we would have trouble using these procedures. For a vague expression, there are no procedures to determine the status of borderline cases.

The opposite of (the technical sense of) 'vague' is 'precise.' A denoting expression which isn't vague is precise. Although many (probably most) expressions which denote objects we experience are vague, this is not a defect of our language. An absolutely precise vocabulary could prove impossibly difficult for conversational use, because we would be unable to learn and remember the precise criteria associated with various words. But there are some occasions where vagueness proves to be a shortcoming. In science and mathematics, precision is an important value. Even in practical affairs, we sometimes find vagueness troublesome. The words 'life,' 'alive,' 'death,' and 'dead' are vague, for cases arise where we cannot decide if an individual is alive or dead. Suppose that due to an accident, the activity of a person's brain ceases, but the heart and lungs continue to operate. Is the *person* alive or not? Insurance companies must have such cases decided one way or the other. We also require a decision to determine the legal liability of the person who caused the accident.

A stipulative definition can be used to make a vague expression more precise. Such a definition should not change the expression's meaning with respect to the clear cases; it should only change the meaning as it concerns borderline cases. A definition used in this way is subject to criticism. If a court decided that a person with no brain activity but whose heart, lungs, and other systems are functioning is alive, it might be told that it is disregarding the most important aspect of human experience. But while the definition would be unsatisfactory, it is not incorrect unless it changes the (already) clear cases which the expression either does or does not denote.

Still another kind of stipulative definition gives technical significance to an ordinary expression. Such a definition gives a new meaning to a term that already belongs to the language. Ordinarily the new meaning is closely related to the old meaning. The new meaning might be "included" in the old, but be more restrictive; or the new meaning might be more precise than the old. (A definition used to give a technical sense to an ordinary expression might also make a vague expression more precise.) In this book, I shall have occasion to give technical meanings to many ordinary expressions. A definition which gives a technical sense to an ordinary word cannot be mistaken, but it will be inappropriate if the technical sense is unrelated to the word's ordinary meaning.

An expression which is given a technical meaning retains its ordinary meaning. The technical meaning is associated with the expression in specialized contexts; its ordinary meaning remains appropriate in other circumstances. Ordinary words are given technical meanings in many academic subjects, and also in legal contexts. Laws and judicial interpretations both serve to give legal definitions to certain expressions. There is no requirement that what legally counts as murder, say, should be identical with what we would ordinarily be inclined to call murder. But we would not expect the meanings to be too far apart. (Where the legal meaning of an expression diverges from the ordinary meaning, there may in time be a change in the ordinary meaning so that it more nearly approximates the legal meaning.)

We have classified definitions on the basis of the status of the expression being defined, and the change (or lack of it) brought about by our definition. Our (incomplete) classification is as follows:

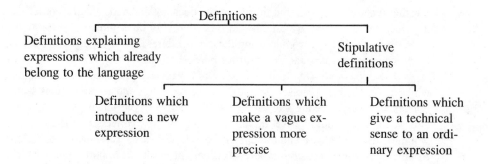

We must not only understand what we hope to accomplish with a definition, but we must also have an understanding of the different ways to explain the meaning of an expression—of the different ways to construct a definition. We will consider techniques for producing single-sentence definitions of nouns and adjectives. These are the expressions we most often have occasion to define, though we will later consider how to define some other kinds of expressions.

An *ostensive* definition provides an experience of the kind of thing the defined expression denotes, and indicates that the expression denotes it. If we explained 'sweet' by giving someone sugar to taste, and telling her that it is sweet, we would be defining 'sweet' ostensively. We would also be making an ostensive definition if we pointed to the sky in explaining 'blue.' Ostensive definitions obviously can't be used for every denoting expression. They wouldn't work for 'electron' or 'justice.' Ostensive definitions work best for expressions whose meanings are closely tied to sense experience—words for colors, shapes, sounds, etc. We *could* define 'automobile' ostensively, but it is difficult to tell from looking just what is important to being an automobile. On the basis of only an ostensive definition, someone might have a hard time determining how 'automobile' is related to other words in the language. Even when they are appropriate, ostensive definitions can easily be misunderstood. If we pointed to a red circle to explain 'round,' our audience might take 'round' to be a word for red.

Denotative definitions list the things or kinds of things that the defined expression denotes. The following is a denotative definition of 'primary color.'

(5) A primary color is one of red, yellow, or blue.

A denotative definition might list everything denoted by an expression, or it might confine itself to a representative selection—as in:

(6) Red is the color of Smith's car, most fire engines, and Sally's hair.

Denotative definitions are most successful for expressions denoting just a few things or kinds of things. Their chief drawback is that they may make it difficult to figure out how the defined expression is related to other expressions in the language. (A definition should enable its audience to use and understand the defined expression. The audience must be aware of the place the word occupies in the system of language.)

A *synonymous* definition provides a synonym for the defined expression. Two expressions are synonyms if they have the same meaning. However, we shall consider synonymous definitions to be only those definitions which give a relatively short synonym that might be used without awkwardness in place of the defined expression. In definition (7):

(7) A square is a four-sided plane figure with equal sides and equal angles.

the expressions 'square' and 'four-sided plane figure with equal sides and equal angles' are synonyms. But the expression 'four-sided plane figure with equal sides and equal angles' is not short; most sentences containing the noun 'square' would be awkward if 'square' were replaced by this synonym. So (7) will not be counted as a synonymous definition. The following is a synonymous definition of 'automobile':

(8) An automobile is a car.

Synonymous definitions are possible only for expressions which have suitable synonyms. Not many expressions qualify.

An *operational* definition is most useful for expressions denoting some feature which can be measured—expressions such as 'length' and 'temperature.' Such a definition describes an operation to measure or detect the denoted feature. The following is an operational definition of 'temperature':

(9) Temperature is a measure of heat which is recorded by placing a thermometer in contact with the object whose heat is being measured.

Operational definitions are frequently useful, but they have several shortcomings. Measurable features can often be measured in different ways. Explaining one operation for measurement can leave the audience in the dark about other operations. In addition, a single operation may be inadequate to measure the whole range of a certain magnitude. We see this when temperature is measured by thermometers; some temperatures are too great to be measured by a thermometer (the thermometer would melt). And an operational definition may not reveal the relations between the defined expression and other expressions in the language. (Whether or not it does depends in part on what the audience for the definition already knows.)

To construct a definition *by genus and difference*, we consider the objects denoted by the defined expression. The genus is a class which contains the denoted objects and other objects as well. ('Genus' is a Latin word meaning *kind*—as in kind of thing.) To define 'chair,' we find a genus which contains chairs and other things. *Pieces of furniture* constitutes a suitable genus. (Any class is a genus, so the class of chairs is a genus. But this class is not suitable for defining 'chair.')

As well as designating a class containing the objects denoted by the defined expression, a definition by genus and difference indicates what makes the denoted objects *different* from other objects in the genus. In this definition of 'chair':

(10) A chair is a piece of furniture which has a back and is designed for one person to sit on.

the genus can be regarded as *pieces of furniture*. The difference (this is the difference between chairs and other pieces of furniture) is *having a back and being designed for one person to sit on*. We could also regard the genus as *pieces of furniture having backs*; then the difference would be *designed for one person to sit on*. Definitions by genus and difference overlap synonymous definitions. The definition 'A bachelor is an unmarried male human' is both a synonymous definition and a definition by genus and difference. But most definitions by genus and difference will not be counted as synonymous definitions, because they don't provide a short synonym which can replace the defined expression without awkwardness.

In defining an expression, there are several shortcomings we want to avoid. In the first place, we don't want to produce a definition that isn't suited to its audience. For example, a chemical definition of 'helium' would not enable a (normal) first-grader to understand the word. A definition should enable its audience to properly situate the defined expression in the system of language.

We normally try to define an expression in positive terms rather than negative ones. Instead of defining 'square' as 'rectangle that does not have unequal sides,' we do better to say that a square is a rectangle having equal sides. However, some expressions require a negative definition. Absence is the state of not being present, and a positive definition of 'absence' would be more cumbersome than a negative one.

If, by mistake, a definition makes the defined expression denote two many things, that definition is too *broad*. This sentence:

(11) A piano is a musical instrument with a keyboard.

is too broad when used to define 'piano.' (But the sentence can be put to some other use, for it *is* true.) A definition that prevents the defined expression from denoting all the right objects is too *narrow*. The sentence:

(12) A chair is a piece of furniture with arms and a back, designed for one person to sit on.

would provide too narrow a definition of 'chair.' The definition excludes armless chairs. A definition might be too broad and too narrow at once:

(13) A chair is a piece of furniture with arms and a back, designed for one or more people to sit on.

If a definition explains an expression by using the same expression, or an expression derived from the defined expression (or an expression from which the defined expression is derived), the definition is *circular*. A circular definition of 'circle' would be:

(14) A circle is a circular figure.

Circular definitions are not very useful. Neither are definitions constructed with obscure, figurative, or ambiguous language. The following definition of 'wine' does not do much to explain the word's meaning:

(15) Wine is liquid sunshine.

Exercise: Section 1

For 1–3, determine which sentences are true.

*1. A definition used to make a vague expression more precise cannot be incorrect if the changes it introduces affect only the (previously) borderline cases.

*2. A stipulative definition might be a definition by genus and difference.

*3. No synonymous definition is a definition by genus and difference.

For 4–6, indicate what kind of definitions these are, with respect to the status of the word being defined, and the changes (or lack of them) accomplished by the definition.

*4. Bill tells his friend, "A ball bearing is a little steel ball used to reduce friction between two surfaces which it helps to separate."

*5. J. K. Logic writes, "In the present paper, 'justification' is the name for the value which sentences have which are known to be true or which follow from sentences known to be true."

*6. The president of the International Fellowship of Advanced Librarians declares, "From now on, no publication containing fewer than ten pages will be counted as a book."

Indicate any shortcomings in definitions 7 and 8.

*7. An organism is alive just in case that organism is not dead.

*8. A rectangle is a four-sided plane figure whose opposite sides are equal and whose adjacent sides are unequal.

9. Explain how 'encyclopedia' might be given an ostensive definition. Provide a denotative definition and a definition by genus and difference of 'encyclopedia.'

10. Define 'door' by genus and difference. What are some borderline cases for 'door' as you have defined it?

11. Note some borderline cases for the word 'table.' How might 'table' be redefined in order to eliminate vagueness?

12. Construct an operational definition of 'length.'

2-2 INFERENCES AND ARGUMENTS

An *inference* is an act of reaching a *conclusion* from certain *premisses*. The premisses are sentences a person begins with. In inferring, the person moves beyond the premisses to a conclusion which they support. Making an inference is reasoning from premisses to a conclusion. A detective might conceivably make an inference like the following:

(1) If Jones killed Baker, then Jones was not in Chicago on Thursday.

(2) But Jones was in Chicago on Thursday.

(3) So Jones must not have killed Baker.

Premisses (1) and (2) support the conclusion, sentence (3).

A person may make an inference to find out something for himself. He may reach a conclusion from premisses he formulates himself, which he accepts. He may also infer a conclusion from someone else's statements. He need not accept the premisses he starts with. He may only be interested in determining their consequences. A person can also make an inference to persuade someone else of something. In such a case, the speaker already accepts the premisses and conclusion. He states premisses which he thinks the other person will accept, and he uses them to support the conclusion he wants that person to accept. An *argument* is an inference made by one person in order to persuade another.

In the inferences we will study, all sentences are used propositionally. The detective's inference used sentences propositionally, and so does the following:

Christmas, 1977 fell on either Saturday or Sunday. It did not fall on Saturday. Therefore, Christmas, 1977 fell on Sunday.

In this inference, the premisses are used to support the truth of the conclusion. But in the following inference:

> Whenever it rains, Thomas, shut the upstairs windows. It is raining now. So, Thomas, shut the upstairs windows.

the first premiss and the conclusion are not used propositionally, for they are commands. The premisses here are not used to support the truth of the conclusion. We might say in this case that they support the conclusion's being "in effect."

An inference or argument has one or more premisses. Theoretically there is no upper limit to the number of premisses, but in practice a person has a hard time "taking in" more than three or four premisses. In our study of inferences, we usually put the premisses at the beginning and the conclusion at the end. But in actual conversations (or written passages) we do not always find this order. The conclusion may come first, followed by the premisses. Or the conclusion may come in the middle of the premisses. The inference attributed to the detective could as well have been presented in one of these ways:

(a) Jones must not have killed Baker, because Jones was in Chicago on Thursday. And if Jones killed Baker, then Jones was not in Chicago on Thursday.

(b) If Jones killed Baker, then Jones was not in Chicago on Thursday. So Jones must not have killed Baker because Jones *was* in Chicago on Thursday.

There are several words which are used to indicate that some sentences are premisses and others are conclusions. The words 'so,' 'thus,' 'hence,' 'therefore,' and 'must' often mark conclusions (but this is not their only function—for instance, 'must' has a variety of jobs.) The word 'because' often indicates that a sentence is a premiss.

Suppose someone makes an inference to extend her knowledge. What does it take for the inference to be successful? In the first place, the premisses should be true or based on good evidence. They should be accepted by the person making the inference. The premisses should really support the conclusion, and the person making the inference should recognize that they do. While these requirements must all be satisfied by a completely successful inference, they are not all logical requirements. In logic we consider the relation between the sentences which serve as premisses and conclusion. We determine if this is an appropriate semantic relation.

In studying inferences in logic, there are several things we usually don't consider. We aren't interested in the person making an inference, or in the situation in which he makes it. So we don't care whether that person is trying to find out something for himself, or is trying to persuade someone else. This is why we find the words 'inference' and 'argument' used interchangeably in logic. And our focus is on the sentences used to make an inference, not on the act of making it. The sequence of premisses and conclusion used to make an inference might be called the content of the inference. This *inference sequence* does not really constitute the inference, but we will often call the sequence of premisses and conclusion an inference or an argument.

One of the principal tasks in logic is developing criteria for determining whether the premisses of an inference support the conclusion. We shall be looking at inferences whose premisses are intended to support the truth of the conclusion—inferences whose premisses and conclusions are used propositionally. But there are different kinds of criteria for evaluating these inferences. Which kind of criteria we employ for a given inference depends on what we expect from that inference. We use *deductive* criteria if we expect an inference to be absolutely conclusive. In a deductively correct inference, the truth of the premisses *guarantees* the truth of the conclusion. The following inference is deductively correct.

Napoleon didn't like both lobster and steak. Then Napoleon must not have liked lobster, because he did like steak.

If the premisses *were* true, then the conclusion would *have* to be true. The truth of the conclusion would *follow* from the truth of the premisses.

Our expectations for an inference must be determined by the situation in which the inference occurs, and by the intentions of the inference maker. Did he intend that his premisses would guarantee the conclusion? Or did he intend to support the conclusion to a lesser degree? *Inductive* criteria are used when the premisses are intended to provide less than conclusive support to their conclusions. An argument is satisfactory by inductive standards if the truth of its premisses is (would be) sufficient to make the conclusion probable. (If the conclusion is probable, it is probably true.) Examples of arguments which satisfy inductive criteria are below.

(a) Seventy per cent of people who have never had chicken pox, and who are exposed to chicken pox, contract the disease. Billy Brown has never had chicken pox, and he has just been exposed to it. So Billy will get chicken pox.

(b) On several occasions Charlie has drunk both beer and bourbon. Each time he has had a terrible headache the next day. So whenever Charlie drinks both beer and bourbon, he will get a terrible headache.

With deductive criteria, everything is black or white. An argument is either deductively satisfactory or deductively worthless. Neither of two deductively satisfactory arguments is better (or worse) than the other. Inductively, arguments range from absolutely terrible to very good, with all shades in between. Two arguments can both be inductively satisfactory, but one be superior to the other.

To compare deductive and inductive criteria, we must understand the difference between truth and probability. If we ask whether a sentence is true, we want to know how the sentence is related to whatever it is about. A sentence is true if things are as it says. The truth of a sentence is fixed once and for all, although a sentence can be true without anyone knowing this. A sentence is probable relative to something; it can be probable with respect to one thing and improbable with respect to something else. We are frequently concerned with the probability of a sentence relative to evidence we have. A single sentence, with respect to a specific propositional use, cannot be both true and false. But a single sentence, used in one way, can be probable on the basis of some evidence, and improbable in the light of other evidence. In practice we try to estimate probability on the basis of all available evidence. But our judgment of probability or improbability is always subject to revision in the light of new evidence. Probability can be combined with truth and with falsity. Because probability is compatible with falsity, an inference which is satisfactory by inductive standards will generally not be satisfactory when judged by deductive standards. (But an argument that satisfies deductive criteria also satisfies inductive criteria.)

Although the deductive/inductive distinction is between different (sorts of) criteria for evaluating inferences, people often speak of a difference between deductive and inductive arguments. This is misleading, because a single argument can be evaluated by both inductive and deductive criteria. When someone speaks of a deductive argument, he must mean one for which he (or its author) has deductive intentions. And similarly for inductive arguments. However, once we realize the true difference between the inductive and the deductive, it is relatively harmless to speak of two kinds of inferences.

In this book we will study deduction but not induction. We simply assume that the inferences we encounter in this book are made by people who have deductive intentions for them. It would be desirable to have courses covering inductive criteria as well as courses treating deductive criteria. But there is no general agreement on criteria for inductively satisfactory inferences. There is no systematic and comprehensive knowledge of induction that is at all comparable to our knowledge of deduction.

An inference which is deductively satisfactory is *valid*. An inference which isn't deductively satisfactory is *invalid*. The validity of an inference depends on the relation between its premisses and conclusion. The premisses of a valid inference *entail* its conclusion. So an inference is valid if it is possible to determine simply on the basis of understanding the premisses and conclusion that it isn't possible for the premisses to be true when the conclusion isn't true.

A valid argument preserves truth from premisses to conclusion, in cases the premisses happen to be true. So if we know that an argument is valid, and we also know that its premisses are true, then we know (we infer) that its conclusion is true. But this *does not work in the opposite direction*. If we know that an argument is valid and its conclusion is true, then we cannot tell (from knowing this alone) whether the premisses are true or not. The following valid argument has a true conclusion and false premisses.

All dogs are birds. All birds are mammals. Hence, all dogs are mammals.

And if a valid argument has some false premisses, we cannot determine whether the conclusion is true or false. (But suppose a valid argument has a false conclusion. What do we know in this case about the truth or falsity of the premisses?)

*Exercise: Section 2

For 1–3, identify the premisses and conclusions of the arguments.

1. Athletes are brave, but no cowards are brave. So some heavy drinkers aren't cowards, because some heavy drinkers are athletes.

2. If Barbara has been to California, then she has stayed in San Francisco. But if Barbara has been to California and stayed in San Francisco, then she knows that Fisherman's Wharf is in San Francisco. But Barbara doesn't know that Fisherman's Wharf is in San Francisco. So she hasn't been to California.

3. Smith doesn't have high blood pressure because Smith has high blood pressure or lung cancer only if he smokes. And Smith smokes only if he isn't a Mormon. But Smith is a Mormon.

For 4–6, select the correct answer.

4. If an inference satisfies inductive criteria and has true premisses, then

    (a) the inference has a true conclusion.
    (b) the inference may have a true conclusion.
    (c) the inference has a false conclusion.

5. A deductively valid inference

    (a) is inductively satisfactory as well.
    (b) is not inductively satisfactory.
    (c) may or may not be inductively satisfactory.

6. If an argument is valid and its conclusion is false, then

- **(a)** the premisses are true.
- **(b)** the premisses may all be true.
- **(c)** at least one premise is false.

2-3 INFORMAL FALLACIES (OPT)

In our study of logic, we will come up with deductive criteria for evaluating inferences, as well as investigate other semantic features of sentences. Deductive criteria typically involve linguistic patterns. The following:

> It isn't true both that Napoleon liked oysters and Julius Caesar liked oysters. But Napoleon liked oysters. So it isn't true that Julius Caesar liked oysters.

is a (deductively) valid inference. This inference exemplifies the following pattern:

> It isn't true both that ___(1)___ and ___(2)___. But ___(1)___.
>
> So it isn't true that ___(2)___.

(The blanks are to be filled-in with sentences. The numerals indicate which blanks must contain the same sentences.) Any inference which examplifies this pattern will be valid.

A *fallacy* is an error in reasoning from premisses to a conclusion. There are many kinds of error for which names have been provided. Some fallacies are marked by linguistic patterns. The following inference is not valid—it is deductively unsatisfactory.

> If George got really drunk last night, then he isn't at school this morning. But George isn't at school this morning. So he got really drunk last night.

This pattern:

> If ___(1)___, then ___(2)___.
>
> But ___(2)___. So ___(1)___.

is not a pattern of valid inferences. An invalid deductive argument which exemplifies this pattern is said to commit the fallacy of *affirming the consequent*. Fallacies marked by linguistic patterns are *formal fallacies*. Other fallacies are *informal*. An understanding of formal fallacies depends on a careful study of language and linguistic forms. Informal fallacies are generally easier to recognize, since they typically depend on features that can be spotted without special training in logic or language.

In introductory logic courses, it has become traditional to include the study of some common informal fallacies. We will follow this tradition. Since one of our major concerns is to recognize cases where the premisses of an inference provide deductive support for its conclusion, it will prove helpful to gain understanding of some cases where the premisses don't support the conclusion. Our study of informal fallacies will also help us to understand the difference between inductive and deductive criteria, for some fallacies are associated with inductive intentions and others with deductive ones.

The conclusion of an argument which commits a fallacy can be either true or false. In the same way, the conclusion of a logically satisfactory inference can be true or false. To say that an argument commits a fallacy is not to speak against its conclusion, but only to note that the argument does not give us good reasons for accepting the conclusion. It is even possible for an argument to have true premisses which genuinely support the conclusion, and still commit a fallacy. One way this might happen is for the arguer to attribute deductive force to an argument that is only satisfactory by inductive standards. This fallacy sometimes occurs when a person regards a scientific proof of some conclusion as the last word possible. Scientific evidence generally provides no more than inductive support for a result. (Even when scientific premises provide deductive support for a conclusion, the premises themselves have support that is at best inductive.)

Many informal fallacies are named 'Appeal to *X*,' where '*X*' is replaced by a word for the distinctive feature of the fallacy. An *Appeal to Force* is a fallacious argument that incorporates a threat. It is common for people, and nations, to make threats to get others to act (or not act) in a certain way. The threat may involve physical force, economic sanctions, or some other painful pressure. When we decide how to act, threats are just one factor among others that we must consider. Do we take the threat seriously? Can we keep it from being carried out? Can we live with whatever sanctions are imposed? It may not be nice for one person to tell another to do something or else, but this isn't a fallacy. We have the fallacy of making an appeal to force if a threat is used to support the truth of a conclusion. The members of a jury might find a defendant innocent because he threatened to kill them if they didn't. We understand their action in finding him innocent, but the threat isn't a legitimate reason for thinking the defendant is innocent. A threat can be a legitimate reason for performing an action, so long as it isn't the act of accepting a sentence as true. People often do accept conclusions "justified" by force, but such beliefs are groundless.

The testimony of an authority can be a reason for accepting a sentence. We must constantly depend on authorities in the course of our lives. We accept the doctor's diagnosis when we are sick, and must often accept a mechanic's diagnosis when the car gives us trouble. That an authority makes a claim can provide inductive support for the claim, but it doesn't guarantee that claim. And authorities often disagree with one another. This is one reason for seeking a second opinion when our doctor recommends surgery. When authorities conflict, we can try to determine which is the greater authority, or we can ask them for the evidence on which their claims are based, and use this to reach our own conclusion. The fallacy of making an *Appeal to Authority* is the mistake of treating a person who isn't an authority as if he were. We commit this fallacy if we use an authority in one field to support a conclusion in a different field. We also commit it if we assign special weight to the claim of a person who is an authority about nothing. This fallacy is common in advertisements. Famous people are often paid to endorse a product whose quality is unrelated to their claims to fame.

The success of a certain practice in the past can provide inductive support for the conclusion that the practice will be successful in the future. Arguing in this way is different from committing the fallacy of making an *Appeal to Tradition*. We err in this direction when we support a belief or practice by citing the fact that it is traditional. For example, the reason given us for supporting a capitalist economy might be that our country has a tradition of free enterprise. Both satisfactory and unsatisfactory practices may be traditional. There is little reason for thinking that traditional beliefs are more likely to be true than false.

The *Appeal to Large Numbers* is the fallacy of an argument which claims that its conclusion is true because it is accepted by a large number of people. If we are told that something must be the right thing to do because "everyone" is doing it, we are the target of an argument which appeals to large numbers. (What counts as large is relative. A child who claims the right to stay up later because all of her friends do has committed the fallacy. But she may be talking about only six or seven friends.)

A person who has experienced bad luck or hard times may have a claim to our sympathy. Religious or humanitarian considerations may prompt us to assist that person. But our feeling sorry for someone is not a reason for thinking that the person did or didn't perform some action. An argument commits the fallacy of making an *Appeal to Pity* if it cites a person's pitiful circumstances to support such a conclusion. Lawyers sometimes commit this fallacy in order to persuade a jury that their client is innocent. The student who claims that he is entitled to a B in a course, because otherwise he will be dropped from school, has also made a fallacious appeal to pity.

Two fallacies are named by the Latin expression '*argumentum ad hominem.*' The *abusive* version cites a person's character or situation to discredit what he says, when his character or situation is not relevant to evaluating his statement. An argument that a certain reporter's account of events in Central America must be false, because she works for *Time* magazine, commits the abusive form of *argumentum ad hominem*. That a person works for *Time* magazine is not a reason for thinking the person will give false reports. However, there are facts about a person's character or situation that can provide inductive evidence that his statements are false or unreliable. If he is known to have frequently lied, or been mistaken, on a certain topic in the past, this evidence can inductively undermine his present statements. Even without knowledge of past prevarication, the fact that a person has a lot to gain from convincing us of a certain claim, together with a lack of other evidence for that claim, may legitimately lead us to be suspicious of the claim.

The abusive version of the *argumentum ad hominem* fallacy talks *about* a person, to argue that his statements are false. The *circumstantial* version talks *to* a person, to convince that person to accept a conclusion. This fallacy cites a person's circumstances as a reason for him to accept the conclusion. The following argument illustrates the circumstantial *argumentum ad hominem* fallacy.

> We need tight restrictions on imported steel. You must accept this conclusion, Mr. Carnegie, because you have large investments in domestic steel corporations.

No evidence is provided which supports the conclusion. Carnegie's situation is given as a reason for him to accept the conclusion, but his situation has nothing to do with the truth or falsity of that conclusion.

A person *argues from ignorance* when he claims that some conclusion is true because he knows of no reason to think it false, or that a conclusion is false because he knows of no reason to think it true—when he is not in a position to know reasons supporting the conclusion or its opposite. He is using his own ignorance as a reason for accepting the conclusion. However, if someone looks for evidence in a reasonable way, but is unable to find any, then he is not appealing to ignorance when he rejects an unsupported statement. The absence of evidence can provide inductive support for a conclusion.

The informal fallacies we have considered are fallacies in arguments for which the arguer would normally have inductive intentions. Each fallacy has some resemblance to a kind of argument in which the premises provide inductive support for a conclusion. There are lots more informal fallacies than the ones we have identified. You should be on the lookout for them when you see advertisements, or read or listen to people who are trying to persuade you to accept a conclusion. In doing this you should understand that an argument can commit more than one fallacy. For example, the arguments presented in advertisements are often incompletely stated. They can sometimes be understood in different ways, as committing different fallacies. (Not all advertisements are fallacious. Nor all arguments you encounter in magazines and books. But it is surprising, and disappointing, to see how often fallacies occur.)

Another informal fallacy is the *Circular Argument*. In a circular argument, the conclusion simply repeats the premiss, or one of the premisses. The conclusion is often worded differently from the premiss, to disguise the circularity. A not-very-serious example is:

You must support your friends, because otherwise they won't enjoy the support which they ought to receive.

A circular argument is unlike the other fallacies we have considered, because the premiss does support the conclusion. A circular argument is deductively valid. But such an argument can't (legitimately) be used to persuade someone who doesn't already accept the conclusion. A person who presents a circular argument is also said to be *begging the question*. Instead of giving his audience a reason to accept the conclusion, he is simply giving his audience the conclusion.

When something is composed of parts, which all have a certain characteristic, we may commit the fallacy of *composition* if we conclude that the something as a whole has that characteristic. Using another silly example, if we argued that because the pieces of a jigsaw puzzle have irregular edges, then the whole puzzle must have irregular edges, we would commit the fallacy of composition. We would also commit this fallacy if we argued that five good players make a good basketball team. However, it isn't always an error to attribute to a whole some property of its parts. If we know that each part of a machine is made of steel, we can correctly conclude that the machine is made of steel. Our premiss deductively supports the conclusion. The fallacy occurs only when we reason about a property that doesn't "carry over" from the parts to the whole.

The fallacy of *division* consists in mistakenly attributing a property of a whole to its parts. An argument that each piece of a jigsaw puzzle must have smooth edges because the puzzle as a whole has smooth edges would commit the fallacy of division.

The last informal fallacies we shall consider are fallacies of *equivocation*, or *ambiguity*. An argument commits this fallacy if an ambiguous expression is used with one meaning in the premisses and a different meaning in the conclusion, where the shift in meaning keeps the premisses from supporting the conclusion. The word 'dumb' is ambiguous, for it means both *unable to speak* and *not very intelligent*. The following argument commits a fallacy of equivocation.

Butler was dumb before the operation, but the operation cured that condition. So it is possible to make a person more intelligent by operating on him.

In the premiss, the word 'dumb' is used with the meaning *unable to speak*. The word isn't used at all in the conclusion, but the conclusion is clearly understanding the occurrence of 'dumb' in the premiss to have the other meaning. However, if the word 'dumb' in the premiss was used with the sense *not very intelligent*, the argument would be valid.

We distinguish two kinds of equivocal terms. The first kind, like 'dumb,' are equivocal in a straightforward way. The second kind of equivocal expressions are *relative adjectives*. The meaning of a relative adjective involves a relation to a class of things. The word 'tall' is a relative adjective. If Sam is a tall third grader, then Sam is tall *with respect to* third graders. A tall third grader, may be a short person. There are fallacies of equivocation which correspond to each kind of equivocal term. If we argued that Jesse would make a better than average ski instructor because he is a better than average skier, we would commit a fallacy of equivocation involving relative adjectives. Being better than most skiers is different from being better than most ski instructors.

The following sums up the informal fallacies we have considered.

More-or-Less Inductive	More-or-Less Deductive
Appeal to Force	Circular Argument
Appeal to Authority	Composition
Appeal to Tradition	Division
Appeal to Large Numbers	Equivocation
Appeal to Pity	Straightforward
Argumentum ad Hominem—abusive	Relative Adjectives
Argumentum ad Hominem—circumstantial	
Argument from Ignorance	

Exercise: Section 3

For 1–10, identify any fallacies.

*1. The November press release for the Turkey Growers Association states, "Eating turkey on Thanksgiving is sanctioned by a long and honorable American tradition. So every good American should eat turkey for Thanksgiving."

*2. Joe's friend tells him, "You shouldn't support gun control legislation, because you ought not to support laws that make it more difficult for people to own guns."

*3. Tom's rich uncle says, "Tom, you'd better believe that anyone who is poor is shiftless and lazy, because I will never leave my money to someone who would waste it in helping those people who won't help themselves."

*4. Professor Jenkins argues, "I know of no reasons to think that Earth is the only place in the universe which supports intelligent life. So there must be intelligent life elsewhere in the universe."

*5. The lobbyist against government-supported medical aid tells Mr. Bradley, "You should oppose anything that smacks of socialized medicine, because you are an executive of the Hospital Payment Insurance Corporation."

*6. Since Paul is a poet, anything he has to say about social and economic conditions will surely be false.

*7. There is no justification for different men earning unequal salaries, because this country is supposed to be based on the principle that all men are created equal.

*8. Anyone who speaks in favor of the present economic system ought to be ignored, for such a person is either corrupt or else he is an unthinking product of this very system.

*9. From the fact that a society is so constituted that everyone must look out for his or her own interests, we can infer that the interests of everyone will be served by that society.

*10. This system transmits messages with very few errors. So the components of this system must be highly reliable.

11. Select advertisements from magazines or newspapers. Try to construe these as abbreviated arguments having some conclusion like (a) everyone ought to buy the advertised product, (b) everyone ought to want to buy the advertised product, (c) everyone ought to prefer the advertised product to its competitors. Determine just what argument is involved. What principle underlies the argument? Is any fallacy involved?

3

Sentences About Individuals

3-0 SUMMARY

This chapter surveys English sentences which we hope to understand better and use more effectively. Our goal is to apply the artificial logical languages we will develop to the study of these sentences. The English sentences are about individuals, and include indefinite sentences, universal sentences, and singular sentences.

3-1 LOOKING AHEAD

In this book, and in the course for which it is the text, we will develop and investigate artificial languages, and apply these artificial languages to portions of English. Our goal is to become more effective in using language. We want to increase our understanding of what it means to say this or that. We want to see the semantic relations between statements more clearly, and to have a greater awareness of the consequences of statements. This will help us use language more accurately and more precisely, to make justified inferences, and to back up the claims that we make. It should also help us to understand which claims we are not in a position to back up.

The artificial languages we will develop don't apply to the whole of the English language. Each artificial language is applicable to a restricted portion of English. In this chapter, we will describe that portion of English which we will try to understand better. We are concerned only with sentences suited to be used propositionally, but we won't consider all of these. Very roughly, we are interested in sentences about individuals. This includes individual persons, trees, tables, and chairs. And also individual places, times, numbers, figures, properties, and relations.

Expressions denoting individuals can be contrasted with expressions for "stuff." The following expressions denote individuals:

person, horse, mountain, planet, number

These expressions denote stuff:

water, air, mud, iron, gold

If *A* is a noun which denotes individuals, then we can speak of each *A* or every *A*. But it makes little sense to speak of each water or every mud (unless we are talking about different kinds of water or mud). We will find ways to determine which sentences about individuals are analytic, which sentences about individuals entail or are incompatible with one another, and which inferences about individuals are valid.

*Exercise: Section 1

Determine which of the following sentences are true.

1. A goal of this course is to improve our ability to use language.

2. Sentences about individuals can be contrasted with sentences about stuff.

3. In this book we will limit our attention to sentences about people.

4. We will use artificial languages as instruments for locating ordinary sentences that have logically important semantic features.

3-2 INDIVIDUALS

To help us know which sentences we are "stalking," we will make a brief survey of the kinds of individuals recognized in English. These are the individuals denoted by ordinary English expressions. One class of denoting expressions are singular terms, expressions suited to denote just one individual. Another class consists of common nouns and noun phrases. Expressions like 'person' and 'tree' denote many individuals. In ordinary English, we have words for rocks, tables, and vegetables. And numbers. And properties, such as wisdom, and relations, like contiguity.

 Concrete individuals are the most familiar kind of individuals. Objects located in space or time are concrete. This includes ordinary substantial individuals like people, tables, and chairs. Events are also located in space and time. An event can be brief, as a birth or a death, or someone's winning a race. An event can be much longer, like the Battle of Gettysburg or World War II. Human acts or actions are events, so a murder or a (specific) game of softball are concrete individuals. A location in space or time is not essential to being concrete. Those of us who accept God regard him as a concrete individual, though in the classical conception God is outside of space and time. An individual which is causally related to other individuals is concrete.

 Fictional and mythical individuals are not real, but, as imagined, many such individuals are concrete. Superman, Sherlock Holmes, and Pegasus are the kind of individuals that would have a spatial and temporal location. However, in developing artificial logical languages, we will not provide a "status" for fictional and mythical individuals. English sentences about these individuals are not fully understood. We will concentrate on sentences about real individuals.

 Concrete individuals are usually contrasted with *abstract* ones. But times and places seem to be intermediate between concrete and abstract individuals. A century, an hour, and a second are individuals. So is a particular instant, like 12:06 P.M. today. These individuals provide the "location" for ordinary concrete individuals. Similarly, a point, an area, or a volume are individuals.

 We talk most easily about fully concrete individuals. The most commonly used denoting expressions stand for them. Fully abstract individuals pose a number of problems. It isn't even easy to say what makes an individual abstract. About the best we can do is say that abstract individuals don't possess the typical characteristics of concrete ones. Fully abstract individuals are not in space or time, they don't cause anything, and they aren't times or places either.

Mathematical objects are abstract individuals. These include numbers, sets, and geometric figures. It is characteristic of these abstract individuals that we don't find several instances of the same object. There are lots of numerals '1,' but there is only one number 1. And the members of a set constitute only that one set. At first, geometric figures may seem to be an exception to this claim. There are lots of triangles, say, and they have spatial relations to one another. But the figures studied in geometry are not located in the space where we find ourselves. The space "housing" geometric figures is abstract; within this space, different figures have different locations.

Some philosophers do not accept mathematical objects as "ultimately real." They claim that we talk about numbers *as if* numbers were real individuals, but that numbers are not part of the "ultimate furniture" of reality. These philosophers then try to show what features of the world make it convenient to talk as if numbers were real individuals, and why we should not take this talk seriously. There are philosophers who feel this way about all abstract individuals, and there are philosophers who accept some kinds of abstract individuals but not others. Problems about what kinds of very basic individuals are real are *ontological* problems; *ontology* is a part of metaphysics. In this book, I am not defending a particular ontological position. At present, we are simply cataloguing some kinds of individuals recognized by ordinary English.

Properties and relations are abstract individuals. A property characterizes individuals. Many individuals can have, or *exemplify*, the same property; for example, many different individuals have the property *red*. However, some properties, like that of being both round and square, are not exemplified by any individuals. Relations have about the same status as properties, but a relation links two or more individuals. *Being married to* is a relation between a husband and his wife. This relation is exemplified by pairs of individuals.

From one perspective, properties and relations are contrasted with individuals. Individuals *have* properties, but we don't say that a property has an individual. However, we have denoting expressions which name properties and relations. In the sentence, 'The car is red,' the adjective 'red' denotes red things. But in 'Red is a color,' the subject 'red' names the property of being red. In English, we can use adjectives to denote individuals which have a property. In sentences like 'Red is a color' and 'Square is a shape,' we use adjectives as names of properties. We can also make names for properties and relations by combining the word 'being' with a suitable expression. *Being wise* is a property and *being older than* is a relation. Single words name some of these abstract individuals. *Wisdom* is the property of being wise. The suffixes 'ity' and 'ness' (as in 'humility' and 'boldness') often indicate that a word names a property. So do 'ship' ('friendship') and 'tion' ('affection').

Another kind of abstract individual is a *type*. To understand types, we will start by considering letters in the alphabet, or words, or longer expressions. Take the letter 'a.' On this page, the letter 'a' occurs many times. The symbols you see printed on the page are *tokens* of the letter 'a.' The letter itself is the *type* of which they are tokens. These tokens are concrete individuals, but types are not located in (intermediate) space or time. Words also come in types and tokens. The word 'madam' is a type. But the preceding sentence contains a 'madam'-token (and so does this sentence). One type can have any number of tokens, but types can also have multiple occurrences in other types. The (type) word 'madam' contains two occurrences of the letter 'a.' Occurrences of symbols in types have some features of types and some features of tokens.

The "type-token" distinction applies only to symbols and their instances. There are other types of things than symbols. In English, the word 'the' is often used to form a name of the *type* of any kind of thing. When we say, "The word 'zebra' begins with 'z,' " we are talking about a word-type and a letter-type. But when we say "The whale is a mammal," we are talking about an animal-type. A type is a *kind* of thing. When a type is a symbol, we call its instances tokens. Otherwise, we simply call them *instances*. Many types have instances, but some don't. Although *the unicorn* is a one-horned animal, there are no instances of the unicorn.

A type is an abstract individual. Types have certain similarities to properties. Just as a property can be exemplified zero or more times, so a type can have zero or more instances. But a property is exemplified *by* an individual. We normally speak of a property as if it were *in* the individuals exemplifying it, or as if it *belonged* to them. The type isn't in its instances, and the instances don't have the type. The type is an abstract representative of its instances.

For any kind of individuals, a *collection* of those individuals is also an individual. A flock of sheep is a collection of sheep, and a platoon is a collection of soldiers. The first five letters of the alphabet constitute a collection; so do the letters which are vowels. A collection of concrete individuals is a concrete individual. A collection of abstract individuals is abstract.

*Exercise: Section 2

For 1–10, determine which of the following name (a) concrete individuals, (b) intermediate individuals, (c) abstract individuals.

1. New York City

2. The Solar System

3. 7

4. June 1, 1937

5. The (American) Civil War

6. The first word defined in the *American Heritage Dictionary*

7. The *American Heritage Dictionary*

8. Christopher Columbus

9. Sincerity

10. The null set

For 11–14, determine which of the following are true.

11. A concrete individual is abstract.

12. A token of an expression is an instance of a type.

13. The property of being green is exemplified by green individuals.

14. Common nouns denote only concrete individuals.

3-3   QUANTIFIED PHRASES

One very important kind of sentences about individuals contains *quantified phrases*. Below are examples of quantified phrases:

all people

every student

each triangle

any even integer

no girl

the pope

a kitten

some wild duck

most diseases

seven neckties

An expression like 'all,' 'every,' etc. is a *quantifier*. A quantified phrase is formed by combining a quantifier with a noun or noun phrase.

Quantified phrases are used in making statements that range from those about specific individuals:

The Governor of Illinois speaks Spanish.

through indefinite statements:

Some student in Professor Rose's class did his homework assignment.

to universal statements:

Every dog is carnivorous.

Some statements that contain quantified phrases fall "between" indefinite and universal statements:

Several customers died from food poisoning.

Seven questions were omitted from the test.

Almost all Sheila's friends are wealthy.

Among sentences formed with quantified phrases, indefinite and universal sentences are especially important. Such sentences are used frequently. An understanding of their logically important features is valuable in itself, and also contributes to achieving an understanding of many other sentences formed from quantified phrases. These sentences:

(1) A student in Mr. Hull's class can speak French.

(2) Some student in Mr. Hull's class can speak French.

seem to be as indefinite as possible, for each sentence means that at least one student in Mr. Hull's class can speak French. Neither sentence is concerned with a specific student; each would be true if several students, or even all students in Mr. Hull's class speak French.

We can contrast (1) and (2) with (3).

(3) Exactly one student in Mr. Hull's class can speak French.

The student in question is unspecified, but the number of such students is fixed. So (3) is less indefinite than (1) and (2). We will also regard sentences like these.

(4) Several students in Mr. Hull's class can speak French.

(5) Seventeen students in Mr. Hull's class can speak French.

(6) Almost all students in Mr. Hull's class can speak French.

as less indefinite than (1) and (2). In each case, their truth requires more than does the truth of (1) and (2). Even this sentence:

(7) Some students in Mr. Hull's class can speak French.

is less indefinite than (1) and (2). For the plural form 'Some students' requires that at least two students in Hull's class speak French.

*Exercise: Section 3

Determine which of the following sentences are true.

1. The truth of this sentence:

> At most two students in Professor Hare's class passed the course.

requires that exactly two students in the class passed the course.

2–3. Consider these sentences for the next two questions:

(a) Exactly one person was killed in the accident.
(b) At least one person was killed in the accident.

2. Sentence (a) entails sentence (b).

3. Sentence (b) entails sentence (a).

4–5. Consider these sentences for the next two questions:

(c) Bill owns a dog.
(d) Bill owns some dogs.

4. Sentence (c) entails sentence (d).

5. Sentence (d) entails sentence (c).

6. The following sentences are incompatible:

No store has a sale on milk this week.
At most one store has a sale on milk this week.

3-4 UNIVERSAL SENTENCES

We are using sentences like:

(1) A student in Mr. Hull's class can speak French.

(2) Some student in Mr. Hull's class can speak French.

as our standard, or paradigm, for indefiniteness. Indefinite sentences can be contrasted with universal sentences. For a universal sentence to be true, every individual of a certain kind must have a specified property. The following sentence:

(3) Each student in Mr. Hull's class can speak French.

is a universal counterpart to (1) and (2).

English (and other languages as well) contains a large variety of universal sentences, and these turn out to be surprisingly complicated. A certain kind of sentence, even a specific sentence, often has a range of possible meanings rather than a single fixed meaning. To understand a sentence, we must understand its range of meanings, and when the sentence is used on a given occasion, we must be able to tell just which meaning it has. Sometimes a kind of sentence can be used to represent things differently on different occasions. For example, a sentence '__(1)__ and __(2)__,' where the blanks are filled with sentences, may represent two separate facts, without representing a relation between them. We have this in:

David is Presbyterian and his wife is Jewish.

Other sentences formed in the same way represent the first situation as occurring before the second:

Brian swung the bat and he missed the ball.

Or a kind of sentence can be used with a different *existential force* on different occasions. This universal sentence:

Any person who can run a mile in three minutes would be amazing.

would not normally be understood as indicating that there is a person who can run a mile in three minutes. But this universal sentence:

Every friend of Mary's would come to the wedding.

would normally be understood as indicating that Mary has a friend.

Some theorists don't agree that most sentences have a range of meanings. They claim that sentences commonly have fixed meanings, but that the circumstances in which a sentence is used provide additional information not found in the sentence. While this can happen, what is represented with a sentence is part of what the sentence means. And the existential force of a sentence also characterizes the act of using the sentence.

Universal sentences are either *affirmative* or *negative*. These are affirmative:

Every person will die.

Each dog has four legs.

All the students in Professor Corcoran's class are frightened.

Any book in the library is listed in the card catalogue.

These universal sentences are negative:

No planets are stars.

Not one guest said "Thank you."

None of the passengers was injured.

It might initially seem that the difference between universal negative and universal affirmative sentences is that the negative sentences rule something out. For example, the sentence 'No planet is a star' rules out something being both a planet and a star. But this does not distinguish negative from affirmative sentences. The sentence 'Each dog has four legs' rules out dogs that don't have four legs.

With indefinite quantified phrases, the difference between singular and plural makes a difference. The phrase 'some student' means at least one student, while 'some students' means at least two. It isn't clear that there is a similar difference with universal phrases. These two sentences:

No planets are stars.

No planet is a star.

don't differ at all in meaning. And I am not convinced that there is an important difference between:

(4) Every child of John's is a boy.

(5) All John's children are boys.

Sentence (4) does not require that John have more than one child. Neither, I think, does (5). Sentence (5) contains a *suggestion* of plurality, but I think that (5) would be regarded as true if John had only one child—who was a boy. However, one child is the minimum that sentence (5) allows John to have. The context in which (5) is used may make it clear that the speaker is taking John to have more than one. But the same can be said of (4).

Many kinds of universal sentences have a range of meanings. The context usually makes clear which meaning is intended. One contrast is between the *unrestricted* and *restricted* understandings of a universal sentence. A statement about every *A*, with the unrestricted understanding, means absolutely all the *A*'s. Given the unrestricted understanding, the following sentence is true:

Every person will die.

But on this understanding, a sentence like:

(6) Every dog has four legs.

isn't true. Some dogs, due to a variety of causes, are missing a leg. However, (6) might be used with the sense 'Every *normal* dog has four legs.' With this restricted understanding the sentence is true. A restricted understanding of this sentence:

(7) All African elephants have tusks.

might be 'All *normal adult* African elephants have tusks.'

Another contrast is between sentences which do and those which don't have *existential force*. Ordinarily, when a person speaks of *every A*, it is to be understood that there is at least one *A*. If someone said one of the following.

Each of John's children is a boy.

All John's children are boys.

we would normally understand the speaker to have indicated that John has a child. But a positive universal sentence doesn't always have existential force. The sentence:

Any trespasser will be prosecuted.

can be used as a warning, to keep people from trespassing. Its truth seems to require that the owner of the property in question *intend* to prosecute any person who trespasses. The owner can intend this even if no one ever trespasses.

Ordinarily, a sentence 'Every *A* is a *B*' does two things:

(i) It rules out an *A* that isn't a *B*.

(ii) It indicates that there is an *A* (indirectly it indicates that there is a *B*).

If the sentence lacks existential force, it does only the first. While universal affirmative sentences without existential force are rare, this isn't true of universal sentences formed with 'no' or 'none.' A sentence 'No *A* is a *B*' rules out there being an *A* which is a *B*, but it may not indicate that there is an *A*. This sentence.

No vampires are in Jesse's closet.

seems to me to be a true and (fairly) ordinary English sentence—though we all know there are no vampires. But it would be natural to understand this sentence:

None of John's children takes drugs.

as indicating that John has a child.

The last contrast that I want to note for universal sentences is between sentences that do and sentences that don't have *modal force*. When we simply say how things are, or were, or will be, our statement does not have modal force. When we say how things are necessarily, or possibly, our statement has modal force. Necessity and possibility are *modalities*; expressions for them are *modal expressions*. The following sentences have modal force:

It is necessary that bats are mammals.

Every whale must live in water.

All frogs can live in water.

It is possible that any of the suspects committed the crime.

Their modal force is indicated by the presence of a modal expression.

Another kind of modal sentence talks about how things would have been if something had happened, or talks about how things would be if something were to happen. Some such sentences are marked by subjunctive expressions (how things *would* have been or *would* be). But some aren't. It would be natural to understand the sentence:

Any student will cheat.

to have modal force. It isn't saying that all students will cheat at some time in the future. Instead it means that every student would cheat if given a suitable opportunity. Similarly, the property owner who announces:

Any trespasser will be prosecuted.

means that if anyone were to trespass, that person would be prosecuted.

Every universal sentence rules something out. We can contrast universal sentences which do and those which don't have modal force by considering what is ruled out. A sentence without modal force rules out the *actual* occurrence of a certain combination. A sentence with modal force, like:

Any trespasser will be prosecuted.

rules out the *possibility* of there being a trespasser who isn't prosecuted. The expressions 'each,' 'every,' and 'all' can be used to form sentences with modal force:

Each trespasser will be prosecuted

Every trespasser will be prosecuted.

All trespassers will be prosecuted.

But it is more common to use 'any.' We can also use negative expressions to form sentences with modal force:

No one will trespass without being prosecuted.

It is most common for sentences with modal force, and no explicit subjunctive expression, to be in the future tense. But not all such sentences are in the future tense:

Any fifteen-year-old who weighs 375 pounds is unhealthy.

Anyone who survived the explosion yesterday was lucky. (We could say this when we didn't know if anyone did survive.)

If a positive universal sentence is understood to have existential force, we will say it is used in the *ordinary* way. Regardless of whether the sentence:

Cats are mammals.

is understood to have modal force, it is used in the ordinary way if the speaker is understood as indicating that there is a cat. A sentence without existential force which is also without modal force is used (and understood) *mathematically*. The mathematical understanding is somewhat artificial; it is only appropriate in special circumstances. With the mathematical understanding, a sentence 'Every A is a B' rules out there actually being an A which isn't a B. On this understanding, if there are no A's, the sentence 'Every A is a B' is true no matter what B is. In such a case, the sentence is said to be *vacuously* true. The mathematical understanding is most often found in technical writing, especially in mathematical or logical writing. In these contexts, it contributes to making true universal statements that have no exceptions.

Even though many universal negative sentences have neither existential force nor modal force, we will not say they are used mathematically. The distinction between a sentence used in the ordinary way and one used in the mathematical way applies only to universal affirmative sentences.

We have considered several distinctions with respect to universal sentences. The distinction between affirmative and negative universal sentences is marked by different expressions. The other distinctions concern different ways to understand a single sentence —though some sentences with modal force are marked by expressions and others aren't. We have noted distinctions between:

(1) The restricted and unrestricted understanding.

(2) Sentences which do and those which don't have existential force.

(3) Sentences which do and which don't have modal force.

We have used these distinctions to characterize the ordinary and the mathematical uses (and understandings) of universal affirmative sentences. We will make further use of these distinctions when we apply artificial logical languages to ordinary English.

*Exercise: Section 4

1. Determine which of the following sentences are universal.

   a. Jack can't be trusted.
   b. None of Jack's friends will lend him money.
   c. Any friend of Jack's knows better than to lend him money.
   d. Jack has no friends who trust him.

2. Of the universal sentences in exercise 1, determine which are affirmative and which are negative.

For 3–4, use these pairs of sentences for the following questions:

   a. All the trespassers were prosecuted.   Nobody was prosecuted.

   b. Each professor in the Economics Department has a national reputation.   All the professors in the Economics Department are totally unknown.

   c. Nobody who failed the final passed the course.   Three students passed the course even though they failed the final.

3. Suppose the universal affirmative sentences above are understood in the ordinary way but have no modal force, and the universal negative sentences are understood to have no modal force, and don't have existential force. Determine which pairs are incompatible.

4. Now suppose the universal affirmative sentences are understood mathematically, but the universal negative sentences are understood the same as before. Determine which pairs are incompatible.

3-5 SOME OTHER UNIVERSAL SENTENCES

An indefinite phrase like 'a salesman' can be used to form an indefinite statement like 'A salesman is at the door.' Such a phrase can also be used to make a sentence which has the sense of a universal sentence. This sentence:

> A salesman is a person who sells something.

would naturally be understood as making a claim about every salesman. This is the *generic* use of the indefinite article (and the indefinite phrase). When an indefinite phrase is used to make a universal statement, the distinctions we made earlier apply. Such a statement can be affirmative or negative, can have existential force or lack it, and can have or not have modal force.

The quantifier 'only' can also be used to make universal statements. This sentence:

> Only students who pass the final will pass the course.

means that every student who passes the course will pass (will have passed) the final. And this sentence:

> The only students who will pass the course are those who pass the final.

means the same thing.

An 'If . . ., then . . .' sentence is a *conditional* sentence. Most conditional sentences that one encounters are not understood to make universal claims. But a conditional sentence can be used with the sense of a universal sentence. The sentence:

> If a student passes the course, then she will have passed the final.

has the sense of 'Any student who passes the course will have passed the final.'

A sentence about a type can be used to make a sentence which is close in meaning to a universal sentence. The sentence:

> The whale is a mammal.

provides information about every whale. However, sentences about types commonly have a modal force. And not all sentences about types "amount" to universal sentences. The sentence:

> The dinosaur is extinct.

does not mean that every dinosaur is extinct. Individual animals cannot be or become extinct. Only a species or a type of animal can be extinct.

There are even sentences without quantified phrases that are understood as universal sentences. Unquantified plural nouns are often used this way. The sentence:

> Whales are mammals.

would naturally be taken to mean that every whale is a mammal. And this sentence:

> Whales are not fish.

would naturally be taken to rule out there being a whale that is a fish.

*Exercise: Section 5

Determine which of the following sentences would naturally be understood as making universal claims.

1. Dogs have knocked over Larry's garbage cans.

2. Snakes are reptiles.

3. If Ralph meets a girl at the party, then he will ask her for a date.

4. If the test is given next Wednesday, then few students will attend class Friday.

5. A lawyer charged Heather $500 for making a will.

6. A lawyer must pass the bar in order to practice.

3-6 SINGULAR SENTENCES

Sentences about some or all individuals of a kind constitute an important class of sentences about individuals. Another important class is sentences formed with *singular terms*. A singular term is an expression for just one individual. Proper nouns are singular terms. So 'George Washington' and 'Napoleon' are singular terms. *Definite descriptions* are also singular terms. A definite description is a quantified phrase formed by prefixing the definite article 'the' to a common noun or noun phrase. The expressions 'the mother of George Washington' and 'the capital of New York State' are definite descriptions. Besides definite descriptions, there are other descriptive singular terms. Examples are 'George Washington's mother' and 'whoever discovered the elliptic orbits of the planets.'

A singular term is an expression for a single individual. This may be a real individual like George Washington or a fictional individual like Sherlock Holmes. We can even find singular terms which don't label any individual. The description 'the king of France in 1920' is one of these, for France had no king in 1920. A singular term is grammatically suited to represent just one individual, even if there doesn't happen to be such an individual (or there happens to be more than one). A singular term must be distinguished from a common noun or noun phrase which just happens to label a single individual. The phrase 'visible natural satellite of earth' labels only the Moon. And 'country which landed men on the Moon' fits only the United States. But these expressions aren't singular terms, because their grammatical role doesn't indicate that they apply to just one individual. (To know this we need extralinguistic information.)

A *singular sentence* is formed with a singular term, and makes a claim about the individual that term denotes. The following are singular sentences:

Chicago is a midwestern city.

The author of *Huckleberry Finn* was famous.

The sum of 7 and 5 is an even number.

Martha's favorite uncle is in the Mafia.

*Exercise: Section 6

Determine which of the following are singular sentences.

1. The President of the United States is a Republican.

2. The President of the United States is elected to a four-year term.

3. Jim asked Nancy to the party.

4. Everybody in his class likes Jesse.

4

The Artificial-
Language Strategy

4-0 SUMMARY

This chapter describes the strategy of the rest of the book: to develop artificial logical languages and use them as instruments to gain an understanding of semantic features in ordinary English. The strategy is described in some detail.

4-1 ARTIFICIAL LANGUAGES

In chapters 1 and 2, we encountered epistemological definitions of some logically important semantic features. The epistemic defintiions were analogous to operational definitions, for they provided criteria we can use to determine if we have a case of one of the features. One of these semantic features is *analytic truth*. A sentence is analytically true if it is true, and can be determined to be true simply on the basis of understanding it. The sentence:

(1) If something is scarlet, then it is red.

is analytically true. So is this sentence:

(2) Either there is an integer greater than 7 or there isn't.

There are also analytically false sentences—sentences which can be determined to be false simply on the basis of understanding them. Sentence (3) is analytically false:

(3) There are integers greater than 7 and there are no integers greater than 7.

However, we shall be more interested in analytic truth than analytic falsity. A sentence described simply as analytic is understood to be analytically true.

One of our main concerns in this logic course is to determine which sentences exemplify the logically important semantic features. We will develop procedures for establishing that we have instances of these features. But we study these procedures to get a better understanding of the semantic features, so that we can eventually recognize sentences which have them without employing the procedures. Another logically important semantic feature is *entailment*. Some sentences entail a further sentence if an understanding of the sentence is sufficient to determine that it isn't possible for the first sentences to be true without the further sentence being true. If one or more sentences entail a further sentence, we can determine on the basis of understanding them that the truth of the first sentences would guarantee the truth of the further sentence. The truth of the sentence that is entailed follows from the truth of the sentences that do the entailing.

A group of sentences are *incompatible* if we can determine on the basis of understanding them that they can't all be true together. And an inference is *valid* just in case its premises entail its conclusion. We can determine simply on the basis of understanding the premises and conclusion that it isn't possible for the premises to be true when the conclusion isn't.

The semantic features analyticity, entailment, incompatibility, and validity will be our concern in the rest of this book. There are some contemporary philosophers, most notably W. V. Quine, who have argued that such concepts as analyticity and entailment are not scientifically legitimate. The semantic concepts cannot be explained in ways these philosophers find satisfactory. However, their view is not accepted in this book. The semantic concepts may resist precise definitions, but they are not difficult to understand.

However, it *is* difficult to give a systematic and comprehensive account of the semantic features for a natural language like English. Natural languages contain a large number of expressions and a great variety of syntactic constructions. They are also subject to ambiguities of various kinds. The historical practice of logicians has been to develop and study artificial languages, much simpler than natural languages, and designed with logical perspicuity in mind. These artificial languages are instruments used to gain understanding of natural languages.

Artificial logical languages may contain expressions from a natural language, or they may be composed of completely new expressions. A logical language containing ordinary expressions is artificial in at least two respects: (1) It is artificially simple compared to a natural language, and (2) the logical expressions in these languages are assigned precise meanings, lacking in ambiguity—this contrasts with the meanings of natural-language expressions. If a logical language also contains expressions not taken from the natural language, this is a third source of artificiality. *Symbolic* logic studies languages in which some or all of the symbols are simply invented, and not borrowed from languages like English or Italian.

The artificial languages used in logic are designed to be logically perspicuous. This means that the logically important semantic features are easy to spot—at least, they are easier to spot in the artificial languages than in natural languages. Another thing that makes artificial logical languages convenient to study is their simplicity. For example, the "verbs" in some artificial languages don't have tenses. And many artificial languages lack plural forms. These simplifications help us focus on what concerns us, allowing us to ignore what is not relevant to a particular investigation.

How a logician regards artificial languages depends on his view of logic. Since I regard logic as a linguistic study, I regard the artificial languages as "modelling" aspects of natural languages. An artificial language isolates a small number of characteristics found in a natural language. A study of the artificial language uncovers the semantic effects of these characteristics.

Someone who thinks logic studies the most general features of reality will regard artificial languages as convenient devices for expressing very general truths. Proponents of this view sometimes claim that certain artificial languages reflect the very "make-up" of reality in a more accurate way than our ordinary language does. The person who thinks logic is a study of reasoning may regard artificial languages as well-suited for highlighting the most important aspects of reasoning. It has even been suggested that we should switch to artificial languages when we wish to reason in much the same way we switch to a mathematical notation when we wish to perform calculations. (This suggestion ignores the fact that we must constantly reason while we only occasionally need to calculate.)

In applied logic, we study artificial languages so that we can use them to understand particular sentences and arguments in English (or some other natural language). Pure logic, logical theory, is the study of artificial languages "for their own sakes." Even in logical theory, we are indirectly concerned with natural languages, for artificial logical languages share features with natural languages. An understanding of these features in an artificial language also gives an understanding of them as they occur in natural languages.

To develop an artificial language, we must give both the syntax and semantics of the language. We specify the elementary syntactic (grammatical) categories of the language, listing or describing the simple expressions that belong to these categories. Then we give rules for combining expressions to form complex expressions. Simple expressions are combined to form complex expressions; very often complex expressions may be combined to form expressions that are even more complex. After we give the syntax of an artificial language, we give a semantic account of the language. We explain the meanings of expressions of the language, and the truth codditions of sentences of the language.

*Exercise: Section 1

Determine which of the following are true.

1. We explain the syntax of an artificial language by explaining which sentences are analytic.

2. In logic, we use artificial languages as replacements for natural languages.

3. All artificial logical languages employ artificial symbols.

4. A semantic account for a language should enable us to determine under what conditions a sentence of the language is true.

4-2   LOGICAL FORM

To set up an artificial logical language, we identify the elementary syntactic categories, and their elements, and give rules for combining expressions. But we also identify distinctively logical expressions. The *logical form* of a sentence is determined by (1) the syntactic categories of its component expressions, (2) the distinctively logical expressions it contains, and (3) the manner in which its components are combined.

The logical form of a sentence is a structural feature of that sentence. Consider this sentence:

(1) Charlie is smart.

The word 'is' is considered to be a distinctively logical expression, but 'Charlie' and 'smart' are not. We can indicate the logical form of (1) like this:

(2) *Proper Noun* is *Adjective*

This gives syntactic information about the structure of (1), and shows which logical expressions occur where. The logical form of (1) is also exemplified by other sentences, as:

(3) Napoleon is French.

Sentences with the same logical form will have similar logical properties and relations.

In studying artificial logical languages, we are especially interested in logical form, and semantic features connected to logical form. We can recognize and describe the logical form of a sentence without bringing in meaning or truth. But a logical form has a meaning, and truth conditions. We can *recognize* a logical form without bringing in semantic considerations. To *understand* a logical form is to grasp its semantic dimension.

One semantic feature connected to logical form is *logical truth*. A logically true sentence can be determined to be true on the basis of (recognizing and) understanding its logical form. Understanding the logical form of a sentence is part of understanding the sentence's meaning. So if we can determine that a sentence is true on the basis of understanding its logical form, we are determining that the sentence is true on the basis of understanding its meaning. Logical truth is a special case of analytic truth. Any logically true sentence is also analytically true. But not every analytic sentence is logically true. The sentence:

(4) If some student is honest, then some student is honest or some student is smart.

is both logically true and analytically true. This sentence has the logical form displayed:

(5) If ____(1)____, then ____(1)____ or ____(2)____

where the blanks are to be filled by sentences.[1] If we reflect on the logical form shown by (5), and the truth conditions of sentences which have this form, we can determine that any such sentence will be true. The sentence:

(7) If a number is even, then it is not odd.

is analytic, but it is not logically true. To determine that it is true, we must consider the meanings of 'even' and 'odd.' But these are not logical words. (The criteria for determining that an expression is logical are controversial. The logical expressions that we shall consider in this book are clear cases of logical expressions. We will not attempt to determine what it is about these expressions that qualifies them as logical.)

Artificial logical languages are made logically perspicuous by making the logical forms of sentences in these languages perspicuous. As well as giving the syntax of an artificial logical language, we must identify specifically logical expressions. Knowledge of the syntax and the logical expressions enables us to recognize and characterize the logical forms of sentences of the language. And the semantic account for an artificial logical language must clearly specify the meanings of the logical expressions. It is often sufficient to

---

[1]Sentence (4), like most sentences, has more than one logical form. The different logical forms are more and less specific. More specific logical forms of (4) involve the structures of the component sentences as well as the structure displayed in (5). A more specific form is displayed by

(6) If some *common noun (i)* is *adjective (i)*, then some *common noun (i)* is *adjective (i)* or some *common noun (i)* is *adjective (ii)*

When someone speaks of *the* logical form of a sentence, he often means the most specific form.

indicate what kinds of meanings nonlogical expressions have. For example, if a logical language contains expressions from a natural language, and these are not logical expressions, then we can assume they have their normal meanings and not make any semantic specifications for them. Even an entirely artificial logical language will normally contain nonlogical expressions which correspond to certain expressions in a natural language. It will often be sufficient to assume that these have the same meanings as corresponding natural-language expressions, without providing specific details.

In studying artificial logical languages, we try to discover cases of semantic features linked to logical form. We start by being interested in a feature like analytic truth in ordinary English. When we set up an artificial language, we look for cases of analytic truth linked to logical form. Such cases of analytic truth are also cases of logical truth. Analytic truth is a *general semantic feature*. Logical truth is the *logical special case* of this general feature. Entailment, incompatibility, and validity are also general semantic features. Each has a logical special case which can be recognized on the basis of understanding logical form. The logical special case of entailment is (*logical*) *implication*. The logical special case of incompatibility is *logical incompatibility*. And the special case of validity is *logical validity*. In studying artificial logical languages, we will develop criteria for recognizing instances of these logical semantic features.

*Exercise: Section 2

Determine which of the following are true.

1. If a sentence is analytic, then it is logically true.

2. Logically true sentences are analytic.

3. If a sentence is false, it might still be logically true.

4. If understanding the logical forms of two sentences enables us to determine that one follows from the second, then the first is logically implied by the second.

4-3 EVALUATION

To determine whether a sentence is analytic, whether two sentences are incompatible, or whether an inference is valid is to *evaluate* the sentence, pair of sentences, or inference (with respect to the semantic feature in question). To evaluate sentences, inferences, etc. in a natural language involves two steps: (1) We translate the natural-language sentences into an artificial language. (2) We evaluate the translated sentences or inferences.

If a sentence in an artificial logical language is logically true, we will say that it is *logically distinguished*. If two or more sentences in an artificial language are related by a logically important semantic relation, this group of sentences is *logically distinguished*. And a logically valid inference in an artificial language is *logically distinguished*. In order to carry out the second step of the evaluation process above, we must develop techniques for recognizing and characterizing the logically distinguished items in a logical language.

In this book, we will develop a number of evaluation techniques for the different languages that we consider. Some techniques are applied to candidates one at a time. An example of this kind of technique is the use of diagrams which represent graphically what a sentence can be used to say. To determine whether two sentences are incompatible, we compare their diagrams to see if they rule each other out. Techniques which can be used to evaluate items one at a time may not contribute to giving us a systematically organized body of knowledge. The technique requires that we "bring" items to it to be checked; it does not enable us to produce (to generate) logically distinguished items. A technique which generates a systematically organized subject matter seems historically to be a goal for knowledge. (It is an interesting philosophical problem to determine the real importance of this goal.)

A *deductive system* can serve as an evaluative device. Such a system will consist of rules and possibly axioms for proving that certain items are logically distinguished, together with the results established according to these rules. A relatively simple set of rules (or rules and axioms) is sufficient to generate a large set of logically distinguished items. This set of rules provides organization, and so characterizes a whole body of knowledge. In this book, we will make use of deductive systems in exploring various logical languages. As well as organizing our knowledge of these languages, the systems will help us improve our ability to make (valid) deductive inferences. In constructing proofs of logically distinguished items, we shall also be making deductively correct inferences.

When we use some technique to evaluate sentences, groups of sentences, or arguments, we must insure that the technique is satisfactory. The technique must not lead us to call an argument valid unless the argument really is valid. There are various ways to justify techniques of evaluation. But at some point a person must rely on his understanding of the expressions involved. He must be able to recognize some simple instances of logically distinguished items. (Anyone who speaks and understands a language can do this. If, impossibly, a language user turned up who could not recognize any logically distinguished items, it would probably not be possible to teach that person to recognize them.) These simple instances of logically distinguished items do not need any further justification. The recognition of these simple instances can then provide a basis for establishing that other items are logically distinguished, and that certain techniques yield correct results.

There are no simple instances of logically distinguished items that must be the starting points for everyone in dealing with logically distinguished sentences, groups of sentences, and inferences. For every logically true sentence, for every group of sentences linked by a logical relation, and for every valid argument, it is possible to prove that these items are logically distinguished by appealing to other principles. There are no ultimate principles which everyone must accept without proof. But for every person, there must be some principles which that person recognizes to be correct, not needing further justification.

In developing techniques for evaluating items in the logical languages, we will start with principles simple enough to be recognized as correct by most people. We will then build on these principles to justify other principles and techniques.

4-4 OTHER LANGUAGES TO BE DEVELOPED

In the rest of the book, we will develop artificial languages we can use to get a better understanding of sentences about individuals. There are four artificial languages we will consider. The *Categorical language* is derived from the language investigated by Aristotle, the founder in the Western world of the study of logic. (In Indian culture, logic was developed independently.) The application of the Categorical language is quite limited. We will overcome some of these limitations by developing the *Extended Categorical* language—an enlarged version of the Categorical language. The two remaining artificial languages are the basic languages of modern logic. The *Propositional Connective* language and the *First-Order* language both belong to *symbolic logic*.

Although our goal is to increase our understanding of sentences about individuals, only the two Categorical languages and the First-Order language contribute directly to this goal. The Propositional Connective language is incorporated in the First-Order language, and forms an essential part of that language. But the Propositional Connective language can be studied on its own. When it is, it helps us to understand compound sentences which contain other sentences as parts.

It probably isn't possible to cover all four artificial languages in a one-semester course. There are several different "paths" that can be taken through the book. If optional sections are included, a one-semester course can be devoted to the Categorical language and the Extended Categorical language. Such a course is well-suited to the goals of an elementary logic course. By skipping optional sections, a one-semester course might cover the Categorical language, the Extended Categorical language, and the Propositional Connective language. Another course covers the Categorical language, the Propositional Connective language, and the First-Order language. And a course which considers only the Propositional Connective and the First-Order languages is both self-contained and complete.

Chapter 5

The Categorical Language

5-0 SUMMARY

This chapter explains the syntax and semantics of the Categorical language. Syntactic relations between sentences are used to characterize simple cases of implication, which are the building blocks of proofs establishing complicated cases. The Categorical deductive system contains proofs of implication and incompatibility. This system organizes our knowledge of the Categorical language, provides an understanding of the inferential meanings of logical expressions, and gives us practice in making deductively valid inferences. Instead of proofs, we use examples to show that sentences aren't linked by implication, or aren't incompatible. Venn diagrams are an alternative technique for detecting cases of implication and incompatibility. An optional section deals with formal fallacies.

5-1 CATEGORICAL SENTENCES

The study of the Categorical language, the simplest artificial language we shall consider, makes a good (and convenient) introduction to logic. The Categorical language is adapted from the artificial language studied by Aristotle. That language was the main focus of logical investigation until late in the nineteenth century. Our version of the Categorical language derives from changes made to Aristotle's language at the beginning of the modern period in logic. However, no version of Aristotle's language is now the main focus of logical investigation. That honor belongs to artificial languages which grow out of the Propositional Connective and First-Order languages.

To explain the syntax of the Categorical language, we give elementary syntactic categories, explain which elements belong, and then explain how to combine expressions from the elementary categories. One elementary category is *common nouns and unquantified noun phrases*. A common noun is a single word, like 'animal' or 'tree.' An unquantified noun phrase is complex, like 'red house' or 'man with a red beard,' but does not begin with a quantifier. (In what follows, I will just speak of noun phrases, and understand them to be unquantified.) A common noun or noun phrase denotes 0 or more individuals. The word 'vampire' denotes no individuals (0 individuals). But 'man' denotes lots of individuals, and 'thing' denotes everything. The common nouns and noun phrases that belong to the Categorical language are in the singular, but a noun phrase might contain a plural component—as 'man with two jobs.'

Although they are not themselves logical expressions, common nouns and noun phrases combine with members of the elementary category of logical expressions to form sentences. The basic logical expressions in the Categorical language are complex, and contain gaps. One of these is:

Every _____ is a(n) _____

The gaps are to be filled with common nouns or noun phrases. The following is a sentence of the Categorical language:

Every student is an agreeable person.

The *subject* is the word filling the first gap, while the second gap is filled by the *predicate*. (This is a special use of the word 'predicate' in relation to the Categorical language. In other contexts, we will regard a predicate as an expression like '____ is a dog.') In ordinary English, sentences can be formed by combining 'Every ____ is a(n) ____' with singular terms, as in:

Every Jim Smith is a person with a common name.

Every military officer is a Napoleon.

These sentences *do not* belong to the Categorical language.

The following are also basic logical expressions:

No _____ is a(n) _____

Some _____ is a(n) _____

Some _____ is not a(n) _____

The four basic logical expressions combine with common nouns and noun phrases to form *categorical sentences*. The Categorical language contains *universal affirmative* sentences:

Every dog is a pet.

and *universal negative* sentences:

No baseball bat is a work of art.

The sentences which aren't universal will be called *particular*. There are *particular affirmative* sentences:

Some hockey player is a man with no teeth.

and *particular negative* sentences:

Some college professor is not an intellectual.

The names for the kinds of categorical sentence are abbreviated by capital letters. A universal affirmative sentence is called an A sentence. A particular affirmative sentence is an I sentence. These letters are the first two vowels in the Latin word 'affirmo' (which means *I affirm*). A universal negative sentence is an E sentence and a particular negative sentence is an O sentence. These letters are from the Latin word 'nego' (*I deny*).

*Exercise: Section 1

For 1–4, determine which sentences are universal, particular, affirmative, and negative.

1. No professional football player is a poorly paid person.

2. Some young radical is not a Marxist.

3. Every European country is a country without foreign colonies.

4. Some youthful politician is a person who is not dishonest.

For 5–8, determine which sentences are A, E, I, and O.

5. Every positive integer is an odd number.

6. Some prime number is not an odd number.

7. No irrational number is an integer.

8. Every even number is a number that isn't odd.

5-2 SEMANTICS

We have identified the elementary syntactic categories of common nouns and noun phrases and of logical expressions. A fancier name for these basic logical expressions is *two-place sentence-forming functors*. A functor is an expression with gaps, which combines with other expressions to form a complex expression. Sentences in the Categorical language also constitute a syntactic category, but not an elementary category.

Common nouns and noun phrases in the Categorical language have their ordinary meanings. We will explain the meanings of the logical expressions by giving the truth conditions of the sentences they form. This semantic account will take care of meaning and truth conditions all at once.

For all four logical expressions, the verb 'is' is understood in a timeless sense. Instead of writing 'No Roman emperor was a good philosopher,' we write 'No Roman emperor is a good philosopher.' A sentence 'No α is a β' (these are lower case Greek letters—'α' is alpha and 'β' is beta) means that no individual in the past, present, or future which is denoted by α (which is, was, or will be denoted by α) is also an individual denoted by β. Only the verb of the logical expression is understood timelessly. To make a statement about a specific time, we can use tenses or dates in the subject or predicate of the sentence. This is illustrated:

Some native of Corsica is a French emperor in 1805.

Every dinosaur is an animal that is now dead.

The sentence 'Some young man in 1800 is an old man in 1850' is true, while 'No young man is an old man' is false. (Some person denoted by 'young man' in 1800 is the same person denoted by 'old man' in 1850.) However, we will often understand a common noun α to mean *individuals that are now* α. With that understanding, the sentence 'No young man is an old man' is true.

Universal sentences in the Categorical language are understood unrestrictedly. The sentence:

Every cow is an animal that gives milk.

means absolutely every cow is a milk-giver, and is false. And this sentence:

No dog is an animal with (exactly) three legs.

is also false. Universal sentences in the Categorical language have no modal force. The logical expressions are used to make claims only about actual individuals. A sentence 'Every α is a β' rules out there being an actual case of an α which isn't a β. It doesn't mean that nothing *could be* an α without being a β.

Universal sentences in the Categorical language have no existential force. The subject of a true universal sentence may not denote any individuals. Since universal affirmative sentences have neither modal nor existential force, they are understood mathematically. In the Categorical language, a sentence 'Every α is a β' is true if there is nothing denoted by the subject which fails to be denoted by the predicate. The sentence 'Every vampire is a kind person' only rules out there being a vampire which isn't a kind person, so it is true—if there aren't any vampires at all, then nothing is both a vampire and not a kind person. The sentence 'Every cow is a mammal' is also true; there are cows, of course, but none of them fails to be a mammal.

If there don't happen to be any α's, then a sentence 'Every α is a β' is *vacuously* true. Because A sentences are understood mathematically, a sentence 'Every α is a β' can't be false unless there is an α. The sentence 'Every dog is a pet' is false. It rules out things which actually exist, for instance, wild dogs. Our reason for adopting the mathematical understanding for universal affirmative sentences is that doing this simplifies the logical features of the Categorical language. It is also possible to develop a logical language in which universal affirmative sentences have the ordinary, existential, meaning.

Although we don't call our understanding of universal negative sentences mathematical, these sentences don't indicate whether their subjects or predicates denote any individuals. The sentence 'No vampire is a kind person' rules out individuals which aren't to be found in the past, present, or future. The sentence is true, even though 'Every vampire is a kind person' is also true. And the sentence 'No cow is a reptile' is true. Cows exist, but cows which are reptiles don't.

For a sentence 'Some α is a β' to be true, at least one individual denoted by the subject must also be denoted by the predicate. It is false otherwise: if not a single thing is both α and β. A sentence 'Some α is not a β' is true just in case at least one individual denoted by the subject is not denoted by the predicate. It is false if there is no such individual. (Both kinds of universal sentence are true when the subject denotes zero individuals. Both kinds of particular sentence are false in that case.)

*Exercise: Section 2

Select the correct answers.

1. Let us agree that there are no vampires. Determine which of the following categorical sentences are true. (Check *all* correct answers.)

   a. Every vampire is a kind person.
   b. No vampire is a kind person.
   c. Some vampire is a kind person.
   d. Some vampire is not a kind person.

2. Suppose there is not a single politician who fails (or failed or will fail) to be a totally honest person. Given this hypothesis, determine which of the following categorical sentences are true.

   a. No politician is an honest person.
   b. No dishonest person is a politician.
   c. Every dishonest person is a person who is not a politician.
   d. Some politician is an honest person.
   e. Some politician is not an honest person.

3. While we continue to agree that there are no vampires (and never were nor will be), determine which of these Categorical-language sentences are true:

   a. Every kind person is a vampire.
   b. No kind person is a vampire.
   c. Some kind person is a vampire.
   d. Some kind person is not a vampire.

5-3   LOGICAL FORM

Before we can use the Categorical language to detect the semantic features of ordinary sentences about individuals, we must learn to detect the semantic features of sentences in the Categorical language. This language is designed to be logically perspicuous. This helps us spot semantic features associated with logical form.

The logical form of a sentence is determined by (1) the syntactic categories of its component expressions, (2) the specifically logical expressions it contains, and (3) the organization of the components to constitute the sentence. The logical form of a sentence is an abstract feature of the sentence. Different sentences can have the same logical form. In the Categorical language, every A sentence has the same logical form. Semantic features like analytic truth and entailment are *general*. In the Categorical language, we look for instances of these features which are linked to logical form. These instances constitute the logical special cases of the general semantic features.

Each kind of categorical sentence has a distinctive logical form. Every A sentence has the same logical form, every E sentence has the same form, etc. As well as having a general logical form in common, sentences of one kind can have more specialized logical forms. Each of the following A sentences shares a logical form:

   Every cow is a mammal.

   Every mammal is a cow.

   Every cow is a cow.

The third sentence also has a form it does not share with the first two. The third sentence is logically true, but the first two are not.

In order to concentrate on the logical form of a sentence, we make use of *variables*. These are letters of some kind which we use to replace expressions. We can highlight the logical form of the following sentence:

   Every cow is a mammal.

like this:

Every S is a P

The variable which replaces an expression *does not* abbreviate that expression. We use variables which have no meaning to replace expressions with meaning, so that we can ignore, or "abstract away from," features of a sentence which are without logical interest. If we start with a sentence, and replace some expressions with variables, the result is *not* a sentence—and is not true or false. The result is a *formula*. (But we will regard sentences as a *special case* of formulas. Every sentence is a formula. Not every formula is a sentence.)

We will use capital Latin letters as variables to replace common nouns and noun phrases. (These are ordinary capital letters.) In the example above, the variables 'S' and 'P' *suggest* the words 'subject' and 'predicate.' This isn't necessary. We can also consider formulas like this:

Every P is an S

Some M is not an N

When a formula contains no nonlogical expressions, we will say that it *displays* a logical form. The following formulas display logical forms:

No A is an A

Some C is not a D

(But this formula:

Some M is an animal

is not said to display such a form.) As well as helping us focus on logical form, variables make it easier to state and establish general results. When we determine that the following sentences imply each other:

No child is a completely honest person.

No completely honest person is a child.

we have a quite specific result. By dealing with formulas, we can determine that any pair of sentences which display this pattern are equivalent:

No M is an N

No N is an M

*Exercise: Section 3

Write formulas which display the logical forms of the following sentences. Show the most specific forms that you can.

1. Some dog is not a pet.

2. Some dog is not a dog.

3. Every famous general is a military leader.

4. No general is a famous general.

5-4 THE COMPLEMENT OF AN EXPRESSION

We will expand the Categorical language by adding a new logical expression. The previous logical expressions combine with two nouns (or noun phrases) to form a sentence. The new expression combines with one noun or noun phrase to form a different noun; it is a *noun-forming functor*. This expression is 'non-_____,' For example, we can take the noun 'person' and obtain the new noun 'non-person.' Or, starting with 'house,' we get 'non-house.' (In ordinary words, the prefix 'non' is frequently attached without a hyphen. But the hyphen is part of the expression we have added to the Categorical language.)

A noun obtained by prefixing 'non-' is the *complement* of the original noun. 'Non-person' is the complement of 'person.' The complement of a term denotes just the individuals not denoted by the term. A term and its complement divide reality. Whatever is not a person is a non-person. Tables, mountains, chairs, and numbers are non-persons. Ordinarily, a noun will denote some individuals and its complement will denote the rest. But if a term denotes all individuals, like 'thing' does, then its complement ('non-thing' in this case) denotes zero individuals. The complement of a term which denotes zero individuals denotes all individuals.

With a complex noun phrase, the prefix 'non-' must apply to the whole expression. We achieve this by using parentheses. The complement of 'white horse' is 'non-(white horse),' and the complement of 'fat lady wearing a wig' is 'non-(fat lady wearing a wig).' You should note that while 'non-horse' is the complement of 'horse,' 'white non-horse' is not the complement of 'white horse.' A white non-horse must be white, but a black horse is a non-(white horse).

The presence of 'non-_____' in a sentence does not affect the classification of the sentence as an A, E, I, or O sentence. The sentence 'Some woman is a non-(logic teacher)' is a particular affirmative sentence, an I sentence; even though it is equivalent to 'Some woman is not a logic teacher,' which is an O sentence.

*Exercise: Section 4

For 1–4, write the complements of these expressions.

1. Methodist

2. Protestant Christian

3. president of the United States

4. non-animal

For 5–8, determine which of the following are true. (Interpret categorical sentences as sentences of the Categorical language).

5. The complement of the complement of an expression denotes the same individuals as the expression does.

6. If 'non-Englishman' is the predicate of a particular sentence, then that sentence is negative.

7. Every white non-horse is a non-(white horse).

8. Every non-(white horse) is a white non-horse.

5-5 SOME SYNTACTIC RELATIONS

There are certain syntactic relations between sentences of the Categorical language for which we shall provide names. Our strategy in investigating the Categorical language is to begin by locating simple cases of semantic features; we are especially concerned to find simple cases of implication. We describe the simple cases in terms of syntactic patterns —for which we need our syntactic vocabulary. Next we establish complicated cases of semantic features by reducing them to simple cases. We combine the syntactic patterns of the simple cases to yield the complex patterns characteristic of the complicated cases.

The first syntactic relation we shall consider is *conversion*. We obtain the *converse* of a categorical sentence by interchanging its subject and predicate. The converse of 'No European city is a capital of an African country' is: No capital of an African country is a European city. When we start with one sentence and then obtain its converse, we have *converted* the first sentence. The converse of any kind of categorical sentence is a sentence of the same kind. (I.e., the converse of a universal affirmative sentence is a universal affirmative sentence, the converse of an E sentence is an E sentence, etc.) And if one sentence is the converse of a second, then the second is the converse of the first.

The relation of *obversion* involves the expression 'non-.' We obtain the *obverse* of a sentence by (1) changing its quality (from affirmative to negative, or vice versa), and (2) replacing its predicate by the complement of the predicate. The obverse of a sentence 'Some *M* is not an *N*' would be 'Some *M* is a non-*N*.' And the obverse of 'Some French restaurant is a three-star restaurant' is this: Some French restaurant is not a non-(three-star restaurant).

If we start with a sentence like 'No chemist is an astrologer,' and obtain its obverse 'Every chemist is a non-astrologer,' the first sentence is *not* the obverse of the second. The obverse of 'Every chemist is a non-astrologer' is this: No chemist is a non-non-astrologer. The obverse of an E sentence is an A sentence, and the obverse of an A sentence is an E sentence, but the obverse-obverse of an E sentence is a different E sentence. (The situation is unlike the case of conversion. The converse-converse of a categorical sentence is the sentence itself.)

The last syntactic relation for which we shall supply a name is *contraposition*. This relation is a combination of obversion and conversion. If we take a categorical sentence, obvert this, then convert the result, and finally obvert that sentence, we have the *contrapositive* of the original. So, for example, we can begin with:

(1) Every statesman is a politician.

Obverting (1) yields:

(2) No statesman is a non-politician.

Then convert:

(3) No non-politician is a statesman.

And, finally, obvert (3) to obtain the contrapositive of (1):

(4) Every non-politician is a non-statesman.

A simpler recipe for obtaining the contrapositive is this: (i) replace the subject and the predicate by their complements, and (ii) interchange them. The contrapositive of 'Some man is an island' is this: Some non-island is a non-man.

*Exercise: Section 5

In this exercise we will use these sentences:

(a) Every war is a human tragedy.
(b) No year is a spatial location.
(c) Some prime number is a small number.
(d) Some property is not a color.

1. Write the converse of each sentence.

2. Write the obverse of each sentence.

3. Write the contrapositive of each sentence.

5-6   IMPLICATION AND EQUIVALENCE

Entailment is a general semantic relation. The logical special case of entailment is *implication*. Some sentences imply a further sentence if an understanding of the logical forms of the sentences is sufficient to determine that the first sentences can't be true when the further sentence isn't. The truth of the first sentences carries over to the further sentence. Now that we have acquired a syntactic vocabulary, we want to use it to describe instances of implication. We know what conversion is, but we want to find out which sentences imply their converses.

Does an A sentence imply its converse? If every *B* is a *C*, does it follow that every *C* is a *B*? It is easier to show that one kind of sentence doesn't imply another than to show that there is implication. If one sentence is true and a second is false, the first cannot imply the second. The A sentence 'Every dog is a mammal' is true, and its converse 'Every mammal is a dog' is false. Since this A sentence does not imply its converse, we know that it isn't true that all A sentences imply their converses.

But some A sentences may imply their converses. An A sentence with the same subject and predicate:

Every *S* is an *S*

is its own converse. There is no way for such a sentence to be true when its converse is false. A sentences do not, *in general*, imply their converses. But those A sentences whose subjects and predicates are the same imply their converses. (An A sentence whose subject differs from the predicate by an even number of 'non-'s, as 'animal' and 'non-non-animal,' will also imply its converse.)

In studying implication, we must not forget the difference between implication and entailment. A sentence that implies another also entails the other. But if one sentence does not imply a second, it may still entail the second. These A sentences:

(1) Every bachelor is an unmarried adult male human.

(2) Every unmarried adult male human is a bachelor.

are related by conversion. Neither implies the other, but they entail one another.

A formula that displays the logical form of a sentence *symbolizes* that sentence. Formula (3) symbolizes sentence (4):

(3) Some *M* is not an *N*

(4) Some person is not a man.

Actually, (3) symbolizes every sentence which has the displayed form. In investigating logical semantic features, we must use two or more formulas to deal with the forms of two or more sentences. To deal with the relation between (5) and (6):

(5) No even number is a square root of 9.

(6) No square root of 9 is an even number.

we might consider these formulas:

(7) No *A* is a *B*

(8) No *B* is an *A*

Which variables we use is not important, but it is important that we use exactly two. When we have several sentences, and formulas displaying the forms of these sentences —where the same expression is replaced by the same variable throughout, and different expressions are replaced by different variables—the formulas *jointly symbolize* the sentences. Formulas (7) and (8) jointly symbolize (5) and (6).

To show that a sentence of one kind does not imply a sentence of a second kind, it is sufficient to find a pair of sentences of the two kinds, where the first sentence is true and the second is false. This technique can't be used to show that there is implication. Though the following sentences are both true, neither implies the other.

(9) Every creature with a heart is a creature with a kidney.

(10) Every creature with a kidney is a creature with a heart.

To show that one kind of sentence implies another, we employ two "procedures": (1) In simple cases, we rely on our understanding of the kinds of sentences involved. (2) We "reduce" complicated cases to simple cases. Let us consider whether particular affirmative sentences imply their converses. Does a sentence having the form (11) imply one with the form displayed by (12)?

(11) Some *A* is a *B*

(12) Some *B* is an *A*

Each sentence is true just in case at least one individual is both *A* and *B*. There is no way for an I sentence to be true when its converse is false. I sentences imply their converses. Similarly, it is easy to see that an E sentence implies its converse. If (13) is true, so must be (14):

(13) No *S* is a *P*

(14) No *P* is an *S*

What about particular negative sentences? Does (15) imply (16)?

(15) Some *M* is not an *N*

(16) Some *N* is not an *M*

Since we can find a true O sentence with a false converse:

(17) Some mammal is not a dog.

(18) Some dog is not a mammal.

there is no implication. O sentences do not, in general, imply their converses. But some O sentences do. A sentence with this form:

(19) Some *S* is not an *S*

can't possibly be true. But (19) is its own converse, and it does imply itself. *Every* sentence implies itself.

E and I sentences imply their converses. A and O sentences don't, in general, imply their converses. And if we know that one sentence doesn't imply another, this doesn't tell us about entailment. Now we shall consider the semantic relation of *equivalence*. Two sentences are equivalent if each entails the other. Two sentences are *logically* equivalent if each implies the other. Which sentences are equivalent to their converses? It is clear that A and O sentences are not, in general, equivalent to their converses. If they have the same subject and predicate, they will be equivalent; *every* sentence is equivalent to itself. But consider an E or I sentence, which implies its converse. If one sentence is the converse of a second, then the second is the converse of the first. Since the converse of an E sentence is also an E sentence, the converse implies *its* converse—this is the original E sentence. Any sentence which implies its converse is equivalent to its converse.

*Exercise: Section 6

Determine which of the following pairs of sentences are logically equivalent.

	a	b
1.	Every giraffe is an animal.	Every animal is a giraffe.
2.	Some animal is a giraffe.	Some giraffe is an animal.
3.	No animal is a giraffe.	No giraffe is an animal.
4.	Some giraffe is not a giraffe.	Some giraffe is not a giraffe.

Consider obversion. Formulas (20) and (21) jointly symbolize an A sentence and its obverse.

(20) Every *S* is a *P*

(21) No *S* is a non-*P*

Does an A sentence imply its obverse? This case is simple enough to rely on our understanding of the two forms. If every *S* is a *P*, then not even one *S* can fail to be a *P*. Not even one *S* can be a non-*P*. Not only does an A sentence imply its obverse, but it is clear that the sentences are equivalent. For if no *S* is a non-*P*, then every *S* must be a *P*. We can also rely on our understanding to determine that an E sentence is equivalent to its obverse:

(22) No *R* is an *S*

(23) Every *R* is a non-*S*

If nothing is both *R* and *S*, then whatever is an *R* must be something other than an *S*—it must be a non-*S*. Similarly, if every *R* is a non-*S*, then nothing can be both *R* and *S*.

It is even easier to see that particular sentences are equivalent to their obverses:

(24) Some *C* is a *D*

(25) Some *C* is not a non-*D*

To be not a non-*D* is the same as being a *D*. And

(26) Some *C* is not a *D*

(27) Some *C* is a non-*D*

must surely have the same truth value. Both E and I sentences imply (and are equivalent to) their converses. Every kind of sentence implies and is equivalent to its obverse.

*Exercise: Section 6 (cont.)

Determine in which cases the sentence in the a column implies the sentence in the b column.

a	b
5. Every secretary is a typist.	Every typist is a secretary.
6. Every stenographer is a secretary.	No stenographer is a non-secretary.
7. Some secretary is not a woman.	Some woman is not a secretary.
8. No professor is a chairman.	Every professor is a non-chairman.

Those cases of conversion and obversion where there is implication (these are *positive* cases of implication) are simple. We will reduce complicated cases of implication to these simple cases. It is important to remember the simple positive cases of implication. We can't remember the complicated cases (there are too many), but we don't need to. We deal with the complicated cases by establishing them when they come up. In this course, memory does not play a central role. We must learn and remember a technical vocabulary. We must remember simple semantic features and some simple techniques. But in investigating and applying artificial languages, the main thing required is that each student develop skills for solving problems.

The instances of contraposition which are positive cases of implication are not simple. They must be justified by reducing them to simple cases. Consider an A sentence and its contrapositive:

(28) Every *F* is a *G*

(29) Every non-*G* is a non-*F*

If this were a *negative* case of implication, we could find a true A sentence and a false contrapositive. But if we look for such a *counterexample* (it would run *counter* to a claim that there is implication), we won't find one. So we will try to use our knowledge of conversion and obversion to show that there is implication. We already know that the contrapositive of a sentence is the obverse of the converse of the obverse of that sentence. We use this knowledge to construct a chain of inferences:

(30) Every *F* is a *G*

(31) No *F* is a non-*G*

(32) No non-*G* is an *F*

(33) Every non-*G* is a non-*F*

Every kind of sentence implies its obverse, so (30) implies (31). Sentence (31) is an E sentence, and E sentences imply their converses. So (31) implies (32). But (32) implies its obverse, which is (33). Since there is a chain of simple implications linking (30) to (33), we know that (30) implies (33). (The truth of (30) would carry down the chain to (33).) Since every pair in this chain is actually linked by equivalence, we can turn the chain over, starting with (33) to reach (30). This shows us that an A sentence is equivalent to its contrapositive.

A genuine inference involves sentences which are premisses and a sentence which is the conclusion. The formulas (30)–(33) are not sentences, so we do not actually have a chain of inferences. Instead we have what might be called a *schematic* chain of inferences, or the outline of a chain of inferences. Considering this schematic chain is sufficient to convince us that an A sentence is equivalent to its contrapositive. A chain of simple inferences is a *proof*. So (30)–(33) is a schematic proof.

We can use examples to show that an E sentence doesn't imply its contrapositive:

(34) No dog is a cat.

(35) No non-cat is a non-dog.

(Any turtle is a non-cat that is a non-dog.) E sentences don't, in general, imply their contrapositives, but some E sentences do. An E sentence like the following implies (and is equivalent to) its contrapositive:

(36) No non-S is an S

I sentences don't imply their contrapositives. It is true that some animals are things, while it is definitely not true that some non-things are non-animals. (There are no non-things.) O sentences are like A sentences in implying their contrapositives. This implication is complicated, and needs to be established by a proof. In constructing a proof, we normally make a column of sentences or formulas. We also write a justification to the right of each sentence or formula, to explain where it comes from. The following proof shows that an O sentence implies its contrapositive:

(37) Some P is not a Q hypothesis

(38) Some P is a non-Q (37), obversion

(39) Some non-Q is a P (38), conversion of I

(40) Some non-Q is not a non-P (39), obversion

The hypothesis (or hypotheses) of a proof is a sentence or formula we assume to be true, in order to determine what follows from it. The steps after the hypothesis in this proof use our knowledge of the simple cases of implication to bridge the gap between an O sentence and its contrapositive. (When we turn the proof over, we get a different proof which requires new reasons to justify the steps.)

The chart below summarizes our study of semantic logical relations in the Categorical language.

Kind of Sentence	Converse (Positive cases are simple cases)	Obverse (These are simple cases)	Contrapositive
Universal Affirmative, A	Does not imply*	Implies Equivalent	Implies Equivalent

Kind of Sentence	Converse (Positive cases are simple cases)	Obverse (These are simple cases)	Contrapositive
Universal Negative, E	Implies Equivalent	Implies Equivalent	Does not imply*
Particular Affirmative, I	Implies Equivalent	Implies Equivalent	Does not imply*
Particular Negative, O	Does not imply*	Implies Equivalent	Implies Equivalent

(*Although these are not, in general, cases of implication, some sentences of this type do imply the related sentences.)

*Exercise: Section 6 (cont.)

Determine which of the following pairs imply each other.

a	**b**
9. Every airplane is a winged vehicle.	Every non-(winged vehicle) is a non-airplane.
10. Some submarine is not a non-(naval vessel).	Some submarine is a naval vessel.
11. Some wagon is an Amish possession.	Some non-(Amish possession) is a non-wagon.
12. Some trailer is not a tractor.	Some tractor is not a trailer.

We have considered semantic relations between sentences related by conversion, obversion, and contraposition. We can deal with other sentences than these. But in doing so, we will continue to regard the positive cases of implication for conversion and obversion as our "official" simple cases. To determine whether (41) implies (42):

(41) Every bus is a train.

(42) No train is a non-bus.

we can consider formulas which display the most specific logical forms of the sentences:

(43) Every B is a T

(44) No T is a non-B

These examples:

(45) Every bus is a vehicle.

(46) No vehicle is a non-bus.

show that sentences like (43) don't, in general, imply sentences like (44). Sentence (41) does not imply (42). Now consider these sentences:

(47) Some car is a taxi.

(48) Some taxi is not a non-car.

If we look for a true sentence with the form of (47) and a corresponding false sentence with the form of (48), we won't find them. But we can construct a proof from (47) to (48):

1	Some car is a taxi.	hypothesis
2	Some taxi is a car.	1, conversion of I
3	Some taxi is not a non-car.	2, obversion

(In a proof we can either use formulas or actual sentences.)

In constructing proofs, we write 'conversion of I' or 'conversion of E' to justify implication based on conversion. We don't need to specify a kind of sentence for obversion. But there is a difference between reasoning from a sentence to its obverse and reasoning to the sentence from its obverse. Going *to* the obverse will be called *Obverse Introduction*. Going *from* the obverse will be called *Obverse Elimination*. The proof above will now be written:

1	Some car is a taxi.	hypothesis
2	Some taxi is a car.	1, conversion of I
3	Some taxi is not a non-car.	2, Obverse Introduction

The following proof involves Obverse Elimination.

1	Every M is a non-N	hypothesis
2	No M is an N	1, Obverse Elimination
3	No N is an M	2, conversion of E
4	Every N is a non-M	3, Obverse Introduction

*Exercise: Section 6 (cont.)

Determine which pairs of sentences are linked by implication from left to right. Either identify the relation as one of conversion, obversion, or contraposition, and rely on our knowledge of implication and equivalence for these syntactic relations, or else use proofs and counterexamples to deal with the sentences.

a	b
13. No pirate is a Buddhist monk.	Some Buddhist monk is not a pirate.
14. Every rustler is a cowboy.	No cowboy is a non-rustler.
15. Every bank robber is a non-(college freshman).	No college freshman is a bank robber.
16. Some burglar is a homeowner.	Some homeowner is a burglar.
17. Some non-(bank owner) is a bandit.	Some bandit is not a bank owner.
18. Some brigand is not a movie star.	Some non-(movie star) is a non-non-brigand.

5-7 LOGICAL TRUTH

A sentence is analytic if it can be determined to be true simply on the basis of understanding it. Analytic sentences which can be determined to be true on the basis of understanding their logical forms are logically true. In the Categorical language, the subject of a true particular sentence must denote at least one individual. But whether or not a common noun denotes at least one individual is not a logical matter. So no particular sentence is logically true. However, some universal sentences are logically true. A sentence having this form:

Every *B* is a *B*

must be true—regardless of whether there is a *B*. Since an A sentence is equivalent to its obverse and to its contrapositive, the following will also be logically true:

No *B* is a non-*B*

Every non-*B* is a non-*B*

(But this last is simply another case where the subject and predicate are the same.) If we start with a logically true sentence and prefix either the subject or the predicate with an even number of 'non-'s, the result will be logically true. This sentence:

Every cow is a non-non-cow.

is logically true.

*Exercise: Section 7

Determine which of the following are logically true.

1. Every acrobat is a non-acrobat.

2. No clown is a non-clown.

3. Some juggler is a juggler.

4. Every non-non-(bareback rider) is a bareback rider.

5-8 VENN DIAGRAMS

There are various kinds of diagrams which can be used to get a better understanding of sentences in the Categorical language, and of their logically important features. The diagrams we shall use are abstract "pictures" of a sentence's logical content. *Venn diagrams* are named for the English logician John Venn. The basic element of Venn diagrams is a circle. These circles represent the individuals denoted by a common noun or noun phrase.

We could represent wolves by this circle:

wolf

Since different circles represent different kinds of thing, we normally label the circles.
An empty circle:

represents wolves but it doesn't tell us anything about them. This circle is like a word
occurring by itself: wolf. A word must normally occur in a sentence before it conveys information. In the Categorical language, there are two things we indicate about individuals
of a certain kind: either (1) there is an individual of that kind, or (2) there is no such individual. To indicate that there is no such individual, we shade the circle:

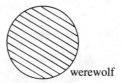

This diagram pictures that "part" of the world made up of werewolves; it shows that there
is nothing there. The werewolf part is empty. (This is what the diagram shows; but it may
not show the true situation.) To indicate that there is a thing of a kind, we place an 'X' in
the circle:

We can think of this 'X' as representing a wolf.
A categorical sentence contains two nouns, and indicates a connection between the
individuals these nouns denote. The diagram for a categorical sentence contains two over-
lapping circles:

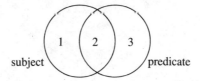

Each section in the diagram represents a different kind of thing. Section 1 represents those
individuals denoted by the subject but not by the predicate. Section 2 represents those individuals denoted by both the subject and the predicate. And section 3 represents the individuals denoted by the predicate but not the subject.

Suppose we have two expressions, *B* and *C*. To indicate the individuals which are not *B* (which are non-*B*), we will place a line over the '*B*.' Then we can show which individuals are represented by the different sections like this:

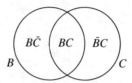

('$B\bar{C}$' indicates individuals which are *B* but not *C*.) Two terms give four combinations: (1) $B\bar{C}$, (2) BC, (3) $\bar{B}C$, (4) $\bar{B}\bar{C}$. The two circles represent only three of the combinations. When we need to represent the fourth combination, we draw a rectangle around the circles:

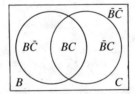

Venn diagrams can represent the logical content of categorical sentences. Consider an A sentence: Every *B* is a *C*. This sentence rules something out but doesn't indicate existence. Its diagram should contain shading but no 'X.' The A sentence rules out a *B* which isn't a *C*:

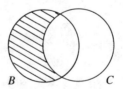

(The rectangle around the circles is omitted when all marking is in the circles.) The sentence declares that the portion of the world for *B*'s which aren't *C*'s is empty.

An E sentence 'No *B* is a *C*' rules out a thing being both a *B* and a *C*:

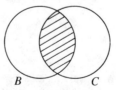

Particular sentences don't indicate that any portions of the world are empty. Particular sentences make existence claims. To show that some *B* is a *C*, we use this diagram:

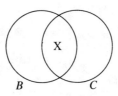

To show that some B is not a C, we need an 'X' in the section $B\bar{C}$:

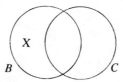

The four "plain" kinds of categorical sentence are easy to diagram. But suppose we want a diagram for 'Every M is a non-N.' This rules out an M which is not a non-N (which is an N):

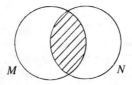

A sentence 'Every non-M is an N' doesn't concern the M circle. Instead it affects a non-M section. The sentence rules out a non-M also being non-N:

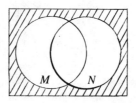

To diagram 'Some M is not a non-N' we need an 'X.' It belongs in the M circle. Since not being a non-N *is* being an N, we diagram it:

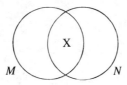

But a sentence 'Some non-M is not an N' requires the rectangle:

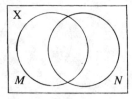

But a sentence 'Some non-*M* is not an *N*' requires the rectangle:

If a categorical sentence contains just one term (or a term and its complement, or a term and the complement of its complement, etc.), we don't need two circles. This sentence:

Every mouse is a mouse.

requires a single circle:

But how do we mark the diagram? The sentence rules out there being a mouse which isn't a mouse. The empty diagram also rules out that combination, by not providing a place for it. There is nothing in the diagram to shade; the empty diagram shows what the sentence says. This indicates that the logically true sentence conveys no information.

The sentence 'No werewolf is a werewolf' has content:

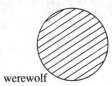

The sentence is true; the diagram is an accurate picture of the world.

The sentence 'Some person is not a person' requires an 'X' in its diagram. But there is no place in this diagram:

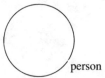

for the 'X' to go. There is no place where the person circle doesn't overlap the person circle. The sentence is impossible to diagram because it makes an impossible claim. The sentence is *logically false*—understanding the sentence's logical form is sufficient for determining that the sentence is false.

*Exercise A: Section 8

Draw Venn diagrams for these sentences.

1. Some non-dog is a tiger.

2. Every dog is an animal.

3. No dog is a non-dog.

4. Every non-dog is a non-animal.

5. Some non-dog is not a dog.

Venn diagrams can be used to discover the logical semantic relations between sentences of the Categorical language. Suppose sentence *p* implies sentence *q*. What should we expect to find in the diagrams for these two sentences? Sentence *p* makes a claim about the way things are. (It can be *used* to make such a claim.) And so does sentence *q*. If *p* implies *q*, the claim made by *p* should "include" the claim made by *q*. We already know that an E sentence implies (and is equivalent to) its converse. Let's take a look at the diagrams for an E sentence and its converse:

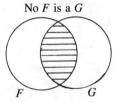

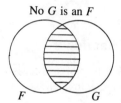

The two sentences have the same diagram. This is a sign that they say the same thing— which means that they are equivalent. Equivalent sentences imply each other.

Now consider two sentences 'Every *M* is an *N*' and 'No non-*N* is an *M*':

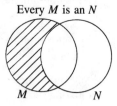

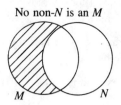

These diagrams also show equivalence (and implication). But in comparing the diagrams for two sentences, as 'Every carpenter is a wood-worker' and 'No wood-worker is a non-carpenter,' it is important that the circles have the same order:

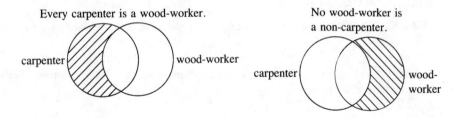

If we reversed the order of either diagram, it would appear that we had a case of equivalence. But the sentences are not equivalent; neither sentence implies the other.

The only cases of implication that we have so far considered are also cases of equivalence. So when we use diagrams to test for implication, we can also look for equivalence. The sign that two sentences are equivalent is that they have the same diagram, if they can be diagramed. (Any two logically false sentences are equivalent, even though they can't be diagramed.)

*Exercise A: Section 8 (cont.)

Draw Venn diagrams for the pairs of sentences below, to determine if they are equivalent.

a	b
6. Some coyote is not a fox.	Some non-fox is a coyote.
7. Some non-girl is a non-boy.	Some non-boy is not a girl.
8. No desk is a table.	No table is a non-desk.
9. Every dictionary is a reference book.	Every non-(reference book) is a non-dictionary.

Exercise B: Section 8

For each pair of sentences below, draw Venn diagrams and determine whether the sentences are equivalent.

a	b
1. Every non-Canadian is a European.	Some European is not a Canadian.
2. Some turkey is not a non-chicken.	Some chicken is not a non-turkey.
3. No non-(hockey player) is a non-athlete.	Every non-athlete is a hockey player.
4. Every professor is a non-(union member).	No non-(union member) is a non-professor.
5. Every sofa is a piece of furniture.	Every non-(piece of furniture) is a non-sofa.
6. Some girl is a college freshman.	Every college freshman is a girl.
7. No island is a continent.	Every continent is a non-island.

5-9   INCOMPATIBILITY

We have used Venn diagrams to test for implication and equivalence. If two sentences have the same diagram, they imply each other; which is what it is for them to be equivalent. We can also use Venn diagrams to test for logical truth, although they are less helpful for detecting this feature. For a logically true sentence, like 'No non-dog is a dog,' has an unmarked diagram:

dog

It is sometimes tricky to tell that a sentence has an unmarked diagram; this is why diagrams aren't so useful for detecting logical truth.

One sentence implies a second if an understanding of their logical forms is sufficient to determine that the first can't be true when the second is false. An understanding of the logical form of a logically true sentence is sufficient to determine that the sentence can't be false at all. No other sentence can be true when a logically true sentence is false. So every sentence implies a logically true sentence. Diagrams can be confusing when we use them to determine how a logically true sentence is related to other sentences. Diagrams are most useful for sentences that are neither logically true nor logically false.

Now suppose we want to know whether sentence (1) implies (2):

(1) No college teacher is a college teacher.

(2) Every college teacher is a wealthy person.

If we diagramed the first sentence by itself, we would use a single circle:

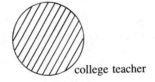

college teacher

But the second diagram requires two circles:

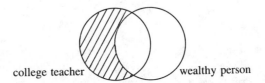

college teacher   wealthy person

It is difficult to compare these diagrams. However, even though sentence (1) contains a single term, we can use these two circles for its diagram:

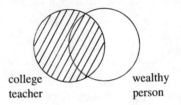

college   wealthy
teacher   person

In diagraming sentence (1), we simply ignored the wealthy person circle. This diagram includes the diagram for sentence (2), but the diagrams are different. This shows that if sentence (1) is true, then (2) must be true—(1) implies (2). But (2) doesn't imply (1); the sentences aren't equivalent.

Venn diagrams can also be used to test for logical incompatibility. Two sentences that are incompatible rule each other out. Diagrams of incompatible sentences do something analogous. If one diagram is shaded where the other contains an 'X,' the diagrams conflict with each other. Consider these diagrams for an A sentence and the corresponding O sentence:

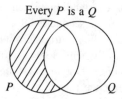

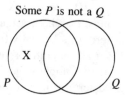

The diagrams show the sentences to be incompatible.

If one diagram is shaded where another has an 'X' (so long as the circles in the diagrams represent the same things), then the sentences which go with these diagrams are incompatible. But not every case of incompatibility gives rise to such diagrams. Consider these sentences:

Some soldier is not a soldier.

Some soldier is a paratrooper.

We can diagram the second sentence:

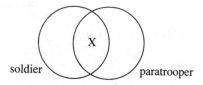

but we cannot diagram the first, for it makes an impossible claim and is logically false. Since the sentence cannot possibly be true, that sentence and any other sentence cannot possibly be true together. The logically false sentence is incompatible with every sentence. The fact that a logically false sentence cannot be diagramed is a sign of incompatibility as well as a sign of logical falsity. But the situation is even worse. Not only is a logically false sentence incompatible with every sentence, it also implies every sentence. A sentence that cannot be diagramed implies any sentence you like.

*Exercise A: Section 9

Use Venn diagrams to determine which of the following pairs of sentences are logically incompatible.

a	b
1. Every baseball bat is a non-(tennis racquet).	Some tennis racquet is a baseball bat.

2. No croquet mallet is a golf club. Every golf club is a croquet mallet.

3. No softball is a non-basketball. Some non-basketball is a basketball.

4. Some non-(military leader) is not a non-(U.S. president). Every U.S. president is a military leader.

5. Some vampire is a living thing. Some non-(living thing) is a vampire.

Exercise B: Section 9

Consider the pairs of formulas and sentences below. For each pair, draw a Venn diagram for each sentence or formula, and indicate whether the sentences (formulas) are related by implication, logical incompatibility, or neither one. If the relation is implication, indicate which implies the other. If each implies the other, say so.

	a	**b**
1.	No M is an N	No C is a non-C
2.	No B is a C	Some non-C is not a non-B
3.	Some D is a C	Every D is a non-D
4.	No D is a non-B	Every D is a non-D
5.	Some S is not a P	Every S is a P
6.	Every Q is a C	No C is a Q
7.	Every bourgeois person is a contemptible person.	Some contemptible person is not a bourgeois person.
8.	No contralto is a soprano.	Every soprano is a non-contralto.
9.	Some bright student is not a non-(logic student).	Some logic student is a bright student.
10.	Some green jewel is an emerald.	No emerald is a green jewel.
11.	Some living thing is not a living thing.	Some thing subject to decay is not a non-(living thing).
12.	No college professor is a happy person.	No non-(happy person) is a non-(college professor).

5-10 SYLLOGISMS

In studying the Categorical language, we have dealt with *two-place* implication and incompatibility. These are neither the most interesting nor the most important cases of these semantic relations. We must learn how to determine whether two or more sentences imply a further sentence, and whether three or more sentences are incompatible. The implication from (1) and (2) to (3):

(1) No cow is a cat.

(2) Some Holstein is a cow.

(3) Some Holstein is not a cat.

is three-place. And these sentences:

(4) No Catholic is a Communist.

(5) Some Jesuit is a Catholic.

(6) Every Jesuit is a Communist.

exemplify three-place incompatibility. If we consider the sentences two at a time, we find each pair to be compatible. This case of three-place incompatibility cannot be reduced to two-place incompatibility.

To begin with, we will consider an extremely simple kind of two-premiss inference. A *syllogism* has two categorical sentences as premisses and a categorical sentence as its conclusion. The sentences of a syllogism contain three terms, each of which occurs twice. The subject of the conclusion is the *minor term* of the syllogism. The predicate of the conclusion is the *major* term of the syllogism. The major term occurs in the *major premiss* (as its subject or predicate), and the minor term occurs in the other premiss, the *minor premiss*. The remaining term of the syllogism is the *middle term*, which occurs in both premisses.

The following inference is a syllogism:

Every meddler is a miserable man.
Every monarch is a meddler.
Therefore, every monarch is a miserable man.

The minor term is 'monarch,' the major term is 'miserable man,' and the middle term is 'meddler.' The first premiss is the major premiss; the minor premiss is second. In a syllogism, it is not required that the three terms be distinct. So the following argument is a syllogism:

Every professor is a generous person.
Some professor is a professor.
Therefore, some professor is a generous person.

In this syllogism, the minor term and the middle term are the same. However, a two-premiss argument with more than three terms is not a syllogism.

*Exercise: Section 10

1. Determine which of the following arguments are syllogisms.

   a. Every miner is a muscular man.
   Every bricklayer is a union member.
   Therefore, every bricklayer is a muscular man.
   b. Every midshipman is a political appointee.
   Every man on that bus is a midshipman.
   Therefore, every man on that bus is a political appointee.
   c. Every married woman is a boring companion.
   Every virtuous woman is a married woman.
   Therefore, no married woman is a virtuous woman.

2. Identify the major, minor, and middle terms in these syllogisms.

   a. Every mountaineer is a mutinous man.
      Every Montanan is a mountaineer.
      Therefore, every Montanan is a mutinous man.
   b. Every misogynist is a magician.
      Every magician is a musician.
      Therefore, every misogynist is a musician.
   c. No politician is a petty person.
      Some politician is a politician.
      Therefore, some politician is not a petty person.

3. Identify the major and minor premisses in these syllogisms.

   a. Every X-ray technician is a xylophone player.
      Some xyster manufacturer is an X-ray technician.
      Therefore, some xyster manufacturer is a xylophone player.
   b. Every Brighton resident is a Briton.
      No Briton is a Breton.
      Therefore, no Brighton resident is a Breton.

Syllogisms are classified (syntactically) according to their structures. To give the *mood* of a syllogism, we indicate the type of the major premiss, then the type of the minor premiss, and then the type of the conclusion. This syllogism:

   Some Berliner is a resident of East Berlin.
   Every resident of East Berlin is an inhabitant of the Russian sector.
   Therefore, some inhabitant of the Russian sector is a Berliner.

has the mood IAI. (The major premiss is an I sentence, the minor is an A sentence, and the conclusion is an I sentence.)

In giving the mood, the type of the major premiss always comes first. But in a syllogism, the major premiss may not occur first. The following syllogism:

   Some Berliner is a resident of East Berlin.
   Every resident of East Berlin is an inhabitant of the Russian sector.
   Therefore, some Berliner is an inhabitant of the Russian sector.

is an AII syllogism. The major premiss occurs after the minor premiss, but this does not affect our classification in terms of mood.

^Exercise: Section 10 (cont.)

4. Give the mood of the following syllogisms.

   a. Every lens grinder is an astronomer.
      No astronomer is an astrologer.
      Therefore, no lens grinder is an astrologer.
   b. Every astronomer is a lens grinder.
      No astrologer is an astronomer.
      Therefore, no astrologer is a lens grinder.

Syllogisms are classified according to *figure* as well as mood. The figure of a syllogism is determined by the position of the middle term in its premisses. In the *first figure*, the middle term is the subject of the major premiss, and the predicate of the minor premiss. Here is an example of a first-figure syllogism:

Every astronomer is a lens grinder.
No astrologer is an astronomer.
Therefore, no astrologer is a lens grinder.

This is an EAE-1 syllogism.

For *second figure* syllogisms, the middle term occurs as the predicate in both premisses. This is an EAE-2 syllogism:

No reptile is a mammal.
Every socialist is a mammal.
Therefore, no socialist is a reptile.

The middle term is the subject of both premisses in the *third figure*. The following argument.

Every miner is a laborer.
Some miner is a digger.
Therefore, some digger is a laborer.

is an AII-3 syllogism.

The *fourth figure* is the last figure. In this figure, the middle term is the predicate of the major premiss and the subject of the minor premiss. The following is an IAI-4 syllogism:

Some wastrel is a wealthy man.
Every wealthy man is an aristocrat.
Therefore, some aristocrat is a wastrel.

The diagram below shows the make-up of syllogisms in the four figures.

FIGURE	1st	2nd	3rd	4th
Major Premiss	Middle Major	Major Middle	Middle Major	Major Middle
Minor Premiss	Minor Middle	Minor Middle	Middle Minor	Middle Minor
Conclusion	Minor Major	Minor Major	Minor Major	Minor Major

In studying syllogisms, we aren't considering real inferences made by real people. We consider sentences that could be used to make an inference. We will call a sequence of sentences that might serve as the premisses and conclusion of an inference an *inference sequence* or *argument sequence*. Both real inferences and inference sequences can qualify as syllogisms. So can *formula sequences*, which present the outlines of inference sequences.

*Exercise: Section 10 (cont.)

5. Give the figure and mood of the syllogisms below.

a. Every *B* is a *C*
Every *D* is a *B*
So every *D* is a *C*

b. No *F* is a *G*
Every *G* is an *H*
So some *H* is not an *F*

c. No *R* is an *S*
Some *T* is an *S*
So some *R* is not a *T*

d. No *J* is a *K*
Every *J* is an *L*
So no *L* is a *K*

e. Every candy is a sweet.
Some sweet is not a healthful food.
So some healthful food is not a candy.

f. Every ranger is a daring man.
No daring man is a dress designer.
So some ranger is not a dress designer.

5-11   THE CATEGORICAL DEDUCTIVE SYSTEM

As well as speaking of inference sequences rather than inferences, we will adopt the practice of writing inference sequences like this:

No puppy is an adult dog. Some dog of Sara's is a puppy. / Some dog of Sara's is not an adult dog.

The slant line separates the premisses from the conclusion. When the slant line is used, we don't need to use a word like 'so' or 'therefore.'

A syllogism can contain formulas as well as sentences:

No *P* is an *A*
Some *D* is a *P*
So some *D* is not an *A*

This syllogism is a formula sequence. It can also be written the second way:

No *P* is an *A*, Some *D* is a *P* / Some *D* is not an *A*

As we have been using the expressions 'valid' and 'logically valid,' only a genuine inference sequence, containing actual sentences, can be valid. For an inference sequence is valid if simply understanding it enables us to determine that it isn't possible for the premisses to be true when the conclusion is false; but only sentences, not formulas with variables, are true or false. However, we will extend our usage for 'valid.' A formula sequence is valid if it is actually a valid inference sequence, or if we obtain only valid inference sequences when we replace its variables (uniformly) by common nouns or noun phrases.

Now that we can classify syllogisms in terms of figure and mood, we want to determine which kinds of syllogism are valid. We will develop the *Categorical deductive system* to establish that certain syllogisms are valid and, more generally, to investigate validity and implication in the Categorical language. A deductive system contains rules, and sometimes axioms, which are used to prove results of some kind. (An axiom is a sentence or formula accepted without proof.) The deductive system consists of the rules and axioms, and the results which can be established with their help. We previously constructed proofs to show that certain sentences imply others. Such proofs also establish that an inference from their hypotheses to their conclusions is valid. Although the same kinds of proofs will be employed in the Categorical deductive system, those earlier proofs were not part of a deductive system. Once we specify the rules of the system, we can construct formal proofs in the system.

A deductive system organizes knowledge. The set of rules is a small "package" which characterizes the infinitely many results obtained by using the rules. Deductive systems are very common in mathematics. Historically, the most famous deductive system is probably that of Euclid, in which he formulated and developed what is now called Euclidean geometry. There are many other mathematical deductive systems. These systems are also employed in science and logic. It is commonly taken to be an ideal that a body of knowledge be organized by means of a deductive system.

In logic, we could have a deductive system to establish logical truths. We might have one for valid inferences or inference sequences. The first known deductive system is Aristotle's, which he designed to prove the valid syllogisms in his system of logic. In the Categorical deductive system, we will also establish that inference sequences are valid. A result which has a proof in a deductive system is a *theorem* of that system. When we construct a proof in our deductive system, we can say that we are proving an inference sequence to be valid. We are also establishing that the inference sequence is a theorem.

We will construct proofs from hypotheses in the Categorical deductive system. A (correct) proof that begins with hypothesis h and reaches conclusion c shows that the inference sequence h / c is logically valid. It also shows that h implies c. Finally, the proof shows that h / c is a theorem of the deductive system. If there is a proof of c from hypothesis h, we can just say so. We will also introduce the symbol '⊢' to abbreviate saying this; '$h \vdash c$' means that there is a proof of c from hypothesis h. A proof from hypotheses can have one or more hypotheses. A proof of conclusion c from hypotheses h_1, h_2, h_3 shows h_1, h_2, h_3 / c to be a theorem (and to be valid). We indicate that there is such a proof by writing this: h_1, h_2, $h_3 \vdash c$.

A proof is a sequence of steps from the hypotheses to the desired conclusion. Each step in the proof must either be (i) an hypothesis, or (ii) obtained according to the rules. We will adopt the practice of listing all hypotheses at the beginning of the proof. Following the hypotheses come the results established according to the rules. As before, we number the steps in a proof, and we insist that each step be accompanied by an explanation, which goes to its right. The explanation of an hypothesis *is* that it is an hypothesis. We could indicate this by writing 'hypothesis' or 'hyp' to the right of each hypothesis. Instead we shall draw a line beneath the last hypothesis; drawing it saves us the trouble of writing 'hyp' over and over. A proof of c from hypotheses h_1, h_2, h_3 would begin like this:

1 h_1

2 h_2

3 h_3

To take a proof beyond its hypotheses, we need rules for adding steps to the proof. Each rule is associated with one or more logical expressions or logical forms. The first rules we shall adopt correspond to the simple cases of implication that we recognized previously. There are two conversion rules:

E-Conversion (E-Conv)

This authorizes us to infer the converse of an E sentence, or of a formula with the form of an E sentence.

I-Conversion (I-Conv)

This authorizes us to infer the converse of an I formula.

And there are two obversion rules:

Obverse Introduction (ObvI)

This authorizes an inference to the obverse of a formula.

Obverse Elimination (ObvE)

This authorizes an inference from the obverse of a formula to the formula.

In explaining steps in proofs, the names of rules will be abbreviated as indicated above. A proof of 'Some A is a B / Some non-non-B is an A' is illustrated:

1	Some A is a B	
2	Some A is not a non-B	1, ObvI
3	Some A is a non-non-B	2, ObvI
4	Some non-non-B is an A	3, I-Conv

Even though step 3 is a special kind of I sentence (formula), we can infer its converse. The rule I conversion applies to any I sentence or formula. The following shows that 'No non-non-dog is a cat'⊢ 'No cat is a dog.'

1	No non-non-dog is a cat.	
2	No cat is a non-non-dog.	1, E-Conv
3	Every cat is a non-dog.	2, ObvE
4	No cat is a dog.	3, ObvE

The rule *Logical Truth (LT)* is unlike the previous rules in requiring no premisses. A formula (or sentence):

Every α is an α

may be added as a step in any proof, and the only explanation we write is 'LT.' A logically true sentence has a form that guarantees its truth; the truth does not depend on assumptions. The following proof:

1 No girl is a boy.
_____
2 Every bird is a bird.   LT

shows that 'No girl is a boy' implies 'Every bird is a bird,' even though the two sentences
are talking about different things. *Every* sentence implies a logically true sentence.

The rule Logical Truth enables us to start a proof with no hypotheses. A formula justified by Logical Truth is not a hypothesis (we *know* it, so we don't need to suppose it),
and it does not require a previous step. The following proof:

1 Every dog is a dog.   LT
2 No dog is a non-dog.   1, ObvI
3 No non-dog is a dog.   2, E-Conv

does not have a line beneath any step. This is a proof from 0 hypotheses. This proof establishes that ' / No non-dog is a dog.' is a theorem, and so is valid. For an argument sequence / *p* to be valid is the same as for the conclusion of that sequence to be logically
true. The above proof establishes that 'No non-dog is a dog' is logically true. (From this
perspective, logical truth is a special, and degenerate, case of validity.) Even though the
Categorical deductive system has been designed to establish cases of logical validity, we
can also use the system to establish cases of logical truth.

*Exercise A: Section 11

Prove the following to be theorems of the Categorical deductive system. (You should
prove that 4 is logically true.)

1. Every non-duck is a bird. / Every non-bird is a duck.

2. Some farmer is not a non-electrician. / Some electrician is not a non-farmer.

3. No *M* is a non-*P* / Every non-*P* is a non-*M*

4. Every non-non-non-*C* is a non-*C*

Our rules are not sufficient for proving the valid syllogisms. We must adopt some
two-premiss rules. There are two kinds of syllogisms whose validity seems especially obvious. These are AAA-1 syllogisms and AII-1 syllogisms:

AAA-1   **AII-1**

Every *B* is a *C*   Every *B* is a *C*
Every *A* is a *B*   Some *A* is a *B*
So every *A* is a *C*   So some *A* is a *C*

We will not prove that these syllogisms are valid. We will simply accept them as valid,
based on our understanding of the logical forms that are involved. The rule AAA-1 allows
us to infer the conclusion of such a syllogism from its premises. The rule AII-1 allows us
to infer the conclusion of an AII-1 syllogism from its premises, when they occur as steps
in a proof.

Suppose we wish to prove that an EAE-2 syllogism is valid. Such syllogisms have this form:

No T is an S
Every R is an S
So no R is a T

The following proof shows such arguments to be valid:

1	No T is an S	
2	Every R is an S	
3	No S is a T	1, E-Conv
4	Every S is a non-T	3, ObvI
5	Every R is a non-T	4, 2, AAA-1
6	No R is a T	5, ObvE

Steps 4, 2, and 5 constitute an AAA-1 syllogism:

4 Every S is a non-T

2 Every R is an S

5 Every R is a non-T

The premisses of the syllogism do not need to be next to each other in a proof. The major premiss does not need to occur first. And a syllogism may contain a complement expression, so long as the same expression occurs twice.

*Exercise A: Section 11 (cont.)

Fill in the reasons for the steps in the following proofs.

5. EIO-3
1 No F is a G

2 Some F is an H

3 Some H is an F

4 Every F is a non-G

5 Some H is a non-G

6 Some H is not a G

6. 1 No camelopard is a leopard.

2 Every giraffe is a camelopard.

3 Every camelopard is a non-leopard.

4 Every giraffe is a non-leopard.

5 No giraffe is a leopard.

6 No leopard is a giraffe.

To prove a syllogism according to the rules we have adopted, we must transform its premisses to yield the premisses of an AAA-1 syllogism or the premisses of an AII-1 syllogism. If we are proving a syllogism whose premisses are both universal, then we try to use the rule AAA-1. If we are proving a syllogism with a particular premiss, we try to use the rule AII-1.

*Exercise A: Section 11 (cont.)

Prove the following syllogisms or kinds of syllogism to be valid. (We prove that a kind of syllogism is valid by proving a formula sequence which symbolizes syllogisms of that kind.)

7. EIO-1

8. OAO-3

9. AEE-2

10. No machine gun is a child's toy. Every crew-served weapon in an infantry platoon is a machine gun. / No crew-served weapon in an infantry platoon is a child's toy.

In setting up a deductive system, it is necessary to be careful about the rules that are adopted. The rules should be relatively simple, and they should be correct. It is possible to set up a deductive system in which the rules are not correct, and still prove results in this system. The results "established" using incorrect rules are not very interesting, for such "proofs" give us no reason to accept the results. For the Categorical deductive system, we desire that the rules not allow proofs of formula sequences that are invalid. A deductive system in which all rules are correct is *sound*. We can be confident that the Categorical deductive system is sound, because we have adopted simple rules that are easily seen to be correct.

Organizing a body of knowledge by means of a deductive system provides a better understanding of that knowledge than we would otherwise have. Such organization facilitates enlarging our knowledge; the organization helps us correct mistakes in what we thought was knowledge. Deductive systems have still more virtues than these from our standpoint. Working in a deductive system gives practice in making deductively correct inferences. We can get a better "feel" for these inferences by making them than by looking at them "from the outside." The study of a deductive system improves our understanding of the meanings of logical expressions. We can distinguish two kinds of meaning that an expression has. The *representational meaning* is what that expression is used to represent. For example, 'blue' is used to represent a certain color, 'square' is used to represent a four-sided shape, and 'older than' is used to represent the relation between two objects such that the first began its existence before the second. As well as having representational meanings, expressions have *inferential* meanings—this consists in the inferences that the expressions "authorize" when they occur in sentences. If we are told that an object is blue, we can infer that it is colored, and that it isn't red. Understanding the inferential meaning of an expression is as important as understanding its representational meaning, though most people don't realize this.

The distinction between representational and inferential meaning also applies to logical expressions. We have considered what we represent by using logical expressions in the Categorical language. For example, a sentence 'Every *A* is a *B*' is used to represent an

A being other than a *B* as never happening. We also need to grasp the inferential meanings of the logical expressions. The rules and the proofs in the Categorical deductive system help us to do this.

Proofs in the Categorical deductive system establish positive cases of implication, validity, and logical truth. But we cannot use proofs for negative cases. Before we developed the deductive system, we established negative cases by finding examples (counter-examples). This is still the way we deal with negative cases. We can show that an EEE-3 syllogism is not valid (that not all syllogisms of this kind are valid) by finding a syllogism of this form with true premises and a false conclusion:

> No man-eating tiger is a household pet.
> No man-eating tiger is a cocker spaniel.
> So no cocker spaniel is a household pet.

Although EEE-3 syllogisms are not, *in general*, valid, there may also be valid syllogisms of that form. This EEE-3 syllogism is valid:

> No man-eating tiger is a man-eating tiger.
> No man-eating tiger is a cocker spaniel.
> So no cocker spaniel is a man-eating tiger.

(Of course, this is a trivial, uninteresting argument. But it *is* valid. And it is an EEE-3 syllogism. It is also an EEE-4 syllogism.)

*Exercise A: Section 11 (cont.)

Determine which of these kinds of syllogism are valid. Construct proofs of valid syllogisms, and find examples to invalidate the others.

11. IOI-3
12. EIO-2
13. EAO-4
14. EOO-2
15. IAI-4

Instead of considering a kind of syllogism, suppose we are given an actual syllogism. Suppose we are given the task of either proving the following, or else showing that it isn't logically valid.

> Every monkey is a language user.
> No mosquito is a monkey.
> So no mosquito is a language user.

If we have no clear intuitions as to whether this is valid, we may choose arbitrarily either to try to prove it, or to try to invalidate it. If we try to prove it, we might get this far:

1	Every monkey is a language user.	
2	No mosquito is a monkey.	
3	No monkey is a mosquito.	2, E-Conv
4	Every monkey is a non-mosquito.	3, ObvI

This approach hasn't succeeded. We could try a different proof, or we can try to show the syllogism to be (logically) invalid. To show that the syllogism isn't valid, it can help to replace terms by variables:

> Every M is an L
> No Q is an M
> So no Q is an L

Now we can replace the variables by words to get this argument:

> Every cocker spaniel is a dog.
> No collie is a cocker spaniel.
> So no collie is a dog.

This is clearly invalid. (We could have skipped the intermediate step, but it can be easier to find a suitable example when we consider variables rather than nouns.)

*Exercise A: Section 11 (cont.)

Determine which of the following are logically valid, and which aren't. Prove the valid syllogisms. Find suitable examples for the others.

16. Every dictionary is a book.
   Some dictionary is a dictionary.
   So some dictionary is a book.

17. Some lion is an octopus.
   Every octopus is a mammal.
   So some mammal is a lion.

18. No snake is a bird.
   Some bird is not a cobra.
   So some cobra is not a snake.

19. No boat is a yacht.
   Every boat is a garbage truck.
   So no garbage truck is a yacht.

The Categorical deductive system enables us to deal with multi-premiss inferences that aren't syllogisms. This formula sequence:

> Every A is a B, Every B is a C, Every C is a D / Every A is a D

has three premisses. But it can be proved as follows:

1	Every A is a B	
2	Every B is a C	
3	Every C is a D	
4	Every A is a C	2, 1, AAA-1
5	Every A is a D	3, 4, AAA-1

*Exercise A: Section 11 (cont.)

Prove those of the following that are valid. Find suitable examples to show that the others aren't logically valid.

20. Some *A* is a *B*, Some *A* is not a non-*C* / Some *B* is a *C*

21. Every *A* is a *B*, Every *B* is a *C*, Some *A* is an *A* / Some *C* is an *A*

22. Every *A* is a *B*, No *B* is a *C*, Every *D* is a *C* / Some *A* is not a *D*

23. Every *F* is a *G*, No *G* is an *H*, Some *H* is an *H* / Some *H* is not an *F*

Exercise B: Section 11

Construct proofs of the valid sequences. Find suitable examples to show that the others are (logically) invalid.

1. Every *F* is a *G*, Every *F* is an *H* / Every *H* is a *G*

2. Some *R* is not an *S*, Every *S* is a *T* / Some *T* is not an *R*

3. Some *A* is a *B*, Some *C* is a *B* / Some *C* is an *A*

4. No *B* is a *C*, Every *C* is a *D*, Some *B* is a *B* / Some *B* is not a *D*

5. Every *H* is an *I*, No *I* is a *J*, Some *H* is an *H* / Some *J* is not an *H*

6. No football player is a weak person. Some boy is a weak person. / Some boy is not a football player.

7. Some person is an overweight person. Some person is an unhappy person. / Some overweight person is an unhappy person.

8. Every friend of Bill's is a weird person. Every weird person is a poet. No poet is a building contractor. Some civil engineer is a building contractor. / Some civil engineer is not a friend of Bill's.

9. No philosopher is a rich person. Some oilman is a rich person. No oilman is a philanthropist. Every philanthropist is a generous person. / Some generous person is not a philosopher.

10. Every pleasure is a thing which contributes to happiness. Some response to Picasso's paintings is a desirable aesthetic experience. Every desirable aesthetic experience is a pleasure. Every thing which contributes to happiness is a suitable ingredient of a good life. / Some response to Picasso's paintings is a suitable ingredient of a good life.

5-12 PROVING INCOMPATIBILITY

We can construct proofs to show that we have a case of implication, or logical validity, or logical truth. But what about logical incompatibility? Is there some way to prove that a group of sentences are incompatible?

It is obvious without using Venn diagrams that corresponding A and O sentences are incompatible:

Every M is an N

Some M is not an N

(By corresponding sentences, I mean sentences whose subjects are the same and whose predicates are the same.) Similarly, corresponding E and I sentences are incompatible:

No M is an N

Some M is an N

These sentences are more than just incompatible, they *contradict* one another. *Contradictory* sentences are sentences for which an understanding of the sentences is sufficient to determine:

(i) that they can't both be true (this makes them incompatible); and (ii) that they can't both be false.

Contradictory sentences must have opposite truth values.

Now suppose we have sentences $p_1, \ldots, p_n$ that are incompatible. These sentences can't all be true. If all but one were true, the last one would have to be false. To show that n sentences are incompatible, we make a proof which takes all but one of these sentences as hypotheses. It doesn't matter how we choose the all but one. Once we have our hypotheses, we construct a proof showing that the remaining sentence is false. We do this by making use of our knowledge of contradictory opposites. To show that an A sentence is false, it is sufficient to show that the corresponding O sentence is true. To show that the O is false, we show that the A is true. Etc.

To prove that these two sentences are logically incompatible:

Every non-fox is a giraffe.

Some non-giraffe is not a fox.

we take all but one of them for our hypotheses. That gives us one hypothesis; let us choose the first sentence. Then we reason to the contradictory opposite of the second sentence:

1	Every non-fox is a giraffe.	
2	No non-fox is a non-giraffe.	1, ObvI
3	No non-giraffe is a non-fox.	2, E-Conv
4	Every non-giraffe is a fox.	3, ObvE

To prove that these three formulas:

No P is a Q, Some R is a Q, Every R is a P

jointly symbolize incompatible sentences, we will take the first and third for hypotheses:

1	No P is a Q	
2	Every R is a P	
3	Every P is a non-Q	1, ObvI
4	Every R is a non-Q	3, 2, AAA-1
5	No R is a Q	4, ObvE

*Exercise A: Section 12

Prove that the following groups are incompatible (or symbolize incompatible sentences).

1. Some dog is not a non-collie. Every collie is a non-dog.

2. No dragon is a unicorn. Every vampire is a unicorn. Some vampire is a dragon.

3. Every non-*A* is a non-*B*, Some *B* is a non-*A*

4. No *A* is a non-*B*, Some *C* is an *A*, No *B* is a *D*, Every *C* is a *D*

We can prove positive cases of logical incompatibility. But what kind of example is required to show that we don't have incompatibility? If these formulas:

No *A* is a *B*, Every *C* is an *A*, Some *C* is not a *B*

symbolize incompatible sentences, then no three sentences like these can all be true. Finding three true sentences which the formulas symbolize would show that the displayed forms don't indicate incompatibility. It isn't hard to do this:

No apple is a peach. Every Ida Red is an apple. Some Ida Red is not a peach.

To show that actual sentences are not logically incompatible:

No dog is an animal. Some collie is a dog. Every animal is a collie.

we find true sentences having the same (specific) logical forms:

No duck is a vampire. Some mallard is a duck. Every vampire is a mallard.

If the original sentences had all been true, that would have shown them to be compatible.

*Exercise A: Section 12 (cont.)

Determine whether the following are logically incompatible. Construct proofs of the positive cases, and find examples for the negative ones.

5. Every dog is a cat. No dog is a cat. Some dog is a dog.

6. Every *A* is a *B*, No non-*C* is a *B*, Every non-*C* is a non-*A*

7. No Western state is a Midwestern state. Every New England state is a non-(Midwestern state). Some non-(Western state) is not a non-(New England state).

8. Every *Q* is a non-*P*, No non-*Q* is an *R*, Every *S* is an *R*, Some *P* is not a non-*S*

Exercise B: Section 12

Determine which of the following groups of sentences are logically incompatible. Give proofs for the positive cases. Find suitable examples to show that the remaining groups of sentences are not logically incompatible.

1. No athlete is a barber. No barber is a chiropractor. No athlete is a chiropractor.

2. Every acrobat is a non-bricklayer. Some relative of Frank is a bricklayer. Some relative of Frank is not a non-acrobat.

3. Every artisan is a ballplayer. No ballplayer is an artisan. Some artisan is an artisan.

4. Every artist is a bully. No bully is a coward. Some artist is an artist. No non-coward is an artist.

5. Every anthropologist is a Baptist. Some Baptist is a Baptist. No Baptist is an anthropologist.

6. Some apple-polisher is a back-slapper. Some non-apple-polisher is a back-slapper. Every apple-polisher is a back-slapper.

7. Every stock broker is an aviator. Every stock broker is a banker. Some aviator is not a banker.

8. Some actor is not a non-butcher. No butcher is an actor. Every butcher is a catcher.

9. Some art dealer is not a baker. No art dealer is an art dealer. Every non-baker is an art dealer.

10. Every astronaut is a boatman. No fat man is an astronaut. Some fat man is a boatman.

5-13 VENN DIAGRAMS FOR MANY-PLACE RELATIONS

We previously used Venn diagrams to test for logical semantic relations between pairs of sentences in the Categorical language. To do this we diagramed each sentence, and compared the diagrams. Using Venn diagrams to test for validity is the same as using them to test for implication, but our previous tests only work for one-premiss inferences. We can also use Venn diagrams to evaluate an inference containing more than one premiss, so long as the inference contains no more than three terms. Consider an EAE-1 syllogism:

No G is an H
Every F is a G
So no F is an H

We need a circle for each term, and they must overlap one another:

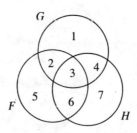

Each of the numbered sections represents a different kind of thing. We can list these as follows:

section 1: $\bar{F}G\bar{H}$

section 2: $F G \bar{H}$

section 3: FGH

section 4: $\bar{F}GH$

section 5: $F\overline{GH}$

section 6: $F\bar{G}H$

section 7: $\overline{FGH}$

The combination $\overline{FGH}$ is not represented by one of these seven sections. If we need to represent that combination, we draw a box around the circles.

In diagramming the syllogism, we focus on one premiss at a time and two circles at a time. To diagram 'No G is an H,' we consider only the G and H circles:

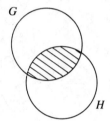

In the whole diagram, this is:

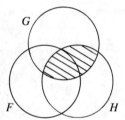

We look at the F and G circles to diagram 'Every F is a G,' which gives us a total diagram like this:

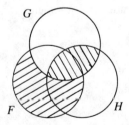

In diagramming an inference, we "enter" all the premisses in the diagram. But we don't make a separate diagram for the conclusion; *we don't diagram the conclusion at all.* After we have diagramed the premisses, we check to see if this diagram already contains the diagram for the conclusion. If it does, the argument is valid. If it does not, the argument is not logically valid. For our example above, the conclusion is 'No F is an H.' So we look at the F and H circles in the diagram:

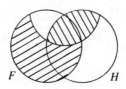

The center section of this diagram is shaded. This is how we diagram 'No F is an H.' So this diagram includes the diagram for the conclusion, and the syllogism is valid. (The diagram indicates *more* than that no F is an H. But this extra information does not "interfere" with the diagram's showing that nothing is both F and H.)

The diagram for this AEE-3 syllogism:

Every C is a D
No C is a B
So no B is a D

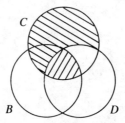

shows that such arguments are not (in general) valid. For the B and D circles:

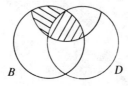

do not contain the diagram for 'No B is a D.'

If an argument contains a particular premiss, it is most convenient to diagram the particular premiss last. Consider this argument:

Some K is not an L
Every K is a J
So some J is not an L

If we diagram the second premiss first, we get:

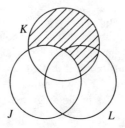

To diagram the major premiss, we need an 'X' in the *K* circle outside of the *L* circle:

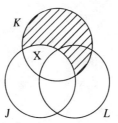

Suppose we diagramed the major premiss first. The sentence 'Some *K* is not an *L*' calls for an 'X' in the *K* circle outside of the *L* circle. There are two sections that meet this description:

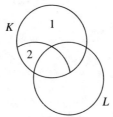

We have no reason for thinking the 'X' goes in 1 rather than 2; neither have we a reason to mark 2. The major premiss only tells us that an 'A' belongs in 1 *or* 2 (or both). To indicate that an 'X' belongs in one of two adjacent sections, we place an 'X' on the line between the sections:

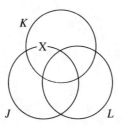

After diagramming the minor premiss we would have:

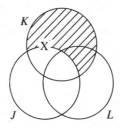

Now the diagram needs to be changed. An 'X' on the line indicates our uncertainty about which of two sections should have an 'X.' Since one of the adjacent sections has been shaded, there is no longer any uncertainty. We need the diagram at the top of the preceding page.

It isn't always possible to avoid placing an 'X' on a line in a three-circle diagram. Consider the following:

> Some non-Q is an R
> No Q is a non-P
> So some P is not an R

If we diagram the second premiss first we get:

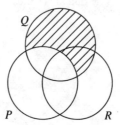

To diagram the first premiss, we must put an 'X' in the R circle outside of the Q circle. But there are two sections in the R circle outside of the Q circle. The 'X' goes on the line between them:

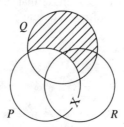

The argument is not a valid one.

Although we did not encounter sentences which put 'X' on a line when we considered two-circle diagrams, we could have. To determine the relation between these formulas (between sentences jointly symbolized by the formulas):

(1) Some A is an A

(2) Some B is an A

we can diagram the formulas. It is helpful to use the same two circles for each one:

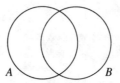

Formula (1) calls for an 'X' in the *A* circle. But the *A* circle has two compartments; formula (1) doesn't indicate which of these compartments gets an 'X.' We diagram the formulas like this:

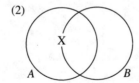 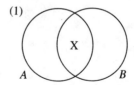

From our previous use of diagrams, it isn't easy to say how the formulas are related. But it should be obvious on reflection that 'Some *B* is an *A*' implies 'Some *A* is an *A*,' though there is no implication in the opposite direction. An 'X' in a compartment "implies" an 'X' on the line of that compartment, but not the reverse. (*p* implies '*p* or *q*,' but '*p* or *q*' does not imply *p*.) To retain the diagram test that we adopted earlier, we will say that an 'X' in a compartment *includes* an 'X' on the line of the compartment.

For arguments containing more than three terms, diagrams constructed with circles don't provide enough compartments. For four terms, there are 2^4 ($= 16$) combinations of terms and complements. For four-term arguments, diagrams can be constructed with ellipses. More complicated figures have been used for arguments having more than four terms. Beyond three terms, the use of Venn diagrams is often more hindrance than help for the purpose of evaluating arguments. (It is, however, interesting to develop more complicated diagrams.)

*Exercise A: Section 13

Use Venn diagrams to evaluate the arguments below.

1. No male is a non-(proud animal).
Some male is a male.
Every male is a colorful animal.
Therefore, some colorful animal is a proud animal.

2. Some vehicle is not a beer keg.
Every wheelbarrow is a vehicle.
Some wheelbarrow is a wheelbarrow.
Therefore, some beer keg is not a wheelbarrow.

3. No chicken is a pheasant.
Every chicken is a fowl.
Some fowl is a chicken.
So some fowl is not a pheasant.

4. Every non-(hardy plant) is a non-weed.
Every ragweed plant is a weed.
Some ragweed plant is a ragweed plant.
So some ragweed plant is a hardy plant.

We can use Venn diagrams to check for multi-sentence incompatibility. But this is only convenient with sentences containing no more than three terms. To show that these sentences:

Every student is an honest person. No student is an honest person. Some student is a student.

are incompatible, we try to diagram them together. If we cannot do this, they are incompatible. In this case, we can diagram the first two sentences together:

No space remains for an 'X' in the student circle. The third sentence requires such an 'X.' We cannot diagram the third sentence. The sentences are incompatible.

*Exercise A: Section 13 (cont.)

Use Venn diagrams to determine whether the following sentences are incompatible.

5. Every park is a marsh. Every marsh is a swamp. Some park is not a swamp.

6. No war is a battle. Every skirmish is a non-battle. Every war is a non-skirmish.

7. No non-lake is a mountain. No lake is a sea. Some mountain is a sea.

8. No man is a non-giant. Some woodcutter is a giant. Some woodcutter is not a man.

Exercise B: Section 13

Use Venn diagrams to determine which of the following arguments are logically valid.

1. No zoo is a store.
Every butcher shop is a store.
Some butcher shop is a butcher shop.
So some butcher shop is not a zoo.

2. Some odd number is a prime number.
Some odd number is not a prime number.
So some prime number is not an odd number.

3. No non-(plane figure) is a triangle.
No plane figure is a non-(mathematical object).
Therefore, every triangle is a mathematical object.

4. Some property is not a virtue.
Every virtue is a good quality.
Hence, some good quality is not a property.

5. Every set is a container.
Every container is a non-set.
So some set is a set.

6. Every war is a disaster.
Every war is a conflict.

Some conflict is a conflict.
So some conflict is a disaster.

7. Every table is a chair.
Every chair is a piece of chalk.
Every piece of chalk is a non-table.
Hence, every table is a non-(piece of chalk).

8. Some woman is a bus driver.
Some bus driver is a bartender.
Therefore, some bartender is a woman.

9. Every square is a rectangle.
Every rectangle is a quadrilateral.
Some square is a square.
Thus, some quadrilateral is a quadrilateral.

10. Every military funeral is a solemn event.
No solemn event is a frivolous frolic.
Some frivolous frolic is a frivolous frolic.
So some frivolous frolic is not a military funeral.

Exercise C: Section 13

Use Venn diagrams to determine which of the following groups of sentences are logically incompatible.

1. Every minnow is a fish. No fish is a non-plant. Some plant is a non-minnow.

2. No non-goat is a frog. Some halibut is not a goat. Every frog is a halibut.

3. Every peach is a pear. Every apple is a peach. Some peach is not an apple.

4. No hamburger is a product made with pork. No sausage is a non-(product made with pork). Some hamburger is a sausage.

5. Every sausage is a non-(hot dog). No sausage is a frankfurter. Every frankfurter is a hot dog.

6. Some non-bear is a non-rabbit. Every polar bear is a bear. Every non-rabbit is a bear.

7. No self-assured person is a freshman. Every freshman is a self-assured person. Some freshman is a nervous wreck.

8. Some unicorn is a unicorn. No vampire is a vampire. Every unicorn is a vampire.

9. Some weapon is a non-(dangerous object). Some weapon is not a non-(dangerous object). No dangerous object is a non-weapon.

10. Every art museum is a target for thieves. No target for thieves is an art museum. Every library is a non-(art museum).

5-14 FORMAL FALLACIES (OPT)

A fallacy is a mistake in an inference. Previously we considered informal fallacies, not linked to specific linguistic forms. In logic we look for formal features which characterize only valid arguments. We can also find formal features characteristic of invalid arguments. However, if a certain form (for example, the form AAA-1) characterizes valid arguments, then *every* argument which has that form is valid. But if a form is characteristic of invalid arguments, then arguments which have that form are not, *in general*, valid. Some arguments which have the form may be valid.

An argument commits a formal fallacy if (1) the argument is invalid, and (2) the argument is characterized by a distinctive logical form. We could probably identify a formal fallacy for every invalid argument. But we shall only consider a relatively small number of formal fallacies committed by syllogisms.

To recognize certain of these formal fallacies, we must know what it means for a term to be *distributed*. We will determine what it is for an expression to be distributed by describing a certain test. To apply this test, we ask whether a sentence containing a term would be used to give information about an arbitrary individual denoted by that term. Consider an A sentence, 'Every α is a β.' If this sentence were asserted, would it give information about an arbitrary α (about each α)? If the answer is "Yes," then the subject is distributed. If every α is a β, then any α chosen at random will be a β. The subject of an A sentence is distributed. But the predicate is not distributed. If we are told that every α is a β, and we pick an arbitrary β, we have no information about this β.

In an E sentence, 'No α is a β' both subject and predicate are distributed. For if no α is a β, then an arbitrary α is not a β. And for an arbitrary β, no α will be that β. Neither term in an I sentence is distributed. If we only know that some α is a β, then we do not know the status of an arbitrary α. Or of an arbitrary β.

It is easy to see that the subject of an O sentence is not distributed. But dealing with the predicate is tricky. Suppose we are told that some α is not a β. And we consider an arbitrary β. We *cannot* say whether or not this β is an α. But we *can* say that some α is not this β. Knowing that at least one α is not a β, we can say that, for any β we choose, at least one α is not this β. So the O sentence does tell us something (rather modest) about an arbitrary individual denoted by its predicate. The predicate of an O sentence is distributed.

The distributed terms in categorical sentences are enclosed in circles:

Every Ⓑ is a *C*

No Ⓑ is a Ⓒ

Some *B* is a *C*

Some *B* is not a Ⓒ

*Exercise: Section 14

1. Indicate the distributed terms in the following sentences.

   a. Some mariner is a mean man.

   b. Every deacon is a daring diver.

   c. Some battalion is not a battered brigade.

   d. No cab is a classy car.

If a syllogism contains three distinct terms (i.e., if the minor, major, and middle terms are different from each other), then to be logically valid it must satisfy certain conditions. Three conditions involve distributed terms:

(i) The middle term must be distributed in at least one premiss.

(ii) If the minor term is distributed in the conclusion, then it must be distributed in the minor premiss.

(iii) If the major term is distributed in the conclusion, then it must be distributed in the major premiss.

Here is an example of a syllogism which violates the first condition:

> Some man is a musician.
> Every jockey is a man.
> So every jockey is a musician.

This syllogism commits the formal fallacy of *undistributed middle*. The following syllogism has the major term distributed in the conclusion but not in the major premiss:

> Every large seagoing mammal is a whale.
> No minnow is a large seagoing mammal.
> Therefore, no minnow is a whale.

The name for this fallacy is *illicit major*. If the minor term is distributed in the conclusion but not the minor premiss, the syllogism commits the fallacy of *illicit minor*.

*Exercise: Section 14 (cont.)

2. Identify any formal fallacies in these syllogisms:

a. Some *P* is an *M*
Some *S* is an *M*
Therefore, some *S* is a *P*

b. Every *A* is a *B*
Every *C* is an *A*
Therefore, every *C* is a *B*

c. Every *F* is a *G*
Some *H* is not an *F*
Therefore, some *H* is not a *G*

d. No *M* is an *N*
Every *M* is an *L*
So no *L* is an *N*

e. Every *R* is an *S*
Every *S* is a *T*
So every *T* is an *R*

f. Some *U* is a *V*
Every *V* is a *W*
Hence, some *W* is a *U*

If a syllogism does not contain three distinct terms, it can violate the conditions for distributed terms and still be logically valid. And a syllogism which is not logically valid may still be (plain) valid. (Remember, we don't accuse a valid argument of committing a formal fallacy, even if it violates one of the conditions for logically valid syllogisms. We reserve the word 'fallacy' for mistakes.)

Some formal fallacies involve negative sentences. Logically valid syllogisms with three distinct terms satisfy these conditions:

(iv) There is at most one negative premiss.

(v) If there is a negative premiss, then the conclusion must be negative.

(vi) If the conclusion is negative, then one premiss must be negative.

*Exercise: Section 14 (cont.)

3. Identify any formal fallacies in the syllogisms below.

a. Some shotgun is not a murder weapon.
Every shotgun is a firearm.
Therefore, some firearm is not a murder weapon.

b. Every hangman is a religious man.
No jockey is a hangman.
So every jockey is a religious man.

c. Every bayonet is a dangerous toy.
Some dangerous toy is a set of brass knuckles.
So every set of brass knuckles is a bayonet.

d. Some petty criminal is a potential gangland leader.
Every petty criminal is a small-time hoodlum.
Therefore, some potential gangland leader is a small-time hoodlum.

e. Some drug addict is not a well-dressed man.
No derelict is a well-dressed man.
Hence, some derelict is not a drug addict.

f. Some smuggler is a dope peddler.
Every dope peddler is a reprehensible person.
So some reprehensible person is not a smuggler.

g. No poisoned apple is a good Christmas present.
Some poisoned apple is an easily hidden object.
So some good Christmas present is not an easily hidden object.

h. Every poisonous substance is a weapon that leaves traces.
Some mushroom product is a poisonous substance.
Therefore, some mushroom product is not a weapon that leaves traces.

The conditions on negative sentences do not apply to syllogisms having fewer than three (distinct) terms. The following (silly) syllogism is valid and has two negative premisses:

No waffle is a pancake.
No pancake is a waffle.
So no pancake is a waffle.

The last conditions for three-term syllogisms involve particular sentences. They are exactly parallel to the conditions on negative sentences.

(vii) There is at most one particular premiss.

(viii) If there is a particular premiss, then the conclusion must be particular.

(ix)   If the conclusion is particular, then one premiss must be particular.

*Exercise: Section 14 (cont.)

4. Indicate any formal fallacies committed by the following kinds of syllogisms — when they have three distinct terms and contain no expressions which make them valid for other than logical reasons.

a. IAI-1

b. AOO-4

c. EEE-2

d. AAI-4

e. EAE-3

f. AII-2

g. AIO-3

h. IAA-3

i. AOI-4

j. IAI-3

k. AAO-2

l. EAE-1

Chapter **6**

Applying an Artificial Language

6-0 SUMMARY

In this chapter we determine how to use an artificial language as an instrument to deal with ordinary English. Sentences in the artificial language are used to translate ordinary sentences. Although we try to provide equivalent translations, we must sometimes settle for translations that aren't equivalent to the ordinary sentences they replace. This chapter explains when nonequivalent translations can be used to test for semantic features it also explains how to carry out and interpret these tests.

6-1 WHAT WE WANT IN A TRANSLATION

Once we achieve a good understanding of an artificial logical language, we can show whether sentences in that language constitute positive or negative cases of logical semantic features. But how can we use the artificial language to answer questions about ordinary sentences and arguments? To do this we must translate ordinary sentences with sentences of the logical language, which we know how to evaluate. Once we evaluate the translations, we try to carry the results of the evaluation "back" to the original sentences. To do this we need both suitable translations and suitable results.

Let's begin by considering what it takes for a translation to be suitable. If we translate an ordinary sentence p by a logical-language sentence $p*$, we would like for $p*$ to "say exactly the same thing" as p. Putting this in terms of entailment, we would like for $p*$ to both entail and be entailed by p — we would like for $p*$ to be *equivalent to p*. Sometimes the artificial language does not possess the resources for producing an equivalent $p*$, but there is a sentence $p*$ entailed by p. If $p*$ is entailed by p but does not entail p, we will say that $p*$ is *weaker than p*. When no equivalent translation is available, we can sometimes employ a weaker translation. A weaker translation can be slightly weaker or very much weaker than the original. In those cases where a weaker translation is allowed, it is still second best to an equivalent translation; and we always prefer a slightly weaker translation to a very much weaker translation.

If $p*$ entails p but is not entailed by p, then $p*$ is *stronger than p*. Just as there are occasions when we can use weaker translations, so we can sometimes make use of stronger translations. A slightly stronger translation is preferable to a very much stronger translation. If we have an ordinary sentence p, but cannot come up with a translation $p*$ which either entails or is entailed by p, then we regard p as a sentence which is "out of bounds" as far as the artificial language is concerned. The sentence p has no suitable translation and cannot be evaluated by means of the artificial language.

Our procedure for detecting semantic features in ordinary sentences may seem paradoxical. We are trying to determine whether we have a case of analytic truth, entailment, incompatibility, or validity. To do this we must be able to come up with suitable translations, and we must be able to tell that they are suitable. This requires that we recognize positive and negative cases of entailment. We cannot test for entailment between ordinary sentences unless we already recognize cases of entailment between ordinary sentences and logical-language sentences. We must make inferences from ordinary to artificial sentences, and back again. There is no getting around this "paradox." The abilities to recognize semantic features and to make deductively valid inferences are absolutely fundamental for understanding and using language. We must exercise these abilities even when we study them.

*Exercise: Section 1

Select the correct answers.

1. If sentence p is equivalent to sentence q, then

    a. p entails q.
    b. q entails p, but p does not entail q.
    c. p may or may not entail q.

2. If p entails q, then

    a. q is weaker than p.
    b. q is not weaker than p.
    c. q may or may not be weaker than p.

3. If p is equivalent to q, then

    a. q is weaker than p.
    b. q is not weaker than p.
    c. q may or may not be weaker than p.

4. If p entails q, then

    a. p is equivalent to q.
    b. if q entails p, then p is equivalent to q.

6-2 THE FEATURES WE TEST FOR

We are concerned with several semantic features of ordinary sentences and arguments. Since any test for validity amounts to the same thing as a test for entailment, we have three semantic features to test for: analyticity, entailment-validity, and incompatibility. We are slightly less interested in analytic truth than the other two. Analytic truth has less practical importance. Some analytic truths can be used to explain what expressions mean; otherwise they aren't informative. And to determine whether a sentence is analytic, we must often recognize entailment relations between the ordinary sentence and its translation that are at least as difficult as the issue of whether the sentence is analytic.

In dealing with ordinary sentences we are concerned with general semantic features. To determine whether ordinary sentences are an instance of a general feature, we ask whether their translations are an instance of the corresponding logical semantic feature. If they are, then the original sentences are an instance of the general semantic feature, *so long as we have employed suitable translations*.

Different semantic features impose different suitability requirements. Consider analytic truth. Suppose we have an ordinary sentence p translated by p^*. We test p^* for logical truth. Suppose p^* *is* logically true. What must its relation be to p, if we are to conclude that p is analytic? If p^* is weaker than p, its truth does not carry over to p. A weaker translation is of no use in testing for analyticity. p^* must entail p. To test for analytic truth, we need an equivalent or a stronger translation.

To determine whether sentences $p_1, \ldots, p_n$ are incompatible, we need translations $p_1^*, \ldots, p_n^*$. Suppose these translations are logically incompatible; what is required for us to conclude that $p_1, \ldots, p_n$ are incompatible? If each translation is equivalent to the sentence it translates, then the original sentences must be incompatible. Equivalent translations can always be used in our tests. Now suppose that some or all of the incompatible translations are stronger. What can we conclude about the originals? If the translations are stronger, their truth would carry back, but what about incompatibility? If the original sentences were all true, then they couldn't be incompatible. Even if they were all true, they might be entailed by sentences that aren't all true. (A false sentence can entail a true one, but not the reverse.) The incompatibility of stronger translations doesn't reveal incompatibility in the original sentences. But if each translation is equivalent or weaker, then the truth of the original sentences must carry over to the translations. In that case, the incompatibility of the translations would carry back. To test for incompatibility we can use equivalent or weaker translations.

However, if we have both a weaker and an equivalent translation available, we will generally make use of the equivalent translation. And we prefer a slightly weaker translation to a much weaker translation. For if the original sentences are incompatible, but their translations are weaker, part of what is lost in the translations might be the incompatibility.

Finally, let's consider requirements that translations must meet if we are to determine that sentences $p_1, \ldots, p_n$ entail q. Suppose we have translations $p_1^*, \ldots, p_n^*$ that imply q^*. What is needed to ensure that $p_1, \ldots, p_n$ entail q? If each of $p_1, \ldots, p_n$ entails its translation among $p_1^*, \ldots, p_n^*$, then if $p_1^*, \ldots, p_n^*$ entail q^* and q^* entails q, we can conclude that there is entailment from $p_1, \ldots, p_n$ to q. Making a requirement out of this, we can say that the sentences that do the entailing (the premises) need equivalent or weaker translations, and the sentence that gets entailed (the conclusion) must have an equivalent or stronger translation.

Elementary logic books do not ordinarily discuss conditions on translations. They frequently give the impression that the same kinds of translations can be used for both premises and conclusions. But if we want implications between translations to be a sure sign of entailment between ordinary sentences, then we must make sure that the requirements on translations are satisfied. I *have* heard it argued that translations need not meet such stern requirements, that it is sufficient for there to be an analogy we can recognize between translations and ordinary sentences. Such an analogy is sometimes sufficient for us to evaluate an argument, but this approach would deprive applied logic of all rigor. We will insist that the requirements be met.

*Exercise: Section 2

Determine which of the following are correct.

1. To determine whether a sentence p is analytic,

    a. we need a translation $p*$ which entails p.
    b. we need a translation $p*$ which is entailed by p.
    c. we need a translation $p*$ which is equivalent to p.

2. If we wish to evaluate an argument from $p_1, \ldots, p_r$ to q,

    a. the premisses and conclusion must receive equivalent translations.
    b. the premisses and conclusion can receive weaker translations.
    c. the premisses can receive weaker translations, but the conclusion cannot.

3. In order to determine whether sentences $p_1, \ldots, p_n$ are incompatible,

    a. the translations $p*, \ldots, p_n^*$ must be equivalent to or weaker than the originals.
    b. the translations $p*, \ldots, p_n^*$ must be equivalent to or stronger than the originals.
    c. the translations $p*, \ldots, p_n^*$ must be equivalent to the originals.

4. If sentences $p_1, \ldots, p_n, q$ are given translations $p*, \ldots, p_n^*, q*$, and each translation is stronger than the original sentence, then if the inference from $p*, \ldots, p_n^*$ to $q*$ is logically valid,

    a. the inference from $p_1, \ldots, p_n$ to q is valid.
    b. the inference from $p_1, \ldots, p_n$ to q may or may not be valid.
    c. the inference from $p_1, \ldots, p_n$ to q is invalid.

6-3 NEGATIVE OUTCOMES

If we are testing ordinary sentences for a semantic feature, come up with suitable translations, and find that these translations are an instance of the logical special case of the general feature, this is a *positive outcome* to our test. A positive outcome carries back to the original sentences. If the translations are not an instance of the logical special case of the general semantic feature, our test has resulted in a *negative outcome*. Negative outcomes are not so conclusive as positive ones.

Suppose we are testing $p_1, \ldots, p_n$ for incompatibility, and suitable translations $p*$, $\ldots, p_n^*$ are not logically incompatible. We *cannot* conclude in this case that $p_1, \ldots, p_n$ are compatible. It can happen that translations possess a general semantic feature even though they don't possess its logical special case. And if translations are not equivalent to the sentences they translate, the changes involved in obtaining stronger or weaker translations can lead to translations not possessing a feature, even though the originals do possess it. A negative outcome to our test is inconclusive.

A positive outcome is conclusive, but a negative one isn't. However, by reflecting on the original sentences and their translations, we can often determine whether or not we have a case of the semantic feature in question. If our translations are not equivalent, we can ask ourselves whether anything important is lost in moving to the translations. We must also ask whether anything important for the semantic feature in question fails to show up in the logical forms of the translations, even though it characterizes the translations. If the answer to both questions is "No," then we can be (fairly) confident that the original sentences constitute a negative case of the semantic feature in question. And if the answer to one or both questions is "Yes," we can frequently tell whether we have a positive or a negative case of the semantic feature.

The different significance of positive and negative outcomes means that we can't consider ourselves as carrying out impartial tests. It is more appropriate to think that we are trying to show that we have a positive case of a semantic feature. If we succeed in our attempt, then we have conclusively established the positive case. When our "test" has a negative outcome, we are reduced to noticing analogies between ordinary sentences and their translations. This is the best we can do, though it isn't so good as we would like. If we abandoned requirements on translations, this would place cases of positive outcomes on the same footing as negative outcomes. This would definitely be a step in the wrong direction.

*Exercise: Section 3

Determine which answers are correct.

1. If we want to know whether $p_1, \ldots, p_n$ entail q, and find suitable translations $p^*_1, \ldots, p^*_n$ which don't imply (suitable translation) q^*, then

   a. $p_1, \ldots, p_n$ don't entail q.
   b. $p_1, \ldots, p_n$ may or may not entail q.
   c. $p_1, \ldots, p_n$ entail q.

2. If artificial-language sentence p^* is not logically true, then

   a. it may be analytically true.
   b. it isn't analytically true either.
   c. it is still analytically true.

3. If sentences $p_1, \ldots, p_n$ are given equivalent translations $p^*_1, \ldots, p^*_n$, but q can only be given a weaker translation q^*, then the inference from $p_1, \ldots, p_n$ to q

   a. cannot be evaluated by means of the logical language.
   b. is invalid.
   c. is valid.

4. If sentence p is logically true, and p entails q, then

   a. q is analytic.
   b. q isn't analytic.
   c. q may not be analytic.

Chapter 7

Applying the Categorical Language to English

7-0 SUMMARY

In this chapter we consider how ordinary English sentences can be translated into the Categorical language. We distinguish between Categorical-language sentences that are equivalent to the ordinary sentences they translate, and sentences that are not equivalent but either entail or are entailed by the ordinary sentences. We determine how to use Categorical-language translations to show that an ordinary argument is valid, or that ordinary sentences are incompatible. Since we have no conclusive tests for establishing negative cases, we strengthen our techniques for establishing positive cases. We do this by adding analytic sentences which bring out important meaning connections between words, and by adding sentences which express assumptions that a speaker takes for granted.

7-1 TRANSLATING ENGLISH SENTENCES

We use the Categorical language to gain an understanding of some semantic features of some English sentences and arguments. Many sentences cannot be adequately translated into the Categorical language, and so cannot be illuminated by the Categorical language. In what follows we will consider some kinds of sentences which *can* be translated into the Categorical language, and we will develop some "rules of thumb" for making these translations. Our "rules" will generally fall short of absolute precision, and many will allow of exceptions. What is most important in making translations is that we have a good understanding of both the English sentences we wish to translate and the logical sentences we use to make translations. We can then do our best to come up with translations that are suitably close to the originals.

In the sentences of the Categorical language, the verbs are either 'is' or 'is not.' To translate a sentence with a different verb, we must eliminate that verb. To translate this sentence:

(1) No man wants to be rich.

we can use the following universal negative sentence:

(2) No man is a person who wants to be rich.

The sentence:

(3) Some woman is running for mayor.

does not belong to the Categorical language, because its verb is 'is running' rather than simply 'is.' But we can translate (3) like this:

(4) Some woman is a person running for mayor.

In translating both (1) and (3), we incorporated the original verb in the predicate of the sentence. We have not changed the meanings of the original sentences.

A sentence may have the right verb but the wrong tense to belong to the Categorical language. Sentence (5) doesn't belong:

(5) Some soldier was a traitor.

This sentence is tricky to translate, because it is ambiguous. It can mean that some person who is now a soldier was a traitor in the past. If it does, then the sentence:

(6) Some soldier is a person who was a traitor.

provides a weaker translation. For, strictly, (6) means that some person who was, is, or will be a soldier was a traitor in the past. We can capture the indicated meaning with sentence (7):

(7) Some person who is now a soldier is a person who was a traitor.

However, we will allow ourselves to understand a plain noun like 'soldier' to mean *soldier now*. With this understanding, both (6) and (7) provide equivalent translations.

Sentence (5) can also mean that at some time in the past, a person who was then a soldier was also a traitor. With this meaning it is difficult to find an equivalent translation. The sentence:

(8) Some person who was a soldier is a person who was a traitor.

gives a weaker translation. For (8) allows the person to have been a soldier at a different time than he was a traitor. The following sentence provides an equivalent but cumbersome translation:

(9) Some person who was a soldier is a person who was a traitor when he was a soldier.

Although sentence (10) has both the wrong verb and wrong tense for a sentence of the Categorical language:

(10) No Green Bay Packer played very well last Sunday.

the most natural way to understand it calls for this translation:

(11) No Green Bay Packer (now) is a person who played very well last Sunday.

As well as having the right verb, a sentence must have the right number to qualify for the Categorical language. This sentence:

(12) No dogs are animals with wings.

doesn't belong to the Categorical language, because the subject and the verb are plural. But we can replace (12) by (13):

(13) No dog is an animal with wings.

The change from (12) to (13) makes no essential difference to what is said.

In English, both 'is' and 'is not' can be followed by an adjective. We see this in the next sentence:

(14) No book of Don's is exciting.

This sentence doesn't belong to the Categorical language, because it doesn't have a common noun for its predicate. We can translate it:

(15) No book of Don's is an exciting book.

or

(16) No book of Don's is an exciting thing.

We shall use the word 'thing' so that every individual, whether concrete, intermediate, or abstract, is a thing.

In supplying a noun for an adjective to modify, we cannot always use a "safe" term like 'thing.' To understand why not, we must distinguish three classes of adjectives:

1. Absolute adjectives. An absolute adjective can be regarded as denoting individuals "on its own." 'Round' is an absolute adjective. To say that a building is a round barn means that the building is round *and* a barn. If the building is something else, say an X, then it is also a round X.

2. Relative adjectives. A relative adjective needs a noun to modify, even if the noun is implicit. For the meaning of a relative adjective involves a relation to the objects denoted by the noun. The adjective 'big' is relative. To say that someone is big means that she is big with respect to the members of some class. A big third-grader is not a big person.

3. Category without a name—from now on, I will call these *radical* adjectives. When an absolute or a relative adjective is applied to a noun, the resulting expression denotes individuals which were already denoted by the noun. Adjectives in this third category produce expressions which denote individuals not denoted by the original noun. The adjective 'counterfeit' belongs to this category. A counterfeit ten-dollar bill is not a (real) ten-dollar bill.

If we supply a noun for an absolute adjective, we can usually use a safe noun like 'thing.' But for adjectives belonging to the remaining two categories, we must be careful to choose an appropriate noun. We cannot translate:

(17) Some ten-dollar bill is counterfeit.

by:

(18) Some ten-dollar bill is a counterfeit thing.

For no individual is a counterfeit thing (a counterfeit thing would pretend to be a thing without really being one). So to translate (17) we need a sentence like one of the following:

(19) Some (apparent) ten-dollar bill is a counterfeit bill.

(20) Some (apparent) ten-dollar bill is a piece of counterfeit currency.

A relative adjective must also be related to the right noun. To translate

(21) Some girl is tall.

we need to know what kind of girl is meant. Is she a young child? An adult? Is she an American? Depending on the answers, we might need to use one or the other of the following for our translation.

(22) Some girl is a tall person.

(23) Some girl is a tall ten-year-old.

(24) Some girl is a tall Japanese.

These translations are obviously not equivalent, and are not equally acceptable. But in different contexts, any of them could provide an equivalent translation.

*Exercise A: Section 1

Translate the following into the Categorical language.

1. No Italian restaurants serve French bread.

2. Some South American countries were originally European colonies.

3. Some prime number is waiting to be discovered.

4. No logicians are dangerous.

5. Some prospectors didn't find gold.

6. No Swiss bankers are currently in jail.

An indefinite statement like these:

(25) A student in Professor Gracia's class speaks Spanish.

(26) Some student in Professor Gracia's class speaks Spanish.

means that at least one student in Professor Gracia's class speaks Spanish. So does this sentence:

(27) There is a student in Professor Gracia's class who speaks Spanish.

All of these sentences can be given an equivalent translation with the same I sentence:

(28) Some student in Professor Gracia's class is a person who speaks Spanish.

Negative indefinite sentences like these:

(29) Some student didn't bring his book to class.

(30) A student didn't bring his book to class.

(31) At least one student didn't bring his book to class.

(32) There is a student who didn't bring his book to class.

have an equivalent translation which is a particular negative sentence:

(33) Some student is not a person who brought his book to class.

Sentences which go beyond indefinite statements, like these:

(34) Some students in Professor Gracia's class speak Spanish.

(35) Ten students in Professor Gracia's class speak Spanish.

(36) Most students in Professor Gracia's class speak Spanish.

must be translated with a particular affirmative sentence:

(37) Some student in Professor Gracia's class is a person who speaks Spanish.

This translation is not equivalent to the sentences it translates. Sentence (37) is slightly weaker than (34), considerably weaker than (35), and much weaker than (36). If the only translation available for a sentence is much weaker, the translation is frequently not useful for evaluating the sentence. However, it is a matter for individual judgment to determine when a much weaker translation can be used.

Sentences which fall "between" indefinite and universal sentences are translated with particular sentences. Universal sentences are translated by universal sentences of the Categorical language. But an ordinary universal sentence is sometimes understood in a restricted sense. For example, the sentence 'Elephants have tusks' might be so understood. If that sentence were taken in such a way that it is true, then we don't want to use 'Every elephant is an animal with tusks' as our translation. To capture the restricted understanding, we want some such translation as this: Every normal adult elephant is an animal with tusks.

A more serious problem in translating universal sentences concerns existential force. In conversation or writing, we normally understand a universal affirmative sentence to indicate existence. If someone told us "All girls in Professor Barber's class think that he is handsome," we would understand that there is a girl in Professor Barber's class—probably there are more than one. To translate this sentence in the Categorical language, we could use this A sentence:

Every girl in Professor Barber's class is a person who thinks that he is handsome.

This translation has no existential force: it rules out there being a girl in the class who doesn't think Barber is handsome, but the sentence doesn't require there to be a girl in the class. An A sentence of the Categorical language provides a weaker translation for a universal affirmative sentence understood in the ordinary way.

These ordinary universal sentences:

Every child of Betty's is a girl.

All Betty's children are girls.

Each child of Betty's is a girl.

Betty's children are girls.

would be given this weaker translation:

Every child of Betty's is a girl.

The ordinary sentences entail the translation, but not the reverse.

To translate this sentence:

(38) Only members of her family are allowed to visit Michelle.

we could use this A sentence:

(39) Every person allowed to visit Michelle is a member of her family.

Whether the translation is equivalent to the original depends on our understanding of the original. Sometimes a sentence 'Only A's and B's does no more than rule out a B which isn't an A. Sometimes such sentences have existential force. Since we usually rely on context to determine if there is existential force, and our examples are not provided with contexts, we will *in this book* understand sentences to have the weakest existential force that they might naturally have. With this convention, I think that (39) provides an equivalent translation for (38). It also provides an equivalent translation for:

(40) The only persons allowed to visit Michelle are members of her family.

Universal affirmative sentences are ordinarily understood to have existential force. Universal negative sentences sometimes have no existential force ("No vampires are in your closet"). But it would not be natural to use this sentence:

None of Rita's friends was invited to the party.

if Rita has no friends. So 'No friend of Rita is a person who was invited to the party' provides a weaker translation. But 'Nobody who got 100 on the logic final failed the course' might be used by a speaker who realizes that nobody got 100 on the final. So we will regard 'No person who got 100 on the logic final is a person who failed the course' as an equivalent translation.

In translating universal sentences, we will presume that these sentences have the weakest existential force they might naturally have. If we translate a sentence p by one of 'Every α is a β' or 'No α is a β,' and the point of asserting p would depend on there being an α, then the universal sentence of the Categorical language provides a weaker translation. Almost all universal affirmative sentences will be assigned existential force, some universal negative sentences will be and and others won't. In those cases where we attribute existential force to universal sentences, this applies to the subjects of these sentences; the predicates are not normally assigned existential force directly. (If we assign existential force to α in 'Every α is a β,' we have indirectly assigned existential force to β.) In the examples and exercises in this book, we will assume that universal sentences about mathematical objects like numbers, sets, or geometrical figures have no existential force. Universal affirmative sentences about mathematical objects will be understood mathematically. You must remember that this is simply a convention adopted in the present book.

Another difference between universal sentences in the Categorical language and ordinary universal sentences concerns modal force. Neither affirmative or negative sentences in the Categorical language are understood to have modal force. This *does not* mean that modal expressions are barred from the Categorical language. This sentence:

Every horse is an animal that must breathe oxygen.

belongs to the Categorical language, and has modal force. The sentence says that each actual horse, if there are any, is an animal for which breathing oxygen is necessary.

This ordinary sentence:

> Any trespasser will be prosecuted.

contains no modal expression, but would naturally be understood to have a modal force. The sentence rules out the possibility of there being a trespasser who isn't prosecuted. With its modal force, this sentence is understood as making a claim about actual and possible trespassers. Expressions in the Categorical language denote only actual individuals —in the past, present, or future. Even putting in explicit modal expressions doesn't change this limitation. In the Categorical language, the following sentence:

> Every horse is an animal that must breathe oxygen.

rules out an actual horse being such that not breathing oxygen is possible. It has a different meaning than the following ordinary sentence:

> It isn't possible for there to be a horse which doesn't breathe oxygen.

This sentence rules out the possibility of a horse that doesn't breathe oxygen. It has no equivalent translation in the Categorical language.

If we understood this sentence:

> None of Dick's children will tell a lie.

to have modal force, we would take it to concern only Dick's actual children—not these plus the children he might have had. So understood, the modal force of the sentence can be captured by this Categorical language translation:

> No child of Dick's is a person for whom telling a lie is possible.

But the translation is weaker, because the original sentence is naturally understood to have existential force.

Even though 'Any trespasser will be prosecuted' has no existential force, we cannot provide an equivalent translation, because we cannot capture its modal force. Our weaker translation is:

> Every trespasser is a person who will be prosecuted.

*Exercise A: Section 1 (cont.)

Translate the following into the Categorical language. Mark weaker translations with an asterisk.

7. Some friends of Ted's have been in jail.

8. There is a man in Julia's law firm who used to be a Catholic priest.

9. None of the bottles of beer in the refrigerator are cold.

10. All even prime numbers are less than ten.

11. There are no vampires.

12. Spiders aren't insects.

13. If someone jumps off the Sears Tower, he will be killed.

14. One of the realtors who showed Kathy a house didn't pressure her to buy.

15. Only friends of the groom got drunk and were obnoxious at the reception.

16. The coral snake is poisonous.

17. Lions are bigger than hyenas.

18. Parrots can't really talk.

Sentences about types can often be translated by universal sentences of the Categorical language. For example, this sentence:

(41) The automobile is self-propelled.

might be translated:

(42) Every automobile is a self-propelled vehicle.

Sentences about types commonly have a modal force. It would be natural to understand (41) as ruling out the possibility of there being an automobile that isn't self-propelled. Since (42) has no modal force, it provides a weaker translation for (41). (In my understanding, sentences about types don't usually indicate the existence of instances of the types, so this isn't a second source of weakness in (42).)

Many sentences about types can be translated by sentences about instances of the types, though the translations usually aren't equivalent. Other sentences about types can't be translated like this. The sentence:

The automobile was an important invention.

can't be replaced by a sentence about automobiles.

Certain kinds of sentences are sometimes translated with universal sentences, and sometimes with particular sentences. It is natural to understand these sentences:

A wolf is carnivorous.

Wolves are carnivorous.

as making a claim about all wolves. We would provide the two sentences with this weaker translation:

Every wolf is a carnivorous animal.

(The original sentences would normally be understood to have existential force.) The originals might also be understood to rule out the very possibility of a wolf that isn't carnivorous. If they are understood like this, then there are two respects in which the translation is weaker than the originals.

This sentence:

A wolf killed the Eskimo's sled dog.

would not be understood universally. We would translate it with this I sentence:

Some wolf is an animal that killed the Eskimo's sled dog.

Similarly, this sentence:

Wolves can be found in Isle Royale Park.

would be given this (weaker) translation:

Some wolf is an animal that can be found in Isle Royale Park.

A plural noun, like 'wolves' in the preceding examples, denotes a collection of individuals. The noun 'wolves' might denote the collection of all wolves, or it might denote a smaller collection. Certain properties are assigned to a collection just in case each member of the collection has the property. For example, we say that whales are mammals just because each whale is a mammal. Such properties (as being a mammal) are *distributive*. Other properties of collections can't appropriately be predicated of the members of a collection. We can't translate:

Whales are numerous.

by:

Every whale is a numerous animal.

because 'numerous' indicates a nondistributive property of collections.
In a similar way, the sentence:

Dogs knocked over David's garbage cans.

is not adequately translated like this:

Some dog is an animal that knocked over David's garbage cans.

The original sentence is most naturally taken to be about a collection of dogs, acting together. We lose this meaning if we give a 'Some dog' translation. In this case, the following seems a better translation:

Some collection of dogs is a collection (group) that knocked over David's garbage cans.

When we translate an ordinary English sentence that contains a negative word like 'no' or 'not,' we try to use a negative expression in the Categorical language. To translate

There is no student who got the answer to question 37.

we would use this E sentence:

No student is a person who got the answer to question 37.

And this sentence:

Somebody didn't finish her ice cream.

would be given a translation like the following:

Some person is not a person who finished her ice cream.

This is a better translation than

Some person is a person who didn't finish her ice cream.

When 'not' or 'n't' is buried in the predicate, it isn't so easy to detect semantic features that depend on this word.
The sentences:

Not all dogs bark.

Not every dog barks.

claim that at least one dog doesn't bark. We provide an equivalent translation like this:

Some dog is not an animal that barks.

In chapter 3, I described English sentences that we hope to understand by using artificial logical languages. These include sentences formed with quantified phrases, and sentences formed with singular terms—singular sentences. We can translate many sentences formed with quantified phrases into the Categorical language. But the Categorical language doesn't possess the resources for translating singular sentences. We will later consider artificial languages that can translate singular sentences.

*Exercise A: Section 1 (cont.)

Translate the following sentences. Mark weaker translations with an asterisk. If a sentence has no adequate translation, say why not.

19. There aren't any generous bankers.

20. Mosquito bites covered Sandra's arms.

21. The mosquito is an insect.

22. A bee stung Michael.

23. The bee lives in a hive.

24. The blue heron is widespread.

25. Millard Fillmore was an undistinguished president.

26. There are students in Professor Cox's class who have never been to DisneyWorld.

27. Not all of John's children have been to college.

7-2 EXPRESSING EXISTENTIAL FORCE

Universal sentences in the Categorical language don't have existential force. But particular sentences do indicate existence. For a particular affirmative sentence 'Some F is a G' to be true, there must be an F and there must be a G. The truth of a particular negative sentence 'Some F is not a G' requires that there be an F, but there need not be any G's. It is true, for example, that some person is not a vampire.

In the Categorical language, we can indicate that a noun R denotes at least one individual by using it twice in an I sentence:

Some R is an R

This sentence tells us that there is an R without telling us what else any R might be.

If we use an A sentence to translate this ordinary sentence:

(1) All the students in Ms. Radner's logic class are smart.

our translation will be weaker, because it lacks existential force. The sentence 'Some student in Ms. Radner's logic class is a student in Ms. Radner's logic class' expresses the missing existential force. We can achieve an equivalent translation for (1) by using two sentences:

(2) Every student in Ms. Radner's logic class is a smart person.
Some student in Ms. Radner's logic class is a student in Ms. Radner's logic class.

If we evaluate an argument, and use a two-sentence translation for a premiss, this doesn't affect our evaluation. Neither does it affect the evaluation if we provide a two-sentence translation for one or more sentences when we are trying to determine if they are incompatible. Things are more complicated if we provide a two-sentence translation for a sentence we are evaluating for analytic truth, or for the conclusion of an argument we are evaluating. However, in such a case we simply treat the two-sentence translation as a unit. An argument with a two-sentence conclusion is valid just in case both sentences follow from the premisses. And for a two-sentence unit to be logically true, both parts must be.

*Exercise A: Section 2

Translate the following into the Categorical language. Mark weaker translations with an asterisk.

1. Every student in Dr. Vesley's calculus class passed the course.

2. The ostrich is a flightless bird.

3. Parrots don't really talk.

4. The only journalists who understand national politics work for the *Chicago Tribune*.

5. Each runner received a T-shirt stamped with his time.

6. Anyone who calls after midnight will hear a recorded message.

7. A squirrel caused the telephone line to break.

8. A maitre d'hotel manages a restaurant.

Exercise B: Section 2

Translate the following sentences by sentences of the Categorical language. Mark weaker translations with an asterisk. If a sentence cannot be given an adequate translation, explain why not.

1. The kangaroo is an animal with a long tail.

2. Only those with invitations will be admitted to the opening.

3. A historical marker is located on Delaware Avenue.

4. The Pope has visited the United States.

5. The pope is elected for life.

6. Prime numbers are integers.

7. No one but members of his family is allowed to visit him.

8. Every person who is successful in studying logic will be successful in life.

9. Wolves are howling in the forest.

10. There are college professors who can scarcely write their own names.

11. There aren't any German red wines that are distinguished.

12. Most students in Professor Barber's classes get A's.

13. If anyone wins a prize in the lottery, he must pay taxes on it.

14. A Buick is a General Motors car.

15. Dinosaurs were not very intelligent animals.

16. Not all students in Professor Hull's class received a passing grade.

17. The people on that bus are making a lot of noise.

18. Not many countries have democratic governments.

19. Anyone who gets a degree in nursing is sure to find a job.

20. The only students who do well in engineering are the mathematically talented ones.

7-3 DETECTING SEMANTIC FEATURES OF EXISTENCE CLAIMS

Since sentences of the form 'Some A is an A' now play an important role in translating (many) universal sentences, it is appropriate to consider how to evaluate arguments and groups of sentences which contain such a sentence. To draw a Venn diagram for a sentence 'Some A is an A' when we aren't considering it with other sentences, we simply put an 'X' in the A circle:

We more commonly diagram these sentences together with others. We diagram these two formulas:

Every A is a B, Some A is an A

like this:

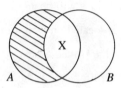

A sentence 'Some A is an A' frequently requires an 'X' on a line. For example, to diagram these:

Every A is a B, Every B is a C, Some B is a B

we need this diagram:

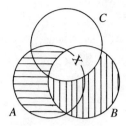

And to diagram the following formulas:

No *A* is a *B*, Every *C* is a *B*, Some *B* is a *B*, Some *C* is a *C*

we would use this:

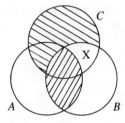

An 'X' in a compartment makes an 'X' on the line of that same compartment redundant. The 'X' that represents 'Some *C* is a *C*' also takes care of 'Some *B* is a *B*.'

In constructing proofs, the two steps:

> Every *A* is a *B*
> Some *A* is an *A*

are premisses for the rule AII-1, yielding the conclusion:

> Some *A* is a *B*

But note that two sentences:

> Every *A* is a *B*
> Some *B* is a *B*

do not yield any conclusion by rule AII-1.

The rules of the Categorical deductive system are not adequate for all reasoning with a sentence 'Some *A* is an *A*.' The following inference sequences are clearly valid:

> Some *F* is a *G* / Some *F* is an *F*

> Some *G* is not an *H* / Some *G* is a *G*

but we can't prove them with the rules that are available.

We will enlarge the Categorical deductive system by making a rule out of these sequences. The rule *Existence Introduction* (ExI) allows us to move from a premiss 'Some *A* is a *B*' or 'Some *A* is not a *B*' to the conclusion 'Some *A* is an *A*.'

The rule Existence Introduction is employed in the following proof:

1	Every A is a B	
2	Some C is an A	
∄	Some A is a C	2, I-Conv
4	Some A is an A	3, ExI
5	Some A is a B	1, 4, AII-1
6	Some B is an A	5, I-Conv

*Exercise: Section 3

For 1–2, use Venn diagrams or proofs and counterexamples to determine whether the following are valid.

1. Every non-A is a B, No B is a non-A, Some A is an A / Some B is an A

2. Every A is a B, No non-C is a B, Every D is a non-C, Some D is a D / Some non-A is a D

For 3–4, use Venn diagrams or proofs and counterexamples to determine whether the formulas are logically incompatible.

3. Every A is a B, No A is a B, Some A is an A

4. Every A is a B, Some non-B is a non-B, No non-B is a non-C, Every D is a C

7-4 EVALUATING ENGLISH SENTENCES AND ARGUMENTS

We are able to test for these features in the Categorical language:

logical truth

implication/logical validity

logical incompatibility

(We can also determine if two sentences are logically equivalent.) In using the Categorical language as an instrument for dealing with ordinary English, we begin by asking a question about an English sentence, group of sentences, or inference. We ask whether the sentence is analytic, whether the inference is valid, or whether the sentences are incompatible. To answer the question about the general semantic feature, we first come up with suitable translations for the ordinary sentences, and then test the translations for the logical special case of the general feature.

We must have an equivalent translation to test an ordinary sentence for analytic truth. The equivalent translation must be logically true in order to show that the original sentence is analytically true. There are not so many ordinary sentences for which we can provide equivalent and logically true translations in the Categorical language. The Categorical language is not very useful for detecting analyticity. We will not use it for this purpose.

However, we will use the Categorical language to uncover cases of entailment, validity, and incompatibility. To determine whether an inference sequence $p_1, \ldots, p_n$ / q is valid (which is to determine whether $p_1, \ldots, p_n$ entail q), we need equivalent or weaker translations for the premises, and an equivalent or stronger translation for the conclusion. If there are no suitable translations, then we can't evaluate the inference.

To determine whether sentence (1) entails (2):

(1) A cow is a mammal.

(2) There is no cow which isn't a mammal.

we can give this two-sentence translation for (1):

(1*) Every cow is a mammal. Some cow is a cow.

If we don't understand (1) to have modal force, then (1*) is equivalent to (1). And if we don't understand (2) to have modal force, then (2*) is an equivalent translation:

(2*) No cow is a non-mammal.

(Since (2) could be used without existential force, we presume that it has no such force.) If the original sentences are both understood to have modal force, we can't determine if (1) entails (2). For in that case, (2*) would be weaker than (2), and we can't "make up the difference." We shall assume that our translations are suitable. But then (2*) is the obverse of the first sentence in (1*); (1*) implies (2*). This positive result about suitable translations carries back to the originals. Sentence (1) entails (2).

We would give each of these sentences:

(3) Bill owns a dog.

(4) Bill owns some dogs.

the same translation:

(3*) Some dog is an animal owned by Bill.

(4*) Some dog is an animal owned by Bill.

These translations are not suitable. Sentence (3) has been given an equivalent translation, but (4)'s translation is weaker. That (3*) implies (4*) is no sign that (3) entails (4). In fact, sentence (3) doesn't entail (4).

If p and q have suitable translations p^*, q^*, but p^* does not imply q^*, we *cannot* say that p fails to entail q. A negative result about suitable translations does not carry back to the originals. But we can frequently determine whether or not the originals are linked by entailment. As an example, consider the question whether (5) entails (6):

(5) Any trespasser will be prosecuted.

(6) Some trespasser will be prosecuted.

These translations are suitable:

(5*) Every trespasser is a person who will be prosecuted.

(6*) Some trespasser is a person who will be prosecuted.

Sentence (5*) does not imply (6*). This doesn't tell us whether (5) entails (6). But sentence (5) doesn't indicate that there is (will be) a trespasser, while the truth of (6) requires this. There is no entailment.

To evaluate this argument:

(7) Only Moslems are allowed to visit Mecca. Christians aren't Moslems. But there are Arabs who are Christians. So some Arab is not allowed to visit Mecca.

We can provide equivalent translations for the first two premisses and the conclusion, and a weaker translation for the third premiss:

(7*) Every person allowed to visit Mecca is a Moslem. No Christian is a Moslem. Some Christian is a Christian. Some Arab is a Christian. So some Arab is not a person allowed to visit Mecca.

It is easy to construct a proof which shows that the premisses of (7*) imply the conclusion. So the original argument is valid. If the conclusion of (7) had been 'Some Arabs are not allowed to visit Mecca,' the translation (7*) would no longer be adequate. For the conclusion of (7*) is weaker than 'Some Arabs are not allowed to visit Mecca.'

*Exercise A: Section 4

For 1–3, determine if the sentence on the left entails the sentence on the right. Translate the sentences into the Categorical language, and use Venn diagrams or proofs and counterexamples to evaluate these translations.

a	b
1. There are no vampires that live in Transylvania.	Vampires don't inhabit Transylvania.
2. There is at least one student who didn't cheat on the exam.	Not all students cheated on the exam.
3. Everyone who heard the fire alarm got out safely.	Only those who heard the fire alarm got out safely.

For 4–6, determine whether the arguments are valid—when they can be tested.

4. No minerals which are metals will fail to conduct electricity. If anything conducts electricity, it is chemically active. So the only minerals which are metals are chemically active substances.

5. If Larry asks a girl to the dance, she will surely turn him down. There are girls who won't turn Larry down. So Larry will ask a girl to the dance.

6. None of Megan's friends will lend her money. The girls on the second floor of Lewis Hall are all Megan's friends. So no girl on the second floor of Lewis Hall will lend Megan money.

In testing ordinary sentences for incompatibility, we can use equivalent or weaker translations. If the only translation available for a sentence is stronger, we can't use the Categorical language to carry out an evaluation. This isn't much of a problem, since all the translations so far have been equivalent to or weaker than the sentences being translated. To determine whether these sentences are incompatible:

(8) The students in the logic class all got passing grades. Twelve students in the logic class didn't get passing grades.

we can use these translations:

(8*) Every student in the logic class is a person who got a passing grade. Some student in the logic class is a student in the logic class. Some student in the logic class is not a person who got a passing grade.

Even though the second translation is weaker than its original, the incompatibility of the translations shows that the original sentences are incompatible.

As with other semantic features, a negative result in testing for logical incompatibility does not mean that we have a negative result about the originals. To test these sentences:

(9) All the men at the table are bachelors. Two men at the table are married.

for incompatibility, we might use these translations:

(9*) Every man at the table is a bachelor. Some man at the table is a man at the table. Some man at the table is a married man.

This completed Venn diagram shows that the translations are not logically incompatible:

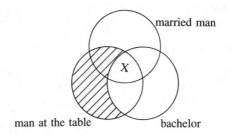

This negative result is not a sign that the original sentences are compatible. In fact, they are obviously incompatible.

*Exercise A: Section 4 (cont.)

For 7–9, determine if the pairs are incompatible.

a	b
7. There is a married couple who have 37 children.	There is no married couple with 37 children.
8. Any trespasser will be prosecuted.	No trespassers will be prosecuted.
9. Somebody at the party is not an invited guest.	There is no one at the party other than invited guests.

For 10–12, determine if the sentences are incompatible.

10. The automobile is self-propelled. Some busses aren't self-propelled. Some busses are automobiles.

11. Only cowards are bullies. Cowards are timid. Bullies aren't timid.

12. There aren't any birds that eat fish, but some birds eat insects. All birds have feathers. If an animal has feathers, then it eats fish.

Exercise B: Section 4

Use the Categorical language to evaluate the arguments below. Show your Categorical-language translations, and show work which justifies your answers. If the Categorical language cannot be used to test for validity, explain why not.

1. The sophomore girls all like Kevin. No one likes Kevin unless they know him. Some girls in geometry don't know Kevin. So there is a girl in geometry class who isn't a sophomore.

2. Mary didn't have fish any day last week. Mary has had fish every Friday. So no day last week was a Friday.

3. The only men who look good in beards are logicians. Some philosophers are logicians. So at least one philosopher looks good in a beard.

4. The cobra is poisonous. The Cleveland zoo has cobras. Hence, there is a poisonous snake in the Cleveland zoo.

5. It takes a brave man to marry a shrew. Many Marines are brave men. So some Marine will marry a shrew.

6. Only animals that can talk can think. Dogs can't talk. So dogs can't think.

7. No one who smokes heavily is in good health. The coaches for the West Side Little League are all heavy smokers. Some of the coaches for the West Side Little League jog regularly. So not all joggers are in good health.

8. A butterfly is not dangerous. A butterfly startled Marie. Anything harmful is dangerous. So something that isn't harmful startled Marie.

Exercise C: Section 4

Use the Categorical language to determine if the following sentences are incompatible. Show your Categorical-language translations, and show work that justifies your answers.

1. Not all students got A's on the midterm. No student failed to pass the midterm. Any student passed the midterm if he got an A on it.

2. Danny is sure to catch some fish this afternoon. If Danny catches a fish this afternoon, he'll eat it for dinner. Danny won't have a fish for dinner.

3. Only adults who are friends of Michael's parents are invited to the reception. Everyone who works for Michael is invited to the reception. Some teenagers work for Michael, and no teenager is an adult friend of Michael's parents.

4. A diesel engine doesn't have spark plugs. Automobile engines have spark plugs, although some automobiles have diesel engines.

5. Only brilliant students major in philosophy. Only philosophy majors think deep thoughts. Nobody who thinks deep thoughts likes country music, though there are brilliant students who like country music.

6. Whatever isn't black isn't a raven. Some ravens are black, but not all black things are ravens.

7. The members of the football team are all big. Some wrestlers are big, but none of them is on the football team.

8. If an animal doesn't use language, then it has no beliefs. Dolphins don't use language, but they have many beliefs. Some dolphins fight sharks.

7-5   ACHIEVING COMPARABLE TRANSLATIONS

When we translate ordinary sentences in the Categorical language, this is preliminary to making an evaluation. To carry out the evaluation, we must be able to *compare* the translations.

Consider the following argument:

> One of the faculty members in the Philosophy Department isn't wise. But all full professors are wise. So not all faculty members in the Philosophy Department are full professors.

The following provides an equivalent translation:

> Some faculty member in the Philosophy Department is not a wise thing. Every full professor is a wise person. Some full professor is a full professor. So some faculty member in the Philosophy Department is not a full professor.

The translation has the form displayed:

> Some F is not a W
> Every P is a Y
> Some P is a P
> So some F is not a P

It is easy to find words that make the premisses true and the conclusion false. Our translation is not logically valid.

But our translation is a poor one, for the original argument is valid. Our translation does not bring this out. The sentences in our translation are not sufficiently *comparable*. In dealing with sentences in the Categorical language, we look for the same terms occurring in different sentences. This is how we compare different sentences, and make satisfactory evaluations of arguments and groups of sentences. In the first sentence of our translation, we find the expression 'wise thing.' In the second sentence, 'wise person' is used. These are different expressions. A better translation, one whose sentences can readily be compared, is the following:

> Some faculty member in the Philosophy Department is not a wise person. Every full professor is a wise person. Some full professor is a full professor. So some faculty member in the Philosophy Department is not a full professor.

We can use this Venn diagram to show that our second translation is logically valid:

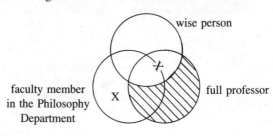

*Exercise: Section 5

For 1–3, determine whether the following arguments are valid, so far as this is possible by using the Categorical language. Justify your answers using proofs, Venn diagrams, or counterexamples.

1. Only college graduates are eligible for honorary degrees from Harvard. A college graduate is a contemptible person. Some football coaches are not contemptible persons. Hence, some football coach is not eligible for an honorary degree from Harvard.

2. The couples who live in apartments on the first floor have no children. Childless couples have lots of time for cultural activities. Bob doesn't know any couples with lots of time for cultural activities. So Bob doesn't know a couple who lives in an apartment on the first floor.

3. Phil doesn't live in a big city. Big cities are cultural centers. So Phil doesn't live in a cultural center.

For 4–6, determine whether the following groups of sentences are incompatible. Justify your answers.

4. Don hasn't visited a single Middle Eastern country. There is some Middle Eastern country which was invaded by the Vikings. Don has visited every country that the Vikings invaded.

5. Paul doesn't own a sailboat. The Sunfish is a sailboat. Paul has two Sunfish.

6. If someone is in college, that person can read. The students in Chemistry 333 are in college. There is someone taking Chemistry 333 who can't read.

7-6 INCORPORATING SEMANTIC FEATURES IN LOGICAL FORM

We test an English sentence, group of sentences, or inference for a general semantic feature by providing Categorical-language translations, and testing them for the logical special case of the general feature. But a positive result of our test carries back to the originals, while a negative result is inconclusive. Our tests are not really suited to determine whether we have or don't have a case of a semantic feature. Instead, we are trying to show that we have a case of the feature. When our test yields a positive result, we have succeeded in showing that the English expressions have the feature we are looking for. A negative result of the test is simply a failure to establish that we have a case of the general feature. It may be that the English expressions don't possess the feature. But the failure may also be due to shortcomings and limitations of our logical techniques.

When an English sentence, group of sentences, or inference has a general semantic feature, but our tests fail to reveal this, the general feature does not "show up" in the logical forms of the translations we use. We would like to overcome some of these limitations of our testing procedure.

Although the following inference:

An uncle of Fred's is a professional baseball player. Professional athletes are well paid. So Fred has an uncle who is well paid.

is clearly valid, if we translate it this way:

> Some uncle of Fred's is a professional baseball player. Every professional athlete is a well-paid person. Some professional athlete is a professional athlete. So some uncle of Fred's is a well-paid person.

our translation is not logically valid. It has this form:

> Some U is a B, Every A is a W, Some A is an A/ Some U is a W

The semantic relation between 'professional baseball player' and 'professional athlete' is one of inclusion, but this is not reflected in the logical form of our translation. The Categorical-language sentence:

> Every professional baseball player is a professional athlete.

is an analytic sentence, though it isn't logically true. If we add this sentence to our translation above, to give us this inference:

> Some uncle of Fred's is a professional baseball player. Every professional baseball player is a professional athlete. Every professional athlete is a well-paid person. Some professional athlete is a professional athlete. So some uncle of Fred's is a well-paid person.

we have a logically valid inference. We will say that the important semantic relation between 'professional baseball player' and 'professional athlete' shows up in the logical form of the sentence 'Every professional baseball player is a professional athlete.'

In making translations from English sentences to Categorical-language sentences, we will allow ourselves to add "extra" Categorical-language sentences, so long as they (1) are either A or E sentences, and (2) are clearly analytic. In translating the argument about Fred's uncle, we allow ourselves to add the extra premiss 'Every professional baseball player is a professional athlete.' This gives us a translation which is logically valid, showing that the original argument is valid. The analytic sentences we add have no existential force. We do not accompany the analytic sentences with 'Some A is an A.' For the analytic character of a sentence is based on the meanings of the words in the sentence. But the fact that a word stands for existing objects is not usually taken to be part of the word's meaning.

If we translate the following inference:

> The students who failed the course all failed the final. One student who passed the final was a freshman girl. So there is a freshman girl who didn't fail the course.

like this:

> Every student who failed the course is a student who failed the final. Some student who failed the course is a student who failed the course. Some student who passed the final is a freshman girl. So some freshman girl is not a person who failed the course.

we cannot show the original inference to be valid. For the relation between 'passed' and 'failed' is an important semantic relation which does not show up in the logical form of the translation. The sentence 'No student who passed the final is a student who failed the final' is an E sentence (a universal negative sentence), and it is obviously analytic. If we add this sentence to our translation, it is easy to show that the expanded translation is logically valid.

When we evaluate an argument, we can "supplement" our translation by adding extra premisses which are analytic A or E sentences. We also supplement our translations in testing sentences for incompatibility. To determine whether these sentences are incompatible:

An uncle of Fred's is a professional baseball player. Professional athletes are well paid. None of Fred's uncles is well paid.

we could use these translations:

Some uncle of Fred's is a professional baseball player. Every professional athlete is a well-paid person. Some professional athlete is a professional athlete. No uncle of Fred's is a well-paid person.

together with this analytic sentence:

Every professional baseball player is a professional athlete.

It is not difficult to construct a proof showing that these sentences are logically incompatible. When we supplement our translations with analytic A and E sentences, we must be careful that the extra sentences we supply really are analytic. If we supply an extra true sentence that isn't analytic, we can make an invalid argument seem valid or compatible sentences seem incompatible. If we supply an extra false sentence, we can obtain any result at all.

By supplementing translations with analytic A and E sentences, we can establish more positive cases of important semantic features than we can without using the analytic sentences. But it is still easier to establish positive cases than it is to establish negative cases. Many sentences can't be adequately translated into the Categorical language. Even for those which can be given adequate translations, a negative result remains inconclusive. There may be some analytic A or E sentences which could be used, but we don't realize this. Or the Categorical language may not be a suitable instrument for getting at a particular instance of a semantic feature. For example, the following argument:

Every carpenter is a union member. Every union member's car is domestic. No Japanese car is domestic. So no carpenter's car is Japanese.

is clearly valid. Each sentence can be given an equivalent translation in the Categorical language:

Every carpenter is a union member. Some carpenter is a carpenter. Every union member's car is a domestic car. Some union member's car is a union member's car. No Japanese car is a domestic car. So no carpenter's car is a Japanese car.

But these translations are not comparable. There are (or seem to be) no analytic sentences we can supply to establish the validity of the argument.

*Exercise A: Section 6

For 1–3, try to show that these arguments are valid, using translations in the Categorical language, and supplying additional analytic premises.

1. Those men wearing yellow hats are carpenters. No one who works with wood likes plastic furniture. Chemical engineers all like plastic furniture. So the men wearing yellow hats aren't chemical engineers.

2. Joe likes to eat whatever Phil likes to eat. But Joe doesn't like to eat any birds. So Phil must not like duck.

3. There is a museum director who isn't stingy, because anthropologists are all generous, and some museum directors are anthropologists.

For 4–6, try to show that these sentences are incompatible, using translations in the Categorical language, and supplying additional analytic sentences.

4. All competent engineers are earning good salaries. There is a competent engineer who is also a theologian.

5. Academics are overworked. Professional philosophers aren't overworked. But all professional philosophers are college professors.

6. All active football players are in good health. Some active football players drink heavily. No one who consumes large quantities of alcohol is in good health.

Exercise B: Section 6

Try to show that the following arguments are valid. Use translations in the Categorical language and supply additional analytic premises if needed. Show work which justifies your answers. In case you cannot show an inference to be valid, try to determine whether it is valid.

1. Doctors all charge too much. Nobody who charges too much is interested in helping people. Ann has a brother-in-law who is a gynecologist. So Ann has a brother-in-law who isn't interested in helping people.

2. It's not true that there is someone who is both a barber and a dentist. There is an Armenian who is an orthodontist. So at least one Armenian isn't a barber.

3. If some individual is a doctor, that individual isn't a chiropractor. Each masseuse is a chiropractor. There isn't any doctor who owns a Mercedes Benz. So no one who owns a Mercedes Benz is a masseuse.

4. Convertibles are heavy cars. But all automobiles use fossil fuel. Nothing which uses fossil fuel is good for the environment. So some convertible isn't good for the environment.

5. There is no newspaper editor who's a doctor. Since George's sons are surgeons, they must not be newspaper editors.

6. Some French kings must not have ruled wisely for there were several kings who levied oppressive taxes while living lavishly themselves. But a king who rules wisely does not levy such taxes unless he avoids lavish living.

7. Professional actors are proud of their looks. Nobody who is proud of his looks is shy. So there isn't a shy professional actor.

8. One of Fran's children is a bachelor. Anyone who isn't married is unhappy about his situation. Nobody who is unhappy about his situation drives a Greyhound bus. So not all of Fran's children drive a Greyhound bus.

Exercise C: Section 6

Try to show that the following groups of sentences are incompatible. Use translations in the Categorical language and supply additional analytic sentences if needed. Show work which justifies your answers. In case you cannot show the sentences to be incompatible, try to determine whether they are incompatible.

1. Scientists belong to a privileged class, but philosophers don't. There are some people who are both scientists and philosophers.

2. No one who plays a sport is a sissy. But anybody who is out of shape is a sissy. And many athletes are out of shape.

3. Auto workers are factory workers. Blue collar workers don't belong to management. But there is an Episcopalian who is an auto worker and an Episcopalian who belongs to management.

4. It isn't true that there is an overweight boxer. But there isn't a boxer who isn't overweight. Mary has a friend who is a fine boxer.

5. The only animals that can think are those that can talk. Dolphins can think but not talk.

6. There is at least one lawyer with a Ph.D. in philosophy. No greedy person has a Ph.D. in philosophy. But if a person wants to get rich, that person is greedy. And there isn't a single lawyer who doesn't want to amass a fortune.

7. Only customers whose orders total $2.00 or more are sitting in a booth. No customer whose order totals $2.00 or more is sitting in a booth.

8. Bruce has a first cousin who is a known criminal. All of Bruce's relatives will be at the family reunion in July. Nobody who is known to be a criminal will attend the reunion.

7-7 ENTHYMEMES

We have allowed ourselves to supply additional analytic A and E sentences in our translations. By supplying additional analytic sentences, we can evaluate more sentences and arguments than we could otherwise. These supplemented translations only make explicit what is implicit in the linguistic practice of English speakers.

When a person makes an inference, he often omits premisses. Though these premisses are essential to the validity of his inference, they are not stated because they are so well known that it seems unnecessary to voice them. Consider this inference:

(1) Any great athlete is sure to have an enlarged heart. So there must be a tennis player with an enlarged heart.

A Categorical-language translation of the inference looks like this:

(2) Every great athlete is a person with an enlarged heart. So some tennis player is a person with an enlarged heart.

This translation is not valid, for nothing in the premiss gives information about tennis players. However, the following argument is valid:

(3) Every great athlete is a person with an enlarged heart. Some tennis player is a great athlete. So some tennis player is a person with an enlarged heart.

Translation (3) would be a "fairer" translation of (1) than (2) would be. Both the speaker and his audience know very well that there are great athletes who are tennis players. This is so well known that it seems unnecessary for the speaker to actually assert it.

An *enthymeme* is an argument with an unstated premiss or premisses. A great many inferences that people actually make are enthymemes. But we cannot use our logical apparatus to evaluate an enthymeme until we supply the missing premisses. Consider this argument:

> Athletic scholarships are not awarded for intellectual achievement. So some college football player has a scholarship that is not awarded for intellectual achievement.

We could translate the argument this way:

> No athletic scholarship is a scholarship awarded for intellectual achievement. Some athletic scholarship is an athletic scholarship. So some college football player's scholarship is not a scholarship awarded for intellectual achievement.

This translation is not logically valid; it is not (plain) valid either. But it is well known that some college football players receive athletic scholarships. If we supplied this additional premiss to the above translation:

> Some college football player's scholarship is an athletic scholarship.

we would obtain a logically valid translation. In actually evaluating the original inference, it would be reasonable to supply the additional premiss. The original inference, with its unstated premiss, provides sufficient support for its conclusion.

The missing premisses of an enthymeme are not analytic sentences. We supply analytic premisses to turn a valid inference into a logically valid inference. The missing premisses of an enthymeme are being taken for granted. It is fair for a speaker (or writer) to do this if the premisses are true and well known. In evaluating real inferences, outside of our logic class, we must be sensitive to the fact that enthymemes occur frequently in ordinary speech. We must be willing to supply reasonable premisses before we evaluate someone's inference. In doing this, we must be careful not to concede too much. Any inference can be turned into a valid inference if we supply strong enough premisses.

*Exercise A: Section 7

Try to show that the following arguments are "valid" enthymemes, by translating them into the Categorical language, supplying additional premisses (if needed) that are true and well known, and evaluating the resulting inferences.

1. There is a city in Washington that doesn't have a harsh winter climate, because no city on the Pacific coast of the 48 contiguous states has a harsh winter climate.

2. Philosophy courses are easy courses. Easy courses have large enrollments. Dave hasn't taken any philosophy courses. So Dave hasn't taken a course which has a large enrollment.

3. Megan hasn't been to any city in Mexico. Megan has visited every city where she has a pen pal. So there is at least one large city where Megan doesn't have a pen pal.

An enthymeme is an inference with an unstated premiss. We might also have a group of sentences which is not incompatible, but which becomes incompatible when a well-known true sentence is added. We might say that such sentences are "enthymematically" incompatible. These two sentences:

> Politicians are honorable. No honorable person is dishonest.

are not incompatible. But it is well known that at least one politician is dishonest. If we translate the above sentences this way:

> Every politician is an honorable person. Some politician is a politician. No honorable person is a dishonest person.

and add this sentence:

> Some politician is a dishonest person.

we get three (logically) incompatible sentences. The original sentences are "enthymematically" incompatible.

*Exercise A: Section 7 (cont.)

Try to find well-known true sentences that can be added to the groups below to yield incompatible sentences. Translate the sentences into the Categorical language, and use the evaluation techniques that have been developed for that language.

4. The large cities on the Great Lakes have large populations of Polish descent. Any city which has a large population of Polish descent has a store which sells pierogis. There are no cities in Illinois that have stores which sell pierogis.

5. Bill doesn't know anybody who lives in Ohio. Bill knows everyone in Ellen's family. One of Ellen's brothers lives in Cincinatti.

6. Communists love caviar. Only well-off people love caviar. No well-off person is a Russian.

Exercise B: Section 7

Use the Categorical language as an instrument to evaluate the inferences stated below. In some cases it may be necessary to supplement the translated premises with analytic A and E sentences or with well-known true sentences. Show work which justifies your answers.

1. Irene must have seen a movie with Peter Lorre in it because Irene has seen every movie in which Humphrey Bogart appeared. And Peter Lorre was in at least one Humphrey Bogart movie.

2. There is a lawyer who lives in Champaign and competes in marathon races. No runners are fat and out of shape. So not all residents of Champaign are fat and out of shape.

3. Bill's sisters must not be fond of Budweiser. For none of Megan's friends likes beer. And all the girls who live on this block are Megan's friends; Bill's sisters live here.

4. A good restaurant won't serve anything that causes food poisoning. It isn't true that there is an expensive restaurant which isn't very good. The restaurants on Anna Ma-

ria Island are all expensive. So none of the restaurants on Anna Maria Island will serve anything that causes food poisoning.

5. No one staying at the Waldorf Astoria is poor. Some college teachers are staying at the Waldorf Astoria. Illegal aliens are all poor. So at least one college teacher is not an illegal alien.

6. Not a single tyrant is well-liked. No dictator is anything but a tyrant. So dictators are not popular.

7. Only profound scholars are philosophers. Only sensitive persons are great artists. Sensitive persons love music. Profound scholars don't love music. Therefore, there is no philosopher who is a great artist.

8. Alsatians are French. And some Basques are French. So there must be an Alsatian who is a Basque.

9. Any student in this logic class who fails the final will fail the course. But nobody will fail the final. So nobody will fail the course.

10. Honest people are unusual. None of Sally's good friends are unusual. They aren't nice either. No one who is trustworthy fails to be honest. So none of Sally's good friends is trustworthy or nice.

Exercise C: Section 7

Use the Categorical language as an instrument to determine whether the following groups of sentences are incompatible. In some cases it may be necessary to supplement the translations with analytic A and E sentences or with well-known true sentences. You must show work which justifies your answers.

1. There are mediums who are residents of Lily Dale, New York. Mediums are spiritualists. But no spiritualists reside in Lily Dale, New York.

2. Some philosophers teach philosophy in college, but not all of them do. Neither is everyone who teaches philosophy in college a philosopher.

3. Ann has a friend who is a famous actress. Any actress is vain. Ann's friends are all humble.

4. Adventurers are brave. Stunt men are oblivious to danger. If a person is oblivious to danger, he is fearless. No fearless person is courageous. But some stunt men are adventurers.

5. The countries with nuclear weapons have them solely for defensive purposes. If a country has nuclear weapons solely for defensive purposes, then that country has not developed nuclear weapons of great accuracy.

6. Mechanical engineers are all both overpaid and over-rated. If a person is over-rated, then he isn't modest. But there is a mechanical engineer who is modest.

7. All fraternity members are poor students, but not conversely. The poor students are all on probation. Every student who's on probation is a fraternity member.

8. Actors love publicity. A person who loves publicity doesn't live on a desert island. Somebody living on a desert island isn't an actor.

9. Carolyn doesn't own a sailboat. Some sailboats have motors. All of Carolyn's boats have motors.

10. Some friend of Dan's mother drinks heavily, even though she belongs to the WCTU. The members of the WCTU are all teetotalers.

7-8 WHAT COMES NEXT

We have developed and investigated the Categorical language, which we then used as an instrument to evaluate sentences and arguments stated in ordinary English. The Categorical language is interesting and useful, but it is a very limited language. What we can say in this language is fairly simple—the *expressive power* of the language is restricted. This restricts the application of the Categorical language. Many English sentences and arguments cannot be evaluated by means of the Categorical language.

In the remainder of this book, we will investigate logical languages with increased expressive power. These are capable of illuminating a larger portion of English. At this point, we have a choice about what to do next. We can proceed to chapter 7, where we will investigate and apply the Extended Categorical language (the EC language). This language builds on the Categorical language by introducing new logical expressions into it. We gain increased expressive power, and wider application, without giving up what we have developed so far.

Or we can move on (starting with chapter 8) to investigate the two fundamental artificial languages of modern logic, the Propositional Connective language and the First-Order language. These languages employ artificial symbols, and so constitute the foundation of *symbolic logic*. The two languages of symbolic logic are more complicated than either the Categorical or the Extended Categorical language, but they have much more expressive power. The Propositional Connective language deals with connectives which join sentences. This is incorporated in the First-Order language, which deals with connectives and quantified phrases.

Chapter 8

The Extended Categorical Language

8-0 SUMMARY

The Categorical language is enriched with new logical expressions, to yield the Extended Categorical language—the ECL. This is more convenient and has greater expressive power than the Categorical language. The ECL can be used to evaluate more ordinary inferences and groups of sentences than can the Categorical language. Venn diagrams are adapted to the ECL, and a new deductive system is developed.

8-1 THE CHANGES WE WANT

The Categorical language is extremely simple, but it can be used to illuminate a surprisingly large portion of ordinary English. However, the Categorical language has some inconvenient features. There are also many kinds of sentences to which the Categorical language can't be applied, and others to which the artificial language is difficult to apply. In this chapter, we will expand the Categorical language to overcome some of these shortcomings.

One inconvenient feature that will be changed is the use of a clumsy sentence 'Some *A* is an *A*' to say that there is an *A*. While this is a very minor irritation, it is easy to fix. A second annoyance is the frequent need to translate one ordinary sentence by separate sentences in the Categorical language. We will make it possible to translate one ordinary sentence by one artificial-language sentence.

The Categorical language enables us to translate these universal sentences:

Bears are carnivorous.

Everybody in the class attended the picnic.

But it isn't easy to translate the denials of universal sentences:

It isn't the case that vampires are dangerous.

It is false that all of Frank's children graduated from college.

In some cases we might translate the denial of a sentence by using a contradictory opposite of the sentence being denied. But we can't always use this technique to translate negative sentences. Even when we can use it, the technique is awkward, and is likely to prove confusing. It will help if we enrich the language with a new expression for making denials.

Singular sentences constitute a very important class of sentences about individuals. Achieving a better understanding of singular sentences is one of our goals in this course. We will enlarge the Categorical language to encompass singular sentences. The language which results from expanding the Categorical language is the *Extended Categorical language*—the *ECL*. The ECL is more convenient than the (plain) Categorical language, and has a wider range of application.

8-2 WHAT WE WILL KEEP

All expressions in the Categorical language also belong to the Extended Categorical language. The Categorical language is a *sublanguage* of the ECL. We obtain the ECL by adding new logical expressions to the Categorical language, together with sentences formed from these new expressions. The new expressions will include two artificial symbols borrowed from symbolic logic. This gives the ECL a mixed character; it contains both ordinary expressions and artificial symbols.

The Venn diagrams we have used for the Categorical language are unchanged in the ECL. But the new logical expressions in the ECL call for some new kinds of diagrams. And the greater complexity of the ECL gives rise to new cases for which diagrams either can't be used or are inconvenient to use.

When we first developed the Categorical deductive system, we used these rules:

E-Conversion

I-Conversion

Obverse Introduction

Obverse Elimination

Logical Truth

AAA-1

AII-1

We will employ these same rules in the Extended Categorical deductive system.

When we applied the Categorical language to English, it proved necessary to enlarge the Categorical deductive system with the rule Existence Introduction. That rule will not be retained in the Extended Categorical deductive system. However, we will use the same name (Existence Introduction) for a new rule. We must also add other rules to capture the inferential meanings of the new logical expressions in the ECL.

*Exercise: Section 2

Determine which of the following sentences are true.

1. Some expressions in the Categorical language will be omitted from the Extended Categorical language.

2. The rule Existence Introduction in the Categorical deductive system will be dropped from the Extended Categorical deductive system.

3. Some logical expressions in the ECL do not belong to the Categorical language.

4. The rule Existence Introduction in the Extended Categorical deductive system is also a rule of the Categorical deductive system.

8-3 SMALL CHANGE

To indicate existence in the ECL, we will use *existence clauses*. These are sentences formed from the logical expression:

There is a(n)_____

by putting a common noun or noun phrase in the blank. Some existence clauses in the Extended Categorical language are:

There is a dog.

There is a non-(college professor).

There is a unicorn.

The logical expression 'There is a(n)_____' is a one-place sentence-forming functor for one common noun or noun phrase. An existence clause 'There is an a' is true just in case there is (or was or will be) at least one a.

The sentence 'Some honest politician is an honest politician' belongs to both the Categorical language and the ECL. But the sentence 'There is an honest politician' is more convenient for indicating existence. To translate this ordinary universal sentence:

All the books on the top shelf are logic books.

we can use two ECL-sentences:

Every book on the top shelf is a logic book.
There is a book on the top shelf.

In the ECL we can make one sentence out of this translation by using the logical expression '&':

Every book on the top shelf is a logic book & There is a book on the top shelf.

The *ampersand* '&' is the sign of *conjunction*. When '&' is used to unite two sentences, the resulting compound sentence is also called a *conjunction*. We *conjoin* two sentences to form a conjunction. In writing, the ampersand is sufficient. But we will say "and" when we read '&.' To read (out loud) the sentence above, we say "Every book on the top shelf is a logic book and there is a book on the top shelf."

Both sentences conjoined with '&' are capitalized. Sentences formed with '&' are enclosed in parentheses:

(Every book on the top shelf is a logic book & There is a book on the top shelf)

When we use parentheses, periods are not placed at the ends of sentences. As an abbreviation, outer parentheses are sometimes omitted; when this is done, a period is restored at the end of the rightmost sentence. We must not omit parentheses when a conjunction is a component of a larger sentence:

[(Every cat is an animal & No dog is a cat) & Some dog is a Collie]

The ampersand is a two-place sentence-forming functor for two sentences. Its meaning is given by this *truth-table*:

p	q	$(p \,\&\, q)$
True	True	True
True	False	False
False	True	False
False	False	False

To translate a universal sentence with existential force, we use a universal sentence of the ECL conjoined to an existence clause for the subject. For example, these sentences:

Alligators don't make good pets.

All Kevin's professors are interesting people.

receive these equivalent translations:

(No alligator is an animal that makes a good pet & There is an alligator)

(Every professor of Kevin's is an interesting person & There is a professor of Kevin's)

Sentences without existential force are translated as they were before. These sentences:

Any trespasser will be prosecuted.

Only a brilliant student deserves an A in logic.

receive these translations:

Every trespasser is a person who will be prosecuted.

Every person who deserves an A in logic is a brilliant student.

We must explain how to reason with the new logical expressions of the ECL—we must explain their inferential meanings. We do this by adding new rules to the Extended Categorical deductive system (from now on we will call this the *EC deductive system*). The new version of Existence Introduction has two forms:

Existence Introduction (ExI)

.			.	
m Some α is a β			m Some α is not a β	
.			.	
n There is an α	m, ExI		n There is an α	m, ExI

We can infer an existence clause for the *subject* of a 'Some' sentence, as is done in the following proof:

1	Some apple is not an orange.	
2	Some apple is a non-orange.	1, ObvI
3	Some non-orange is an apple.	2, I-Conv
4	There is a non-orange.	3, ExI

This proof establishes 'Some apple is not an orange. / There is a non-orange.' as a theorem of the EC deductive system.

The rule *Conjunction* is a two-premiss rule for reasoning with '&':

Conjunction (Conj)

.

m p

.

n q

.

r $(p \& q)$ m, n, Conj

In the illustration above, the first formula (at step m) was put on the left side of step r. Using the premisses from steps n and m, we could also infer:

t $(q \& p)$ n, m, Conj

Using Conjunction, a single step can be "taken" twice. A proof of 'There is an M / (There is an M & There is an M)' can be constructed like this:

1	There is an M	
2	(There is an M & There is an M)	1, 1, Conj

There are two *Simplification (Simp)* rules. From a premiss $(p \& q)$ we can infer p by Simplification, and we can infer q by Simplification. Simplification is used in the following proof:

1	(Every F is a G & There is an F)	
2	Every F is a G	1, Simp
3	No F is a non-G	2, ObvI
4	No non-G is an F	3, E-Conv

The rule *Existential Subalternation* involves both '&' and existence clauses. This rule has two forms:

Existential Subalternation (ExS)

.

m (Every α is a β & There is an α)   m   (No α is a β & There is an α)

.

n Some α is a β m, ExS n Some α is not a β m, ExS

To use this rule, the existence clause must contain the *subject* of the universal sentence. (In logical systems where universal sentences have existential force, the inference from a universal sentence to the corresponding particular is called 'Subalternation.' Our rule Existential Subalternation is like Subalternation with the addition of an explicit existence clause.) Existential Subalternation is used in the following proof:

1	There is a dog.	
2	No cat is a dog.	
3	No dog is a cat.	2, E-Conv
4	(No dog is a cat & There is a dog)	3, 1, Conj
5	Some dog is not a cat.	4, ExS
6	Some dog is a non-cat.	5, ObvI

It was necessary to convert step 2 before conjoining it with step 1. If 1 had simply been combined with 2 to obtain this:

(No cat is a dog & There is a dog)

it could not serve as a premiss for the rule Existential Subalternation. It would also be a mistake to start the proof like this:

1	There is a dog.	
2	No cat is a dog.	
3	(No cat is a dog & There is a dog)	2, 1, Conj
4	(No dog is a cat & There is a dog)	3, E-Conv

Step 3 is correct, but step 4 is mistaken. Our conversion and obversion rules are only used on sentences standing alone; we do not use them on the components of larger sentences.

*Exercise A: Section 3

For 1–2, fill in the reasons which justify the steps.

1.
1	(There is a *B* & Every *B* is a *C*)
2	There is a *B*
3	Every *B* is a *C*
4	(Every *B* is a *C* & There is a *B*)
5	Some *B* is a *C*
6	Some *C* is a *B*

2.
1	There is a cow.
2	Every cow is a non-horse.
3	No cow is a horse.
4	(No cow is a horse & There is a cow)
5	Some cow is not a horse.

For 3–4, prove the formula sequences to be theorems.

3. There is an *A* / Some *A* is an *A*

4. Every *L* is an *M*, No *M* is an *N*, There is an *N* / Some *N* is not an *L*

The Venn diagram for a sentence 'There is an α' calls for an 'X' in the α circle. We diagram the sentence 'There is a student' like this:

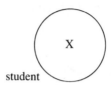

If the circle for the noun in the existence clause is combined with other circles, it may be necessary to place the 'X' on a line. To diagram 'There is a student' in two circles, we put an 'X' on the line which cuts the student circle:

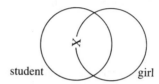

The diagram for 'There is an α' is the same as the diagram for 'Some α is an α.'

To diagram a sentence (*p* & *q*), we simply combine the diagrams for *p* and for *q*—unless the two sentences contain too many terms. The diagram for:

(Every college freshman is a girl & There is a college freshman)

is the following:

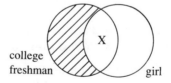

And the diagram for:

(Every *A* is a *B* & No *C* is a *B*)

is:

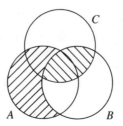

We do not try to diagram:

(Every A is a B & No C is a D)

because we don't diagram sentences or groups of them containing more than three terms.

*Exercise A: Section 3 (cont.)

For 5–6, use Venn diagrams to determine if the sentence on the left implies the sentence on the right.

a	b
5. (No A is a B & There is an A)	Some B is not an A
6. (Every A is a B & There is a non-B)	Some non-B is a non-A

For 7–8, use Venn diagrams to test for incompatibility.

7. Every A is a B, Every A is a non-B, There is an A

8. (Some A is a non-B & Some B is a non-A), No A is a B, No B is a non-B

Exercise B: Section 3

Use the ECL as an instrument to evaluate the inferences stated below. In some cases it may be necessary to supplement the translated premises with analytic A and E sentences or with well-known true sentences. Show work which justifies your answers.

1. Each full professor in the English Department has published at least one book. All full professors are members of the graduate faculty, but not all members of the graduate faculty have published a book. So there is a member of the graduate faculty who has published a book and a member who hasn't.

2. Jane's good friends are all generous. So none of the people in the blue house across the street can be a good friend of Jane, because they are extremely selfish.

3. Not all college professors are elitist snobs, but some of them are. One of Norma's uncles is a college professor. So Norma has an uncle who isn't an elitist snob.

4. Some of Jorge's cousins live in Mexico. Edith's relatives all live in Canada. Clearly, not all of Jorge's cousins are related to Edith.

5. None of Fran's children will eat mushrooms. One of Fran's children is a computer programmer. People who have good taste will eat mushrooms. So there is a computer programmer who doesn't have good taste.

6. If Neil sees a painting he likes at the art festival, he will buy it. Neil will buy a painting. So he must be going to see a painting he likes at the art festival.

7. The engineering majors who will graduate this semester have all gotten good jobs. The graduating students who have gotten good jobs will be asked to make a pledge to the alumni fund. Mr. Devin has a son who is in mechanical engineering, and will graduate this semester. So Mr. Devin has a son who will be asked to make a pledge to the alumni fund.

8. Bruce has an uncle who won a Nobel Prize. Only brilliant people have won Nobel Prizes. Professional wrestlers aren't brilliant. So one of Bruce's uncles doesn't wrestle professionally.

Exercise C: Section 3

Use the ECL to determine if the following groups of sentences are incompatible. In some cases it may be necessary to supplement the translation with analytic A and E sentences or with well-known true sentences. Show work which justifies your answers.

1. Several guests asked Carolyn for her recipe for cheesecake. The guests were all on diets. Nobody who asked Carolyn for her recipe for cheesecake was on a diet.

2. The students in Professor Barber's seminar are all senior philosophy majors, but not all the senior philosophy majors are taking the seminar. Every senior philosophy major is taking an honors seminar. The only students in Professor Barber's seminar are those who are taking an honors seminar.

3. Sheri doesn't know any boys who are good at math. One of Rocco's roommates is a boy who is a mathematical genius. But Sheri knows Rocco's roommates.

4. None of Mary's children graduated from a midwestern university. But one of Mary's daughters was in the senior class of Rantoul High School in 1974. The entire senior class from Rantoul High School in 1974 entered the University of Illinois the next fall. And every person from Rantoul High School who entered the University of Illinois in fall, 1974 graduated.

5. Only ghost stories have frightened Marian, but not all the ghost stories she has read or heard have done so. Sally told a story that frightened Marian, but Sally has never told a ghost story.

6. The teachers in the Oakland public schools are all union members. If someone is a union member, then that person has job security. But not everyone with job security has a savings account. However, there is a person who teaches in the Oakland public schools and has a savings account.

7. FBI agents are college graduates. Some FBI agents are lawyers. One of Marcia's children is an FBI agent. But Marcia's children all took Jane's advice, and no one who took Jane's advice graduated from college.

8. Gothic cathedrals have (exclusively) pointed arches, but the arches in Romanesque cathedrals are round. Dick went into some Romanesque cathedrals last summer. All the cathedrals that Dick has visited are Gothic.

8-4   THE SIGN OF NEGATION

In this section, we introduce the sign of negation '~.' It is prefixed to a sentence; we might write:

> ~Every student is a girl.

> ~(No vampire is a student & There is a vampire)

The sign of negation is a sentence-forming functor which applies to a single sentence (or formula). By introducing the sign of negation together with '&,' we have very much increased the expressive power of the ECL.

A sentence $\sim p$ is negative, but it isn't categorical. In the negative sentence '$\sim$Every girl is a model,' the component 'Every girl is a model' is the *negated part*. This part is a universal (affirmative) sentence, but the whole sentence is neither universal nor particular.

The sign of negation is used to deny the claim made by the negated part. It is very important to understand what is being denied. For example, this sentence:

(1) ($\sim$Every dog is a Collie & There is a dog)

makes a different claim from this one:

(2) $\sim$ (Every dog is a Collie & There is a dog)

The *scope* of the negation sign is the sentence that is negated. In (1), the scope of '$\sim$' is just 'Every dog is a Collie.' So (1) claims two things:

(i) It isn't true that every dog is a Collie.

(ii) (It is true that) there is a dog.

In (2), the scope of the negation sign is the whole sentence in parentheses. The compound sentence makes more than one claim: (2) does not single out any specific claim as the mistaken one. What (2) claims is that *either* it isn't true that every dog is a Collie *or* it isn't true that there is a dog (*or* both).

The meaning of the negation sign is explained by the following truth-table:

p	$\sim p$
True	False
False	True

Since it is true that every dog is a mammal, the sentence '$\sim$Every dog is a mammal' is false. Similarly, the sentence:

$\sim$(Every vampire is a goat & There is a vampire)

is true. But this sentence:

($\sim$Every vampire is a goat & There is a vampire)

is false. (Why?)

In order to read a sentence beginning with '$\sim$,' we can say one of the following for '$\sim$':

It is false that

It is not true that

It is not the case that

We might read ' ~ No college student is a boy' as "It is not true that no college student is a boy."

*Exercise A: Section 4

For 1–4, determine which sentences are true.

1. The negation of a universal negative sentence is not a particular affirmative sentence.

2. If a sentence $\sim p$ is false, then p is true.

3. A sentence $\sim(p \,\&\, q)$ is equivalent to $(\sim p \,\&\, q)$.

4. A negative sentence $\sim p$ is incompatible with p.

Sentences 5–8 belong to the ECL. Determine which are true.

5. $\sim$ Some vampire is a nice person.

6. $\sim$(No student is a puppy & There is a student)

7. ($\sim$No student is a puppy & There is a student)

8. $\sim(\sim$No student is a puppy & $\sim$There is a student)

In this sentence:

(3) $\sim$ No man is a fish.

the diagram for the negated part of (3) is:

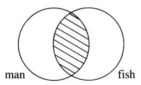

The diagram for sentence (3) should "cancel" the diagram for the negated part. Since the diagram for 'No man is a fish' is only marked in one section, we can (and must) deny this by using a diagram with the opposite marking in that same section:

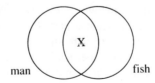

This is also the diagram for the sentence:

(4) Some man is a fish.

The diagram indicates that (3) is equivalent to (4).

To diagram a sentence beginning with ' $\sim$,' we think of (or draw) the diagram for the negated part. Then we draw a diagram which cancels the diagram for the negated part. It is easy to diagram a sentence beginning with '~' when the diagram for the negated part is marked in just one section. It is also easy to diagram a negative sentence when the diagram for the negated part has an 'X' on the line—if this is the only marking in the diagram. Suppose we are considering vampires and bats, and diagram the sentence 'There is a vampire' in this two-circle diagram:

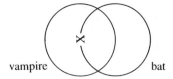

To diagram (5):

    (5) ~There is a vampire.

in a two-circle diagram, we must cancel the 'X' on the line:

    Difficulties arise when the diagram for the negated part is marked in two or more sections. In this sentence:

    (6) ~(No jockey is a heavyweight & There is a jockey)

the diagram for the negated part is:

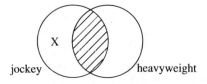

    Sentence (6) denies the compound sentence in parentheses. The diagram for (6) should cancel the diagram for the negated part. If the sentence 'No jockey is a heavyweight & There is a jockey' is incorrect, there are two possibilities for error in its diagram: (i) The 'X' in the left section, and (ii) the shading in the center section. We cannot draw just one diagram which represents the content of (6). We need two diagrams—one for each possible error. And we must say that one *or* the other diagram (or, possibly, both) is correct:

The diagrams above were obtained by thinking about the diagram for the negated part, and making a separate diagram for each thing that might be wrong with it. Instead of thinking about the diagram for the negated part, we can think about the negated part itself. Sentence (6) says that the conjunction in parentheses is false. Either it is false that no jockey is a heavyweight or it is false that there is a jockey:

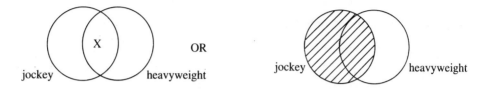

This pair of diagrams differs from those above. Either pair can be used to represent the claim made by the negative sentence. However, to obtain correct results about semantic relations, it is necessary to consistently use one style of representation. In this book I will make use of the pair obtained by considering the diagram for the negated sentence.

The diagrams for:

(7) ~(Every apple is an orange & There is an apple) are the following:

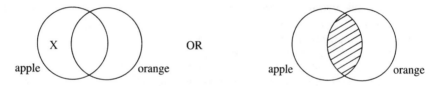

However, we use a single diagram for:

(8) (~Every apple is an orange & There is an apple)

The diagram is:

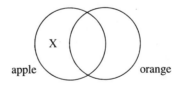

Given the left conjunct:

(9) ~Every apple is an orange.

and its diagram, the right conjunct is redundant. Since there is already an 'X' in the apple circle, we do not add another 'X' for the existence clause.

To diagram this sentence:

(10) ~(Some vampire is a person & Some vampire is not a person)

we use these diagrams:

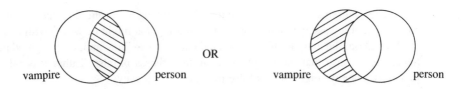

*Exercise A. Section 4 (cont.)

Draw Venn diagrams for the sentences (and formulas) below.

9. ~Every *M* is a non-*N*

10. (~No *M* is an *N* & There is an *N*)

11. ~(Every patriot is scoundrel & Some scoundrel is a patriot)

12. ~(No philosopher is a statesman & Every philosopher is a statesman)

For a sentence with a single diagram, we can test for logical semantic features as we did before. It is more difficult to test sentences which have multiple diagrams. Suppose we wish to know whether sentence *p* implies *q*, but *p* has two diagrams while *q* has only one. Each diagram for *p* represents one way in which *p* might be true. But for *p* to imply *q*, any way to make *p* true must also make *q* true. For *p* to imply *q*, each diagram for *p* must show implications to the diagram for *q*.

To determine whether (11) implies (12):

(11) ~(No tiger is a feline & There is a tiger)

(12) Some tiger is a feline.

we can draw these diagrams:
(11)

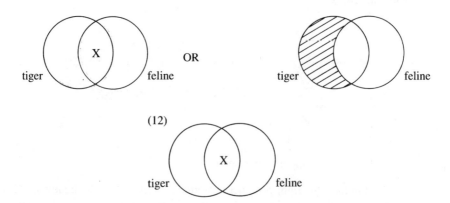

The left diagram for (11) shows implication to the single diagram for (12). But the right diagram does not show implication. Sentence (11) might be true because the right diagram is correct and the left isn't. (In actuality, of course, both are correct.) In such a case, (12) wouldn't be true. Sentence (11) does not imply (12).

Each diagram for:

(13) ~(There is a vampire & There is a unicorn)

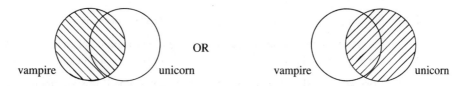

shows implication to the single diagram for (14):

(14) No vampire is a unicorn.

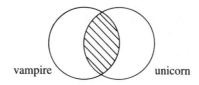

Sentence (13) implies (14).

The same principles apply when we consider *n*-place implication, where $n > 2$. To evaluate this argument:

> ~(Every man is a college graduate & There is a man) Some man is an attorney. So some man is not a college graduate.

we require two separate diagrams for the premisses:

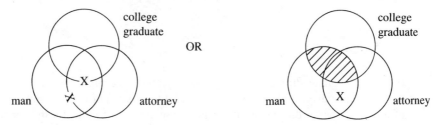

If the premisses imply the conclusion, each diagram for the premisses must contain the diagram for the conclusion. In this case, then, the argument is logically valid.

To determine whether *p* implies *q* when *p* has a single diagram but *q* has two diagrams, we recall that *q* is true if either diagram is correct. *p* implies *q* if the diagram for *p* shows implication to either diagram for *q*. If *p* and *q* both have multiple diagrams, then *p* implies *q* if every diagram for *p* shows implication to at least one diagram for *q*.

*Exercise A: Section 4 (cont.)

Use Venn diagrams to determine whether the sentences on the left imply those on the right.

a	b
13. ~No dog is a cat.	~Some dog is not a cat.
14. ~Some turkey is a cow.	~(Every turkey is a cow & There is a turkey)

15. ~(No dog is a cat & There is a cat),   Some dog is a cat.
    Some cat is a Siamese.

16. ~Some turkey is a cow.   ~(Every turkey is a cow & There is a cow)

17. ~(Every chicken is a horse & Some   ~(~No non-chicken is a horse & ~Some
    horse is not a chicken)   non-horse is a chicken)

Suppose we wish to use Venn diagrams to determine if this argument is valid:

~(Every D is a G & Every G is a D)
~Some D is not a G
So ~(No G is a non-D & Some D is a G)

We need two diagrams for the first premiss:

   OR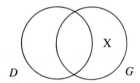

The diagram for the second premiss conflicts with the left diagram for the first premiss. This combination is impossible. We continue with the right diagram:

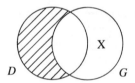

(If all the diagrams drop out, the argument is valid—we might say that such an argument is valid "vacuously.") The argument is valid if the diagram for the premisses contains one of the diagrams for the conclusion. Since these are the diagrams for the conclusion:

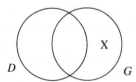   OR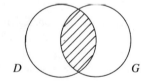

the argument is valid.

If we are testing sentences for incompatibility, we try to complete at least one diagram in which all the sentences are represented. If we can do this, the sentences are not incompatible.

*Exercise A: Section 4 (cont.)

Use Venn diagrams to determine which groups of sentences are incompatible.

18. ~Some rabbi is a priest. (Every priest is a rabbi & There is a priest)

19. No parson is a clergyman. ~(Every clergyman is a parson & There is a clergyman)

20. ~No nun is a priest. ~Some priest is a woman. Every nun is a woman.

21. ~(Some mullah is a rabbi & Some mullah is not a rabbi), No mullah is a rabbi. Every rabbi is a mullah.

22. (~No monk is an abbot & ~Every monk is an abbot), ~(~Every non-abbot is a non-monk & ~Every abbot is a non-monk)

Exercise B: Section 4

Use Venn diagrams to determine whether the following formula sequences are logically valid.

1. ~(Every A is a B & There is a B) / ~(~There is an A & Some B is a non-A)

2. ~There is an M / No M is an N

3. ~(No F is a G & There is an F) / ~Some F is not a G

4. ~(No P is a Q & There is a P), No R is a Q, Some P is an R / Some P is a Q

5. ~Some L is not a non-M / Every M is an L

6. Some A is not a B / (~Every A is a B & there is a B)

7. (No satisfactory martini is a cocktail made with vodka & There is a satisfactory martini) / ~Every cocktail made with vodka is a satisfactory martini.

8. Every Italian wine is a subtle wine, ~No non-(subtle wine) is a non-(subtle wine). / Some non-(subtle wine) is a non-(Italian wine).

9. Every ski instructor is a poor teacher & There is a poor teacher. / ~Every poor teacher is a ski instructor.

10. Some existentialist philosopher is a German, ~Some existentialist philosopher is a Russian. / Some existentialist philosopher is not a Russian.

11. (Every Marxist is a radical & There is a Marxist) / ~(No Marxist is a radical & Every Marxist is a person of limited intelligence)

12. ~(No Frenchman is a European & Every European is a non-Frenchman), Every European is a profound scholar. / ~No profound scholar is a Frenchman.

Exercise C: Section 4

Use Venn diagrams to determine whether the following groups of sentences and formulas are logically incompatible.

1. ~Some A is a B, Some B is not a non-A

2. No M is a non-N, ~Every non-N is an M, Some N is a non-M

3. ~(Some P is a Q & Some P is not a Q), ~No P is a Q, Some Q is a non-P

4. ~Some F is not a G, ~(Some H is a non-F & There is an H), ~Every H is a G

5. (Every non-*A* is a *B* & ~There is an *A*), No non-*B* is a non-*A*

6. ~(Every square is a rectangle & There is a square), ~Some square is a non-rectangle. Some square is a quadrilateral.

7. (~Some joker is a playing card & There is a joker), ~Some joker is not a playing card.

8. ~There is a square circle. No square circle is a square circle. Some circle is a square circle.

9. ~(Every motorcycle is a dangerous vehicle & There is a motorcycle), Some motorcycle is a dangerous vehicle. ~Every dangerous vehicle is a motorcycle.

10. No macaroni sandwich is a gourmet's delight. (There is a macaroni sandwich & ~Some macaroni sandwich is not a gourmet's delight)

8-5 REASONING WITH NEGATIVE SENTENCES

Now is a good time to return to the basic technique for establishing positive cases of semantic features. We will enlarge the EC deductive system to include rules based on the sign of negation. Until we can reason (correctly) with sentences containing this expression, we won't understand it completely.

The first rules for negation are based on our knowledge about contradictory opposites. The *A-O Transformation (AOT)* allows us to use a formula:

(i) Every α is a β

as a premiss to infer:

(ii) ~Some α is not a β

The same rule allows us to infer (i) from (ii). Using AOT, we can also move from:

(iii) ~Every α is a β

to:

(iv) Some α is not a β

and from (iv) to (iii). The following proof uses A-O Transformation.

1	Every *M* is an *M*	LT
2	~ Some *M* is not an *M*	1, AOT

A sentence '~Some *M* is not an *M*' is logically true.

The *E-I Transformation (EIT)* is analogous to AOT: From:

(i) No α is a β

we can infer:

(ii) ~Some α is a β

We can also use EIT to move from (ii) to (i). And we can infer either of the following from the other:

(iii) ~No α is a β

(iv) Some α is a β

*Exercise A: Section 5

Prove the following to be theorems of the EC deductive system.

1. / $\sim$ Some non-A is an A

2. $\sim$ Some M is an N / Every N is a non-M

3. There is a B, $\sim$ Some B is a C / Some B is not a C

In order to deal with the remaining rules which involve negation, we must allow proofs from hypotheses to have more complicated structure. We will allow a whole proof to occur as a step in another proof. The proofs within proofs are *conditional subproofs*. A conditional subproof has *exactly one hypothesis*, which is the first step of the subproof. Suppose we are developing a proof from hypotheses p_1, p_2, and have gotten this far:

1 p_1

2 p_2
$\overline{}$
3 p_3

4 p_4

At this point we want to start a conditional subproof with hypothesis q_1. We continue the numbering of the steps in the proof from hypotheses—so q_1 will be step 5. But we shift the conditional subproof slightly to the right, and we draw a vertical line to separate the conditional subproof from the *main proof*:

.

.

4 p_4

5 $\quad\big|\,q_1$

The following illustrates an actual proof containing a conditional subproof:

1	No A is a B	
2	Every A is a B	
3	$\sim$ Some A is a B	1, EIT
4	$\sim$ Some A is not a B	2, AOT
5	$\big|$ There is an A	
6	$\big|$ (Every A is a B & There is an A)	2, 5, Conj
7	$\big|$ Some A is a B	6, ExS
8	$\big|$ (Some A is a B & $\sim$ Some A is a B)	7, 3, Conj

A conditional subproof which is a step in a larger proof is *subordinate to* the larger proof. We can also have a conditional subproof within a second conditional subproof, which is itself a step in the main proof. To cover this, we say that if one conditional subproof is subordinate to a second, and the second is subordinate to a third proof (or subproof), then the first is *subordinate to* the third. Finally, a conditional subproof is *subordinate to* itself. In a conditional subproof, any previous step can serve as a premiss, *so long as it occurs in a proof or subproof to which the conditional subproof is subordinate*.

In the EC deductive system, the reason for having conditional subproofs is to demonstrate that their hypotheses are mistaken. Either we have a hypothesis p, and we really wish to justify $\sim p$. Or we have a hypothesis $\sim p$, and we wish to justify p. We can show that a hypothesis is mistaken if we show that it leads to some false consequence. For our purposes, we will insist that the hypothesis must lead to a logically false consequence having the form either $(p \,\&\, \sim p)$ or $(\sim p \,\&\, p)$.

The rules *Negation Introduction* ($\sim I$) and *Negation Elimination* ($\sim E$) are rules for which a whole conditional subproof serves as premiss. Negation Introduction uses a premiss:

$$\begin{array}{ll} p & \qquad\qquad\text{or:} \qquad\quad p \\ \cdot & \qquad\qquad\qquad\qquad\qquad \cdot \\ \cdot & \qquad\qquad\qquad\qquad\qquad \cdot \\ (q \,\&\, \sim q) & \qquad\qquad\qquad\quad (\sim q \,\&\, q) \end{array}$$

to infer the conclusion $\sim p$. This conclusion *must not* be written in the conditional subproof. It is written as a step in the first proof or subproof (other than the conditional subproof itself) to which the conditional subproof is subordinate. An illustration of Negation Introduction is the following:

1	No A is a B	
2	Every A is a B	
3	$\sim$ Some A is a B	1, EIT
4	$\sim$ Some A is not a B	2, AOT
5	$\quad$ There is an A	
6	$\quad$ (Every A is a B & There is an A)	2, 5, Conj
7	$\quad$ Some A is a B	6, ExS
8	$\quad$ (Some A is a B & $\sim$ Some A is a B)	7, 3, Conj
9	$\sim$ There is an A	5 – 8, $\sim$ I

The rule Negation Elimination uses a premiss

$$\begin{array}{ll} \sim p & \qquad\qquad\text{or} \qquad\quad \sim p \\ \cdot & \qquad\qquad\qquad\qquad\qquad \cdot \\ \cdot & \qquad\qquad\qquad\qquad\qquad \cdot \\ (q \,\&\, \sim q) & \qquad\qquad\qquad\quad (\sim q \,\&\, q) \end{array}$$

to reach the conclusion p. This rule is illustrated in the following:

1	~ There is an *A*	
2	~ Every *A* is a *B*	
3	Some *A* is not a *B*	2, AOT
4	There is an *A*	3, ExI
5	(There is an *A* & ~ There is an *A*)	4, 1, Conj
6	Every *A* is a *B*	2 – 5, ~ E

Whenever Negation Elimination is used, the rule Negation Introduction could also be used. In this proof, for example, instead of the step 6 that actually appears, we could have inferred:

6   ~~ Every *A* is a *B*   2 – 5, ~ I

A conditional subproof cannot be the last item in a proof. Every successful proof must end with a formula which is a step in the main proof. And once a conditional subproof is completed, the steps in it are no longer available as premisses for the later steps. The whole subproof is available as a premiss in the next proof to the left, but the individual steps are not available. For this reason, the following "proof" is mistaken:

1	~ There is an *A*	
2	~ Every *A* is a *B*	
3	Some *A* is not a *B*	2, AOT
4	There is an *A*	3, ExI
5	(There is an *A* & ~ There is an *A*)	4, 1, Conj
6	Every *A* is a *B*	2 – 5, ~ E
7	(Every *A* is a *B* & There is an *A*)	6, 4, Conj

Step 7 is in error. For step 4 is no longer available as a premiss following step 5.

We know that a proof from hypotheses can begin with no hypotheses when the first step is justified by the rule Logical Truth. A proof that begins with a conditional subproof is also a proof with no hypotheses. The hypothesis of the conditional subproof does not count as a hypothesis of the main proof. So the following proof:

1	(Every *A* is a non-*A* & Some *A* is an *A*)	
2	Every *A* is a non-*A*	1, Simp
3	No *A* is an *A*	2, ObvE
4	~ Some *A* is an *A*	3, EIT
5	Some *A* is an *A*	1, Simp
6	(Some *A* is an *A* & ~ Some *A* is an *A*)	5, 4, Conj
7	~(Every *A* is a non-*A* & Some *A* is an *A*)	1 – 6, ~ I

establishes that a sentence having the form of step 7 is logically true.

*Exercise A: Section 5 (cont.)

For 4–6 fill in the reasons justifying the steps in the proofs.

4. 1   ~ There is an *A*

     2   Some *A* is a *B*

     3 | Every *A* is a *B*

     4 | (Every *A* is a *B* & There is an *A*)

     5 | Some *A* is a *B*

     6 | (Some *A* is a *B* & ~ Some *A* is a *B*)

     7   ~ Every *A* is a *B*

5. 1   ~ ~ No *B* is a *C*

     2 | ~ No *B* is a *C*

     3 | (~ No *B* is a *C* & ~ ~ No *B* is a *C*)

     4   No *B* is a *C*

6. 1 | (There is an *F* & ~ There is an *F*)

     2   ~(There is an *F* & ~ There is an *F*)

Construct proofs for 7–9.

7. ~ There is a *C* / ~ Some *C* is a *C*

8. Some *B* is a *C*, ~ Some *B* is a *D* / Some *B* is not a *D*

9. No *F* is a *G*, Some *F* is a *G* / No *P* is a *Q*

Previously, we proved that a group of sentences is incompatible by proving that all but one of the sentences imply the contradictory opposite of the remaining sentence. This is still the right idea. But in the ECL, the sign of negation provides a convenient way to obtain the contradictory opposite of a sentence. Any two sentences *p* and ~*p* are contradictory opposites.

To prove that sentences *p*, *q*, *r* are logically incompatible, we can prove *p*, *q* / ~*r* (or *q*, *r* / ~*p* or *p*, *r* / ~*q*). And to prove that *p*, *q*, ~ *r* are incompatible, we can prove *p*, *q* / *r* (or *q*, ~*r* / ~*p* or *p*, ~*r* / ~*q*). From now on, in proving incompatibility we will make use of contradictory opposites formed with '~ .'

*Exercise A: Section 5 (cont.)

Prove that the following groups of formulas symbolize incompatible sentences.

10. ~(Every *A* is a *B* & No *B* is a *C*), ~ Some *A* is not a *B*, ~ Some *C* is a *B*

11. Every *A* is a *B*, No *B* is a *C*, Some *C* is a *C*, Every *C* is an *A*

12. (Every *A* is a *B* & Some *A* is not a *B*), ~ Some *C* is a *D*

Exercise B: Section 5

Determine which of the following formula sequences are valid. Construct proofs in the EC deductive system of the valid sequences. Produce counterexamples to show that the remaining sequences are invalid.

1. No *N* is an *M* / ~Some *N* is not a non-*M*

2. ~Every *R* is an *S*, ~Some *R* is an *S* / (No *R* is an *S* & There is an *R*)

3. No non-*G* is an *F*, Every *G* is an *H*, There is an *H* / ~No *H* is an *F*

4. ~(Every *P* is a *Q* & Every *Q* is a *P*), ~Some *P* is not a *Q* / Some *Q* is not a *P*

5. ~(Some *R* is an *S* & Some *T* is a *Q*) / (~Some *R* is an *S* & ~Some *T* is a *Q*)

6. Every *A* is a *B*, Every *C* is a *B*, There is a *C* / Some *A* is a *C*

7. / ~(No *A* is a non-*B* & Some *A* is not a *B*)

8. ~(No *A* is a *B* & No *C* is a *B*), ~Some *B* is an *A*, Every *C* is a *D* / Some *D* is a *B*

Exercise C: Section 5

Determine which of the following groups of formulas symbolize incompatible sentences. Construct proofs in the EC deductive system to show incompatibility. Produce counterexamples to show that the remaining groups do not symbolize logically incompatible sentences.

1. Every *F* is a *G*, Every *G* is an *H*, Every *H* is an *F*, ~There is an *F*

2. ~(Every *L* is an *M* & No *L* is an *M*), ~(Some *L* is not an *M* & Some *L* is an *M*)

3. ~(Every *A* is a *B* & No *A* is a *C*), Every *A* is a *D*, ~Some *A* is a *D*

4. Some *X* is a *Y*, ~Some *X* is not a *Z*, ~Some *Y* is a *Z*

5. (~Some *D* is an *E* & ~ Some *D* is an *F*), ~(No *D* is an *E* & No *D* is a *G*), Every *G* is an *F*

6. Some *R* is not an *S*, Some *S* is not a *T*, ~Some *R* is not a *T*

7. ~[(Every *T* is an *E* & There is a *T*) & Every *E* is a *C*], Every *E* is a *C*, Some *E* is a *T*, ~Some non-*E* is a *T*

8. (No *J* is a *K* & There is a *K*), Every *K* is an *L*, ~Some *L* is a non-*J*

8-6   TRANSLATING NEGATED SENTENCES

There are three kinds of negative logical expressions in the ECL. (1) There are the sentence-forming functors which yield E and O sentences:

(E) No _____ is a(n) _____

(O) Some _____ is not a(n) _____

(2) There is the complement-forming functor 'non-.' (3) There is the sentence-forming functor '~.' It is important to understand all three kinds of negating expressions in translating ordinary English sentences.

Negative universal sentences formed with 'no' or 'none' are often translated by E sentences of the ECL. We can also use E sentences to translate negative universal sentences formed with a 'not' in the verb, as:

A bird is not a mammal.

Cows are not carnivorous.

But a 'not' in the verbs of other sentences often calls for an O translation. These sentences:

One sailor wasn't rescued.

Some sailors weren't rescued.

Seven sailors weren't rescued.

would get this translation:

Some sailor is not a person who was rescued.

When a 'not' occurs in a noun phrase, this can sometimes be translated with 'non-.' For example, the sentence

Something that wasn't alive frightened Gary.

could be translated:

Some non-(living thing) is a thing that frightened Gary.

But many phrases containing a 'not' can't be exactly translated with 'non-.' The sentence:

Some student who didn't pass the logic final understands logic very well.

is not equivalent to:

Some non-(student who passed the logic final) is a person who understands logic very well.

The original sentence is stronger than its translation. (Why?)

When the word 'not' begins an English sentence, we do not ordinarily use '$\sim$' to translate the sentence. The following:

(1) Not one student was excused from the final.

would be translated:

(2) No student is a person who was excused from the final.

Of course, (2) is equivalent to:

(3) $\sim$ Some student is a person who was excused from the final.

But (3) seems strained as a translation for (1). The sentence:

(4) Not all students passed the final.

is translated:

(5) Some student is not a person who passed the final.

This is equivalent to:

(6) ~ Every student is a person who passed the final.

But (5) provides a more "direct" translation than (6) does.

When an English sentence contains an expression like 'It is not true that' or 'is not true,' 'It is false that' or 'is false,' then we ordinarily translate this expression with ' ~ .' If we have an ordinary sentence 'It is not true that p,' and p is translated by an equivalent p^*, then $\sim p^*$ is equivalent to 'It is not true that p.' But suppose p^* is weaker than p. In case p^* is false, p will be false. But then, if $\sim p^*$ is true, the ordinary sentence 'It is false that p' must also be true. $\sim p^*$ entails 'It is false that p.' In case p^* is weaker than p, $\sim p^*$ is stronger than 'It is false that p.' Similarly, if p^* is stronger than p, then $\sim p^*$ is weaker than 'It is false that p.' Having the negation sign in the ECL produces many translations that are stronger than their originals.

This ordinary universal sentence:

(7) Bats all have rabies.

would be understood to have existential force, and would be translated:

(8) (Every bat is an animal with rabies & There is a bat)

When a universal sentence with existential force is denied:

(9) It isn't true that bats all have rabies.

the denial is not usually understood to "cover" the existential force. We would not translate (9) like this:

(10) ~ (Every bat is an animal with rabies & There is a bat)

Instead, (9) would itself be understood to have existential force. An equivalent translation for (9) is:

(11) ~ Every bat is an animal with rabies.

Since (11) already indicates that there is a bat, no existence clause is needed.

*Exercise A: Section 6

Translate the following into the ECL. Mark weaker translations with an asterisk. Mark stronger translations with a double asterisk. If no acceptable translation can be provided, explain what causes the problem.

1. It isn't true that some of Michelle's professors are famous.

2. Not all college professors have shifty eyes.

3. Not a single person recovered from the infection.

4. There is no such thing as a square circle.

5. Not many college students aim for a military career.

6. It isn't the case that no students are attractive.

7. Terrorists are people who have no consciences.

8. Some person who didn't vote in the last election is running for Congress.

9. Some girls in Joel's class didn't pass the driving test.

10. It isn't true that the unicorn is a winged animal.

11. It is false that lawyers are all both honest and intelligent.

12. Not a soul discovered Freddy's secret.

Exercise B: Section 6

Determine which of the following arguments are valid. Show your translations (or their abbreviations), and show work to justify your answers. In some cases, it may be necessary to supplement the translations with analytic A or E sentences or with well-known true sentences. If the ECL cannot be used to evaluate some argument, explain why not.

1. Not all college professors have shifty eyes because nobody who can be trusted has shifty eyes. But any friend of Jim's can be trusted, and he has friends who are college professors.

2. Birds are winged animals. But it isn't true that the unicorn is a winged animal. So some unicorn isn't a bird.

3. Anybody who recovered from the infection is a person who received a shot of the new antibiotic. But no one received a shot of the new antibiotic. So not a single person recovered from the infection.

4. It is false that vampires make good companions. If a person has lots of friends, that person makes a good companion. So some vampire doesn't have lots of friends.

5. Those who have committed crimes deserve to be punished. It isn't true that some innocent victim deserves punishment. Innocent victims are entitled to sympathy. Martin has an uncle who isn't entitled to sympathy. So Martin has an uncle who has committed a crime.

6. Whenever Carolyn gets paid, she eats dinner in a restaurant. She never eats dinner in a restaurant on any other day. Carolyn is never paid on Saturday or Sunday. So Carolyn never eats dinner in a restaurant on a weekend.

7. There is no freshman in Dillworth High School who isn't taking biology. All the students who are selling ads for the yearbook are in Mr. Fox's home room. Since one of the students selling ads for the yearbook isn't taking biology, there must be a student in Mr. Fox's home room who isn't a freshman.

8. Kevin has read all the books that Mark Twain wrote, but he doesn't like all of them. So there is a book written by Samuel Clemens that Kevin doesn't like.

Exercise C: Section 6

Determine which of the following groups of sentences are incompatible. Show your translations (or their abbreviations), and show work to justify your answers. In some cases, it may be necessary to supplement the translations with analytic A or E sentences or with well-known true sentences. If the ECL cannot be used to evaluate some sentences, explain why not.

1. It isn't true that some students in his class visited Professor Franklin in the hospital. The girls at the next table are in Professor Franklin's class, and one of them visited him in the hospital.

2. It is false that John's children are all both courteous and helpful. His children all volunteer to do work around the house. Anyone who does that is helpful. And John doesn't have even one child who fails to be courteous.

3. Many Marxists teach economic theory, although no Marxist understands it. No one teaches economic theory without understanding it.

4. Ruthie has a brother who lives in Chicago. Everyone who lives in Illinois is a midwesterner. None of Ruthie's siblings is a midwesterner.

5. Dave isn't pleased with any of his children. When Dave isn't pleased with someone, he has a hard time being polite to that person. Dave has no trouble being polite to his daughters.

6. Only husbands have wives. No belly dancer is a man. It isn't true that no belly dancer has a wife.

7. Any manuscript accepted for publication by SUNY Press is excellent. Some of Bob's manuscripts have been accepted by SUNY Press. But some of his manuscripts have been terrible.

8. Nobody who hangs around Cosentino's is a nice person. Robert has friends who hang around Cosentino's. Robert's friends all meet with his mother's approval. But she doesn't approve of anyone who isn't nice.

8-7 SINGULAR SENTENCES

The last addition to the ECL incorporates singular sentences. This requires a new elementary syntactic category: singular terms which denote real individuals. Singular terms include names, like 'George Washington,' definite descriptions, like 'the capital of France,' and other descriptive singular terms, like 'Whistler's mother.' Not all descriptive singular terms are allowed in the ECL. If there is more than one φ (the symbol is a lower case Greek phi), then the definite description 'the φ' does not denote a single real individual. The expression is grammatically suited to denote a single individual, but it fails to do so and fails to qualify for membership in the Extended Categorical language. The description 'the man who was a president of the United States' doesn't belong to the ECL.[1] Neither does 'the king of France in 1920,' for France didn't have a king in 1920.

English has names for real individuals, fictional individuals, and mythical individu-

---

[1] In conversations, we often use definite descriptions which don't strictly and literally denote a single individual. If we are sitting around a table, and someone says, "The table is scratched," we understand her to be talking about the table in front of us. The context in which the sentence is spoken enables us to recognize which table is intended. In the ECL, we will consider sentences containing such descriptions; we will understand these descriptions as if they had their denotations fixed by a particular context.

als. We have, for example, 'George Washington,' 'Othello,' and 'Santa Claus.' Only names of real individuals are allowed in the ECL. This is a *semantic* restriction on singular terms of the ECL. We impose this restriction to keep the artificial language simple and easy to study. But there are real individuals in the past, present, and future (though we don't know enough to name very many future individuals). And the individuals we name aren't limited to people or physical objects. We have names for people, cities, planets, numbers, and a variety of abstract individuals.

Two sentence-forming functors are used to form singular sentences:

_____ is a(n) _____

_____ is not a(n) _____

The first is affirmative, the second negative. In both functors, the first blank is filled with a singular term, and the second with a common noun or noun phrase. The following singular sentences belong to the ECL:

7 is a prime number.

Napoleon is not an English king.

The capital of New York State is not a city in Western New York.

We need a new kind of variable to symbolize singular sentences. These *individual variables*:

$x, y, z, x_1, \ldots$

replace singular terms to obtain formulas like these:

x is an A

z is not a non-B

A singular sentence 'x is an A' is true just in case the individual denoted by the subject is one of the individuals denoted by the predicate. And 'y is not a B' is true if the individual denoted by the subject is not denoted by the predicate. Now consider how to draw a Venn diagram for a sentence like this: John F. Kennedy is a U.S. president. A circle in a Venn diagram represents things of a kind. But a singular term labels just one individual, not things of a kind. *We do not use a circle for a singular term.* Instead, a single mark or letter will represent a single individual. We can diagram 'John F. Kennedy is a U.S. president' like this:

Here the 'J' represents John F. Kennedy. This diagram shows him in the U.S. president circle. To diagram the sentence 'Aaron Burr is not a U.S. president' we can use this:

U.S. president

An important principle governing diagrams for singular sentences is this: *A single individual (or its mark) cannot occupy different locations in a Venn diagram.* If we are diagramming the following two sentences:

Bruce is a football player.

Bruce is an English major.

we would diagram the first sentence like this:

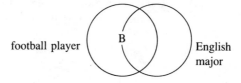

The football player circle is divided into two parts. We put Bruce on the line between them to show that he could be in either one. If we began by diagraming the second sentence, we would get:

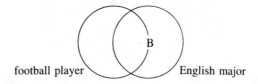

But we don't want to represent the two sentences by combining these two diagrams. We must find one location (for Bruce) that satisfies both sentences—which gives us this:

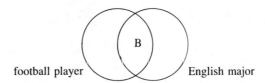

The following sentences are incompatible:

No football player is an English major. Bruce is a football player. Bruce is an English major.

After we diagram the first sentence:

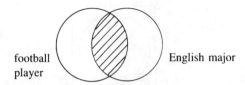

there is no place to put Bruce that will represent both of the remaining sentences—we cannot finish the diagram. If we show him being a football player:

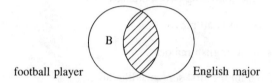

he isn't an English major. And if we show him being an English major, he isn't a football player. The following diagram represents an impossible situation:

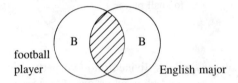

We can diagram two particular sentences:

Some dog is a Collie.

Some dog is not a Collie.

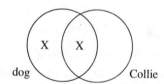

because each 'X' represents a different dog. But these two sentences:

Lassie is a Collie.

Lassie is not a Collie.

are incompatible. With singular sentences we have a new diagram test for incompatibility. Two diagrams (whose circles represent the same things) which show one individual in different locations indicate incompatible sentences. However, these sentences:

Lassie is a Collie.

~There is a Collie.

are also incompatible. Their diagrams:

can't be combined.

To diagram the negation of a sentence whose diagram has an 'X,' we use shading. The diagram for '~Some cat is a monkey' is:

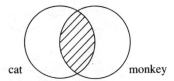

But we don't use shading for the negation of a singular sentence, we simply move the individual out of the forbidden area. The diagram for '~Napoleon is an English king' is this:

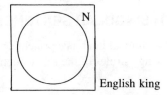

If we used a diagram to evaluate the following argument sequence:

Lassie is a Collie. Lassie is a pet. / Some Collie is a pet.

we would make a diagram of the premisses:

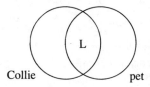

This diagram shows Lassie being both a Collie and a pet. If we made a separate diagram for the conclusion, we would have an 'X' in the area where the circles overlap. This is different than the diagram for the premisses, but the premisses imply the conclusion. If we have a specific individual, like Lassie, in a compartment, then we have *an* individual in that compartment.

*Exercise: Section 7

For 1–3, use Venn diagrams to test for validity.

1. Every bus driver is a non-(softball umpire). Don is a softball umpire. Every member of

Teamsters Local 7572 is a bus driver. So Don is not a member of Teamsters Local 7572.

2. Fran is a regular churchgoer. ~Fran is a pious little old lady. So ~Every regular churchgoer is a pious little old lady.

3. Every doctor is a well-off person. No garbage collector is a doctor. Ron is a garbage collector. So ~Ron is not a well-off person.

For 4–6, use Venn diagrams to test for incompatibility.

4. ~(Roger is a person who wants french fries & Roger is a person who wants onion rings) Every person who wants french fries is a person who wants onion rings. Every boy who is hungry after swimming is a person who wants french fries. Roger is a boy who is hungry after swimming.

5. ~(Some college professor is an overpaid person & Some college professor is not an overworked person)~ Every college professor is an overworked person. (Ken is a college professor & Ken is an overpaid person)

6. Anne is a person with a Ph.D. in English. Anne is a person who has written a book. Every person with a Ph.D. in English is an English teacher. Some English teacher is not a person who has written a book.

8-8 REASONING WITH SINGULAR SENTENCES

We must now adopt additional inference principles concerning singular sentences. We already have the following as rules of the EC deductive system:

I Conversion

.

m Some α is a β

.

n Some β is an α m, I-Conv

E Conversion

.

m No α is a β

.

n No β is an α m, E-Conv

Obverse Introduction

We can infer the obverse of a categorical sentence (or formula).

Obverse Elimination

We can infer a categorical sentence (or formula) from its obverse.

Logical Truth

At any step in a proof or subproof, we can add a formula (or sentence)

    Every α is an α

Existence Introduction

.

m Some α is a β

.

n There is an α m, ExI

.

m Some α is not a β

.

n There is an α m, ExI

Existential Subalternation

.

m (Every α is a β & There is an α) m (No α is a β & There is an α)

.

n Some α is a β m, ExS n Some α is not a β m, ExS

Simplification   **Conjunction**

.

m $(p \mathrel{\&} q)$ m p

.   .

n p m, Simp n q

.   .

m $(p \mathrel{\&} q)$ r $(p \mathrel{\&} q)$ m, n, Conj

.

n q m, Simp

A-O Transformation

.

m Every α is a β m $\sim$ Every α is a β

.   .

n $\sim$ Some α is not a β m, AOT n Some α is not a β m, AOT

.   .

m $\sim$ Some α is not a β m Some α is not a β

.   .

n Every α is a β m, AOT n $\sim$ Every α is a β m, AOT

E-I Transformation

.

m No α is a β m $\sim$ No α is a β

.   .

n $\sim$ Some α is a β m, EIT n Some α is a β m, EIT

.   .

m $\sim$ Some α is a β m Some α is a β

.   .

n No α is a β m, EIT n $\sim$ No α is a β m, EIT

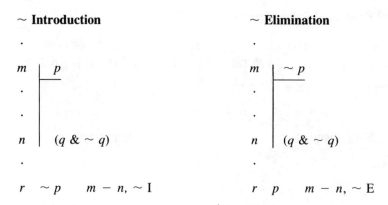

It is clear that there should be no conversion rules for singular sentences, for singular sentences don't have converses (in the ECL). However, singular sentences do have obverses. These sentences are related by obversion:

George Washington is a U.S. president.

George Washington is not a non-(U.S. president).

It is easy to see that a singular sentence is equivalent to its obverse, so the rules *Obverse Introduction* and *Obverse Elimination* are amended to cover singular sentences.

We will also amend *Existence Introduction*. From a singular affirmative sentence:

x is an *A*

we can conclude:

There is an *A*

A singular negative sentence is not a premiss for Existence Introduction.

The following proof uses some of the new rules:

1	Every non-politician is a non-(U.S. president).	
2	George Washington is not a non-(U.S. president).	
3	George Washington is a U.S. president.	2, ObvE
4	No non-politician is a U.S. president.	1, ObvE
5	No U.S. president is a non-politician.	4, E-Conv
6	There is a U.S. president.	3, ExI
7	(No U.S. president is a non-politician & There is a U.S. president)	4, 6, Conj
8	Some U.S. president is not a non-politician.	7, ExS
9	Some U.S. president is a politician.	8, ObvE
10	Some politician is a U.S. president.	9, I-Conv

We will add a *Transformation* rule for singular sentences:

Singular Transformation (SingT)

From:

(1) x is an A

we infer:

(2) $\sim x$ is not an A

And we can infer (1) from (2).

From:

(3) x is not a B

we infer:

(4) $\sim x$ is a B

And we can infer (3) from (4).

You should note how singular sentences differ from particular sentences with respect to negation. These two sentences:

Chicago is not a French city.

$\sim$Chicago is a French city.

are equivalent. But the following sentences are definitely not equivalent:

Some city in the U.S. is not a city in Illinois.

$\sim$Some city in the U.S. is a city in Illinois.

The last rules we need for singular sentences enable us to link them to categorical sentences. The rule *A Elimination (AE)* is illustrated:

  .

m Every A is a B

  .

n x is an A

  .

r x is a B m, n, AE

This rule is used in the following proof:

1	Every city in New York is a U.S. city.	
2	Berlin is not a U.S. city.	
3	Berlin is a city in New York.	
4	Berlin is a U.S. city.	1, 3, AE
5	$\sim$ Berlin is a U.S. city.	2, SingT
6	(Berlin is a U.S. city & $\sim$ Berlin is a U.S. city)	4, 5, Conj

7   ~ Berlin is a city in New York.   3 − 6, ~ I

8   Berlin is not a city in New York.   7, SingT

To combine E sentences and singular sentences, we can use one of two forms of *E Elimination (EE)*:

m	No *A* is a *B*		*m*	No *A* is a *B*	
n	*x* is an *A*		*n*	*y* is a *B*	
r	*x* is not a *B* *m, n*, EE		*r*	*y* is not an *A* *m, n*, EE	

This rule permits a different proof of result established above:

1   Every city in New York is a U.S. city.

2   Berlin is not a U.S. city.
___
3   No city in New York is a non-(U.S. city).   1, ObvI

4   Berlin is a non-(U.S. city).   2, ObvI

5   Berlin is not a city in New York.   3, 4, EE

We also have rules that allow us to infer particular sentences from singular sentences:

I Introduction (II)   **O Introduction (OI)**

m	*x* is an *A*	*m*	*y* is an *A*
n	*x* is a *B*	*n*	*y* is not a *B*
r	Some *A* is a *B* *m, n*, II	*r*	Some *A* is not a *B* *m, n*, OI

*Exercise A: Section 8

Construct proofs of the following inference sequences.

1. No soldier is a politician., Frank is a politician., Every non-civilian is a soldier. / Frank is a civilian.

2. Every *A* is a *B*, No *B* is a *C*, *x* is a *D*, *x* is a *C* / Some *D* is not an *A*

3. No freshman is a person passing logic., David is a freshman., David is a person passing logic. / Chicago is a city in Illinois.

When we come up with examples to invalidate an inference sequence containing singular sentences, or find examples to show that sentences are not incompatible, we must be sure that the subject of a singular sentence (or formula) is replaced by a singular term. If we want an example to make this formula come out false:

x is an A

we CANNOT replace 'x' by 'apple' and 'A' by 'orange.' For 'apple' is not a singular term. We need to do something like replace 'x' by 'Paris' and 'A' by 'U.S. city.'

*Exercise A: Section 8 (cont.)

For 4–6, determine if the formula sequences are valid. Construct a proof in the EC deductive system for the valid sequences, and find examples to show that the rest are invalid.

4. Every A is a B, No C is a B, x is not a C / x is an A

5. ~(Peggy is a physics major & Peggy is a psychology major), Every student taking Physics 437 is a physics major, Peggy is a student taking Physics 437. / Peggy is not a psychology major.

6. Every famous actor is a talented performer, No skillful lion tamer is a non-(talented performer), No clumsy person is a talented performer, (Mark is not a famous actor & Mark is not a skillful lion tamer) / Mark is a clumsy person.

For 7–9, determine if the sentences are incompatible, or the formulas symbolize (only) incompatible sentences. Construct proofs of the incompatible sentences, and find examples to show that the rest are not incompatible.

7. ~(Some actor is a bridge player & Some actor is not a bridge player), Hugh is an actor. Hugh is not a bridge player. Every intellectual is a bridge player. Chuck is an actor. Chuck is an intellectual.

8. ~(John is not a lawyer & John is not a doctor), No son of Martha's is a doctor. John is a son of Martha's. ~John is not a doctor.

9. Every person who likes broccoli is a person who likes Brussels sprouts. No person who likes Brussels sprouts is a non-(person who likes asparagus). Jesse is not a person who likes broccoli. Jesse is a person who likes asparagus.

Exercise B: Section 8

Use the ECL as an instrument to evaluate the inferences stated below. In some cases it may be necessary to supplement the translations of the premises with analytic A or E sentences or with well-known true sentences. Show work which justifies your answers.

1. If a person has good taste, she won't serve red wine with fish. People who serve white wine with fish have good taste. Jim's best friend serves red wine with fish. So Jim's best friend doesn't have good taste and doesn't serve white wine with fish.

2. Napoleon must not have been a French emperor. For it isn't true that some French emperors were from Corsica. But all the members of Napoleon's family were from Corsica. And, of course, Napoleon was a member of his own family.

3. Megan doesn't want both pizza and chicken wings. She must not want pizza, because she does want chicken wings.

4. Every Western state irrigates its crops. No state with sufficient rainfall irrigates its crops. Indiana is not a Western state. So Indiana gets sufficient rainfall.

5. The only boys whom Betty likes are intelligent. Betty doesn't like anyone whom Marcia likes. It is false that Bill is a boy liked by neither Betty nor Marcia. Marcia must like Bill, then, for he's not very smart.

6. Tom is a carpenter. No one who works with wood likes plastic furniture. Chemical engineers all like plastic furniture. So Tom isn't a chemical engineer.

7. Alsatians are French. And some Basques are French. So it isn't true that no Alsatians are Basques.

8. Carolyn has been to every one of the state capitals. Whenever Carolyn visits a city, she eats in an expensive restaurant in that city. So Carolyn must have eaten in an expensive restaurant in Albany, New York.

9. It isn't true that all ghosts are kind. Anyone who is thoughtful and helpful is kind. So not all ghosts are thoughtful and helpful.

10. Jane hasn't seen both *Key Largo* and *Casablanca*. She must not have seen *Key Largo*, for all Humphrey Bogart fans have seen *Casablanca*, and Jane is certainly a Humphrey Bogart fan.

Exercise C: Section 8

Use the ECL as an instrument to determine whether the following groups of sentences are incompatible. In some cases it may be necessary to supplement the translations with analytic A or E sentences or with well-known true sentences. You must show work which justifies your answers.

1. Nobody with asthma is comfortable in a city that has serious air pollution problems. Dr. Reach's patients all have asthma, and Danny is one of his patients. But Danny is perfectly comfortable living in a city with serious air pollution problems.

2. It isn't true that there is an overweight boxer. Neither is it true that there is a boxer who isn't overweight. Max is a fine boxer.

3. One of Shirley's mother's sisters graduated from Yale. Anyone who graduated from an Ivy League school appreciates the importance of a college education. None of Shirley's aunts or uncles thinks it is important to go to college.

4. Auto workers are factory workers. Blue collar workers don't belong to management. But there is an Episcopalian who is an auto worker and an Episcopalian who belongs to management.

5. None of the teachers in Jim's school likes him. It isn't true that Jim has an uncle who doesn't like him. But one of his uncles teaches in Jim's school.

6. It isn't true that if a student fails the logic final, then that student will fail the course though, in fact, there is no one who will fail the final without failing the course.

7. A boy Jane knew in high school is a hit man for the Mafia. Nobody who is a good citizen is a hit man for the Mafia. Everybody who works to uphold the laws is a good citizen. It isn't true that no boy Jane knew in high school works to uphold the laws.

8. No one who plays a sport is a sissy. But it isn't true that Stacey is neither out of shape nor a sissy. Stacey is an athlete and she isn't out of shape.

9. George's mother is a college graduate. It isn't true that George's mother both received a college education and was a famous actress. But it is false that his mother wasn't a famous actress.

10. It isn't true that Joel likes a girl in his Ethics class. Michele is taking calculus from Mr. Goodman and she is in Mr. Wickert's poetry class. Joel likes the girls in Mr. Wickert's poetry class. Any girl who is taking calculus from Mr. Goodman is also in Joel's Ethics class.

Chapter 9

The Propositional Connective Language

9-0 SUMMARY

This chapter introduces and examines the Propositional Connective language. The syntax of the language is described, then a semantic account of the logical connectives is presented. Propositional variables are introduced so that formulas displaying logical forms can be constructed. Truth-tables are used to determine which sentences, groups of sentences, and arguments are logically distinguished.

9-1 A MIXED LANGUAGE

The *Propositional Connective language,* which will also be called the *PC language,* focusses on compound sentences formed with connectives. The PC language will be incorporated in the *First-Order language* which is developed later in this book. But the PC language can also stand on its own. As an independent logical language, the PC language has a *mixed* character, for it contains some English expressions and some artificial symbols.

The ordinary English expressions in the PC language are true and false English sentences. The artificial symbols of the PC language are its distinctively logical expressions. These symbols are called *connectives,* because most of them connect sentences to form larger sentences. Two of these connectives were employed in the Extended Categorical language:

    ~   the negation sign

    &   the symbol of conjunction

The remaining connectives are:

    v   the wedge, the symbol of disjunction

    ⊃   the horseshoe, the symbol of material implication

    ≡   the triple bar, the symbol of material equivalence

Compound sentences of the PC language are formed with connectives. Ordinary English compound sentences, like

The fire spread rapidly because the forest was dry.

are not regarded as compound sentences *of the PC language*. A compound English sentence can be a simple sentence of the artificial language.

In addition to ordinary English sentences and symbolic connectives, the PC language contains three styles of parentheses:

( )   round parentheses

[ ]   brackets

{ }   braces

Pairs having different styles are interchangeable. With complicated sentences it is helpful to alternate styles. A sentence having this structure:

$$(((A \ \& \ B) \ v \ C) \supset ((A \ v \ (B \equiv C)) \equiv (C \supset D)))$$

is easier to understand if it is written like this:

$$([(A \ \& \ B) \ v \ C] \supset \{[A \ v \ (B \equiv C)] \equiv (C \supset D)\})$$

Here are some sentences of the PC language:

Denver is the capital of Colorado.

~Denver is the capital of Colorado.

Denver or Boulder is the capital of Colorado.

[~(Denver is the capital of Colorado ≡ Boulder is the capital of Colorado) & Denver is the capital of Colorado]

*Exercise: Section 1

Determine which of the following are simple sentences of the PC language and which are compound sentences of the PC language.

1. France is in Europe and Russia is in Africa.

2. [France is in Europe & Russia is in Africa]

3. ~ Russia is in Africa.

4. France is not in Europe.

9-2   THE SYNTAX AND SEMANTICS OF THE PC LANGUAGE

We will give a definition of 'sentence of the PC language' that contains directions for constructing sentences.

(1) A true or false English declarative sentence is a *sentence of the PC language*; it is a *simple* (or *atomic*) sentence of the PC language.

(2) If ρ is a sentence of the PC language, then ∼ ρ is a *sentence of the PC language*; it is a *compound* sentence of the PC language. (The symbol employed as a variable is a lower case Greek rho.)

(3) If ρ, σ are sentences of the PC language, then so are (ρ & σ), (ρ v σ), (ρ ⊃ σ), (ρ ≡ σ); they are *compound* sentences. The round parentheses may be replaced by brackets or braces. (The symbols employed are rho and lower case Greek sigma.)

(4) Every sentence of the PC language is obtained by (1) - (3).

This is an inductive definition. Clause (1) is the *base* clause; it indicates the sentences we have to begin with. Clauses (2) and (3) are *inductive* clauses. They indicate how to get more sentences once we already have some. And clause (4) is the *closure* clause. It "closes" the set of sentences by keeping out additional candidates.

If we start with these sentences:

Albany is the capital of New York.

Buffalo is the capital of New Jersey.

we can follow the directions in the definition to obtain the following:

∼Albany is the capital of New York.

(Albany is the capital of New York ⊃ Buffalo is the capital of New Jersey)

[∼ Albany is the capital of New York & Buffalo is the capital of New Jersey]

[(Albany is the capital of New York ⊃ Buffalo is the capital of New Jersey) v (∼ Albany is the capital of New York & Buffalo is the capital of New Jersey)]

The definition of 'sentence of the PC language' gives the syntax of the PC language. The basic syntactic, or grammatical, categories of the PC language are *sentences* and *sentence-forming functors which take sentences into sentences*. (A *functor* is an expression which combines with other expressions to form a complex expression. The functor is the expression we think of as having gaps which are filled by the other expressions.)

When an English sentence is followed by a connective or enclosed in parentheses, periods will be omitted. We write:

(Albany is the capital of New York ⊃ Buffalo is the capital of New Jersey)

But the period stays in:

∼Albany is the capital of New York.

Simple English sentences will be capitalized even when they occur in compound sentences. The definition of 'sentence of the PC language' requires that every compound sentence formed with a two-place connective be enclosed in parentheses:

[Albany is the capital of New York ⊃ (Buffalo is the capital of New Jersey & ∼Albany is the capital of New York)]

As an abbreviation, we often omit the outer pair of parentheses. We might write:

Albany is the capital of New York ⊃ (Buffalo is the capital of New Jersey & ∼Albany is the capital of New York)

The PC language is primarily a written language. But we need something to say when we read the connectives. We might just use the expressions 'negation,' 'wedge,' 'ampersand,' 'horseshoe,' 'triple bar.' But the practice of logicians is to use ordinary expressions as readings for the connectives. For the sign of negation we use 'It is false that' or 'It is not the case that.' So:

~Cheyenne is in Pennsylvania.

is read

"It is false that Cheyenne is in Pennsylvania." or "It is not the case that Cheyenne is in Pennsylvania."

For the '&' we say "and." To read:

Springfield is in Illinois & Springfield is in Massachusetts.

we say "Springfield is in Illinois and Springfield is in Massachusetts." The reading for 'v' is 'or.' The sentence:

David is in prison v David is out of the country.

is read "David is in prison or David is out of the country." The reading for '$\supset$' contains two separated words. The sentence $(A \supset B)$ is read "If A, then B." The sentence:

Seattle is in Washington $\supset$ Washington is the first president of the United States.

is read "If Seattle is in Washington, then Washington is the first president of the United States." And for '$\equiv$' we say "if, and only if" (this is sometimes abbreviated: iff). The sentence:

Montgomery is the capital of Alabama $\equiv$ Jackson is the capital of Mississippi.

is read "Montgomery is the capital of Alabama if, and only if, Jackson is the capital of Mississippi."

We use these readings for convenience, but we give the meanings of the connectives by giving their *truth conditions*. The following *truth-table* for '$\sim$':

p	$\sim p$
true	false
false	true

indicates that if 'p' is replaced by a true sentence, then '$\sim p$' will be false. And if 'p' is replaced by a false sentence, then '$\sim p$' will be true. The negation sign "interchanges" truth and falsity. Instead of writing 'true' and 'false' in truth-tables, we will normally use their abbreviations, 't' and 'f.' So the truth-table will be constructed:

p	$\sim p$
t	f
f	t

The truth-table for '&' is:

p	q	$p \& q$
t	t	t
t	f	f
f	t	f
f	f	f

A sentence $(\rho \;\&\; \sigma)$ is true just in case both ρ, σ are true. The sentence:

(Chicago is in Illinois & Milwaukee is in Florida)

is false. But:

(Chicago is in Illinois & $\sim$ Milwaukee is in Florida)

is true. To determine the *value* of a sentence like:

($\sim$ Chicago is in Illinois & $\sim$ Milwaukee is in Florida),

we begin by determining the values of the simple components. Then we take these values and consult the truth-tables for the relevant connectives to determine the values of compound sentences. In this case, 'Chicago is in Illinois' is true and 'Milwaukee is in Florida' is false. Consulting the truth-table for '$\sim$,' we find that:

~Chicago is in Illinois.

is false, while:

~Milwaukee is in Florida.

is true. By the truth-table for '&,'

($\sim$ Chicago is in Illinois & $\sim$ Milwaukee is in Florida)

is false. Consulting the truth-table for '$\sim$' again, we find that the whole sentence is true.

When the negation sign is applied to a sentence, the sentence that is negated is its *scope*. The scope of the first '$\sim$' in:

~Chicago is in Illinois & $\sim$ Milwaukee is in Florida.

is very different from the scope of the first '$\sim$' in the following:

~(Chicago is in Illinois & $\sim$ Milwaukee is in Florida)

The "idea" of the PC language is for the language to be composed of atomic sentences and compound sentences formed with connectives that can be explained by means of truth-tables. Such connectives are called *truth-functional*, because the (truth) *value of a* compound sentence is always a *function* of the values of the simple components. Once we know which simple sentences are true and which false, we can compute the value of a compound sentence in a mechanical fashion.

The wedge is the sign of disjunction. Its truth-table looks like this:

p	q	$p \vee q$
t	t	t
t	f	t
f	t	t
f	f	f

The wedge is sometimes said to capture the *inclusive* sense of 'or.' The *exclusive* sense of 'or' rules out the possibility that both disjuncts are true. There is no connective in the PC language for the exclusive sense of 'or.' To show that either ρ is true or σ is true, but not both, we could write: (ρ v σ) & ~(ρ & σ).

The connectives '~,' '&,' and 'v' have meanings that are very close to the meanings of the English expressions we read for them. But the meaning of '⊃' is not close to the meaning of 'If . . . , then . . .' The English reading only approximates the meaning of the symbolic connective. The full meaning of the connective is given by this truth-table:

p	q	$p \supset q$
t	t	t
t	f	f
f	t	t
f	f	t

The sentence:

Washington D. C. is the capital of the United States ⊃ Philadelphia is the capital of the United States.

is false. But:

Philadelphia is the capital of the United States ⊃ Washington D. C. is the capital of the United States.

is true.

The triple bar is used to indicate that two sentences have the same truth value. The sentence:

France is in Europe ≡ George Washington is the first president of the United States.

is true. So is:

France is in Australia ≡ France is in South America.

A *semantic account* of a language explains the meanings of expressions in the language. The English sentences in the PC language have their normal meanings. We take these for granted, and focus on the meanings of the logical expressions. The following truth-table summarizes their meanings:

p	q	$\sim p$	$p \,\&\, q$	$p \lor q$	$p \supset q$	$p \equiv q$
t	t	f	t	t	t	t
t	f	f	f	t	f	f
f	t	t	f	t	t	f
f	f	t	f	f	t	t

*Exercise: Section 2

Determine which of the following are true and which are false.

1. ~ Denver is in Colorado.

2. ~ Atlanta is in Georgia ⊃ Boston is in Massachusetts.

3. Alaska is in Canada ≡ (Toronto is in Canada ≡ ~ Vancouver is in Canada)

4. ~(Snakes are mammals & Cows are reptiles) ⊃ Bats are birds.

5. ~ (~ India is in Asia v ~ Argentina is in South America)

6. [The earth orbits the sun ⊃ ~ The earth orbits the sun) ⊃ The earth orbits the sun] ⊃ The earth orbits the sun.

9-3 VARIABLES AND FORMULAS

We want to recognize instances of analyticity, entailment, and incompatibility. But in an artificial logical language, we are especially concerned with the instances of these semantic features that can be traced to logical form. The logical form of a sentence is determined by (1) the syntactic categories of its component expressions, (2) the distinctively logical expressions it contains, and (3) the organization of its component expressions. The following two sentences:

Washington D. C. is in Virginia ⊃ Chicago is in Massachusetts.

New York City is in New York ⊃ Cairo is in Illinois.

have the same logical form. For they both consist of two simple sentences connected by the horseshoe. Our artificial languages are designed to be *logically perspicuous*: The logical forms of their sentences are easy to recognize and understand.

An analytic sentence which can be determined to be true on the basis of (recognizing and) understanding its logical form is *logically true*. This sentence:

Chicago is in Illinois v ~ Chicago is in Illinois.

is logically true. Any other sentence with the same logical form is also true. A logically true sentence is an analytically true sentence. But not every analytic sentence is logically true. The sentence:

Today is Tuesday ⊃ Tomorrow is Wednesday.

is analytic without being logically true.

In order to focus on the logical forms of sentences of the PC language, we will introduce *propositional variables*. These are the letters: p, q, r, s. If we should need more variables than four, we affix numerical *subscripts*: $p_1, q_1, r_1, s_1, p_2, \ldots$ We use propositional variables to replace sentences of the PC language. We might, for example, begin with

(1) Chicago is in Illinois ⊃ Boston is in Massachusetts.

and then obtain:

(2) $p \supset q$

We could also obtain:

(3) Chicago is in Illinois ⊃ r

(4) p ⊃ Boston is in Massachusetts.

(5) $r \supset p$

Propositional variables don't have any meaning. We replace sentences by variables so that we can concentrate on the remaining expressions and their meanings, and on logical form and its meaning.

The result of replacing sentences by variables is not a sentence; it is a *formula*. But sentences are a special case of formulas. The formulas we employ must be constructed properly—they must be *well-formed formulas*. (The expression 'well-formed formula' is abbreviated 'wff.') An inductive definition of 'well-formed formula' goes like this:

(1) A true or false English declarative sentence or a propositional variable standing alone is a (*simple*) *well-formed formula of the PC language*.

(2) If ρ is a wff, then $\sim \rho$ is a *wff*.

(3) If ρ, σ are wffs, then so are $(\rho \vee \sigma)$, $(\rho \,\&\, \sigma)$, $(\rho \supset \sigma)$, $(\rho \equiv \sigma)$. In this clause, round parentheses may be replaced by brackets or braces.

(4) All wffs of the PC language are obtained by (1)–(3).

A sentence of the PC language is a wff that contains no propositional variables. (An English sentence might mention a propositional variable without using it as a variable. So, strictly speaking, a sentence is a wff that contains no propositional variable other than one which is mentioned.) A wff that contains no sentences is a *pure* wff. The following are pure wffs:

(5) $(p \supset q) \supset p$

   $(\sim p \vee q) \supset (p \supset q)$

A pure wff *displays* a logical form.

If we begin with an English sentence:

(6) (The Empire State Building is in New York City $\supset$ The Sears Tower is in Chicago) & The Empire State Building is in New York City.

and replace sentences by variables to obtain a pure formula:

(7) $(p \supset q) \,\&\, p$

then the formula displays a logical form of the original sentence. We cannot say that (7) displays *the* logical form of (6), for (6) has more than one logical form. This formula:

(8) $p \,\&\, q$

also displays one of the logical forms of (6). Formula (8) shows less about sentence (6) than formula (7) does, so (8) is less adequate, and generally less useful, than (7).

In the PC language, the significance of a logical form is determined by its truth conditions. It is convenient to give these truth conditions by constructing truth-tables for pure formulas. To begin with, consider the elementary formula '$(p \supset q)$.' The truth-table which explains the meaning of the horseshoe also gives the truth conditions of this formula:

p	q	$p \supset q$
t	t	t
t	f	f
f	t	t
f	f	t

In any formula, there is one occurrence of a connective which is the *principal*, or *main*, occurrence in the formula. The column under this occurrence gives the value of the whole formula (for each row). In '$(p \supset q)$,' the only occurrence of a connective is the main occurrence.

Now consider this formula: $(p \supset q) \vee q$. To make the truth-table for this formula, we begin by listing the variables on the left:

p q $(p \supset q) \vee q$

Next we add the rows which give the different truth-values that are possible for sentences replacing the variables:

p	q	$(p \supset q) \vee q$
t	t	
t	f	
f	t	
f	f	

Now we want to determine the value of the formula for each row. We begin by making truth-tables for component formulas:

p	q	$(p \supset q) \vee q$
t	t	t
t	f	f
f	t	t
f	f	t

The next step is to fill-in the column under 'v.' To do this we must consult (or remember) the truth-table which gives the meaning of 'v.' That truth-table is a recipe for determining the value of a 'v.' It tells us what to put under 'v' for various combinations on the left and right sides of 'v.' In our truth-table above, the first row has a 't' on the left of 'v' (under '$(p \supset q)$'), and a 't' on the right—the variable 'q' has value t even though we have not written this in. The combination 't,' 't' corresponds to the first row in the truth-table for 'v.' So we get this:

p	q	$(p \supset q)$	$\vee$	q
t	t	t	t	
t	f	f		
f	t	t		
f	f	t		

If we continue to follow the directions implicit in the truth-table for 'v,' we get this result:

p	q	$(p \supset q)$	$\vee$	q
t	t	t	t	
t	f	f	f	
f	t	t	t	
f	f	t	t	

The single occurrence of the wedge is the principal occurrence of this wff. The column under the wedge gives the value of the whole formula for the different combinations of values assigned to 'p' and 'q.' The truth-table is finished.

If we make a truth-table for '$[(q \supset p) \vee p]$,' the column under '$(q \supset p)$' will not be the same as the column under '$(p \supset q)$.' To construct the column under '$(q \supset p)$,' we must use the truth-table giving the meaning of '$\supset$' as our recipe. When we use it as a recipe, it tells us how the values on the left and right sides of '$\supset$' determine the value under '$\supset$.' We start:

p	q	$(q \supset p) \vee p$
t	t	t
t	f	t
f	t	f
f	f	t

Then we finish:

p	q	$(q \supset p)$	$\vee p$
t	t	t	t
t	f	t	t
f	t	f	f
f	f	t	t

In making a truth-table, we fill-in the columns under component formulas for only one reason: to be of assistance in determining the values of the complex formulas. Once the truth-table is completed, we could eliminate every column but that under the main occurrence:

p	q	$(q \supset p) \vee p$
t	t	t
t	f	t
f	t	f
f	f	t

(This is easy to do on a blackboard, but not on a sheet of paper.)

To construct a truth-table for a formula, we begin by listing all distinct variables occurring in the formula. Then we make rows giving every possible combination of 't' and 'f' for these variables. The previous examples contained two variables and four rows. For this formula:

$$[(p \supset q) \vee (r \supset q)] \supset [(p \,\&\, r) \supset q]$$

we need three variables and eight rows:

p	q	r	[(p ⊃ q) v (r ⊃ q)] ⊃ [(p & r) ⊃ q]
t	t	t	
t	t	f	
t	f	t	
t	f	f	
f	t	t	
f	t	f	
f	f	t	
f	f	f	

The order in which the variables are listed is unimportant. The order of the rows is also unimportant, but it is important that none is left out. The pattern exemplified in this truth-table is convenient to ensure that no combinations are omitted. A truth-table with n distinct variables requires 2^n rows to exhaust all possible assignments of t and f to the variables.

To complete the truth-table, we begin by making columns for the smallest component formulas other than variables. In the example above, each of these components contains two distinct variables. To construct the columns for one of these components, we only consider the values of the variables in the component. This gives us:

p	q	r	[(p ⊃ q) v (r ⊃ q)] ⊃ [(p & r) ⊃ q]		
t	t	t	t	t	t
t	t	f	t	t	f
t	f	t	f	f	t
t	f	f	f	t	f
f	t	t	t	t	f
f	t	f	t	t	f
f	f	t	t	f	f
f	f	f	t	t	f

Once we have columns under the component formulas, we keep working up. Next we get:

p	q	r	[(p ⊃ q) v (r ⊃ q)] ⊃ [(p & r) ⊃ q]				
t	t	t	t	t	t	t	t
t	t	f	t	t	t	f	t
t	f	t	f	f	f	t	f
t	f	f	f	t	t	f	t
f	t	t	t	t	t	f	t
f	t	f	t	t	t	f	t
f	f	t	t	t	f	f	t
f	f	f	t	t	t	f	t

The last occurrence of a connective (i.e., the only occurrence without a column beneath it) is the principal occurrence (as an abbreviation we will sometimes call this the *principal connective*, or the *main connective*). We are now able to complete the truth-table for the formula:

p	q	r	[(p ⊃ q) v (r ⊃ q)] ⊃ [(p & r) ⊃ q]
t	t	t	t t t t t t
t	t	f	t t t t f t
t	f	t	f f f t t f
t	f	f	f t t t f t
f	t	t	t t t t f t
f	t	f	t t t t f t
f	f	t	t t f t f t
f	f	f	t t t t f t

The column under the horseshoe connecting the bracketed formulas is the one that counts. The truth-table shows that any sentence with the displayed form is true regardless of the values of its component sentences. Such a sentence is logically true.

In constructing a truth-table for a formula containing '~,' we must be careful to note the scope of the negation. In this formula:

$$(p \supset \sim p) \supset p$$

the negation sign applies to a single variable. To make the truth-table, we start:

p	(p ⊃ ~ p) ⊃ p
t	f
f	t

To continue, we use the column under '~ p' together with the column giving the value of 'p':

p	(p ⊃ ~ p) ⊃ p
t	f f
f	t t

Finally, we get:

p	(p ⊃ ~ p) ⊃ p
t	f f t
f	t t f

In the following formula, the negation has a greater scope than in the formula just considered:

$$\sim(p \supset q) \text{ v } q$$

We start:

p	q	~(p ⊃ q) v q
t	t	f t
t	f	t f
f	t	f t
f	f	f t

It is the column under ' ~ ' that we consult to determine the values under 'v':

p	q	$\sim(p \supset q) \vee q$		
t	t	f	t	t
t	f	t	f	t
f	t	f	t	t
f	f	f	t	f

In constructing truth-tables for complex formulas, it is very important that all the parentheses by included in the formula (except for the pair enclosing the entire formula). Consider this formula:

(9) $[(p \supset q \supset q) \vee r]$

Formula (9) is not well-formed, because a pair of parentheses is missing inside the round parentheses. If we tried to construct a truth-table for (9), we wouldn't know what values to consider. We might first consider '$p \supset q$' and make its truth-table:

p	q	$[(p \supset q \supset q) \vee q]$
t	t	t
t	f	f
f	t	t
f	f	t

If we consider '$q \supset q$' first, we get:

p	q	$[(p \supset q \supset q) \vee q]$
t	t	t
t	f	t
f	t	t
f	f	t

No matter which procedure we adopt, we will be stuck when it comes to constructing the column under 'v.' We can't say which column to use for the formula in the round parentheses. There are two ways to "correct" formula (9) to obtain a formula with the right number of parentheses:

(10) $[((p \supset q) \supset q) \vee q]$

(11) $[(p \supset (q \supset q)) \vee q]$

Formulas (10) and (11) have different truth tables.
The formula:

(12) $[p \supset (q \supset p)] \supset \sim\{[(r \supset s) \supset r] \supset r\}$

contains four distinct variables. Its truth-table must contain $2^4 = 16$ rows. The left side of a formula or sentence constructed with the horseshoe is called the *antecedent*. The right side is called the *consequent*. In formula (12), the antecedent is: $[p \supset (q \supset p)]$. And the consequent is:

$\sim\{[(r \supset s) \supset r] \supset r\}$.

Each formula has a main connective (a main occurrence of a connective). The column in the truth-table under the main connective of the antecedent gives the values of the antecedent as a whole. And the column under the main connective of the consequent gives the values of the consequent as a whole. In order to fill in the column under the main connective of formula (12), we must first obtain the columns under the main connectives of the antecedent and consequent of (12). We consult these columns to obtain the final column. The completed truth-table for (12) looks like this:

p	q	r	s	$[p$	$\supset$	$(q \supset p)]$	$\supset$	$\sim\{[(r$	$\supset$	$s)$	$\supset$	$r]$	$\supset$	$r\}$
t	t	t	t		t		t	f	f		t		t		t
t	t	t	f		t		t	f	f		f		t		t
t	t	f	t		t		t	f	f		t		f		t
t	t	f	f		t		t	f	f		t		f		t
t	f	t	t		t		t	f	f		t		t		t
t	f	t	f		t		t	f	f		f		t		t
t	f	f	t		t		t	f	f		t		f		t
t	f	f	f		t		t	f	f		t		f		t
f	t	t	t		t		f	f	f		t		t		t
f	t	t	f		t		f	f	f		f		t		t
f	t	f	t		t		f	f	f		t		f		t
f	t	f	f		t		f	f	f		t		f		t
f	f	t	t		t		t	f	f		t		t		t
f	f	t	f		t		t	f	f		f		t		t
f	f	f	t		t		t	f	f		t		f		t
f	f	f	f		t		t	f	f		t		f		t

*Exercise: Section 3

For 1–4, circle the principal occurrence of a connective in each formula.

1. $\sim p \mathbin{\&} q$

2. $\sim (p \mathbin{\&} q)$

3. $\{[(p \supset q) \supset r] \supset s\}$

4. $\{p \supset [q \supset (r \equiv \{s \lor \sim q\})]\}$

For 5–8, construct truth-tables for the following formulas.

5. $[(p \supset p) \supset p] \lor \sim p$

6. $[(p \mathbin{\&} q) \lor (p \mathbin{\&} \sim q)]$

7. $\sim (p \supset \sim q) \supset (\sim p \supset q)$

8. $\sim [(p \lor q) \equiv (q \mathbin{\&} r)]$

9-4   EVALUATING SENTENCES OF THE PC LANGUAGE

We wish to determine which sentences of the PC language are logically true. As well as considering logically true sentences, we can also consider those that are *logically false*—these can be determined to be false on the basis of understanding their logical form.

To detect logically true or logically false sentences of the PC language, we focus on their logical forms. We can do this most easily if we replace sentences by formulas with variables. Let α' be obtained from a sentence α of the PC language by replacing each simple component of α by a propositional variable in such a way that (i) occurrences of the same sentence are replaced by occurrences of the same variable, and (ii) occurrences of distinct sentences are replaced by occurrences of distinct variables. Then α' *symbolizes* α.

A formula which symbolizes a sentence must be a pure formula. The formula will display a logical form of the sentence. This sentence:

(1) Chicago is in Illinois $\supset$ [$\sim$ Chicago is the capital of Wisconsin & $\sim$ Chicago is the capital of Indiana]

is symbolized by both of:

(2) $q \supset (\sim r \,\&\, \sim s)$

(3) $p \supset (\sim q \,\&\, \sim s)$

The sentence:

(4) $\sim$ Boston is in Iowa $\supset$ [Boston is in Iowa $\supset$ $\sim$ Boston is in Iowa]

is symbolized by:

(5) $\sim s \supset (s \supset \sim s)$

But (4) is not symbolized by either of:

(6) $\sim p \supset (q \supset \sim p)$

(7) $p \supset (q \supset p)$

Formulas (6) and (7) display logical forms of sentence (4), but they fail to symbolize (4). (Why?)

In logic, there are two general procedures for determining that a sentence or group of sentences is logically distinguished: (1) For sufficiently simple cases, we rely on our understanding of the logical forms involved. (2) We reduce complicated cases to simple cases. Reduction is normally accomplished by using proofs. But in the PC language, knowledge of the meanings of connectives is simple. In constructing the truth-table for a complicated formula, we use knowledge of simple cases to reach an understanding of the complicated case.

Suppose we want to determine if a sentence α is logically true. We can begin by constructing a truth table for a formula α' which symbolizes α. The sentence α is logically true if the truth conditions of its logical form rule out the possibility that α is false. α is logically true if the truth-table for α' contains all 't's under the principal occurrence of a connective. Let us see if sentence (4) is logically true. Sentence (4) is symbolized by formula (5), and the truth-table for (5) is:

s	$\sim s \supset (s \supset \sim s)$		
t	f	t	f
f	t	t	t

The column that "counts" is under the first '⊃.' Any sentence which has the logical form displayed by formula (4) will be true.

A formula whose truth-table contains all 't's in the column under the main connective is a *tautology*. Formula (5) is a tautology. Any sentence symbolized by a tautology is logically true. Indeed, any sentence which has a form displayed by a tautology is logically true.

The use of formulas and truth-tables provides a partial test for analyticity in the PC language. But a sentence can be analytic without being symbolized by a tautology. The use of formulas and truth-tables is a complete test for logical truth, *so long as we confine our attention to the symbolic connectives of the PC language.* Ordinary English sentences have structures which we are ignoring in the PC language. And some English sentences contain distinctively logical English expressions. The sentence:

(8) It isn't true that Christmas, 1934 occurred on Sunday and didn't occur on Sunday.

is a logical truth of English. But (8) is a simple sentence of the PC language. A logically true English sentence won't be counted as a logical truth of the PC language.

A test a sentence α for logical falsity, we construct a truth-table for a formula α' which symbolizes α. Instead of the truth-table showing all 't's beneath the main connective, it must show all 'f's. This sentence:

(9) (Cairo is in Egypt v ~ Cairo is in Egypt) ≡ (Rome is in Italy & ~ Rome is in Italy)

is symbolized by: $(q \lor \sim q) \equiv (r \,\&\, \sim r)$. Its truth-table is:

q	r	$(q$	$\lor$	$\sim q)$	$\equiv$	$(r$	$\&$	$\sim r)$
t	t		t		f		f	
t	f		t		f		f	
f	t		t		f		f	
f	f		t		f		f	

Since no sentence with this form can be true, sentence (9) is logically false.

*Exercise: Section 4

For 1-3, determine which of these formulas are tautologies. In constructing truth-tables in a hurry, it is often difficult to make 't's and 'f's sufficiently distinct. One way to get around this problem is to use '1's instead of 't's and '0's instead of 'f's. '1's and '0's are easy to distinguish.

1. $(p \equiv q) \equiv p$

2. $\sim(p \,\&\, q) \equiv (\sim p \lor \sim q)$

3. $[p \supset (q \supset r)] \supset [(p \supset q) \supset r]$

For 4–6, determine which of the following sentences are logically true, and which are logically false.

4. Chicago is in California ⊃ (Chicago is in Illinois ⊃ ~ Chicago is in California)

5. ~ (Judas Iscariot is honest v ~ Judas Iscariot is honest)

6. [(2 > 1) ⊃ (3 >1)] ⊃ {[(2 > 1) v (3 > 1)] ⊃ (3 > 1)}

9-5   TWO-PLACE RELATIONS

Logical truth and logical falsity are properties of sentences. We are also interested in relations linking two or more sentences. We shall begin by considering semantic relations that connect one sentence to a second sentence. Two-place entailment is a general semantic relation. Sentence ρ entails sentence σ if understanding ρ and σ is sufficient for determining that ρ cannot be true when σ is untrue. The sentence:

(1) The White House is yellow.

entails:

(2) The White House isn't purple.

Sentence (1) isn't true, but understanding (1) and (2) is all it takes to realize that there is no way for (1) to be true when (2) isn't.

The special logical case of entailment is (*logical*) *implication*. (I shall always use 'implication' for the logical special case of entailment. But the word is sometimes used, even technically, for other relations. This is why I have prefixed the parenthetical qualification.) One sentence implies a second if an understanding of their logical forms is sufficient to determine that the first can't be true when the second isn't. We want to use truth-tables to test for logical implication. Suppose we want to determine whether sentence (3) implies sentence (4):

(3) Aluminum is a metal & Helium is an inert element.

(4) Silicon is a metal v Aluminum is a metal.

The following wffs symbolize the sentences:

(3′) $q \& p$

(4′) $r \vee s$

But these formulas are not helpful for determining whether (3) implies (4). The sentence which (3) and (4) have in common is crucial for the implication relation joining (3) to (4). The formulas do not share a variable.

We need to recognize a new kind of symbolizing. Let $\rho_1, \ldots, \rho_n$ be sentences of the PC language. Let $\rho'_1, \ldots, \rho'_n$ be obtained from these sentences by replacing each simple sentence in $\rho_1, \ldots, \rho_n$ by a propositional variable in such a way that (i) occurrences of the same sentence in $\rho_1, \ldots, \rho_n$ are replaced by occurrences of the same variable, and (ii) occurrences of distinct sentences in $\rho_1, \ldots, \rho_n$ are replaced by occurrences of distinct variables. Then $\rho'_1, \ldots, \rho'_n$ (in that order) *jointly symbolize* $\rho_1, \ldots, \rho_n$ (in that order).

Formulas (3′) and (4′) do not jointly symbolize sentences (3) and (4). But the following wffs do:

(3″) $p \& s$

(4″) $r \vee p$

To determine whether (3) implies (4), we can investigate (3″) and (4″). To do this, we make a *joint* truth-table. At the left of this table, we list the variables that occur in any of the formulas we are concerned with. Then we list the formulas:

p	*r*	*s*	*p* & *s*	*r* ∨ *p*

As before, the next thing we do is list all possible combinations of values for the variables; then we construct the columns under each wff:

p	*r*	*s*	*p* & *s*	*r* ∨ *p*
t	t	t	t	t
t	t	f	f	t
t	f	t	t	t
t	f	f	f	t
f	t	t	f	t
f	t	f	f	t
f	f	t	f	f
f	f	f	f	f

Since we are testing for implication, we must be careful to distinguish the sentence (and its formula) which does the implying from the sentence which gets implied. In the joint truth-table, we are looking for implication from (3″) to (4″). Remember, if (3) implies (4), there is no way for (3) to be true when (4) is false. So we look at the joint truth-table to see if every 't' under (3″) is matched by a 't' under (4″). There are two 't's under (3″); these *are* matched by 't's under (4″). So (3) implies (4).

We can also ask whether (4) implies (3). This time the answer is "No." There are six 't's under (4″). Four of them are not matched by 't's under (3″)—even if there were just one unmatched 't,' we would know that there is no implication. Now consider these sentences:

(5) George Washington is the first president of the U.S. & ~ George Washington is the first president of the U.S.

(6) Thomas Jefferson is the first president of the U.S.

We want to know if (5) implies (6). The following wffs jointly symbolize the sentences:

(5′) *q* & ~ *q*

(6′) *r*

The joint truth-table looks like this:

q	*r*	*q* & ~ *q*	*r*
t	t	f	t
t	f	f	f
f	t	f	t
f	f	f	f

We look for 't's under the main connective of (5′), to see if they are matched. Since there are no 't's at all under (5′), there is no way for (5) to be true when (6) is false. There is no way for (5) to be true. This is the test for implication, so (5) implies (6). (Some logicians object to this. They deny that a logically false sentence implies every sentence. But we shall understand 'imply' so that a logically false sentence does imply every sentence.) The following truth-table shows implication in both directions:

s	p	$s \vee p$	$\sim(\sim p\ \&\ \sim s)$
t	t	t	t
t	f	t	t
f	t	t	t
f	f	f	f

Two sentences which imply each other are *logically equivalent*. (Sentences which entail each other are simply *equivalent*.) If the columns under the main connectives of two formulas in a joint table are exactly the same, the formulas symbolize logically equivalent sentences.

*Exercise: Section 5

For 1–4, determine whether the sentences on the right imply those on the left.

	a	**b**
1.	Chocolate ice cream causes cancer ⊃ Vanilla ice cream cures cancer.	∼Vanilla ice cream cures cancer ⊃ ∼Chocolate ice cream causes cancer.
2.	Abraham Lincoln preferred Coke to Pepsi ⊃ U.S. Grant preferred Pepsi to Coke.	Abraham Lincoln preferred Coke to Pepsi ⊃ [George Washington didn't like cola beverages ⊃ U.S. Grant preferred Pepsi to Coke]
3.	Snails taste better than steak.	[(Rich people like snails ⊃ Snails are more expensive than beef) ⊃ Snails taste better than steak] & Snails are more expensive than beef.

For 4–6, determine which pairs of sentences are logically equivalent.

4.	∼(∼ Buffalo is famous for chicken wings and beef on weck v ∼ Peking is famous for Chinese food)	∼∼Buffalo is famous for chicken wings and beef on weck.
5.	Louis XIV preferred chocolate to vanilla shakes ⊃ (Cardinal Richelieu wouldn't eat hamburgers without french fries ⊃ Louis XIII refused to eat fast food)	(Louis XIV preferred chocolate to vanilla shakes ⊃ Cardinal Richelieu wouldn't eat hamburgers without french fries) & (Louis XIV preferred chocolate to vanilla shakes ⊃ Louis XIII refused to eat fast food)
6.	Cottage cheese is an aphrodisiac ⊃ (∼ Cottage cheese is an aphrodisiac v ∼ Tomato juice is an aphrodisiac)	∼Tomato juice is an aphrodisiac v ∼ Cottage cheese is an aphrodisiac.

The logical special case of two-place incompatibility is (two-place) logical incompatibility. Two sentences are logically incompatible if an understanding of their logical forms is sufficient to determine that it isn't possible for the sentences to be both true. To test

(7) Chicago is bigger than Milwaukee & Milwaukee is nicer than Chicago.

(8) Milwaukee is nicer than Chicago ⊃ ~ Milwaukee is nicer than Chicago.

for incompatibility, we can use these formulas:

(7′) $p \& q$

(8′) $q \supset \, \sim q$

and this joint truth-table:

p	q	$p \& q$	$q \supset \, \sim q$
t	t	t	f
t	f	f	t
f	t	f	f
f	f	f	t

Incompatible sentences can't both be true. If there is no row where both formulas come out true, the truth-table indicates incompatibility. Sentence (7) is incompatible with sentence (8).

*Exercise: Section 5 (cont.)

Determine which of the following pairs are logically incompatible.

a	b
7. (Calculus is an easy course & Electrical Engineering is an easy major) ⊃ Sociology is very difficult.	Electrical Engineering is an easy major & ~ Sociology is very difficult.
8. (Logic is part of philosophy v Logic is part of mathematics) ⊃ Logic is confusing.	Logic is part of mathematics & ~ Logic is confusing.
9. Law School is demanding ≡ (~Graduate study in English is a picnic v Graduate study in English is a picnic)	~Law School is demanding.

Determine whether the following pairs of sentences are linked by implication, logical equivalence, or logical incompatibility. For any cases of implication, indicate which sentence implies the other. Determine which pairs of pure formulas reveal which relations for sentences they jointly symbolize.

10. Napoleon liked steak & Napoleon liked lobster.	~[Napoleon liked steak v Napoleon liked lobster]
11. Chicago is in California ⊃ Chicago is in Illinois.	[Chicago is in California ⊃ ~ Chicago is in Illinois] & Chicago is in Illinois.

12. Buffalo is the capital of Florida ⊃   ~Buffalo is the capital of Florida ⊃
    Houston is the capital of Texas.   ~Houston is the capital of Texas.

13. $q \supset \sim p$ $[p \supset (q \supset r)] \& \sim r$

14. $p \supset (q \vee r)$ $(\sim q \& p) \& \sim r$

15. $[p \supset (q \supset r)] \& q$ $\sim r \supset \sim p$

9-6 MANY-PLACE RELATIONS

In order to test for many-place implication, when 'many' is more than two, we must extend our test for two-place implication. To see whether:

(1) Napoleon liked steak v (Napoleon liked snails ⊃ ~ Napoleon liked snails)

(2) Napoleon liked snails.

imply:

(3) Napoleon liked steak.

we first come up with formulas which jointly symbolize the sentences:

(1′) $s \vee (r \supset \sim r)$

(2′) r

(3′) s

Then we construct a joint truth-table:

r	s	$s \vee (r \supset \sim r)$	r	s
t	t	t	t	t
t	f	f	t	f
f	t	t	f	t
f	f	t	f	f

We look for a row where (1′) and (2′) each have value t, but (3′) has value f. There is no such row. This shows that we have a case of three-place implication.

Consider these three sentences:

(4) (Daniel Boone lived in Missouri ⊃ ~ Davey Crockett lived in Miami) v (Merriwether Lewis lived in St. Louis ⊃ ~ Davey Crockett lived in Miami)

(5) Daniel Boone lived in Missouri v Merriwether Lewis lived in St. Louis.

(6) ~ Davey Crockett lived in Miami.

Do (4) and (5) imply (6)? If we use these formulas:

(4′) $(p \supset \sim r) \vee (q \supset \sim r)$

(5′) $p \vee q$

(6′) $\sim r$

to (jointly) symbolize the sentences, we can construct this truth-table:

p	q	r	$(p \supset \sim r) \lor (q \supset \sim r)$			$p \lor q$	$\sim r$
t	t	t	f	f	f	t	f
t	t	f	t	t	t	t	t
t	f	t	f	t	t	t	f
t	f	f	t	t	t	t	t
f	t	t	t	t	f	t	f
f	t	f	t	t	t	t	t
f	f	t	t	t	t	f	f
f	f	f	t	t	t	f	t

In looking at this table, we must be sure to pay attention to the proper columns. Only the column which gives the value for a whole formula counts. In this table, there are two rows where (4′) and (5′) have value t but (6′) has value f. There is no implication based on the logical forms displayed by the formulas.

The fact that the truth-table test does not show implication cannot be taken as evidence that (4) and (5) fail to entail (6). For there can be entailment without logical implication. The truth-table test only evaluates the logical forms displayed by formulas; other factors are not taken into account.

The test for implication can also be used to determine if an inference or argument is *logically* valid. An inference is valid if its premisses entail its conclusion. It is logically valid if its premisses (logically) imply its conclusion.

An inference or argument is an act performed by one or more persons. (Someone has to *make* an inference.) In logic we are primarily concerned with the sentences which constitute the content of an inference. To mark the difference between an act and its content, we will say that a sequence of premisses and a conclusion is an *inference sequence* or an *argument sequence*. If we have premisses $\rho_1, \ldots, \rho_n$ and conclusion σ, we write the inference sequence (argument sequence) this way $\rho_1, \ldots, \rho_n / \sigma$. The elements of an inference sequence must be sentences, but we also consider sequences of formulas, like this one: $p \supset (q \supset r)$, $\sim q / \sim r \supset \sim p$. Such a sequence is a *formula sequence*. (Since sentences are one kind of formulas, an inference sequence is also a formula sequence.) If a formula sequence contains nothing but pure formulas, and these formulas in order jointly symbolize the sentences in an inference sequence (in order), then the formula sequence *symbolizes* the inference sequence.

An inference sequence is valid in the same circumstances that an inference is valid: when its premisses entail its conclusion. An inference sequence is logically valid if its premisses imply its conclusion. We will also speak of formula sequences as logically valid and invalid. A formula sequence is logically valid if it is itself a logically valid inference sequence or it yields only logically valid inference sequences when sentences are substituted (uniformly) for its variables.

Like implication and entailment, incompatibility is not limited to two sentences at a time. Any number of sentences can be linked by incompatibility. If several sentences are mutually incompatible, it isn't possible for them to be simultaneously true. Consider the following sentences:

(7) Today is Thursday v Today is Friday.

(8) $\sim$ Today is Thursday.

(9) $\sim$ Today is Friday.

It should be clear that no two of these are incompatible, even though all three are. The following truth-table shows that the sentences are logically incompatible:

p	q	$p \vee q$	$\sim p$	$\sim q$
t	t	t	f	f
t	f	t	f	t
f	t	t	t	f
f	f	f	t	t

There is no row where all three formulas have value t. The logical forms displayed by the formulas "prevent" the three sentences from being true together.

*Exercise: Section 6

For 1–3, determine which of the following inference sequences and formula sequences are logically valid.

1. There is a greatest integer $\equiv$ There is an integer which has no successor., There is an integer which has no successor $\supset$ Peano's postulates are mistaken. / $\sim$ Peano's postulates are mistaken $\supset$ $\sim$ There is a greatest integer.

2. Red wine goes well with roast beef $\supset$ (Daniel will serve roast beef tonight $\supset$ Daniel will serve red wine tonight), Red wine goes well with beef $\supset$ Daniel will serve roast beef tonight. / Red wine goes well with beef $\supset$ Daniel will serve red wine tonight.

3. $p \supset q, q \supset \sim p$ / $\sim p$

For 4–6, determine which groups of sentences are logically incompatible. Determine which groups of formulas display incompatible forms.

4. (John lives in Champaign v John lives in Urbana) v John lives in Danville. $\sim$ John lives in Champaign & $\sim$ John lives in Urbana. John lives in Danville $\supset$ John lives in Urbana.

5. $(p \supset q) \equiv p, p \equiv q, \sim q$

6. $(p \supset q) \& (\sim p \supset r), \sim p \vee \sim q, \sim r \vee p$

9-7   INDIRECT TESTS

The truth-table tests we have considered are *direct* tests for the logical semantic features. Each test is designed to answer a question about one feature. We can also develop *indirect* tests for these features. An indirect test answers a question about one feature on the basis of a test for a different feature. Our indirect tests reduce the tests for other features to a test for logical truth. Because of the fundamental role of logical truth, we won't have an indirect test for logical truth.

Suppose we want to know if sentence ρ implies sentence σ. What sentence should we test for logical truth to determine if there is implication? If the sentence (ρ $\supset$ σ) is logically true, the truth-table for a formula symbolizing it has no 'f' in the column under the principal connective. But then no 't' under the antecedent is matched by an 'f' under the consequent. This indicates implication. So ρ implies σ just in case (ρ $\supset$ σ) is logically true.

To determine whether:

(1) (Chicago is in Oklahoma $\supset$ Peoria is in Oklahoma) & $\sim$ Peoria is in Oklahoma.

implies:

(2) $\sim$ Chicago is in Oklahoma.

we can construct:

(3) [(Chicago is in Oklahoma $\supset$ Peoria is in Oklahoma) & $\sim$ Peoria is in Oklahoma] $\supset$ $\sim$ Chicago is in Oklahoma.

Then we obtain a suitable formula:

(4) $[(p \supset q) \& \sim q] \supset \sim p$

(It wasn't really necessary to construct (3). We could have moved from (1) and (2) to (4).) The truth-table is:

p	q	$[(p \supset q]$	$\& \sim q]$	$\supset \sim p$
t	t	t	f	t
t	f	f	f	t
f	t	t	f	t
f	f	t	t	t

Since the formula is a tautology, sentence (3) is logically true. But then (1) implies (2).

As an indirect test to see if ρ_1, ρ_2 imply σ, we can check $[(\rho_1 \& \rho_2) \supset \sigma]$ for logical truth. To determine whether ρ_1, ρ_2, ρ_3 imply σ, we can test $\{[(\rho_1 \& \rho_2) \& \rho_3] \supset \sigma\}$. Etc. The indirect test for logical validity is the same as the indirect test for implication (from premises to conclusion).

There are two indirect tests to determine whether sentences $\rho_1, \ldots, \rho_{n+1}$ are logically incompatible: (i) We can take any n sentences, conjoin them (supplying enough parentheses), and connect them with the horseshoe to the negation of the remaining sentence. Then we can test that for logical truth. Or (ii) we can negate the conjunction of all $n + 1$ sentences, and test this negation for logical truth. Consider these sentences:

(5) Madison is in Minnesota $\supset$ $\sim$ Madison is in Minnesota.

(6) (Milwaukee is in Illinois & Green Bay is in Iowa) $\supset$ Madison is in Minnesota.

(7) $\sim$ Milwaukee is in Illinois $\supset$ Green Bay is in Iowa.

(8) Green Bay is in Iowa $\equiv$ Milwaukee is in Illinois.

If we use the first indirect test for incompatibility, we can take any three sentences, conjoin them, and like them with the horseshoe to the negation of the fourth. So we can test this formula:

(9) $\{[(p \equiv q) \& (\sim q \supset p)] \& [(q \& p) \supset r]\} \supset \sim (r \supset \sim r)$

If we apply the second indirect test, we can test this formula:

(10) $\sim \{[(r \supset \sim r) \& [(q \& p) \supset r]] \& [(\sim q \supset p) \& (p \equiv q)]\}$

If either formula is a tautology, the other is too. If either formula is a tautology, the sentences are incompatible. (You can make a truth-table to test this.)

*Exercise: Section 7

For 1–3, use indirect tests to check the following groups of sentences for logical incompatibility. Use indirect tests to determine whether the groups of pure formulas would jointly symbolize incompatible sentences.

1. Bill will graduate in June ≡ Bill gets an A in Logic, ∼ Bill will get an A in Logic, ∼Bill will graduate in June.

2. Kentucky has an outstanding basketball team ⊃ ∼ UCLA has a good basketball team, Kentucky has an outstanding basketball team v UCLA has a good basketball team.

3. p & $(q$ & $r)$, $p ≡ s$, $s ⊃ (r ⊃ ∼ q)$

For 4–6, use indirect tests to check the following argument sequences for logical validity. Use indirect tests to see if the formula sequences are valid.

4. Albert passed the test ⊃ ∼ Albert will fail the course., (Albert is stupid v ∼ Albert has been studying) ⊃ Albert will fail the course., Albert passed the test. / ∼ Albert is stupid.

5. $p ⊃ (q ⊃ r)$, $r ⊃ (q$ & $p)$ / $(p$ & $q) ≡ r$

6. $p ⊃ (q$ v $r)$, ∼ r / ∼ $p ⊃ ∼ q$

9-8 THE QUICK METHOD OF DETERMINING IF A FORMULA IS A TAUTOLOGY

There seem to be few reasons for using the indirect tests for logical semantic features. Both direct and indirect tests yield the same results. The indirect tests involve more work, since the truth-tables constructed in these tests contain the truth-tables of the direct tests together with other symbols and columns. The indirect tests also give more chance for error.

For the indirect tests, we eventually put together a single wff which we test for being a tautology. There are different ways to determine if a formula is a tautology. The way we have learned previously requires the construction of an entire truth-table. Now we shall learn the *quick method*. When this is employed, indirect tests are sometimes superior to direct tests.

A (pure) formula is a tautology if its truth-table has all 't's in the column under the principal connective. The quick method of determining if a formula is a tautology is a systematic procedure for constructing a row in the truth-table for which the formula has value f. Consider this formula: $(p ⊃ q) ⊃ [q ⊃ (p ⊃ r)]$. We shall try to complete this row in which there is an 'f' under the main horseshoe:

$$(p ⊃ q) ⊃ [q ⊃ (p ⊃ r)]$$
$$\text{f}$$

Only one row in the truth-table which defines '⊃' has the value f. For $(ρ ⊃ σ)$ to have f, ρ must have value t and σ have f. We proceed:

$$(p ⊃ q) ⊃ [q ⊃ (p ⊃ r)]$$
$$| \quad \text{f} \quad |$$
$$\text{t} \quad\quad \text{f}$$

We write the 't's and 'f's on different levels to keep track of the order in which we assign values. We draw lines to insure that the 't's and 'f's are associated with the correct symbols. Three rows in the truth-table defining the horseshoe give value t to the horseshoe. This makes it difficult to follow up the value t assigned to the antecedent of our formula. Since f is assigned to the consequent, we continue working with the consequent:

$$(p \supset q) \supset [q \supset (p \supset r)]$$

$$\begin{array}{c} \quad \text{f} \\ \text{t} \quad \quad \text{f} \\ \quad \quad \text{t} \quad \text{f} \\ \quad \quad \quad \text{t} \quad \text{f} \end{array}$$

Different occurrences of a single variable receive the same value in one row of a truth-table. The values assigned to 'p' and 'q' in the consequent are also assigned in the antecedent:

$$(p \supset q) \supset [q \supset (p \supset r)]$$

$$\begin{array}{c} \quad \text{f} \\ \text{t} \quad \quad \text{f} \\ \quad \quad \text{t} \quad \text{f} \\ \quad \quad \quad \text{t} \quad \text{f} \\ \text{t} \quad \text{t} \end{array}$$

This gives us a row in the truth-table for which the formula has value f:

$$(p \supset q) \supset [q \supset (p \supset r)]$$

$$\text{t} \quad \text{t} \quad \text{t} \quad \text{f} \quad \text{t} \quad \text{f} \quad \text{t} \quad \text{f} \quad \text{f}$$

The existence of this row guarantees that the formula is not a tautology.

To use the quick method, we write 'f' under the main connective and then "work backwards," assigning values to symbols (according to the relevant truth-tables) until a single value is assigned to every symbol. If we succeed in doing this, the formula is not a tautology. But what happens if we carry out this procedure with a formula that is a tautology? Let's try this formula: $[(p \And q) \supset r] \supset [p \supset (q \supset r)]$. We can assign values like this:

It appears that we have found a row for which the formula has value f. But if we look more carefully, we will see that we are not done with our allocation of 't's and 'f's. The antecedent of our formula is the '$\supset$'-formula '$[(p \And q) \supset r]$.' But the antecedent of *this* formula, '$(p \And q)$, has been assigned t and the consequent assigned f. So the formula '$[(p \And q) \supset r]$' should have value f. It has already been assigned t. We must assign a second value to the antecedent:

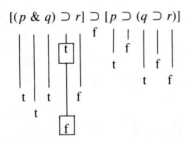

The boxes around the two values assigned a single symbol are to call attention to them. Something has gone wrong in our search for a row where the formula has value f, for an occurrence of a single symbol should receive a single value. Our being required to assign two values to one symbol shows that there is no row like the one we are looking for.

It is a shortcoming of the quick method that a person can easily think he has constructed a false row of a formula that is really a tautology. We must be more careful in using the quick method than in constructing the entire truth-table.

The order of steps in carrying out the quick method is not unique. We could have proceeded like this:

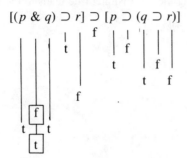

It doesn't matter which symbol both 't' and 'f' are written beneath.

When the values assigned to a certain point don't determine what values must be assigned to remaining symbols, the quick method is not quite so quick. Consider this formula:

$$(p \lor q) \supset (p \& q)$$

If we begin:

```
(p v q) ⊃ (p & q)
 |     f     |
 t           f
```

we must now make an arbitrary choice. But our choice of further values must be consistent with the values already assigned. Consider the antecedent. We might choose values for both disjuncts at once. But a disjunction is true if either disjunct is true; so we can consider the disjuncts one at a time. Suppose we assign t to 'p':

```
(p v q) ⊃ (p & q)
 |  |   f    |
 |  t        f
 t
```

If we carry this value to the other occurrence of '*p*,' we will be able to continue and *falsify* the formula:

$(p \vee q) \supset (p \& q)$

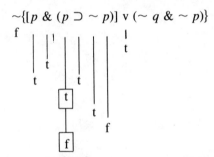

When we must make a choice, we try to complete a row where the formula has value f.

Now consider a choice which fails to lead to a row where the formula has value f. In this case:

$\sim\{[p \& (p \supset \sim p)] \vee (\sim q \& \sim p)\}$

we are required to make a choice. Making the left disjunct true leads to the following:

$\sim\{[p \& (p \supset \sim p)] \vee (\sim q \& \sim p)\}$

We *cannot* take this as evidence that the formula is a tautology. We have discovered that our choice does not lead to a row in which the formula has value f. We must see if another choice would lead to such a row. And it does:

$\sim\{[p \& (p \supset \sim p)] \vee (\sim q \& \sim p)\}$

This falsifying assignment shows that the formula is not a tautology.

The quick method is quickest when we use it on formulas that don't require a choice. If we make a choice, and our choice leads to a row where the formula has value f, then we are done—the formula is not a tautology. If we make a choice which does not lead to a falsifying assignment, we must try the other choices. If any choice leads to a falsifying assignment, the formula is not a tautology. If no choice leads to such an assignment, the formula is a tautology.

*Exercise: Section 8

Use the quick method to determine which of the following formulas are tautologies.

1. $[(p \supset q) \& (s \supset p)] \supset (s \supset q)$

2. $[(p \supset q) \supset (q \supset r)] \supset (p \supset r)$

3. $[(p \supset r) \lor (q \supset r)] \supset [(p \lor q) \supset r]$

4. $[(p \& \sim q) \lor (\sim p \& q)] \supset (\sim p \lor \sim q)$

5. $(p \supset q) \equiv \sim(p \lor q)$

6. $(\sim p \lor \sim q) \equiv (p \supset \sim q)$

Exercise B: Section 8

Determine which of the following sentences are logically true and logically false, to the extent that this can be ascertained with truth-tables. For the formulas, determine which symbolize logical truths and logical falsehoods. Show your work.

1. [Bill likes beer v ($\sim$ Bill likes beer & $\sim$ Bill likes ale)] v Bill likes ale.

2. German white wine is generally better than French white wine $\supset$ [French white wine is usually superior to German white wine & $\sim$ German white wine is generally better than French white wine]

3. No after-dinner drink is better than a fine cognac & [(The best after-dinner drink in the world is a properly aged calvados $\supset$ $\sim$ No after-dinner drink in the world is better than a fine cognac) & (No after-dinner drink in the world is better than a fine cognac $\supset$ The best after-dinner drink in the world is a properly aged calvados)]

4. The per capita consumption of beer is higher in Belgium than in any other country $\equiv$ $\sim$ (The per capita consumption of beer in Germany is higher than in any other country v The per capita consumption of beer is higher in Belgium than in any other country)

5. (The best wines from the Loire valley are less expensive than the best wines from Bordeaux $\supset$ The best wines from the Loire valley are less good than the best wines from Bordeaux) v ($\sim$ The best wines from the Loire valley are less good than the best wines from Bordeaux & The best wines from the Loire valley are less expensive than the best wines from Bordeaux)

6. $\{[(p \supset q) \supset q] \supset \sim p\} \supset \sim p$

7. $[p \equiv (q \equiv r)] \equiv (\sim p \equiv \sim r)$

8. $[(p \& q) \supset r] \supset [p \supset (q \supset r]$

9. $\sim p \supset \{[(p \supset p) \supset p] \supset [(p \supset p) \supset p]\}$

10. $[(p \& q) \equiv (p \lor q)] \& (p \equiv \sim q)$

Exercise C: Section 8

Determine which pairs of sentences are linked by implication, logical equivalence, or logical incompatibility. Determine which pairs of formulas would jointly symbolize sentences linked by one of the relations. For cases of implication, specify the "direction" of implication. Show your work.

	a	**b**
1.	(White wine goes with chicken & ~Red wine goes with fish) v (~ White wine goes with chicken & ~Red wine goes with fish)	~Red wine goes with fish.
2.	Betty can type ⊃ (She will type Sally's paper v Sally will turn-in a hand-written copy)	Betty can type & ~ Sally will turn-in a hand-written copy.
3.	Anderson will win the election ≡ ~Butler will win the election.	~(Anderson will win the election ≡ Butler will win the election)
4.	~ Chuck will win the race ⊃ ~Andy will hurt his ankle.	[Andy will hurt his ankle ⊃ (Bob will get the flu ⊃ Chuck will win the race)] & Bob will get the flu.
5.	(~ Niagara Mohawk will raise their rates this year & The Public Service Commission will refuse their request) & ~ Niagara Mohawk will request a rate hike next year.	Niagara Mohawk will raise their rates this year v (The Public Service Commission will refuse their request ⊃ Niagara Mohawk will request a rate hike next year)
6.	$p \supset (q \supset r)$	$(\sim p \; \& \sim q) \supset \sim r$
7.	$(q \equiv r) \supset p$	$[(q \; \& \; r) \; v \sim (r \; v \; q)] \; \& \sim p$
8.	$[p \; \& \; (q \supset r)] \; \& \; q$	$p \supset (q \supset \sim r)$
9.	$(p \; \& \; q) \supset r$	$(p \supset \sim r) \; v \; (q \supset \sim r)$
10.	$\sim q$	$[q \supset (r \supset p)] \; \& \; [(\sim p \supset \sim r) \supset \sim q]$

Exercise D: Section 8

For 1–6, determine which argument sequences and formula sequences are valid. Show your work.

1. 2 is even ⊃ 3 is a prime number., ~ 2 is even ⊃ 3 is a prime number. / 3 is a prime number.

2. Milwaukee is larger than Seattle ⊃ (There are a lot of Germans in Milwaukee v They drink a lot of beer in Milwaukee), There are a lot of Germans in Milwaukee ⊃ They drink a lot of beer in Milwaukee. / ~ They drink a lot of beer in Milwaukee ⊃ ~ Milwaukee is larger than Seattle.

3. (Cheeseburgers are more popular than plain hamburgers & Grilled cheese sand-wiches are very popular) ⊃ Restaurants buy a lot of cheese., ~ Restaurants buy a lot of cheese., ~ Cheeseburgers are more popular than plain hamburgers. / Grilled cheese sandwiches are very popular.

4. $p \equiv (q \ \& \ r)$, ~ $q / p \equiv r$

5. $(p \supset q) \lor (r \supset q)$, $p \lor r$, ~ $p / r \supset q$

6. ~$(p \ \& \ q)$, $r \supset q / p \supset \ \sim r$

For 7–12, determine which of the following groups of sentences are incompatible. Deter-mine which formulas would jointly symbolize incompatible sentences. Show your work.

7. Jones will go to the fish fry Friday ≡ (Jones will get over his cold by Friday & Jones will get paid Friday) Jones will get over his cold by Friday ⊃ ~ Jones will get paid Friday. Jones will go to the fish fry Friday.

8. Mesa Verde is in the Four Corners area ≡ ~(Mesa Verde is in Montana v Mesa Verde is in Kansas) ~ Mesa Verde is in the Four Corners area. Mesa Verde is in Montana.

9. Normandy is north of Brittany v (Brittany is north of Normandy ⊃ Belgium is part of France) ~ Normandy is north of Brittany. ~ Brittany is north of Normandy.

10. $(p \ \& \ q) \lor (p \ \& \sim q)$, $(\sim q \supset \ \sim p)$, $(\sim q \ \& \ r)$

11. $(p \ \& \ q) \equiv (r \lor s)$, $r \supset \ \sim p$, $s \supset \ \sim q$

12. ~$(p \supset p)$, $q \lor \sim p$, $r \supset \ \sim q$

Exercise E: Section 8

It sometimes happens that symbols developed for one purpose are found to be suitable for another. This is the case with the symbols and formulas we have been studying. For we can use the formulas to represent electric switching circuits.

To understand how formulas can represent circuits, we will consider some simple circuits. In the circuit drawn here:

p is a switch. The arrows indicate the direction of the current. In the circuit, shown, p is open, so no current flows through the wires.

The circuit drawn.

is represented by '$p \ \& \ q$.' In a circuit like this, p and q are said to be connected *in series*. When '$p \ \& \ q$' represents a circuit instead of symbolizing a sentence, we can think of '$p \ \& \ q$' as indicating that current flows through the circuit when p is closed *and* q is closed. In the truth-table for the ampersand, we now think of 't' as indicating that current flows, and 'f' as indicating that no current flows. In the following:

p	q	$p \,\&\, q$
t	t	t
t	f	f
f	t	f
f	f	f

the first row indicates that when p is closed (so current can flow through p) and q is closed, then current flows through the circuit. The second row indicates that when p is closed and q is open, current does not flow. The third row indicates that current does not flow when p is open and q is closed. The fourth row indicates that current does not flow when both switches are open.

1. What formula can we use to represent the circuit shown below? (These switches are connected *in parallel*.)

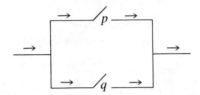

2. If p is a switch that is open when q is closed, and p is closed when q is open, what formula can we use to represent the relation between them?

3. If two or more switches are always open and closed together, then we can use the same letter (variable) to represent them. In the formula representing a circuit, the number of times that the "same" switch occurs must be reflected in the number of occurrences of the variable representing the switch. How can we represent the circuit drawn below?

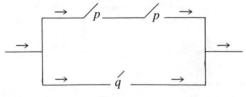

4. Draw a circuit where current flows whenever current flows through the circuit drawn in 3, but which uses the fewest possible switches.

5. How can we represent the circuit drawn below?

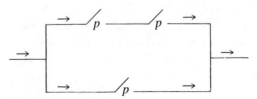

6. Draw a circuit where current flows whenever current flows through the circuit drawn below, but which uses the fewest possible switches.

7. In the drawings, switches are always drawn as if they were open, so that we can tell where the switches are. But the drawings do not indicate whether or not the switches are open; the same drawing will be used for both cases. How can we represent the circuit drawn below?

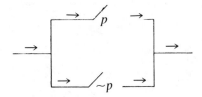

8. When does the circuit drawn in 7 conduct current?

9. How can we represent the following?

10. When does the circuit drawn in 9 conduct current?

11. How can we represent the following circuit?

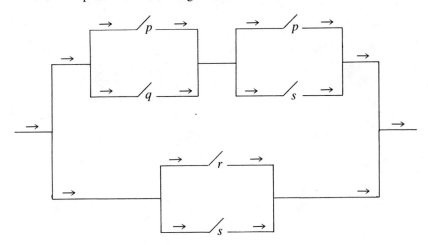

12. Draw a circuit represented by '(p & q) v (q & r).'

13. Draw a circuit represented by '(p v q) v (r & ~ p).'

14. Draw a circuit represented by '[(p & ~ q) & (r v s)] v (q & s).'

15. Draw a circuit that does the same job as the one drawn below, but which uses the fewest possible switches.

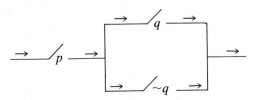

16. Draw a circuit that does the same job as the one drawn below, but which uses the fewest switches possible.

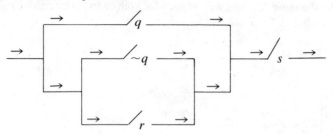

Chapter 10

The PC Deductive System

10-0 SUMMARY

In this chapter, the Propositional Connective deductive system is developed to prove that inference sequences are logically valid. We can also prove that a sentence is logically true, and, indirectly, that sentences are logically incompatible. Proofs from hypotheses are used to establish results in the deductive system. We make assignments of values to show that a sentence, group of sentences, or inference sequence is not a case of a logical semantic feature. Optional sections prove results about the Propositional Connective deductive system.

10-1 A DEDUCTIVE SYSTEM

We have used truth-tables to determine whether we have or don't have a case of a logical semantic feature. Now we will learn to *prove* that an inference is logically valid or a sentence is logically true. Our proofs will belong to the *Propositional Connective* deductive system—the *PC* deductive system.

A deductive system consists of rules for proving results, proofs of results, and the results that can be established by proofs. Some deductive systems contain *axioms,* which are sentences or formulas accepted without proof, but the PC deductive system has no axioms. The results proved in a deductive system constitute a body of knowledge. The set of rules of the system *characterizes* the body of knowledge.

Proofs in the PC deductive system establish exactly the same results that can be established using truth-tables. But the deductive system gives an understanding of the meanings of logical expressions that can't be gained from truth-tables. For most expressions, we can distinguish two kinds of meaning:

  (i) Representational meaning

  (ii) Inferential meaning

The representational meaning of an expression is what the expression can be used to represent. Take 'blue'; this is a color word, it represents the color blue (or else it represents blue objects). We understand the representational meaning of this word if we know what color it is used to represent. (Even a word like 'unicorn' has a representational meaning. We understand what it is used to represent if we understand what unicorns are supposed to be like.)

The inferential meaning of a word consists in the contribution that the word makes to (deductively valid) inferences. In the inference from:

Bill's car is blue.

to:

Bill's car isn't red.

the color words 'blue' and 'red' are crucial. Understanding these words enables us to recognize that the inference is correct (valid). Every word with a representational meaning also has an inferential meaning. We must understand both meanings to understand the word.

We use truth-tables to explain the representational meaning of a connective. The truth-table explains what we are saying "about the world" when we use the connective. In the PC deductive system, we find that most rules are associated with this or that connective. The PC deductive system provides an account of the inferential meanings of the connectives. Since inferences and inferential meanings are a central concern of logic, it is appropriate that we consider the deductive system to be more useful than truth-tables.

10-2 PROOFS FROM HYPOTHESES

If we wish to show that an inference sequence p_1, p_2 / c is valid by means of a *proof from hypotheses,* we begin by supposing that p_1 and p_2 are true. This makes them *hypotheses* of the proof. Then we try to reason from these hypotheses to the conclusion c. Starting with hypotheses p_1, p_2 and reasoning correctly to conclusion c shows that p_1, p_2 (together) imply c. A proof from p_1, p_2 to conclusion c also establishes that p_1, p_2 / c is logically valid.

Results that can be proved in the PC deductive system are called *theorems* of the system. (Actually, any result which has a proof can be called a theorem. The word is not confined to results proved within deductive systems.) A proof which shows $p_1, \ldots, p_n$ / c to be valid establishes that $p_1, \ldots, p_n$ / c is a theorem of the PC deductive system.

Steps in a proof from hypotheses are written vertically (one beneath the other). The hypotheses are first. Next come the steps obtained from the hypotheses by reasoning. The last step is the conclusion. A proof of the sequence p_1, p_2 / c would look like this:

1   p_1

2   p_2

.

.

.

m c

In a proof from hypotheses, each step is numbered. And each step must be provided with an explanation which justifies that step being in the proof. The explanation for an hypothesis *is* that it is an hypothesis. A proof of p_1, p_2 / c might start:

1   p_1 hyp(othesis)

2   p_2 hyp

Instead of writing 'hypothesis' or its abbreviation 'hyp,' we will adopt the practice of listing all the hypotheses at the beginning of a proof, then drawing a line beneath the last hypothesis:

> 1 p_1
>
> 2 p_2

The line is a substitute for writing 'hyp' beside each hypothesis.

The steps which follow the hypotheses are reached by inferences. We need rules which authorize us to infer steps from steps already available. Each rule for adding steps to a proof from hypotheses is a rule for making a certain kind of inference. We explain a step which isn't an hypothesis by giving the name of the rule used to infer that step, and the number(s) of the step(s) used as a premiss in the inference. If we obtain a step by starting with step 4 and reasoning according to rule α, we explain the step by writing: 4, α.

*Exercise: Section 2

Determine which of the following are true.

1. Proofs from hypotheses enable us to establish some valid inference sequences that cannot be shown to be valid using truth-tables.

2. If an inference sequence is a theorem of the PC system, then it is valid.

3. In constructing a proof, an explanation must be provided for every step.

4. The hypotheses of a proof from hypotheses don't need to be explained.

10-3   THE EASY RULES

The first rules are associated with '&.' The rule *Simplification (Simp)* allows us to start with a premiss:

> (A & B)

and infer either *A* or *B* as a conclusion. There are really two rules called Simplification. One authorizes us to infer the left side of a conjunction; the other authorizes us to infer the right side. Suppose we want to prove this inference sequence to be valid: $(p \ \& \ q) \ / \ p$. Since the sequence has one premiss, our proof from hypotheses begins with a single hypothesis:

> 1 $(p \ \& \ q)$

To complete this proof, we must reason beyond the hypothesis until we reach the conclusion '*p*.' This is easy to do:

> 1 $(p \ \& \ q)$
>
> 2 p 1, Simp

This proof establishes that '$(p \ \& \ q) \ / \ p$' is a theorem of the PC deductive system. It also shows (1) that the inference sequence is valid, and (2) that a sentence of the form $(p \ \& \ q)$ implies a sentence *p*.

To prove this inference sequence: $[p \ \& \ (q \ \& \ r)] \ / \ q$, we need another proof with just one hypothesis:

1 $[p \ \& \ (q \ \& \ r)]$

We cannot reach the desired conclusion in a single step. Only one occurrence of '&' in the hypothesis is the principal occurrence. The rule Simplification applies only to this occurrence. The rule allows us to break a conjunction into two halves. We can have a proof:

1 $[p \ \& \ (q \ \& \ r)]$

2 p 1, Simp

or:

1 $[p \ \& \ (q \ \& \ r)]$

2 $(q \ \& \ r)$ 1, Simp

Once we break our hypothesis in two, we can further simplify the half in which '&' is the principal connective:

1 $[p \ \& \ (q \ \& \ r)]$

2 $(q \ \& \ r)$ 1, Simp

3 q 2, Simp

Simplification is a rule for taking a conjunction apart. *Conjunction (Conj)* is a rule for putting one together. This is a two-premiss rule. It allows us to move from premisses A, B to a conclusion $(A \ \& \ B)$. The rule Conjunction is illustrated in the following proof of '$(p \ \& \ q), (r \ \& \ s) \ / \ (p \ \& \ r)$':

1 $(p \ \& \ q)$

2 $(r \ \& \ s)$

3 p 1, Simp

4 r 2, Simp

5 $(p \ \& \ r)$ 3, 4, Conj

Since the inference sequence has two premisses, the proof from hypotheses must have two hypotheses. The hypotheses of the proof must be the same as the premisses of the inference sequence, but their order is not important. In using the rule Conjunction in the proof above, the step that came earlier formed the left side of the conclusion, and the step that came later formed the right side. This isn't important either.

The rule *Addition (Add)* is associated with the wedge, the symbol for disjunction. The two forms of this rule are illustrated:

m A

n $(A \lor B)$ m, Add

m   *A*

.

n   *(B* v *A)*   *m,* Add

The formula "added" to the original formula using 'v' can be any formula at all—it need not occur earlier in the proof. The rule Addition is used in proving '$(q \& p) / (r$ v $p)$':

1    $(q \& p)$

2   *p*   *1, Simp*

3   *(r* v *p)* *2, Add*

In going from step 2 to step 3, the new formula '*r*' was added to the left side of step 2. The other form of Addition is used in this proof of '$[q \& (p \& r)] / [(p \& r)$ v $(q \supset p)]$':

1    $[q \& (p \& r)]$

2    $(p \& r)$ *1, Simp*

3    $[(p \& r)$ v $(q \supset p)]$ 2, Add

Dilemma is associated with two connectives, the wedge and the horseshoe. It is a two-premiss rule:

.

m $(A \supset C)$

.

n $(B \supset C)$

.

r $[(A$ v $B) \supset C]$ *m, n,* Dil

The rule Dilemma is used in the following proof:

1    $(p \supset p)$

2    $(q \supset p)$

3    $[(q$ v $p) \supset p]$ 1,2, Dil

It may seem that this use of Dilemma does not fit the pattern illustrated above. In the illustration there are three different variables '*A*,' '*B*,' and '*C*,' while in the proof there are only two formulas, '*p*' and '*q*.' However, to use the rule, we need three formulas *A*, *B*, and *C*. These formulas can be, but need not be, distinct.

We will introduce a symbol to abbreviate 'is a theorem.' We will use '⊢,' and write it to the left of the theorem like this: ⊢ $(p \supset p)$, $(q \supset p) / [(q$ v $p) \supset p]$. (When we use this symbol, we will not enclose the sequence in single quotes.) As well as writing ⊢ *A, B / C* to say that *A, B / C* is a theorem, we will write *A, B* ⊢ *C* to say that there is a proof of *C* from hypotheses *A, B*. It is clear that ⊢ *A, B / C* if, and only if, *A, B* ⊢ *C*.

Modus Ponens (MP) is a two-premiss rule for reasoning with the horseshoe. It is illustrated:

.

$m \quad (A \supset B)$

.

$n \quad A$

.

$r \quad B \qquad m, n, \text{MP}$

The rule Modus Ponens is used in this proof:

1   $(p \supset p)$

2   $(q \supset p)$

3   $(q \lor p)$

───────────

4   $[(q \lor p) \supset p] \qquad 3, 1, \text{Dil}$

5   $p \qquad\qquad\qquad 4, 3, \text{MP}$

This proof shows that $\vdash (p \supset p), (q \supset p), (q \lor p) \mathbin{/} p$ and also that $(p \supset p), (q \supset p), (q \lor p)$ $\vdash p$.

*Exercise: Section 3

For 1 and 2, fill in the reasons for the steps in the proofs:

1. 1 $[p \supset (q \supset r)]$

2   $(s \supset r)$

3   p

─────

4   $(q \supset r)$

5   $[(q \lor s) \supset r]$

6   $[(s \mathbin{\&} p) \lor [(q \lor s) \supset r]]$

2. 1 p

2   q

─────

3   $(p \lor r)$

4   $(r \lor q)$

5   $[(r \lor q) \mathbin{\&} (p \lor r)]$

For 3–6, construct proofs of the inference sequences.

3. $[p \mathbin{\&} (p \supset q)], r \mathbin{/} [(p \supset q) \lor r]$

4. $p, (q \supset r), (s \supset r) \mathbin{/} \{[(s \lor q) \supset r] \mathbin{\&} p\}$

5. $p, (p \supset q) [(q \lor r) \supset s] \mathbin{/} s$

6. $[p \mathbin{\&} (p \supset q)] \mathbin{/} (p \mathbin{\&} q)$

10-4 MORE RULES

To prove an inference sequence $P_1, \ldots , P_n / C$, we start a proof with hypotheses P_1, $\ldots , P_n$ and reason according to the rules until we reach the conclusion C. But what if the conclusion C is one of the hypotheses we begin with? Suppose we want to prove 'p, $(q \supset r)$, s / s.' We start the proof by listing the hypotheses:

1 p

2 $(q \supset r)$

3 s

Our proof will be done when we obtain 's' as the last step. But 's' already is the last step. In this case, we have proved the inference sequence to be a theorem once we have listed the hypotheses.

We can prove the inference sequence 'p, $(q \supset r)$, $s / (q \supset r)$' by listing the hypotheses in a different order than the premisses are listed:

1 p

2 s

3 $(q \supset r)$

In general, we can prove an inference sequence $P_1, \ldots , P_n / P_i$ for $1 \leq i \leq n$ by listing the hypotheses in such a way that P_i is last.

Of the rules considered so far, Simplification and Addition are one-premiss rules. And Conjunction, Modus Ponens, and Dilemma are two-premiss rules. We cannot use two premisses for a one-premiss rule. The following "proof" is mistaken:

1 p

2 q

3 $(p \vee q)$ 1, 2, Add

What is mistaken in this proof is the explanation for step 3. Two premisses are listed, then the abbreviation of the name of the rule. But Addition is a one-premiss rule. This proof can be corrected by changing the explanation for step 3 to either:

1, Add

or:

2, Add

The following "proof" is also mistaken:

1 r

2 $(p \supset q)$

3 q 2, MP

4 $(q \& r)$ 3, 1, Conj

Step 3 is incorrect, because Modus Ponens is a two-premiss rule. There is no legitimate way to obtain '*q*' from the hypotheses that are given.

A two-premiss rule requires two premisses, but we don't always need two distinct premisses. To prove the sequence '*p* / (*p* & *p*),' we would start with this hypothesis:

> 1   *p*
> ___

This hypothesis is "half" of the desired result. We allow ourselves to "take" the hypothesis twice to get this proof:

> 1   *p*
> ___
> 2   (*p* & *p*)   1, 1, Conj

Repetition is a one-premiss rule that is not associated with any connective; it allows us to repeat a step in a proof. It can be illustrated:

> *m*   *A*
>
> *n*   *A*   *m*, Rep

The two-step proof above is a perfectly satisfactory proof of '*p* / (*p* & *p*),' but the rule Repetition gives us a different way to prove the same result:

> 1   *p*
> ___
> 2   *p*   1, Rep
> 3   (*p* & *p*)   1, 2, Conj

The rule *Equivalence Introduction* (≡*I*) is illustrated:

> *m*   (*A* ⊃ *B*)
>
> *n*   (*B* ⊃ *A*)
>
> *r*   (*A* ≡ *B*)   *m*, *n*, ≡I

Strictly speaking, the rule should be called *Material Equivalence Introduction*. We shall not be so strict. This two-premiss rule is used in the following proof:

> 1   (*p* ⊃ *q*)
> 2   (*q* ⊃ *p*)
> 3   [(*p* ≡ *q*) ⊃ *r*]
> ___
> 4   (*p* ≡ *q*)   1, 2, ≡I
> 5   *r*   3, 4, MP

The rule *Equivalence Elimination* ($\equiv$E) has two forms:

  .

m $(A \equiv B)$

  .

n $(A \supset B)$ $m, \equiv$E

  .

m $(A \equiv B)$

  .

n $(B \supset A)$ $m, \equiv$E

This rule is used in the following proof:

1 $(p \equiv q)$

2 p

3 $(p \supset q)$ $1, \equiv$E

4 q 3, 2, MP

Replacement is a two-premiss rule associated with the triple bar. It has two forms:

  .

m $(A \equiv B)$

  .

n $\ldots A \ldots$ A can occur once or many times in the formula at step n.

  .

r $\ldots B \ldots$ m, n, Repl   The formula at step r is obtained from the formula at step n by replacing A by B at some or all of its occurrences.

  .

m $(A \equiv B)$

  .

n $\ldots B \ldots$ B can occur once or many times in the formula at step n.

  .

r $\ldots A \ldots$ m, n, Repl   The formula at step r is obtained from the formula at step n by replacing B by A at some or all of its occurrences.

The abbreviation for 'Replacement' is 'Repl.' In the illustrations, the expression '$\ldots A \ldots$' represents a formula in which A is a component. A might be the whole formula. But A might just be a small part of a big formula. The rule Replacement is used in the following proof:

1 $(p \equiv q)$

2 $\sim\sim p$

3 $\sim\sim q$ 1, 2, Repl

The replacement in step 2 is "authorized" by step 1 (and the rule Replacement). Another proof which uses Replacement is this one:

1 $\sim(p \& q) \equiv (\sim p \vee \sim q)$

2 $\sim p$

3 $\sim p \vee \sim q$ 2, Add

4 $\sim(p \& q)$ 1, 3, Repl

The whole formula at step 3 is replaced to get step 4.

If a formula A occurs more than once in $\ldots A \ldots$, then Replacement (together with the premiss $(A \equiv B)$) allows fewer than all occurrences to be replaced. It is also possible to replace them all.

*Exercise: Section 4

For 1 and 2, fill in the reasons for the steps in the proofs.

1. 1 $r \equiv (s \supset p)$

   2 $(s \supset p) \supset q$

   3 r

   4 $s \supset p$

   5 q

2. 1 $[p \supset (r \supset s)]$

   2 $(p \vee q)$

   3 $(q \supset p)$

   4 $(s \supset r)$

   5 $(p \supset p)$

   6 $[(p \vee q) \supset p]$

   7 p

   8 $(r \supset s)$

   9 $(s \equiv r)$

For 3 - 6, prove the inference sequences to be theorems.

3. $(p \& q), (\sim q \supset p), (p \supset \sim q) / (q \& \sim q)$

4. $[r \equiv (s \supset p)], [\sim(s \supset p) \supset q], \sim r / q$

5. $[p \& (q \equiv \sim r)], \sim q / (\sim\sim r \& p)$

6. $[p \supset (p \vee q)], (p \supset p), (q \supset p) / [p \equiv (p \vee q)]$

10-5 PROOFS WITHIN PROOFS

So far we have considered relatively simple proofs from hypotheses. We will now consider proofs which contain other proofs as ingredients.

A proof within another proof is a *conditional subproof*. The subproof must contain exactly one hypothesis. A conditional subproof is separated by a vertical line from the proof in which it is an ingredient. A proof from hypotheses which contains a conditional subproof might look like this:

$$
\begin{array}{ll}
1 & B_1 \\
\underline{2 \quad B_2} \\
\quad \cdot \\
r & B_r \\
r+1 & \big| A_1 \\
\quad \cdot \quad \big| \cdot \\
\quad \cdot \quad \big| \cdot \\
r+m & \big| A_m \\
r+m+1 & B_{r+1} \\
\quad \cdot \\
r+m+s & B_{r+s}
\end{array}
$$

In this proof, the whole proof from B_1 to B_{r+m+s} is the *main proof*. Steps 1 - r, and steps $(r+m+1)$ - $(r+m+s)$ are steps *in* (or *of*) *the main proof*. Steps $(r+1)$ - $(r+m)$ are not steps in the main proof; they are steps *in the conditional subproof*. Steps in the subproof are numbered consecutively with steps in the main proof. The hypothesis of the subproof is not counted among the hypotheses of the main proof. The main proof is a proof from its hypotheses to its conclusion. A subproof *cannot* be the last ingredient of a (complete) main proof, because the main proof must end with a step in the main proof.

As well as a subproof being an element of the main proof, one subproof can also be an element of another. We need a special terminology for discussing subproofs. A subproof which occurs in a main proof is an *element of* the main proof. If we have two subproofs, one within the other, the first subproof (counting from the left) is an *element of* the main proof; the second subproof is an *element of* the first, but the second is not an element of the main proof. In this proof (where the reasons are omitted):

$$
\begin{array}{ll}
1 & \underline{(p \supset q)} \\
2 & \big| (p \supset r) \supset s \\
3 & \big| \big| q \supset r \\
4 & \big| \big| \big| \underline{p} \\
5 & \big| \big| \big| q \\
6 & \big| \big| \big| r
\end{array}
$$

$$
\begin{array}{ll}
7 & \quad\ \ p \supset r \\
8 & \quad\ \ s \\
9 & \quad (q \supset r) \supset s \\
10 & [(p \supset r) \supset s] \supset [(q \supset r) \supset s]
\end{array}
$$

the subproof from 2–9 is an element of the main proof; the subproof from 3–8 is an element of the first subproof, but is not an element of the main proof. The subproof from 4–6 is an element of the subproof from 3–8, but not of the first subproof (from 2–9) or the main proof.

Any subproof is *subordinate to* itself. If a subproof is an element of a proof or subproof, then it is *subordinate to* that proof or subproof. And if one subproof is subordinate to a second subproof, and the second subproof is subordinate to a third proof or subproof, then the first subproof is *subordinate to* the third proof or subproof. In the proof above, the first subproof is subordinate to the main proof and to itself. The second subproof is subordinate to the first and to the main proof, as well as to itself. The innermost subproof is subordinate to the proof and to all the subproofs, including itself.

Each step in a proof must either be an hypothesis or follow from previous steps according to a rule. In developing a conditional subproof, we must know what previous steps can serve as premisses. A previous step can serve as a premiss to a step in a conditional subproof *so long as the previous step is in a proof or subproof to which the developing subproof is subordinate.* Earlier steps in a subproof can serve as premisses to later steps, since a subproof is subordinate to itself. And if a subproof is an element of a main proof, earlier steps in the main proof can be used. In the following (incomplete) proof, we see how steps in a subproof have premisses inside and outside of the subproof:

$$
\begin{array}{lll}
1 & (p \supset q) \\
2 & (q \supset r) \\
3 & \quad p \\
4 & \quad q & 1,3,\text{MP} \\
5 & \quad r & 2,4,\text{MP}
\end{array}
$$

If one subproof is an element of a second, the inner proof is subordinate to the first subproof; the inner subproof is also subordinate to the main proof. So in the inner subproof, it is legitimate to use premisses from three places: (1) the inner subproof, (2) the first subproof, (3) the main proof. We see this in the following (incomplete) proof:

$$
\begin{array}{lll}
1 & p \supset (q \supset r) \\
2 & \quad q \\
3 & \quad\quad p \\
4 & \quad\quad q \supset r & 1,3,\text{MP} \\
5 & \quad\quad r & 4,2,\text{MP}
\end{array}
$$

If there are two separate subproofs, neither of which is within the other, then neither is subordinate to the other. In that case, the second subproof cannot make use of premisses from the first.

When a subproof is finished, we cannot use its steps as premisses for getting steps in the main proof. The following is NOT allowed:

$$
\begin{array}{ll}
1 & p \\
2 & q \,\&\, (p \supset s) \\
3 & (p \supset s) \qquad 2,\ \text{Simp} \\
4 & s \qquad\qquad 3, 1, \text{MP}
\end{array}
$$

Similarly, if one subproof is within another, the innermost subproof can use premisses from the subproof which contains it. But the reverse is not allowed.

I have explained what a conditional subproof is, and how to construct one. But I have not explained what conditional subproofs are good for. To make use of conditional subproofs, we need additional rules. The premisses for these rules are not formulas, they are subproofs.

The first new rule concerns the horseshoe. The rule *Horseshoe Introduction* ($\supset I$) is illustrated:

$$
\begin{array}{ll}
m & A \\
\cdot & \\
n & B \\
\cdot & \\
r & (A \supset B) \qquad m - n,\ \supset I
\end{array}
$$

A subproof with hypothesis A and conclusion B serves· as a premiss for obtaining the conclusion $(A \supset B)$. *This conclusion must not occur within the subproof.* The conclusion $(A \supset B)$ must occur in the next proof or subproof to the left of the subproof from A to B.

This proof makes use of Horseshoe Introduction:

$$
\begin{array}{lll}
1 & p \supset (q \supset r) & \\
2 & q & \\
3 & p & \\
4 & (q \supset r) & 1, 3,\ \text{MP} \quad \text{This shows: } p \supset (q \supset r) \vdash q \supset (p \supset r) \\
5 & r & 4, 2,\ \text{MP} \\
6 & (p \supset r) & 3 - 5,\ \supset I \\
7 & q \supset (p \supset r) & 2 - 6,\ \supset I
\end{array}
$$

The next rules involve the negation sign. The two forms of *Negation Introduction* ($\sim I$) are illustrated:

$$
\begin{array}{ll}
m & \quad A \\
\cdot & \\
n & \quad (B\ \&\ \sim B) \\
\cdot &
\end{array}
\qquad
\begin{array}{ll}
m & \quad A \\
\cdot & \\
n & \quad (\sim B\ \&\ B) \\
\cdot &
\end{array}
$$

$$
r \quad \sim A \qquad m - n,\ \sim \mathrm{I} \qquad r \quad \sim A \qquad m - n,\ \sim \mathrm{I}
$$

If A is the hypothesis of a subproof, and the conclusion of the subproof is a formula having the form $(B\ \&\ \sim B)$ or $(\sim B\ \&\ B)$, then we can conclude that A is false—i.e., we can conclude $\sim A$. The "idea" of this rule is that any hypothesis that leads to an impossible result must be false. As with the rule Horseshoe Introduction, the concludion reached by Negation Introduction must occur in the next proof or subproof to the left of the subproof which is the premiss for this rule.

The rule Negation Introduction is used in the following proof:

$$
\begin{array}{lll}
1 & (p \supset \sim q) & \\
2 & q & \\
3 & \quad p & \\
4 & \quad \sim q & 1,\ 3,\ \mathrm{MP} \\
5 & \quad (q\ \&\ \sim q) & 2,\ 4,\ \mathrm{Conj} \\
6 & \sim p & 3 - 5,\ \sim \mathrm{I}
\end{array}
$$

The rule *Negation Elimination* ($\sim E$) also has two forms:

$$
\begin{array}{ll}
m & \quad \sim A \\
\cdot & \\
n & \quad (B\ \&\ \sim B) \\
\cdot &
\end{array}
\qquad
\begin{array}{ll}
m & \quad \sim A \\
\cdot & \\
n & \quad (\sim B\ \&\ B) \\
\cdot &
\end{array}
$$

$$
r \quad A \quad m - n,\ \sim \mathrm{E} \qquad r \quad A \quad m - n,\ \sim \mathrm{E}
$$

The rule Negation Elimination is very similar to Negation Introduction. In both rules, we have a subproof whose hypothesis leads to an impossible result. In Negation Introduction, we infer that the hypothesis is false. In Negation Elimination, the hypothesis is that a certain sentence (formula) is false; we infer that the sentence must not be false.

The rule Negation Elimination is used in this proof of ' $\sim \sim p\ /\ p$ ':

$$
\begin{array}{lll}
1 & \sim \sim p & \\
2 & \quad \sim p & \\
3 & \quad (\sim p\ \&\ \sim \sim p) & 2,\ 1,\ \mathrm{Conj} \\
4 & p & 2 - 3,\ \sim \mathrm{E}
\end{array}
$$

Whenever we are in a position to use Negation Elimination, we can also use Negation Introduction. In the example above, instead of the step 4 that we got, we could infer:

$$4 \sim \sim p \qquad 2 - 3, \sim I$$

*Exercise: Section 5

For 1 and 2, fill in the reasons for the steps.

1. 1 $\sim p$

2 | p

3 | | $\sim q$

4 | | $(p \ \& \sim p)$

5 | q

6 $(p \supset q)$

2. 1 $(p \supset q)$

2 | q

3 | q

4 $(q \supset q)$

5 $(p \lor q) \supset q$

For 3–6, construct proofs of the inference sequences.

3. $(p \supset \sim p) / \sim p$

4. $(p \supset q), \sim q / \sim p$

5. $[p \supset (q \supset r)], q / (\sim r \supset \sim p)$

6. $(p \supset q), (p \& r) \supset s / \supset [(q \& r) \supset s]$

10-6 PROPERTIES OF THE PC SYSTEM

A deductive system is *sound* if it can only be used to establish correct results. The PC system is sound if its only results are valid inference sequences.

If someone constructs a deductive system that isn't sound, then he has made a mistake. If we added the following rule to the PC system:

Horseshoe Elimination

.

$m \quad (A \supset B)$

.

$n \quad B$

.

$r \quad A \qquad m, n, \supset E$

the system wouldn't be sound.

We can see why this rule is undesirable if we consider the following proof:

$$
\begin{array}{lll}
1 & p & \\
2 & (q \ \& \sim q) & \\
3 & p & 1, \text{Rep} \\
4 & (q \ \& \sim q) \supset p & 2 - 3, \supset\text{I} \\
5 & (q \ \& \sim q) & 4, 1, \supset\text{E}
\end{array}
$$

This proof "establishes" that an arbitrary sentence p implies a logically false sentence $(q \ \& \sim q)$. (In some systems, the rule Modus Ponens is called Horseshoe Elimination; *that* rule Horseshoe Elimination is satisfactory.)

To prove that the PC system is sound, we would first show that proofs which contain only pure formulas all establish valid sequences. This means that it isn't possible to assign values to the variables occurring in the proof so that the hypotheses all come out true but the conclusion is false. We could easily extend this result to cover proofs which contain sentences, for a proof with a true sentence is like a proof containing a formula which has value t for a certain assignment, and a proof with a false sentence is like a proof with a formula that has value f.

To prove soundness for the subsystem of the PC system which contains pure wffs, we can first say that a step in a proof or subproof is *subject to* the hypotheses of the main proof and to the hypotheses of any subproof to which its subproof (if it is a step in a subproof) is subordinate. Next we show that if A is the last step of a complete or incomplete proof, and an assignment of values to the variables in the proof makes true all the hypotheses to which A is subject, then that assignment also makes A true. We would prove this result by *induction on the size of the proof:* we first show it to be true for all one-step proofs, and then we show that if it is true for all proofs up to a certain size, it is also true for proofs one step longer. In the course of carrying out this proof, we would consider each rule and show that it is truth-preserving. Finally, we would show that when this result about complete and incomplete proofs is applied to complete proofs, it guarantees that complete proofs establish valid inference sequences.

The details of a soundness proof are somewhat involved. The proof is more complicated than the proofs we carry out in the PC deductive system. (The soundness proof is a proof *about* the PC system, not a proof *in* the system. It is typical of proofs that are studied in logical theory.) The soundness proof will not be presented here. But that proof *can* be carried out, for the PC system is sound.

It is essential for a deductive system to be sound. It is also desirable for a deductive system to be *complete*. A system is complete if all correct "items" are theorems of the system. The PC system is designed to prove inference sequences of the PC language. It is complete if every valid inference sequence of the PC language is a theorem. The PC system is both sound and complete. But we will not carry out the completeness proof, because it is a difficult proof.

Since the PC system is sound, it is useful to our goal of getting a better understanding of deductively valid inferences. When we construct correct proofs, we are making deductively valid inferences; we get a better understanding of the inferences by getting better at making them.

*Exercise: Section 6

Determine which of the following are true.

1. A deductive system might be sound without being complete.

2. A deductive system might be complete without being sound.

3. A sound deductive system might contain proofs which establish incorrect results.

4. If a deductive system is both sound and complete and we add a new rule to the system, then the system with the new rule might establish more correct results than the original system.

10-7   PROOFS WITHOUT HYPOTHESES

The inference sequences we have proved so far have one or more premises and a single conclusion. It is also possible to establish a result which has a conclusion but no premisses. Such a result would be an inference sequence $/ B$.

The following proof:

```
1    │ p
     ├──
2    │ p        1, Rep

3  p ⊃ p        1 − 2, ⊃I
```

has no hypothesis. It starts with a subproof, but the hypothesis of a subproof doesn't count as an hypothesis of the main proof. Actually, the proof above is longer than necessary. The following is sufficient to establish the result:

```
1    │ p
     ├──
2  p ⊃ p        1 − 1, ⊃I
```

Both proofs establish that '$/ (p \supset p)$' is a theorem of the PC system. Using the symbol '⊢,' we can write either:

$$⊢ / (p \supset p) \qquad \text{or} \qquad ⊢ (p \supset p)$$

to indicate what has been proved.

When a sequence $A_1, \ldots, A_n / B$ is logically valid, then either (1) $A_1, \ldots, A_n, B$ are sentences, and it isn't possible for $A_1, \ldots, A_n$ to be true when B isn't—this can be determined on the basis of understanding the logical forms of the sentences; or (2) at least some of $A_1, \ldots, A_n, B$ are not sentences, but any result of replacing variables (uniformly) by sentences will be logically valid. If B is a sentence and $/ B$ is valid, then it isn't possible for the premises to be true and B not to be true. Since there aren't any premises, $/ B$ is logically valid if it isn't possible for B not to be true, and this can be determined on the basis of understanding B's logical form.

A sentence B is logically true just in case the inference sequence $/ B$ is logically valid. Logical truth can be regarded as a special case of logical validity—the special case where there are no premises. When we have a proof from hypotheses $A_1, \ldots, A_n$ to conclusion B, we will say that this proof establishes $A_1, \ldots, A_n / B$ as a *sequence-theorem*. When $n = 0$, we will still say that $/ B$ is a sequence-theorem. But we will also say that B (by itself, without the slant line) is a *sentence-theorem* or a *formula-theorem*.

Since every logically true sentence is the conclusion of a logically valid inference sequence with no premises, and the PC deductive system is complete with respect to valid inference sequences, the PC system is also complete with respect to logically true sentences of the PC language. Every logically true sentence of the PC language is a sentence-theorem of the PC system.

We have shown '$(p \supset p)$' to be a sentence-theorem of the PC system. The formula '$(p \supset p)$' is the *Law of Self-Implication*—abbreviated 'LSI.' (It would be more appropriate to have the law be "Any sentence which has the form displayed by '$(p \supset p)$' is true." We will continue to say that the formula itself is the law.) There are two other formulas displaying important forms that have names of their own. These are:

The Law of Contradiction (LC): $\sim (p \ \& \sim p)$

The Law of Excluded Middle (LEM): $(p \ v \sim p)$

The Law of Contradiction is sometimes called the *Law of Noncontradiction*. The Law of Excluded Middle is understood as saying that there is no "middle" between truth and falsity; either p is true or p is false. Proofs of these two laws are below:

1	$(p \ \& \sim p)$	
2	$\sim(p \ \& \sim p)$	$1 - 1, \sim$ I

1	$\sim(p \ v \sim p)$	
2	p	
3	$(p \ v \sim p)$	2, Add
4	$(p \ v \sim p) \ \& \sim(p \ v \sim p)$	3, 1, Conj
5	$\sim p$	$2 - 4, \sim$ I
6	$(p \ v \sim p)$	5, Add
7	$(p \ v \sim p) \ \& \sim(p \ v \sim p)$	6, 1, Conj
8	$(p \ v \sim p)$	$1 - 7, \sim$ E

*Exercise: Section 7

Construct proofs of the following formulas and sequences.

1. $(p \equiv p)$

2. $(p \supset q) / (\sim p \ v \ q)$

3. $[(p \ \& \sim p) \supset q]$

4. $(p \supset q), (\sim p \supset q) / q$

5. $[(p \supset \sim p) \supset \sim p]$

10-8 METATHEOREMS AND DERIVED RULES

The PC deductive system is sound and complete. No additional rules are needed. However, it would often be convenient to have additional rules that make possible shorter proofs.

We don't want to clutter up the PC system with redundant rules. But we can adopt some new rules simply as shortcuts. A rule is a shortcut if every result of using the rule could be gotten (in several steps) without using the rule. We regard any proof using a shortcut rule as an abbreviation for a longer proof that doesn't use it.

To make certain that our new rules don't give new results, we will provide proofs to this effect. A proved result in the PC system is a theorem of the PC system. A proved result about the PC system is a *metatheorem*. Metatheorems are stated in English. And the proof of a metatheorem is carried out in English. Such a proof must consist in a chain of simple inferences which are justified by the inferential meanings of the expressions used.

A new rule which is regarded as a shortcut, whose use is justified by a metatheorem, is a *derived rule*. It is derived from the original rules. In sections 9, 10, and 11, metatheorems will be proved which justify several derived rules. These sections are optional sections. In section 12, the derived rules justified by these metatheorems are stated and illustrated. Section 12 is not optional. Even those who omit the optional sections will make use of the derived rules. It is preferable to read and work through the optional sections. For someone who doesn't do this, the derived rules won't have the character of shortcuts. To adopt them without understanding their justification is like adding new official rules to the PC system.

10-9 OUR FIRST METATHEOREMS (OPT)

Once we have proved a formula theorem, it would sometimes be convenient to use that theorem in further proofs. Consider number 4 in the exercises at the end of section 7:

$(p \supset q), (\sim p \supset q) / q$

When we start the proof, it is easy to get this far:

1 $(p \supset q)$

2 $(\sim p \supset q)$

3 $(p \vee \sim p) \supset q$ 1, 2, Dil

In order to continue, we might try to obtain a step '$(p \vee \sim p)$.' For once we get this, we can use Modus Ponens to obtain 'q.' But the formula '$(p \vee \sim p)$' is the Law of Excluded Middle, The following proof:

1 $(p \supset q)$

2 $(\sim p \supset q)$

3 $(p \vee \sim p) \supset q$ 1, 2, Dil

4 | $\sim(p \vee \sim p)$

5 | | p

6 | | $(p \vee \sim p)$ 5, Add

7 | | $(p \vee \sim p) \mathbin{\&} \sim(p \vee \sim p)$ 6, 4, Conj

8 | $\sim p$ 5 – 7, $\sim$ I

9 | $(p \vee \sim p)$ 8, Add

10 | $(p \lor \sim p)$ & $\sim(p \lor \sim p)$ 9, 4, Conj

11   $(p \lor \sim p)$ 4 − 10, $\sim$ E

12   q 3, 11, MP

incorporates the proof of the Law of Excluded Middle in the proof of the inference sequence '$(p \supset q)$, $(\sim p \supset q)$ / q.' It seems wasteful to "re-prove" the Law of Excluded Middle once it has already been proved.

What we would like to have is the following rule:

Theorem Repetition (T-Rep) If $\vdash A$, then A can simply be added as a step in the proof from hypotheses.

We will prove a metatheorem that justifies us in using Theorem Repetition as a shortcut rule. Since we will later prove other metatheorems, we will number them. And we will abbreviate 'Metatheorem' as 'MT.' The statement of MT1 is:

MT1 Let A be a formula theorem (i.e., $\vdash A$). In a proof from hypotheses, A can be obtained both as a step in the main proof and as a step in any subproof that is subordinate to the main proof.

In proving a metatheorem, we will simply write sentences that follow easily from the statement of the problem or are inferred from earlier sentences. The proof must always be such that it is obvious that a given conclusion follows from what has gone before. MT1 is a simple result, and its proof is very easy:

Proof of MT1   Since A is a theorem, it has a proof from no hypotheses. We can simply incorporate any such proof in the proof being developed in such a way that A is a step in the proof or subproof where it is wanted.

Our second metatheorem has a name of its own; it is the *Deduction Theorem*.

MT2 THE DEDUCTION THEOREM If $A_1, \ldots, A_n \vdash B$, then $A_1, \ldots, A_{n-1} \vdash (A_n \supset B)$.

Proof Suppose $A_1, \ldots, A_n \vdash B$. And let

1   A_1

$\cdot$

$\cdot$

$\cdot$

$\underline{n \quad A_n}$

$\cdot$

$\cdot$

$r \quad B$

be a proof of this result. We can easily adapt this proof to yield a proof of the desired result:

1   A_1

$$
\begin{array}{ll}
n-1 & \underline{A_{n-1}} \\
n & \left| A_n \right. \\
\cdot & \\
\cdot & \\
r & \left| B \right. \\
r+1 & (A_n \supset B) \qquad n-r, \supset \text{I}
\end{array}
$$

original proof

When there is an important result that follows from a theorem by a simple inference or is a special case of a general result stated by the theorem, then the important result is called a *corollary*. The Deduction Theorem has a corollary that we will note.

COROLLARY If $A \vdash B$, then $\vdash (A \supset B)$.

*Exercise: Section 9

1. Prove the following : $(p \supset q), (q \supset r) / (p \supset r)$

2. Using the Deduction Theorem, list all the other theorems that can be based on the theorem proved in exercise 1.

10-10 MORE METATHEOREMS (OPT)

The derived rules we have justified above enable us to use earlier theorems in proving later theorems. It is also helpful to add rules authorizing various patterns of inference.

MT3 (i) Suppose we are developing a proof from hypotheses, and, either in the main proof or a subproof, there are two steps $(A \supset B)$, $\sim B$ available as premisses. Then we can obtain $\sim A$ as a step in the proof or subproof for which the two steps are available as premisses. (ii) Suppose $(A \supset \sim B)$, B are available as premisses. Then we can obtain $\sim A$. (iii) Suppose $(\sim A \supset B)$, $\sim B$ are available as premisses. Then we can obtain A. (iv) Suppose $(\sim A \supset \sim B)$, B are available as premisses. Then we can obtain A.

Proof (i) Suppose the proof from hypotheses has been developed as far as step r. Whether we are in the main proof or a subproof, we can continue as follows:

$$
\begin{array}{lll}
r+1 & \left| A \right. & \\
r+2 & \left| B \right. & (A \supset B), r+1, \text{MP} \\
r+3 & \left| (B \,\&\, \sim B) \right. & r+2, \sim B, \text{Conj} \\
r+4 & \sim A & (r+1) - (r+3), \sim \text{I}
\end{array}
$$

The proofs of (ii)–(iv) are similar.

MT3 justifies the four forms of the derived rule *Modus Tollens (MT)*.

MT4   Suppose that in a proof from hypotheses there are two steps $(A \supset B)$ and $(B \supset C)$ available as premisses. Then we can obtain $(A \supset C)$ as a step.

Proof Suppose the proof from hypotheses has been developed as far as step r. We can continue:

$$
\begin{array}{lll}
r + 1 & \big|\, A & \\
r + 2 & \big|\, B & (A \supset B),\ r + 1,\ \mathrm{MP} \\
r + 3 & \big|\, C & (B \supset C),\ r + 2,\ \mathrm{MP} \\
r + 4 & (A \supset C) & (r + 1) - (r + 3),\ \supset\mathrm{I}
\end{array}
$$

MT4 justifies the derived rule *Hypothetical Syllogism (HS)*.

MT5 (i) Suppose that in a proof from hypotheses, there are two steps $(A \vee B)$, $\sim A$ available as premises. Then in the proof or subproof for which the steps are available as premises, we can obtain B as a step. (ii) If $(A \vee B)$, $\sim B$ are available as premises, then we can obtain A as a step. (iii) If $(\sim A \vee B)$, A are available as premises, then we can obtain B as a step. (iv) If $(A \vee \sim B)$, B are available as premises, then we can obtain A as a step.

Proof (i) Suppose the proof from hypotheses has been developed as far as step r. We can continue:

$$
\begin{array}{lll}
r + 1 & \big|\, B & \\
r + 2 & (B \supset B) & (r + 1) - (r + 1),\ \supset\mathrm{I} \\
r + 3 & \big|\, A & \\
r + 4 & \big|\big|\, \sim B & \\
r + 5 & \big|\big|\, (A\ \&\ \sim A) & r + 3,\ \sim A,\ \mathrm{Conj} \\
r + 6 & \big|\, B & (r + 4) - (r + 5),\ \sim\mathrm{E} \\
r + 7 & (A \supset B) & (r + 3) - (r + 6),\ \supset\mathrm{I} \\
r + 8 & (A \vee B) \supset B & (r + 7),\ (r + 2),\ \mathrm{Dil} \\
r + 9 & B & (r + 8),\ (A \vee B),\ \mathrm{MP}
\end{array}
$$

The proofs of (ii)–(iv) are similar.

MT5 justifies the four forms of the derived rule *Disjunctive Syllogism (DS)*.

MT6   Suppose that in a proof from hypotheses a formula $(A \vee B)$ and two conditional subproofs

$$
\begin{array}{ll}
\big|\, A & \big|\, B \\
\ \ \cdot & \ \ \cdot \\
\ \ \cdot & \ \ \cdot \\
\ \ \cdot & \ \ \cdot \\
\big|\, C & \big|\, C
\end{array}
$$

are available as premises. Then in the proof or subproof for which these are available as premises, we can obtain C as a step.

Prove this metatheorem as an *Exercise.

MT6 justifies the derived rule *Disjunction Elimination* (∨E).

10-11   STILL MORE METATHEOREMS (OPT)

MT7 Let A, B, C be wffs. Then the following are theorems of the PC system:

Law of Self-Implication (LSI)

1. $(A \supset A)$

Law of Excluded Middle (LEM)

2. $(A \vee \sim A)$

Law of Contradiction (LC)

3. $\sim(A \,\&\, \sim A)$

De Morgan's Laws (DE M)

4. $\sim(A \,\&\, B) \equiv (\sim A \vee \sim B)$

5. $\sim(A \vee B) \equiv (\sim A \,\&\, \sim B)$

Double Negation (DN)

6. $A \equiv \sim \sim A$

Commutative Laws (COMM)

7.   For Conjunction: $(A \,\&\, B) \equiv (B \,\&\, A)$

8.   For Disjunction: $(A \vee B) \equiv (B \vee A)$

Associative Laws (ASSOC)

9.   For Conjunction: $[(A \,\&\, B) \,\&\, C] \equiv [A \,\&\, (B \,\&\, C)]$

10.   For Disjunction: $[(A \vee B) \vee C] \equiv [A \vee (B \vee C)]$

Definitional Equivalences

Disjunction (DEF v)

11. $(A \vee B) \equiv \sim(\sim A \,\&\, \sim B)$

12. $(A \vee B) \equiv (\sim A \supset B)$

Conjunction (DEF &)

13. $(A \,\&\, B) \equiv \sim (\sim A \vee \sim B)$

14. $(A \,\&\, B) \equiv \sim(A \supset \sim B)$

Material Implication (DEF ⊃)

15. $(A \supset B) \equiv (\sim A \vee B)$

16. $(A \supset B) \equiv \sim(A \,\&\, \sim B)$

Material Equivalence (DEF ≡)

17. $(A \equiv B) \equiv [(A \supset B) \,\&\, (B \supset A)]$

18. $(A \equiv B) \equiv [(A \& B) \lor (\sim A \& \sim B)]$

19. $(A \equiv B) \equiv \sim [(A \& \sim B) \lor (\sim A \& B)]$

Variables like 'p' and 'q' belong to the PC language, as do formulas constructed from these variables. The letters 'A,' 'B,' and 'C' are not variables of the PC language. In the statement of Metatheorem 7, these letters are used as variables in English to represent formulas of the PC language. In this use, the letters serve as variables of the *metalanguage* English.

Each formula constructed with the variables 'A,' 'B,' and 'C' is a *schema* representing an infinite number of formulas in the PC language. A proof of MT7 will give us an infinite number of results in the PC system.

To prove that $(A \supset A)$ is a theorem, we can use this proof:

1 | A
2   $(A \supset A)$ $1 = 1, \supset I$

This is not a proof in the PC system, because 'A' is not a formula of the PC language. Instead this is a schematic proof. It is like a recipe for constructing a real proof. Looking at the schematic proof, we can see that the recipe will work for any formula A. The schematic proof is sufficient to prove part 1 of MT7.

Exercise: Section 11

Prove parts 2–19 of MT7.

MT8 Suppose that either $\vdash (A \equiv B)$ or $\vdash (B \equiv A)$. Let . . . A . . . be a formula in which A occurs one or more times. Let . . . B . . . be obtained from . . . A . . . by replacing one or more occurrences of A by B. Then if . . . A . . . is available as a premiss in a proof from hypotheses, we can obtain . . . B . . . as a step in the proof or subproof in which . . . A . . . is available.

Proof Consider the proof or subproof in which . . . A . . . is available as a premiss. By MT1, we can obtain $(A \equiv B)$ or $(B \equiv A)$ as a step in this proof or subproof. By Replacement we can obtain . . . B . . . as a step.

MT8 justifies the derived rule *Theorem Replacement (T-Repl)*.

If we "put together" Metatheorems 7 and 8, we can justify a derived rule for each of the results 4–19 of MT7. For example, for any formula A, the formula $(A \equiv \sim \sim A)$ is an instance of the Law of Double Negation. By MT7, this is a theorem. By MT8, if a proof contains a step . . . A . . . , we can replace this by . . . $\sim \sim A$ . . . Similarly, we can replace a step . . . $\sim \sim A$ . . . by . . . A . . . We will use the names of the '$\equiv$'-laws as names of the derived rules associated with the laws.

10-12   RULES TO SHORTEN PROOFS

Our metatheorems justify two kinds of derived rules. One kind authorizes us to simply accept a formula or sequence as a theorem, without providing a new proof for it. MT2 justifies such a rule:

Deduction Theorem (DT) If $A_1, \ldots, A_n \vdash B$, then we can simply accept $A_1, \ldots, A_{n-1} / (A_n \supset B)$ as a theorem. To illustrate the use of the Deduction Theorem, consider

Exercise 4 at the end of section 7:$(p \supset q)$, $(\sim p \supset q) / q$. This has already been proved. Now suppose we want to prove the following: $(p \supset q) / [(\sim p \supset q) \supset q]$. We can get this result immediately, by Exercise 4, DT.

MT7 justifies our accepting an infinite number of theorems. If A, B, C are any wffs, the following are theorems of the PC system:

Law of Self-Implication (LSI)

$(A \supset A)$

Law of Excluded Middle (LEM)

$(A \vee \sim A)$

Law of Contradiction (LC)

$\sim(A \mathbin{\&} \sim A)$

Commutative Laws (COMM)

$(A \mathbin{\&} B) \equiv (B \mathbin{\&} A)$

$(A \vee B) \equiv (B \vee A)$

Associative Laws (ASSOC)

$[(A \mathbin{\&} B) \mathbin{\&} C] \equiv [A \mathbin{\&} (B \mathbin{\&} C)]$

$[(A \vee B) \vee C] \equiv [A \vee (B \vee C)]$

De Morgan's Laws (DE M)

$\sim(A \mathbin{\&} B) \equiv (\sim A \vee \sim B)$.

$\sim(A \vee B) \equiv (\sim A \mathbin{\&} \sim B)$

Double Negation (DN)

$A \equiv \sim \sim A$

Definitional Equivalences

Disjunction (DEF v)

$(A \vee B) \equiv \sim (\sim A \mathbin{\&} \sim B)$

$(A \vee B) \equiv (\sim A \supset B)$

Conjunction (DEF &)

$(A \mathbin{\&} B) \equiv \sim (\sim A \vee \sim B)$

$(A \mathbin{\&} B) \equiv \sim (A \supset \sim B)$

Material Implication (DEF ⊃)

$(A \supset B) \equiv (\sim A \vee B)$

$(A \supset B) \equiv \sim (A \mathbin{\&} \sim B)$

Material Equivalence (DEF ≡)

$(A \equiv B) \equiv [(A \supset B) \& (B \supset A)]$

$(A \equiv B) \equiv [(A \& B) \vee (\sim A \& \sim B)]$

$(A \equiv B) \equiv \sim [(A \& \sim B) \vee (\sim A \& B)]$

Previously we identified '$(p \supset p)$' as the Law of Self-Implication. Now we say that any formula $(A \supset A)$ is an instance of the law. So the following are instances of LSI:

$(r \supset r)$

$\{[p \vee (r \& \sim s)] \supset [p \vee (r \& \sim s)]\}$

*Exercise: Section 12

Identify the laws of which the following are instances.

1. $(p \supset p) \vee \sim(p \supset p)$

2. $\sim[(q \& \sim r) \vee s] \equiv [\sim(q \& \sim r) \& \sim s]$

3. $[(q \& \sim r) \vee s] \equiv \sim [\sim(q \& \sim r) \& \sim s]$

4. $\{[(p \& q) \vee r] \vee s\} \equiv [(p \& q) \vee (r \vee s)]$

5. $(\sim p \supset \sim q) \equiv (\sim \sim p \vee \sim q)$

The remaining derived rules are for adding a step in proof from hypotheses. One of these is the following:

Theorem Repetition (T-Rep) If ⊢ A, then A can simply be added as a step in a proof from hypotheses.

We will use an earlier example to illustrate how Theorem Repetition is used:

1 $(p \supset q)$

2 $(\sim p \supset q)$

3 $(p \vee \sim p) \supset q$ 1, 2, Dil

4 $(p \vee \sim p)$ LEM

5 q 3, 4, MP

Step 4 is not inferred from previous steps. If Theorem Repetition is used to introduce a theorem which has a name, we simply give the name of the theorem. If the rule is used to introduce a theorem without a name of its own, we can refer to its proof, or to the place where it is proved.

MT3 justifies four forms of the derived rule *Modus Tollens (MT)*:

(i)   ·   (iii)   ·

    m $(A \supset B)$ m $(A \supset \sim B)$

    ·   ·

    n $\sim B$ n B

    ·   ·

    r $\sim A$ m, n, MT r $\sim A$ m, n, MT

(ii)   ·

    m $(\sim A \supset B)$

    ·

    n $\sim B$

    ·

    r   *A*   *m, n,* MT

(iv)   ·

    m $(\sim A \supset \sim B)$

    ·

    n   *B*

    ·

    r   *A*   *m, n,* MT

MT4 justifies *Hypothetical Syllogism (HS)*:

    ·

    m $(A \supset B)$

    ·

    n $(B \supset C)$

    ·

    r $(A \supset C)$ *m, n,* HS

MT5 justifies four forms of the derived rule *Disjunctive Syllogism (DS)*:

(i)   ·

    m $(A \vee B)$

    ·

    n $\sim A$

    ·

    r   *B*   *m, n,* DS

(iii)   ·

    m $(A \vee B)$

    ·

    n $\sim B$

    ·

    r   *A*   *m, n,* DS

(ii)   ·

    m $(\sim A \vee B)$

    ·

    n   *A*

    ·

    r   *B*   *m, n,* DS

(iv)   ·

    m $(A \vee \sim B)$

    ·

    n   *B*

    ·

    r   *A*   *m, n,* DS

The rule Disjunctive Syllogism can really help to shorten a proof. It is used in the following proof:

1	$(\sim p \vee q)$	
2	p	
3	q	1, 2, DS
4	$(p \supset q)$	2 − 3, ⊃I

MT6 justifies the derived rule *Disjunction Elimination* (vE):

m $(A \vee B)$

.

n | A

.

.

r | C

.

s | B

.

.

t | C

.

u C $m, n - r, s - t,$ vE

MT8 justifies the rule *Theorem Replacement* (*T-Repl*):

If ⊢ $(A \equiv B)$ or ⊢ $(B \equiv A)$, then this proof is justified:

m . . . A . . . A occurs one or more times in this formula.

.

n . . . B . . . m, ⊢ $(A \equiv B)$ or ⊢ $(B \equiv A)$, T-Repl
                            The formula at step n is obtained from . . . A . . . by
                            replacing one or more occurrences of A by B.

Our last derived rules are associated with the logical laws whose principal connective is '≡.' For each of these laws, there is a derived rule with the same name. These rules authorize us to replace occurrences of the left or right side of a law by occurrences of the other side. For example, the rule *Double Negation (DN)* is the following:

A formula A can be replaced at some or all of its occurrences in . . . A . . . by ~ ~ A (to yield . . . ~ ~ A . . .). Similarly, ~ ~ A can be replaced at some or all of its occurrences in . . . ~ ~ A . . . by A (to yield . . . A . . .).

The following proof makes use of derived rules based on logical laws.

1   $(\sim p \supset q)$

2   $(\sim\sim p \vee q)$ 1, Def ⊃

3   $(p \vee q)$ 2, DN

Step 2 is obtained from step 1 by the rule based on the first definitional equivalence for material implication.

*Exercise: Section 12 (cont.)

Prove the following.

6. $\{[(p \supset q) \supset p] \supset p\}$ 8. $[(p \equiv q) \equiv q] \, / \, p$

7. $[(p \supset q) \supset q] \, / \, [(q \supset p) \supset p]$ 9. $(p \,\&\, q) \, / \sim [q \supset \sim(q \supset p)]$

10-13   PROVING INCOMPATIBILITY

For convenience, a list of the original and the derived rules is found at the end of this chapter.

The PC deductive system was set up to prove that formula sequences are logically valid. So long as there is at least one premiss, any result about logical validity is also a result about implication—and conversely. And when there is no premiss, a result about logical validity is at the same time a result about logical truth.

We are also interested in logical incompatibility. To prove that m sentences are logically incompatible, we can take all but one of these sentences, and show that they imply the negation of the remaining sentence. (If the remaining sentence is already a negation, we can show that the $(m - 1)$ sentences imply the remaining sentence minus its negation sign.) To show that any three sentences jointly symbolized by these formulas:

$(p \supset q), (q \supset r), (p \,\&\, \sim r)$

are logically incompatible, we can prove this inference sequence: $(p \supset q), (q \supset r) \, / \sim(p \,\&\, \sim r)$. The following proof establishes incompatibility:

1	$(p \supset q)$	
2	$(q \supset r)$	
3	$\quad (p \,\&\, \sim r)$	
4	$\quad p$	3, Simp
5	$\quad q$	1, 4, MP
6	$\quad r$	2, 5, MP
7	$\quad \sim r$	3, Simp
8	$\quad (r \,\&\, \sim r)$	6, 7, Conj
9	$\sim(p \,\&\, \sim r)$	$3 - 8, \sim$ I

We could as well establish incompatibility by proving this inference sequence: $(p \supset q)$, $(p \,\&\, \sim r) \, / \sim (q \supset r)$.

Another way to prove that m sentences are incompatible is to prove that the conjunction of these m sentences is logically false.

*Exercise: Section 13

Prove that the following symbolize incompatible sentences.

1. $q, [p \supset (q \supset r)], [q \supset (p \,\&\, \sim r)]$

2. $(p \lor q), (p \supset q), (q \supset \sim p), (\sim p \supset \sim q)$

3. $[(p \supset q) \supset p]$, $(q \supset \sim p)$, $(\sim q \supset \sim p)$

4. $\sim [p \,\&\, (q \equiv \sim r)]$, p, $(p \supset q)$, $\sim r$

10-14 REFUTATION

The PC deductive system is sound. An inference sequence which isn't valid can't be proved. But the PC system doesn't possess the resources to prove that such a sequence isn't valid. To show that an inference sequence isn't valid, we *invalidate* the inference sequence. We invalidate this inference sequence:

$$(p \supset q), [p \supset (q \supset r)] \,/\, r$$

by showing how to make the premises true and the conclusion false:

$(p \supset q), [p \supset (q \supset r)] \,/\, r$

     t   t   f

f   t   f   t   f   f

Invalidating an inference sequence is similar to using the quick method to show that a formula isn't a tautology.

If an argument sequence to be invalidated contains some English sentences, these must be replaced by variables. The replacement must be uniform. To invalidate this sequence:

(Paul will be late $\supset$ Ellie will be angry), (Ellie will be angry $\supset$ Ellie will burn the dinner), $\sim$ Paul will be late. / $\sim$ Ellie will burn the dinner.

we can assign values to this formula sequence:

$(p \supset q), (q \supset r), \sim p \,/\, \sim r$

     t   t   t   f

f   f   f   t   f   t

If we try to invalidate a logically valid inference sequence, we will end up with an impossible assignment:

$[(p \,v\, q) \supset (r \,\&\, s)]$, $p \,/\, r$

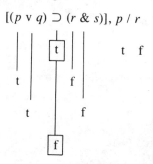

This is the same result we got when we used the quick method to show that a formula is a tautology. If we have been directed to prove the sequence in case it is valid, the above result is not sufficient. But it *does* show the sequence to be valid.

When dealing with a single formula or an inference sequence with no premisses, the invalidating is exactly like using the quick method. (We invalidate a sequence and *falsify* a formula.)

If we invalidate a sequence or formula made up of pure formulas, we have shown it is not valid. There is no difference between validity and logical validity for sequences that consist of pure formulas. If we invalidate a sequence containing sentences, we have shown that the sequence is not logically valid. This leaves open the possibility that the sequence might be valid anyway. Some valid inference sequences are not logically valid. The following sequence:

(John is unmarried ⊃ John is a bachelor), (John is unmarried ⊃ John is well-to-do), John is a bachelor. / John is well-to-do.

can be invalidated:

$(p \supset q), (p \supset r), q / r$

$$
\begin{array}{c c c c c}
 & t & & t & t \quad f \\
f & f & f & f
\end{array}
$$

This only shows that the sequence is not *logically* valid; if it is valid, its validity is not a matter of its logical form. The inference sequence *is* valid. It owes its validity (in part) to the meanings of 'bachelor' and 'unmarried.' These are not logical expressions. Since John is a bachelor, he must be unmarried. But if he is unmarried, then he is well-to-do. So he must be well-to-do.

*Exercise: Section 14

Prove the theorems below. Falsify or invalidate the nontheorems.

1. $[(p \supset q) \supset q] / p$
2. $(p \ \& \ q) / (p \equiv q)$
3. $[\sim(p \equiv q) \supset (p \supset \sim q)]$
4. $[\sim p \supset \sim(p \lor q)]$
5. $[(p \ \& \ q) \supset r], q / (\sim p \supset r)$
6. $[(p \supset q) \supset r] / (\sim p \supset r)$

We have used proofs in the PC system to establish that we have positive cases of each of the following:

Implication-Logical Validity

Logical Truth

Logical Incompatibility

An argument that isn't logically valid, sentences that aren't related by implication, etc., constitute a *negative case* of the feature. We assign values to show that we have a negative case of a semantic feature. If we actually replaced variables by true and false sentences "matching" the values, the resulting sentence or sequence would be an obvious *counter-example* with respect to the semantic feature. It *counters* the claim that all instances of the formulas are positive cases of the semantic feature.

We know how to prove that we have a positive case of any of the logical semantic features. We can produce counter-examples which show that we have negative cases of logical truth, implication, and logical validity. To show that a group of formulas does not represent logically incompatible sentences, we construct an assignment which makes all the formulas come out true. Sentences jointly symbolized by these formulas:

$$[p \supset (q \lor r)], (q \supset s), (r \supset \sim s), (p \& \sim s)$$

are not logically incompatible (with respect to the forms considered in the PC language), as the following assignment makes clear:

$$[p \supset (q \lor r)], (q \supset s), (r \supset \sim s), (p \& \sim s)$$

*Exercise: Section 14 (cont.)

Determine whether the following groups of formulas symbolize logically incompatible sentences. For those which do, construct proofs in the PC deductive system. For those which don't, show this by making a suitable assignment of values.

7. $[p \equiv (q \equiv r)], (q \equiv r), [p \equiv (r \& \sim r)]$

8. $[p \supset (q \supset r)], p, (\sim r \supset \sim q)$

9. $[p \& (q \lor \sim r)], \sim (p \& q), (r \supset q)$

10. $\{p \supset [q \supset (r \equiv s)]\}, (q \supset r), [s \supset (q \equiv \sim q)], (q \supset \sim p)$

10-15   WHAT TO DO NEXT

Before you proceed to Chapter 11, you should go back and read (or reread) Chapter 6. This presents material you need in order to understand Chapter 11.

Exercise A: Section 15

Prove that the following are theorems of the PC deductive system.

1. $(p \supset q), (q \supset \sim p) / \sim p$

2. $[p \lor (q \& r)] / (p \lor q)$

3. $\{[p \lor (q \& r)] \supset [(p \lor q) \& (p \lor r)]\}$

4. $p, q, \sim r / \sim [p \supset (q \supset r)]$

5. $(p \& q), (\sim p \& r) / (s \equiv \sim s)$

6. $\sim p / [\sim q \supset (p \equiv q)]$

7. $\{[(p \equiv q) \equiv p] \supset q\}$

8. $\sim [p \& (q \& r)] / [q \supset (\sim r \lor \sim p)]$

Exercise B: Section 15

For those of the following which are theorems, give proofs in the PC deductive system. Invalidate or falsify the others.

1. $(\sim p \supset q) / [(p \supset q) \supset q]$

2. $\{(\sim p \lor q) \supset [(p \supset q) \supset q] \supset q]\}$

3. $p, q / \sim [q \supset \sim (q \supset p)]$

4. $[(p \& q) \supset r] / [(p \supset r) \& (q \supset r)]$

5. $[(p \supset p) \supset p] / (\sim p \supset q)$

6. $[(p \supset r) \lor (q \supset r)] / [(p \lor q) \supset r]$

7. $[(p \supset q) \lor (p \supset r)], \sim q / (p \supset r)$

8. $[p \lor (p \supset q)]$

9. $[p \lor (\sim p \& r)]$

10. $\sim (p \& q), q / (p \supset r)$

Exercise C: Section 15

Construct proofs for those of the following which are logically valid. For those which aren't logically valid, invalidate a formula sequence which symbolizes the inference sequence.

1. [(Dorothy speaks Chinese v Dorothy speaks Japanese) ⊃ Dorothy is at home in East Asia], (Dorothy speaks Chinese ⊃ Dorothy speaks Japanese), (∼ Dorothy speaks Japanese ⊃ Dorothy speaks Chinese) / Dorothy is at home in East Asia.

2. [Plato taught Aristotle ⊃ (Aristotle was a Platonist v Aristotle developed his own theories)], ∼ Aristotle was a Platonist. / (∼ Aristotle developed his own theories ⊃ ∼Plato taught Aristotle)

3. [Don will take Fran to dinner Saturday ≡ (Don will get paid Friday & Don will finish grading his students' tests by Saturday afternoon)], ∼ Don will take Fran to dinner Saturday. / (∼ Don will get paid Friday & ∼ Don will finish grading his students' tests by Saturday afternoon)

4. [Descartes was a rationalist ⊃ (Hobbes was an empiricist ⊃ Locke was an empiricist)], (Montaigne was a skeptic ⊃ Descartes was a rationalist) / (Montaigne was a skeptic ⊃ Locke was an empiricist)

5. Bill has a cocker spaniel , [(Bill has a dog & Bill has a cat) ⊃ Bill likes animals], (Bill has a cocker spaniel ⊃ Bill has a cat) / Bill likes animals.

6. [Patrick has a child ≡ (Patrick has a son v Patrick has a daughter)], (∼ Patrick has a child ⊃ Patrick has plenty of money), (∼ Patrick has a son v ∼ Patrick has a daughter) / Patrick has plenty of money.

7. [(We will have pork chops for dinner v We will have Chicken Kiev for dinner) v We will have crab for dinner], ∼ We will have Chicken Kiev for dinner., (∼ We will have pork chops for dinner v We will have crab for dinner) / We will have crab for dinner.

8. [(Descartes invented analytic geometry & ~ Leibniz invented analytic geometry) v (~ Descartes invented analytic geometry & Leibniz invented analytic geometry)] / (Descartes invented analytic geometry ≡ ~ Leibniz invented analytic geometry)

Exercise D: Section 15

For those groups of sentences below which are logically incompatible, construct proofs in the PC deductive system to show this. For those which are not logically incompatible, find formulas which symbolize the sentences and assign suitable values to the variables in the formulas to show that the sentences are logically compatible.

1. [(Marilyn will get an A in calculus & Keith will get an A in physics) v (~ Marilyn will get an A in calculus & Bruce will get a B in calculus)], (Bruce will get a B in calculus ⊃ Keith will get an A in physics), (~ Bruce will get a B in calculus ⊃ ~ Keith will get an A in physics)

2. John owns a dairy farm., (John owns a farm ⊃ John votes Republican), (~ John owns a dairy farm v ~ John votes Republican)

3. [Next winter will be severe ⊃ (Frank will move to Arizona v Frank will move to Florida)], (Frank will move to Arizona ⊃ ~ Next winter will be severe), ~(~ Next winter will be severe v Frank will move to Florida)

4. [Teresa is a good logic student ⊃ (Chris is a good logic student ⊃ Dawn is a good logic student)], (Chris is a good logic student & ~ Dawn is a good logic student), (Dawn is a good logic student ⊃ Teresa is a good logic student)

5. [Cream sherry is an after-dinner drink ≡(Amontillado is an aperitif ≡ Aperitifs are appropriate before dinner)], (Cream sherry is an after-dinner drink ≡ Aperitifs are appropriate before dinner), (Amontillado is an aperitif ⊃ ~ Cream sherry is an after-dinner drink)

6. (Necessity is the mother of invention v A stitch in time saves nine), (A fool and his money are soon parted v A stitch in time saves nine), [~(Necessity is the mother of invention & A fool and his money are soon parted) v ~ A stitch in time saves nine]

7. (Roses are red v Violets are blue), (Daffodils are yellow v Lilies are white), (Daffodils are yellow ⊃ ~ Violets are blue), [Lilies are white ⊃ (~ Roses are red & ~ Violets are blue)], (Roses are red ⊃ ~ Daffodils are yellow)

8. [(Philosophers make too much money v Political leaders make too little money) ⊃ The world is a strange place], (~ Philosophers make too much money & ~ The world is a strange place), (Political leaders make too little money ⊃ Philosophers make too much money)

10-16 THE ORIGINAL AND DERIVED RULES OF THE PC DEDUCTIVE SYSTEM

The Original Rules

    Simplification (Simp)   **Conjunction (Conj)**

    m (*A* & *B*)   *m* (*A* & *B*)   *m* *A*

$\cdot$ $\cdot$ $\cdot$

n A m, Simp n B m, Simp n B

                                           $\cdot$

                                        r $(A \,\&\, B)$ m, n, Conj

Addition (Add)   **Dilemma (Dil)**

$\cdot$ $\cdot$ $\cdot$

m A m A m $(A \supset C)$

$\cdot$ $\cdot$ $\cdot$

n $(A \lor B)$ m, Add n $(B \lor A)$ m, Add n $(B \supset C)$

                                           $\cdot$

                                           r $[(A \lor B) \supset C]$ m, n, Dil

Modus Ponens (MP)   **⊃ Introduction (⊃I)**

$\cdot$ $\cdot$

m $(A \supset B)$ m |A

$\cdot$ $\cdot$

n A $\cdot$

$\cdot$ n |B

r B m, n, MP $\cdot$

                                    r $(A \supset B)$ $m - n$, ⊃I

Repetition (Rep)

$\cdot$

m A

$\cdot$

n A m, Rep

≡ Introduction (≡I)   **≡ Elimination (≡E)**

$\cdot$ $\cdot$ $\cdot$

m $(A \supset B)$ m $(A \equiv B)$ m $(A \equiv B)$

$\cdot$ $\cdot$ $\cdot$

n $(B \supset A)$ n $(A \supset B)$ m, ≡E n $(B \supset A)$ m, ≡E

$\cdot$ $\cdot$

r $(A \equiv B)$ m, n, ≡I

Replacement (Repl)

.

m $(A \equiv B)$

.

n $\dots A \dots$ A occurs one or more times in this formula.

.

r $\dots B \dots$ m, n, Repl   This formula is obtained from $\dots A \dots$ by replacing one or more occurrences of A by B.

.

m $(A \equiv B)$

.

n $\dots B \dots$ B occurs one or more times in this formula.

.

r $\dots A \dots$ m, n, Repl   This formula is obtained from $\dots B \dots$ by replacing one or more occurrences of B by A.

$\sim$ Introduction ($\sim$ I) $\sim$ Elimination ($\sim$ E)

.   .

m | A m | $\sim A$

.   .   The conclusions of

.   .   the subproofs can

                                                      also be: $(\sim B \,\& \,B)$

n | $(B \,\& \sim B)$ n | $(B \,\& \sim B)$

.   .

r $\sim A$ $m - n, \sim$ I r A $m - n, \sim$ E

Derived Rules

For adding a step in a proof from hypotheses

Theorem Repetition

If $\vdash A$, then A can be added as a step in a proof from hypotheses.

Modus Tollens (MT)

.   .   .   .

m $(A \supset B)$ m $(A \supset \sim B)$ m $(\sim A \supset B)$ m $(\sim A \supset \sim B)$

.   .   .   .

n	$\sim B$		n	B		n	$\sim B$		n	B
.			.			.			.	
r	$\sim A$	m, n, MT	r	$\sim A$	m, n, MT	r	A	m, n, MT	r	A	m, n, MT

Hypothetical Syllogism (HS)

.

$m \quad (A \supset B)$

.

$n \quad (B \supset C)$

.

$r \quad (A \supset C) \qquad m, n, \text{HS}$

Disjunctive Syllogism (DS)

.			.			.			.	
m	$(A \lor B)$		m	$(A \lor B)$		m	$(\sim A \lor B)$		m	$(A \lor \sim B)$
.			.			.			.	
n	$\sim A$		n	$\sim B$		n	A		n	B
.			.			.			.	
r	B	m, n, DS	r	A	m, n, DS	r	B	m, n, DS	r	A	m, n, DS

∨ Elimination (∨E)

.

$m \quad (A \lor B)$

.

$n \quad \big|\ A$

.

.

$r \quad \big|\ C$

.

$s \quad \big|\ B$

.

.

$t \quad \big|\ C$

.

$u \quad C \qquad m, n-r, s-t, \lor\text{E}$

Theorem Replacement (T-Repl)

If $\vdash (A \equiv B)$ or $\vdash (B \equiv A)$,

.

$m \quad \ldots A \ldots$

.

$n \quad \ldots B \ldots \qquad m, \vdash (A \equiv B)$ or

$\qquad\qquad\qquad\qquad \vdash (B \equiv A), \text{T-Repl}$

For each of the '$\equiv$'-logical laws listed below, there is a rule allowing replacement of an instance of one side of the law by the corresponding instance of the other side.

Rules for Obtaining a Theorem Directly

Deduction Theorem (DT)

If $A_1, \ldots, A_n \vdash B$, then we can simply accept $A_1, \ldots, A_{n-1} / (A_n \supset B)$ as a theorem.

If A, B, C are wffs, then we can simply accept the following as theorems.

Law of Self-Implication (LSI)

$(A \supset A)$

Law of Contradiction (LC)

$\sim(A \& \sim A)$

Commutative Laws (Comm)

$(A \& B) \equiv (B \& A)$

$(A \vee B) \equiv (B \vee A)$

Associative Laws (Assoc)

$[(A \& B) \& C] \equiv [A \& (B \& C)]$

$[(A \vee B) \vee C] \equiv (A \vee (B \vee C))$

De Morgan's Laws (De M)

$\sim(A \& B) \equiv (\sim A \vee \sim B)$

$\sim(A \vee B) \equiv (\sim A \& \sim B)$

Double Negation (DN)

$A \equiv \sim \sim A$

Law of Excluded Middle (LEM)

$(A \vee \sim A)$

Definitional Equivalences

Conjunction (Def &)

$(A \& B) \equiv \sim(\sim A \vee \sim B)$

$(A \& B) \equiv \sim(A \supset \sim B)$

Disjunction (Def v)

$(A \vee B) \equiv \sim(\sim A \& \sim B)$

$(A \vee B) \equiv (\sim A \supset B)$

Material Implication (Def $\supset$)

$(A \supset B) \equiv (\sim A \vee B)$

$(A \supset B) \equiv \sim(A \& \sim B)$

Material Equivalence (Def $\equiv$)

$(A \equiv B) \equiv [(A \supset B) \& (B \supset A)]$

$(A \equiv B) \equiv [(A \& B) \vee (\sim A \& \sim B)]$

$(A \equiv B) \equiv \sim[(A \& \sim B) \vee (\sim A \& B)]$

Chapter 11

Applying the PC Language to English

11-0 SUMMARY

In this chapter we use the PC language as an instrument for dealing with ordinary English. We find translations in the PC language for many kinds of ordinary sentences. An optional section explores the connection between horseshoe sentences and ordinary conditional sentences. We test ordinary sentences and arguments, through their translations, for analytic truth, entailment, incompatibility, and validity. Some techniques are considered for incorporating semantic features in the logical forms of translations. These include giving exclusive translations for certain occurrences of 'or,' and supplying analytic '⊃'-sentences. Translations are also supplemented by well-known true sentences.

11-1 TRANSLATIONS WITHIN A SINGLE LANGUAGE

To evaluate an ordinary English sentence, group of sentences, or inference, we first translate the ordinary sentences into sentences of the PC language, then we evaluate the translations. In doing this, we try for equivalent translations. If we can't obtain them, we will often settle for weaker or stronger translations.

But ordinary true-or-false English sentences already belong to the PC language. Why translate a sentence of the PC language into the PC language? The techniques we have developed don't enable us to uncover semantic features of sentences that don't have symbolic connectives. This sentence:

It will rain tomorrow or it won't.

belongs to the PC language. Although it is analytic, we can't show this by means of a truth-table or a proof in the PC deductive system. If we translate the sentence like this:

(It will rain tomorrow v ~ It will rain tomorrow)

we can use a truth-table to show that the translation is logically true:

p	$(p \text{ v} \sim p)$
t	t
f	t

11-2 TRANSLATING WITH THE NEGATION SIGN

The symbol '~' is used to say that a propositional act isn't true. Sentences like these:

It is false that A

It is not true that A

It is not the case that A

are normally translated: $\sim A$. The translation will be equivalent to the original sentence. We would translate:

It is false that Chicago is the capital of Illinois.

by: ~Chicago is the capital of Illinois.

Some sentences containing 'not' can also be translated with '~.' The sentence:

Chicago is not the capital of Illinois.

is equivalent to:

~Chicago is the capital of Illinois.

We can replace an internal 'not' by a prefixed '~' only when the sentence is about a single individual, like Chicago, George Washington, or the number three. We DO NOT want to translate this sentence:

(1) Some student is not passing Economics 101.

with this one:

(2) ~ Some student is passing Economics 101.

Sentence (2) means that not even one student is passing, while (1) only means that at least one student is not passing. Sentence (1) can't be given a translation using connectives; it is its own best translation. Here are other sentences that can't be translated using '~':

Most dogs are not friendly.

Some good logic students are not girls.

Seven incumbent governors were not reelected.

With a sentence:

Single individual is not this or that

we can just delete the 'not' and prefix '~':

~Single individual is this or that

But with a sentence like this one:

Jesse does not drink milk.

the phrase 'does not' acts as a unit. The best translation is:

~Jesse drinks milk.

We could have simply removed the 'not' and prefixed '~':

> ~Jesse does drink milk.

This is an awkward translation. In English, an internal 'not' needs to be preceded by a verb, but the 'does' in 'does not' makes no important semantic contribution. We delete the whole phrase in translating with '~.'

Suppose we want to translate 'It is false that A,' where A is complex. If A is translated by an equivalent sentence $A*$, then $\sim A*$ is equivalent to 'It is false that A.' But suppose $A*$ is weaker than A: A entails $A*$, but $A*$ doesn't entail A. If $\sim A*$ is true, then A can't be true—because if it were, $A*$ would also be true. So $\sim A*$ entails 'It is false that A.' But 'It is false that A' doesn't entail $\sim A*$. When $A*$ is weaker than A, this makes $\sim A*$ *stronger* than 'It is false that A.' Similarly, if $A*$ is stronger than A, then $\sim A*$ is weaker than 'It is false that A.'

It would be possible to use '~' to translate some sentences containing words with negating prefixes—prefixes like 'un,' 'in,' and 'ir.' But our policy will be to leave these negating prefixes untouched. We won't translate:

> Don is unlucky.

by:

> ~Don is lucky.

This translation is weaker than the original (why?), but we will treat the original sentence as its own translation.

*Exercise: Section 2

Translate the following sentences into the PC language, using the connective '~' when this is possible.

1. David is not married to Rosemary.

2. Some state capitals are not large cities.

3. It isn't true that John isn't passing logic.

4. It is false that some state capitals are small cities.

5. Clare is an unhappy girl.

6. Jorge won't visit Cuba next year.

11.3 TRANSLATING WITH '&'

The reading for '&' is 'and.' Normally, we will use '&' to replace 'and' between two sentential clauses. This sentence:

> Bill went to Harvard as an undergraduate and he attended Yale Law School.

would be translated:

> Bill went to Harvard as an undergraduate & He attended Yale Law School.

This translation is equivalent to the original sentence. But sometimes an 'and'-sentence is used to indicate temporal order, as:

Pat swung the bat and he missed the ball.

Our translation:

(Pat swung the bat & He missed the ball)

leaves out part of the meaning of the original sentence. The translation is weaker than the original. Although 'and'-sentences are sometimes used to indicate temporal order, sentences formed with '&' are never used to indicate temporal order.

Other words than 'and' get translated with '&.' We would translate this sentence:

Michele is smart but her grades are poor.

like this:

(Michele is smart & Her grades are poor)

The word 'but' is used to signal a contrast. We might think of the first clause in the original sentence as generating certain expectations; the word 'but' indicates that these expectations are not met. The '&' gives no such indication. We might take this to show that a sentence with '&' provides a weaker translation for a sentence with 'but.' However, I think that the function of 'but' is primarily stylistic. Even when 'but' is used inappropriately, a sentence 'A but B' is true just in case both A and B are true. We will regard the translation with '&' as equivalent to the sentence with 'but.'

There are some sentences formed with 'but' which indicate temporal order:

Pat swung the bat but he missed the ball.

In this case, the translation:

Pat swung the bat & He missed the ball.

is weaker than the original sentence.

English contains other words which function like 'but.' These include 'yet,' 'however,' and 'although.' The sentences:

Kathy is a popular teacher, although she is very sarcastic.

Richard is wealthy, however he is very unhappy.

Atlanta is a large city, yet it is a pleasant one.

would be translated:

Kathy is a popular teacher & She is very sarcastic.

Richard is wealthy & He is very unhappy.

Atlanta is a large city & It is a pleasant one.

When one of these expressions is translated with '&,' the translation will be equivalent unless the original sentence indicates temporal order. Even a semicolon can be translated with '&.' The sentence:

Springfield is the capital of Illinois; Madison is the capital of Wisconsin.

becomes:

>(Springfield is the capital of Illinois & Madison is the capital of Wisconsin)

This is equivalent to the original. But if a semicolon-sentence indicates temporal order from the first clause to the second, the ampersand provides a weaker translation.

We can sometimes use '&' to translate sentences in which 'and' occurs between nouns, adjectives, or verbs. These sentences:

>Larry and Don are Electrical Engineers.

>Cows and bats are mammals.

>Dan plays tennis and golf.

are translated:

>Larry is an Electrical Engineer & Don is an Electrical Engineer.

>Cows are mammals & Bats are mammals.

>Dan plays tennis & Dan plays golf.

Although 'and' can join expressions which aren't sentences, the symbol '&' can only join sentences. And we can't always translate a sentence containing 'and' with '&.' This sentence:

>Sally and Mark are the same age.

doesn't mean the same as this one:

>Sally is the same age & Mark is the same age.

This "translation" makes no sense. Instead of attributing a certain property to both Sally and Mark, the first sentence indicates that there is a relation between them—*being the same age as*.

>The sentence:

>Frank and Kathy are married.

is ambiguous. In one meaning, the following provides an equivalent translation:

>(Frank is married & Kathy is married)

In the other meaning, the sentence indicates that they are married to each other, and can't be translated with '&.' The sentence:

>Lucy sang and danced.

is also ambiguous. Its meaning might be captured in this translation:

>Lucy sang & Lucy danced.

If the original sentence means that Lucy sang while she danced, this translation is weaker than the original.

>Since this translation:

>Pat swung the bat & Pat hit the ball.

is weaker than:

> Pat swung the bat and hit the ball.

the sentence:

> ~(Pat swung the bat & Pat hit the ball)

is stronger than

> 'It isn't true that Pat swung the bat and hit the ball.'

Instead of just 'and,' an English sentence sometimes contains the two-part expression 'both. . .and. . .' as these sentences do:

> Both Mary and Beth sell real estate.

> Jesse got both Matt and Josh into trouble.

The word 'both' doesn't change or add to the meaning of 'and.' These are equivalent translations:

> Mary sells real estate & Beth sells real estate.

> Jesse got Matt into trouble & Jesse got Josh into trouble.

Sometimes 'both' serves the function for which we use a left parenthesis. We see this especially when negation is present. In this sentence:

> It isn't true that both John and Jesse are skiers.

'both' follows the negating expression, and shows that this expression applies to the whole of what follows. We can translate it:

> ~(John is a skier & Jesse is a skier)

When 'not both' occurs in a sentence, then in the translation, the negation sign should have a greater scope than the ampersand. The sentence:

> (1) Elana and Jane are not both Catholics.

is translated:

> (2) ~ (Elana is a Catholic & Jane is a Catholic)

We must not confuse (1) with either of:

> Neither Elana nor Jane is a Catholic.

> Elana and Jane are both not Catholics.

These last two sentences are equivalent to:

> (~ Elana is a Catholic & ~ Jane is a Catholic)

This PC-sentence is definitely not equivalent to (2).

*Exercise: Section 3

Translate the following sentences with connectives when this is possible. Place an asterisk by those translations which are weaker than the sentences they translate. Place a double asterisk by stronger translations.

1. Cats and dogs fight.

2. Andrea pushed Megan; Megan fell down.

3. Jack both jogs and jumps rope.

4. Tom and Bob are not both doctors.

5. Bob is a doctor, but Tom isn't.

6. Helen and Ruth are sisters.

7. Even though Peter got a special invitation, he won't attend the reception.

8. Tom is not only a great athlete, but he's also a very gracious person.

11-4 TRANSLATIONS WITH 'v'

The reading for the wedge is 'or.' We use the wedge to translate sentences in which two clauses are connected with 'or.' This sentence:

Mary knows the answer or Steve knows the answer.

would be translated:

Mary knows the answer v Steve knows the answer.

A sentence '*A* or *B*' has a range of meanings. Such a sentence can mean that at least one, and possibly both, of *A, B* are true. It can mean that exactly one of *A, B* is true. Whether the sentence is to be understood inclusively or exclusively is determined by the words in the sentence and the circumstances in which it is used. In this sentence:

The test will be on Tuesday or it will be on Thursday.

the expression 'the test' indicates that a single test is involved. It must be given on a single day. The test will be on Tuesday or Thursday, but not on both days. A sentence '*A* v *B*' is always understood inclusively. If '*A* or *B*' means that one of the two is true, but not both, then '*A* v *B*' provides a weaker translation. To provide an equivalent translation for an exclusive disjunction, we use:

$(A \text{ v } B) \& \sim (A \& B)$.

We use the wedge to translate 'or' between clauses. We can also use the wedge to translate sentences in which 'or' connects other expressions. These sentences:

John had a headache on Tuesday or Wednesday.

Bill or Margaret knows the answer to your question.

can be given equivalent translations with the wedge:

(John had a headache on Tuesday v John had a headache on Wednesday)

(Bill knows the answer to your question v Margaret knows the answer to your question)

We often use the circumstances of its use to determine whether an ordinary disjunctive sentence is to be understood inclusively or exclusively. The sentences we translate in exercises are not actually being used. We cannot let the circumstances of their use guide our translations. We will understand these sentences to have the weakest sense that they might naturally have. We regard an inclusive translation as equivalent unless a sentence demands to be understood exclusively. The sentence:

Bill is married to Mary or Lynn.

calls for an exclusive translation:

(Bill is married to Mary v Bill is married to Lynn) &

~(Bill is married to Mary & Bill is married to Lynn)

because, in our culture, a man can have only one wife. But the sentence:

Bill has met Mary or Lynn.

receives this equivalent translation:

(Bill has met Mary v Bill has met Lynn)

Nothing about the original sentence rules out the possibility of Bill having met both.

If it is understood that Sacramento is different from San Francisco, someone might argue that the sentence:

(1) (Sacramento is the capital of California v San Francisco is the capital of California)

provides an equivalent translation for:

(2) Either Sacramento or San Francisco is the capital of California.

Even in (1), the expression 'the capital of California' indicates that there is only one capital, so that both disjuncts can't be true. But if (1) is equivalent to (2), the fact that only one disjunct of (1) can be true is not indicated by the logical form of (1). One of the goals of our translations is to have as much of the semantic content of the original sentences as possible show up in the logical forms of our translations. Even if (1) provides an equivalent translation for (2), the following is a better translation:

[(Sacramento is the capital of California v San Francisco is the capital of California) & ~ (Sacramento is the capital of California & San Francisco is the capital of California)]

It seems to make no difference whether a sentence contains simply 'or' or the two-part expression 'either . . .or . . .' Both sentences:

Sally or Stacey will get an A in logic.

Either Sally or Stacey will get an A in logic.

receive this equivalent translation:

(Sally will get an A in logic v Stacey will get an A in logic)

Both 'either' and 'both' sometimes function like a left parenthesis in the PC language. But 'either' does not combine with negative expressions in the same way that 'both' does. We can easily say 'not both' but it is awkward to say 'not either.'

*Exercise: Section 4

Translate the following sentences with connectives when this is possible. Mark weaker translations with an asterisk. Mark stronger translations with a double asterisk.

1. That car is not worth $6000.

2. Mr. Smith and Mr. Pollock are college teachers.

3. Mary and Bill are partners.

4. Bob will clean up his room or he will be punished.

5. It isn't true that Al slipped on a rug and broke his ankle.

6. Neither Bill nor Tom likes spinach.

7. Molly hasn't visited France and Italy.

8. It isn't true that girls do poorly in logic.

9. Bill will visit Yugoslavia or Spain.

10. Either Kevin or Sam is the tallest boy in the freshman class.

11. A few members have not paid their dues.

11-5 TRANSLATIONS WITH THE HORSESHOE

In the PC language, a horseshoe sentence is a *conditional* sentence. It is a *material* conditional sentence. In English, and 'if . . . , then . . .' -sentence is a conditional sentence. These sentences:

> If Sunday is a nice day, then we will go for a drive.

> If the Germans had invaded England in 1940, then they would have won World War II.

are conditional sentences. In English, the consequent of a conditional need not begin with 'then.' The following is a conditional sentence:

> If Sunday is a nice day, we will go for a drive.

An English conditional sentence can even begin with the consequent:

> The Germans would have won World War II, if they had invaded England in 1940.

No matter whether it comes first or second, the 'if'-clause in a conditional sentence is the antecedent. The other clause is the consequent.

In the PC language, the antecedent must always occur to the left of the horseshoe. The consequent always follows the horseshoe.

English also contains very different kinds of conditionals. One kind is *subjunctive*. And one kind of subjunctive conditional is *counterfactual*. The earlier example:

> If the Germans had invaded England in 1940, then they would have won World War II.

is a counterfactual conditional. In such a sentence, the antecedent describes a situation which did not occur. The antecedent runs *counter to the facts*. When the antecedent runs counter to the facts, the consequent may also do so, as above. But the consequent need not run counter to the facts:

> If there had been no depression in the thirties, then there would still have been World War II.

Other subjunctive conditionals than counterfactual ones have no special name. These conditionals are concerned with what might happen, as in:

> If Dale were to call Charlene, then she would hang up.

This does not indicate that Dale will not or has not called. A subjunctive conditional sentence talks about what *would* happen if something else did, not simply about what will happen (or has happened).

We will try to translate some English conditional sentences with the horseshoe. BUT WE WILL NOT TRANSLATE SUBJUNCTIVE CONDITIONALS THIS WAY. To understand the reason, consider these sentences:

> (1) If there had been no depression in the thirties, then there would have been no World War II.

> (2) If there had been no depression in the thirties, then there would (still) have been World War II.

I am not sure which sentence is true, but I feel confident that one is true and the other is false. Suppose we try to use the horseshoe to translate them. The symbol '$\supset$' joins independently significant sentences. In (1) and (2), the antecedents and consequents are inappropriate to stand alone. To translate them with the horseshoe, we need to get rid of their subjunctive expressions. For the antecedent, we will write 'there was no depression in the thirties.' And for the consequent, we will use 'there was (no) World War II.' If we translate (1) and (2) like this:

> (1') (There was no depression in the thirties $\supset$ There was no World War II)

> (2') (There was no depression in the thirties $\supset$ There was World War II)

both translations are true. While I don't know which, one of (1), (2) *is* true and the other false. The "translations" (1') and (2') obliterate the important difference between the two subjunctive (and counterfactual) conditionals. The horseshoe sentences are too much weaker than the subjunctive conditionals to be useful. Since the horseshoe cannot provide an adequate translation for a subjunctive conditional sentence, we usually avoid such sentences when we employ the PC language. If we much consider a subjunctive conditional, we will regard it as its own best translation.

A plain conditional sentence is an *indicative* conditional. An indicative conditional says that if one thing was, is, or will be the case, then another thing (or even the same thing) was, is, or will be the case. These sentences are indicative conditionals:

> If Al was in Seattle Tuesday, then he didn't commit the crime.

> If it is snowing in Miami Beach today, then the natives are astonished.

> If the skiing is good in January, then it won't be good in March.

Let us consider whether we can use '⊃' to translate them.

Suppose that on Thursday, John tells Jane, "If Sunday is a nice day, then I will take you for a drive." We want to compare this sentence to the following:

(Sunday is a nice day ⊃ I will take you for a drive)

With the PC sentence, we have this truth-table:

Nice	Drive	(Nice ⊃ Drive)
t	t	t
t	f	f
f	t	t
f	f	t

Once we know whether or not Sunday is (will be) nice, and whether or not John will take Jane for a drive, we can determine whether the PC sentence is true or false. Let us consider the value of the English conditional sentence. Suppose it is true that Sunday is (will be) nice, and true that John takes Jane for a drive. Then what John told Jane on Thursday is true. If it is true that Sunday is nice, but false that John takes Jane for a drive, then the English conditional sentence is false. There may be good reasons for not going (the car broke down, John got sick, etc.), but Thursday's statement is false. So far, the English (indicative) conditional agrees with the horseshoe sentence:

Nice	Drive	(Nice ⊃ Drive)	If Nice, then Drive
t	t	t	t
t	f	f	f

Now suppose that Sunday isn't nice. And suppose John takes Jane for a drive anyway. I don't think this tells us anything about the truth of Thursday's statement. If Sunday isn't nice, we must know what would have happened if Sunday were nice. It might be that John had secretly made other plans. He had no intention of going for a drive if the weather were nice. If that were so, then I believe that Thursday's statement was false. On the other hand, if John fully intended to go for a drive, and he was able to, then Thursday's statement was true. With the English conditional, if the antecedent is true, the value of the consequent determines the value of the conditional. But if the antecedent is false, the value of the consequent is irrelevant. We can't explain English conditional sentences by using a truth-table. We can only make some such table as this:

p	q	If p, then q
t	t	t
t	f	f
f	t	?
f	f	?

The question mark indicates that the value could be either t or f.

Connectives in the PC language are *truth-functional*. A certain combination of values for the components yields a unique value for the compound sentence. The English conditional expression isn't truth-functional.

Now consider whether we can use the horseshoe to give weaker or stronger translations of indicative conditional sentences. Suppose we have an indicative conditional 'If A, then B' and a tentative translation '$(A \supset B)$.' And suppose the indicative conditional is true. The only way for the horseshoe sentence to be false is for A to be true and B to be false. In that case, the indicative conditional would also be false. But we already said that it is true. If the indicative conditional is true, the horseshoe sentence is sure to be true. The indicative conditional entails the horseshoe sentence. Since they aren't equivalent, the horseshoe sentence provides a weaker translation.

An indicative conditional sentence:

If A, then B

If A, B

is translated: $(A \supset B)$. And this sentence:

Don paid Social Security, if he worked last year.

gets the following translation:

(Don worked last year $\supset$ He paid Social Security)

If we translate a sentence:

It is false that if A, then B

like this:

$\sim(A \supset B)$,

our translation is stronger than the original. The negation of a weaker translation is stronger than the negation of the original.

Now consider the expression 'only if.' This time, let John tell Jane (on Thursday), "I will take you for a drive Sunday only if Sunday is a nice day." There is an important difference between 'only if' and just plain 'if.' The sentence '. . .drive. .if. .nice. . .' tells Jane what to expect if Sunday is a nice day. But the sentence '. . .drive. .only if. . nice. . .' doesn't guarantee Jane a ride if Sunday is nice. It only tells her what must have happened in case they do go for a drive.

Suppose it is true that John takes Jane for a drive, and false that Sunday is a nice day. In that case, the sentence is clearly false. So far, we have this truth-table:

p	q	p only if q
t	f	f

The remaining cases are more difficult. Suppose Sunday is nice and John takes Jane for a drive. These facts give us no evidence that John's statement was false. But it might have been false. Suppose John really intended to go for a drive no matter what the weather was like. In that case I think that his statement was false, even though the weather cooperated to keep this from being evident. The first two rows of the truth-table look like this:

p	q	p only if q
t	t	?
t	f	f

We can similarly see that, if they don't go for a drive, then regardless of the weather, the value of John's statement is undetermined. For if Sunday is nice and they don't go for a drive, we can't say that John's statement was false. John's statement might have been false because he intended to go if the weather weren't nice. The statement might have been true because John had two requirements for a drive: (i) nice weather, (ii) money for gas. Not having money for gas stopped the trip, but nice weather was one of the requirements for a drive.

Now suppose they don't go for a drive and the weather isn't nice. John's original statement might have been true. But if John actually intended to ignore the weather and go for a drive once he got money for gas, then his original statement was false. We end up with this truth-table for 'only if':

p	q	p only if q
t	t	?
t	f	f
f	t	?
f	f	?

This shows that $(A \supset B)$ provides a weaker translation for 'A only if B.'

The horseshoe is used to translate both these sentences:

(3) I will take you for a drive Sunday if Sunday is a nice day.

(4) I will take you for a drive Sunday only if Sunday is a nice day.

but the translations are very different:

(3') (Sunday is a nice day $\supset$ I will take you for a drive Sunday)

(4') (I will take you for a drive Sunday $\supset$ Sunday is a nice day)

If the components of a conditional sentence are complex, then the principles governing the PC translation are complicated. Suppose the components of 'If A, then B' are translated by A^*, B^*. If both components receive equivalent translations, then the conditional is translated by the weaker $(A^* \supset B^*)$. But suppose A^* is weaker than A. In this case, A^* might be true and B^* be false, without A being true. The ordinary conditional might be true when $(A^* \supset B^*)$ is false. In this case, $(A^* \supset B^*)$ doesn't provide a weaker translation; we can't be sure that it is stronger either. Similarly, if B^* is stronger than B, this keeps $(A^* \supset B^*)$ from being a weaker translation without guaranteeing that it is stronger. So to translate 'If A, then B' by $(A^* \supset B^*)$, we require:

(i) that A^* be equivalent to or stronger than A,

(ii) that B^* be equivalent to or weaker than B.

If we can't find a suitable A^* or B^*, we simply use the original sentence. These same principles govern the translation of 'only if' sentences. This means that to translate sentences:

If (If A, then B), then C

If (A only if B), then C

we would use:

(If A, then B) $\supset C$

(A only if B) $\supset C$

*Exercise: Section 5

Translate the following with connectives when this is possible. Mark weaker translations with an asterisk. Mark stronger translations with a double asterisk.

1. Don won't come to dinner if Mary doesn't apologize.

2. If Alabama had beaten Nebraska, Alabama would have been ranked number one.

3. If UCLA is on probation, then UCLA isn't eligible for a post-season tournament.

4. Kevin will attend Notre Dame only if he receives a full athletic scholarship.

5. Neither Joe Namath nor Jack Kemp was a fullback.

6. It isn't true that if Jesse passes his logic course, he will be eligible for spring sports.

7. If either Larry or Joan calls, Jim will pretend he isn't home.

8. Mary won't be at the party, if she will come only if Delia gives her a ride.

11-6 SOME ADDITIONAL TRANSLATIONS

The reading for '≡' is 'if, and only if.' An English sentence which contains the expression 'if, and only if' amounts to the same as two sentences, one containing 'if' and the other containing 'only if.' So the sentence:

> Ken will attend the party if, and only if, he gets an apology from Ed.

is equivalent to:

> Ken will attend the party if he gets an apology from Ed and

> Ken will attend the party only if he gets an apology from Ed.

Since we translate both (indicative) 'if'-sentences and 'only if'-sentences with the horseshoe, we could use the horseshoe to translate 'if, and only if'-sentences. But a sentence '$(A \equiv B)$' is equivalent to '$[(A \supset B) \ \& \ (B \supset A)]$.' The first sentence above would be translated:

> (Ken will attend the party ≡ He gets an apology from Ed)

The triple bar provides a weaker translation for 'if, and only if'-sentences.

We can also (sometimes) use the triple bar to translate a sentence that contains the expression 'just in case.' The sentence:

> Joe will go to Florida in April just in case he gets his income tax refund by that time.

can be translated:

> (Joe will go to Florida in April ≡ He gets his income tax refund by that time)

This translation is weaker than the original sentence. A 'just in case'-sentence needs to be distinguished from an 'in case'-sentence. The sentence:

> The doors will shut automatically in case there is a fire.

is not translated with '≡.' Instead we would translate this with '⊃':

(There is a fire $\supset$ The doors will shut automatically)

This is a weaker translation.

To ensure that we get suitable translations using '$\equiv$,' if we translate either '*A* if, and only if *B*' or '*A* just in case *B*' by ($A* \equiv B*$), we require that both $A*$, $B*$ be equivalent to the sentences they translate.

Now consider the expression 'unless.' Suppose Leonard says, "I will go to Florida in March unless my car breaks down." Suppose that Leonard doesn't go to Florida in March and his car doesn't break down. In this case, his statement is definitely false. This give us:

p	q	p unless q
f	f	f

Now suppose that Leonard does go to Florida even though his car breaks down. The original sentence doesn't rule this out; it only explains his not going to Florida—in case he doesn't go. But the original sentence would be false if there was something else that would have kept Leonard from going. The truth of both component expressions does not uniquely determine the value of the 'unless'-sentence:

p	q	p unless q
t	t	?
f	f	f

If Leonard goes to Florida and his car doesn't break down, then his statement might be true. But if there was something besides the car's breaking down that would have kept him from going, his statement is (was) false. Again, if he doesn't go and the car does break down, his statement might be true. But if the car's breaking down is not the only thing that would keep him from Florida, his statement is false. This gives us:

p	q	p unless q
t	t	?
t	f	?
f	t	?
f	f	f

Different translations for an 'unless'-sentence are possible, but the simplest uses the wedge. The wedge provides a weaker translation, for the wedge sentence might be true when the 'unless'-sentence is false.

*Exercise: Section 6

Translate the following sentences with connectives when this is possible. Mark weaker translations with an asterisk. Mark stronger translations with a double asterisk.

1. If Bill doesn't call by 7, then Mary won't come along.

2. Mary won't come along unless Bill calls by 7.

3. Sally will pass the course only if she passed the final.

4. Shirley won't go to the movie if she doesn't get over her headache.

5. John will go out to dinner tonight if, and only if, he gets a check in the mail today.

6. If Tom didn't win the race, he won't want to go out tonight.

7. If some students are not passing, then either some students will fail the course or some students will resign.

8. It isn't true that if Tom wins the race, he will be happy.

9. Tom won't lose the race unless he feels sick.

10. Sam will marry Barbara only if Sam gets a job and Barbara's father doesn't disapprove.

11. If Leonard will drive to Florida unless his car breaks down, then we will vacate the condominium by Sunday.

12. John will fail the course only if he doesn't study if, and only if, John is smart enough to pass the course.

11-7 THE SCOPE OF A CONNECTIVE

The *scope* of a connective is the expression or expressions to which the connective applies. In:

~Tom lives in Cincinnati.

the scope of the negation sign is the sentence 'Tom lives in Cincinnati.' In this formula: $[\sim (p \ \& \ q) \supset r]$, the scope of the negation sign is '$(p \ \& \ q)$.' The scope of the ampersand is the two expressions (variables) 'p,' 'q.' And the scope of the horseshoe is the two expressions '$\sim (p \ \& \ q)$,' 'r.' Parentheses are essential in the PC language for determining the scopes of connectives.

We might think of ordinary expressions like 'and,' 'or,' and 'if. . . , then. . .' as also having scope. But ordinary English does not contain a simple device like parentheses for determining scope. English contains a variety of devices for this purpose. In writing, there is punctuation: commas, semicolons, periods. In speaking, we use pauses and intonation. The context may also be important for determining the scope of an expression. Consider this sentence:

College professors are not overpaid.

If this sentence is used as a rejoinder to someone who claims that college professors are overpaid, then we would naturally construe the 'not' as having the rest of the sentence for its scope. We would want this translation:

~College professors are overpaid.

Used in a different setting, the sentence might be understood as saying that no college professor is overpaid. With this understanding, the 'not' has a smaller scope; we would not use '$\sim$' to translate this sentence.

In making translations, it is necessary to ensure that the scope of the connectives comes out right in our translations. To translate:

> If Bill agrees to take Stan's place, then if Stan can borrow enough money, he will go to the convention.

we don't want this sentence:

> [(Bill agrees to take Stan's place ⊃ Stan can borrow enough money) ⊃ He will go to the convention]

In this translation, the second horseshoe has a greater scope than the first. It should be the other way around:

> [Bill agrees to take Stan's place ⊃ (Stan can borrow enough money ⊃ He will go to the convention)]

*Exercise: Section 7

Translate the following with connectives when this is possible. Mark weaker translations with an asterisk. Mark stronger translations with a double asterisk.

1. If Bill knows the answer and Tom doesn't, Bill will win the contest.

2. If you call before you leave, then if you go out, you will know you are expected.

3. Tom can expect to be met at the airport only if he calls his parents the day before and arrives before 9:30.

4. If Chicago is on Lake Michigan, then Lake Michigan is polluted; but Chicago is on Lake Michigan.

5. If the phone rings in the evening, either Sally or Marge will answer it.

6. Either Fred will keep his promise, or if he doesn't, he will have a good excuse.

7. If you announce that you are coming, neither Kevin nor Jesse will be there when you arrive.

8. If the ice will melt only if the temperature is raised, then if the temperature isn't raised, the ice won't melt.

9. If the president and the governor don't both speak at the graduation, then the ceremony won't take a long time.

10. The student government will improve next year if, and only if, either Margaret or Anne is elected.

11-8 IDENTIFYING SENTENCES

In translating ordinary sentences into the PC language, it is important to note when we have multiple occurrences of a single sentence. For example, two sentences having the forms p, $(p \supset q)$ imply a sentence with form q. For this implication, it is essential that the single sentence p also occurs as antecedent of the material conditional $(p \supset q)$.

It is sometimes difficult to determine when to count two sentences as occurrences of different sentences (of different sentence types) and when to count them as occurrences of a single sentence. Consider these sentences:

Bill went to London yesterday.

If Bill went to London yesterday, then he won't be home tonight.

We want to determine whether these sentences, together, entail this one:

Bill won't be home tonight.

If we translate the sentences with connectives, we get:

Bill went to London yesterday. (Bill went to London yesterday ⊃

~He will be home tonight) ~ Bill will be home tonight.

It may seem obvious that the first two sentences of our translations imply the third. But now suppose that in the first sentence, the London is London, England. And in the second sentence, the London is London, Ontario. In that case, we have no implication. The sentence 'Bill went to London yesterday' is ambiguous; when it occurs with different meanings, we will regard the occurrences as occurrences of different sentences. To symbolize the translations above (to jointly symbolize them), we would use:

$p, (q \supset \sim r), \sim r$

With these formulas, it is easy to show that we do not have logical implication from the first two to the third. For two sentences to count as occurrences of the same sentence (type), it is not always sufficient that they be composed of the same words, in the same order.

There are also cases where we want to count sentences containing different words as instances of the same sentence (type). In these sentences:

(Bill went to London yesterday ⊃ ~ He will be home tonight)

~Bill will be home tonight.

the consequent of the first sentence contains 'He' where the second sentence contains 'Bill.' But we understand 'He' to signify Bill. So we regard this occurrence of 'He will be home tonight' to be an instance of the same sentence (type) as 'Bill will be home tonight.' And we use these formulas to symbolize the sentences above:

$(q \supset \sim r), \sim r$

When one sentence is like another except for containing a pronoun where the other contains a name, and the pronoun could be replaced by the name with no loss, we regard the two as occurrences of the same sentence; we use the same variable to symbolize them. We can only do this if the name is a name (or singular term) for a single individual. In these sentences:

If a man is in the kitchen, he is my uncle. A man is my uncle.

the second sentence is NOT an occurrence of the same sentence as the consequent of the conditional sentence. The expression 'a man' is not the name of a single individual.

In these sentences:

(Ernest has visited Paris & He wants to live there)

Ernest wants to live in Paris.

there are two differences between:

He wants to live there.

Ernest wants to live in Paris.

The first contains 'He' where the second contains 'Ernest'; the first contains 'there' where the second contains 'in Paris.' But in this context we would regard these as occurrences of the same sentence, and would symbolize the original two sentences:

$$(p \,\&\, q), q$$

We will regard English sentences which are obviously saying the "same thing," and which have only slight grammatical differences, as different occurrences of the same sentence. This convention requires judgment on our part. It is needed because the PC language is a mixed language, combining ordinary expressions with artificial symbols.

Another example of this phenomenon is provided by the following argument:

If Bill goes to California next summer, he will not attend summer school.

Bill will go to California next summer. So Bill will not attend summer school.

To determine whether this is a valid argument, we could translate it:

(Bill goes to California next summer $\supset$ ~ He will attend summer school)

Bill will go to California next summer. So ~ Bill will attend summer school.

The antecedent of the first premiss is 'Bill goes to California next summer.' The second premiss is 'Bill will go to California next summer.' These are different strings of words, but we count them as occurrences of a single sentence. The antecedent of an indicative conditional sentence can be in the present tense and still be understood as concerned with the future. This fact about English syntax entitles us to use these formulas to symbolize the argument:

$$(p \supset {\sim}q), p \,/ \sim q$$

*Exercise: Section 8

Translate the following into the PC language. Produce formulas which jointly symbolize the sentences you have translated.

1. Either Bill wants french fries or he wants onion rings. Bill does not want french fries. Bill does want onion rings.

2. If Rachel knows the answer to this question, then she will pass the test. Rachel won't pass the test. Rachel did not know the answer to this question.

3. If Rachel answers this question correctly, then she will pass the test. Rachel will answer this question correctly. Rachel will pass the test.

4. Rachel will pass the test only if she answers this question correctly. Rachel will answer this question correctly. Rachel will pass the test.

5. If Rachel passes the test, then she will have answered this question correctly. Rachel will pass the test. Rachel will answer the question correctly.

11-9 A FURTHER LOOK AT THE DIFFERENCE BETWEEN ORDINARY CONDITIONAL SENTENCES AND HORSESHOE SENTENCES (OPT)

We know that the truth-table for '$\supset$' is:

p	q	$(p \supset q)$
t	t	t
t	f	f
f	t	t
f	f	t

In trying to make a truth table for ordinary indicative conditions, we came up with this:

p	q	If p, then q
t	t	t
t	f	f
f	t	?
f	f	?

The question marks indicate that the values of component sentences are not sufficient to determine the value of the conditional sentence.

If we consider inferential meaning rather than representational meaning, the two kinds of conditional sentences seem more similar. The rules for the '$\supset$' in the PC deductive system are Modus Ponens, Dilemma, and Horseshoe Introduction. I will ignore Dilemma, since that chiefly concerns the wedge. The derived rule Modus Tollens also gives an important feature of the horseshoe.

Now consider what inferences are authorized by 'If. . . , then. . .' Modus Ponens is clearly correct:

If it snowed Saturday, then Paul went skiing.
It snowed Saturday. So Paul went skiing.

Modus Tollens is also correct for 'If. . . , then. . .':

If it snowed Saturday, then Paul went skiing.
Paul didn't go skiing. So it didn't snow Saturday.

And if we suppose that A is true, and then reason (correctly) to B, we are entitled to claim that if A, then B. The rules for the horseshoe are valid for 'If. . . , then. . .'

This fact may be a consequence of a partial agreement in meaning between the two expressions. Let us consider other inferential features of the horseshoe. In its truth-table, only one row gives a horseshoe formula the value falsity. It is this feature of the horseshoe's meaning that accounts for the validity of these sentences:

$\sim(p \supset q) / p$

and:

$\sim(p \supset q) / \sim q$

Corresponding sequences should not be valid for 'If. . . , then. . . ,' because other combinations (than a true antecedent and false consequent) are compatible with a false indicative conditional.

Consider the following proof of the sequence '$\sim(p \supset q)$ / p':

1	$\sim(p \supset q)$	
2	$\sim p$	
3	p	
4	$\sim q$	
5	$(p \, \& \sim p)$	3, 2, Conj
6	q	$4 - 5$, $\sim$ E
7	$(p \supset q)$	$3 - 6$, $\supset$I
8	$[(p \supset q) \, \& \sim (p \supset q)]$	7, 1, Conj
9	p	$2 - 8$, $\sim$ E

Let us see if there is any reasoning that becomes invalid upon replacing '$\supset$' by 'If. . . , then. . .' The only possibility would be a step obtained by a rule for the horseshoe. The only step obtained by a rule for the horseshoe is step 7, obtained by $\supset$ Introduction. I have already said that this rule is correct for 'If. . . , then. . .' as well as the horseshoe. So upon replacing all the horseshoes in the proof by 'If. . . , then. . . ,' we have a correct proof that '$\sim$(If p, then q) / p' is valid. Intuitively, this sequence isn't valid.

The interested reader should stop at this point and try to make sense of things. Are we wrong to think that '$\supset$' is different in meaning from 'If. . . , then. . .'? Are we wrong to think that the rules for the horseshoe are correct for 'If. . . , then. . .'? What is our trouble?

To resolve this difficulty, we must try to get clearer about the meaning of ordinary indicative conditionals. I think that a conditional 'If A, then B' is relative to the speaker's knowledge and beliefs. The speaker means that, given what he knows and believes, the occasion won't arise for accepting A without accepting B. Either A *and* B are both true. Or the speaker's current knowledge and beliefs are incompatible with A. Or A is false, but not incompatible with the knowledge and beliefs, and if A were true, then B would be true. We can determine the value of the conditional without taking much account of the speaker's knowledge and beliefs if the antecedent is true. If the antecedent is false, they play an important role. If the antecedent is incompatible with the knowledge and beliefs, we might regard the conditional as "vacuously" true. An example is a sentence:

If p, then I'm a monkey's uncle.

This is a colorful, somewhat old-fashioned way to deny that A is true. The speaker is indicating that A is incompatible with his knowledge and beliefs. If the antecedent is false but not incompatible, the truth or falsity of the indicative conditional is tied to the value of the corresponding subjunctive conditional. This is a complicated and difficult topic, which can't now be explored further.

There is an important difference between a simple conditional and a conditional embedded in another. A sentence 'If A, then B' indicates that a world described by the speaker's knowledge and beliefs doesn't correspond to A without matching B. In 'If A, then if B, then C,' the main conditional still means that exactly one of: (1) the antecedent and consequent are true, or (2) the antecedent is incompatible with the speaker's knowledge and beliefs, or (3) if the antecedent were true, so would be the consequent. But the embedded conditional 'if B, then C' is not simply relative to the speaker's knowledge and beliefs. It is relative to the knowledge and beliefs *supplemented with A*; for the purpose of the embedded conditional, we think of A as additional knowledge.

Let us consider our proof again. When I took $\supset$I to be correct for 'If. . . , then. . . ,' I was thinking of the case where A is the only hypothesis. When we combine this sentence we suppose true with sentences we actually accept as true, and reason to B, we have shown that A isn't true without B being true. In case A isn't true, we have shown that if it were true, then so would be B. There is an important difference between the hypothesis of a proof or subproof and the antecedent of a conditional. To make an hypothesis is like adding the hypothesis to the class of true sentences. To make a sentence the antecedent of an indicative conditional is like adding that sentence to the class of sentences that are both true and known. A proof from one hypothesis A to B justifies both $(A \supset B)$ and 'If A, then B.' A proof from hypotheses A_1, A_2 to B justifies $(A_2 \supset B)$ with respect to hypothesis A_1. In case A_1 is true, so will be $(A_2 \supset B)$. The proof does not justify 'If A_2, then B' with respect to A_1. In case A_1 simply happens to be true, it need not be the case that 'If A_2, then B' is true. For A_1 might be true without being known (or believed).

In this proof:

1	$\sim(p \supset q)$	
2	$\sim p$	
3	p	
4	$\sim q$	
5	$(p \;\&\; \sim p)$	3, 2, Conj
6	q	$4 - 5$, $\sim$ E
7	$(p \supset q)$	$3 - 6$, $\supset$I
8	$(p \supset q) \;\&\; \sim (p \supset q)$	7, 1, Conj
9	p	$2 - 8$, $\sim$ E

if we replace step 7 by 'If p, then q,' the inference is not valid. Nor is it valid if we replace step 1 by '$\sim$ (If p, then q)' as well as replacing step 7. The truth of 'If p, then q' does not follow from the truth of '$\sim$ (If p, then q)' and '$\sim p$.' What is justified is a sentence like this:

If $\sim$(If p, then q), then If $\sim p$, then If p, then q.

If we suppose our knowledge supplemented with '$\sim$(If p, then q)' and '$\sim p$,' then we won't have occasion to accept p but not q. This is trivial, since once we suppose our knowledge is supplemented with '$\sim p$,' this knowledge is incompatible with p.

Replacing the '$\supset$'s in the proof above with 'If. . . , then. . .'s keeps steps 7, 8, and 9 from being justified. As a replacement for step 8, we could validly infer:

If $\sim$(If p, then q), then If $\sim p$, then

[(If p, then q) $\&$ $\sim$(If p, then q)]

It is contradictory to suppose our knowledge is supplemented with both '~(If p, then q)' and '~ p.' If we suppose that our knowledge is supplemented with '~(If p, then q),' then it follows that '~ p' is not known. It does not follow that '~ p' is not true. A sentence 'If ~(If p, then q), then p' is not invariably true (though some instances of this formula are true). And an inference sequence '~(If p, then q) / p' is not valid.

Exercise A: Section 9

Translate the following sentences with connectives, where this is possible. Mark weaker translations with an asterisk. Mark stronger translations with a double asterisk.

1. Carolyn hit Victor as hard as she could, but this didn't bother him at all.

2. Either Carolyn or Paul is in the kitchen.

3. Henry will drink sherry only if there is no more gin.

4. If neither Isabelle nor Bruce smokes, then they have no use for ashtrays.

5. Frank will be at the dance unless he has to prepare a grant application.

6. Megan won't practice the flute if her mother doesn't make her practice.

7. David and Deborah are lawyers; Rosemary is a physical therapist.

8. It is false that Alan will make a living only if he joins the Army.

9. If John will take his family to dinner Saturday if he gets a check in the mail, then he won't get a check in the mail.

10. Jane isn't very tall; neither is Megan.

11. Janet will be here for dinner if, and only if, her show is over early and she doesn't have trouble with her car.

12. If Norma is making hors d'oeuvres and dessert, then if Jane is preparing the main course, the meal will be outstanding.

13. John will win the tournament just in case neither Dale nor Jim enters.

14. If either Kevin or Jesse is the starting quarterback, the team will have a balanced attack.

15. At least one of Kathy and Rosemary has a Ph.D.

Exercise B: Section 9

Translate the following groups of sentences into the PC language. Produce formulas which jointly symbolize the translations.

1. Kathy didn't like the movie; neither did Frank. If Frank didn't like the movie, it was boring.

2. Alice will lead the discussion only if Bill gets sick. Bill won't get sick. So Alice won't lead the discussion.

3. Victor is at home; Carolyn is too. If Victor is at home, the TV set isn't on. But if Carolyn is at home, the set is on.

4. If it is false that Julie will go to the dance only if Sean asks her, then Julie may go to the dance. But Sean won't ask her.

5. The mayor will go swimming if he finds his suit. He hasn't found his suit. So he won't go swimming.

6. Henry and Linda are Christians, but neither is a Presbyterian. If Henry becomes a Presbyterian, then Linda will too.

7. Leonard will go to Florida unless his car breaks down. Leonard won't go. His car will break down.

8. Jim will go to Florida, but not Leonard. If Leonard goes to Florida, Jim will have a good time. Otherwise, he won't.

11-10   TESTING FOR ANALYTICITY

In dealing with English sentences and arguments, we will test for the general semantic features of analytic truth, validity-entailment, and incompatibility. To make a test, we use connectives to translate ordinary sentences, then we test the translations for the logical case of the general feature that concerns us.

In carrying out these tests, we must have suitable translations. What it takes for translations to be suitable depends on the feature we are testing for. To determine whether a sentence is analytically true, we require an equivalent or stronger translation. Once we test a suitable translation for the logical special case of the general semantic feature, we can get either a positive or negative outcome. A positive outcome carries back to the original sentences. A negative outcome is inconclusive.

Suppose we ask whether the following sentence is analytically true:

It won't both rain and not rain tomorrow.

We can provide an equivalent translation:

~(It will rain tomorrow & ~ It will rain tomorrow)

This is (a form of) the Law of Contradiction; it is logically true. Since this is an equivalent translation, the original sentence is analytic.

If we try to determine whether this sentence:

It will rain tomorrow unless it doesn't rain tomorrow.

is analytic, we can begin by translating it into the PC language:

(It will rain tomorrow v ~ It will rain tomorrow)

This sentence is (an instance of) the Law of Excluded Middle. Although our translation is logically true, it is weaker than the original sentence. We cannot use it to test the original sentence for analytic truth. In fact, we cannot use the PC language to evaluate the original sentence for analyticity.

This sentence:

(1) John's house is not both yellow (all over) and blue.

is equivalent to:

(2) ~ (John's house is yellow & John's house is blue)

The translation is symbolized by the formula ' ~ (p & q),' which has the truth-table:

p	q	~ (p & q)	
t	t	f	t
t	f	t	f
f	t	t	f
f	f	t	f

The translation is not logically true. When we get a negative result, we must consider whether some semantic content in the original sentence fails to show up in the logical form of the translation, and is relevant to the question of analytic truth. If the answer is "No," the sentence is not analytic. In the present case, the nonlogical expressions in (2) do determine that the sentence is analytic, though it isn't logically true. And sentence (1) is analytically true. (Although we have determined that the English sentence is analytic, its analyticity is traced to features that can't be analyzed using the PC language.)

*Exercise: Section 10

Determine whether the English sentences are analytically true. Write or abbreviate your translations, and use proofs or truth-tables (or counter-examples) to justify your answers.

1. Either it will rain or snow Sunday, or else it will do neither one.

2. Tom doesn't both like beer and not like beer.

3. If Mary can do the homework assignment, then if Bill can't do the homework assignment, then Mary can't do the homework assignment.

4. Either it will rain and snow Sunday, or else it won't rain and it won't snow.

11-11 INCOMPATIBILITY

To test for incompatibility, we need equivalent or weaker translations. Consider the following sentences:

Leonard will go to Florida unless his car breaks down. Leonard won't go to Florida. Leonard's car won't break down.

These sentences have suitable translations:

(Leonard will go to Florida v His car will break down), ~ Leonard will go to Florida ~ Leonard's car will break down.

Since these translations are logically incompatible:

p	q	(p v q)	~ p	~ q
t	t	t	f	f
t	f	t	f	t
f	t	t	t	f
f	f	f	t	t

the original sentences are incompatible.

*Exercise: Section 11

Determine whether the English sentences are incompatible. Write or abbreviate your translations, and justify your answers.

1. Chuck likes Greek food and Italian food. Chuck either doesn't like Greek food or he doesn't like Italian food.

2. If too much salt contributes to heart disease, then Frank has heart disease. Too much salt contributes to heart disease. Frank doesn't have heart disease.

3. Bill will be on the football team unless his grades make him ineligible. Bill won't be on the football team. Bill's grades will make him ineligible.

4. If fish is served tonight, then lamb won't be served tonight. Lamb will be served tonight only if fish isn't served tonight. If we won't have white wine, then lamb will be served tonight. If we will have white wine, then fish will be served tonight. Neither lamb nor fish will be served tonight.

11-12   ENTAILMENT AND VALIDITY

To determine whether English sentences $A_1, \ldots, A_n$ entail B is the same as determining whether the inference sequence $A_1, \ldots, A_n \,/\, B$ is valid. We need translations $A^*_1, \ldots,$ A^*_n, B^* Each of $A^*_1, \ldots, A^*_n$ must be equivalent to or weaker than the sentence it translates. B^* must be equivalent to or stronger than B.

Consider the following argument:

Bill knows the answer only if Lynn told it to him. If Lynn told Bill the answer, he didn't learn it from Mary. But Bill does know the answer. So Lynn told Bill the answer; he didn't learn it from Mary.

We want to know whether the premises entail the conclusion. We can translate the sentences:

(Bill knows the answer ⊃ Lynn told it to him), (Lynn told Bill the answer ⊃ ~ He learned it from Mary), Bill knows the answer. So (Lynn told Bill the answer & ~He learned it from Mary)

The first two premises receive weaker translations, which is allowed. The third premiss is its own translation; this is an equivalent translation. And the conclusion receives an equivalent translation. The translation is a suitable one to use. This proof:

1   $(p \supset q)$

2   $(q \supset {\sim} r)$

3   p
   _____

4   q 1, 3, MP

5   ${\sim} r$ 2, 4, MP

6   $(q \,\&\, {\sim} r)$ 4, 5, Conj

shows that the translation is logically valid. Hence, the original argument is valid.

To evaluate the following argument:

Sally will pass logic only if she studies logic all day Wednesday and Thursday. If Sally studies logic all day Wednesday and Thursday, she will get at least a B on the final. So Sally will pass logic only if she gets at least a B on the final.

we can translate the sentences like this:

[Sally will pass logic ⊃ (She will study logic all day Wednesday & She will study logic all day Thursday)], [(Sally studies logic all day Wednesday & Sally studies logic all day Thursday) ⊃ She will get at least a B on the final], So (Sally will pass logic ⊃ She will get at least a B on the final)

The translation is logically valid; but this doesn't show that the original is valid. The translation of the conclusion is weaker than the conclusion. We can't use the PC language to evaluate the argument.

Now we shall try to evaluate this argument:

If Lynn isn't married, then he's happy. Lynn is happy. So he isn't married.

We can translate it:

(~ Lynn is married ⊃ He's happy) Lynn is happy. So ~ He is married.

This truth-table:

p	q	$(\sim p \supset q)$	q	$\sim p$
t	t	t	t	f
t	f	t	f	f
f	t	t	t	t
f	f	f	f	t

shows that the translation isn't logically valid. Or reflection, we can see that nothing important fails to show up in the logical form of the translation. The original argument isn't valid.

*Exercise: Section 12

Determine whether the English arguments are valid. Write or abbreviate your translations, and justify your answers.

1. Bill or his brother will deliver the message. If Bill delivers the message, then Barry will bring extra ski gloves. Barry won't bring extra ski gloves. So Bill's brother won't deliver the message.

2. Either San Francisco or Sacramento is the capital of California. Sacramento is the capital of California. So San Francisco isn't the capital of California.

3. Leonard will go to Florida for spring vacation unless he spends all his money fixing his car. Leonard won't spend all his money fixing his car. So he will go to Florida for spring vacation.

4. If Leonard doesn't spend all his money fixing his car, then he will go to Florida for spring vacation. So Leonard will go to Florida for spring vacation unless he spends all his money fixing his car.

11-13   AN IMPORTANT EXCEPTION

To use the PC language to evaluate an English argument, we need an equivalent or stronger translation for the conclusion. This requirement keeps us from dealing with an important class of English arguments. It is common for the conclusion of an argument to be a conditional sentence, as in:

> If the convention is in either Seattle or San Francisco, then Sharon can't afford to attend. If Sam gets his way, the convention will be in Seattle. So if Sam gets his way, then Sharon can't afford to attend the convention.

We translate indicative conditionals with the horseshoe, which gives weaker translations. Even though our requirement tells us to stay away from them, we would like to find some way to deal with arguments having conditional conclusions. (An 'only if'-sentence is not counted as a conditional, even though we use a material conditional to translate it.)

This translation for the argument above:

> [(The convention is in Seattle v The convention is in San Francisco) ⊃ ~ Sharon can afford to attend the convention], (Sam gets his way ⊃The convention will be in Seattle), So (Sam gets his way ⊃ ~ Sharon can afford to attend the convention)

is logically valid. This means that the original premisses entail:

So (Sam gets his way ⊃ ~ Sharon can afford to attend the convention)

But this conclusion is weaker than 'If Sam gets his way, then Sharon can't afford to attend the convention.' A '⊃'-sentence can be true without the corresponding indicative conditional being true. But if we accept the analysis in section 9 of this chapter, the person who says 'If A, then B' means that, given what he at that time knows and believes, he won't have occasion to accept A without accepting B. A person who knows that '$(A ⊃ B)$' is true is justified in claiming that If A, then B.

When someone seriously advances an argument, that person accepts (or pretends to) the premisses. The premisses count as part of the person's knowledge and beliefs. So once we reason from these premisses to a conclusion $(A ⊃ B)$, we are further justified in reasoning to 'If A, then B.'

This rationale would allow us to use the PC language to evaluate an argument whose conclusion is 'If A, then B.' With suitable translations for the premisses, we could translate the conclusion as '$(A ⊃ B)$.' However, there is a qualification to be made here. Consider this argument:

> Bill is going skiing tomorrow. So if Bill breaks his leg today, he will go skiing tomorrow.

This argument is intuitively unsatisfactory. Of course, if the premiss is really true, and known, the conclusion is sure to be true. But a person (perhaps Bill) who accepts the premiss is not likely to accept the conclusion. In the earlier example of an argument with a conditional conclusion, we understood the antecedent of the conclusion to simply add more information to what we know and believe. In the present case, the antecedent is intended to call into question the information given in the premiss. Instead of supplementing the information given in the premiss, the antecendent is challenging this information.

We will use the PC language to evaluate arguments with conditional conclusions—*but only when the antecedent of the conclusion is intended to supplement the information in the premisses, and not to call (some of) it into question.* This adds uncertainty to our evaluations of arguments, for we must now assess the intentions of the person advancing an argument. In practice this does not cause difficulties. It is customary for a person advancing a serious argument with a conditional conclusion to regard the antecedent of the conclusion as supplementing the premises.

In general, when evaluating an argument $A_1, \ldots, A_n / B$, the translations $A_1^*, \ldots,$. A_n^* *can be weaker than the sentences they translate, but* B^* must be equivalent to or stronger than B. However, if B is an indicative conditional 'If C, then D' (or 'If C, D' or 'D if C'), then we allow this sentence to be translated by '$(C \supset D)$,' so long as the antecedent C is not intended to call the premises into question. This exception allows us to use the PC translation to evaluate the argument on page 272. This proof:

1	$[(p \lor q) \supset \sim r]$	
2	$(s \supset p)$	
3	s	
4	p	2, 3, MP
5	$(p \lor q)$	4, Add
6	$\sim r$	1, 5, MP
7	$(s \supset \sim r)$	3 – 6, $\supset$I

shows the translation to be logically valid. This positive result shows that the original argument is valid.

We ordinarily do not allow the translation for a conclusion to be weaker than the conclusion. As an exception, we allow a conditional conclusion 'If C, then D' to be translated by '$(C \supset D)$.' We will embellish this exception as follows: Suppose C, D are themselves complex, having translations C^*, D^*. We will allow C^* to be weaker than C, so long as D^* is equivalent to or stronger than D. But if the conclusion is a conditional 'If C, then if D, then E,' we will allow C and D to have weaker translations C^*, D^*, so long as E^* isn't weaker than E, and we translate the conclusion '$[C^* \supset (D^* \supset E^*)]$.' (We are treating the antecedents as if they were premises, and the consequent as if it were the conclusion.)

The exception (or exceptions) to the rule that the conclusion of an inference needs an equivalent or stronger translation causes certain problems for our understanding of validity. We originally took an argument to be valid if we could determine simply on the basis of understanding it, that it isn't possible for the premises to be true when the conclusion isn't. This conception of validity doesn't take account of the person making an argument, or his knowledge. If we make use of this conception of validity, we must say that the following argument:

> Either Francis or Frederick committed the crime. So if Francis didn't commit the crime, then Frederick did.

is invalid. For suppose the premise is true but not known to us. Further, suppose that Francis, not Frederick, committed the crime. It may well be that with respect to our knowledge and beliefs, the conclusion isn't true. So the premise could be true (the premiss's truth is unaffected by our knowledge and belief) when the conclusion isn't. However, this, intuitively, is an acceptable argument. It makes good sense to infer the conclusions from the premiss.

It seems appropriate to adopt a different conception of validity, rather than to reject the argument. We shall distinguish between our previous concept of validity, the *narrow concept of validity*, and a new concept, the *more generous concept of validity*. Every argument that is valid on the narrow concept of validity is also valid on the more generous concept. To explain the more generous concept, we say that an argument is valid in this new sense *if accepting the premisses commits one to accepting the conclusion*. We understand this in such a way that if the premisses couldn't possibly be true, then accepting them commits one to accepting every sentence. The more generous concept of validity makes the concepts of accepting a sentence and being committed to accept a sentence fundamental.

Some logicians have objected to the more generous concept of validity by noting that a person who accepts certain premisses may not accept a conclusion that follows from them. For the person may know that the conclusion is false, in which case the argument will cause him to reject one or more of the premisses. This is an irrelevant objection. The more generous concept of validity makes the argument valid so long as continuing to accept the premisses commits a person to accepting the conclusion.

We will similarly distinguish narrow and more generous concepts of entailment and incompatibility. For the more generous concept of entailment, sentences $A_1, \ldots, A_n$ entail sentence B if accepting $A_1, \ldots, A_n$ commits one to accepting B. For the more generous concept of incompatibility, sentences $A_1, \ldots, A_n$ are incompatible, if accepting all but one of the sentences commits one to rejecting the remaining sentence. From now on we will adopt the more generous semantic concepts rather than the narrow ones. But the differences between the narrow concepts and the more generous concepts will not usually be important to us. For theoretical purposes, both the narrow and the more generous concepts need to be investigated.

*Exercise A: Section 13

Determine whether the following arguments are valid. Write or abbreviate your translations, and justify your answers.

1. If Leonard goes to Florida, he will spend all his money. If Leonard's car breaks down, he will spend all his money. So if Leonard will go to Florida unless his car breaks down, then he will spend all his money.

2. John will be happy if his book is published. John will be happy only if his book is published. So John will be happy if, and only if, his book is published.

3. Kathy and Isabelle aren't both studying philosophy. If Kathy is intellectually curious, then she is studying philosophy. So if Isabelle isn't studying philosophy, then Kathy isn't intellectually curious.

4. Megan fell down. If Andrea was angry, she pushed Megan. Andrea was angry. So Andrea pushed Megan, and Megan fell down.

5. It isn't true both that Scott doesn't speak French and Donna doesn't speak French. If Donna speaks French, then she will understand Andre's note. So if Scott doesn't speak French, then Donna will understand Andre's note.

Exercise B: Section 13

Determine which of the following sentences are analytically true. Show your translations, and show work which justifies your answers.

1. Either Jimmy is neither Polish nor German, being Irish, or else he is Polish or German or not Irish.

2. It isn't true that (if Alfreda is Polish, she isn't German; but Alfreda is both Polish and German).

3. Mario is Italian but not Spanish, or Spanish but not Italian.

4. It isn't true that, although Pierre isn't French and isn't English, he is either French or English.

5. If Jean is French, he's French or Italian—but Jean is French or Italian only if he's Italian; however, Jean is French, not Italian.

Exercise C: Section 13

Determine which of the following inferences are valid. Show your translations and show work which justifies your answers.

1. Either Frank or Isabelle is the person who committed the crime. If Isabelle was in Rochester Thursday, then Frank committed the crime. So if Isabelle was in Rochester Thursday, then she isn't the person who committed the crime.

2. Sally won't graduate unless she passes German. She won't graduate if she doesn't pay her library fines. So Sally will graduate only if she passes German and pays her library fines.

3. If Paul gets paid Friday, then if Carolyn doesn't work late Friday, they will go to dinner at Hoak's on Friday. Carolyn won't work late Friday only if Paul gets paid Friday. Paul and Carolyn won't go to dinner at Hoak's on Friday. Hence, Carolyn will work late Friday.

4. Dick will be in class Thursday if, and only if, he gets over the flu and he cancels his doctor's appointment. If Dick gets over the flu, he will cancel his doctor's appointment. So Dick will be in class Thursday.

5. Ruth but not Anne will take the Civil Service Exam. If Ruth and Anne don't both take the Civil Service Exam, then they won't both get government jobs. Ruth will get a government job just in case Anne gets a government job. So neither Ruth nor Anne will get a government job.

6. Larry lives in Cambridge or Boston. If he lives in Cambridge, his car has a Massachusetts license. In case his car doesn't have a Massachusetts license, he doesn't live in Boston. So Larry's car has a Massachusetts license.

7. It isn't true that there will be an accident unless Ken stops driving. So Ken won't stop driving.

8. If today is sunny, then Carolyn will get a tan if she goes to the beach. Today will be sunny. And Carolyn will get a tan. So she's going to the beach.

Exercise D: Section 13

Determine if the following groups of sentences are incompatible. Show your translations, and show work which justifies your answers.

1. Shirley will go to Florida at Christmas unless her car costs more than $250 to fix. Shirley won't go to Florida at Christmas. Her car won't cost more than $250 to fix.

2. It isn't true that if Richard is elected, there will be a nuclear war. If Richard is elected, there won't be a nuclear war. But Richard won't be elected.

3. If Buffalo builds a new baseball stadium, then if Buffalo gets a major league baseball team, War Memorial Stadium will be torn down. Buffalo will get a major league baseball team. War Memorial Stadium won't be torn down.

4. If fish or chicken is served, we will have a white wine with dinner. If Jeanne got paid today, fish will be served. If Jeanne didn't get paid today, chicken will be served. We won't have a white wine with dinner.

5. Phil has a full house only if deuces are wild. If Phil hasn't got a full house, then he drew three cards. Phil didn't draw three cards. Deuces aren't wild, but threes are.

6. George has two kings or three of a kind. If he has two kings, he will see Joe's bet. George will raise if he has three of a kind. George will neither see Joe's bet nor raise.

7. Jeff isn't both a lawyer and a government employee. He's a lawyer only if he's a government employee. But Jeff is a government employee.

8. Don went skiing just in case both Billy and Joan went skiing. Billy or Joan did go skiing. Don didn't go skiing.

11-14 INCORPORATING SEMANTIC FEATURES IN LOGICAL FORM

Many English sentences and arguments can't be evaluated using the PC language. Some valid English arguments can't be adequately translated in the PC language. Others can be translated, but they can't be given translations that are logically valid. The limitations on the use of the PC language are responsible for the difference between positive and negative outcomes of tests for various features.

We can't overcome all the limitations of the PC language, but it is possible to overcome some of them. We have done this in translating 'or'-sentences. Even though this sentence:

(1) Either Morgan or Roger is the tallest boy in the class.

is equivalent to:

(2) (Morgan is the tallest boy in the class v Roger is the tallest boy in the class)

if we understand Morgan to be a different boy than Roger, we prefer this translation:

(3) [(Morgan is the tallest boy in the class v Roger is the tallest boy in the class) & ~ (Morgan is the tallest boy in the class & Roger is the tallest boy in the class)]

More of the semantic content of (1) "shows up" in the logical form of (3) than in the logical form of (2).

Another possibility for overcoming limitations of the PC language involves an argument like this:

Bill is a bachelor. If Bill owns a house, then he is married. So Bill doesn't own a house.

This translation:

> Bill is a bachelor. (Bill owns a house ⊃ He is married) So ~ Bill owns a house.

is not logically valid. But it is part of the meaning of 'bachelor' that a bachelor isn't married. Since Bill is a bachelor, he isn't married. But if he's not married, then he must not own a house.

The sentence:

> (Bill is a bachelor ⊃ ~ Bill is married)

is a true sentence. It is analytically true. If we add this to the premisses of our translation, we get:

> Bill is a bachelor. (Bill is a bachelor ⊃ ~ Bill is married) (Bill owns a house ⊃ He is married) So ~ Bill owns a house.

This argument is symbolized: p, $(p \supset \sim r)$, $(q \supset r) / \sim q$. The following proof shows it to be valid:

$$
\begin{array}{lll}
1 & p & \\
2 & (p \supset \sim r) & \\
3 & \underline{(q \supset r)} & \\
4 & \sim r & 2, 1, \text{MP} \\
5 & \sim q & 3, 4, \text{MT}
\end{array}
$$

The added premiss doesn't add any content to the argument it translates. In translating arguments, we will allow ourselves to supply additional premisses so long as:

(1) These are horseshoe sentences $(A \supset B)$ or $(A \supset \sim B)$;

(2) The A and B sentences are simple sentences, containing no symbolic connectives;

(3) The horseshoe sentences are clearly analytic.

If we evaluate this argument:

> Larry is either an engineer or an accountant, but not both. Larry is an accountant if he took lots of deductions on his income tax. But Larry is a civil engineer. So Larry didn't take lots of deductions on his income tax.

by dealing with this translation:

> [(Larry is an engineer v Larry is an accountant) & ~ (Larry is an engineer & Larry is an accountant)], (Larry took lots of deductions on his income tax ⊃ Larry is an accountant), Larry is a civil engineer. So ~ Larry took lots of deductions on his income tax.

we will not be able to show that the argument is valid. However, it is part of the meaning of 'civil engineer' that a civil engineer is an engineer. The following sentence is analytically true:

> (Larry is a civil engineer ⊃ Larry is an engineer)

If we add this analytic premiss to our translation, we get an argument with this form: [(p v q) & ~ (p & q)], (r ⊃ q), s, (s ⊃ p) / ~ r. This is the form of a logically valid argument, as you can easily prove.

Allowing ourselves to add extra analytic premisses enables us to establish the validity of more arguments than we otherwise could. But we still can't deal with an argument like this:

> Every Scandanavian has blue eyes. Olaf doesn't have blue eyes. So Olaf isn't Scandanavian.

Since negative results of an evaluation are less useful than positive results, we can regard ourselves as trying to show that an argument is a positive case, rather than as trying to determine whether or not it is. Allowing ourselves to add analytic '⊃'-premisses doesn't make it easier to determine that an argument isn't valid. When we don't succeed in showing that an argument is valid, our failure may be due to (1) the lack of ingenuity on on our part, (2) the inadequacy of the PC language, or (3) the fact that the argument is invalid. We can only decide that the argument is invalid after discounting the first two possibilities.

Suppose we are trying to show that a group of sentences is incompatible. We will allow ourselves to supplement the translations with additional analytic '⊃'-sentences. If we wish to show that these sentences are incompatible:

> Noble is Jane's dog. Either Noble isn't a dog or he is a cat.

and use these translations:

> Noble is Jane's dog. (~ Noble is a dog v He is a cat)

we will find that they are not logically incompatible. Adding this analytic '⊃'-sentence:

> (Noble is Jane's dog ⊃ Noble is a dog)

gives us translations that aren't logically incompatible either. But we can add another analytic '⊃'-sentence:

> (Noble is a dog ⊃ ~ Noble is a cat)

Now our translations have these forms: p, (~ q v r), (p ⊃ q), (q ⊃ ~ r). We finally have translations we can show to be logically incompatible. (*You* show it.)

*Exercise A: Section 14

For 1–4, determine if these arguments are valid. Write or abbreviate your translations, supply additional analytic premisses if needed, and use truth-tables or proofs to establish validity.

1. If Joe's mother sent him money and some neckties, then he will go out to dinner. Joe's mother sent him thirty dollars. So Joe will go out to dinner if his mother sent him some neckties.

2. If Sal is a millionaire, then either he has an education or he graduated from college. But if Sal has an education, then he isn't a millionaire. So Sal isn't a millionaire.

3. If Smith owns his own house, then he's paying off a mortgage. Smith has trouble paying his bills if he's putting his daughter through college. Smith does own his own house. So Smith is paying off a mortgage, and has trouble paying his bills.

4. If that animal is a bat and a mammal, then it doesn't have feathers. The animal does have feathers. So the animal isn't a bat.

For 5–8, determine if these sentences are incompatible. Write or abbreviate your translations, supply additional analytic '⊃'-sentences if necessary, and justify your answers.

5. Carol will get a new dress if Ben takes her to the dance. Carol will get a new dress even if Ben doesn't take her to the dance. Carol won't get a new dress unless Ben takes her to the dance, and he won't take her.

6. Either Michele or Megan is Jane's oldest child. Michele is Jane's oldest child if Megan isn't. Megan isn't Jane's oldest child if Michele isn't. Megan is Jane's oldest child.

7. Dick will shave his beard if Elaine asks him to. Elaine won't ask Dick to shave his beard, but he'll shave it anyway.

8. Julie said "No" when David asked her out. If Julie gave a negative answer to David's request, then David is unhappy. But David is happy.

Exercise B: Section 14

Determine if the following arguments are valid. Write or abbreviate your translations, supply additional analytic premises if needed, and show work which justifies your answers.

1. If everyone is obliged to pay taxes on his income, then it is wrong to conceal one's income from the government. But if it is wrong either to conceal one's income or to file a false tax return, there are many businessmen who are guilty of unethical behavior. Since everyone is obliged to pay taxes on his income, many businessmen are guilty of unethical behavior.

2. If this year's red wines from Burgundy are distinguished, then if the red wines from Bordeaux are distinguished, this will be an excellent year for red wine. But the red wines from either Burgundy or Bordeaux are distinguished this year. So this will be an excellent year for red wine.

3. If Don plays football, then if he is on the offense, he isn't likely to receive an athletic scholarship for college. But Don is the quarterback on his high school's football team. So Don isn't likely to receive an athletic scholarship for college.

4. Leonard's father is a captain in the Navy, and he graduated from Annapolis. If Leonard's father is a pacifist, then he isn't a military officer. Leonard's father will be promoted to admiral if he is an Annapolis graduate and not a pacifist. So if Leonard's father lives long enough, he will be promoted to admiral.

5. Kathy will get a good grade on the Philosophy midterm unless she is asked questions about Aristotle's logical writings. Kathy can't answer questions about the logical

works of Aristotle. If Kathy gets a good grade on the midterm, she will get a good grade in the course. If Kathy is asked questions about the logical works of Aristotle on the midterm, she will get a good grade in the course if, and only if, she produces a super term paper. She will produce a super term paper in any case. So Kathy will get a good grade in the Philosophy course.

6. Harry raises corn and soybeans on his farm in Illinois. A farmer in Illinois makes a lot of money only if he raises either corn or soybeans. So Harry makes a lot of money.

7. It isn't true that if Tony asks Sally for a date, she will turn him down. Tony is going to ask Sally for a date. So she won't turn him down.

8. Either lobster or filet mignon is Kevin's favorite food. Lobster is Kevin's favorite food if Kevin likes fish. Kevin likes filet mignon better than any other food. So Kevin doesn't like fish.

Exercise C: Section 14

Determine if the following groups of sentences are incompatible. Write or abbreviate your translations, supply additional analytic sentences if needed, and show work which justifies your answers.

1. Danny won't sell his house unless he is offered his full price. Danny will sell his house if he receives an offer for the full price. Danny will receive an offer for the full price.

2. If Michele speaks any foreign language, then she speaks French. But Michele doesn't speak German if she speaks French. It isn't true that Michele either doesn't speak German or doesn't speak the language of a non-English speaking foreign country.

3. Morgan is either a dentist or an optician. He's a dentist even if he's an optician. But if Morgan is a dentist, then he's neither an optician nor an investor. However, Morgan is an investor if he's a dentist.

4. Don is playing tennis only if Billy promised to cut the grass and Joan promised to make sure that Billy does cut it. If Don isn't playing tennis, then Billy is jogging in Delaware Park. But if Billy promised to cut the grass, then he's not jogging.

5. It isn't true that logic is both a difficult and an important subject. Logic isn't important. But logic is the opposite of easy unless it's important.

6. Allen isn't into both pottery and health foods. Allen is into pottery. But if Allen isn't into health foods, then he doesn't eat any citrus fruit. Allen eats lots of oranges.

7. Either Megan or Sheila has the car. If Megan has a dental appointment, then if she has the car, she will be home in time for dinner. Megan will be home in time for dinner unless she has a dental appointment. It is true neither that Sheila has the car nor that Megan will be home in time for dinner.

8. Roger is a professional tennis player, but he is a professional athlete only if he is a golf pro. Roger gives golf lessons if he's a golf pro. But he doesn't give golf lessons.

11-15 ENTHYMEMES

When a person makes an ordinary-language inference, it is common to leave some things unsaid. For example, if we take this inference at "face value":

If Tom was in the Midwest Saturday, then he missed the Southern California game. Tom was in Chicago Saturday. So he missed the Southern California game.

we must conclude that it isn't valid. For this translation isn't logically valid:

(Tom was in the Midwest Saturday ⊃ He missed the Southern California game)
Tom was in Chicago Saturday. So Tom missed the Southern California game.

There is no analytic sentence we can add to obtain a valid argument. However, it is a well known fact that Chicago (Illinois) is a Midwestern city. To give a fair analysis of the argument that the speaker intended, we should add this premiss:

(Tom was in Chicago Saturday ⊃ Tom was in the Midwest Saturday)

This is not an analytic sentence. But it is reasonable to think that the person making the argument intends for some such sentence to function as a premiss in his argument.

An *enthymeme* is an argument with an unstated premiss. A large number of arguments that people actually make are enthymemes. If we evaluate an enthymeme without supplying its missing premiss, then we are not dealing fairly with the enthymeme. This argument:

If Harry grew up on a dairy farm, then cows don't give milk. So it's not true that Harry both grew up on a dairy farm and is a country boy.

can be translated:

Harry grew up on a dairy farm ⊃ ~ Cows give milk. So ~ (Harry grew up on a dairy farm & Harry is a country boy)

It is easy to show that this translation isn't logically valid. It doesn't seem to be valid either. While it is true that cows give milk, it isn't analytic. The truth of 'Cows give milk' depends (in part) on there being cows, which isn't usually regarded as "given" by the meaning of 'cow.' Since it is true and well known that cows give milk, it is reasonable to supply an additional premiss:

Harry grew up on a dairy farm ⊃ ~ Cows give milk. Cows give milk. So ~ (Harry grew up on a dairy farm & Harry is a country boy)

Since the supplemented argument is (logically) valid, we can regard the original argument as satisfactory. The arguer has provided sufficient support for the conclusion.

In evaluating arguments encountered outside our logic class, we must be ready to supply missing premises when this is appropriate. For it is quite common to encounter arguments with missing premisses—which are intended to support the conclusion. However, we must be sure that the premisses we supply are both true and well known. Any argument at all can be transformed into a valid argument by adding extra premisses.

*Exercise A: Section 15

Try to show that the following arguments are "valid" enthymemes. Translate them into the PC language, supply true and well-known premisses (if needed), and evaluate the resulting inferences.

1. If Paula attends college in the nation's capital, then if Washington, D.C. is the capital of the United States, then Paula attends Georgetown. Paula doesn't go to Georgetown. So Paula doesn't attend college in the nation's capital.

2. If either Jim or Anne doesn't smoke less than a pack of cigarettes a day, then they spend a lot of money on cigarettes. They don't each smoke less than a pack a day. So Jim and Anne spend a lot of money on cigarettes and Jim or Anne has a higher probability than average of contracting lung cancer.

3. Victor has steak more often than hot dogs only if hot dogs aren't cheaper than steak. If Victor doesn't have steak more often than hot dogs, then he doesn't prefer steak to hot dogs. So if Victor prefers steak to hot dogs, then he prefers hot dogs to steak.

4. Either Janet is in Rochester or she is in Detroit and will be gone for the Fourth of July. If Janet will be gone for the Fourth of July, she isn't in Rochester. So Janet is in Detroit if she will be gone for the Fourth of July.

An enthymeme is an argument with one or more unstated premisses. But we can consider what might be called "enthymematic incompatibility." We will say that sentences $p_1, \ldots, p_n$ are enthymematically incompatible if there are true, well-known sentences $q_1, \ldots, q_r$ such that $p_1, \ldots, p_n, q_1, \ldots, q_r$ are incompatible.

*Exercise A: Section 15 (cont.)

Try to show that the following groups of sentences are enthymematically incompatible. Translate the sentences into the PC language, supply true and well-known sentences (if needed), and use truth-tables or proofs to establish incompatibility (if the original sentences *are* enthymematically incompatible).

5. If Tom drinks more whiskey than coffee, then either Tom is sometimes drunk or Tom drinks no coffee at all. It isn't true both that Tom drinks no coffee at all and that whiskey contains alcohol. If whiskey contains alcohol, then Tom drinks more whiskey than coffee but it isn't true that he is sometimes drunk.

6. Either Jim plays tennis every Tuesday and Thursday or else he doesn't play every Tuesday but he runs ten miles every Tuesday. Jim runs ten miles every Tuesday if, and only if, he plays tennis every Thursday. If Jim runs ten miles every Tuesday, then the moon is made of green cheese.

7. Either Tom or Rachel is Anne's oldest child. Tom is Anne's oldest child, if her oldest is a boy. And if Anne's oldest child has dark hair, then Rachel is the oldest. But it is false that Anne's oldest child either isn't a boy or doesn't have dark hair.

8. Most people who are in prison deserve to be there. Most people who deserve to be in prison aren't there. The judicial system is unjust if most people who are in prison don't deserve to be there. The judicial system isn't unjust but it is ineffective. If there are many people who are guilty of crimes, then if the judicial system is ineffective, then the judicial system is unjust.

Exercise B: Section 15

Try to show that the premisses of the following arguments provide adequate support for the conclusions. Translate these arguments into the PC language. Supply analytic ⊃-premisses or well known, true premisses if these are needed. Show work which justifies your answer. (If the arguments are not valid, not even enthymematically, you must show the translations to be logically invalid.)

1. Bill will pass his logic course only if he gets more than 100 points on the final. Bill will get more than 100 points on the final of his logic course only if he understands the material. But Bill doesn't understand the material. So Bill won't pass logic.

2. If Marie either drinks alcoholic beverages or beverages containing caffeine, then if Marie is a Mormon, she isn't a good one. Marie must not be a good Mormon, because she drinks beer, though she doesn't drink beverages containing caffeine.

3. If David is in trouble, he will ask his friends for help. If David isn't in trouble, he won't ask his friends for help. So David is in trouble if, and only if, he will ask his friends for help.

4. If Count Dracula lived in Transylvania, then there are vampires if he really drank the blood of living people. If Bram Stoker based his novel on historical facts, then Count Dracula lived in Transylvania. So if Dracula didn't really drink the blood of living people, then Bram Stoker didn't base his novel on historical facts.

5. Buffalo is in New York, but Albany is the capital of New York State. The capital of New York is in the Mohawk Valley if Albany is the capital of New York. If the capital of New York is the largest city in New York, then New York City isn't the largest city in New York State. So the capital of New York isn't the largest city in the state, but it is located in the Mohawk Valley.

6. David got his degree in Arts and Letters only if he majored in Philosophy or English. David will go on to graduate school if he got his degree in Arts and Letters. Since David majored in Philosophy, he is going to attend graduate school.

7. Bill is a water skier or a scuba diver if, and only if, Bill both is a good swimmer and is athletically inclined. He is a good swimmer. So if Bill skis in Florida or scuba dives, then he is athletically inclined.

8. John must not play golf. For he either plays golf, tennis, and polo, or he plays tennis, but neither golf nor polo. And if John plays tennis, he doesn't play polo.

9. If Jane visits Japan, she will also visit India unless the weather is very hot in India. Jane will fail to visit India only if she is running short of funds and the weather is very hot. So if Jane doesn't visit Japan, she will be running short of funds.

10. If Don doesn't accept the invitation for Sunday dinner, we'll have a normal meal on Sunday. We'll have wine with Sunday dinner if we have a normal meal. And if Don isn't a vegetarian, we'll have a normal meal Sunday even if he does accept the invitation. So if Don eats meat or if he doesn't accept the invitation, we'll have wine with Sunday dinner.

Exercise C: Section 15

Try to show that the following groups of sentences are incompatible. Translate the sentences into the PC language. Supply analytic ⊃-sentences or well-known, true sentences if these are needed. Show work which justifies your answer.

1. If Al supports nuclear energy, then he works for Niagara Mohawk. Al doesn't support nuclear energy if he works for Niagra Mohawk. But if nuclear energy is used to generate electricity, then Al supports nuclear energy.

2. The O'Brians are Irish only if Dick's parents are Irish. The O'Briens aren't Irish even though Dick's parents are Irish.

3. Michele will sleep all Sunday morning unless her father comes to visit. If Michele's father comes to visit, Michele will go to church Sunday morning. If Michele sleeps all Sunday morning, she won't go to church. Michele's father will come to visit, but she will sleep all Sunday morning.

4. Either Kevin plays a sport—he plays tennis—or he plays a sport, but it's golf, or else he doesn't play a sport. Kevin plays tennis only if he doesn't play a sport. Keven plays baseball, not golf.

5. If Karen puts that salt in water, it will dissolve if, and only if, salt is water soluble. Salt is water soluble. That salt won't dissolve. If salt is water soluble, then Karen will put that salt in water.

6. It isn't true that if Larry asks Joan for a date, she will turn him down. Larry will ask Joan for a date, but she will turn him down.

7. Jorge will lose his job or Jorge's employer will lose money, if Jorge drinks too much. Jorge won't lose his job. But Jorge's employer won't lose money if Jorge drinks too much.

8. John will go to college in Bozeman or Helena, and John is a resident of Colorado unless Denver is in New Mexico. John won't go to college in Bozeman if he is a resident of Colorado. Nor will he go to college in Helena if he resides in Colorado.

9. The convention will be held in either Chicago or San Francisco. Don and Jim will both attend the convention if, and only if, it is held in Chicago or San Francisco. Don will attend the convention if, and only if, it is held in Chicago. Jim will attend the convention just in case it is held in San Francisco.

10. Either Jesse likes salmon and hates all fish or else he likes tuna but not salmon. If Jesse likes even one kind of fish, he likes salmon.

Chapter 12

The First-Order Language

12-0 SUMMARY

This chapter presents the syntax and semantics of the First-Order language, a completely artificial language containing names, predicates, connectives, and quantifiers. We learn how to determine whether a sentence in the First-Order language is true or false.

12-1 A PURELY ARTIFICIAL LANGUAGE

Before reading this chapter, you should reread chapter 3, especially sections 1 and 2. That chapter describes a goal of this book (and course): to gain a better understanding of a large class of ordinary English sentences about individuals. By itself, the PC language does not contribute to this goal, for the PC language helps us get a better understanding of compound sentences. But the *First-Order language* is based on the PC language, and provides the understanding we are looking for.

The First-Order language contains the same propositional connectives as the PC language: $\sim$, v, &, $\supset$, $\equiv$. It also contains *singular terms* and *predicates* for constructing simple sentences. A singular term is an expression used to designate a single individual. Proper names are singular terms. And *definite descriptions* such as 'the president of the United States' and 'the positive square root of 4' are singular terms. Still other expressions, like 'George Washington's mother,' are singular terms.

In the First-Order language, the following will be used as singular terms: a, b, c, d, a_1, b_1, . . . These expressions are *individual constants*. An individual constant which replaces an English singular term has the same significance (if any) as the English expression. (There is a controversy among logicians and other students of language as to whether proper names have meanings.) In the First-Order language, only singular terms which label real individuals are allowed. This restriction enables us to keep the First-Order language simpler and more perspicuous than it would be otherwise.

Singular terms (individual constants) are used to pick out individuals for the rest of the sentence to say something about. *Predicates* are used to characterize these individuals. In the First-Order language, the predicates will be capital letters with numerical superscripts. (A superscript is a symbol higher than the other symbols on the same line, as '2' is higher in '5^2.') We also use the symbol ' $=$ ' as a predicate. Suppose we want to say that Lassie is a dog. We can introduce 'a' as a name for Lassie, but we need a predicate if we are to characterize Lassie as a dog. Let 'D^1' be used to say that something is a dog. Then '$D^1(a)$' is read "Lassie is a dog." In the First-Order language, predicates other than ' $=$ ' are written to the left of parentheses enclosing singular terms.

The numerical superscript indicates how many places the predicate has. So 'D^1' is a one-place predicate: it is combined with one individual constant at a time. A two-place predicate applies to pairs of individuals. Let 'b' name Napoleon and 'c' name Josephine. And let 'M^2' mean that one individual was married to the second. Then '$M^2(b, c)$' is read "Napoleon was married to Josephine." With a predicate having more than one place, commas separate names in the different places. Using the predicate 'M^2,' we can say both '$M^2(b, c)$' and '$M^2(c, b)$.' These two First-Order sentences are equivalent. Not all two-place predicates are like this. Suppose 'B^2' means that the first individual is bigger than the second. Let 'd_1' name New York City and 'd_2' name Chicago. Then the sentence '$B^2(d_1, d_2)$' is true, but '$B^2(d_2, d_1)$' isn't. (But this is true: $\sim B^2(d_2, d_1)$.)

When we explain a predicate by using an English expression, the predicate has the same meaning as the English expression. And when we read a First-Order sentence like '$M^2(b, c)$,' we normally use the corresponding English expressions: Napoleon was married to Josephine. The usefulness of the First-Order language for helping us understand English comes at the written level. There is no need to adopt special locutions for reading First-Order expressions.

The First-Order language also contains three-place predicates. Let 'G^3' mean that the first individual gave the second to the third. Let 'a' name Sally, 'b' name Sally's logic book, and 'c' name Megan. Then '$G^3(a, b, c)$' is: Sally gave her logic book to Megan. (In this example, we have changed the objects denoted by 'a,' 'b,' 'c' from the examples above. In using the First-Order language, the assignments we make to nonlogical expressions will not have much permanence.) 'G^3' is a three-place predicate. For any number n, we can introduce n-place predicates. In practice, we shall not have much use for predicates with more than three places.

The numerical superscript reveals how many places are associated with the predicate. These superscripts allow us to use 'B^2' for *bigger* and 'B^3' to say that one thing is between two others. Since 'B^2' is clearly different from 'B^3,' there is no danger of ambiguity in using 'B' for both predicates. However, when a predicate is combined with singular terms, we can tell by counting singular terms how many places the predicate has. As an abbreviation, we will often omit superscripts from predicates in sentences. Using the vocabularly above, we can say that Napoleon was married to Josephine by writing '$M(b, c)$.'

Predicates in the First-Order language are used to translate English verbs or phrases which contain verbs. Verbs in English have tenses. One verb can occur (different times) with different tenses. In these sentences:

(1) Mary sees John.

(2) Mary saw John.

the verb is the same—it is the verb *to see*. But in (1) this verb occurs in the present tense, while it is past tense in (2). In the First-Order language, one predicate cannot have different tenses. If we use 'a' for Mary and 'b' for John, we can use 'S^1' for *sees*, so that '$S(a, b)$' is *Mary sees John*. But then we cannot use 'S^1' to translate sentences (2). We need a different predicate for the past tense. We might use 'T^1' for *saw*, and translate (2) as '$T(a, b)$.' We cannot tell from looking at their translations that the two sentences contain the same verb; the translations do not contain the same predicate.

The equals sign which is a predicate of the First-Order language is unlike other predicates in two respects: (i) It does not officially have a numerical superscript—it is always understood to be two-place. (ii) It is written between two individual constants rather than to their left, as in: ($a = b$). In the First-Order language, the symbol ' = ' is NEVER read "equals." For us, ' = ' will be the sign of *identity*. It is read "is the same individual as," "is the same as," or (sometimes) even "is." If 'a' names Albany and 'b' translates 'the capital of New York State,' then '($a = b$)' is "Albany is the capital of New York State."

In reading sentences that contain ' = ,' we use an English expression in the present tense to read ' = .' But the English expression must be understood in a timeless sense. Let 'c' name George Washington, and let 'd' mean *the first president of the United States*. Then '($c = d$)' comes out "George Washington is the first president of the United States." This sentence is true because George Washington is (timelessly) the first president of the United States. If it is important to indicate time or tense with an identity sentence, this must be made part of the meaning of one of the singular terms.

*Exercise: Section 1

Let 'a' name 0, 'b' name 1, and 'c' name 2. Let 'E^1' mean *is an even number*. Let 'L^2' mean that the first individual is a number less than the second individual (which is also a number). And let 'P^3' mean that the product of the first two numbers is the third number. Determine which of the following sentences are true.

  1. $[E(c) \mathbin{\&} \sim E(b)]$

  2. $(b = c)$

  3. $[L(a, b) \lor L(a, c)]$

  4. $[L(a, a) \supset L(a, c)]$

  5. $[L(c, b) \supset L(b, a)]$

  6. $P(a, a, a)$

  7. $[P(a, b, b) \supset (a = b)]$

  8. $[P(a, c, a) \supset (a = c)]$

  9. $[L(a, a) \lor L(b, b)]$

  10. $\{E(b) \equiv [E(a) \mathbin{\&} E(c)]\}$

12-2   THE TRUTH CONDITIONS OF ATOMIC SENTENCES

The simple sentences of the First-Order language are also called *atomic* sentences. If ϕ (this is a lower case Greek phi) is an n-place predicate other than ' = ,' and $\alpha_1, \ldots, \alpha_n$ are individual constants, then $\phi(\alpha_1, \ldots, \alpha_n)$ is an *atomic sentence*. And if α_1, α_2 are individual constants, then $(\alpha_1 = \alpha_2)$ is an *atomic sentence* (and so are $[\alpha_1 = \alpha_2]$ and $\{\alpha_1 = \alpha_2\}$. There are no other atomic sentences. (In this definition, the α_i's are not required to be distinct—so that '$F^3(a, b, a)$' and '($a = a$)' are atomic sentences.)

In the First-Order language, each singular term must denote exactly one individual. (Recall that we don't allow singular terms that fail to denote genuine individuals; and, of course, an expression can't be an unambiguous singular term if it denotes more than one individual.) Predicates also denote. A one-place predicate denotes all the individuals of which it can be truly predicated. If 'R^1' means (*is*) *red*, then 'R^1' denotes all red things. A one-place predicate might not denote any individuals. Suppose 'S^1' means *is a square circle*. There are no square circles, so 'S^1' denotes no individuals. A one-place predicate denotes zero or more individuals. (In some treatments, one-place predicates denote sets of individuals rather than individuals, but this difference makes no difference to the truth and falsity of sentences in the First-Order language, except that we are also allowing predicates that denote individuals too numerous to be members of a single set.) If ϕ is a one-place predicate and α is an individual constant, then $\phi(\alpha)$ is true just in case the individual denoted by α is among the individuals denoted by ϕ. (So no matter what individual is denoted by 'a,' the sentence '$S^1(a)$' will be false.)

It is easy to understand how a one-place predicate denotes zero or more individuals. But suppose 'O^2' means that the first individual is older than the second. The predicate 'O^2' will denote *pairs* of individuals. But it denotes these pairs in a certain order: it denotes *ordered* pairs of individuals. So let 'a' name London and 'c' name Chicago. London *is* older than Chicago, so '$O(a, c)$' is true. The ordered pair which consists of London first and Chicago second is denoted by 'O^2.'

Mathematicians have a convention for writing about ordered pairs that we will adopt. To designate a pair like the pair London first and Chicago second, they write '$<$ London, Chicago $>$.' The angular parentheses indicate that we are denoting the ordered pair of the two objects. Let ϕ be a two-place predicate and let α_1, α_2 be individual constants that denote γ (gamma) and δ (delta), respectively. Then $\phi(\alpha_1, \alpha_2)$ is true if, and only if, $< \gamma, \delta >$ is among the pairs denoted by ϕ.

The capital-letter predicates are not specifically logical symbols, though they belong to our artificial logical language. But the two-place predicate ' $=$ ' is a logical symbol. With nonlogical symbols, we consider the *kind* of meanings they have, and their contributions to the truth conditions of sentences. With logical symbols, we must give their meanings. Let α_1, α_2 be individual constants which denote γ, δ respectively. Then $(\alpha_1 = \alpha_2)$ is true if, and only if, γ is the same individual as δ. So the predicate ' $=$ ' denotes those ordered pairs $< \beta_1, \beta_2 >$ in which β_1 is the same individual as β_2. Another way to say the same thing is this: ' $=$ ' denotes ordered pairs $< \beta, \beta >$. (This sentence brings out the difference between a plain pair of individuals and an ordered pair. To have a plain pair of things, we need two things. But for an ordered pair, one thing is enough. For we can "take" it once as first member, and again as second member.)

If a two-place predicate denotes individuals, in order, two at a time, then a three-place predicate will denote individuals, in order, three at a time. A three-place predicate denotes *ordered triples* of individuals. In general, an n-place predicate will denote zero or more *ordered n-tuples* of individuals.

*Exercise: Section 2

Let 'a' denote 1, 'b' denote 2, and 'c' denote 0. Let

F^1 denote 0, 2, 4

G^1 denote 2

H^1 denote 3, 1

L^2 denote $< 0, 1 >$, $< 0, 2 >$, $< 1, 2 >$

M^2 denote $< 0, 0 >$, $< 1, 1 >$, $< 2, 2 >$, $< 0, 1 >$, $< 0, 2 >$, $< 1, 2 >$.

A^3 denote $< 0, 1, 1 >$, $< 0, 2, 2 >$, $< 0, 0, 0, >$, $< 1, 0, 1 >$, $< 2, 0, 2 >$, $< 1, 1, 2 >$, $< 1, 2, 3 >$, $< 2, 1, 3 >$

Determine which of the following sentences are true.

1. $F(a)$

2. $[F(a) \text{ v } F(c)]$

3. $L(a, c)$

4. $[L(a, b) \supset M(a, b)]$

5. $[A(c, c, c) \equiv A(c, b, b)]$

6. $\{[H(a) \& G(b)] \text{ v } A(a, a, a)\}$

7. $\{A(b, c, a) \supset [M(b, a) \& M(c, a)]\}$

8. $\sim\{[G(b) \text{ v } H(a)] \text{ v } F(c)\}$

9. $[A(b, b, b) \supset (b = c)]$

10. $\{[G(a) \& \sim G(c)] \supset \sim (a = c)\}$

12-3 NEW VARIETIES OF VARIABLES

In the First-Order language, propositional variables will still be used to replace whole sentences. And we will use the same propositional variables as before: $p, q, r, s, p_1, \ldots$ If 'a' names Paris and 'F^1' means *is in France*, then '$[F(a) \text{ v } \sim F(a)]$' is a sentence of the First-Order language. This sentence is symbolized by the formula '$p \text{ v } \sim p$.' The formula '$p \text{ v } \sim p$' does not show everything that is logically important about the sentence '$F(a) \text{ v } \sim F(a)$.' But the formula reveals enough so that we can tell that the sentence is logically true. Additional information cannot "cancel" this knowledge.

But we want other kinds of variables besides propositional variables. *Predicate variables* will replace predicates. For predicate variables, we will use lower case 'f,' 'g,' and 'h' with numerical superscripts. So 'f^1' might replace 'F^1.' In case we need more n-place predicate variables than 'f^n,' 'g^n,' 'h^n,' we will manufacture more by adding numerical subscripts: $f_1^n, g_1^n, h_1^n, f_2^n, \ldots$ Numerical superscripts indicate the number of places, while numerical subscripts serve only to distinguish one variable from another. (We can often omit the superscripts from predicate variables. In '$f(a, b, c)$,' it is clear that the predicate variable must be 'f^3.')

Individual variables will replace singular terms. For individual variables, we use these symbols: $x, y, z, x_1, \ldots$ Now the sentence '$F(a \text{ v } \sim F(a)$' can be symbolized by a new kind of formula: $g(x) \text{ v } \sim g(x)$. Both '$p \text{ v } \sim p$' and '$g(x) \text{ v } \sim g(x)$' symbolize the same sentence, but the second formula reveals more about the sentence's logical form than the first formula does. For the First-Order language, the expression 'formula' will be taken broadly so that sentences are counted as formulas. But a pure formula does not contain nonlogical expressions. The expression '$F(a) \text{ v } \sim F(a)$' is both a sentence and a formula. But '$p \text{ v } \sim p$' and '$g(x)$' are pure formulas. We also have mixed formulas, as '$p \text{ v } \sim F(a)$,' '$F(x) \text{ v } \sim F(x)$,' and '$g(a) \text{ v } \sim g(a)$.'

In the PC language, we treated propositional variables as place-holders for sentences.

If we started with a pure formula and replaced the variables by sentences, the resulting sentence would have the logical form displayed by the formula. A truth-table gave the results of replacing variables by combinations of true and false sentences.

Now we will regard a variable as a significant expression, whose significance is *to have a range of values*. The range of values for a propositional variable consists of truth and falsity. A formula has a certain truth-value when values are *assigned* to its variables. Each row in a truth-table shows the value of a formula for one *assignment* of values to its variables.

Each kind of variable has a different kind of value in its range. Truth and falsity are the values assigned to propositional variables. Since individual constants denote individuals, these same individuals should constitute the values assigned to individual variables. Similarly, a predicate variable will have collections of individuals or collections of n-tuples of individuals for values. Because propositional variables only take two values, truth-tables are practical when all variables are propositional variables. If we consider all the individuals we might deal with, there are an infinite number. There are also an infinite number of values to be assigned to predicate variables. We cannot use tables (or matrices) for dealing with individual and predicate variables.

All variables *take*, or are assigned, values of one sort or another. And a formula will have some value when its variables are assigned values. The formula '$p \supset (q \lor r)$' has value truth (or t) when 'p' is assigned f, 'q' is assigned f, and 'r' is assigned t. It has value f when 'p' is assigned t and both 'q' and 'r' are assigned f. The formula '$[(x = y) \& f(x)] \supset f(y)$' has value t when '$x$' is assigned 2, '$y$' is assigned 4, and '$f^1$' is assigned the collection of all even numbers.

*Exercise: Section 3

Consider this First-Order formula: $\{f(x, y) \supset [f(y, z) \supset f(x, z)]\}$ Determine what values it has for the assignments described below.

1. Let 'f^2' be assigned: $< 1, 1 >, < 2, 2 >, < 3, 3 >, < 1, 2 >, < 1, 3 >, < 2, 3 >$. Let '$x$' be assigned 1, '$y$' be assigned 1, and '$z$' be assigned 3.

2. Let 'f^2' be assigned: $< 1, 2 >, < 2, 1 >, < 1, 3 >, < 3, 1 >, < 2, 3 >, < 3, 2 >$. Let '$x$' be assigned 2, '$y$' be assigned 3, and '$z$' be assigned 2.

3. Let 'f^2' be assigned: $< 0, 0 >$. Let 'x,' 'y,' and 'z' be assigned 0.

4. Let 'f^2' be assigned the collection containing every pair of positive integers $< n, n + 1 >$. Let 'x' be assigned 12, 'y' be assigned 13, and 'z' be assigned 14.

5. Let 'f^2' be assigned the same value as in problem 4. Let 'x' be assigned 2, 'y' be assigned 4, and 'z' be assigned 6.

12-4 QUANTIFIERS

So far we can construct complicated sentences about specific individuals. But the First-Order language does not possess the resources for making general statements. We cannot say that all persons are mortal, or that every even number is divisible by two.

Suppose 'F^1' means *is a French person* and 'E^1' means *is a European*. Consider the formula '$F(x) \supset E(x)$.' Different individuals can be assigned as value to 'x.' If we choose an individual who is a French person, that individual will also be a European. Since the antecedent and consequent will be true, the whole formula will be true. If we choose an individual which is not a French person, the antecedent will be false. No matter what the value of the consequent is, the whole formula will have value t. For every value of 'x,' the formula has value t. If we add an expression to indicate that a formula is invariably true, we will have the capacity to make general statements. Then we can say that for *every-thing*, if it is a French person, it is (also) a European. This would also be a statement about every French person. It would say that everything which is a French person is a European.

The symbol '$\forall$' is the *universal quantifier*. It can be combined with an individual variable α to form a *quantified phrase* $(\forall\alpha)$. So '$(\forall x)$,' '$(\forall y)$,' '$(\forall z)$' are quantified phrases. Only round parentheses will be used to construct quantified phrases. (In many treatments, the whole expression '$(\forall x)$' is called a universal quantifier. But that terminology usually provides no name for the symbol '$\forall$.') A universally quantified phrase $(\forall\alpha)$ is prefixed to formulas containing α. If we consider the example above, we can use '$(\forall x)$' to obtain: $(\forall x)[F(x)\supset E(x)]$. (It was necessary to supply the brackets—or some other parentheses—around '$F(x)\supset E(x)$.' Otherwise the quantified phrase would not apply to the whole formula.) The universal quantifier is used to indicate that a formula has value t for every value of the quantified individual variable. The sentence '$(\forall x)[F(x)\supset E(x)]$' might be read (1) For everything x, if x is a French person, then x is a European; (2) For every individual x, if x is a French person, then x is a European; or, simply, (3) For every x, if x is a French person, then x is a European. The third reading is probably the most common.

In many logic books the symbol '$\forall$' is not used. Instead an expression like '(x)' is used as a universally quantified phrase. So instead of a sentence '$(\forall x)[F(x) \supset E(x)]$,' these books would have '$(x)[F(x)\supset E(x)]$.' But the meaning of the two sentences is the same.

Consider this sentence: $(\forall z)[F(z) \lor E(z)]$. This is: For every z, either z is a French person or z is a European. I.e., everything is either a French person or a European. This sentence is clearly false. A sentence $(\forall\alpha)[\ldots]$ is true if the formula $[\ldots]$ has value t for every value of α. The sentence is false if there is even one value of α for which $[\ldots]$ has value f.

There is another quantifier in the First-Order language. The symbol '$\exists$' is the *existential* quantifier, or the *particular* quantifier. A quantified phrase $(\exists\alpha)$ is used to indicate that a formula has value t for at least one value of α. So while the sentence '$(\forall y)[F(y) \lor E(y)]$' is false, the following is true: $(\exists y)[F(y) \lor E(y)]$. This sentence might be read: (1) For some individual y, either y is a French person or y is a European; (2) There is (there exists) an individual y such that either y is a French person or y is a European; or (3) There is a y such that either y is a French person or y is a European. The third reading is the most common.

A sentence $(\exists\alpha)[\ldots]$ is true if the formula $[\ldots]$ is true for at least one value of α. Such a sentence is false if $[\ldots]$ is false for every value of α.

Let us consider some more examples, using the predicates 'F^1' and 'E^1.' The sentence '$(\forall z)[F(z)\supset E(z)]$' is true, but the following sentence isn't: $(\forall z)[E(z)\supset F(z)]$. This last sentence says that for everything, if it is a European, then it is a French person. To show that this is false, it is sufficient to find a European who isn't a French person. Any such European will do. Suppose we choose the (present) mayor of Rome (Italy) as the value of 'z.' Then '$E(z)$' has value t, but '$F(z)$' has a value f. Since there is (at least) one value of 'z' for which '$[E(z)\supset F(z)]$' has value f, the sentence '$(\forall z)[E(z)\supset F(z)]$' is false (has value f). The sentence '$(\exists z)[E(z) \supset F(z)]$' is true if there is a value of 'z' for which '$[E(z) \supset F(z)]$' is true. It is easy to find such a value. For (i) any value of 'z' which makes '$E(z)$' false will make the formula true (the number two is such a value), and (ii) any value of 'z' which makes '$F(z)$' true will make '$[E(z) \supset F(z)]$' true (the current prime minister of France is such a value).

Since the number two is sufficient to make the sentence '$(\exists z)[E(z) \supset F(z)]$' true, this sentence must not mean that some European is a French person. To make it true that some European is a French person, we must have an individual who is both French and European. The sentence '$(\exists x)[E(x) \mathrel{\&} F(x)]$' is the one we would use to say that some European is a French person.

In order to talk carefully about quantifiers and quantified phrases, we need technical terminology. In dealing with the PC language, we spoke of the *scope* of the logical connectives. Quantifiers also have scope. In a formula $(\forall \alpha)[\ldots]$, the part $[\ldots]$ is the *scope* of the universal quantifier. And [———] is the *scope* of '$\exists$' in $(\exists \alpha)[$———$]$. As well as speaking of the scope of quantifiers, we will also speak of the scope of quantified phrases. So $[\ldots]$ is the scope of $(\forall \alpha)$ in $(\forall \alpha)[\ldots]$. (Strictly speaking, it is occurrences of a quantifier or quantified phrase which have scope.)

If A is a formula containing occurrences of individual variable α, and A contains no occurrences of the quantified phrases $(\forall \alpha)$ and $(\exists \alpha)$, then the occurrences of α in A are *free* occurrences. If A contains free occurrences of individual variable α, and B is a formula, then the free occurrences of α in A are also *free* occurrences of α in $\sim A$, $(A \mathrel{\&} B)$, $(B \mathrel{\&} A)$, $(A \vee B)$, $(B \vee A)$, $(A \supset B)$, $(B \supset A)$, $(A \equiv B)$, and $(B \equiv A)$. If α and β are distinct individual variables, and A contains free occurrences of both α, β, then the free occurrences of α in A are also *free* occurrences of α in $(\forall \beta)A$, $(\exists \beta)A$.

A free occurrence of an individual variable is one that is not "covered" by a quantifier. The opposite of free is *bound*. If α is an individual variable, the occurrences of α in the quantified phrases $(\forall \alpha)$ and $(\exists \alpha)$ are *bound* occurrences. If α is an individual variable which occurs free in a formula A, the free occurrences of α in A are *bound* occurrences of α in $(\forall \alpha)A$ and $(\exists \alpha)A$. These bound occurrences are *bound by* the (occurrence of the) quantifier; the quantifier *binds* the occurrences of the variables. (The occurrence of α in $(\forall \alpha)$ or $(\exists \alpha)$ is also bound by the quantifier.) Any bound occurrences of α in A are also *bound* occurrences of α in the formulas $\sim A$, $(A \mathrel{\&} B)$, $(B \mathrel{\&} A)$, $(A \vee B)$, $(B \vee A)$, $(A \supset B)$, $(B \supset A)$, $(A \equiv B)$, and $(B \equiv A)$, $(\forall \beta)A$, $(\exists \beta)A$.

The sentence '$(\forall x)[F(x) \mathrel{\&} E(x)]$' has no free occurrences of individual variables. Each occurrence of 'x' is bound by the occurrence of '$\forall$.' In the formula '$(\exists x)[F(x) \mathrel{\&} E(y)]$,' the occurrences of '$x$' are bound occurrences, but the occurrence of 'y' is free. This formula:

$$(\exists x)F(x) \mathrel{\&} E(x)$$

has both bound and free occurrences of the same variable. The first two occurrences of 'x' are bound by the existential quantifier. The third occurrence of 'x' (in '$E(x)$') is not within the scope of the existential quantifier. The third occurrence of 'x' is free. All occurrences of individual variables are bound in this formula:

$$(\exists y)F(y) \mathrel{\&} (\exists y)E(y).$$

Although the distinction between bound and free occurrences of variables applies to all variables, not just to individual variables, we will not employ quantifiers for propositional variables and predicate variables. All occurrences of propositional and predicate variables are free occurrences.

*Exercise: Section 4

For 1–6, let 'D^1' mean that an individual is a dog, 'C^1' mean that an individual is a cat, and 'A^1' mean that an individual is an animal. Determine which of the following sentences are true.

1. $(\forall y)[D(y) \supset \sim C(y)]$

2. $(\exists z)D(z) \supset (\forall y)C(y)$

3. $(\forall z)\{[C(z) \;\&\; D(z)] \supset \sim A(z)\}$

4. $(\forall x)\{[C(x) \vee D(x)] \supset A(x)\}$

5. $(\exists y)\,[C(y) \;\&\; D(y)] \supset (\forall x)A(x)$

6. $(\exists y)A(y) \;\&\; [(\exists y)D(y) \;\&\; (\exists y)C(y)]$

For 7–12, in the formulas below, circle the free occurrence of individual variables. Draw lines beneath the formulas to connect quantifiers to the occurrences of individual variables which they bind.

7. $f(x) \supset (\exists x)f(x, x)$

8. $F(a) \supset [G(x, a) \vee G(a, x)]$

9. $(\forall x)[F(x) \supset [p \vee F(y)]]$

10. $[f(x) \;\&\; (\exists x)g(x)] \vee (\forall y)[f(y) \equiv g(x)]$

11. $(\forall x)(\exists y)[x = y]$

12. $(\forall x)[F(x) \vee (\exists x)G(x)]$

12-5 MULTIPLE QUANTIFICATION

The expressive power of the First-Order language is much greater than that of either the Categorical language or the Extended Categorical language (considered earlier in this book); it approaches the power of English. However, the increased expressive power brings complications with it.

Although it isn't difficult to understand sentences where no quantifier occurs within the scope of another, what can we make of a sentence like this one:

$(\forall x)(\exists y)[E(x) \supset F(y)]$?

To understand this, we must remove the quantifiers one at a time. The sentence is true if the formula '$(\exists y)[E(x) \supset F(y)]$' is true for every value of 'x.' Given this particular formula, the only difference that matters between different values of 'x' is that some values make '$E(x)$' true and other values make it false. Suppose we first consider a value which makes it true. Let 'x' be assigned the (present) mayor of Rome as value. Now we are considering '$(\exists y)[E(\text{the mayor of Rome}) \supset F(y)]$.' This is true if there is a value of 'y' which satisfies '$[E(\text{the mayor of Rome}) \supset F(y)]$.' But any value of '$y$' for which '$F(y)$' is true will do—there are many such values. So '$(\exists y)[E(\text{the mayor of Rome}) \supset F(y)]$' is true. Now consider some value of 'x' for which '$E(x)$' is false. Assign the (present) mayor of Chicago as value of 'x.' This leaves us with '$(\exists y)[E(\text{the mayor of Chicago}) \supset F(y)]$.' But this is true if '$[E(\text{the mayor of Chicago}) \supset F(y)]$' is true for some value of 'y.' Any value of 'y' will do, for the antecedent is false. So '$(\exists y)[E(\text{the mayor of Chicago}) \supset F(y)]$' is true. No matter what we choose for 'x,' the formula '$(\exists y)[E(x) \supset F(y)]$' will have value t. So the sentence '$(\forall x)(\exists y)[E(x) \supset F(y)]$' is true.

Suppose we now consider the sentence '$(\forall x)(\forall y)[E(x) \supset F(y)]$.' This is true if '$(\forall y)[E(x) \supset F(y)]$' is true for every value of 'x.' If we proceed as before, we can consider '$(\forall y)[E(\text{the mayor of Rome}) \supset F(y)]$.' This is true if '$[E(\text{the mayor of Rome}) \supset F(y)]$' is true for every value of 'y.' But let 'y' be assigned the number two. It is false that two is a French person. So '$[E(\text{the mayor of Rome}) \supset F(y)]$' is false when two is assigned to 'y.' But then '$(\forall y)[E(\text{the mayor of Rome}) \supset F(y)]$' is false—which means that $(\forall x)(\forall y)[E(x) \supset F(y)]$' is false.

*Exercise: Section 5

Let 'M^2' mean that the first individual is married to the second. Let 'H^2' mean that the first individual is husband to the second. Let 'F^1' mean that the individual is a female human, and 'M^1' mean *is a male human*. Determine which of the following sentences are true.

1. $(\forall x)(\forall y)[H(x, y) \supset H(y, x)]$

2. $(\forall x)(\forall y)[H(x, y) \supset M(x, y)]$

3. $(\forall x)(\forall y)[[M(x, y) \& F(x)] \supset M(y)]$

4. $(\forall x)[(\exists y)[M(y, x) \& M(y)] \supset F(x)]$

5. $(\forall x)(\exists y)[F(x) \supset [M(y) \& \sim M(x, y)]]$

6. $(\forall x)]M(x) \supset (\exists y)[F(y) \& H(x, y)]]$

7. $(\exists x)[M(x) \& (\forall y)[H(x, y) \supset F(y)]]$

8. $(\exists x)(\forall y)[M(x) \supset F(y)]$

12-6   RESTRICTED DOMAINS

So far, we have considered every individual there is when we assign values to individual variables. We have been taking the universal quantifier to really mean *everything*, and the existential quantifier to really mean *something*. When the quantifiers are understood in this way, they are given the *unrestricted interpretation*.

There are some situations in which we restrict our attention to a limited class of things. Perhaps we are considering just people, or numbers, or positive integers. In such a case, the class we are considering is a *universe of discourse*. (For the purposes of a certain discussion, the limited class counts as the universe.) In connection with the First-Order language, a universe of discourse is a *domain of interpretation*. A *restricted* interpretation of the quantifiers limits the values to be denoted by individual constants and the values to be assigned to individual variables to the individuals in the limited class. With a restricted interpretation, the universal quantifier no longer means *really everything*; it now means *everything in the selected domain*. And the existential quantifier means *something in the selected domain*.

Let '$E(x)$' mean x *is an even integer*, and '$O(x)$' mean x *is an odd integer*. The sentence '$(\forall x)[E(x) \lor O(x)]$' is false, if we give the quantifiers the unrestricted interpretation. For the sentence says that everything is either an even integer or an odd integer. Since neither you nor I are integers of any kind, we can use ourselves as values of '*x*' for which '[*E*(*x*) v *O*(*x*)]' is false. But if we restrict our domain of interpretation to the positive integers, the sentence will be true. For then it says that every positive integer is even or odd. (Given the unrestricted interpretation, 'O^1' doesn't denote the same things as it does on this restricted interpretation. On the restricted interpretation described above, 'O^1' denotes only odd integers in the domain of interpretation—these are just the odd positive integers. We can see from this that a restricted interpretation of the quantifiers is really a restricted interpretation of the whole First-Order language.)

In studying mathematics, it is often convenient to deal with a limited domain of interpretation. We don't very often want to consider numbers and, say, people together. Outside of a mathematics context it is often difficult to choose an appropriate restricted domain. In what follows, quantifiers will be given the unrestricted interpretation·unless an explicit restriction is stated.

*Exercise: Section 6

Let the domain of interpretation be restricted to: 1, 2, 3, 4, 5, 6, 7, 8, 9, 10. Let

O^1 denote 1, 3, 5, 7, 9

E^1 denote 2, 4, 6, 8, 10

L^2 denote every ordered pair of individuals in the domain in which the first individual is · less than or equal to the second.

A^3 denote every ordered triple of individuals in the domain such that the sum of the first two individuals is the third.

Determine which of the following sentences are true.

1. $(\forall x)[E(x) \supset (\exists y)[O(y) \& L(y, x)]]$

2. $(\forall x)[O(x) \supset \sim(\exists z)L(x, z)]$

3. $(\forall x)(\exists y)L(x, y)$

4. $(\exists x)(\exists y) \sim (\exists z)A(x, y, z)$

5. $(\forall x)(\exists y)[\sim(x = y) \& L(x, y)]$

6. $(\forall x)(\exists y)[\sim(x = y) \supset L(x, y)]$

7. $(\forall x)(\forall y)(\forall z)[A(z, y, x) \supset L(z, x)]$

8. $(\forall x)(\forall z)[[E(z) \& E(x)] \supset (\exists y)[E(y) \& A(z, x, y)]]$

12-7 A MORE CAREFUL DESCRIPTION OF THE FIRST-ORDER LANGUAGE

So far the syntax and semantics of the First-Order language have been developed piecemeal. Now it is appropriate to give comprehensive definitions of some important expressions.

The *well-formed formulas* (*wffs*) of the First-Order language are the formulas constructed properly. 'Well-formed formula' is defined:

(1) A propositional variable is an *atomic wff*.

(2) If ϕ is an *n*-place predicate other than ' = ,' or an *n*-place predicate variable, and $\alpha_1, \ldots, \alpha_n$ are individual expressions (either constants or variables), then $\phi(\alpha_1, \ldots, \alpha_n)$ is an *atomic wff*. (In these atomic wffs, only round parentheses are used.)

(3) If α_1, α_2 are individual expressions, then $(\alpha_1 = \alpha_2)$ is an *atomic wff*. (In these wffs, the round parentheses may be replaced by brackets or braces.)

(4) If A, B are wffs, then so are $\sim A$, $(A \vee B)$, $(A \& B)$, $(A \supset B)$, $(A \equiv B)$. (In these wffs, the round parentheses may be replaced by brackets or braces.)

(5) If A is a wff in which individual variable α occurs free, then $(\forall\alpha)A$ and $(\exists\alpha)A$ are *wffs*. (Only round parentheses are used to form quantified phrases.)

(6) All wffs are obtained by (1) – (5).

A *sentence* of the First-Order language is a wff that has no free occurrences of variables.

A *pure* wff is a wff that contains no individual constants and no predicates other than ' = .'

Let A be a pure wff and let A^* be a sentence of the First-Order language. Then A *symbolizes* A^* iff (1a) each occurrence of an *n*-place predicate variable in A is replaced by an *n*-place predicate in A^*, (1b) occurrences of the same predicate variable are replaced by occurrences of the same predicate, and occurrences of distinct predicate variables are replaced by occurrences of distinct predicates, (2a) each free occurrence of an individual variable in A is replaced by an individual constant in A^*, (2b) free occurrences of the same individual variable in A are replaced by occurrences of the same individual constant in A^* and free occurrences of distinct individual variables in A are replaced by occurrences of distinct individual constants, (3a) each occurrence of a propositional variable in A is replaced by a sentence in A^*, (3b) occurrences of the same propositional variable in A are replaced by occurrences of the same sentence in A^* and occurrences of distinct propositional variables in A are replaced by occurrences of distinct sentences in A^*.

This definition allows one sentence to be symbolized by different kinds of formulas. For example, the sentencé '$[H(a) \vee \sim H(a)]$' is symbolized by (1) $[f(x) \vee \sim f(x)]$, (2) $(p \vee \sim p)$, (3) $[p \vee \sim f(x)]$, (4) $[f(x) \vee \sim p]$. Both formulas (1) and (2) reveal important features of the sentence. Formulas (3) and (4) are less useful.

As well as having one formula symbolize a sentence, we want to allow for several formulas jointly symbolizing several sentences. Let $A_1, \ldots, A_n$ be pure wffs and let $A_1^*, \ldots, A_n^*$ be sentences of the First-Order language. Then $A_1, \ldots, A_n$ *jointly symbolize* $A_1^*, \ldots, A_n^*$ (in that order) iff (1) each A_i symbolizes A_i^*, (2) each free occurrence of any variable in $A_1, \ldots, A_n$ is replaced by the same expression in $A_1^*, \ldots, A_n^*$ and free occurrences of distinct variables in $A_1, \ldots, A_n$ are replaced by occurrences of distinct expressions in $A_1^*, \ldots, A_n^*$.

Let $A_1, \ldots, A_n \, / \, B$ be a formula sequence in which every member is a pure wff. And let $A_1^*, \ldots, A_n^* \, / \, B^*$ be an argument sequence (so that each member is a sentence). The formula sequence *symbolizes* the argument sequence iff the formulas $A_1, \ldots, A_n, B$ jointly symbolize the sentences $A_1^*, \ldots, A_n^*, B^*$.

A description of the semantics of the First-Order language should cover all formulas of the language, not just the sentences. But a formula that contains free occurrences of variables isn't simply true or false. Instead it has value truth or falsity for a certain assignment of values to its free variables. And if it has value t for one assignment, it might have value f for some other. Suppose A is a formula. This formula might contain different sorts of variables; but different kinds of variables are assigned different kinds of values. In speaking about the value of a formula A for an assignment, we will consider only *appropriate* assignments of values to the variables occurring free in A. These assign the right kinds of values to the variables in A.

A statement of the semantics of the First-Order language will explain how the value of a formula A is determined for an appropriate assignment of values to the variables occurring free in A. In this connection, if α is an individual variable and α is assigned the individual β as value, we will say that α *denotes* β *on this assignment*. Similarly, when a collection of individuals or n-tuples is assigned to a predicate variable, that variable *denotes those individuals or n-tuples on this assignment*.

Our statement of the evaluation conditions of formulas begins with atomic formulas and works up to longer formulas.

(1) Suppose A is an atomic formula. There are three possibilities:

    (a) A is just a propositional variable. In this case A has whatever value it is assigned.

    (b) A is a wff $\phi(\alpha_1, \ldots, \alpha_n)$ where ϕ is an n-place predicate or predicate variable other than ' $=$.' Given an appropriate assignment of values to the variables in A, let α_1 denote β_1, α_2 denote β_2, $\ldots$, and α_n denote β_n. Then (i) if $n = 1$, A has value t iff β_1 is one of the individuals denoted by ϕ, and (ii) if $n > 1$, then A has value t iff $< \beta_1, \ldots, \beta_n >$ is one of the n-tuples denoted by ϕ.

    (c) A is a wff $(\alpha_1 = \alpha_2)$. Given an appropriate assignment of values to the variables in A, let α_1 denote β_1 and α_2 denote β_2. Then A has value t iff β_1 is the same individual as β_2.

(2) Suppose A, B are wffs. And suppose we have an appropriate assignment of values to the variables occurring free in either A or B. Then the values for this assignment of the wffs $\sim A$, $(A \lor B)$, $(A \& B)$, $(A \supset B)$, $(A \equiv B)$ are determined by the values of A, B and the truth-tables for the connectives.

(3) Suppose A is a wff containing free occurrences of individual variable α. And suppose we have an appropriate assignment of values to the variables *other than* α which occur free in A. Then $(\forall \alpha)A$ has value t for this assignment iff for every individual β, A has value t for the given assignment supplemented with the assignment of β to α. (This gives the truth conditions of $(\forall \alpha)A$ on the unrestricted interpretation. For the restricted interpretation, we don't consider every individual β. Instead we consider every individual β in the domain of interpretation.)

(4) Suppose A is a wff containing free occurrences of individual variable α. And suppose we have an appropriate assignment of values to the variables *other than* α which occur free in A. Then $(\exists \alpha)A$ has value t for this assignment iff there is an individual β such that A has value t for the given assignment supplemented with the assignment of β to α.

The above semantic description covers all formulas of the First-Order language. But when A is a sentence (so that A contains no free occurrences of variables), the parts of the description which mention appropriate assignments do not apply. A sentence is simply true or false, not true for one assignment and false for some other.

If we consider the logical semantic features we studied previously, we can now provide new characterizations for sentences (and arguments) which possess these features. Take logical truth. A sentence is logically true if it can be determined to be true simply on the basis of recognizing (and understanding) its logical form. But now suppose A is a pure wff, and A symbolizes the sentence A^*. If there is no way to assign values to the variables of A so that A comes out false, then there is no falsifying assignment for A. (A PC tautology is just one kind of pure formula for which there is no falsifying assignment.) But if A can't be falsified, then A^* must be true—and true for logical reasons. So if B is a sentence of the First-Order language, then B is logically true iff B is symbolized by some (pure) wff A that can't be falsified.

Similarly, an argument $A_1, \ldots, A_n / B$ (in the First-Order language) is logically valid iff it is symbolized by a formula sequence that can't be invalidated.

*Exercise A: Section 7

Construct formulas or sequences of them which symbolize or jointly symbolize the following sentences and arguments.

1. $[H(a) \equiv \sim H(b)]$

2. $[F(a, b) \text{ v } F(b, c)] \supset F(b)$

3. $(\forall x)(\exists y)[F(x, y) \text{ v } G(x, y)]$

4. $(\forall z)(\forall x)[[M(x) \text{ \& } W(z)] \supset \sim (z = x)]$

5. $(\forall x)[H(x) \supset M(x)], H(c) / M(c)$

6. $(\forall y) \sim V(y), \sim (\exists x)U(x) / (\forall x)[V(x) \equiv U(x)]$

7. $(\forall x)[M(x) \supset D(x)], (\exists z)[G(z) \text{ \& } M(z)] / (\exists z)[G(z) \text{ \& } D(z)]$

8. $\{T(a) \text{ v } [D(a) \text{ v } H(a)]\}, [G(b) \text{ \& } \sim T(a)] / [H(a) \supset D(a)]$

Exercise B: Section 7

Let '$I(x)$' mean x *is an integer* (i.e., x is one of $\ldots, -3, -2, -1, 0, 1, 2, 3, \ldots$).

Let '$G(x, y)$' mean x *is greater than* y.

Let '$A(x, y, z)$' mean $x + y = z$.

Let 'a' name 0 and 'b' name 1.

Determine which of the following are true.

1. $(\forall x)[I(x) \supset (\exists y)[I(y) \text{ \& } G(x, y)]]$

2. $(\forall x)(\exists y)[I(x) \supset [I(y) \text{ \& } G(x, y)]]$

3. $(\forall z)[[I(z) \text{ \& } G(a, z)] \supset (\exists y)[[I(y) \text{ \& } G(a, y)] \text{ \& } G(y, z)]]$

4. $(\forall y)(\forall x)[[I(y) \text{ \& } I(x)] \text{ \& } G(y, x)] \supset (\exists z)[[I(z) \text{ \& } G(z, x)] \text{ \& } G(y, z)]]$

5. $(\forall x)(\forall y)[I(x) \supset [A(x, b, y) \supset I(y)]]$

6. $(\forall x)[I(x) \supset (\exists y)[I(y) \& A(x, y, a)]]$

7. $(\forall x)(\forall y)[A(x, y, a) \supset [(x = a) \lor (y = a)]]$

8. $(\forall x)(\forall y)[[G(x, y) \lor (x = y)] \supset \sim [G(y, x) \lor (x = y)]]$

Exercise C: Section 7

Let the domain of interpretation consist of the following individuals:

Beloit, Wisconsin

Terre Haute, Indiana

Dubuque, Iowa

Big Rapids, Michigan

Let 'a' name Beloit

'b' name Terre Haute

'c' name Dubuque

'd' name Big Rapids

Let 'F^1' be assigned: Beloit, Terre Haute, Dubuque, Big Rapids

'N^1' be assigned: Beloit, Big Rapids

'N^2' be assigned: $<$ Beloit, Dubuque $>$, $<$ Beloit, Terre Haute $>$,

$<$ Big Rapids, Dubuque $>$, $<$ Big Rapids, Terre Haute $>$

'E^2' be assigned no ordered pairs (this predicate is assigned an empty collection of ordered pairs).

Determine which of the following are true:

1. $F(c)$

2. $\sim N(c)$

3. $(\forall x)[(x = a) \supset E(x, x)]$

4. $(\forall x)[(\exists z)E(x, z) \supset N(x, x)]$

5. $(\exists y)[F(y) \supset (\forall z)N(z)]$

6. $(\forall x)(\forall z)[N(x, z) \lor N(z, x)]$

7. $(\forall x)[N(x, b) \supset [(x = a) \lor (x = d)]]$

8. $(\forall z)F(z)$

9. $(\forall y)[(b = y) \supset (\exists z)N(z, y)]$

10. $(\exists y)(\exists x)[[N(x) \& N(y)] \supset E(y, x)]$

Chapter 13

The First-Order Deductive System

13-0 SUMMARY

In this chapter, the PC deductive system is modified and enlarged to constitute the First-Order deductive system. Theorems are established in the system. Metatheorems about the system are also proved; these justify "short cut" (derived) rules for the First-Order system. We consider how to refute (invalidate or falsify) formula sequences and formulas.

13-1 ADAPTING THE PC SYSTEM

To fully understand the First-Order language, we must understand the inferential meanings of its logical expressions. We will develop the *First-Order deductive system* to achieve this understanding. Since the logical expressions of the PC language belong to the First-Order language, we will adapt the PC system to obtain (part of) the First-Order system.

Proofs from hypotheses in the First-Order deductive system establish (1) formula sequences and (2) formulas (including sentences). *Except for the rule Replacement*, all the rules of the PC system are rules of the First-Order system. But this statement applies only to the original and authentic rules of the PC system, *not* to the derived rules that were justified as shortcuts.

The rule Replacement in the PC system gives way to the following rule REPLACEMENT in the First-Order system:

Let $\alpha_1, \ldots, \alpha_n$ ($n \geq 0$) be the distinct individual variables which occur free in either of the formulas A, B.

.

$m \ (\forall \alpha_1) \ldots (\forall \alpha_n)[A \equiv B]$

.

$r \ldots A \ldots$ A occurs one or more times in the formula at step r.

.

$s \ldots B \ldots$ *m, r*, Repl   A may be replaced at some or all of its occurrences in the formula at step *r*, *so long as the result of this replacement is a wff.*

$m \; (\forall \alpha_1) \ldots (\forall \alpha_n)[A \equiv B]$

$r \ldots B \ldots$ *B* occurs one or more times in the formula at step *r*.

$s \ldots A \ldots$ *m, r*, Repl   B may be replaced at some or all of its occurrences in the formula at step *r*, *so long as the result of this replacement is a wff.*

In this (new) rule Replacement, the requirement that the result of the replacement be a wff is very important. In the following "proof":

1   $(\forall x)(\forall y)[F(x, x) \equiv G(x, y)]$

2   $(\forall x)(\exists y)G(x, y)$

---

3   $(\forall x)(\exists y)F(x, x)$ 1, 2, Repl

step 3 is not a wff. The "proof" violates the restriction in the rule Replacement.

For this new rule, the formula which "authorizes" the replacement must not contain free occurrences of individual variables. However, if the two formulas joined by '≡' do not contain free occurrences of individual variables, then quantifiers are not required at the beginning of the '≡'-formula. The following is a correct proof:

1   $p \equiv (q \vee r)$

2   q

---

3   $q \vee r$ 2, Add

4   p 1, 3, Repl

In the illustrations of the new rule Replacement, *n* is greater than *or equal to* zero.

In dealing with formulas which don't contain individual variables, the new rule Replacement amounts to the same as the old one. Every theorem of the PC system which contains only pure wffs is also a theorem of the First-Order system.

*Exercise: Section 1

Prove that the following are theorems of the First-Order system.

1. $(\forall z)(\forall y)[f(z, z, y) \equiv g(y, z)]$, $(\exists y)(\exists z)[p \vee f(z, z, y)] / (\exists y)(\exists z)[p \vee g(y, z)]$

2. $\sim[f(x, y) \vee g(x)] \equiv [\sim f(x, y) \& \sim g(x)]/ \sim[\sim f(x, y) \& \sim g(x)] \supset [f(x, y) \vee g(x)]$

3. $(\exists x)[g(x) \vee h(x)] \equiv (\forall z)\sim f(z), [p \supset (\forall z) \sim f(z)]/ [p \supset (\exists x)[g(x)) \vee h(x)]]$

13-2 SOME DERIVED RULES

In developing the PC deductive system, we made use of many derived rules. The meta-theorems which justified derived rules for the PC system were proved with respect to that system. Some proofs of those metatheorems are also correct with respect to the First-Order system; others are not. The following derived rules were justified by proofs which do not hold for the First-Order system:

Theorem Repetition

Theorem Replacement

The rules corresponding to the logical laws

We are NOT justified in using these rules for the First-Order system. (We are not at present justified in using them. If we can construct new proofs, we may later be justified in using them.)

The proofs which justified the remaining derived rules also hold for the First-Order system. We ARE justified in using the following:

Deduction Theorem

Modus Tollens

Hypothetical Syllogism

Disjunctive Syllogism

v Elimination

Each instance of the following logical laws can be accepted as a theorem:

Law of Self Implication

Law of Excluded Middle

Law of Contradiction

Commutative Laws

Associative Laws

De Morgan's Laws

Dougle Negation

Definitional Equivalences

*Exercise: Section 2

Prove the following to be theorems.

1. $[F(a) \supset {\sim}F(a)] \supset F(a) \;/\; F(a)$

2. $p \;\&\; [(\forall x)f(x) \;v\; (\forall x)g(x)] \;/\; [p \;\&\; (\forall x)f(x)]v\,[p \;\&\; (\forall x)g(x)]$

3. $(\forall x)[M(x) \equiv (\exists z)M(x, z)],(\exists x)[B(x) \;\&\; (\exists z)M(x, z)] \supset {\sim}(\exists y)E(y),\; (\exists y)E(y)\;/$ ${\sim}(\exists x)[B(x) \;\&\; M(x)]$

13-3 A NOTATION FOR SUBSTITUTION

In order to write about the quantifier rules, it is convenient to have a notation for the result of substituting one expression in another. This notation belongs to English, not the First-Order language. If A is a formula (or sentence) in the First-Order language, and α and β are expressions of the First-Order language, then 'S $^{\alpha}_{\beta}$ $A|$' is a name for the result of replacing every occurrence of α in A by β. If we write 'S $_{(r \,\&\, s)}^{\,p}$ $[p \supset (q \supset p)]|$,' this names the following formula:

$$\{(r \,\&\, s) \supset [q \supset (r \,\&\, s)]\}$$

We can use the new notation to indicate the replacement of any kind of expression. The formula S $^{a}_{b}$ $[F(a) \lor G(x)]|$ is: $[F(b) \lor G(x)]$. We can also indicate the result of replacing more than one component at a time. S $^{\alpha}_{\beta}$ $^{\gamma}_{\delta}$ $A|$ is the result of replacing every occurrence of α in A by β *and* every occurrence of γ by δ. (It only makes sense to write this if α and γ are different symbols.) The expression 'S $_{(r \,\&\, s)}^{\,p}$ $_{(r \,\lor\, s)}^{\,q}[p \supset (q \supset p)]|$' names this formula:

$$\{(r \,\&\, s) \supset [(r \lor s) \supset (r \,\&\, s)]\}$$

In substituting for distinct components in a formula, we must think of the substitution as taking place "all at once" (simultaneously). For example, if we wanted to write the formula S $_{(q \,\&\, r)}^{\,p}$ $_s^q[p \supset (q \supset p)]|$, it would be a MISTAKE to proceed like this:

1 $\{(q \,\&\, r) \supset [q \supset (q \,\&\, r)]\}$ This results from replacing 'p's.

2 $\{(s \,\&\, r) \supset [s \supset (s \,\&\, r)]\}$ This results from replacing 'q's.

In moving to the second step, two kinds of (occurrences of) 'q's were replaced: (i) the occurrences that were in the original formula, and (ii) the occurrences that were introduced by the first step. In carrying out the substitution, only the occurrences in the original formula should be replaced. So S $_{(q \,\&\, r)}^{\,p}$ $_s^q [p \supset (q \supset p)]|$ is actually this formula:

$$\{(q \,\&\, r) \supset [s \supset (q \,\&\, r)]\}$$

We will also provide a way to understand S $^{\alpha}_{\beta}$ $A|$ when α does not occur in A. We could decide that the notation makes no sense in this case. Instead, we will say that S $^{\alpha}_{\beta}$ $A|$ just names A when α does not occur in A.

When we use the symbolic notation for substitution, we can actually write the original formula. But if this formula has a name (or a numeral), we can write that instead. If we have this labelled formula:

I $(\forall x)[f(x, y) \supset f(x, x)]$

then S $_{G^2}^{f^2}I|$ is the following: $(\forall x)[G(x,y) \supset G(x, x)]$.

*Exercise: Section 3

These formulas are referred to below:

(1) $[p \supset (q \supset r)] \supset [(p \supset q) \supset (p \supset r)]$

(2) $(\forall x)f(x) \supset f(y)$

(3) $(\exists x)[f(x) \supset p] \supset [(\forall x)f(x) \supset p]$

(4) $(\forall x)(\forall y)(\exists z)f(x, y, z) \supset (\exists z)f(a, y, z)$

For 1 – 5, write out the formulas that are named.

1. S $_{f(x,\ y)}^{p}\ _{p}^{r}$ (1)|

2. S $_{z}^{x}\ _{(q\ \&\ r)}$ (2)|

3. S $_{G'}^{f'}$(2)|

4. S $_{[q\ \supset\ _{(\exists y)g(y)}^{p}]}\ _{r}^{q}$ (3)|

5. S $_{x}^{z}$ (4)|

For 6 – 10, use the notation for substitution to indicate how the following formulas were obtained from the formulas at the beginning of this exercise.

6. $[p \supset (p \supset p)] \supset [(p \supset p) \supset (p \supset p)]$

7. $(\forall x)F(x) \supset F(a)$

8. $[r \supset (p \supset q)] \supset [(r \supset p) \supset (r \supset q)]$

9. $(\forall x)(\forall y)(\exists z)h(x, y, z) \supset (\exists z)h(a, y, z)$

10. $(\exists x)[f(x) \supset (\exists x)f(x)] \supset [(\forall x)f(x) \supset (\exists x)f(x)]$

13-4 AN ADDITIONAL NOTATION

The notation in the previous section indicates the result of replacing any kind of expression in a formula. If we consider this formula:

II $(\exists x)f(x) \vee g(x)$

the notation 'S $_{a}^{x}$ II|' names:

III $(\exists a)f(a) \vee g(a)$

Our symbolic notation designates the result of a certain manipulation of symbols. There is no guarantee that we will end with a wff if we start with one.

If we replace just the free occurrences of 'x' in II by 'a,' we obtain this result:

IV $(x)f(x) \vee g(a)$

This is a wff. It is convenient to have a notation we can use to indicate the relation between II and IV. The new notation is obtained from the old by writing a dot under the 'S' as in: Ṣ. If α is a variable, then Ṣ $_{\beta}^{\alpha} A$| is the result of replacing all *free* occurrences of α by β. If α is a variable but there are no free occurrences of α in A, then Ṣ $_{\beta}^{\alpha} A$| is just A. If α is not a variable, then Ṣ $_{\beta}^{\alpha} A$| is the same formula as S $_{\beta}^{\alpha} A$|.

Using our new notation, we can denote IV by writing 'Ṣ $_{a}^{x}$ II|.'

*Exercise: Section 4

Use these formulas to answer the questions below.

(1) $(\forall z)[f(y) \supset h(z)] \supset [f(y) \supset (\forall z)h(z)]$

(2) $h(x, y, z) \supset (\exists y)(\exists z)h(x, y, z)$

(3) $[q \lor (\forall y)h(y)] \supset [q \lor h(y)]$

For 1 – 6, write out the formula that is denoted.

1. $\underset{x}{\overset{y}{S}}(1)|$

2. $\underset{a\ b\ c}{\overset{x\ y\ z}{S}}(2)|$

3. $S\,\underset{h^1}{\overset{f^1}{}}\,\underset{b\ c}{\overset{y\ z}{S}}(1)|$

4. $S\,\underset{h(b)}{\overset{q}{}}\,\underset{b}{\overset{y}{S}}(3)|$

5. $\underset{x}{\overset{y}{S}}(2)|$

6. $S\,\underset{h(y)}{\overset{q}{}}(3)|$

For 7 – 10, use the notation for substitution to indicate how these formulas were obtained from the formulas at the beginning of the exercise.

7. $h(x,\ x,\ x) \supset (\exists y)(\exists z)h(x,\ y,\ z)$

8. $[(\forall x)f(x) \lor (\forall y)h(y)] \supset [(\forall x)f(x) \lor h(a)]$

9. $(\forall z)[h(c) \supset h(z)] \supset [h(c) \supset (\forall z)h(z)]$

10. $h(z,\ x,\ y) \supset (\exists x)(\exists y)h(z,\ y,\ x)$

13-5 CHANGE OF BOUND VARIABLES

The first rule for quantifiers allows us to replace one bound variable by another. It permits us, for instance, to infer '$(\forall x)f(x,\ x)$' from '$(\forall z)f(z,\ z)$.' The rationale for this rule is that the bound variable serves only to mark the places "affected" by the quantifier—one place-marker is as good as another.

In stating this rule, there are certain difficulties to look out for. The inference from (1) to (2) below is not justified:

(1) $(\exists y)[f(x) \supset (\forall y)g(y,\ x)]$

(2) $(\exists y)[f(y) \supset (\forall y)g(y,\ y)]$

In (1), the existential quantifier "affects" two positions in the bracketed formula. In (2), the existential quantifier only "concerns" one position. The rule we wish to state here is intended to leave quantificational structure unchanged.

Change of Bound Variable (CBV)

Let Q be one of '$\forall$' or '$\exists$.' Let $(Q\alpha)A$ be a wff. Let β be an individual variable which does not occur free in A. And let no free occurrence of α in A be within the scope of a quantifier binding occurrences of β.

$m \ldots (Q\alpha)A \ldots$ The wff $(Q\alpha)A$ may occur once or many times in the formula at step m.

$n \ldots (Q\beta)S^{\alpha}_{\beta}A| \ldots \qquad m,$ CBV   The wff $(Q\alpha)A$ may be replaced by $(Q\beta)$ $S^{\alpha}_{\beta}A|$ at some or all of its occurrences in the formula at step m.

(In this rule, the 'Q' must represent the same quantifier throughout.)
Using the rule Change of Bound Variable, we can prove the following:

$(\forall x)(\exists y)f(x, y) / (\forall y)(\exists x)f(y, x)$

1	$(\forall x)(\exists y)f(x, y)$	
2	$(\forall x)(\exists z)f(x, z)$	1, CBV
3	$(\forall y)(\exists z)f(y, z)$	2, CBV
4	$(\forall y)(\exists x)f(y, x)$	3, CBV

We should note that the rule CBV does not authorize the following "proof":

1	$(\forall x)[g(x) \supset (\exists y)f(x, y)]$	
2	$(\forall x)[g(x) \supset (\exists x)f(x, x)]$	1, CBV

In moving from step 1 to 2, we have replaced '$(\exists y)f(x, y)$' by '$(\exists x)f(x, x)$.' The variable 'y' has been replaced by 'x.' In terms of the statement of the rule, α is 'y' and β is 'x.' But β ('x') occurs free in A ('$f(x, y)$'). So the rule CBV forbids this move.

Similarly, the following is incorrect:

1	$(\forall x)[g(x) \supset (\exists y)f(x, y)]$	
2	$(\forall y)[g(y) \supset (\exists y)f(y, y)]$	1, CBV

This time, there is a free occurrence of α ('x') in A ('$[g(x) \supset (\exists y)f(x, y)]$') within the scope of a quantifier ('$\exists$') binding occurrences of β ('y'). The same quantifiers must be linked to the same locations after applying the rule as they were before.

*EXERCISE: Section 5

Prove the following.

1. $(\forall y)[(\exists x)g(x) \vee f(y)] / (\forall x)[(\exists x)g(x) \vee f(x)]$

2. $(\forall x)(\forall y)[f(x, y) \equiv g(x, x, y)], p \supset (\exists y)(\exists z)f(y, z) / p \supset (\exists y)(\exists z)g(y, y, z)$

3. $[H(a) \supset (\exists z)M(a, z)], (\exists x)M(a, x) \supset (\exists x)W(x, a) / [H(a) \supset (\exists y)W(y, a)]$

13-6 UNIVERSAL QUANTIFIER ELIMINATION

This rule allows us to make an inference from a statement about everything to a statement about one particular thing—or to a formula which represents such a statement.

Universal Quantifier Elimination ($\forall$E)

.

$m \ (\forall\alpha)A$

.

n Ṣ $^{\alpha}_{\beta}$ A| m, ∀E   β is an individual constant or β is an individual variable such that no free occurrence of α in A is within the scope of a quantifier binding occurrences of β.

In the following proof, Universal Quantifier Elimination is used to infer a sentence containing a name:

1   $(\forall x)F(x)$ & $G(a)$

2   $(\forall x)F(x)$ 1, Simp

3   $F(a)$ 2, ∀E

The rule ∀E can only be used when '∀' is the principal operator of the premiss. It would not be permissible to use ∀E directly on the formula at step 1. And the formula '$(\forall x)F(x) \supset G(x)$' cannot be the premiss for ∀E.

When ∀E is used to replace the bound variable by an individual constant, there is no restriction on the constant that may be used. The following is a satisfactory proof:

1   $(\forall x)F(x, a)$

2   $F(a, a)$ 1, ∀E

When ∀E is used to replace the bound variable by an individual variable, there are some restrictions on the variable that may be introduced. It is *always* permissible to drop the quantifier and leave the variable unchanged—as in:

1   $F(a)$ v $(\forall y)G(y)$
2   $\sim F(a)$

3   $(\forall y)G(y)$ 1, 2, DS
4   $G(y)$.   3, ∀E

But when ∀E is used to change the bound variable to a new variable, we must not pick a variable that will be bound by some other quantifier. The following "proof" violates the restriction in the rule ∀E:

1   $(\forall x)(\exists y)[f(x) \supset g(y)]$

2   $(\exists y)[f(y) \supset g(y)]$ 1, ∀E

The following is a correct application of the rule:

1   $(\forall x)(\exists y)[f(x) \supset g(y)]$

2   $(\exists y)[f(z) \supset g(y)]$ 1, ∀E

So is this:

1   $(\forall x)[f(x) \supset g(y)]$

2   $f(y) \supset g(y)$ 1, ∀E

(Go back and re-read the restriction in the rule ∀E, to be sure that this last proof is correct.)

*Exercise: Section 6

Prove that the following are theorems.

1. $(\forall x)[B(x) \supset C(x)]$, $B(c)$ / $C(c)$

2. $(\forall x)f(x)$, $[f(x) \vee g(x)] \supset p$ / p

3. $(\forall x)[N(x) \supset (\exists y)L(x, y)]$, $N(b)$ / $(\exists x)L(b, x)$

13-7 UNIVERSAL QUANTIFIER INTRODUCTION

It is easy to understand how an inference *from* a universally quantified sentence to a statement about a particular individual is justified. But when can we legitimately make an inference *to* a universally quantified sentence?

A rule that was "opposite" to $\forall$E might allow us to move from a formula A to $(\forall \alpha)A$ — where α is an individual variable having free occurrences in A. But this does not seem legitimate. It is like reasoning from a statement about one thing to a statement about everything.

However, if A occurs as a step in a proof, and if, without changing the hypotheses of the proof, we could change the proof to replace the free occurrences of α in A by the name of *any* individual, then we would be justified in introducing $(\forall \alpha)$. In this proof:

1   $(\forall x)f(x, x)$

2   $f(y, y)$ 1, $\forall$E

if we replace the free 'y's by the name of *any* individual, the result remains a proof — and the change does not affect the hypothesis. So we are entitled to continue:

1   $(\forall x)f(x, x)$

2   $f(y, y)$ 1, $\forall$E

3   $(\forall y)f(y, y)$

For such a move to be justified, the hypotheses must make no special assumptions about the variable that is generalized. To accomplish this, we can require that this variable not occur free in the hypotheses of the proof.

In order to give a careful statement of the rule Universal Quantifier Introduction, we must first give a definition explaining when a step in a proof is *subject to* an hypothesis. (1) If $A_1, \ldots, A_n$ are the hypotheses of a proof from hypotheses, then every step in the main proof is *subject to* these hypotheses. (2) Every step in a subproof is *subject to* the hypotheses of every proof or subproof to which its subproof is subordinate.

In the following proof:

1   $p \supset q$

2   $p \supset \sim q$

3 | p

4 | q 1, 3, MP

5 | $\sim q$ 2, 3, MP

6 | $q \,\&\, \sim q$ 4, 5, Conj

7   $\sim p$ 3 − 6, $\sim$ I

every step is subject to the hypotheses in steps 1 and 2. In addition, steps 3–6 are subject to the hypothesis 'p.' Step 7 is subject only to the hypotheses of the main proof.

Universal Quantifier Introduction (∀I)

.

m A

.

n (∀α)*A*   *m*, ∀I   α is an individual variable which occurs free in *A* but does not occur free in any hypothesis to which the formula at step *m* is subject.

The following proofs employ the rule Universal Quantifier Introduction.

(i) (∀*x*)(∀*y*)*f*(*x*, *y*) /(∀*x*)*f*(*x*, *x*)   (ii) [*p* ⊃ (∀*x*)*f*(*x*)] / (∀*x*) [*p* ⊃ *f*(*x*)]

1	(∀*x*)(∀*y*)*f*(*x*, *y*)			1	[*p* ⊃ (∀*x*)*f*(*x*)]	
2	(∀*y*)*f*(*x*, *y*)	1, ∀E		2	*p*	
3	*f*(*x*, *x*)	2, ∀E		3	(∀*x*)*f*(*x*)	1, 2, MP
4	(∀*x*)*f*(*x*, *x*)	3, ∀I		4	*f*(*x*)	3, ∀E
				5	*p* ⊃ *f*(*x*)	2 – 4, ⊃I
				6	(∀*x*)[*p* ⊃ *f*(*x*)]	5, ∀I

The following "proof" is not legitimate:

1	(∀*x*)*f*(*x*, *y*)	
2	*f*(*y*, *y*)	1, ∀E
3	(∀*y*)*f*(*y*, *y*)	2, ∀I

The variable 'y' occurs free in the hypothesis. It cannot be generalized by ∀I.

*Exercise:Section 7

Prove that the following are theorems.

1. (∀*z*)[*f*(*z*) ⊃ *g*(*z*)] / (∀*y*)*f*(*y*) ⊃ (∀*y*)*g*(*y*)

2. [*p* v (∀*x*)*f*(*x*)] / (∀*x*)[*p* v *f*(*x*)]

3. (∀*x*)[*A*(*x*) ⊃ *B*(*x*)], (∀*x*) [*B*(*x*) ⊃ *C* (*x*)] / (∀*x*)[*A*(*x*) ⊃ *C*(*x*)]

4. (∀*y*)[*f*(*x*) ⊃ *g*(*y*)] / [*f*(*x*) ⊃ (∀*x*)*g*(*x*)]

13-8 EXISTENTIAL QUANTIFIER INTRODUCTION

The situations in which we are entitled to infer (∃α)*A* are fairly clear. If we have a premiss about a specific individual, we can reach a conclusion about *something*:

1	(∀*x*)*F*(*a*, *x*)
2.	(∃*y*)(∀*x*) *F*(*y*, *x*)

And if we have a premiss which uses a free individual variable as if it were a name for an individual, we can reach a similar conclusion.

Existential Quantifier Introduction ($\exists$I)

$m \; \text{S} \, {}^{\alpha}_{\beta} \, A|$ α is an individual variable and β is an individual constant or

                                             an individual variable. α must not occur free in A within the

$n \; (\exists \alpha)A \quad\quad m, \exists\text{I}$ scope of a quantifier binding β.

It might at first seem that this statement of the rule is "backwards," for we must substitute in the conclusion to obtain the premiss. But the substitution notation indicates only a relation between two formulas. It does not indicate the direction in which the inference must move.

Consider these formulas:

(i) $f(x, y) \supset (\exists z)f(z, x)$

(ii) $f(y_1, y) \supset (\exists z)f(z, y_1)$

Each of these can be obtained from the other by a substitution for free occurrences of individual variables. So each could serve as a premiss to a conclusion prefixing the existential quantifier to the other—as in:

1   $f(y_1, y) \supset (\exists z)f(z, y_1)$
2   $(\exists x)[f(x, y) \supset (\exists z)f(z, x)] \quad\quad 1, \exists\text{I}$

In using Existential Quantifier Introduction, it isn't necessary to change the variable in the original formula—since any wff can be thought of as a substitution instance of itself. The following proof is correct.

1   $f(y_1, y) \supset (\exists z)f(z, y_1)$
2   $(\exists y_1)[f(y_1, y) \supset (\exists z)f(z, y_1)] \quad\quad 1, \exists\text{I}$

The statement of $\exists$I incorporates a restriction. Consider these formulas:

(iii) $f(x, y) \supset (\exists y)[g(y) \lor f(y)]$

(iv) $f(x, z) \supset (\exists y)[g(y) \lor f(z)]$

Formula (iii) is a substitution instance of (iv). Indeed, (iii) is both $\text{S}^z_y (\text{iv})|$ and $\text{S}^z_y (\text{iv})|$. But (iii) cannot be a premiss to a conclusion which prefixes an existential quantifier to (iv). You can see this by noticing that the 'y' in '$f(y)$' that is bound by '$(\exists y)$' in (iii) is "taken away" from this quantified phrase in (iv). While (iii) is a substitution instance of (iv), the variable 'z' occurs free in (iv) within the scope of a quantifier binding 'y'—this violates the restriction in the statement of this rule.

Notice that the following proof is correct:

1   $f(x, x)$
2   $(\exists y)f(x, y) \quad\quad 1, \exists\text{I}$

For '$f(x, x)$' is $\text{S}^y_x f(x, y)|$. So in using $\exists$I to quantify the places occupied by an individual *expression, it is not necessary to bind every position where the individual expression has a free occurrence.*

The following proof uses $\exists$I:

$f(x, x) \supset (\exists x) (\exists y) f(x, y)$

1	$f(x, x)$	
2	$(\exists y) f(x, y)$	1, $\exists$I
3	$(\exists x) (\exists y) f(x, y)$	2, $\exists$I
4	$f(x, x) \supset (\exists x) (\exists y) f(x, y)$	1 − 3, $\supset$I

The two existential quantifiers in a row, '$(\exists x)(\exists y)$,' don't mean *there exists an individual x and a different individual y*. They mean *there exists an individual x and an individual y, which may be the same individual as x.*

*Exercise: Section 8

Prove the following to be theorems.

1. $(\forall x)g(x) \supset (\exists x)g(x)$

2. $(\exists y)[h(y) \vee \sim h(y)]$

3. $(\forall z)[(\exists y)f(y) \supset g(z)] / [f(a) \supset (\forall z)g(z)]$

4. $(\forall x)(\forall y)[f(x, y) \supset p] / (\forall x)(\exists y)[f(x, y) \supset p]$

13-9 EXISTENTIAL QUANTIFIER ELIMINATION

This last rule is associated with a subproof. We can illustrate it like this:

Existential Quantifier Elimination ($\exists$E)

$m \quad (\exists \alpha)A$

n	$S\,^{\alpha}_{\beta}\,A$	β must be an individual constant which does not occur earlier in the proof.
r	C	C must not contain β.

$s \quad C \quad m, n - r, \exists$E

In using this rule, we begin with a step $(\exists \alpha)A$. This tells us that there is something which satisfies the formula A. In the subproof, it is as if we are choosing a name for one such something. But it must be a name not already used in the proof, and we think of our "choice" as temporary—it lasts no longer than the subproof. If we can reason to a conclusion which does not contain the name, we can "keep" the conclusion. The subproof shows that from a premiss about an arbitrary individual which satisfies A, we can infer C. So C must follow from step m.

The following proof illustrates Existential Quantifier Elimination.

$(\forall x)[f(x) \supset g(x)], (\exists x)f(x) / (\exists x)g(x)$

1 $(\forall x)[f(x) \supset g(x)]$

2 $(\exists x)f(x)$

3 | $f(a)$

4 | $f(a) \supset g(a)$ 1, $\forall$E

5 | $g(a)$ 4, 3, MP

6 | $(\exists x)g(x)$ 5, $\exists$I

7 $(\exists x)g(x)$ 2, 3 – 6, $\exists$E

In this proof, the subproof is started before the rule $\forall$E is used. It is important that the subproof be started first. The following:

1 $(\forall x)[f(x) \supset g(x)]$

2 $(\exists x)f(x)$

3 $f(a) \supset g(a)$ 1, $\forall$E

4 | $f(a)$

5 | $g(a)$ 3, 4, MP

6 | $(\exists x)g(x)$ 5, $\exists$I

7 $(\exists x)g(x)$ 2, 4 – 6, $\exists$E

is not correct. The use of $\exists$E to obtain step 7 is not allowed, because the constant '*a*' in the subproof is not one that is new to the proof.

*Exercise: Section 9

Prove that the following are theorems.

1. $(\exists x)[f(x) \& \sim f(x)] / p$

2. $(\forall x)[H(x) \supset M(x)], (\exists x)[G(x) \& H(x)] / (\exists x)[G(x) \& M(x)]$

3. $(\exists x)[f(x) \& g(x)] / (\exists x) f(x) \& (\exists x)g(x)$

4. $(\forall x)[f(x) \supset \sim g(x)], (\exists x)g(x) / (\exists x)[g(x) \& \sim f(x)]$

13-10 IDENTITY RULES

In the First-Order deductive system we now have rules for reasoning with the connectives and quantifiers. But we don't have rules which explain how to make inferences involving the sign of identity. The first rule for identity is a rule for inferring a conclusion from no premisses.

Identity Axioms (Id Ax)

If α is an individual variable or an individual constant, then $(\alpha = \alpha)$ can be added as a step in a proof from hypotheses.

The rule Identity Axioms is illustrated in this proof:

$(\forall x)(x = x)$

1   $x = x$ Id Ax

2   $(\forall x)(x = x)$ 1, $\forall$I

The first step in this proof is not an hypothesis, since it is justified by the rule Identity Axioms. Since this proof has no hypotheses, the last step, by itself, is a theorem.

The next rule for identity is a two-premiss rule.

Identity Replacement (Id R)

.

$m\ (\alpha = \beta)$

.

$n \ldots \alpha \ldots$ The formula at step n contains one or more free occurrences of the individual symbol α.

.

$r \ldots \beta \ldots$ m, n, Id R   Some or all of the free occurrences of α in the formula at step n may be replaced by β. No occurrence of α may be replaced which is within the scope of a quantifier binding β.

.

$m\ (\alpha = \beta)$

.

$n \ldots \beta \ldots$ The formula at step n contains one or more free occurrences of the individual symbol β.

.

$r \ldots \alpha \ldots$ m, n, Id R   Some or all of the free occurrences of β in the formula at step n may be replaced by α. No occurrence of β may be replaced which is within the scope of a quantifier binding α.

The following proof makes use of Identity Replacement.

$D(a)$, $(a = b)$ / $D(b)$

1   $D(a)$

2   $(a = b)$

3   $D(b)$ 2, 1, Id R

Identity Replacement is also used in this proof:

$$(\forall x)(\forall y)[(x = y) \supset (y = x)]$$

1	$(x = y)$	
2	$(x = x)$	Id Ax
3	$(y = x)$	1, 2, Id R
4	$(x = y) \supset (y = x)$	1 – 3, $\supset$I
5	$(\forall y)[(x = y) \supset (y = x)]$	4, $\forall$I
6	$(\forall x)(\forall y)[(x = y) \supset (y = x)]$	5, $\forall$I

In using the rule Identity Replacement, if it is a variable that is being replaced, only the free occurrences of the variable can be replaced. But not all free occurrences can be replaced; the following is incorrect:

1	$f(x) \supset (\exists y)[\sim(x = y) \& f(y)]$	
2	$(x = y)$	
3	$f(y)$	
4	$f(y) \supset (\exists y)[\sim(y = y) \& f(y)]$	2, 1, Id R
5	$(\exists y)[\sim(y = y) \& f(y)]$	4, 3, MP

In step 1, the second free occurrence of 'x' is within the scope of a quantifier binding 'y.' This free occurrence of 'x' cannot be replaced by 'y.'

*Exercise: Section 10

Prove that the following are theorems.

1. $[f(x) \supset [\sim f(y) \supset \sim(x = y)]]$

2. $(x = y), (y = z) / (x = z)$

3. $(\forall z)\{f(z) \supset [(z = x) \vee (z = y)]\}, \sim f(x), (\exists x)f(x) / f(y)$

13-11 MORE DERIVED RULES

For developing the PC deductive system, we made use of the derived rule Theorem Repetition (T-Rep). The metatheorem which justified this derived rule was proved in a way that doesn't hold for the First-Order system. It isn't always possible to incorporate the proof of one theorem in a proof of a second theorem. The proof of the first might use the rule $\forall$I to generalize a variable that occurs free in a hypothesis of the second proof. Or the proof of the first might have a subproof premiss for $\exists$E that uses a constant which has already been used in the second proof.

Even though the proof which justified T-Rep for the PC system doesn't work for the First-Order system, we can justify this rule for the First-Order system with a new proof. We will develop a new series of metatheorems to justify derived rules for the First-Order system, and we will number them starting from 1.

The first metatheorem will justify Theorem Repetition. The proof which establishes this result is complicated. Before proving the metatheorem, we will prove a *lemma*. A lemma is a "minor" result which is preliminary to proving a major result.

LEMMA Let Γ be a proof of (formula theorem) A. Let $\alpha_1, \ldots, \alpha_r$ be the distinct individual variables which occur in steps of Γ. Let $\beta_1, \ldots, \beta_r$ be distinct individual variables which do not occur in Γ. And let Γ^* be obtained from Γ by replacing $\alpha_1, \ldots, \alpha_r$ by $\beta_1, \ldots, \beta_r$. Then Γ^* is a proof of

$$S \begin{matrix} \alpha_1 \ldots \alpha_r \\ \beta_1 \ldots \beta_r \end{matrix} A|.$$

Proof If we consider each rule that might be used to obtain a step of Γ, we can see that the same rule will justify the corresponding step of Γ^*. This systematic substitution turns one proof into another.

MT1 Let $\vdash A$. And suppose we are constructing a proof of $B_1, \ldots, B_n / C$. Then we can extend this proof to obtain A as a step.

Proof Let Γ be a proof of A.

First consider every subproof used as a premiss for $\exists$E in Γ. Select new individual constants which occur neither in Γ nor in the proof being developed. Replace the original constants in Γ by the new ones, yielding Γ'. It is clear (it *should be) that* Γ' is also a proof of A.

Now follow the procedure of the lemma, and transform Γ' into Γ^*, making sure that variables $\beta_1, \ldots, \beta_r$ are chosen which don't (yet) occur in the proof under construction.

The proof Γ^* can be incorporated in the proof under construction. The changes in constants and variables ensure that the inferences in Γ^* don't violate restrictions due to the proof under construction.

The conclusion of Γ^* is $S \begin{smallmatrix} \alpha_1 \ldots \alpha_r \\ \beta_1 \ldots \beta_r \end{smallmatrix} A \mid$. We can change the bound variables of this conclusion to the bound variables found in A by repeated use of CBV. Suppose we do this and obtain A^*. Let $\rho_1, \ldots, \rho_s$ be the distinct individual variables occurring free in A^*. None of $\rho_1, \ldots, \rho_s$ occurs free in any hypothesis to which A^* is subject. We can extend the proof under construction by s applications of $\forall$I to obtain $(\forall \rho_1) \ldots (\forall \rho_s)A^*$. Now by s applications of $\forall$E we obtain A.

The derived rule Theorem Repetition is used in this proof:

1	$(\forall x)[F(a) \supset G(x)]$	
2	$(\forall x)[\sim F(a) \supset G(x)]$	
3	$[F(a) \supset G(x)]$	1, $\forall$E
4	$[\sim F(a) \supset G(x)]$	2, $\forall$E
5	$[F(a) \vee \sim F(a)] \supset G(x)$	4, 3, Dil
6	$[F(a) \vee \sim F(a)]$	LEM
7	$G(x)$	5, 6, MP
8	$(\forall x)G(x)$	7, $\forall$I

The next metatheorem justifies Theorem Replacement.

MT2 Let $\vdash A \equiv B$. *Let* $\ldots A \ldots$ be a wff in which A occurs one or more times. Let $\ldots B \ldots$ be a wff obtained from $\ldots A \ldots$ by replacing one or more occurrences of A by

B. Then if either is available as a premiss in a proof from hypotheses, we can obtain the other.

Proof Let $\alpha_1, \ldots, \alpha_r$ be the distinct individual variables occurring free in either *A* or *B*. Let Γ be a proof of $[A \equiv B]$. Suppose Γ has *s* steps. We can extend Γ as follows:

$s + 1 \ (\forall\alpha_r) \ [A \equiv B] \quad s, \forall\text{I}$

.

.

$s + r \ (\forall\alpha_1) \ldots (\forall\alpha_r)[A \equiv B) \quad s + r - 1, \forall I$

This shows that $(\forall\alpha_1) \ldots (\forall\alpha_r) \ [A \equiv B]$ is a theorem.

Now suppose we have proof from hypotheses in which . . . *A* . . . is available as a premiss. Suppose it has been developed as far as step *m*. We can continue:

$m + 1 \ (\forall\alpha_1) \ldots (\forall\alpha_r)[A \equiv B] \qquad$ Since this is a theorem, it is justified by T-Rep.

$m + 2 \ldots B \ldots \quad (m + 1), \ldots A \ldots, \text{Repl}$

Similarly, if . . . *B* . . . is available as a premiss we can obtain . . . *A* . . .

Even though the (plain) rule Replacement is different in the First-Order system than in the PC system, the derived rule Theorem Replacement is the same—except that in the First-Order system there is the additional requirement that the result of the replacement be well-formed.

Now that Theorem Replacement is a derived rule, we can add an additional derived rule for each '$\equiv$'-logical law. We can replace instances of one side of a law by instances of the other side.

*Exercise A: Section 11

Prove the following to be theorems.

1. $(\forall x)f(x), (\forall x)g(x) / (\forall x)[f(x) \ \& \ g(x)]$

2. $(\forall y)[f(y \ \& \ g(y)] \supset (\forall y)[f(y) \equiv g(y)]$

3. $(\forall x)\{[f(x) \lor g(x)] \equiv \sim[\sim f(x) \ \& \sim g(x)]\}$

4. $p \supset [f(x) \lor g(x)], p \supset [\sim f(x) \ \& \sim g(x)] / \sim p$

The next result is our final metatheorem.

MT3 Let α be an individual variable which occurs free in the wff *A*. Then the following are theorems of the First-Order deductive system:

(1) $(\forall\alpha)\sim A \equiv \sim(\exists\alpha)A$

(2) $(\exists\alpha)\sim A \equiv \sim(\forall\alpha)A$

(3) $(\forall\alpha)A \equiv \sim(\exists\alpha)\sim A$

(4) $(\exists\alpha)A \equiv \sim(\forall\alpha)\sim A$

Exercise B: Section 11

Prove MT3.

Metatheorem 3, combined with T-Repl, allows us to replace formulas containing one quantifier by formulas containing the other. The derived rule corresponding to MT3 is *Quantificational Equivalence (QEq)*. It is used in the following proof:

$$
\begin{array}{lll}
1 & (\forall x)[F(x) \supset G(x)] & \\
\hline
2 & (\forall x) \sim [F(x) \, \& \sim G(x)] & 1, \text{Def} \supset \\
3 & \sim (\exists x)[F(x) \, \& \sim G(x)] & 2, \text{QEq}
\end{array}
$$

*Exercise C: Section 11

Prove the following to be theorems of the First-Order system.

1. $(\forall y)h(y) \, \text{v} \, (\exists z) \sim h(z)$

2. $(\forall z)[g(z) \supset \sim f(z)] \supset \sim (\exists z)[f(z) \, \& \, g(z)]$

3. $\sim (\exists x)g(x), (\forall x)[f(x) \supset g(x)] \, / \sim (\exists x)f(x)$

4. $(\forall x)[f(x) \supset (x = a)] \, / \, (\forall x)(\forall y)[[f(x) \, \& \, f(y)] \supset (x = y)]$

At the end of this chapter is a list of the rules and derived rules that are different from those for the PC system. The rules and derived rules for the PC system are found at the end of Chapter 9.

13-12 REFUTATION

The First-Order deductive system is sound. Every theorem that is an inference sequence is valid. Every formula theorem is either logically true—if it is a sentence—or it presents the form of logically true sentences. The First-Order system is also complete. All valid inference sequences in the First-Order language are theorems of the system. All logically true sentences and all formulas that present the forms of logically true sentences are theorems. But if a formula sequence isn't valid, then it can't be proved. To show that a sequence isn't valid, we must invalidate it. If we do this, we have refuted the sequence.

In considering refutation, we will begin with pure formulas and sequences constructed from pure formulas. A sequence which contains only propositional variables can be invalidated as it was in the PC language. We can show that this sequence:

$$p \supset q, \sim p \, / \sim q$$

isn't valid by making this assignment:

$$p \supset q, \sim p \, / \sim q$$

$$\text{f t t} \qquad \text{t f} \qquad \text{f t}$$

If we want to refute a single formula, we try to falsify it.

Now suppose we want to refute this sequence:

$$f(x) \supset g(y), g(y) \supset f(z) \, / \, f(z) \supset f(x)$$

We can begin by assigning truth values to the sequence like this:

$f(x) \supset g(y), \; g(y) \supset f(z) \; / \; f(z) \supset f(x)$

    f   t   t   t   t   t   t   f   f

This assignment does not invalidate the sequence. We have assigned values to whole (atomic) formulas, but not to individual and predicate variables. We won't have invalidated the sequence until we assign further values to the variables in such a way that we can "keep" the values assigned already. In the present case, this is easy to do. We can assign all women to 'f^1' and all men to 'g^1.' Next we assign George Washington as value for 'x,' Abraham Lincoln for 'y,' and Queen Elizabeth I for 'z.' Now '$f(x)$' "says" that George Washington is (was, or will be) a woman; this is false. '$g(y)$' "says" that Abraham Lincoln is a man—true. And '$f(z)$' "says" that Queen Elizabeth I is a woman—true. This assignment of values to the predicate and individual variables invalidates the formula sequence.

In a similar fashion, to falsify:

$[f(x, y) \; \& \; f(y, z)] \supset f(x, z)$

we can begin

$[f(x, y) \; \& \; f(y, z)] \supset f(x, z)$

     t   t   t   f   f

To finish, we can assign to 'f^2' all ordered pairs of integers $<m, n>$ such that $n = m + 1$. Then we can assign 1 to 'x,' 2 to 'y,' and 3 to 'z.' This makes the antecedent true and the consequent false.

*Exercise Section 12

Refute those sequences and formulas for which this is possible. Prove the others to be theorems.

1. $\sim [f(x, y, z) \supset f(y, x)], \; \sim f(x, y, z) \; / \; f(y, x)$

2. $\sim [f(y, z) \; \& \; g(z, x)], \; \sim g(z, x) \; / \; f(y, z)$

3. $[[h(x, y) \; \text{v} \; h(y, z)] \; \text{v} \; [h(y, x) \; \text{v} \; h(z, y)]] \; \text{v} \; [h(x, z) \; \text{v} \; h(z, x)]$

Refuting formulas and sequences is more difficult when we consider those containing quantified phrases. To invalidate:

$(\forall x)[f(x) \supset g(x)], \; \sim f(y) \; / \sim g(y)$

we can begin like this:

$(\forall x)[f(x) \supset g(x)], \; \sim f(y) \; / \sim g(y)$

     t   t   f   f   t

But the quantifier is an operator that isn't explained by a truth-table. We can't proceed from the 't' under the universal quantifier to truth values beneath the scope of the quantified phrase. We must at this point assign values to the free variables in the first premiss in such a way that we can keep the truth value already assigned. To keep the 't' under the universal quantifier, we must pick suitable values for 'f^1' and 'g^1.' We don't need to pick a value for 'x,' because 'x' does not occur free. So we want values for 'f^1' and 'g^1' so that:

$[f(x) \supset g(x)]$

will be true for every value of 'x.' This is easy to do. Let every dog (in the past, present, and future) be assigned to 'f^1' and every mammal be assigned to 'g^1.' Since every dog is a mammal, the formula '$(\forall x)[f(x) \supset g(x)]$' is true for this assignment. We must now pick a value for the free 'y' in '$\sim f(y)$' and '$\sim g(y)$.' This needs to be an individual which isn't a dog and is a mammal. We can easily find such an individual. If we pick the oldest cow in Wisconsin on January 1st, 1932, we will have a suitable value for 'y.'

*Exercise: Section 12 (cont.)

Refute those sequences and formulas for which this is possible. Prove the others to be theorems.

4. $(\forall x)[x = y], (\exists x)[f(x) \& \sim g(x)] / \sim g(y)$

5. $\sim (\forall y)[f(y) \supset g(y)], f(x) / \sim g(x)$

6. $(\forall z)[f(z) \supset [g(y) \& \sim g(y)]] / (\exists y)[f(y) \& g(y)]$

Refutation can be much more difficult when one quantified phrase is within another's scope. Suppose we want to falsify this formula:

$(\forall x)(\exists y)[f(x) \supset f(y)]$

We can start like this:

$(\forall x)(\exists y)[f(x) \supset f(y)]$

f

This isn't much help. To falsify the formula, we must pick a value for 'f^1' so that '$(\exists y) [f(x) \supset f(y)]$' has value f for some value of 'x.' Suppose we had a suitable value for 'f^1' and α was an individual such that the formula '$(\exists y)[f(x) \supset f(y)]$' is false for α as value of x.' We can think of this "formula":

$(\exists y)[f(\alpha) \supset f(y)]$

as being false for our chosen value of 'f^1.' In that case, the "formula" '$[f(\alpha) \supset f(y)]$' must be false for every value of 'y.' So for every value of 'y,' '$f(\alpha)$' must be true and '$f(y)$' false. We can't accomplish this, because α is a value such that '$f(x)$' is true for α as value of 'x.' So '$f(y)$' would also be true for α as value of 'y.' The original formula can't be falsified; it presents the form of logically true sentences. We can prove this formula as follows:

1   $[f(x) \supset f(x)]$ LSI

2   $(\exists y)[f(x) \supset f(y)]$ 1, $\exists$I

3   $(\forall x)(\exists y)[f() \supset f(y)]$ 2, $\forall$I

To invalidate this sequence:

$$(\exists x)(\forall y)[\sim(y = x) \supset (\exists z)g(z, y)], (\forall x)(\exists y)\sim(y = x) \, / $$
$$(\forall x)(\exists z)[f(x) \supset g(z, x)]$$

we must find an assignment that makes both premisses true and the conclusion false. It is easy to "make" the second premiss true. This premiss says that for every individual, there is an individual different from it. So this premiss says that there are at least two different individuals. This is already true if we make the unrestricted interpretation; no assignment is needed to give this a value, since it contains no free variables. To make the first premiss true, we need only make an assignment to 'g^2.' We must make an assignment so that the formula:

$$(\forall y)[\sim(y = x) \supset (\exists z)g(z, y)]$$

is true for some value of 'x.' There are lots of choices of values for 'g^2' that will make this formula true for some individual x. But the same choice must also make the conclusion false.

When we are dealing with a complicated example like this one, and trying to refute a formula or sequence, it is often convenient to work with a restricted domain. Instead of considering things in general, let us restrict attention to the domain of positive integers —i.e., to the domain whose members are 1, 2, . . . The second premiss remains true for this domain, since the domain contains at least two members. Now we want to choose a value for 'g^2' so that:

$$(\forall y)[\sim(y = x) \supset (\exists z)g(z, y)]$$

is true for some value of 'x.' Suppose we had such a value for 'g^2,' and the formula was true for α as value of 'x.' This means that the "formula":

$$\sim(y = \alpha) \supset (\exists z)g(z, y)$$

is true for every value of 'y.' For every integer that is different from α, some integer has relation g^2 to the integer. If 'g^2' denoted every pair of positive integers $<m, n>$ such that m is less than n, then α could be the number 1. If we assign every pair $<m, n>$ such that m is less than n to 'g^2,' the first premiss is true. Now we want to see if we can make a further assignment to 'f^1' so that the conclusion is false. If the conclusion is false, then the formula:

$$(\exists z)[f(x) \supset g(z, x)]$$

must be false for some value of 'x.' Suppose β is such a value. Then this:

$$f(\beta) \supset g(z, \beta)$$

must be false for every value of 'z.' For every value of 'z,' we must have '$f(\beta)$' true and '$g(z, \beta)$' false. Regardless of what we assign to 'f^1,' the only number that β can be is 1. And '$f(1)$' must be true. We can bring things out as we want them if we assign all odd positive integers to 'f^1.' Our assignment of values to 'g^2' and 'f^1' has invalidated the sequence. It does not matter that we have invalidated it only in a restricted domain. For purposes of refutation, it makes no difference whether we consider the unrestricted interpretation or an interpretation whose domain is limited.

*Exercise: Section 12 (cont.)

Refute those sequences and formulas for which this is possible. Prove the others to be theorems.

7. $[(\forall x)[f(x) \supset (\exists y)g(y)] \ \& \ (\forall x) \sim f(x)] \supset (\forall y) \sim g(y)$

8. $(\forall x)(\forall y)[f(x, y) \supset (\exists z)[f(x, z) \ \& \ f(z, y)]]$

9. $(\forall x)(\forall y)(\forall z)[\ [f(x, y) \& f(y, z) \supset f(x, z)], \ (\forall x)\ (\forall y)\ [f(x, y) \supset f(y, x)]\ /$
$(\forall x)\ (\forall y)\ [f(x, y) \supset f(x, x)]$

So far, we have considered refutation for pure formulas, and for sequences which consist of pure formulas. If instead of pure formulas, we were considering sentences or mixed formulas, we would carry out refutation in the same way. In doing this, we treat predicates and individual constants as if they were variables.

13-13 INCOMPATIBILITY

We can adopt the strategy we used with the PC system to establish results about logical incompatibility. To prove that n sentences are logically incompatible, we can take all but one of these as premises, and prove that these imply the negation of the remaining sentence. We can prove that:

$$(\exists x)f(x), \ (\forall x)[f(x) \supset g(x)], \ (\forall x)[f(x) \supset \sim g(x)]$$

present the forms of logically incompatible sentences like this:

1	$(\forall x)[f(x) \supset g(x)]$	
2	$(\forall x)[f(x) \supset \sim g(x)]$	
3	$(\exists x)f(x)$	
4	$f(a)$	
5	$f(a) \supset g(a)$	1, $\forall$E
6	$f(a) \supset \sim g(a)$	2, $\forall$E
7	$g(a)$	5, 4, MP
8	$\sim g(a)$	6, 4, MP
9	$\sim g(a) \ v \ (p \ \& \sim p)$	8, Add
10	$g(a) \supset (p \ \& \sim p)$	9, Def $\supset$
11	$p \ \& \sim p$	10, 7, MP
12	$p \ \& \sim p$	3, 4 − 11, $\exists$E
13	$\sim(\exists x)f(x)$	3 − 12, $\sim$I

To show that sentences are not logically incompatible (or that formulas don't present the forms of logically incompatible sentences), we must assign values so that all come out true. These sentences:

$$(\forall x)[D(x) \supset \sim S(x)], \ (\forall x)[S(x) \supset \sim M(x)], \ (\forall x)[D(x) \supset M(x)]$$

are not logically incompatible. For if we assign all dogs to 'D^1,' all sharks to 'S^1,' and all mammals to 'M^1,' then all three sentences are true.

*Exercise A: Section 13

If a group of formulas presents the forms of logically incompatible sentences, prove this. If it doesn't, show this by assigning suitable values.

1. $(\forall x)[f(x) \supset \sim f(x)]$; $(\exists y)f(y)$

2. $(\forall x)(\exists y) \sim g(x, y)$; $(\exists x)(\forall y)g(y, x)$

3. $(\forall x) \sim f(x, x)$; $(\forall x)(\forall y)[f(x, y) \supset (\exists z)[f(x, z) \,\&\, f(z, y)]]$; $f(a, b)$; $(\forall x)[f(a, x) \supset (x = b)$

Exercise B: Section 13

Prove the following to be theorems.

1. $(\forall x)(\exists y)[f(x) \supset g(y)]$ / $(\exists x)f(x) \supset (\exists y)g(y)$

2. $(\forall x)[f(x) \,\&\, g(x)] \equiv [(\forall y)f(y) \,\&\, (\forall z)g(z)]$

3. $(\forall x)f(x) \lor (\forall y)g(y)$ / $(\forall z)[f(z) \lor g(z)]$

4. $(\forall x) [f(x) \supset (x = a)]$, $(\exists x)g(x)$, $(\exists x)[h(x) \,\&\, f(x)]$, $(\forall x)[g(x) \supset f(x)]$ / $(\exists x)[g(x) \,\&\, h(x)]$

5. $(\exists x)g(x)$ / $(\exists x)[f(x) \supset g(x)]$

6. $(\exists x)(\forall y)f(x, y) \supset (\exists z)f(,z, z)$

7. $(\forall x)(\exists y)g(x, y)$, $(\forall z) \sim g(z, z)$ / $(\exists x)(\exists y) \sim (x = y)$

8. $(\forall x)(\exists y)(\forall z)f(x, y, z)$ / $(\forall x)(\exists y)f(x, y, y)$

Exercise C: Section 13

Refute those sequences and formulas for which this is possible. Prove the other theorems.

1. $(\forall y)(\exists z)f(y, z)$ / $(\exists z)(\forall y)f(y, z)$

2. $(\exists x)(\forall z)B(x, z)$ / $(\forall y)(\exists z)B(z, y)$

3. $(\exists z)(\exists y)F(y, z)$ / $(\exists y)(\exists z)F(y, z)$

4. $(\forall y)[f(y) \supset g(y)] \supset (\exists z)[f(z) \,\&\, g(z)]$

5. $(\exists x)[P(x) \,\&\sim (\forall z)[P(z) \supset L(x,z)]]$ / $(\exists x)(\forall y)[P(x)\&[P(y) \supset \sim L(x, y)]]$

6. $(\forall x)(\exists y)[f(x, y) \lor \sim f(y, x)]$

7. $(\forall x)[f(a, x) \supset (\exists y)[f(y, a) \lor f(x, y)]]$

8. $(\forall x)(\exists y)[F(x) \supset G(y)]$ / $(\exists y)(\forall x)[F(x) \supset G(y)]$

Exercise D: Section 13

Determine which groups of formulas present the forms of logically incompatible sentences. Construct proofs to establish incompatibility. If a group is not logically incompatible, show this by suitable assignments of values.

1. $\sim f(x, y)$; $(\forall z)[f(x, z) \supset (z = y)]$

2. $(\forall x)(\exists y) [f(x) \supset [g(y) \& f(x, y)]]$; $f(z)$; $(\forall y)[g(y) \supset \sim f(z, y)]$

3. $(\forall x)(\forall y)[\sim(x = y) \supset [f(x, y) \vee f(v, x)][[; (\forall x)(\forall y)[f(x, y) \supset f(y, x)];$
$(\exists x)(\exists y)[[f(x) \& \sim f(y)] \& \sim f(x, y)]$

4. $\forall x[f(x) \supset g(x)]$; $(\exists y)f(y)$; $(\exists z) \sim g(z)$

5. $(x = y)$; $(y = z)$; $\sim(x = z)$

6. $(\forall y)[f(y) \supset [h(y) \vee (y = z)]]$; $h(z)$; $(\exists x)[f(x) \& \sim h(x)]$

7. $(\forall x)[f(x) \vee g(x)]$; $(\forall x)[f(x) \supset g(x)]$; $\sim(\exists x)f(x)$

8. $(\forall x) (\forall y)[f(x, y) \supset \sim f(y, x)]$; $f(y, x)$; $(\forall z)[f(z, x) \supset (x = z)]$

13-14 RULES AND DERIVED RULES OF THE FIRST-ORDER DEDUCTIVE SYSTEM

Official Rules

Every official rule of the PC system, except the rule Replacement, is a rule of the First-Order system. In addition, there are the following:

Replacement (Repl)

Let $\alpha_1, \ldots, \alpha_r$ be the distinct individual variables occurring free in either A or B.

.

m $(\forall\alpha_1) \ldots (\forall\alpha_r)[A \equiv B]$

.

n $\ldots A \ldots$ A occurs one or more times in this wff.

.

s $\ldots B \ldots$ $m, n,$ Repl $\ldots B \ldots$ is a wff obtained from the formula at step n by replacing one or more occurrences of A by B.

.

m $(\forall\alpha_1) \ldots (\forall\alpha_r)[A \equiv B]$

.

n $\ldots B \ldots$ B occurs one or more times in this wff.

.

s . . . A . . . m, n, Repl   . . . A . . . is a wff obtained from the formula at step n by replacing one or more occurrences of B by A.

Change of Bound Variable (CBV)

Let Q be one of '$\forall$' or '$\exists$.' Let $(Q\alpha)A$ be a wff. Let β be an individual variable which does not occur free in A. And let no free occurrence of α in A be within the scope of a quantifier binding occurrences of β.

.

m . . . $(Q\alpha)A$ . . .   The wff $(Q\alpha)A$ may occur once or many times in the formula at step m.

.

.

n . . . $(Q\beta)S^{\alpha}_{\beta}A|$ m, CBV   The wff $(Q\alpha)A$ may be replaced by $(Q\beta)S^{\alpha}_{\beta}A|$ at some or all of its occurrences in the formula at step m.

$\forall$ Elimination ($\forall E$)

.

m $(\forall\alpha)A$

.

n $S^{\alpha}_{\beta}A|$ m, $\forall$E β is an individual constant or β is an individual variable such that no free occurrence of α in A is within the scope of a quantifier binding occurrences of β.

$\forall$ Introduction ($\forall I$)

.

m A

.

n $(\forall\alpha)A$ m, $\forall$I α is an individual variable which occurs free in A but does not occur free in any hypothesis to which the formula at step m is subject.

$\exists$ Introduction ($\exists I$)

.

m $S^{\alpha}_{\beta}A|$ α is an individual variable and β is an individual constant or an individual variable. α must not occur free in A within the scope of a quantifier binding β.

.

n $(\exists\alpha)A$ m, $\exists$I

∃ Elimination (∃E)

.

m $(\exists\alpha)A$

.

n $S^{\alpha}_{\beta}A|$ β must be an individual constant which does not occur earlier in the proof.

.

.

r C C must not contain β.

.

s C $m, n - r$, ∃E

Identity Axioms (Id Ax)

If α is an individual variable or an individual constant, then $(\alpha = \alpha)$ can be added as a step in a proof from hypotheses.

Identity Replacement (Id R)

.

m $(\alpha = \beta)$

.

n $\ldots \alpha \ldots$ The formula at step n contains one or more free occurrences of the individual symbol α.

.

r $\ldots \beta \ldots$ m, n, Id R   Some or all of the free occurrences of α in the formula at step n may be replaced by β. No occurrence of α may be replaced which is within the scope of a quantifier binding β.

.

m $(\alpha = \beta)$

.

n $\ldots \beta \ldots$ The formula at step n contains one or more free occurrences of the individual symbol β.

.

r $\ldots \alpha \ldots$ m, n, Id R   Some or all of the free occurrences of β in the formula at step n may be replaced by α. No occurrence of β may be replaced which is within the scope of a quantifier binding α.

DERIVED RULES

Every derived rule of the PC system is a derived rule of the First-Order system. These derived rules are found at the end of Chapter 9. The derived rule Theorem Replacement is changed to require that the result of the replacement be a wff. (In the PC system, the replacement can't help resulting in a wff.) In addition, there is the following derived rule:

Quantification Equivalence (*QEq*)

Instances of either member of the following pairs can be replaced by instances of the other member.

(1) $(\forall\alpha)\sim A; \sim(\exists\alpha)A$

(2) $(\exists\alpha)\sim A; \sim(\forall\alpha)A$

(3) $(\forall\alpha)A; \sim(\exists\alpha)\sim A$

(4) $(\exists\alpha)A; \sim(\forall\alpha)\sim A$

Chapter 14

Applying the First-Order Language to English

14-0 SUMMARY

In this chapter, we consider how to provide suitable translations in the First-Order language for ordinary English sentences. The First-Order language is used as an instrument to evaluate English sentences, groups of sentences, and inferences. There is a discussion of ways to provide comparable translations. And translations are supplemented with obviously analytic sentences and well-known true sentences.

14-1 THE EXPRESSIVE POWER OF THE FIRST-ORDER LANGUAGE

Before reading this chapter, it is helpful to review sections 3 – 6 of Chapter 3, and to reread Chapter 6. These explain the English sentences we will deal with, and the requirements for suitable translations.

   The First-Order language has great expressive power—much more than the PC language. Many arguments and groups of sentences that cannot be evaluated by means of the PC language can be dealt with using the First-Order language. The First-Order language is also much more powerful than either the Categorical language or the Extended Categorical language. The First-Order language owes this expressive power to the fact that the scope of quantified phrases can vary, as well as to the possibility that one quantified phrase can occur within the scope of another.

   Since the First-Order language contains the same connectives as the PC language, our discussion of translation for the PC language also applies to the First-Order language. We translate 'and' by '&,' 'or' by 'v,' and 'If . . . , then . . . ' by '⊃.' If the symbolic connective already gives a weaker translation than the English expression, our translation will be weaker. It is also possible to have a connective which doesn't make the translation weaker, but still derive a weaker translation because the components have weaker translations. For example, [A & B] might be equivalent to 'A and B.' But if A, B are translated by weaker sentences A^*, B^*, then [A^* & B^*] will be weaker than 'A and B' (or [A & B]).

*Exercise: Section 1

Select the correct answers.

1. If ordinary sentence A has a First-Order translation $A*$, then

  a. we insist that $A*$ be equivalent to A.
  b. $A*$ can be equivalent to A or weaker or stronger than A.
  c. we can use $A*$ if A is not related to $A*$ by entailment.

2. If A has a weaker translation $A*$, then

  a. $\sim A*$ is stronger than 'It is false that A.'
  b. $\sim A*$ is weaker than 'It is false that A.'
  c. $\sim A*$ may be equivalent to 'It is false that A.'

3. If A, B have equivalent translations $A*$, $B*$, then

  a. $[A* \supset B*]$ is equivalent to 'If A, then B.'
  b. $[A* \supset B*]$ is weaker than 'If A, then B.'
  c. $[A* \supset B*]$ entails 'If A, then B'.

4. If $A*$ is equivalent to A, and $B*$ is weaker than B, then

  a. 'If A, then B' is entailed by $[A* \supset B*]$.
  b. 'If A, then B' is equivalent to $[A* \supset B*]$.
  c. 'If A, then B' entails $[A* \supset B*]$.

14-2 PREDICATES AND SINGULAR TERMS

In translating an English sentence into the First-Order language, we will begin by looking for singular terms. In this sentence:

  Abraham Lincoln was assassinated.

there is only one singular term, the proper name 'Abraham Lincoln.' The sentence:

  Seattle is north of San Francisco.

contains two names, 'Seattle' and 'San Francisco.' We might use 'a' for 'Abraham Lincoln,' 'b' for 'Seattle,' and 'c' for 'San Francisco.' When we are dealing with one sentence or group of sentences, one individual constant must replace only one name. But on some other occasion, we might use 'a' to replace 'George Washington.'

While a proper name for a person or place is easy to recognize, the situation is more complicated with numerals. In many sentences, numerals can be regarded as proper names of numbers. To translate a sentence like:

  7 plus 5 is equal to 12.

we might use 'a' for '7,' 'b' for '5,' and 'c' for '12.' Numerals are also used for counting or measuring; in such a use they do not name individuals to which we ascribe properties or relations. The sentence:

  7 students passed the test.

is not used to say something about the number seven (except indirectly). In a sentence like this, we will not ordinarily replace the numeral by an individual constant.

After we pick individual constants, we must choose predicates to replace the expressions which characterize the named individuals. If we use '*a*' for 'Abraham Lincoln,' and '*A*(*x*)' to say that *x* was assassinated, then we can translate the sentence:

Abraham Lincoln was assassinated.

by:

A(*a*).

The translation has the same meaning as the original sentence; it is just written differently.
To translate the following:

Seattle is north of San Francisco.

we have already chosen '*b*' for 'Seattle' and '*c*' for 'San Francisco.' We need a predicate for saying that one individual is north of another. If we use '*N*(*x*, *y*)' to say that *x* is north of *y*, then we can provide an equivalent translation: *N*(*b*, *c*).

*Exercise: Section 2

Translate the following sentences into the First-Order language. Mark with an asterisk those translations that are weaker than the original sentences. Mark stronger translations with a double asterisk. The same First-Order expression can be used to replace different English expressions in different exercises.

1. Megan is playing tennis, but Michelle isn't; Michelle will play tennis.

2. If Plato is a philosopher, then Socrates is a haberdasher.

3. Chuck introduced Dave to Andrea.

4. Frank knows neither Ken nor Dick; however, Dick knows Ken.

5. It isn't true that Isabelle will become a mechanical engineer unless Frank is a mechanical engineer.

Individual constants replace not only names, they are also used to replace other singular terms. But in the First-Order language, individual constants label only real individuals. There are no First-Order names for Sherlock Holmes, the capital of Atlantis, or the Wizard of Oz.
To translate this sentence:

The capital of Wyoming is not a large city.

we can use '*a*' for 'the capital of Wyoming,' and '*L*(*x*)' to say that *x* is a large city. Then the First-Order translation is:

~*L*(*a*).

If we want a translation for:

The capital of Wyoming is Cheyenne.

we can use '*c*' for 'Cheyenne.' Then our translation can be:

(*a* = *c*).

We could also use '$W(x)$' to say that x is the capital of Wyoming, and translate the sentence this way:

$W(c)$.

Both translations are equivalent to the original sentence (and also to one another), but the syntactic structure of the first translation brings out more of the syntactic structure of the original sentence than does the syntactic structure of the second translation. It is desirable to bring out as much of the syntactic structure of the original as we can. We often go farther and incorporate semantic content from the original sentence in the logical form of our translation. To translate this sentence:

Either Cheyenne or Laramie is the capital of Wyoming.

we can use 'a' for 'capital of Wyoming,' 'b' for 'Laramie,' and 'c' for 'Cheyenne.' The original sentence would most naturally be understood as claiming that exactly one of Cheyenne or Laramie is the capital. This content is incorporated in the logical forms of these (equivalent) translations:

$[(c = a) \lor (b = a)] \,\&\, \sim[(c = a) \,\&\, (b = a)]$

$[(c = a) \lor (b = a)] \,\&\, \sim(c = b)$

When we replace a descriptive singular term by an individual constant, something is lost. For example, if we replace 'the mayor of Chicago' by 'a,' the individual constant doesn't contain a name of Chicago. Even though our general policy is to bring out as much structure as possible, we will make an exception for descriptive singular terms. Ordinarily, we will translate a sentence like:

The mayor of Chicago is a Democrat.

by a sentence like this:

$D(a)$.

But if the structure of a singular term is important to an argument, we can produce an expanded translation. We might use 'c' for Chicago and '$M(x, y)$' to say that x is mayor of y. Then we could translate the sentence like this:

$[D(a) \,\&\, M(a, c)]$.

One kind of descriptive singular term is like a title that applies to different individuals at different times. Examples are 'the president of the United States' and 'Napoleon's wife.' The second kind of descriptive singular term is permanent; it labels the same individual whenever it is used. Examples are 'Napoleon's mother' and 'the author of *Huck Finn.*' Permanent singular terms can be translated into the First-Order language without difficulty. The sentence:

Napoleon's mother lived on Corsica.

can be translated '$L(a, c)$,' if we use 'a' for 'Napoleon's mother,' 'c' for 'Corsica,' and let '$L(x, y)$' mean x *lived on* y.

When we translate a nonpermanent descriptive singular term, we must supply a date. To translate this sentence:

Uncle Henry ate dinner with the president of the U.S.

using two individual constants, we can let '*a*' denote Uncle Henry, but we can't simply use '*b*' for 'the president of the U.S.' We must indicate which president ate with Uncle Henry. If the dinner took place in 1950, we could use '*b*' for 'the president of the U.S. in 1950.' This would allow us to translate the sentence '*D(a, b)*'—where '*D(x, y)*' means *x ate dinner with y*. But now our translation contains more information than the original sentence. This makes it a stronger translation. To avoid this, we could use '*P(x)*' to say that *x* was a president of the U.S., and translate the sentence as follows:

(∃*x*)[*P(x)* & *D(a, x)*].

*Exercise: Section 2 (cont.)

Translate the following sentences into the First-Order language. Explain the individual constants and predicates that you use. Mark weaker translations with an asterisk. Mark stronger translations with a double asterisk.

6. Franklin Roosevelt was the president of the U.S. in 1936, but not in 1946.

7. If Jimmy wins this election, he will be the governor of Idaho.

8. Myra is Betsy's mother if, and only if, Betsy is Myra's daughter.

9. Jorge didn't lend his tennis racquet to Dale.

10. Either Mark Twain or Samuel Clemens is the author of *Tom Sawyer*.

11. Springfield is in Ohio, but Springfield is the capital of Illinois.

The problem of picking singular terms to be replaced by individual constants has a counterpart in the problem of determining what predicates to use. One predicate can be used to "sum up" a very involved sentence. We could translate:

If Tom and Rachel go to the beach, they will be sunburned.

by using '*S(x)*' to say that if *x* and Rachel go to the beach, they will be sunburned, and using '*a*' for Tom. Then this First-Order sentence:

S(a)

provides an equivalent translation. But the structure of the translation does not reflect the structure of the original. Nor does any important semantic content of the original show up in the logical form of the translation.

A more successful translation can be provided with this vocabulary:

a - Tom   *b* - Rachel   *c* - the (relevant) beach

G(x, y) - *x* will go to *y*   *S(x)* - *x* will be sunburned

Given this vocabulary, the following is a suitable translation:

[[*G(a, c)* & *G(b, c)*] ⊃ [*S(a)* & *S(b)*]]

unless the original is understood to mean that Tom and Rachel go to the beach together. Then we could use '*G(x, y, z)*' to say that *x* and *y* together will go to *z*, and our translation would be:

$[G(a, b, c) \supset [S(a) \& S(b)]]$

Whichever translation we use will be weaker than the original, but the structures of the translations reflect the structure of the original sentence.

To translate:

(1) Victor is married and a college professor.

we could use 'd' for Victor, and let '$M(x)$' mean *x is married and a college professor*. Then the sentence can be translated like this:

$M(d)$.

This translation brings out less structure than we would like. It is preferable to let '$M(x)$' mean *x is married*, and '$C(x)$' mean *x is a college professor*. This gives '$[M(d) \& C(d)]$' for a translation. However, with the sentence:

(2) Victor is a married college professor.

we would normally use one predicate for 'is a married college professor.' We will not ordinarily try to bring out adjective + noun structure in our translations. However, if it seemed desirable, we could translate (2) like this:

$[M(d) \& C(d)]$

We couldn't use the same strategy to translate:

Leonard is a tall fifth grader.

*Exercise: Section 2 (cont.)

Translate the following into the First-Order language. Explain the individual constants and predicates that you use. Mark weaker translations with an asterisk. Mark stronger translations with a double asterisk.

12. David is his mother's son.

13. If Fred is Frank's brother, then Fred's father is Frank's father.

14. If 5 times 7 is 35, then 35 divided by 7 is 5.

15. Jim's current wife is not his first.

16. Dan refuses to pay Stacey the five dollars that he borrowed.

14-3 QUANTIFIED PHRASES IN ENGLISH

We want to use quantified phrases in the First-Order language to bring out, as far as possible, the quantificational structure of English sentences. But quantified phrases in the First-Order language are quite different from quantified phrases in English. In the First-Order language, there are really only two quantified phrases—the variable used doesn't affect the significance of the phrase.

In English, a quantified phrase consists of a quantifier combined with a common noun or noun phrase. The following are English quantified phrases: Every flower, All planets, Each girl, No dragon, Some oak tree, Some students, A desk, The capital of England, Seven horses, a few doughnuts, Most Russians. It is a problem to render the great variety of English quantifiers by two First-Order quantifiers. Another problem is due to the fact that English quantified phrases contain nouns or noun phrases, while quantified phrases in the First-Order language do not. In English we have the phrase 'every man.' In the First-Order language, we can read '$(\forall x)$' as "every x," but the quantifier '$\forall$' really means every*thing*. The 'x' signals the places that are "affected" by the quantifier. To translate an English quantified phrase, we must first "break" it into two parts. To translate:

Every man is rational.

we use '$\forall$' for 'every' and introduce a predicate for being a man—say, 'M^1.' We need another predicate for 'rational'; we can use '$R(x)$' to say x *is rational*, and translate the sentence like this:

$(\forall x)[M(x) \supset R(x)]$

The 'every' in 'every man' has been turned into 'every*thing*.' The 'man' has been taken away from the quantifier and used to form a separate phrase. Our translation has the sense *For everything, if it is a man, then it is rational.*

To translate this sentence:

A girl is at the front door.

we can determine that this is a sentence about some girl—so it is about something. We can paraphrase it:

For something, it is a girl, and it is at the front door.

(Or: There is something which is a girl and which is at the front door.) If we use this vocabulary:

$G(x)$ - x is a girl

$A(x, y)$ - x is at y

d - the (relevant) front door

we can make this translation:

$(\exists x)[G(x) \& A(x, d)]$

It is important that we don't paraphrase these sentences:

A girl is at the front door.

Some girl is at the front door.

like this:

For something, *if* it is a girl, *then* it is at the front door.

This paraphrase says that if the something, which may not be a girl, is a girl, then etc. The original sentences definitely claim that something is a girl, which is why we paraphrase and translate them as in the preceding paragraph.

Another difference between English and the First-Order language concerns positions occupied by quantified phrases. In English, a quantified phrase can occupy the same position as a proper noun:

Margaret is at the front door.

Some girl is at the front door.

Megan watched Jesse ski down the hill.

Megan watched a boy ski down the hill.

Janet has read *Moby Dick*.

Janet has read every book.

In the First-Order language, a quantified phrase must always precede the clause (formula) that it governs. Quantified phrases can also occupy such positions in English sentences, but this is not common:

For some girl, she is at the front door.

For some boy, Megan watched him ski down the hill.

For every book, Janet has read it.

If we are going to use a quantified phrase in the First-Order language to translate an English quantified phrase, we must:

(1) Split up the quantified phrase so that the noun is separated from the quantifier.

(2) Paraphrase the quantifier in terms of 'everything' or 'something.'

(3) Prefix the quantified phrase to a clause which it governs.

Once we have paraphrased the original English sentence by a suitable English sentence, it isn't so hard to come up with a translation. Consider this sentence:

Clare doesn't like any boy.

This contains only one quantified phrase, 'any boy.' We want to separate 'any' from 'boy.' We want to replace 'any' by either 'everything' or 'something.' Suppose we try to use 'everything'; then we want to prefix 'everything' (or 'for everything') to a clause which it governs. We might try:

For everything which is a boy, Clare doesn't like it.

This paraphrase retains the meaning of the original sentence, but it isn't suitable. For the quantified phrase in our paraphrase is 'everything which is a boy,' not simply 'everything.' But the following paraphrase seems all right:

For everything, if it is a boy, then Clare doesn't like it.

This is a sentence which is easy to translate once we have a suitable vocabulary. Suppose we use this:

c - Clare

$B(x)$ - x is a boy

$L(x, y)$ - x likes y

Now we can use this translation:

$(\forall x)[B(x) \supset \sim L(c, x)]$.

If we had chosen 'something' rather than 'everything,' we could have produced this paraphrase: It isn't true that for something, it is a boy and Clare likes it. (It isn't true that there is something such that it is a boy and Clare likes it.) That would give us the following translation:

$\sim(\exists x)[B(x) \;\&\; L(c, x)]$.

*Exercise: Section 3

Translate the following sentences into the First-Order language. Explain the individual constants and predicates that you use.

1. No one is at the door.

2. Any student who correctly answers the fourth question will please Professor Lambros.

3. Kevin doesn't own a car.

4. Each member of the Union voted in favor of the new contract.

14-4 INDEFINITE SENTENCES

In Chapter 3, indefinite and universal sentences were contrasted as "extremes" of sentences formed from quantified phrases. The following were used as examples of the most indefinite sentences:

A student in Mr. Hull's class can speak French.

Some student in Mr. Hull's class can speak French.

It is easy to see that these sentences have the same meaning as this paraphrase:

For something, it is a student in Mr. Hull's class and it can speak French.

With this vocabulary:

a - Mr. Hull's class

$S(x, y)$ - x is a student in y

$F(x)$ - x can speak French

we obtain this equivalent translation:

$(\exists x)[S(x, a) \;\&\; F(x)]$.

When 'some' is combined with a plural noun, translations become more complicated. To translate the sentence:

Some dogs are in the back yard.

we can use this vocabulary:

c - the (appropriate) back yard

$D(x)$ - x is a dog $I(x, y)$ - x is in y

This First-Order sentence:

$$(\exists x)[D(x) \ \& \ I(x, \ c)]$$

is weaker than the original sentence, which means that two or more dogs are in the back yard. The following:

$$(\exists x)(\exists y)[[D(x) \ \& \ D(y)] \ \& \ [I(x, \ c) \ \& \ I(y, \ c)]]$$

doesn't provide an equivalent translation either; it doesn't indicate that there are at least two dogs in the back yard. However, this First-Order translation is equivalent to the original sentence:

$$(\exists x)(\exists y)[[\sim(x = y) \ \& \ [D(x)\&D(y)]] \ \& \ [I(x, \ c) \ \& \ I(y, \ c)]]$$

This is a cumbersome translation. It is more convenient to say some things in English than it is in a language with only singular forms.

This sentence:

Some girls are making a lot of noise.

proves even more difficult to translate. If '$G(x)$' means *x is a girl*, and '$N(x)$' means *x is making a lot of noise*, then one meaning of the sentence is captured by this translation:

$$(\exists x)(\exists y)[[\sim (x = y) \ \& \ [G(x) \ \& \ G(y)]] \ \& \ [N(x) \ \& \ N(y)]]$$

But this is not the most natural meaning to assign to the original sentence. We would ordinarily take the original sentence to be talking about some group, or collection, of girls. A group might be noisy without even one member of the group being noisy. If '$C(x)$' means *x is a collection of girls*, then our translation can be:

$$(\exists x)[C(x) \ \& \ N(x)].$$

In the First-Order language, it is difficult to relate a sentence about a collection of girls to some other sentence about girls.

We often translate 'some,' 'a,' and 'an' with an existential quantifier. But we don't always use a quantified phrase. For this sentence:

Jean is an administrative assistant.

we need a name, say 'b,' for Jean, and a predicate, say 'A^1,' for 'is an administrative assistant.' Our translation, '$A(b)$,' does not contain a quantified phrase, although the original sentences does. If someone demanded a translation with a quantified phrase, we could use this one:

$$(\exists x)[A(x) \ \& \ (b = x)].$$

This translation is needlessly complicated. When 'a' or 'an' immediately follows 'is' (or 'was' or 'will be'), we ordinarily "incorporate" it in a predicate.

*Exercise: Section 4

Translate the following into the First-Order language. Mark weaker translations with an asterisk and stronger translations with a double asterisk.

1. Some high school student is a millionaire.

2. Leonard doesn't own a Cadillac; he owns a Mercedes Benz.

3. Martha bought some copies of Tom's book.

4. If a policeman is at the front door, then John will sneak out the back door.

5. Some of Kathy's students put on a play after school.

A singular or plural indefinite sentence can (usually) be given an equivalent translation in the First-Order language. If a sentence falls "between" an indefinite and a universal sentence, it isn't always convenient or even possible to provide an equivalent translation. Sometimes no satisfactory translation is available.

Sentences with numerical quantifiers can, in principle, be given equivalent translations. In making these translations, it is important to distinguish sentences which say there are *at least n* things of a kind from sentences which say there are *exactly n*. It is natural to understand this sentence:

There are nine players on a baseball team.

to mean *exactly* nine. But in this sentence:

Kevin owns two baseball gloves.

it isn't clear whether Kevin owns at least two or exactly two.

Sentences in the First-Order language are not ambiguous between at least *n* and exactly *n*. If we want to say that there is at least one F, we can simply use the existential quantifier:

$(\exists x) F(x)$.

To say that there is exactly one F, we must say that there is at least one, and this one is the only one:

$(\exists x)[F(x) \mathrel{\&} (\forall y)[F(y) \supset (y = x)]]$.

To say there are at least four F's, we need four existential quantifiers and four individual variables:

$(\exists x)(\exists y)(\exists z)(\exists x_1)$.

We must say that each individual is an F, and that each is different from all the others:

$(\exists x)(\exists y)(\exists z)(\exists x_1)[[[[F(x) \mathrel{\&} F(y)] \mathrel{\&} [F(z) \mathrel{\&} F(x_1)]] \mathrel{\&}$

$[[\sim(x = y) \mathrel{\&} \sim(x = z)] \mathrel{\&} [\sim(x = x_1) \mathrel{\&} \sim(y = z)]]] \mathrel{\&}$

$[\sim(y = x_1) \mathrel{\&} \sim(z = x_1)]]$

Think how cumbersome it would be to say that there are 57 F's! We can say that there are exactly four F's like this:

$(\exists x)(\exists y)(\exists z)(\exists x_1)[[[[[F(x) \mathrel{\&} F(y)] \mathrel{\&} [F(z) \mathrel{\&} F(x_1)]] \mathrel{\&}$

$[[\sim(x = y) \mathrel{\&} \sim(x = z)] \mathrel{\&} [\sim(x = x_1) \mathrel{\&} \sim(y = z)]]] \mathrel{\&}$

$[\sim(y = x_1) \mathrel{\&} \sim(z = x_1)]] \mathrel{\&} (\forall x_2)[F(x_2) \supset [[(x_2 = x) \vee (x_2 = y)] \vee$

$[(x_2 = z) \vee (x_2 = x_1)]]]]]$

We will not use the First-Order language to translate sentences which say that there is a certain large number of things of a kind. If we were concerned to investigate such sentences, it would make sense to expand the First-Order language with additional numerical quantifiers.

We will translate sentences involving relatively small numbers (one, two, or three) into the First-Order language, but not those involving larger numbers. However, we must distinguish sentences with numerical quantifiers from sentences about numbers. To translate sentences about numbers into the First-Order language, we would translate numerals by individual constants. However, from now on, we will enlarge the First-Order language by including the ordinary arabic numerals among the individual constants. (These are: 0, 1, 2, . . .) These numerals will name the corresponding numbers.

When a sentence contains a quantified phrase constructed with 'few,' 'many,' 'most,' or 'almost all,' it is difficult to find a suitable translation. To translate:

Mary invited a few friends to dinner.

we must know how many it takes to constitute a few. If we understand a few to be at least three, we can use this vocabulary:

a - *Mary* $F(x, y)$ - x is a friend of y $I(x, y)$ - x invited y to dinner

and provide this (equivalent?) translation:

$(\exists x)(\exists y)(\exists z)[[[[\sim(x = y) \mathbin{\&} \sim(x = z)] \mathbin{\&} \sim(y = z)] \mathbin{\&}$

$[[F(x, a) \mathbin{\&} F(y, a)] \mathbin{\&} F(z, a)]] \mathbin{\&} [[I (a, x)]] \mathbin{\&} I(a, y)] \mathbin{\&} I(a, z)]]$

We aren't able to provide such a definite translation for this sentence:

Mary has few friends.

This would not normally be understood as saying that Mary has no more than three friends. This sentence just can't be given a structure-preserving translation into the First-Order language. We are also unable to deal with these:

Many students are poor spellers.

Most congressmen are lawyers.

Almost all people like beer.

The First-Order language is an instrument we can use to deal with a large variety of English sentences. But the First-Order language is a limited instrument. We must simply recognize those cases where we can't provide satisfactory First-Order translations, and restrict our use of the First-Order language to those cases we can deal with.

*Exercise: Section 4 (cont.)

Translate the following sentences. Mark weaker translations with an asterisk and stronger translations with a double asterisk. If some sentence cannot be adequately translated, explain why not.

6. If 7 times 5 is 35, then 35 divided by 5 is 7.

7. The Smiths have two daughters and one son.

8. No more than three candidates will run for vice president.

9. The majority of towns in Texas are very small.

10. Dawn bought a couple of books.

11. There are 278 students in the senior class.

14-5 UNIVERSAL SENTENCES

To make a universal sentence, we combine the universal quantifier with the horseshoe. For example, we paraphrase a sentence:

Every dog is . . .

like this:

For everything, if it is a dog, then . . .

which gives a translation:

$(\forall x)[D(x) \supset \ldots$

Earlier, we distinguished affirmative from negative universal sentences. In the First-Order language we mark this difference with '$\sim$.' To translate 'Every dog is a pet,' we use:

$(\forall x)[D(x) \supset P(x)]$

and for 'No dog is a pet' we come up with:

$(\forall x)[D(x) \supset \sim P(x)]$

In Chapter 3, we distinguished three different kinds of ambiguity with respect to universal sentences: A universal sentence can be understood

(1) in a restricted or unrestricted sense,

(2) as having or not having existential force,

(3) as having or not having modal force.

One way to understand universal sentences in a restricted sense is to interpret the First-Order language with respect to a limited domain. However, our practice is to give the unrestricted interpretation. If we are translating a universal sentence which is understood in a restricted sense, we try to capture the original meaning by the predicates we use. If this sentence:

Every dog has four legs.

is understood in such a way that it is true, it is understood in a restricted sense. To translate it, we might use this vocabulary:

$D(x)$ - x is a normal dog $F(x)$ - x has four legs.

The translation '$(\forall x)[D(x) \supset F(x)]$' is restricted in an appropriate way.

A universal sentence '$(\forall x)[F(x) \supset G(x)]$' has no existential force. It has no modal force either. It says that all actual F's, if there are any, are G's. A universal affirmative sentence which has neither existential nor modal force is said to be understood *mathemat-*

ically. It is a peculiarity of such sentences that if there are no *F*'s, they are true—they are *vacuously* true in such a case.

Ordinary universal affirmative sentences commonly have existential force. If we use this vocabulary:

> *a* - the final exam   *b* - the course (in question)
>
> *S*(*x*) - *x* is a student (in the relevant class)
>
> *P*(*x*, *y*) - *x* passed *y*

and translate this sentence:

> Every student who passed the final passed the course.

like this:

> $(\forall x)[[S(x) \,\&\, P(x, a)] \supset P(x, b)]$

our translation is weaker than the original. The translation doesn't indicate that there is a student who passed the final, but the original does. We can supply the missing existential force by conjoining an existence statement:

> $(\forall x)[[S(x) \,\&\, P(x, a)] \supset P(x, b)] \,\&\, (\exists x)[S(x) \,\&\, P(x, a)]$

This is an equivalent translation.

If a sentence is used to make a statement with existential force, this force may be indicated by expressions in the sentence, or it may be indicated by the context in which the sentence is used. In translating sentences in this book, there are no actual contexts to determine existential force. We will assume that the sentences we translate have the weakest existential force that they might naturally have. Ordinarily when we translate a universal affirmative sentence formed with 'every,' 'each,' or 'all,' like these sentences:

> Every student in Prof. Brady's class has been to DisneyWorld.
>
> Each student in Prof. Brady's class has been to DisneyWorld.
>
> All the students in Prof. Brady's class have been to DisneyWorld.

we will supply existential force:

> $(\forall x)[S(x, b) \supset D(x)] \,\&\, (\exists x)S(x, b)$

We take the original sentences to indicate the existence of at least one individual of the relevant kind. In some circumstances, these same sentences might be used to indicate the existence of more than one individual. But they could naturally be used with the existential force *at least one*—this is the weakest force they might naturally have. So long as the original sentences lack modal force, we will regard such translations as equivalent. However, *as a convention in this book*, we will suppose that universal sentences about mathematical objects are understood mathematically. Our equivalent translation for:

> All prime numbers greater than two are odd.

will be:

> $(\forall x)[[P(x) \,\&\, G(x, 2)] \supset O(x)]$

The indefinite article is sometimes used to make a universal statement:

A bat is a mammal.

Our translation for this sentence requires existential force:

$(\forall x)[B(x) \supset M(x)]$ & $(\exists x)B(x)$

If the original sentence means that bats are necessarily mammals, our translation is weaker. If the original sentence has no modal force, the translation is equivalent.

A plural noun can also be used to make a universal statement. The sentence 'Bats are mammals' is translated the same way as 'A bat is a mammal.'

We can supply existential force to our translations by adding a statement (clause) of existence. We can't do the same thing with modal force. If we translate a universal sentence which is understood to have modal force (but lacks a modal expression), our translation must be weaker. There is a branch of logic called *modal logic* which explores modal force; in modal logic it is possible to give equivalent translations of sentences that have modal force.

For many universal sentences formed with 'any,' especially those in the future tense, we don't supply existential force in our translations. If '$T(x)$' means x *is or will be a trespasser* and '$P(x)$' means x *will be prosecuted*, we would translate:

Any trespasser will be prosecuted.

like this:

$(\forall x)[T(x) \supset P(x)]$.

These 'any'-sentences typically have modal force, so their translations will be weaker.

This universal sentence:

Any basketball player over ten feet tall is remarkable.

doesn't seem (to me) to have existential force. However, it does have modal force: it covers possible basketball players as well as actual ones. But in this sentence:

Any basketball player over six feet six inches tall in 1920 was remarkable.

it does seem natural to understand the speaker to be expressing his commitment to there being a basketball player over 6'-6" tall in 1920. Using this vocabulary:

$B(x)$ - x was a basketball player over 6'-6" tall in 1920

$R(x)$ - x was remarkable.

we get this translation:

$(\forall x)[B(x) \supset R(x)]$ & $(\exists x)B(x)$.

In this case, I don't feel the original would be taken to have modal force. If I am right, we have an equivalent translation.

In translating sentences about types into the First-Order language, our strategy is to replace talk about types by talk about instances of types. But it isn't always possible to carry out this strategy. We may sometimes introduce expressions for types into the First-Order language. If we wanted to translate this sentence:

The letter 'a' is the first letter of the alphabet.

we might use this vocabulary:

a - the letter 'a' b - the alphabet

$M(x, y)$ - x is the first member of the ordered sequence y

This gives the following translation: $M(a, b)$.

Other sentences about types are easier to deal with. This sentence:

The whale is a mammal.

comes to nearly the same thing as the sentence 'Whales are mammals.' However, we will not understand a sentence like 'The whale is a mammal' as indicating that there is a whale. For we can talk about the type of both real and fictional individuals. Types are abstract individuals whose status is not affected by the status of their instances.

Using this vocabulary:

$W(x)$ - x is a whale $M(x)$ - x is a mammal

we translate 'The whale is a mammal' like this:

$(\forall x)[W(x) \supset M(x)]$

This is a weaker translation, because an English sentence about a type usually has a modal force. When we say "The unicorn is an animal that resembles a horse with a horn in the middle of its forehead," our statement says more than that any unicorn which actually exists resembles a horse, etc. It also says that if any unicorn were to exist, it would resemble a horse with a horn in the middle of its forehead.

*Exercise: Section 5

Translate the following sentences into the First-Order language. Mark weaker translations with an asterisk and stronger translations with a double asterisk.

1. Everyone who drives a Ferrari is happy.

2. Each positive integer is greater than zero.

3. Kevin doesn't know everyone in his class.

4. All who have met Fran like her.

5. Every student in the college knows a freshman.

6. Some freshman knows every student in the college.

7. The oak tree develops from an acorn.

8. The bird evolved from the dinosaur.

9. Anyone who jumps off a twelve-story building is sure to be killed.

10. It isn't true that anyone who asked Dale for help received it.

Universal sentences formed with 'no' or 'none' don't always have existential force. If Mary tells us, "No vampire is to be found in the attic," she isn't committed to there being a vampire someplace else. But it would not be natural for a speaker to use this sentence:

None of Paul's children went to college.

if he believes that Paul has no children. This sentence is most naturally understood to have existential force. With this vocabulary:

> b - Paul $C(x)$ - x is a college $C(x, y)$ - x is a child of y
>
> $A(x, y)$ - x attended y

we can make this (equivalent) translation:

> $(\forall x)[C(x, b) \supset \sim(\exists y)[C(y) \,\&\, A(x, y)]] \,\&\, (\exists x)C(x, b)$

When an indefinite phrase or a plural noun is used to make a universal negative sentence:

> A spider is not an insect.
>
> Spiders are not insects.

we normally understand these sentences to have existential force:

> $(\forall x)[S(x) \supset \sim I(x)] \,\&\, (\exists x)S(x)$

*Exercise: Section 5 (cont.)

Translate the following sentences. Mark weaker translations with an asterisk and stronger translations with a double asterisk.

11. Nobody likes a tattletale.

12. None of Professor Hood's students gave him a favorable recommendation.

13. Chuck found no cans of tunafish in the pantry.

14. A penguin can't fly.

> When a universal sentence with existential force is denied:
>
> It isn't true that all of David's children are girls.

the denial is not normally understood to "cover" the existential force. The denial itself has existential force. An equivalent translation for this sentence is:

> $\sim(\forall x)[C(x, d) \supset G(x)]$

No existence claim is needed, since this translation already has existential force. It is equivalent to:

> $(\exists x)[C(x, d) \,\&\, \sim G(x)]$

*Exercise: Section 5 (cont.)

Translate the following sentences. Mark weaker translations with an asterisk and stronger translations with a double asterisk.

15. It is false that bats all have rabies.

16. It isn't true that boys don't make passes at girls who wear glasses.

14-6 ONLY

The word 'only' is used in a variety of situations in English. We might have a sentence 'Only F's will be G's.' For example, 'Only students with an A average will be excused from the final exam.' This sentence does not say that every student with an A will be excused. Instead it says that every student who will be excused has (will have) an A average. But the function of 'only' in such a sentence is to rule something out, not to indicate that there actually will be things of a certain kind. Using this vocabulary:

> a - the final exam $A(x)$ - x has an A average in that class
>
> $S(x)$ - x is a student in the class in question
>
> $E(x, y)$ - x will be excused from y

we can provide this equivalent translation:

> $(\forall x)[E(x, a) \supset [S(x) \,\&\, A(x)]]$

If someone said, "Only students who cheated received an F," it would be natural to understand him as indicating that someone did receive an F. Using this vocabulary:

> $S(x)$ - x is (was) a student $C(x)$ - x cheated
>
> $F(x)$ - x received an F

we would get this translation:

> $(\forall x)[[S(x) \,\&\, F(x)] \supset C(x)] \,\&\, (\exists x)[S(x) \,\&\, F(x)]$

With a sentence 'The only F's that are (were) G are (were) H' the speaker is normally committed to the existence of F's that are (were) G. The sentence:

> 'The only students who failed are those who cheated'

would be translated:

> $(\forall x)[[S(x) \,\&\, F(x)] \supset C(x)] \,\&\, (\exists x)[S(x) \,\&\, F(x)]$

using the obvious vocabulary.

Another kind of sentence with 'only' is the following:

> Only John failed the test.

With this vocabulary:

> a - John b - the test $F(x, y)$ - x failed y

we can translate the sentence like this: $F(a, b) \,\&\, (\forall x)[F(x, b) \supset (x = a)]$ The first conjunct says that John failed the test. The second says that everything that failed the test is John—nothing other than John failed. If we wanted to say that *nobody* other than John failed, we could replace the second conjunct by '$(\forall x)[[P(x) \,\&\, F(x, b)] \supset (x = a)]$,' where '$P(x)$' means *x is a person*.

*Exercise: Section 6

Translate the following into the First-Order language. Explain the predicates and individual constants that you use. Mark weaker translations with an asterisk and stronger translations with a double asterisk.

1. All and only members of the freshman class are invited to the President's reception.

2. Only Mexicans like tequila.

3. Only nonsmokers can buy life insurance from David's company.

4. The only people who can buy life insurance from David's company are nonsmokers.

5. Isabelle invited only Bruce to dinner.

14-7 ANOTHER USE OF 'ANY'

An important use of 'any' is in connection with a negative or a conditional expression. In this sentence:

> Jim doesn't know any Russians.

the use of 'any' depends on the 'n't' in 'doesn't.' For if we take out the negative expression, the resulting "sentence" doesn't make sense. Neither of:

> Jim does know any Russians.

> Jim knows any Russians.

would be used in normal circumstances. There are two ways to understand 'any' in the sentence above. We can note that that sentence means (very nearly) the same as this one:

> Jim doesn't know a Russian.

We can paraphrase this:

> It is false that, for something x, x is a Russian and Jim knows x.
> With this vocabulary:

> a - Jim $R(x)$ — x is a Russian

> $K(x, y)$ - x knows y

we get the following translation:

> $\sim(\exists x)[R(x)\ \&\ K(a, x)]$.

This is equivalent to the original sentence.
> Even when it occurs in:

> Jim doesn't know any Russians.

the word 'any' has a universal "flavor." It seems appropriate to capture this by using a universal quantifier in our translation. Another paraphrase for our original sentence is:

> For everything, if it is a Russian, then Jim doesn't know it.

This yields the following translation:

> $(\forall x)[R(x) \supset\ \sim K(a, x)]$.

We don't supply an existence claim, because the speaker of the original sentence could naturally use it without indicating a commitment to there being Russians.
> An example of the use of 'any' in a conditional sentence is:

> If Tommy eats any cookies, he will be punished.

We should note that the antecedent, 'Tommy eats any cookies,' doesn't make sense as a separate sentence. The 'any' is appropriate only because of its connection with the conditional expression 'if.' Since the above conditional sentence means about the same as this one:

If Tommy eats a cookie, he will be punished.

we can paraphrase it:

If for something, it is a cookie and Tommy eats it, then Tommy will be punished.

With the following vocabulary:

a - Tommy $C(x)$ - x is a cookie $E(x, y)$ - x will eat y

$P(x)$ - x will be punished

we get this translation:

$(\exists x)[C(x) \, \& \, E(a, x)] \supset P(a)$

The translation is weaker than the original sentence because the conditional sentence is translated by the horseshoe.

To translate the sentence with a universal quantifier, we can use this paraphrase:

For everything, if it is a cookie and Tommy eats it, then Tommy will be punished.

Our translation:

$(\forall x)[[C(x) \, \& \, E(a, x)] \supset P(a)]$

does not employ an existence claim. It is essential in this translation that the scope of the universal quantifier extends to the end of the sentence.

Not all uses of 'any' in conditional sentences are connected to the conditional expressions. In this sentence:

If Diane will cheat, then any student will cheat.

the consequent makes sense as a separate sentence. So we translate the consequent as a separate sentence. With this vocabulary:

d - Diane $C(x)$ - x will cheat

$S(x)$ - x is a student

we get this translation:

$C(d) \supset (\forall x)[S(x) \supset C(x)]$.

The following sentence is ambiguous:

If any student will cheat, then Diane will cheat.

For we can regard the 'if'-clause as independently significant. If we regard it that way, we could produce this weaker translation for the antecedent:

$(\forall x)[S(x) \supset C(x)]$

But now we cannot translate the whole sentence into the First-Order language, for if the antecedent of a conditional sentence receives a weaker translation, we cannot determine if the horseshoe sentence is related by entailment to the original sentence. When we regard the antecedent as independently significant, the following is not a suitable translation:

$(\forall x)[S(x) \supset C(x)] \supset C(d)$

There is no suitable First-Order translation. When we don't regard the antecedent as independently significant, then the sentence has the sense of:

If even one student will cheat, then Diane will cheat.

Either of the following provides a suitable translation:

$(\forall x)[[S(x) \,\&\, C(x)] \supset C(d)]$

$(\exists x)[S(x) \,\&\, C(x)] \supset C(d)$

*Exercise: Section 7

Translate the following sentences into the First-Order language. Mark weaker translations with an asterisk and stronger translations with a double asterisk.

1. Barbara hasn't purchased any book.

2. If Clare meets anyone she knows at the party, she will feel relieved.

3. If Jesse hasn't visited any art gallery, then he doesn't know what he has missed.

4. Jack's soccer team hasn't won any games.

14-8 GENERALIZED CONDITIONALS

In the First-Order language, a sentence '$(\forall x)[\ \ldots \supset \ldots\ ]$' is a *generalized conditional* sentence. We use such sentences in translating general (universal) sentences like these:

Every dog is an animal.

Cats are felines.

We can give these sentences the following translations:

$(\forall x)[D(x) \supset A(x)] \,\&\, (\exists x)D(x)$

$(\forall x)[C(x) \supset F(x)] \,\&\, (\exists x)C(x)$

There is another kind of sentence that we translate with a generalized conditional. This kind contains an indefinite article. In this sentence:

If Don encounters a grizzly bear, he (Don) will be terrified.

we can translate the antecedent and consequent by independently significant sentences:

$(\exists x)[G(x) \,\&\, E(d, x)] \supset T(d)$

But in this sentence:

If Dan meets a girl, he will ask her for a date.

we cannot translate antecedent and consequent by independently significant sentences. Suppose we use this vocabulary:

d - Dan $G(x)$ - x is a girl

$M(x, y)$ - x will meet y $A(x, y)$ - x will ask y for a date

There is no trouble translating the antecedent:

$(\exists x)[G(x) \mathbin{\&} M(d, x)]$

But we cannot handle the consequent. For the 'her' in the consequent is linked to 'a girl' in the 'if'-clause. In this First-Order formula:

$(\exists x)[G(x) \mathbin{\&} M(d, x)] \supset A(d, x)$

the final 'x' is a free variable. It is not bound by the existential quantifier. Since this formula contains a free variable, it is not a sentence, and so cannot be a translation for the original English sentence.

It won't do to give the existential quantifier a greater scope like this:

$(\exists x)[[G(x) \mathbin{\&} M(d, x)] \supset A(d, x)]$

The meaning of this First-Order sentence is very different from the meaning of the original sentence. To translate 'If Dan meets a girl, he will ask her for a date' we give up our tactic of translating the indefinite article with the existential quantifier. In this case, we employ a generalized conditional. We can paraphrase the sentence:

For everything x, if x is a girl and Dan meets x, then Dan will ask x for a date.

This yields the following:

$(\forall x)[[G(x) \mathbin{\&} M(d, x)] \supset A(d, x)]$

We do not incorporate an existence claim about girls in our translation, for the original sentence does not make such a claim about girls.

*Exercise A: Section 8

Translate the following sentences into the First-Order language. Mark weaker translations with an asterisk and stronger translations with a double asterisk.

1. If Barbara owns a car, then she won't need a ride to the meeting.

2. If a person owns a car, then the person must buy a license for it.

3. Victor's cat bit an old lady, and she bit the cat right back.

4. If he has any sense, a boy will get a good education.

5. If Mary passes any classmates who are walking, she will give them a ride.

Exercise B: Section 8

Translate the following sentences into the First-Order language. Explain the predicates and individual constants that you use. Mark weaker translations with an asterisk and stronger translations with a double asterisk.

1. Chuck lent his car to his mother.

2. If Albany is the capital of New York, then Buffalo isn't.

3. Manchester is in England, but it isn't the capital of England.

4. Don saw Alice with Bill, but Alice didn't see Don.

5. Although Jorge isn't in his office, he will be.

6. Judy will call Paul and Marvin if they don't come to the faculty meeting.

7. Kevin will go out for baseball or track; in either case, he will make the team.

8. Fred not only insulted Harry, but he also broke Harry's camera.

9. The governor was a Republican four years ago; he's a Democrat now.

10. If Indiana isn't between Illinois and Iowa, then Illinois is between Iowa and Indiana.

Exercise C: Section 8

Translate the following sentences into the First-Order language. Explain the predicates and individual constants that you use. Mark weaker translations with an asterisk. Mark stronger translations with a double asterisk.

1. Sally knows everyone who is important.

2. The lion is the king of beasts.

3. Spiders aren't insects unless insects have eight legs.

4. There is only one null set; it has no members.

5. The mayor won't see any reporters today.

6. Alan will have a martini before dinner only if he isn't giving a talk after dinner.

7. Each woman at the party wore a mink coat, and all of them kept their coats with them.

8. Some students in Professor McBride's logic class came to his office to get help.

9. John drinks at least three cups of coffee every day.

10. There will be no survivors of a nuclear war.

11. The polar bear is an enormous animal.

12. If two is a prime number, then some even number is prime.

13. There is a number which, when multiplied by any number, leaves that number unchanged.

14. The owner of every dairy wants to sell it.

15. Every number is divisible (without remainder) by some number, and some number divides every number.

Exercise D: Section 8

Translate the following sentences into the First-Order language, if this is possible. Explain the expressions that you use. Mark weaker translations with an asterisk and stronger translations with a double asterisk. If some sentence cannot be translated, explain why not.

1. If Larry asks someone to the dance, she will turn him down.

2. Twenty-seven students failed Mr. Kearns' logic class last semester.

3. It isn't the case that if Sam didn't eat any roast beef at dinner, he must not feel well.

4. Scotch and bourbon are whiskies, but cognac isn't.

5. 27 plus 32 is 59 only if 27 plus 33 is 60.

6. If Mr. Foster intends to prosecute any trespassers, then no one should trespass on Foster's property.

7. No one knows anyone who owns every painting by Picasso.

8. If Nelson has more money than anyone, then he has more money than himself; but no one has more money than himself.

9. Cows are cattle; so are bulls and steers.

10. Jack will eat peanut butter sandwiches and nothing else.

11. Only a Mercedes Benz is a good enough car for Karl.

12. If the only people who like okra are from Louisiana, then Larry doesn't like okra.

13. Not many college students have grandchildren.

14. Some doctors examined Dorothy, but couldn't discover what is wrong with her.

15. If a secretary answers when you call Carolyn, then she has gotten a promotion.

16. Take a paragraph from a newspaper or magazine, and translate it into the First-Order language.

14-9 ANALYTIC SENTENCES

Analytic truth has less practical importance than the other general semantic features. In addition, the First-Order language is not well suited to discovering interesting cases of analytic truth. However, we shall see just what we can do by way of uncovering analytic sentences with the First-Order language.

To determine whether an ordinary sentence p is analytic, we need a First-Order translation $p*$ that is either equivalent to or stronger than the original. If the following sentence is understood in the mathematical sense:

Triangles are triangles.

then we can provide this equivalent translation:

$(\forall x)[T(x) \supset T(x)]$

Since it is easy to prove that this First-Order sentence is logically true, we know that the original sentence is analytic. But if we understand this sentence:

Every dog is a dog.

in the ordinary way, we get this equivalent translation:

$$(\forall x)[D(x) \supset D(x)] \ \& \ (\exists x)D(x)$$

The left conjunct is logically true, but the right one is not. The translation isn't logically true. This doesn't show that the original sentence fails to be analytic. But the original sentence does entail that there is a dog. This truth is not one we can discover simply by understanding a sentence claiming that dogs exist. The original sentence is not analytic.

*Exercise A: Section 9

Use the First-Order language to determine which of the following are analytically true. You must do work (either give a proof or a counter-example) which justifies your answers. If some sentence cannot be evaluated, explain why not.

1. A positive integer is either prime or else it isn't.

2. Either it's false that whales aren't fish or there is some fish which isn't a whale.

3. If the grapefruit is a citrus fruit, and the fruit on Molly's dish is a grapefruit, then the fruit on Molly's dish is a citrus fruit.

4. It isn't true that Newton will order a steak only if he doesn't order a steak.

Exercise B: Section 9

Use the First-Order language to determine whether the following are analytically true. Show your translations and explain the predicates and individual constants you use. You must show work which justifies your answers. If some sentence cannot be evaluated, explain why not.

1. The following sentence is to be understood mathematically: Each red barn is red.

2. It isn't true both that students from Mr. Link's epistemology class are complaining to the chairman and that there aren't even two students in his class.

3. Either Leonard isn't good, or he isn't a lawyer, or he's a good lawyer.

4. It isn't true that nothing is the same as itself.

5. If Phil won't come if his car breaks down, then he won't come unless his car doesn't break down.

6. Either there aren't at least two students in Professor Hare's office, or Sheila isn't the only student in his office.

7. Either everything is bigger than something or something is at least as small as everything else.

8. In the following sentence, 'every' is used mathematically: Either no one hates everyone or someone hates himself/herself.

14-10 INCOMPATIBILITY

In testing English sentences and arguments for incompatibility, entailment, and validity, we shall continue our practice of supplementing translations with obviously analytic sentences and well known true sentences. However, we will begin by considering unsupplemented translations. Once we can deal with them, we will enlarge the translations.

To test English sentences $A_1, \ldots, A_n$ for incompatibility, we must provide translations that are equivalent to or weaker than the English sentences. To determine whether these sentences:

> Everyone is selfish. An altruistic person is one who isn't selfish. Carol is one person who is truly altruistic.

are incompatible, we can use this vocabulary:

c - Carol

$S(x)$ - x is selfish

$P(x)$ - x is a person

$A(x)$ - x is altruistic

This gives the following translations:

$(\forall x)[P(x) \supset S(x)]$ & $(\exists x)P(x)$, $(\forall x)[[A(x) \& P(x)] \supset \sim S(x)]$ &

$(\exists x)[A(x) \& P(x)]$, $[P(c) \& A(c)]$

(There is no difference between being altruistic and being truly altruistic.) We can show that these translations are logically incompatible by taking any two and proving that they imply the negation of the one that is left. The following proof does this:

1	$(\forall x)[P(x) \supset S(x)]$ & $(\exists x)P(x)$	
2	$(\forall x)[[A(x) \& P(x)] \supset \sim S(x)]$ & $(\exists x)[A(x) \& P(x)]$	
3	$(\forall x)[P(x) \supset S(x)]$	1, Simp
4	$(\forall x)[[A(x) \& P(x)] \supset \sim S(x)]$	2, Simp
5	$P(c)$ & $A(c)$	
6	$P(c)$	5, Simp
7	$P(c) \supset S(c)$	3, $\forall$E
8	$S(c)$	7, 6, MP
9	$[A(c) \& P(c)] \supset \sim S(c)$	4, $\forall$E
10	$A(c)$	5, Simp
11	$A(c) \& P(c)$	10, 6, Conj
12	$\sim S(c)$	9, 11, MP
13	$S(c) \& \sim S(c)$	8, 12, Conj
14	$\sim[P(c) \& A(c)]$	5 − 13, $\sim$ I

*Exercise A: Section 10

Use the First-Order language as an instrument to determine whether these sentences are incompatible. If the sentences cannot be evaluated by means of the First-Order language, explain why not.

1. Everyone knows at least one lawyer. Lawyers must be college graduates. Somebody doesn't know any college graduates.

2. The only students who will be excused from the final exam are those with an A average. Not a single student will be excused from the final.

3. It isn't true that Jane will go to Florida only if she gets a check before Saturday. But either Jane won't be going to Florida or she will get a check before Saturday. Jane will surely go to Florida.

Exercise B: Section 10

Use the First-Order language to determine whether the following groups of sentences are incompatible. You must show your translations and show work to justify your answers. If the sentences cannot be evaluated by means of the First-Order language, explain why not.

1. Only athletes belong to Delta Iota Pi. There isn't any athlete with a 4.0 average. Mark not only belongs to Delta Iota Pi, but he also has a 4.0 average.

2. The councilmen who attended the conference all bought gifts for their wives. Virgil is a councilman, and he attended the conference, but he didn't buy his wife anything.

3. It isn't true that if Kevin doesn't get new boots, he won't ski this year. If Kevin does get new boots, he won't be able to buy lift tickets. And if he can't buy lift tickets, he won't ski. But Kevin will get new boots.

4. George had fish for dinner Sunday. George had dinner at the Hall's Sunday. The Hall's have never served fish for dinner.

5. It isn't true that some boys called Stephanie last night. Watson is one of the boys in the Spanish Club; last night he called Stephanie and asked her for a date.

6. Jim's children all entered the military or attended a college. One of Jim's children didn't enter the military and didn't graduate from high school. There is no college that was attended by someone who didn't graduate from high school.

7. Michelle knows how to drive, but she doesn't have a license. Jane doesn't let someone drive her car unless that person has a license. Jane lets all of her children drive her car. Michelle is Jane's oldest child.

8. Each contestant won a prize, and only contestants won prizes. It's not true that one contestant won all the prizes. Some prizes weren't won by any contestant.

14-11 ENTAILMENT AND VALIDITY

If we want to determine whether sentences $A_1, \ldots, A_n$ entail B, then we must come up with translations $A_1^*, \ldots, A_n^*, B^*$. We always prefer our translations to be equivalent to the originals, but it is possible to make use of weaker translations for $A_1, \ldots, A_n$. We require that B^* be equivalent to or stronger than B.

To evaluate this argument:

> Bill is a carpenter, and he owns a car. Any carpenter is a union member. So every car of Bill's belongs to a union member.

we can use this vocabulary:

> b - Bill $C(x)$ - x is a carpenter
>
> $A(x)$ - x is a car $U(x)$ - x is a union member
>
> $O(x, y)$ - x owns y

and translate the argument like this:

> $C(b)$ & $(\exists x)[A(x)$ & $O(b, x)]$, $(\forall x)[C(x) \supset U(x)]$ /
>
> $(\forall x)[[A(x)$ & $O(b, x)] \supset (\exists y)[U(y)$ & $O(y, x)]]$ & $(\exists x)[A(x)$ & $O(b, x)]$

We can easily prove that our translation is logically valid:

1	$C(b)$ & $(\exists x)[A(x)$ & $O(b, x)]$	
2	$(\forall x)[C(x) \supset U(x)]$	
3	$C(b)$	1, Simp
4	$C(b) \supset U(b)$	2, $\forall$E
5	$U(b)$	4, 3, MP
6	$(\exists x)[A(x)$ & $O(b, x)]$	1, Simp
7	$\quad A(x)$ & $O(b, x)$	
8	$\quad O(b, x)$	7, Simp
9	$\quad U(b)$ & $O(b, x)$	5, 8, Conj
10	$\quad (\exists y)[U(y)$ & $O(y, x)]$	9, $\exists$I
11	$[A(x)$ & $O(b, x)] \supset (\exists y) [U(y)$ & $O(y, x)]$	7 – 10, $\supset$I
12	$(\forall x)[[A(x)$ & $O(b, x)] \supset (\exists y)[U(y)$ & $O(y, x)]]$	11, $\forall$I
13	$(\forall x)[[A(x)$ & $O(b, x)] \supset (\exists y)[U(y)$ & $O(y, x)]]$ & $(\exists x)[A(x)$ & $O(b, x)]$ 12, 6, Conj	

Since we are unable to provide a suitable translation for 'Any carpenter is a union member,' the following argument:

> Any carpenter is a craftsman. Craftsmen are union members. So any carpenter is a union member.

is not one we can evaluate. (But what about it—is the argument valid?)

In evaluating an argument, we allow the premises to receive weaker translations, but insist that the conclusion have an equivalent or stronger translation. However, we allow the same exception for the First-Order language that we did for the PC language. If the conclusion of an argument is a sentence 'If A, then B,' and A, B have suitable translations A^*, B^*, we will allow ourselves to make use of the translation $(A^* \supset B^*)$—so long as the antecedent A is not intended to call (one or more of) the premisses into question. For A^*, B^* to be suitable, A^* can be weaker than A, but B^* must be equivalent to or stronger than B.

In allowing the exception for arguments with conditional conclusions, we have replaced our original concepts of validity and entailment by new ones. With our original concepts, an argument from $A_1, \ldots, A_n$ to B is valid, and $A_1, \ldots, A_n$ entail B, if we can determine on the basis of understanding the sentences that it isn't possible for $A_1, \ldots, A_n$ to be true when B isn't. For the original concepts, if the argument is valid, then the truth conditions of $A_1, \ldots, A_n$ can't be satisfied without also satisfying those of B. If we adhered to the original concepts, then the exception which allows us to translate an 'If $\ldots$, then $\ldots$' conclusion by a horseshoe sentence would not be justified. In many of the cases covered by this exception, it is possible for the truth conditions of the premisses to be satisfied when the truth conditions of the conclusion are not. The significance of a conditional sentence is relative to a particular person, and that person's knowledge and beliefs. The same indicative conditional sentence can have one significance, and one truth value, for person P and a different significance and truth value for person Q. The premisses of an argument might be true, but not believed by person P; the conditional conclusion 'If A, then B' might be true for anyone who believes the premisses, but not true for P. So the premisses could be true when the conclusion is false for P. With respect to P, then, the argument would not be valid according to the original concept of validity.

However, it seems unreasonable to evaluate the conclusion with respect to a person who doesn't accept the premisses. It makes more sense to ask whether a person who accepts the premisses of an argument is justified in accepting the conclusion. In asking this, we are asking whether accepting the premisses of an argument commits one to accepting its conclusion. This is the basis for the new, *more generous* concepts of entailment and validity. With respect to the more generous concepts, our exception for conditional conclusions is acceptable and correct.

*Exercise A: Section 11

Use the First-Order language to determine whether the following arguments are valid. If an argument cannot be evaluated by means of the First-Order language, explain why not.

1. There is a positive integer which is less than every other. If some positive integer is less than every positive integer, then this positive integer is also greater than every positive integer. So there is a greatest positive integer.

2. Ruth ate something which gave her indigestion. Whatever gave Ruth indigestion was either improperly stored or improperly cooked. So if Ruth didn't eat something that was improperly stored, she did eat something that was improperly cooked.

3. William is a pediatrician, and he belongs to the AMA. Doctors who belong to the AMA are more conservative than those who don't. Neil is a doctor who doesn't belong to the AMA. So William is more conservative than Neil.

4. No one will buy a lottery ticket unless she thinks she might win. Emily is a person who doesn't like to gamble. So Emily will buy a lottery ticket only if she thinks she has a chance of winning.

Exercise B: Section 11

Use the First-Order language to determine whether the following arguments are valid. You must show your translations and show work to justify your answers. If the First-Order language cannot be used to evaluate an argument, explain why not.

1. Everyone knows someone he dislikes. So there is someone that everyone who knows dislikes.

2. Whatever causes another thing is different from the thing it causes. If one thing causes a second, and the second causes a third, then the first also causes the third. So either something had no cause, or whenever a thing has one cause, it is sure to have another.

3. No one in Lee's department supports him for dean. Lee's department is the Civil Engineering Department, and he is its most distinguished member. Everyone who doesn't support Lee for dean supports Keith instead. So the members of the Civil Engineering Department all support Keith for dean.

4. Anyone who won a letter in a spring sport at Mallory High School is either on the track team or plays baseball. Nobody who isn't an excellent pitcher or a good batter plays baseball at Mallory. When Robert is at bat, he's an easy out. So if Robert isn't on the track team, he didn't win a letter in a spring sport at Mallory.

5. The French restaurants in Cincinatti are all very good, but they are quite expensive. Sheila will eat in a restaurant in Cincinatti only if it serves chili. So if Sheila eats in a Cincinatti restaurant, it won't be French, because none of the restaurants that serve chili qualify as quite expensive.

6. No one in Betty's office will go to her party unless they get an apology from her. Betty won't apologize to anyone. Ruth is in Betty's office. So Ruth will go to Betty's party only if Ruth gets an apology from Betty, but she won't get it.

7. The only people who live in California are eccentrics. So Mary isn't an eccentric, because she doesn't live in California.

8. It isn't true that all of the Barker's neighbors hate them. And it isn't true that none of them do. So some neighbor does, and some doesn't.

14-12 COMPARABLE TRANSLATIONS

Suppose we have an argument $A_1, \ldots, A_n / B$, and we translate it $A_1^*, \ldots, A_n^* / B^*$. It can happen that each A_i^* is a good translation for A_i, and B^* is a good translation for B, but $A_1^*, \ldots, A_n^* / B^*$ is a bad translation for $A_1, \ldots, A_n / B$.

As an example consider this argument:

Zachary is a student in Professor Hull's class, and he's not passing. If a student is not passing a class, then the instructor will give the student extra help. So Professor Hull will give Zachary extra help.

Suppose we use this vocabulary:

a - Professor Hull c - Zachary

b - Professor Hull's class $I(x, y)$ - x is in y $S(x)$ - x is a student

$P(x, y)$ - x is passing y $C(x)$ - x is a class $T(x, y)$ - x teaches y

$G(x, y)$ - x will give y extra help

Then we might give this translation:

$[S(c) \mathbin{\&} I(c, b)] \mathbin{\&} {\sim} P(c, b), (\forall x)(\forall y)(\forall z)[[[[S(x) \mathbin{\&} C(y)] \mathbin{\&}$

$\sim P(x, y)] \mathbin{\&} T(z, y)] \supset G(z, x)] / G(a, c)$

This translation is not logically valid. We can reinterpret the vocabulary so that the premisses are true and the conclusion is false.

However, the original argument is obviously valid. Our translation is a poor one, because we can't readily *compare* the two premisses and the conclusion. Since the conclusion talks about Professor Hull, it would be a good idea to translate the first premiss so that it also talks about him. If we use the following vocabulary:

a - Professor Hull c - Zachary

b - Professor Hull's class $P(x, y)$ - x is passing y

$S(x, y, z)$ - x is a student in y which is taught by z

$G(x, y)$ - x will give y extra help

we get this translation:

$[S(c, b, a) \mathbin{\&} {\sim} P(c, b)[, (\forall x)(\forall y)(\forall z)[[S(x, y, z) \mathbin{\&} {\sim} P(x, y)] \supset G(z, x)] / G(a, c)$

The translated sentences are readily comparable. It is easy to show that this translation is valid:

1   $S(c, b, a) \mathbin{\&} {\sim} P(c, b)$

2   $(\forall x)(\forall y)(\forall z)[[S(x, y, z) \mathbin{\&} {\sim} P(x, y)] \supset G(z, x)]$

3   $(\forall y)(\forall z)[[S(c, y, z) \mathbin{\&} {\sim} P(c, y)] \supset G(z, c)]$ 2, $\forall$E

4   $(\forall z)[[S(c, b, z) \mathbin{\&} {\sim} P(c, b)] \supset G(z, c)]$ 3, $\forall$E

5   $[S(c, b, a) \mathbin{\&} {\sim} P(c, b)] \supset G(a, c)$ 4, $\forall$E

6   $G(a, c)$ 5, 1, MP

In making translations, we try to obtain equivalent translations. We also try to obtain translations that bring out the syntactic structures of the original sentences. But this isn't enough. For we must have comparable translations in order to carry out evaluations. We will sometimes sacrifice syntactic structure, or equivalence, to get comparable translations.

A common problem in obtaining comparable translations is choosing the right individual constants. Which names and descriptive terms should be translated by individual constants? Consider this inference:

Dick owns exactly one car, which is a Pontiac. Pontiacs are General Motors products. So Dick's car is a General Motors product.

To translate the first premiss, we need a name for Dick and predicates for being a car, being a Pontiac, and owning:

d - Dick $C(x)$ - x is a car

$P(x)$ - x is a Pontiac $O(x, y)$ - x owns y

If we use '$G(x)$' to mean x *is a General Motors product*, we can translate the premises:

$(\exists x)[[[C(x) \,\&\, O(d, x)] \,\&\, (\forall y)[[C(y) \,\&\, O(d, y)] \supset (x = y)]] \,\&\, P(x)],$

$(\forall x)[P(x) \supset G(x)] \,\&\, (\exists x)P(x)$

But the conclusion contains a descriptive singular term, 'Dick's car.' If we use an individual constant for this term, our translated conclusion will not be readily comparable with the translations of the premises. Instead of using an individual constant for 'Dick's car,' we can give an analysis of 'Dick's car' in our translation without using a constant. Our analysis will follow that provided by Bertrand Russell in the article "On Denoting." According to Russell, when we say that Dick's car is a General Motors product, we mean that:

(i)   There is an individual which is Dick's car,

(ii) There is only one such individual,

(iii) That individual is a General Motors product.

Using this analysis, we could translate the conclusion:

$(\exists x)[[[C(x) \,\&\, O(d, x)] \,\&\, (\forall y)[[C(y) \,\&\, O(d, y)] \supset (x = y)]] \,\&\, G(x)]$

We can now prove that our translation is logically valid:

1	$(\exists x)[[[C(x) \,\&\, O(d, x)] \,\&\, (\forall y)[[C(y) \,\&\, O(d, y)] \supset (x = y)]] \,\&\, P(x)]$	
2	$(\forall x)[P(x) \supset G(x)] \,\&\, (\exists x)P(x)$	
3	$(\forall x)[P(x) \supset G(x)]$	2, Simp
4	$[[C(a) \,\&\, O(d, a)] \,\&\, (\forall y)[[C(y) \,\&\, O(d, y)] \supset (a = y)]] \,\&\, P(a)$	
5	$[C(a) \,\&\, O(d, a)] \,\&\, (\forall y)[[C(y) \,\&\, O(d, y)] \supset (a = y)]$	4, Simp
6	$P(a)$	4, Simp
7	$P(a) \supset G(a)$	3, $\forall$E
8	$G(a)$	7, 6, MP
9	$[[C(a) \,\&\, O(d, a) \,\&\, (\forall y)[[C(y) \,\&\, O(d, y)] \supset (a = y)]] \,\&\, G(a)$	5, 8, Conj
10	$(\exists x)[[[C(x) \,\&\, O(d, x)] \,\&\, (\forall y)[[C(y) \,\&\, O(d, y)] \supset (x = y)]] \,\&\, G(x)]$	9, $\exists$I
11	$(\exists x)[[[C(x) \,\&\, O(d, x)] \,\&\, (\forall y)[[C(y) \,\&\, O(d, y)] \supset (x = y)]] \,\&\, G(x)]$	1, 4 $-$ 10, $\exists$E

Not all problems in achieving comparable translations concern singular terms. Consider this argument:

Sharon is a red-haired teacher of Economics, and the only female faculty member of the Economics Department. Anyone who teaches either Economics or Statistics is mathematically gifted. So there is a mathematically gifted female faculty member.

If we use this vocabulary:

a - Sharon b - the Economics Department

$F(x)$ - x is a female faculty member $M(x, y)$ - x is a member of y

$E(x)$ - x is a person who teaches Economics

$G(x)$ - x is mathematically gifted

$S(x)$ - x is a person who teaches Statistics

we get the following translation:

$R(a)$ & [[$F(a)$ & $M(a, b)$] & $(\forall x)[[F(x) \& M(x, b)] \supset (x = a)]$],

$(\forall x)[[E(x) \lor S(x)] \supset G(x)]$ / $(\exists x)[F(x) \& G(x)]$

It should be clear that this translation is not logically valid, because the connection between being a red-haired teacher of Economics and simply being a teacher of Economics does not "show up" in the logical form of the translation. To achieve a comparable translation, we must analyze what it is to be a red-haired teacher of Economics. This is to be both red-haired and a teacher of Economics. (The same sort of analysis would not work for 'popular teacher of Economics.') So if we let '$R(x)$' mean simply x *is red-haired*, we can translate the first premiss like this:

[$R(a)$ & $E(a)$] & [[$F(a)$ & $M(a, b)$] & $(\forall x)[[F(x) \& M(x, b)] \supset (x = a)]$]]

Now it is easy to construct a proof showing that our translation is valid.

*Exercise A: Section 12

For 1 – 3, use the First-Order language to determine whether the arguments are valid.

1. It is false that Barry will go to the beach Saturday just in case Saturday is a nice day, because Barry is going to the beach Saturday no matter what kind of day it is.

2. The tenants on the first floor are all unmarried lawyers or doctors. Judy is a tenant in the building, and she's a lawyer. So if Judy is unmarried, then she lives on the first floor.

3. Carol is Tom's wife. Any wife of Tom's knows a lot about both baseball and football. But if someone knows a lot about either baseball or football, then that person reads *Sports Illustrated*. So Tom's wife reads *Sports Illustrated*.

For 4 – 6, use the First-Order language to determine if the sentences are incompatible.

4. Diane is tall and slender, and she has bright red hair. No female bus driver who works for the City Transit Line is slender; they are all overweight. But if Diane has a job, she works for the City Transit Line. She does have a job—she is a bus driver.

5. Any hunter who trespasses on Newton's property during the hunting season will be arrested. No one who trespasses on Newton's property will be arrested.

6. If Nick owns a car, it certainly isn't a Mercedes. If Nick's car isn't a Mercedes, it isn't a car at all.

Exercise B: Section 12

Use the First-Order language to determine if the following arguments are valid. Show your translations and show work to justify your answers. If some argument cannot be evaluated, explain why not.

1. Nobody enjoys working as a clerk in a supermarket. Anyone who doesn't enjoy his or her work will look for another job. So Sara isn't working as a clerk in a supermarket unless she is also looking for another job.

2. Barbara's Porsche is a car that cost $22,000. But any car of Barbara's is bound to be expensive, and any Porsche is expensive. If the owner of an expensive car has any sense, he or she has insured it against theft. So Barbara has insured her Porsche against theft.

3. It isn't true that only white wine has been used to fill the glasses on the table. Any glass that isn't filled with white wine is filled with rosé. So some glass on the table is filled with rosé.

4. All but one of Frank's children are girls. John is one of Frank's children, and he isn't a girl. Julie is one of Frank's children too. Julie isn't John. So Julie is a girl.

5. Newton's oldest child is his daughter. Since daughters are children, Newton's oldest child is his oldest daughter.

6. Dinosaurs are extinct. Extinct animals no longer exist, so there are no dinosaurs in the St. Louis Zoo.

7. Jesse hasn't burned all the hamburgers, because some of them still look pink. Burned hamburgers look like charcoal: black on both sides. Hamburgers that look that way don't look pink and they aren't still juicy.

8. Lionel doesn't even have two friends. But Susan is Lionel's friend, and she is both smart and good looking. Sandra isn't smart, though she is good looking. So Sandra must not be Lionel's friend.

Exercise C: Section 12

Use the First-Order language to determine if the following sentences are incompatible. Show your translations, and show work to justify your answers. If some sentences cannot be evaluated, explain why not.

1. There is only one house on this block that doesn't have a big front porch; Chuck lives in a house on this block, but not that house. The houses with big front porches all have porch swings. Chuck's house doesn't have a porch swing.

2. Only honest and capable men ought to be elected to public office. Honest and capable men aren't business partners of known criminals. There is a known criminal whose business partner ought to be elected to public office.

3. One of Ken's children is a priest, another is a surgeon; one is also a college professor. The oldest child is the surgeon, and his daughter is the priest. Ken has exactly two children.

4. Everyone Sally invited will be at the party. Gary's friends won't be there. But there is no one in her chemistry lab whom Sally didn't invite, and some of them are friends of Gary.

5. Everyone knows someone she doesn't like. Julie doesn't know anyone she likes, and she doesn't like anyone she knows. Julie doesn't know anyone or like anyone.

6. Marie's boyfriend is pretty cheap, if he will take her to dinner only if she pays her share. If Marie's boyfriend takes her to dinner, she will pay her share. Marie's boyfriend isn't cheap.

7. There is exactly one barber who lives in Farmer City. The barber shaves every male who lives in Farmer City and who doesn't shave himself, and he only shaves males who don't shave themselves.

8. It isn't true that some students from his programing course visited Mr. Murphy while he was in the hospital. Michele is the only student in his programing course who likes Mr. Murphy, and she visited him while he was in the hospital.

14-13 SUPPLEMENTING OUR TRANSLATIONS

In the PC language, we supplemented our translations with analytic sentences that had the form [$A \supset B$] or [$A \supset \sim B$]. We will now allow ourselves to add extra sentences if:

(1) These have the form $(\forall \alpha_1) \ldots (\forall \alpha_n)[\ldots \supset \text{------}]$, for $n \geq 0$;

(2) They are analytic;

(3) Their analytic character is obvious.

In order to evaluate this argument:

Chuck gave Colleen an expensive present. Anyone polite who received an expensive gift thanked the person who gave it. Colleen is polite. So she thanked Chuck.

we can use this vocabulary:

c - Chuck d - Colleen

$T(x, y)$ - x thanked y $F(x)$ - x is an expensive present

$R(x, y, z)$ - x is a person who received y from person z

$G(x, y, z)$ - x is a person who gave y to person z

$P(x)$ - x is a polite person

This vocabulary yields the following translation:

$(\exists x)[E(x) \& G(c, x, d)], (\forall x)(\forall y)(\forall z)[[[P(x) \& E(y)[\&$

$R(x, y, z)] \supset T(x, z)], P(d) / T(d, c)$

This translation is not logically valid. But it is valid; the semantic connection between giving and receiving fails to show up in the logical form of our translation. The following sentence:

$$(\forall x)(\forall y)(\forall z)[G(x, y, z) \supset R(z, y, x)]$$

has the prescribed form, and is obviously analytic. If we supply this sentence as an additional premiss, we can prove the argument to be valid. (*You* prove it.)

It often happens that we talk about particular people, and make inferences involving 'everybody,' 'anybody,' or 'somebody.' An example is the following:

> Anyone who isn't extravagant doesn't own a Mercedes Benz.
> David owns a Mercedes Benz. So David is extravagant.

If we translate the argument with this vocabulary:

d - David

$P(x)$ - x is a person

$E(x)$ - x is extravagant

$M(x)$ - x owns a Mercedes Benz

we get the following:

$$(\forall x)[[P(x) \& \sim E(x)] \supset \sim M(x)], M(d) \,/\, E(d)$$

However, this translation is not logically valid. The problem is that the first premiss concerns people (persons), and we aren't given a premiss saying that David is a person. We can't say that anything named David is a person, because the name might be given to an animal or to a famous statue. But in a normal conversation, it would ordinarily be clear whether the speaker is concerned with persons or something else. We will say that either a particular use of a name or the linguistic context itself makes it clear whether we are dealing with persons. *In such a context*, if we are dealing with persons, we will regard it as analytic that a certain individual is a person. In this book, we will assume that the use of an ordinary personal name is a sign that the named individual is a person, unless there is some indication to the contrary. So we can translate the above argument like this:

$$(\forall x)[[P(x) \& \sim E(x)] \supset \sim M(x)], M(d), P(d) \,/\, E(d)$$

Now we can prove that the argument is valid:

1	$(\forall x)[[P(x) \& \sim E(x)] \supset \sim M(x)]$	
2	$M(d)$	
3	$P(d)$	
4	$[P(d) \& \sim E(d)] \supset \sim M(d)$	1, $\forall$E
5	$\quad \sim E(d)$	
6	$\quad P(d) \& \sim E(d)$	3, 5, Conj
7	$\quad \sim M(d)$	4, 6, MP
8	$\quad M(d) \& \sim M(d)$	2, 7, Conj
9	$E(d)$	$5 - 8$, $\sim$ E

*Exercise A: Section 13

For 1 – 3, determine which of the following are valid. You can supply additional analytic premisses if required.

1. Anne got at least a B from each of her professors. Anyone who gave Anne a B or better thinks she is intelligent. But none of Anne's relatives think she is intelligent. So none of Anne's professors is a cousin of Ed's, for his cousins are all related to Anne.

2. Nobody had a helping of Martha's potato salad. Anyone who made a dish and didn't have a helping of his or her own dish isn't a good cook. So Martha must not be a good cook.

3. Anyone who has visited Tampa has been either to Busch Gardens or to DisneyWorld. Arlene thinks that DisneyWorld is vulgar and overly commercial, although she has never been there. She doesn't like Busch Gardens either. So Arlene hasn't visited Tampa.

For 4 – 6, determine whether the following groups of sentences are incompatible. You may supplement the translations with additional analytic sentences if required.

4. Jose never drinks alcoholic beverages. Whenever Jose eats at the Gracia's, he is served wine. Invariably polite, Jose eats whatever food and drinks whatever beverage he is served.

5. U.S. Army Rangers are soldiers. But only those who have been trained to kill people are soldiers, and U.S. Army Rangers haven't been trained to kill people.

6. Everybody on the cross country team except Ed Monnelly got a letter this year. Ed ran in twelve meets and never placed worse than tenth. Anyone who placed in the top ten in at least four meets got a letter.

Exercise B: Section 13

Use the First-Order language to determine whether the following arguments are valid. You may supplement the premisses in your translations with additional analytic premisses if required. You must show your translations and show work to justify your answers.

1. A normal summer in St. Louis is both hot and humid; being hot and humid is what it takes for a summer to be normal. No summer in St. Louis is hot without being humid. So if a summer in St. Louis isn't normal, it is humid but not hot.

2. Every successful person owes his success to someone else. Whenever one person owes his success to another, the other person ought to be compensated by the first. But if one person ought to be compensated by a second, then there is something that the second ought to give the first. So if there is nothing that someone ought to be given by Jim, then Jim isn't successful.

3. Mary's jewelry is insured against loss and theft. Mary's engagement ring is either on the kitchen window sill or else it has been stolen. If Mary is missing something that is covered by insurance, it will be replaced. So if Mary's engagement ring isn't replaced, then it is on the kitchen window sill.

4. Allan, Brian, and Carla had reason to want Murdock dead; no one else did. Murdock was killed on Tuesday evening by a person who was waiting for him in his apartment

in San Diego. Allan couldn't have killed Murdock, if he was in Chicago Tuesday. But someone saw Allan in Chicago Tuesday. Whoever killed Murdock had both a motive and the opportunity. Carla has never been in San Diego. So Brian did it.

5. It isn't true that a worker will quit unless she is adequately paid. But a worker who isn't adequately paid will quit if she doesn't need her job. Sally is a worker who doesn't need her job. So Sally will quit unless she is adequately paid.

6. Herb is very abrasive; no one likes him. Herb regards anyone who doesn't like him as an enemy. So Herb must regard everyone as an enemy.

7. If Gene isn't guilty, he won't be convicted unless he has a terrible lawyer defending him. But Carolyn is Gene's defense attorney, and she isn't terrible. So if Gene is convicted, we can be sure he's guilty.

8. Every camper wrote a letter to his parents on Sunday night. The letters written on Sunday were mailed on Monday and received by Friday. So no camper's parents received a letter from the camper on Saturday.

Exercise C: Section 13

Use the First-Order language to determine if the following sentences are incompatible. Show your translations and show work to justify your answers. You may supplement your translations with additional analytic sentences if required.

1. There is no bricklayer who is also a concert pianist. Some friend of Jack's is a concert pianist. But all of Jack's friends are bricklayers.

2. If George buys a new car, it will be a Chrysler product. George won't buy a Chrysler product, unless it is a new car. George isn't buying a car, but he will buy a Chrysler product.

3. Gill and Dan are the only persons who could have taken the money. Someone took the money, but Gill didn't. Neither did Dan.

4. Bob didn't ask anyone to the prom. Bob went to the prom, and he didn't go alone, he took Cheryl.

5. Human beings are rational animals. Barney is human, and he's an animal all right. But Barney is incapable of being rational.

6. Not all undergraduate philosophy majors will become rich or famous. Those undergraduate philosophy majors who specialize in logic will become rich and famous. Undergraduate philosophy majors all specialize in logic.

7. It isn't true that a match will light if it is struck. A match won't light if it isn't dry. Any match that won't light hasn't been struck.

8. Swiss Army Knives are made of stainless steel, which doesn't rust. Henry has a Swiss Army Knife with a saw blade. The knife of Henry's which has a saw blade is rusty.

In evaluating arguments, we not only add analytic sentences, but we also add well-known true sentences. If we translate this argument:

None of Bill's relatives lives in California.
So Bill hasn't any relatives living in Los Angeles.

with this vocabulary:

b - Bill

c - California

d - Los Angeles

$R(x, y)$ - *x* is a relative of *y*'s

$L(x, y)$ - *x* lives in *y*

we obtain:

$(\forall x)[R(x, b) \supset \sim L(x, c)] / (\forall x)[R(x, b) \supset \sim L(x, d)]$

This translation is neither logically valid nor valid. But it is well known that Los Angeles is in California, and also that anyone who lives in Los Angeles lives in California. If we add this to the premiss above:

$(\forall x)[L(x, d) \supset L(x, c)]$

we get a valid argument. It is reasonable to add the extra premiss, for the person making the argument surely intended that information to figure in his argument.

*Exercise D: Section 13

Determine which of the following are valid, or become valid when supplemented with well-known true premises.

1. Food containing salt contributes to high blood pressure. Anyone who has hypertension has reason to avoid things which contribute to high blood pressure. So Jane either has reason to avoid food containing salt or else she doesn't have hypertension.

2. *Huck Finn* is a great novel. Only outstanding writers have written great novels. Some of Mark Twain's books are mediocre. So not all the books written by an outstanding writer are outstanding.

3. None of the clerks who works on the first floor has a college degree. The employees who are on lunch break now are either clerks who work on the first floor or management trainees. Bradley must not be on lunch break, because he's an employee who graduated from Princeton, but he's not a management trainee.

Determine whether the following sentences are incompatible, or become so when supplemented with well-known true sentences.

4. George will never travel to a place that isn't in the U.S. or Canada. Fran will marry George only if he will take her to Bermuda for their honeymoon. Fran won't marry anyone but George, although she will get married.

5. Every middle class adult American has played *Monopoly*. Henri doesn't own a *Monopoly* set, although he is certainly middle class. Henri has never even heard of *Monopoly*; he should have. After all, he has lived in Montreal for all of his 27 years.

6. Mathematically gifted people really appreciate classical music. Nobody who really appreciates classical music also likes country music. It is the people who lack aesthetic sensibility who like country music. Engineers are one group of people who lack aesthetic sensibility.

Exercise E: Section 13

Use the First-Order language to determine whether the premises below provide adequate (deductive) support for the conclusions. In evaluating these inferences, you may supply obviously analytic premises or well-known true premises. You must show your translations and show work to justify your answers.

1. The cause of the food poisoning was one of the tuna fish casserole or the pot of baked beans or the macaroni salad. The only ones who got sick were those who ate some of the substance that caused food poisoning, but all of them got sick. Everyone who ate some of all three dishes got sick. Someone who didn't get sick ate the macaroni but not the tuna or the beans. Those who had tuna and macaroni but not beans got sick. So the tuna fish casserole caused the food poisoning.

2. Only the members of Trinity Church are eligible to borrow from the Trinity Credit Union; the Trinity Credit Union won't grant a loan to anyone who isn't eligible. Mark doesn't know anyone who can pay cash for a new car. Betty is going to buy a new four door sedan. Betty will either pay cash for it or borrow from the Trinity Credit Union to pay for it. So if Betty is a friend of Mark's, she is a member of Trinity Church.

3. No sane person would let his or her young child play with a loaded revolver. Nick's daughter is playing with a loaded revolver. So Nick must be crazy, because his daughter is seven.

4. Jane's children forgot about April Fool's Day, and didn't play any tricks that day. If one of her children had remembered, that child would have put salt in the sugar bowl on April Fool's Day. Jane wouldn't have been able to eat her cereal if there were salt in the sugar bowl. So Jane was able to eat her cereal on April Fool's Day.

5. Either there is a McDonald's Restaurant to which Bob told Rosemary he would take her to lunch, or else there is a Pizza Hut where he said he would take her to lunch. Bob will certainly take Rosemary to lunch, if he said he would, and he will take her to whatever restaurant he said. Rosemary will have salad if they go to Pizza Hut. So Rosemary is sure to have salad, because Bob never goes to restaurants that specialize in hamburgers.

6. The only people who have survived a trip over Niagara Falls have gone over on the Canadian side. Sandra went over Niagara Falls in a small boat. When the motor stalled, she tried to guide the boat to the Canadian side. If she wasn't successful, she must be dead.

7. The butterflies on display were all selected by Dr. Cohen. Each butterfly illustrates a distinctive coloration, and some are brightly colored. Not all of the butterflies are native to this area; those that aren't come from South America. All of the insects on display that aren't native to this area were collected by Dr. Cohen, on scientific expeditions to their native habitats. So either Dr. Cohen has collected a colorful butterfly in South America, or else there is a colorful butterfly native to this area.

8. The product of two odd integers is odd. The product of an even integer and any integer is an even integer. So if an integer squared is even, the integer is even. (Hint: It is analytic, or at least well known, that every integer is even or odd.)

Exercise F: Section 13

Use the First-Order language to determine whether the sentences below are incompatible, either as they stand or when supplemented with well-known true sentences. You must show your translations, and show work to justify your answers.

1. Only female mosquitos bite, male mosquitos don't need blood. Gary does research on mosquitos, and he put his arm in a compartment that contained only male mosquitos. He got mosquito bites from doing that.

2. The girls that Jack likes don't like him. But some girls do like Jack—Peggy, for one. Jack likes any girl who is slender and good looking. Peggy is certainly good looking; and she is slender if anyone is.

3. People who study ethics will learn how to rationalize behavior they know is wrong. The only people who will become really successful criminals will be able to rationalize behavior they know is wrong. But not everyone who studies ethics will become a really successful criminal.

4. Technological advances are always based on scientific advances; technology depends on scientific knowledge. But the windmill and the water wheel were developed independently of scientific knowledge.

5. Those children who watch two or more hours of television every day are more prone to aggression and violence than children who watch less. Some of the most aggressive and violent children watch television less than an hour each day.

6. No students in Professor Hall's Ethics course had done the reading for Monday's class. Professor Hall gave a quiz on the reading Monday; her quizzes always provide a good indication of whether students have read and understood their assignments. Professor Hall's students all did well on her quiz Monday.

7. Every student who scored more than 100 points on the logic final has a satisfactory knowledge of logic. There are students (in that logic class) who don't have a satisfactory knowledge of logic. Only one student failed to score more than 100 points on the logic final.

8. The only people who lead rich, rewarding lives are those who have achieved an understanding of logic. Not everyone who has studied logic has achieved an understanding of logic, but the only ones with an understanding of logic are those who have studied it. No one whose life is rich and rewarding has ever made use of an artificial language.

AFTERWORD: REFLECTIONS ON LOGIC

1. Applied Logic

This book, and the course for which it is the text, deals with applied logic. We have developed and investigated various artificial languages, then used them as instruments to increase our understanding of ordinary English. We have considered specific English sentences, groups of sentences, and arguments, which we evaluate by translating them into an artificial language, and evaluating their translations.

In applying the artificial languages to ordinary English, we have been concerned to detect instances of analytic truth, entailment, validity, and incompatibility. Our primary interest has been directed to the last three semantic features, because they have more practical importance than does analyticity. Being able to recognize an analytic sentence shows that we understand the sentence and the expressions in it. But this understanding precedes the ability to recognize analyticity. About the only thing an analytic sentence might be good for is to explain expressions to someone else.

It is different with entailment. The ability to recognize entailment is necessary in order to recognize the consequences of statements made by oneself or someone else. This is important if we are to use language effectively. We must also recognize entailment if we are to recognize validity and make valid inferences. This ability is required to do something as simple as following directions. Making valid inferences gives us a way to increase our knowledge and to convince others.

We know that someone is mistaken if she makes incompatible assertions. Incompatibility is a sure sign of error. Being able to spot incompatibility enables us to recognize and to avoid error. This is also part of the effective use of language.

There is nothing particularly logical about the general semantic features analyticity, entailment, validity, and incompatibility. We have made use of logic to get at these features. We have studied logically perspicuous artificial languages. The logical forms in these languages are easy to detect. This makes it easier to tell when we have a logical special case of a general semantic feature.

We have dealt with logical semantic features in artificial logical languages as a means to detect plain semantic features in ordinary English. This makes it seem that we have been concerned with what is logical by default. We aren't really interested in logical features. What really concerns us are the general features. If we had some more direct way to get at these general semantic features—without taking a detour through logical languages and logical features—then we would have no interest in logic and logical features. However, it is no accident that logical semantic features are more accessible than the general features.

Logical expressions and logical concepts are among the most fundamental expressions and concepts of a language. They are linked to various grammatical categories, so that an understanding of the logical concepts is necessary for the correct use of expressions in the related categories. Consider the quantifiers 'every' and 'some' (or '∀' and '∃' in the First-Order language). These are linked to the category of common nouns and noun phrases in English, and to nouns or predicates in the artificial languages. We don't understand nouns or predicates unless we understand how they are used to denote one or more individuals (and sometimes zero individuals). We must also understand how different nouns (predicates) can denote the same individual—this is to understand what it is for some F to be a G. And we must understand how the objects denoted by one expression can be included among those denoted by a second expression—which is to understand what it means for every F to be a G.

2. Logical Theory

This book has emphasized the application of logic to ordinary English. A reader who is interested in the further study of logic should look for courses in logical theory. In such a course, one studies artificial languages and deductive systems for establishing results in these languages. Little or no attention is paid to translating ordinary sentences into the logical languages. The emphasis in a course on logical theory is on metatheorems which establish results about the language and deductive system. With respect to a deductive system, the most important metatheorems are those which show that the system is sound and complete.

In the next course after this one, it is appropriate to study one or more deductive systems for the basic languages of modern logic, the Propositional Connective language and the First-Order language. After getting a good grounding in these languages and systems, you can move on to more specialized areas in logic, such as modal logic, tense logic, or the logic of questions or imperatives.

Even though logical theory doesn't deal with specific sentences or arguments from a natural language, logical theory is related to natural languages. Artificial languages are much simpler than the languages people speak, but they incorporate various features from these languages. The understanding of an artificial language carries over to the natural language which has features in common with it. Logical theory explains those features of a natural language which it shares with the artificial one.

Logic is a very old subject of study, but it isn't a closed or finished one. Instead, logic is currently expanding and developing. New "departments" are being added, old ones are being redeveloped. Logic is an interesting and challenging field. There is plenty of opportunity for readers of this book to make important contributions to its further development.

Answers
to Starred
Questions

CHAPTER ONE

Section 2
1. False. A word can be both mentioned and used. It can also be mentioned without being used.
2. True
3. False
4. 'To be or not to be' is a line in *Hamlet*.
5. 'Short' is longer than 'long.'

Section 3
1. False
2. True
3. True

4 and **5** are an example of a paradoxical pair of sentences. If either is true, then it is false. And, apparently, if either is false, then it is true. There is no universally accepted explanation of these sentences. Some logicians have called the sentences meaningless. Others claim they are significant, but neither true nor false. What do you think?

Section 4
1. Each expression is included in the other.
2. Incompatible
3. Neither inclusion nor incompatibility.
4. Neither inclusion nor incompatibility.
5. 'logician' is included in 'human being.'

Section 5
1. False
2. False. Both a true and a false sentence can entail a true sentence.
3. True

CHAPTER TWO

Section 1
1. True
2. True
3. False
4. This definition is used to explain an expression already in the language.
5. This definition is used to assign a technical sense to an ordinary expression.
6. This definition is used to make a vague expression more precise.
7. This definition is negative when it might helpfully be affirmative. It is also subject to a further difficulty. Before an organism is born, it is surely not dead. But it isn't alive either. So the definition is too broad.
8. This definition is too narrow, for it excludes squares. It is also too broad, for it includes parallelograms that don't have right angles.

Section 2
For 1–3, the arguments are rewritten with the premisses first and the conclusion at the end.
1. Athletes are brave, but no cowards are brave. Some heavy drinkers are athletes. Therefore, some heavy drinkers aren't cowards.
2. This argument doesn't need rewriting. The premisses precede the conclusion in the original exercise.
3. Smith has high blood pressure or lung cancer only if he smokes. And Smith smokes only if he isn't a Mormon. But Smith is a Mormon. Therefore, Smith doesn't have high blood pressure.
4. (b) If an inference is satisfactory by inductive criteria, and the inference has true premisses, then the inference *may* have a true conclusion.
5. (a) A deductively valid inference is inductively satisfactory as well. An argument which guarantees the truth of its conclusion provides conclusive evidence for the conclusion. It gives the conclusion the highest possible probability.
6. (c) If an argument is valid and its conclusion is false, then at least one premiss is false, for if all the premisses were true, the conclusion couldn't be false.

Section 3
1. Appeal to tradition
2. Circular argument
3. Appeal to force
4. Appeal to ignorance
5. *Argumentum ad hominem*, circumstantial
6. *Argumentum ad hominem*, abusive
7. Equivocation. The word 'equal' is a relative adjective; people can be equal in one respect but not another.
8. *Argumentum ad hominem*, abusive
9. Composition
10. Division

CHAPTER THREE

Section 1
1. True
2. True

3. False
4. True

Section 2
1. Concrete
2. Concrete
3. Abstract
4. Intermediate
5. Concrete
6. Abstract
7. Abstract
8. Concrete
9. Abstract
10. Abstract
11. False
12. True
13. True
14. False

Section 3
1. False. To say at most two passed is compatible with no students passing.
2. True
3. False. If at least one was killed, there might have been more than one.
4. False
5. True
6. False. To say 'at most one' means no more than one. But there might not even be one.

Section 4
1. Sentences b and c are clearly universal. Sentence d is universal in one respect but not another. Considered as a sentence about Jack, it is not universal—it is a singular sentence. Considered as a sentence about Jack's friends, it is universal.
2. Sentence c is affirmative. Sentences b and d are negative.
3. With the understanding indicated, every pair is incompatible.
4. With the universal affirmative sentences understood mathematically, c is an incompatible pair. But pairs a and b are not incompatible.

Section 5
1. This would not be understood universally.
2. It is natural to undersand this universally.
3. This would be understood as a universal statement about every girl Ralph meets at the party.
4. This would not be understood universally.
5. This would not be understood universally.
6. This would be understood as a universal statement about all lawyers.

Section 6
1. This is a singular sentence.
2. This sentence is ambiguous. It could be used to make a statement about the current

president; understood this way, the sentence is singular. It could also be used to make a statement about every president.
3. This is a singular sentence.
4. This sentence is both universal and singular. It is a universal sentence with respect to persons in Jesse's class. It is a singular sentence with respect to Jesse.

CHAPTER FOUR

Section 1
1. False. Analyticity is a semantic feature. It does not belong to syntax.
2. False
3. False
4. True

Section 2
1. False
2. True
3. False. If a sentence is logically true, then it is true. A sentence cannot be both true and false.
4. True

CHAPTER FIVE

Section 1
1. Universal negative
2. Particular negative
3. Universal affirmative
4. Particular affirmative. The predicate of this sentence contains 'not,' but a negative predicate does not affect the classification of the sentence.
Sentences **5–8** are as follows: 5. A   6. O   7. E   8. A

Section 2
The correct answers are as follows:
1. a, b
2. b, c, d
3. b, d

Section 3
The formulas below symbolize sentences 1– 6. But the variables chosen are not important. Any others might be used.
1. Some B is not a D
2. Some B is not a B
3. Every G is an F
4. No G is an F (The expressions 'general' and 'famous general' are different, and must be replaced by different variables.)

Section 4
The complements of 1–4 are:
1. non-Methodist

2. non-(Protestant Christian)
3. non-(president of the United States)
4. non-non-animal
The true sentences are 5 and 7.

Section 5
1. Converse   (a) Every human tragedy is a war.
                (b) No spatial location is a year.
                (c) Some small number is a prime number.
                (d) Some color is not a property.
2. Obverse   (a) No war is a non-(human tragedy).
                (b) Every year is a non-(spatial location).
                (c) Some prime number is not a non-(small number).
                (d) Some property is a non-color.
3. Contrapositive (a) Every non-(human tragedy) is a non-war.
                (b) No non-(spatial location) is a non-year.
                (c) Some non-(small number) is a non-(prime number).
                (d) Some non-color is not a non-property.

Section 6
The following are the equivalent pairs of sentences: 2, 3
The following sentences are linked by implication from left to right: 6, 8
The following pairs of sentences are equivalent: 9, 10
The explanations for 13–18 are as follows:
13. There is no implication. The sentences are symbolized by
          No P is a B Some B is not a P
If we replace 'P' by 'politician' and 'B' by 'vampire,' the left sentence will be true and the right sentence false.
14. The (a) sentence does not imply the (b) sentence. The sentences are symbolized:
          Every R is a C No C is a non-R
If we replace 'R' by 'rake' and 'C' by 'tool,' the left sentence is true and the right sentence false.
15. The (a) sentence implies the (b) sentence. A proof is:
          1   Every B is a non-C hypothesis
          2   No B is a C 1, Obverse Elimination
          3   No C is a B 2, Conversion of E
16. The (a) sentence implies the (b) sentence. They are related by conversion, and I sentences imply their converses.
17. The (a) sentence implies the (b) sentence. A proof follows.
          1   Some non-O is a B hypothesis
          2   Some B is a non-O 1, Conversion of I
          3   Some B is not an O 2, Obverse Elimination
18. The (a) sentence implies the (b) sentence. A proof follows.
          1   Some B is not an M hypothesis
          2   Some B is a non-M 1, Obverse Introduction
          3   Some non-M is a B 2, Conversion of I
          4   Some non-M is not a non-B 3, Obverse Introduction
          5   Some non-M is a non-non-B 4, Obverse Introduction

Section 7
The following sentences are logically true: 2, 4

Section 8
1. Some non-dog is a tiger.

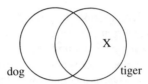

2. Every dog is an animal.

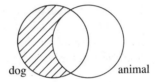

3. No dog is a non-dog.
The unmarked diagram represents the sentence, which is logically true.

4. Every non-dog is a non-animal.

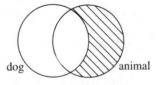

5. Some non-dog is not a dog.
This indicates that something which isn't a dog isn't a dog—i.e., that there is a non-dog.

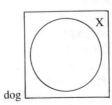

6. These sentences are equivalent. They can both be diagramed with this diagram:

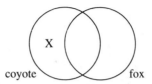

7. These sentences are equivalent. Their diagram is the following:

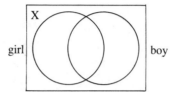

8. These sentences are not equivalent. They have these diagrams:

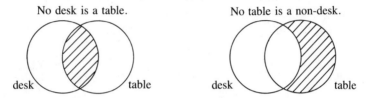

9. These sentences are equivalent. They have this diagram:

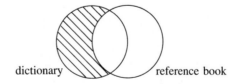

Section 9
1. The diagrams are:

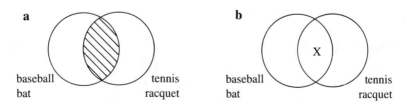

The diagrams show the sentences to be incompatible.

2. The diagrams are:

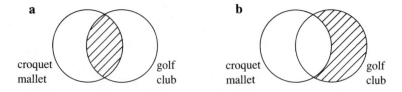

The sentences are not incompatible.

3. The diagram for the left sentence is:

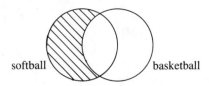

The right sentence cannot be diagramed; it makes an impossible claim. The two sentences are incompatible; the right sentence is incompatible with every sentence (including itself).

4. The diagrams are:

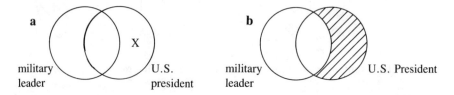

The sentences are incompatible.

5. The diagrams are:

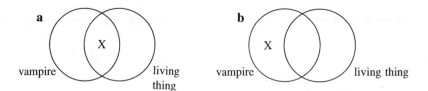

The sentences are not incompatible.

Section 10

1. a is not a syllogism; it contains too many terms.
 b is a syllogism.
 c is not a syllogism; the terms are not organized properly.
2. a. Middle term: mountaineer
 Minor term: Montanan
 Major term: mutinous man

    b. Middle term: magician
       Minor term: misogynist
       Major term: musician
    c. Middle term: politician
       Minor term: politician
       Major term: petty person.

3. a. Minor premiss: Some xyster manufacturer is an X-ray technician.
       Major premiss: Every X-ray technician is a xylophone player.
    b. Minor premiss: Every Brighton resident is a Briton.
       Major premiss: No Briton is a Breton.

4. a. EAE
    b. AEE

5. a. AAA-1
    b. EAO-4
    c. IEO-2
    d. EAE-3
    e. AOO-4
    f. EAO-1

Section 11

1. 1   Every non-duck is a bird.

    2   No non-duck is a non-bird.   1, ObvI

    3   No non-bird is a non-duck.   2, E-Conv

    4   Every non-bird is a duck.   3, ObvE

2. 1   Some farmer is not a non-electrician.

    2   Some farmer is an electrician.   1, ObvE

    3   Some electrician is a farmer.   2, I-Conv

    4   Some electrician is not a non-farmer.   3, ObvI

3. 1   No M is a non-P

    2   No non-P is an M 1, E-Conv

    3   Every non-P is a non-M 2, ObvI

4. 1   Every non-non-non-C is a non-non-non-C LT

    2   No non-non-non-C is a non-non-C 1, ObvE

    3   Every non-non-non-C is a non-C 2, ObvE

5. 1   No F is a G

    2   Some F is an H

    3   Some H is an F 2, I-Conv

    4   Every F is a non-G 1, ObvI

    5   Some H is a non-G 4, 3, AII-1

    6   Some H is not a G 5, ObvE

6. 1   No camelopard is a leopard.

    2   Every giraffe is a camelopard.

    3   Every camelopard is a non-leopard.   1, ObvI

    4   Every giraffe is a non-leopard.   3, 2, AAA-1

    5   No giraffe is a leopard.   4, ObvE

    6   No leopard is a giraffe.   5, E-Conv

7. EIO-1

    1   No A is a B

    2   Some C is an A

    3   Every A is a non-B 1, ObvI

    4   Some C is a non-B 3, 2, AII-1

    5   Some C is not a B 4, ObvE

8. OAO-3

    1   Some F is not a G

    2   Every F is an H

    3   Some F is a non-G 1, ObvI

    4   Some non-G is an F 3, I-Conv

    5   Some non-G is an H 2, 4, AII-1

    6   Some H is a non-G 5, I-Conv

    7   Some H is not a G 6, ObvE

9. AEE-2

    1   Every M is an N

    2   No L is an N

    3   No N is an L 2, E-Conv

    4   Every N is a non-L 3, ObvI

    5   Every M is a non-L 4, 1, AAA-1

    6   No M is an L 5, ObvE

    7   No L is an M 6, E-Conv

10. 1   No machine gun is a child's toy.

    2   Every crew-served weapon in an infantry platoon is a machine gun.

    3   Every machine gun is a non-(child's toy).   1, ObvI

    4   Every crew-served weapon in an infantry
       platoon is a non-(child's toy).   3, 2, AAA-1

5 No crew-served weapon in an infantry
platoon is a child's toy.   4, ObvE

11. A clearly invalid IOI-3 syllogism is the following:

Some duck is a bird.
Some duck is not a truck.
So some truck is a bird.

12. An EIO-2 syllogism is valid. We can prove this as follows:

1 No *R* is an *S*

2 Some *T* is an *S*

3 No *S* is an *R*   1, E-Conv

4 Every *S* is a non-*R*   3, ObvI

5 Some *T* is a non-*R*   4, 2, AII-1

6 Some *T* is not an *R*   5, ObvE

13. The following shows that EAO-4 syllogisms are not (in general) valid.

No mammal is a vampire.
Every vampire is a donkey.
So some donkey is not a mammal.

14. The following shows that EOO-1 syllogisms are not (in general) valid.

No cow is a bird.
Some duck is not a cow.
So some duck is not a bird.

15. We can prove that IAI-4 syllogisms are valid.

1 Some *P* is a *Q*

2 Every *Q* is an *R*

3 Some *P* is an *R*   2, 1, AII-1

4 Some *R* is a *P*   3, I-Conv

16. This is valid. One way to prove it is the following:

1 Every dictionary is a book.

2 Some dictionary is a dictionary.

3 Some dictionary is a book.   1, 2, AII-1

17. This is valid. A proof is:

1 Some lion is an octopus.

2 Every octopus is a mammal.

3 Some lion is a mammal.   2, 1, AII-1

4 Some mammal is a lion.   3, I-Conv

18. This is invalid. The premisses are already true and the conclusion is false. This makes it obvious that the argument isn't valid.

19. This is not valid. The argument has this form:

> No *B* is a *Y*
> Every *B* is a *G*
> So no *G* is a *Y*

If we replace '*B*' by 'book,' '*Y*' by 'yacht,' and '*G*' by 'physical object,' we get true premisses and a false conclusion.

20. This is invalid. If we replace '*A*' by 'animal, '*B*' by 'bear,' and '*C*' by 'cat,' the premisses will be true and the conclusion false.

21. This is valid. It can be proved like this:

1	Every *A* is a *B*	
2	Every *B* is a *C*	
3	Some *A* is an *A*	
4	Every *A* is a *C*	2, 1, AAA-1
5	Some *A* is a *C*	4, 3, AII-1
6	Some *C* is an *A*	5, I-Conv

22. This is not valid. If we replace '*A*' by 'vampire,' '*B*' by 'bear,' '*C*' by 'fish,' and '*D*' by 'shark,' the premisses will be true and the conclusion false.

23. This is valid. It can be proved as follows:

1	Every *F* is a *G*	
2	No *G* is an *H*	
3	Some *H* is an *H*	
4	Every *G* is a non-*H*	2, ObvI
5	Every *F* is a non-*H*	4, 1, AAA-1
6	No *F* is an *H*	5, ObvE
7	No *H* is an *F*	6, E-Conv
8	Every *H* is an non-*F*	7, ObvI
9	Some *H* is a non-*F*	8, 3, AII-1
10	Some *H* is not an *F*	9, ObvE

Section 12

1.

1	Some dog is not a non-collie.	
2	Some dog is a collie	1, ObvE
3	Some collie is a dog.	2, I-Conv
4	Some collie is not a non-dog.	3, ObvI

2. 1   Every vampire is a unicorn.

2   Some vampire is a dragon.

———————————————

3   Some dragon is a vampire.   2, I-Conv

4   Some dragon is a unicorn.   1, 3, AII-1

3. 1   Every non-*A* is a non-*B*

———————————————

2   No non-*A* is a *B*   1, ObvE

3   No *B* is a non-*A*   2, E-Conv

4.   1   No *A* is a non-*B*

2   No *B* is a *D*

3   Every *C* is a *D*

———————————————

4   No *D* is a *B*   2, E-Conv

5   Every *D* is a non-*B*   4, ObvI

6   Every *C* is a non-*B*   5, 3, AAA-1

7   No non-*B* is an *A*   1, E-Conv

8   Every non-*B* is a non-*A* 7, ObvI

9   Every *C* is a non-*A*   8, 6, AAA-1

10   No *C* is an *A*   9, ObvE

5. These are incompatible. This can be proved:

1   Every dog is a cat.

2   Some dog is a dog.

———————————————

2   Some dog is a cat   1, 2, AII-1

6. These are not incompatible. If we replace '*A*' by 'cow,' '*B*' by 'mammal,' and '*C*' by 'animal,' all three sentences will be true.

7. The three sentences are all true. This shows they are not incompatible.

8. These symbolize incompatible sentences. We can prove this:

1   Every *Q* is a non-*P*

2   No non-*Q* is an *R*

3   Every *S* is an *R*

———————————————

4   No *R* is a non-*Q*   2, E-Conv

5   Every *R* is a *Q*   4, ObvE

6   Every *S* is a *Q*   5, 3, AAA-1

7   Every *S* is a non-*P*   1, 6, AAA-1

8   No *S* is a *P*   7, ObvE

9   No *P* is an *S*   8, E-Conv

10   Every *P* is a non-*S*   9, ObvI

Section 13

1. The argument is valid.

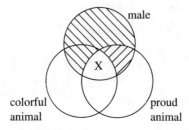

2. The argument is not logically valid.

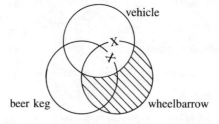

3. This argument is valid.

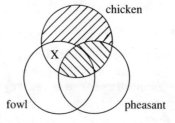

4. This argument is valid.

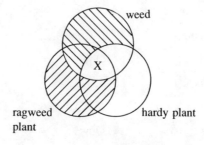

5. The sentences are incompatible. Once we diagram the first two sentences:

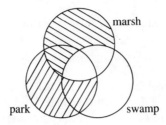

it is not possible to diagram the third sentence.

6. The sentences are not logically incompatible. They can all be diagramed:

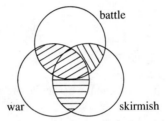

7. The sentences are incompatible. Once we diagram the first two:

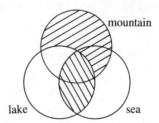

it is not possible to diagram the third.

8. The sentences are not logically incompatible. We can diagram all three:

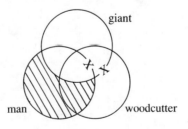

Section 14

1. a No term is distributed
   b The distributed term is 'deacon.'

    c The distributed term is 'battered brigade.'

    d The distributed terms are 'cab' and 'classy car.'

2. a Undistributed middle

    b There is no formal fallacy in this syllogism; it is valid.

    c Illicit major

    d Illicit minor

    e Illicit minor

    f There is no formal fallacy; this syllogism is valid.

3. a There is no formal fallacy; this syllogism is valid.

    b This syllogism has a negative premiss but no negative conclusion.

    c Illicit minor; undistributed middle

    d There is no formal fallacy; this syllogism is valid.

    e Two negative premisses; illicit major

    f Illicit major; negative conclusion without a negative premiss

    g Illicit major

    h Illicit major; negative conclusion without a negative premiss

4. a Undistributed middle

    b Undistributed middle

    c Two negative premisses

    d Particular conclusion without a particular premiss

    e Illicit minor

    f Undistributed middle

    g Illicit major; negative conclusion without a negative premiss

    h Illicit minor; particular premiss without a particular conclusion

    i Undistributed middle; negative premiss without a negative conclusion

    j Valid .

    k Particular conclusion without a particular premiss; negative conclusion without a negative premiss; undistributed middle

    l Valid

CHAPTER 6

Section 1

1. a

2. c. The statement does not say whether q entails p.

3. b

4. b

Section 2

1. a   **2.** c   **3.** a   **4.** b

Section 3

1. b   **2.** a   **3.** c   **4.** a

CHAPTER 7

Section 1

The sentences can be translated:

1. No Italian restaurant is a restaurant that serves French bread.

2. Some South American country is a country that was originally a European colony.

3. Some prime number is a number waiting to be discovered.
4. No logician is a dangerous person.
5. Given the most natural understanding of the sentence, the following translation fails to capture the temporal significance:

   Some prospector is not a person who found gold.

   A more adequate translation is:

   Some prospector is not a person who found gold while he was a prospector.

6. No Swiss banker is a person currently in jail.
*7. Some friend of Ted's is a person who has been in jail.
8. Some man in Julia's law firm is a person who used to be a Catholic priest.
*9. No bottle of beer (currently) in the refrigerator is a cold bottle (now).
10. Every even prime number is a number less than ten.
11. No vampire is a thing.
*12. No spider is an insect.
*13. Every person who jumps off the Sears Tower is a person who will be killed.
14. Some realtor who showed Kathy a house is not a person who pressured her to buy.
*15. Every person who got drunk and was obnoxious at the reception is a friend of the groom.
*16. Every normal coral snake is a poisonous animal.
*17. Every normal adult lion is an animal bigger than a normal adult hyena.
*18. No parrot is a bird that can really talk.
19. No person (thing) is a generous banker.
20. Some collection of mosquito bites is a collection that covered Sandra's arms.
*21. Every mosquito is an insect.
22. Some bee is an insect that stung Michael.
*23. Every normal bee is an insect that lives in a hive.
24. No adequate translation can be given for 24. Being widespread is a nondistributive property of the collection of currently existing blue herons.
25. Sentence 25 is a singular sentence, and has no adequate translation in the Categorical language.
*26. Some student in Professor Cox's class is a person who has never been to Disney-World.
27. Some child of John's is not a person who has been to college.

Section 2
1. Every student in Dr. Vesley's calculus class is a person who passed the course. Some student in Dr. Vesley's calculus class is a student in Dr. Vesley's calculus class.
*2. Every ostrich is a flightless bird.
3. No parrot is an animal that really talks. Some parrot is a parrot.
4. Every journalist who understands national politics is a person who works for the *Chicago Tribune*. Some journalist who understands national politics is a journalist who understands national politics.
5. Every runner is a person who received a T-shirt stamped with his time. Some runner is a runner.
*6. Every person who calls after midnight is a person who will hear a recorded message.
7. Some squirrel is an animal that caused the telephone line to break.

8. Every maitre d'hotel is a person who manages a restaurant. Some maitre d'hotel is a matire d'hotel.

Section 3

1. This inference sequence is invalid:

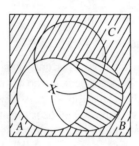

2. The proof below shows the inference sequence to be valid:

1	Every *A* is a *B*	
2	No non-*C* is a *B*	
3	Every *D* is a non-*C*	
4	Some *D* is a *D*	
5	Every non-*C* is a non-*B*	2, ObvI
6	Every *D* is a non-*B*	5, 3, AAA-1
7	No *A* is a non-*B*	1, ObvI
8	No non-*B* is an *A*	7, E-Conv
9	Every non-*B* is a non-*A*	8, ObvI
10	Every *D* is a non-*A*	9, 6, AAA-1
11	Some *D* is a non-*A*	10, 4, AII-1
12	Some non-*A* is a *D*	11, I-Conv

3. These formulas are incompatible. If we diagram the first two:

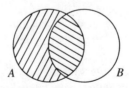

there is no place for the third.

4. The formulas are not incompatible (they do not symbolize only incompatible sentences). The true sentences below are jointly symbolized by the formulas:

Every ant is an insect. Some non-insect is a non-insect.
No non-insect is a non-thing. Every duck is a thing.

Section 4

1. The sentences can be given equivalent translations:

    (a) No vampire is an inhabitant of Transylvania.

    (b) No vampire is an inhabitant of Transylvania. Some vampire is a vampire.

These diagrams show the (a) translation does not logically imply the (b) translation:

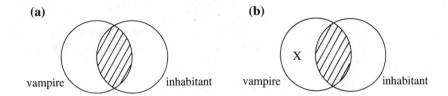

This result is inconclusive with respect to the original sentences. But on reflection we can see that the (a) sentence does not entail the (b) sentence—the (a) sentence does not indicate that there is a vampire, but the (b) sentence does.

2. Both the (a) sentence and the (b) sentence can be given this equivalent translation:

    Some student is not a person who cheated on the exam.

This makes it obvious that the (a) sentence entails the (b) sentence.

3. The sentences can be given equivalent translations:

    (a) Every person who heard the fire alarm is a person who got out safely. Some person who heard the fire alarm is a person who heard the fire alarm.

    (b) Every person who got out safely is a person who heard the fire alarm. Some person who got out safely is a person who got out safely.

The (a) translation does not imply the (b) translation:

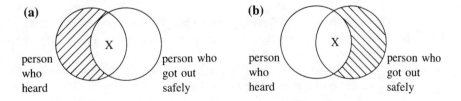

This is an inconclusive result about the original sentences, but we can see that the (a) sentence does not entail the (b) sentence.

4. If the first premise is not understood to have existential force, the argument can be translated:

    No mineral which is a metal is a non-(conductor of electricity). Every conductor of electricity is a chemically active substance. So: Every mineral which is a metal is a chemically active substance. Some mineral which is a metal is a mineral which is a metal.

This translation is not logically valid, as we can see from the following diagram:

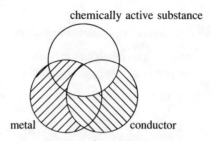

This inconclusive result does not tell us whether the original argument is valid.

If the first premiss does have existential force, we must add this to our translation of the premisses:

Some mineral which is a metal is a mineral which is a metal.

The added premiss calls for an 'X' in the metal circle, indicating that the argument is valid.

5. One way to translate the argument is the following:

Every girl Larry will ask to the dance is a girl who will turn Larry down. Some girl is not a girl who will turn Larry down. So some girl is a girl Larry will ask to the dance.

This diagram shows that the translation is not logically valid:

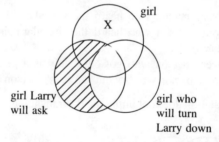

This is an inconclusive result, but it is clear that the argument isn't valid.

6. If the conclusion is not understood to have existential force, the argument can be translated:

No friend of Megan is a person who will lend Megan money. Every girl on the second floor of Lewis Hall is a friend of Megan. Some girl on the second floor of Lewis hall is a girl on the second floor of Lewis Hall. So no girl on the second floor of Lewis hall is a person who will lend Megan money.

The following shows the translation, and hence the original argument, to be valid:

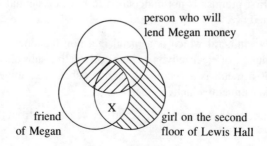

If the conclusion does have existential force, we need a two-sentence translation for the conclusion. Understood this way, the argument is still valid.

7. The sentences can be translated:

   (a) Some married couple is a couple with 37 children.
   (b) No married couple is a couple with 37 children.

Since the translations are corresponding E and I sentences, it is clear that they are logically incompatible. Diagrams also reveal this. Hence, the original sentences are incompatible.

8. The sentences can be translated:

   (a) Every trespasser is a person who will be prosecuted.
   (b) No trespasser is a person who will be prosecuted.

These translations are logically compatible. Although this result is inconclusive, it is clear that the original sentences are compatible.

9. The sentences can be translated:

   (a) Some person at the party is not an invited guest.
   (b) No person at the party is a non-(invited guest). Some person at the party is a person at the party.

The translations are logically incompatible:

The original sentences are incompatible.

10. The sentences can be translated:

Every automobile is a self-propelled vehicle. Some bus is not a self-propelled vehicle. Some bus is an automobile.

It is easy to construct a diagram which shows the translations to be logically compatible. This is an inconclusive result for the original sentences.

11. We can translate the sentences like this:

Every bully is a coward. Every coward is a timid person. Some coward is a coward. No bully is a timid person. Some bully is a bully.

If we diagram the universal sentences:

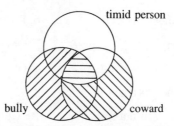

we cannot diagram 'Some bully is a bully.' The sentences are incompatible.

12. We can translate the sentences:

> No bird is a fish eater. Some bird is an insect eater. Every bird is an animal with feathers. Every animal with feathers is a fish eater.

The following proof shows the translation (and hence the original sentences) to be incompatible:

1	No bird is a fish eater.	
2	Some bird is an insect eater.	
3	Every bird is an animal with feathers.	
4	Some bird is a bird.	2, ExI
5	Some bird is an animal with feathers.	3, 4, AII-1
6	Some animal with feathers is a bird.	5, I-Conv
7	Every bird is a non-(fish eater).	1, ObvI
8	Some animal with feathers is a non-(fish eater)	7, 6, AII-1
9	Some animal with feathers is not a fish eater	8, ObvE

Section 5

1. The argument can be translated:

> Every person eligible for an honorary degree from Harvard is a college graduate. Every college graduate is a contemptible person. Some college graduate is a college graduate. Some football coach is not a contemptible person. So some football coach is not a person eligible for an honorary degree from Harvard.

The following proof (in which expressions are replaced by variables) shows this argument to be valid:

1	Every E is a G	
2	Every G is a C	
3	Some G is a G	
4	Some F is not a C	
5	Every E is a C	2, 1, AAA-1
6	No E is a non-C	5, ObvI
7	No non-C is an E	6, E-Conv
8	Every non-C is a non-E	7, ObvI
9	Some F is a non-C	4, ObvI
10	Some F is a non-E	8, 9, AII-I
11	Some F is not an E	10, ObvE

2. The argument can be translated:

> Every couple in a first-floor apartment is a childless couple. Some couple in a first-floor apartment is a couple in a first-floor apartment. Every childless couple is a couple with lots of time for cultural activities. No couple known by Bob is a couple with lots of time for cultural activities. So no couple known by Bob is a couple in a first-floor apartment.

The argument is valid, as the following proof establishes:

1	Every *F* is a *C*	
2	Some *F* is an *F*	
3	Every *C* is an *L*	
4	No *B* is an *L*	
5	Every *F* is an *L*	3, 1, AAA-1
6	No *L* is a *B*	4, E-Conv
7	Every *L* is a non-*B*	6, ObvI
8	Every *F* is a non-*B*	7, 5, AAA-1
9	No *F* is a *B*	8, ObvE
10	No *B* is an *F*	9, E-Conv

3. The argument can be translated:

> No big city is a place where Phil lives. Every big city is a cultural center. Some big city is a big city. So no cultural center is a place where Phil lives.

It is easy to show that the translation is not logically valid. This is an inconclusive result, but it is clear that the original argument isn't valid.

4. The sentences can be translated:

> No Middle Eastern country is a country visited by Don. Some Middle Eastern country is a country that was invaded by the Vikings. Every country that was invaded by the Vikings is a country visited by Don. Some country that was invaded by the Vikings is a country that was invaded by the Vikings.

It is easy to use a Venn diagram to show that the translations are logically incompatible. Hence the original sentences are incompatible.

5. The sentences can be translated:

> No sailboat is an object owned by Paul. Every Sunfish is a sailboat. Some Sunfish is an object owned by Paul.

Since the translations are logically incompatible, the original sentences are incompatible.

6. The sentences can be translated:

> Every person in college is a person who can read. Every student in Chemistry 333 is a person in college. Some student in Chemistry 333 is a student in Chemistry 333. Some student in Chemistry 333 is not a person who can read.

It is easy to show that the translations are logically incompatible (we can use a Venn diagram). So the original sentences are incompatible.

Section 6

1. The argument can be translated:

> Every one of those men wearing a yellow hat is a carpenter. Some one of those men wearing a yellow hat is one of those men wearing a yellow hat. No person who works with wood is a person who likes plastic furniture. Every chemical engineer is a person who likes plastic furniture. Some chemical engineer is a chemical engineer. So: No one of those men wearing a yellow hat is a chemical engineer. Some one of those men wearing a yellow hat is one of those men wearing a yellow hat.

The translation is not logically valid. But if we add the following analytic sentence to the premisses:

> Every carpenter is a person who works with wood.

we obtain a logically valid argument. It can be proved:

1	Every Y is a C	
2	Some Y is a Y	
3	No W is a P	
4	Every E is a P	
5	Some E is an E	
6	Every C is a W	
7	Every Y is a W	6, 1, AAA-1
8	Every W is a non-P	3, ObvI
9	Every Y is a non-P	8, 7, AAA-1
10	No E is a non-P	4, ObvI
11	No non-P is an E	10, E-Conv
12	Every non-P is a non-E	11, ObvI
13	Every Y is a non-E	12, 9, AAA-1
14	No Y is an E	13, ObvE
15	Some Y is a Y	2, ExI

The two sentences of the "double conclusion" are the last two steps in the proof.

2. The argument can be translated:

> Every thing Phil likes to eat is a thing Joe likes to eat. Some thing Phil likes to eat is a thing Phil likes to eat. No bird is a thing Joe likes to eat. So no duck is a thing Phil likes to eat.

This translation is not logically valid. But the following sentence is an obviously analytic A sentence:

Every duck is a bird.

If we add this to the premisses, the resulting argument is logically valid, as you can easily prove. So the original argument is valid.

3. The argument can be translated:

Every anthropologist is a generous person. Some anthropologist is an anthropologist. Some museum director is an anthropologist. So some museum director is not a stingy person.

This translation isn't logically valid, but we can add this analytic premiss:

No generous person is a stingy person.

The resulting inference can easily be proved valid.

4. The sentences can be translated:

Every competent engineer is a person earning a good salary. Some competent engineer is a theologian.

These sentences are not logically incompatible. There is no analytic sentence we can add which yields an incompatible set.

5. The sentences can be translated:

Every academic is an overworked person. Some academic is an academic. No professional philosopher is an overworked person. Some professional philosopher is a professional philosopher. Every professional philosopher is a college professor.

These sentences are not logically incompatible. If we add this analytic sentence:

Every college professor is an academic.

we can prove the sentences to be incompatible.

6. The sentences can be translated:

Every active football player is a person in good health. Some active football player is an active football player. Some active football player is a heavy drinker. No person who consumes large quantities of alcohol is a person in good health.

If we add the following analytic sentence:

Every heavy drinker is a person who consumes large quantities of alcohol.

we can prove that the resulting sentences are logically incompatible.

Section 7

1. The argument can be translated:

No city on the Pacific coast of the 48 contiguous states is a city with a harsh winter climate. So some city in Washington is not a city with a harsh winter climate.

This argument is not valid. But it is true, and should be well known, that the state of Washington is on the Pacific coast and has cities on the coast. If we add this true sentence to the premisses:

> Some city in Washington is a city on the Pacific Coast of the 48 contiguous states.

we can easily show the resulting argument to be valid.

2. The argument can be translated:

> Every philosophy course is an easy course. Some philosophy course is a philosophy course. Every easy course is a course with a large enrolment. Some easy course is an easy course. No philosophy course is a course taken by Dave. So no course with a large enrolment is a course taken by Dave.

This argument is not logically valid. there is no analytic sentence nor well-known true sentence we can add to yield a logically valid argument.

3. The argument can be translated:

> No city in Mexico is a city where Megan has been. Every city where Megan has a pen pal is a city where Megan has been. Some city where Megan has a pen pal is a city where Megan has a pen pal. So some large city is not a city where Megan has a pen pal.

This argument is not valid. But the following true sentence is well known:

> Some city in Mexico is a large city.

If we add this to the premisses, we can prove the resulting argument to be valid.

4. The sentences can be translated:

> Every large city on the Great Lakes is a city with a large population of Polish descent. Some large city on the Great Lakes is a large city on the Great Lakes. Every city with a large population of Polish descent is a city with a store selling pierogis. No city in Illinois is a city with a store selling pierogis.

These sentences are not incompatible. But we can add this well-known true sentence:

> Some city in Illinois is a large city on the Great Lakes.

Now we can prove the sentences to be incompatible.

5. The sentences can be translated:

> No person Bill knows is a person who lives in Ohio. Every person in Ellen's family is a person Bill knows. Some person in Ellen's family is a person in Ellen's family. Some brother of Ellen is a person who lives in Cincinatti.

These sentences are not incompatible. But if we add this analytic sentence:

> Every brother of Ellen is a person in Ellen's family.

and this well-known true sentence:

> Every person who lives in Cincinatti is a person who lives in Ohio.

we can prove the sentences to be incompatible:

1	No *B* is an *O*	
2	Every *F* is a *B*	
3	Some *F* is an *F*	
4	Every *E* is an *F*	
5	Every *C* is an *O*	
6	Every *E* is a *B*	2, 4, AAA-1
7	Every *B* is a non-*O*	1, ObvI
8	No *C* is a non-*O*	5, ObvI
9	No non-*O* is a *C*	8, E-Conv
10	Every non-*O* is a non-*C*	9, ObvI
11	Every *B* is a non-*C*	10, 7, AAA-1
12	Every *E* is a non-*C*	11, 6, AAA-1
13	No *E* is a *C*	12, ObvE

6. The sentences can be translated:

> Every communist is a person who loves caviar. Some communist is a communist. Every person who loves caviar is a well-off person. Some person who loves caviar is a person who loves caviar. No well-off person is a Russian.

These sentences are not incompatible. If we add this true sentence:

> Some Russian is a communist.

the resulting sentences are incompatible.

CHAPTER 8

Section 2
1. False
2. True
3. True
4. False. There is a different rule with this name in the Categorical deductive system.

Section 3

1.

1	(There is a *B* & Every *B* is a *C*)	
2	There is a *B*	1, Simp
3	Every *B* is a *C*	1, Simp
4	(Every *B* is a *C* & There is a *B*)	3, 2, Conj
5	Some *B* is a *C*	4, ExS
6	Some *C* is a *B*	5, I-Conv

2. 1   There is a cow

    2   Every cow is a non-horse.

    ———————————————

    3   No cow is a horse.   2, ObvE

    4   (No cow is a horse & There is a cow)   3, 1, Conj

    5   Some cow is not a horse   4, ExS

3. 1   There is an *A*

    ———————————————

    2   Every *A* is an *A*   LT

    3   (Every *A* is an *A* & There is an *A*)   2, 1, Conj

    4   Some *A* is an *A*   3, ExS

4. 1   Every *L* is an *M*

    2   No *M* is an *N*

    3   There is an *N*

    ———————————————

    4   Every *M* is a non-*N*   2, ObvI

    5   Every *L* is a non-*N*   4, 1, AAA-1

    6   No *L* is an *N*   5, ObvE

    7   No *N* is an *L*   6, E-Conv

    8   (No *N* is an *L* & There is an *N*)   7, 3, Conj

    9   Some *N* is not an *L*   8, ExS

5. The Venn diagram for the left formula is: This does not show a *B* which isn't *A*. There is no implication.

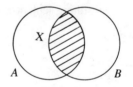

6. The Venn diagram for the left formula is: The 'X' for 'There is a non'*B* ' is in the outer portion of the diagram. This 'X' represents an individual which is both non-*A* and non-*B*. The left formula implies the right one. (The formulas jointly symbolize sentences linked by implication.)

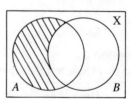

7. If we diagram the first two formulas: we cannot diagram the third. This is a sign of incompatibility.

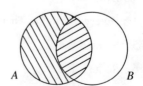

8. We can diagram all three formulas:
(The third formula symbolizes logically true
sentences. It makes no contribution to the
diagram.)

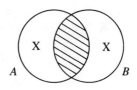

Section 4
  1. True
  2. True
  3. False
  4. True
  5. True
  6. False
  7. False
  8. True
  9. ~ Every *M* is a non-*N*

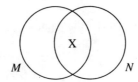

10. (~ No *M* is an *N* & There is an *N*)

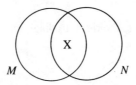

11. ~(Every patriot is a scoundrel & Some scoundrel is a patriot)

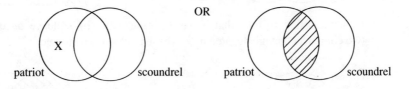

12. ~(No philosopher is a statesman & Every philosopher is a statesman)
We can diagram the sentence like this:

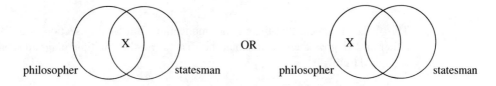

But we can also use a single diagram: The 'X' on the line *means* that there is an 'X' in the left *or* the center compartment.

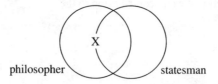

13. There is no implication. The diagrams are:

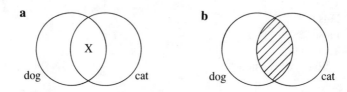

14. There is implication. The (a) diagram:

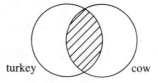

shows implication to the right (b) diagram:

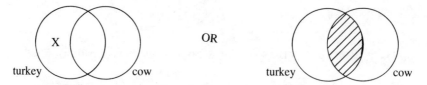

It is interesting to note that if we diagramed the (b) sentence by considering the two conjuncts that are negated in the (b) sentence, we would get:

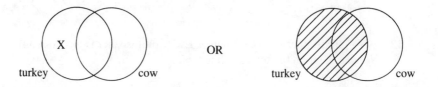

This makes it appear that there is no implication. But for any section of a diagram, either an 'X' goes there or it should be shaded. So this multiple diagram represents a "logical truth":

Every sentence implies a logical truth. And combining a logical truth with a sentence adds nothing to the content of the sentence. Adding the representation for '~ Some turkey is a cow' to this logical truth gives:

This multiple diagram shows implication to the second multiple diagram for the (b) sentence.

15. There is implication. Both diagrams for the left sentences contain the diagram for the right sentence:

16. There is no implication. The diagram for the (a) sentence:

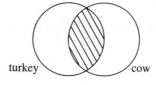

does not show implication to either of the diagrams for the (b) sentence:

17. There is implication. Each diagram for the (a) sentence:

shows implication to a diagram for the (b) sentence:

18. The sentences are incompatible. The diagram for the right sentence:

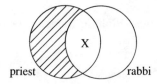

cannot accommodate the diagram for the (a) sentence, which shades the middle section.

19. The sentences are not incompatible. Both are represented by this diagram:

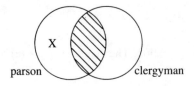

20. The sentences are incompatible. When the first two sentences are diagramed:

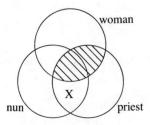

the third cannot be accommodated.

21. The sentences are not incompatible. They are both accommodated in this multiple diagram:

OR

22. The sentences are incompatible. Neither of these two diagrams for the right sentence:

OR

will accommodate the diagram for the left sentence.

Section 5

1. 1   Every *A* is an *A*   LT

    2   No *A* is a non-*A*   1, ObvI

    3   No non-*A* is an *A*   2, E-Conv

    4   ~ Some non-*A* is an *A*   3, EIT

It would not be correct to prove this as follows:

    1   Every *A* is an *A*   LT

    2   ~ Some *A* is not an *A*   1, AOT

    3   ~ Some *A* is a non-*A*   2, ObvI

    4   ~ Some non-*A* is an *A*   3, I-Conv

The obversion and conversion rules are not used on a formula which is part of a larger formula. They must be used on a formula which stands alone. In the second "proof," both steps 3 and 4 are mistaken.

2. 1   ~ Some *M* is an *N*

    2   No *M* is an *N*   1, EIT

    3   No *N* is an *M*   2, E-Conv

    4   Every *N* is an non-*M*   3, ObvI

3. 1   There is a *B*

    2   ~ Some *B* is a *C*

    3   No *B* is a *C*   2, EIT

    4   (No *B* is a *C* & There is a *B*)   3, 1, Conj

    5   Some *B* is not a *C*   4, ExS

4. 1   There is an *A*

    2   ~ Some *A* is a *B*

    3 | Every *A* is a *B*

    4 | (Every *A* is a *B* & There is an *A*)   3, 1, Conj

    5 | Some *A* is a *B*   4, ExS

    6 |(Some *A* is a *B* & ~ Some *A* is a *B*)   5, 2, Conj

    7   ~ Every *A* is a *B*   3 − 6, ~ I

5. 1   ~~ No *B* is a *C*

    2 |~ No *B* is a *C*

    3 |(~ No *B* is a *C* & ~~ No *B* is a *C*)   2, 1, Conj

    4   No *B* is a *C*   2 − 3, ~ E

6. 1 |(There is an *F* & ~ There is an *F*

    2   ~(There is an *F* & ~ There is an *F*)   I, ~ I

7. 1   ~ There is a *C*

    2 | Some *C* is a *C*

    3 | There is a *C*   2, ExI

    4 |(There is a *C* & ~ There is a *C*)   3, 1, Conj

    5   ~ Some *C* is a *C*   2 − 4, ~ I

8. 1   Some *B* is a *C*

    2   ~ Some *B* is a *D*

    3   No *B* is a *D*   2, EIT

    4   There is a *B*   1, ExI

    5   (No *B* is a *D* & There is a *B*)   3, 4, Conj

    6   Some *B* is not a *D*   5, ExS

9. 1   No *F* is a *G*

    2   Some *F* is a *G*

    3 |~ No *P* is a *Q*

    4 |~ No *F* is a *G*   2, EIT

    5 |(No *F* is a *G* & ~ No *F* is a *G*)   1, 4, Conj

    6   No *P* is a *Q*   3 − 5, ~ E

10. 1   ~ Some *A* is not a *B*

     2   ~ Some *C* is a *B*

3	Every A is a B	1, AOT
4	No C is a B	2, EIT
5	No B is a C	4, E-Conv
6	Every A is a B & No B is a C	3, 5, Conj

11.

1	Every A is a B	
2	No B is a C	
3	Every C is an A	
4	Every C is a B	1, 3, AAA-1
5	Every B is a non-C	2, ObvI
6	Every C is a non-C	4, 5, AAA-1
7	No C is a C	6, ObvE
8	$\sim$ Some C is a C	7, EIT

12.

1	(Every A is a B & Some A is not a B)	
2	$\sim$ Some C is a D	
3	Every A is a B	1, Simp
4	Some A is not a B	1, Simp
5	$\sim$ Every A is a B	4, AOT
6	(Every A is a B & $\sim$ Every A is a B)	3, 5, Conj
7	Some C is a D	2 – 6, $\sim$ E

Section 6

**1. $\sim$ Some professor of Michele's is a famous person.

2. Some college professor is not a person with shifty eyes.

3. (No person is a person who recovered from the infection & There is a person)

4. We could use:

> No thing is a square circle.

or

> $\sim$ There is a square circle.

5. This sentence cannot be given an adequate translation in the ECL. The best we can do is this weaker translation:

> (Some college student is a person aiming for a military career &
> Some college student is not a person aiming for a military career)

6. $\sim$ No student is an attractive person.

7. (Every terrorist is a person with no conscience & There is a terrorist)

8. Some non-(person who voted in the last election) is a person running for Congress.

*9. Some girl in Joel's class is not a person who passed the driving test.

**10. ~ Every unicorn is a winged animal.

11. ~ (Every lawyer is an honest person & Every lawyer is an intelligent person)

or: ~ Every lawyer is an honest and intelligent person.

12. No person is a person who discovered Freddy's secret.

Section 7

1. Valid

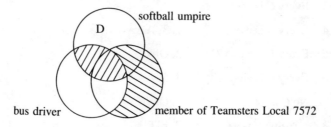

2. The diagram for the premises is this:

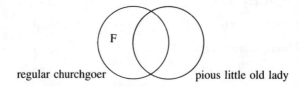

The diagram for the conclusion is:

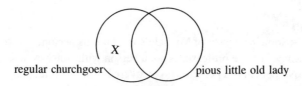

The diagrams are different, but a specific individual (Fran) in a compartment implies *an* individual in that compartment. The argument is valid.

3. Not logically valid

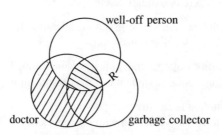

4. The sentences are incompatible; if we diagram the last three sentences:

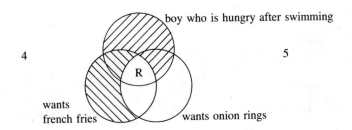

we cannot diagram the first.

5. Not incompatible

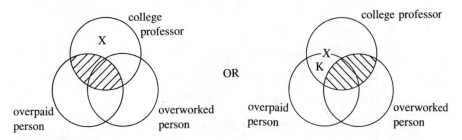

OR

The left diagram cannot be completed, but the right diagram has been completed.

6. Not incompatible

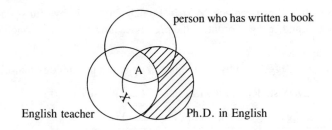

Section 8

1. 1 No soldier is a politician.

  2 Frank is a politician.

  3 Every non-civilian is a soldier.

  ———————————————————————

  4 Frank is not a soldier.   1, 2, EE

  5 No non-civilian is a non-soldier.   3, ObvI

  6 Frank is a non-soldier.   4, ObvI

  7 Frank is not a non-civilian.   5, 6, EE

  8 Frank is a civilian.   7, ObvE

2. 1 Every A is a B

  2 No B is a C

3	x is a D	
4	x is a C	
5	x is not a B	2, 4, EE
6	x is a non-B	5, ObvI
7	No A is a non-B	1, ObvI
8	x is not an A	7, 6, EE
9	Some D is not an A	3, 8, OI

3.

1 No freshman is a person passing logic.

2 David is a freshman.

3 David is a person passing logic.

4 | ~ Chicago is a city in Illinois.

5 | David is not a person passing logic.   1, 2, EE

6 | ~ David is a person passing logic.   5, SingT

7 | (David is a person passing logic & ~ David is a person passing logic)
                                                 3, 6, Conj

8 Chicago is a city in Illinois.   4 − 7, ~ E

4. Invalid. If we replace 'A' by 'French city,' 'B' by 'European city,' 'C' by 'U.S. city,' and 'x' by 'Toronto,' the premises are true and the conclusion is false.

5. Valid

1 ~ (Peggy is a physics major & Peggy is a psychology major)

2 Every student taking Physics 437 is a physics major.

3 Peggy is a student taking Physics 437.

4 Peggy is a physics major.   2, 3, AE

5 | Peggy is a psychology major.

6 | (Peggy is a physics major & Peggy is a psychology major)
                                                 4, 5, Conj

7 | [Peggy is a physics major & Peggy is a psychology major) &
   | ~(Peggy is a physics major & Peggy is a psychology major]
                                                 6, 1, Conj

8 ~ Peggy is a psychology major.   5 − 7, ~ I

9 Peggy is not a psychology major.   8, SingT

6. Not valid. If we replace 'famous actor' by 'French city,' 'skillful lion tamer' by 'German city,' 'talented performer' by 'European city,' 'clumsy person' by 'U.S. city,' and 'Mark' by 'Toronto,' we get true premises and a false conclusion.

7. These are incompatible.

1   ~ (Some actor is a bridge player & Some actor is not a bridge player)

2   Hugh is an actor.

3   Hugh is not a bridge player.

4   Every intellectual is a bridge player.

5   Chuck is an actor.

6   Some actor is not a bridge player.   2, 3, OI

7 | Chuck is an intellectual.

8 | Chuck is a bridge player.   4, 7, AE

9 | Some actor is a bridge player.   5, 8, II

10 | (Some actor is a bridge player & Some actor is not a bridge player)
            9, 6, Conj

11 | [Some actor is a bridge player & Some actor is not a bridge player) &
      | ~ (Some actor is a bridge player & Some actor is not a bridge player)]
            10, 1, Conj

12   ~ Chuck is an intellectual.   7 − 11, ~ I

8. Not incompatible. If we replace 'lawyer' by 'European city,' 'doctor' by 'German city,' 'son of Martha's' by 'French 'city,' and 'John' by 'Paris,' all the sentences will be true.

9. Not incompatible. If we replace 'person who likes broccoli' by 'city in the South of France,' 'person who likes Brussels sprouts' by 'French city,' 'person who likes asparagus' by 'European city,' and 'Jesse' by 'London,' all the sentences will be true.

CHAPTER 9

Section 1
1. Simple
2. Compound
3. Compound
4. Simple

Section 2
1. False
2. True
3. True
4. False
5. True
6. True

Section 3
1. $\sim p \textcircled{\&} q$
2. $\ominus(p \mathbin{\&} q)$

3. $\{[(p \supset q) \supset r]\bigcirc s\}$

4. $\{p\bigcirc[q \supset (r \equiv \{s \vee \sim q\})]\}$

In these truth-tables, only the column under the main connective is shown.

5.

p	$[(p \supset p) \supset p] \vee \sim p$
t	t
f	t

6.

p	q	$[(p \& q) \vee (p \& \sim q)]$
t	t	t
t	f	t
f	t	f
f	f	f

7.

p	q	$\sim(p \supset \sim q) \supset (\sim p \supset q)$
t	t	t
t	f	t
f	t	t
f	f	t

8.

p	q	r	$\sim[(p \vee q) \equiv (q \& r)]$
t	t	t	f
t	t	f	t
t	f	t	t
t	f	f	t
f	t	t	f
f	t	f	t
f	f	t	f
f	f	f	f

Section 4

1. Not a tautology

2. Tautology

3. Not a tautology

4. Neither logically true nor logically false

5. Logically false

6. Logically true

Section 5

1. Implication

2. No implication

3. Implication

4. Not logically equivalent

5. Not logically equivalent

6. Logically equivalent

7. Not logically incompatible

8. Logically incompatible

9. Logically incompatible

10. Logically incompatible

11. Right implies left
12. No two-place relation
13. Right implies left
14. Logically incompatible
15. Logically equivalent

Section 6
1. Logically valid
2. Logically valid
3. Logically valid
4. Logically incompatible
5. Logically incompatible
6. Logically incompatible

Section 7
1. Not logically incompatible
2. Not logically incompatible
3. Logically incompatible
4. Logically valid
5. Logically valid
6. Not logically valid

Section 8
1. Tautology
2. Not a tautology
3. Not a tautology
4. Tautology
5. Not a tautology
6. Tautology

CHAPTER TEN

Section 2
1. False
2. True
3. True
4. False

Section 3
1. 1 $[p \supset (q \supset r)]$

   2   $(s \supset r)$

   $\underline{3 \quad p}$

   4   $(q \supset r)$ 1, 3, MP

   5   $[(q \lor s) \supset r]$ 4, 2, Dil

   6   $\{(s \,\&\, p) \lor [(q \lor s) \supset r]\}$ 5, Add

2. 1 p

  2 q
  ___

  3 $(p \lor r)$ 1, Add

  4 $(r \lor q)$ 2, Add

  5 $[(r \lor q) \& (p \lor r)]$ 4, 3, Conj

3. One proof of the inference sequence is:

  1 $[p \& (p \supset q)]$

  2 r
  ___

  3 $[(p \supset q) \lor r]$ 2, Add

There are any number of different but correct proofs of this inference sequence. There is no such thing as *the* proof of a theorem.

4. Here is one proof:

  1 p

  2 $(q \supset r)$

  3 $(s \supset r)$
  ___

  4 $[(s \lor q) \supset r]$ 3, 2, Dil

  5 $\{[(s \lor q) \supset r] \& p\}$ 4, 1, Conj

5. A proof follows:

  1 p

  2 $(p \supset q)$

  3 $[(q \lor r) \supset s]$
  ___

  4 q 2, 1, MP

  5 $(q \lor r)$ 4, Add

  6 s 3, 5, MP

6. 1 $[p \& (p \supset q)]$
  ___

  2 p 1, Simp

  3 $(p \supset q)$ 1, Simp

  4 q 3, 2, MP

  5 $(p \& q)$ 2, 4, Conj

Section 4

1. 1 $r \equiv (s \supset p)]$

  2 $[(s \supset p) \supset q]$

  3 r
  ___

   4   $(s \supset p)$ 1, 3, Repl

   5   q 2, 4, MP

2. 1 $p \supset (r \supset s)]$

   2   $(p \vee q)$

   3   $(q \supset p)$

   4   $(s \supset r)$

   5   $(p \supset p)$
   _____
   6   $[(p \vee q) \supset p]$ 5, 3, Dil

   7   p 6, 2, MP

   8   $(r \supset s)$ 1, 7, MP

   9   $(s \equiv r)$ 4, 8, $\equiv$I

3. 1 $(p \& q)$

   2   $(\sim q \supset p)$

   3   $(p \supset \sim q)$
   _____
   4   p 1, Simp

   5   $\sim q$ 3, 4, MP

   6   q 1, Simp

   7   $(q \& \sim q)$ 6, 5, Conj

4. 1 $[r \equiv (s \supset p)]$

   2   $[\sim(s \supset p) \supset q]$

   3   $\sim r$
   _____
   4   $\sim(s \supset p)$ 1, 3, Repl

   5   q 2, 4, MP

5. 1 $[p \& (q \equiv \sim r)]$

   2   $\sim q$
   _____
   3   $(q \equiv \sim r)$ 1, Simp

   4   $\sim \sim r$ 3, 2, Repl

   5   p 1, Simp

   6   $(\sim \sim r \& p)$ 4, 5, Conj

6. 1 $[p \supset (p \vee q)]$

   2   $(p \supset p)$

   3   $(q \supset p)$
   _____

4   $[(p \lor q) \supset p]$ 2, 3, Dil

5   $[p \equiv (p \lor q)]$ 1, 4, $\equiv$I

Section 5

1. 1 $\sim p$

   2   p

   3   $\sim q$

   4   $(p \,\&\, \sim p)$ 2, 1, Conj

   5   q 3 $-$ 4, $\sim$ E

   6   $(p \supset q)$ 2 $-$ 5, $\supset$I

2. 1 $(p \supset q)$

   2   q

   3   q 2, Rep

   4   $(q \supset q)$ 2 $-$ 3, $\supset$I

   5   $[(p \lor q) \supset q]$ 1, 4, Dil

3. 1 $(p \supset \sim p)$

   2   p

   3   $\sim p$ 1, 2, MP

   4   $(p \,\&\, \sim p)$ 2, 3, Conj

   5   $\sim p$ 2 $-$ 4, $\sim$ I

4. 1 $(p \supset q)$

   2   $\sim q$

   3   p

   4   q 1, 3, MP

   5   $(q \,\&\, \sim q)$ 4, 2, Conj

   6   $\sim p$ 3 $-$ 5, $\sim$ I

5. 1 $[(p \supset (q \supset r)]$

   2   q

   3   $\sim r$

   4   p

   5   $(q \supset r)$ 1, 4, MP

   6   r 5, 2, MP

   7   $(r \,\&\, \sim r)$ 6, 3, Conj

$$8 \quad |\sim p \qquad\qquad 4-7, \sim \text{I}$$

$$9 \quad (\sim r \supset \sim p) \qquad 3-8, \supset \text{I}$$

6. 1 $(p \supset q)$

    2 $[(p \,\&\, r) \supset s\,]$

    3 $|p$

    4 $\quad |(q \,\&\, r)$

    5 $\quad |r \qquad\qquad\qquad$ 4, Simp

    6 $\quad |(p \,\&\, r) \qquad\qquad$ 3, 5, Conj

    7 $\quad |s \qquad\qquad\qquad$ 2, 6, MP

    8 $|[(q \,\&\, r) \supset s] \qquad$ 4 – 7, $\supset$I

    9 $\{p \supset [(q \,\&\, r) \supset s]\} \qquad$ 3 – 8, $\supset$I

Section 6

1. True. A sound deductive system establishes only correct results. But it need not establish all correct results.

2. True. A deductive system can be complete without being sound. This means that it establishes all the correct results and some incorrect results as well. Even though a system can be complete without being sound, such a system is not very interesting.

3. False

4. False. If the system is complete, then adding a new rule won't yield any new correct results. It might yield some new incorrect results, if the extra rule destroys the soundness of the system.

Section 7

1. 1 $|p$

    2 $(p \supset p) \qquad$ 1 – 1, $\supset$I

    3 $(p \equiv p) \qquad$ 2, 2, $\equiv$I

2. 1 $(p \supset q)$

    2 $|\sim(\sim p \vee q)$

    3 $\quad |p$

    4 $\quad |q \qquad\qquad\qquad$ 1, 3, MP

    5 $\quad |(\sim p \vee q) \qquad\qquad$ 4, Add

    6 $\quad |[(\sim p \vee q) \,\&\, \sim(\sim p \vee q)] \qquad$ 5, 2, Conj

    7 $\quad |\sim p \qquad\qquad$ 3 – 6, $\sim$I

    8 $|(\sim p \vee q) \qquad\qquad$ 7, Add

    9 $|(\sim p \vee q) \,\&\, \sim(\sim p \vee q) \qquad$ 8, 2, Conj

    10 $(\sim p \vee q) \qquad\qquad$ 2 – 9, $\sim$E

3.
1	$(p \& \sim p)$	
2	$\sim q$	
3	$(p \& \sim p)$	1, Rep
4	q	$2 - 3, \sim E$
5	$[(p \& \sim p) \supset q]$	$1 - 4, \supset I$

4.
1	$(p \supset q)$	
2	$(\sim p \supset q)$	
3	$\sim q$	
4	p	
5	q	1, 4, MP
6	$\sim q \& q$	3, 5, Conj
7	$\sim p$	$4 - 6, \sim I$
8	q	2, 7, MP
9	$q \& \sim q$	8, 3, Conj
10	q	$3 - 9, \sim E$

5.
1	$(p \supset \sim p)$	
2	p	
3	$\sim p$	1, 2, MP
4	$(p \& \sim p)$	2, 3, Conj
5	$\sim p$	$2 - 4, \sim I$
6	$[(p \supset \sim p) \supset \sim p]$	$1 - 5, \supset I$

Section 9

1.
1	$(p \supset q)$	
2	$(q \supset r)$	
3	p	
4	q	1, 3, MP
5	r	2, 4, MP
6	$(p \supset r)$	$3 - 5, \supset I$

2. By one application of the Deduction Theorem, we have these results:

$$(p \supset q) \vdash [(q \supset r) \supset (p \supset r)]$$
$$(q \supset r) \vdash [(p \supset q) \supset (p \supset r)]$$

By a second application, we have:

$$\vdash \{(p \supset q) \supset [(q \supset r) \supset (p \supset r)]\}$$
$$\vdash \{(q \supset r) \supset [(p \supset q) \supset (p \supset r)]\}$$

Section 10

A proof for MT10 is as follows:

Suppose the proof from hypotheses has been developed as far as step r.

We can continue:
$r+1$	$(A \supset C)$	$\begin{vmatrix} A, \supset I \\ \dot{C} \end{vmatrix}$
$r+2$	$(B \supset C)$	$\begin{vmatrix} B, \supset I \\ \dot{C} \end{vmatrix}$
$r+3$	$[(A \lor B) \supset C]$	$(r+1), (r+2)$, Dil
$r+4$	C	$(r+3), (A \lor B)$, MP

Section 12

1. LSI
2. De M
3. Def v
4. Assoc
5. Def $\supset$
6.

1	$[(p \supset q) \supset p]$	
2	$\sim p$	
3	$\sim (p \supset q)$	1, 2, MT
4	$\sim\sim(p \,\&\, \sim q)$	3, Def $\supset$
5	$(p \,\&\, \sim q)$	4, DN
6	p	5, Simp
7	$(p \,\&\, \sim p)$	6, 2, Conj
8	p	$2 - 7, \sim$ E
9	$\{[(p \supset q) \supset p] \supset p\}$	$1 - 8, \supset I$

7.

1	$[(p \supset q) \supset q]$	
2	$(q \supset p)$	
3	$\sim p$	
4	$\sim q$	2, 3, MT
5	$\sim (p \supset q)$	1, 4, MT
6	$\sim \sim(p \,\&\, \sim q)$	5, Def $\supset$
7	$(p \,\&\, \sim q)$	6, DN
8	p	7, Simp
9	$(p \,\&\, \sim p)$	8, 3, Conj

10	p	$3 - 9, \sim E$
11	$[(q \supset p) \supset p]$	$2 - 10, \supset I$

8.

1	$(p \equiv q) \equiv q]$	
2	$\sim p$	
3	q	
4	$p \equiv q$	3, 1, Repl
5	p	4, 3, Repl
6	$p \,\&\sim p$	5, 2, Conj
7	$\sim q$	$3 - 6, \sim I$
8	$\sim(p \equiv q)$	1, 7, Repl
9	$\sim p \,\&\sim q$	2, 7, Conj
10	$(p \,\& q) \vee (\sim p \,\&\sim q)$	9, Add
11	$p \equiv q$	10, Def $\equiv$
12	$(p \equiv q) \,\&\sim(p \equiv q)$	11, 8, Conj
13	p	$2 - 12, \sim E$

9.

1	$(p \,\& q)$	
2	$[q \supset \sim(q \supset p)]$	
3	q	1, Simp
4	$\sim(q \supset p)$	2, 3, MP
5	$\sim \sim(q \,\&\sim p)$	4, Def $\supset$
6	$(q \,\&\sim p)$	5, DN
7	$\sim p$	6, Simp
8	p	1, Simp
9	$(p \,\&\sim p)$	8, 7, Conj
10	$\sim [q \supset \sim(q \supset p)]$	$2 - 9, \sim I$

Section 13

1.

1	$[(p \supset (q \supset r)]$	
2	$[q \supset (p \,\&\sim r)]$	
3	q	
4	$(p \,\&\sim r)$	2, 3, MP
5	p	4, Simp
6	$(q \supset r)$	1, 5, MP

7	r	6, 3, MP
8	$\sim r$	4, Simp
9	$r \,\&\, \sim r$	7, 8, Conj
10	$\sim q$	$3-9, \sim$ I

2.

1	$(p \lor q)$	
2	$(p \supset q)$	
3	$(q \supset \sim p)$	
4	$(\sim p \supset \sim q)$	
5	p	
6	q	2, 5, MP
7	$\sim p$	3, 6, MP
8	$(p \,\&\, \sim p)$	5, 7, Conj
9	$\sim p$	$5-8, \sim$ I
10	q	1, 9, DS
11	$\sim q$	4, 9, MP
12	$(q \,\&\, \sim q)$	10, 11, Conj
13	$\sim (\sim p \supset \sim q)$	$4-12, \sim$ I

3. Incompatibility can be proved:

1	$[(p \supset q) \supset p]$	
2	$(q \supset \sim p)$	
3	$(\sim q \supset \sim p)$	
4	$[(q \lor \sim q) \supset \sim p]$	2, 3, Dil
5	$(q \lor \sim q)$	LEM
6	$\sim p$	4, 5, MP
7	$\sim (p \supset q)$	1, 6, MT
8	$\sim \sim (p \,\&\, \sim q)$	7, Def $\supset$
9	$(p \,\&\, \sim q)$	8, DN
10	p	9, Simp
11	$(p \,\&\, \sim p)$	10, 6, Conj
12	$\sim (\sim q \supset \sim p)$	$3-11, \sim$ I

4. One proof is:

1	p	
2	$(p \supset q)$	

$$\frac{3 \quad \sim r}{}$$

4	q	2, 1, MP
5	$(q\ \&\sim r)$	4, 3, Conj
6	$[(q\ \&\sim r) \vee (\sim q\ \&\sim\sim r)]$	5, Add
7	$(q \equiv\ \sim r)$	6, Def $\equiv$
8	$[p\ \&\ (q \equiv\ \sim r)]$	1, 7, Conj

Section 14

1. This is not a theorem: $[(p \supset q) \supset q] / p$

$$\quad\quad\quad\quad\quad t \quad\quad f$$
$$\quad\quad\quad f\ t\ t \quad\quad t$$

2. This is a theorem:

1	$(p\ \&\ q)$	
2	$[(p\ \&\ q) \vee (\sim p\ \&\sim q)]$	1, Add
3	$(p \equiv q)$	2, Def $\equiv$

3. This is a theorem:

1	$\sim(p \equiv q)$	
2	p	
3	q	
4	$(p\ \&\ q)$	2, 3, Conj
5	$[(p\ \&\ q) \vee (\sim p\ \&\sim q)]$	4, Add
6	$(p \equiv q)$	5, Def $\equiv$
7	$(p \equiv q)\ \&\sim(p \equiv q)$	6, 1, Conj
8	$\sim q$	3 – 7, $\sim$I
9	$(p \supset\ \sim q)$	2 – 8, $\supset$I
10	$[\sim(p \equiv q) \supset (p \supset\ \sim q)]$	1 – 9, $\supset$I

4. This is not a theorem: $[\sim p \supset\ \sim(p \vee q)]$

$$\quad\quad\quad\quad f \quad\quad\quad\quad$$
$$\quad t \quad\quad\quad f \quad\quad\quad$$
$$\quad\quad f \quad\quad\quad\quad t \quad$$
$$\quad\quad\quad\quad\quad\quad f \quad t$$

5. This is not a theorem: $[(p\ \&\ q) \supset r],\ q / (\sim p \supset r)$

$$\quad\quad\quad\quad\quad\quad t \quad\quad t \quad\quad\quad f$$
$$\quad\quad\quad f\ f\ t \quad\quad f \quad\quad t\ f \quad f$$

6. This is a theorem:

1	$[(p \supset q) \supset r]$	
2	$\sim p$	
3	$(\sim p \vee q)$	2, Add

4	$(p \supset q)$	3, Def $\supset$
5	r	1, 4, MP
6	$(\sim p \supset r)$	$2 - 5$, $\supset$I

7. These formulas symbolize incompatible sentences:

1	$[p \equiv (q \equiv r)]$	
2	$(q \equiv r)$	
3	$[p \equiv (r \,\&\, \sim r)]$	
4	p	1, 2, Repl
5	$\sim(r \,\&\, \sim r)$	LC
6	$\sim p$	3, 5, Repl
7	$(p \,\&\, \sim p)$	4, 6, Conj
8	$\sim[(p \equiv (r \,\&\, \sim r)]$	$3 - 7$, $\sim$I

8. These formulas do not symbolize incompatible sentences:

$$[p \supset (q \supset r)], p, (\sim r \supset \sim q)$$

9. These formulas do not symbolize incompatible sentences:

$$[p \,\&\, (q \vee \sim r)], \sim(p \,\&\, q), (r \supset q)$$

10. These formulas do not symbolize incompatible sentences:

$$\{p \supset [q \supset (r \equiv s)]\}, (q \supset r), [s \supset (q \equiv \sim q)], (q \supset \sim p)$$

CHAPTER ELEVEN

Section 2

1. $\sim$ David is married to Rosemary.
2. This sentence cannot be translated with '$\sim$.' It is its own best translation.
3. $\sim \sim$ John is passing logic. Even though (semantically) the second negation "cancels" the first, we need two negation signs to reflect the fact that the original sentence has two negative expressions.
4. $\sim$ Some state capitals are small cities.
5. We will not use the negation sign to translate this sentence. We are regarding it as its own translation.
6. $\sim$ Jorge will visit Cuba next year.

Section 3

1. It is most reasonable to understand this sentence as claiming that cats and dogs fight each other. A translation with connectives is not useful.

*2. (Andrea pushed Megan & Megan fell down)
3. (Jack jogs & Jack jumps rope)
4. ~(Tom is a doctor & Bob is a doctor)
5. (Bob is a doctor & ~ Tom is a doctor).
6. This sentence is ambiguous. If it means that the two women are nuns, then it can be translated: (Helen is a sister & Ruth is a sister). If the sentence means that they are sisters to one another, then the sentence is its own best translation.
7. (Peter got a special invitation & ~ He will attend the reception)
8. (Tom is a great athlete & Tom is a very gracious person)

Section 4

1. ~ That car is worth $6000.
2. (Mr. Smith is a college teacher & Mr. Pollock is a college teacher)
3. This sentence is its own best translation; it seems they are partners to one another.
4. (Bob will clean up his room v He will be punished)
**5. ~(Al slipped on a rug & Al broke his ankle)
6. ~(Bill likes spinach v Tom likes spinach)
7. ~(Molly has visited France & Molly has visited Italy)
8. ~ Girls do poorly in logic.
9. (Bill will visit Yugoslavia v Bill will visit Spain)
10. [(Kevin is the tallest boy in the Freshman class v Sam is the tallest boy in the Freshman class) & ~(Kevin is the tallest boy in the Freshman class & Sam is the tallest boy in the Freshman class)]
11. This sentence is its own translation.

Section 5

*1. (~ Mary apologizes ⊃ ~ Don will come to dinner)
2. This is a counterfactual conditional. It is not translated with connectives.
*3. UCLA is on probation ⊃ ~ UCLA is eligible for a post-season tournament.
*4. Kevin will attend Notre Dame ⊃ He will receive a full athletic scholarship.
5. ~(Joe Namath was a fullback v Jack Kemp was a fullback)
   We could also use:
        (~ Joe Namath was a fullback & ~ Jack Kemp was a fullback)
**6. ~(Jesse passes his logic course ⊃ He will be eligible for spring sports)
*7. [(Larry calls v Joan calls) ⊃ Jim will pretend he isn't home]
*8. (Mary will come only if Delia gives her a ride) ⊃ ~ Mary will be at the party.

Section 6

*1. (~ Bill calls by 7 ⊃ ~ Mary will come along)
*2. (~ Mary will come along v Bill will call by 7)
*3. (Sally will pass the course ⊃ She passed the final)
*4. ~ Shirley gets over her headache ⊃ ~ Shirley will go to the movie.
*5. (John will go out to dinner ≡ He gets a check in the mail today)
*6. ~ Tom won the race ⊃ ~ He will want to go out tonight.
*7. [Some students are not passing ⊃ (Some students will fail the course v Some students will resign)]
**8. ~(Tom wins the race ⊃ He will be happy)
*9. (~ Tom will lose the race v He feels (will feel) sick)

*10. [Sam will marry Barbara ⊃ (Sam gets (will get) a job & ~ Barbara's father disapproves (will disapprove))]

*11. [Leonard will drive to Florida unless his car breaks down ⊃ We will vacate the condominium by Sunday] The antecedent is not translated, because the only translation available to us is weaker. A weaker translation is not used for the antecedent of a conditional.

*12. (John will fail the course only if he doesn't study ≡ John is smart enough to pass the course) The left side is not translated with connectives, because the translation would be weaker.

Section 7

*1. [(Bill knows the answer & ~ Tom knows the answer) ⊃ Bill will win the contest]

*2. [You call before you leave ⊃ (You go out ⊃ You will know you are expected)]

*3. [Tom can expect to be met at the airport ⊃ (He calls his parents the day before & He arrives before 9:30)]

*4. [(Chicago is on Lake Michigan ⊃ Lake Michigan is polluted) & Chicago is on Lake Michigan]

*5. [The phone rings in the evening ⊃ (Sally will answer it v Marge will answer it)]

*6. [Fred will keep his promise v (~ Fred keeps his promise ⊃ He will have a good excuse)]

*7. [You announce that you are coming ⊃ ~(Kevin will be there when you arrive v Jesse will be there when you arrive)]

*8. [The ice will melt only if the temperature is raised ⊃ (~ The temperature is raised ⊃ ~ The ice will melt)] The antecedent is not translated with connectives, because of the restriction on translations with '⊃.'

*9. [~(The president speaks at the graduation & The governor speaks at the graduation) ⊃ ~ The ceremony will take a long time]

*10. [The student government will improve next year ≡ (Margaret is elected v Anne is elected)]

Section 8

1. (Bill wants french fries v He wants onion rings) ~ Bill wants french fries. Bill does want onion rings. $(p \vee q)$, ~ p, q

2. (Rachel knows the answer to this question ⊃ She will pass the test) ~ Rachel will pass the test. ~ Rachel knew the answer to this question. $(p \supset q)$, ~ q, ~ r. The third sentence is in the past tense, talking about past time. None of the other sentences is saying the same thing as the third sentence.

3. (Rachel answers this question correctly ⊃ She will pass the test) Rachel will answer this question correctly. Rachel will pass the test. $(p \supset q), p, q$

4. (Rachel will pass the test ⊃ She answers this question correctly) Rachel will answer this question correctly. Rachel will pass the test. $(p \supset q), q, p$

5. (Rachel passes the test ⊃ She will have answered this question correctly) Rachel will pass the test. Rachel will answer the question correctly. $(p \supset q)$, p, r The third sentence is in the (plain) future tense. The consequent of the first sentence is in the future perfect tense. They are not occurrences of a single sentence.

Section 10

1. The sentence can be translated:

[(It will rain Sunday v It will snow Sunday) v ~(It will rain Sunday v It will snow Sunday)]

This sentence is symbolized by a tautology:

p	q	$[(p \lor q) \lor \sim(p \lor q)]$		
t	t	t	t f	
t	f	t	t f	
f	t	t	t f	
f	f	f	t t	

The translation is logically true. Since it is equivalent to the original sentence, that sentence is analytic.

2. The sentence can be given an equivalent translation:

~(Tom likes beer & ~ Tom likes beer)

Since '~(p & ~ p)' is an instance of the Law of Contradiction, we know that the translation is logically true. Hence, the original is analytic.

3. If we translate the original sentence with connectives, we get:

[Mary can do the homework assignment ⊃ (~ Bill can do the homework assignment ⊃ ~ Mary can do the homework assignment)]

This weaker translation cannot be used to test for analytic truth.

4. An equivalent translation is the following:

[(It will rain Sunday & It will snow Sunday) v (~ It will rain Sunday & ~ It will snow Sunday)]

This truth table:

p	q	$[(p \,\&\, q) \lor (\sim p \,\&\, \sim q)]$		
t	t	t	t	f
t	f	f	f	f
f	t	f	f	f
f	f	f	t	t

shows that the translation is not logically true. This negative result leaves it up in the air whether the original is analytic. On reflection, it is clear that the original is not analytic.

Section 11

1. The sentences are translated:

(Chuck likes Greek food & Chuck likes Italian food) (~ Chuck likes Greek food v ~ Chuck likes Italian food)

The translations are logically incompatible; the original sentences are incompatible.

2. The sentences are translated:

(Too much salt contributes to heart disease ⊃ Frank has heart disease) Too much salt contributes to heart disease. ~ Frank has heart disease.

These suitable translations are logically incompatible. The original sentences are incompatible.

3. The sentences have these translations:

> (Bill will be on the football team v His grades will make him ineligible) ~ Bill will be on the football team. Bill's grades will make him ineligible.

This truth-table:

p	q	$(p \vee q)$	$\sim p$	q
t	t	t	f	t
t	f	t	f	f
f	t	t	t	t
f	f	f	t	f

shows that the translations are not logically incompatible. This does not tell us that the original sentences are compatible. On reflection, it is clear that they are compatible.

4. The sentences are translated:

> (Fish is served tonight $\supset$ ~ Lamb will be served tonight) (Lamb will be served tonight $\supset$ ~ Fish will be served tonight) (~ We will have white wine $\supset$ Lamb will be served tonight) (We will have white wine $\supset$ Fish will be served tonight) ~(Lamb will be served tonight v Fish will be served tonight)

The translations are logically incompatible. The original sentences are thus incompatible.

Section 12

1. The argument can be translated:

> (Bill will deliver the message v His brother will deliver the message) (Bill delivers the message $\supset$ Barry will bring extra ski gloves) ~ Barry will bring extra ski gloves. So ~ Bill's brother will deliver the message.

The following assignment shows that the translation is not logically valid:

$(p \vee q), (p \supset r), \sim r / \sim q$
f t t   f t f   t f   f t

The translation's being logically invalid does not show the original to be invalid. But we can see that everything important about the original argument shows up in the logical form of the translation. The original is invalid.

2. The argument can be translated like this:

> [(San Francisco is the capital of California v Sacramento is the capital of California) & ~(San Francisco is the capital of California & Sacramento is the capital is the capital of California)] Sacramento is the capital of California. So ~ San Francisco is the capital of California.

This truth-table:

p	q	$[(p \vee q)$	$\&\sim$	$(p \& q)]$	q	$\sim p$
t	t	t	f f	t	t	f
t	f	t	t t	f	f	f

```
f  t    t    t t   f     t  t
f  f    f    f t   f     f  t
```

shows the translation to be logically valid. Hence, the original argument is valid.

3. We can translate the argument:

> (Leonard will go to Florida for spring vacation v He will spend all his money fixing his car) ~Leonard will spend all his money fixing his car. So He will go to Florida for spring vacation.

It is easy to show that the translation is logically valid. So the original argument is valid.

4. We cannot provide an equivalent or stronger translation for the conclusion of this argument. We cannot use the PC language to evaluate this argument.

Section 13

1. The argument can be translated:

> (Leonard goes to Florida ⊃ He will spend all his money) (Leonard's car breaks down ⊃ He will spend all his money) So [(Leonard will go to Florida v His car will break down) ⊃ He will spend all his money]

This proof:

$$1\ (p \supset q)$$
$$\underline{2\ (r \supset q)}$$
$$3\ [(p \lor r) \supset q] \qquad 1, 2, \text{Dil}$$

shows the translation to be logically valid, and this shows the original to be valid.

2. Even though this argument is obviously valid, we can't use the PC language to evaluate it for we can't provide a suitable translation for the conclusion. (The conclusion of the argument is not a conditional sentence.)

3. The argument is translated like this:

> ~(Kathy is studying philosophy & Isabelle is studying philosophy) (Kathy is intellectually curious ⊃ She is studying philosophy) So (~ Isabelle is studying philosophy ⊃ ~ Kathy is intellectually curious)

The following assignment:

$$\sim (p\ \&\ q), (r \supset p), (\sim q \supset \sim r)$$
```
t  t f f    t t t    t f  f  f t
```

shows that the translation is not logically valid. This does not show that the original is invalid. But nothing important about the original argument fails to show up in the logical form of its translation. The original argument isn't valid.

4. We cannot use the PC language to evaluate this argument, because we can't provide an equivalent or stronger translation for the conclusion. When understood in the most natural way, the conclusion indicates the temporal order between the pushing and the falling down.

5. We can translate the argument this way:

~(~ Scott speaks French & ~ Donna speaks French) (Donna speaks French ⊃ She will understand Andre's note) So (~ Scott speaks French ⊃ Donna will understand Andre's note)

The following proof:

1 ~(~ p & ~ q)

2 (q ⊃ r)
_____

3 │~ p

4 │ │~ q

5 │ │(~ p & ~q)   3, 4, Conj

6 │ │[(~ p & ~ q) & ~(~ p & ~ q)]   5, 1, Conj

7 │q   4 – 6, ~ E

8 (~ p ⊃ q)   3 – 7, ⊃I

shows that the translation is logically valid. Since the translation is a suitable one, the original argument is valid.

Section 14

1. The argument can be translated:

> [(Joe's mother sent him money & Joe's mother sent him some neckties) ⊃ He will go out to dinner] Joe's mother sent him thirty dollars. So (Joe's mother sent him some neckties ⊃ Joe will go out to dinner)

This translation is not logically valid, but the following sentence can be added to the premisses of the translation:

> (Joe's mother sent him thirty dollars ⊃ Joe's mother sent him money)

This sentence is analytic. The translation supplemented with the analytic premiss can easily be shown to be logically valid. The original is valid.

2. The argument can be translated:

> [Sal is a millionaire ⊃ (He has an education v He graduated from college)] (Sal has an education ⊃ ~ He is a millionaire) So ~ Sal is a millionaire.

This translation is not logically valid. But the following sentence:

> (Sal graduated from college ⊃ He has an education)

is analytically true (or is it?). When we supplement the premisses of the translation with this sentence, we can prove that the supplemented translation is logically valid. The original argument is valid.

3. The argument can be translated:

> (Smith owns his own house ⊃ He's paying off a mortgage) (Smith is putting his daughter through college ⊃ Smith has trouble paying his bills) Smith owns his own house. So (Smith is paying off a mortgage & Smith has trouble paying his bills)

It is easy to show that this translation is not logically valid. There is no analytic sentence that we can add to yield a valid argument.

4. The argument can be translated:

[(That animal is a bat & That animal is a mammal) ⊃ ~ That animal has feathers] That animal has feathers. So ~ That animal is a bat.

This translation is not logically valid, but if we add this analytic sentence to the premisses:

(That animal is a bat ⊃ That animal is a mammal)

the resulting argument is logically valid. The original is valid.

5. The sentences can be translated:

(Ben takes Carol to the dance ⊃ Carol will get a new dress) (~ Ben takes Carol to to the dance ⊃ Carol will get a new dress) [(~ Carol will get a new dress v Ben will take Carol to the dance) & ~ Ben will take Carol to the dance]

These sentences are logically incompatible, as this proof shows:

```
1  (p ⊃ q)
2  (~ p ⊃ q)
─────────────
3  [(p v ~ p) ⊃ q]        1, 2, Dil
4  (p v ~ p)              LEM
5  q                      3, 4, MP
6  │[(~ p v q) & ~ q]
7  │~ q                   6, Simp
8  │(q & ~ q)             5, 7, Conj
9  ~[(~ p v q) & ~ q]     6 – 8, ~ I
```

The original sentences are incompatible.

6. The sentences can be translated:

[(Michele is Jane's oldest child v Megan is Jane's oldest child) & ~(Michele is Jane's oldest child & Megan is Jane's oldest child)] (~ Megan is Jane's oldest child ⊃ Michele is Jane's oldest child) (~ Michele is Jane's oldest child ⊃ ~ Megan is Jane's oldest child) Megan is Jane's oldest child.

These translations are logically incompatible, so the original sentences are incompatible.

7. The sentences can be translated:

(Elaine asks Dick to shave his beard ⊃ Dick will shave his beard) (~ Elaine will ask Dick to shave his beard & Dick will shave his beard)

The translations are not logically incompatible. There are no analytic '⊃'-sentences we can add to obtain logically incompatible sentences.

8. The sentences can be translated:

Julie said "No" when David asked her out. (Julie gave a negative answer to David's request ⊃ David is unhappy) David is happy.

These sentences are not logically incompatible. But the following sentences are analytic:

(Julie said "No" when David asked her out ⊃ Julie gave a negative answer to David's request) (David is unhappy ⊃ ~ David is happy)

If we add these to the sentences above, the resulting sentences are logically incompatible.

Section 15

1. The argument can be translated like this:

[Paula attends college in the nation's capital ⊃ (Washington, D.C. is the capital of the United States ⊃ Paula attends Georgetown)] ~ Paula attends Georgetown. So ~ Paula attends college in the nation's capital.

If we add the following true, well-known sentence as a premiss:

Washington, D.C. is the capital of the United States.

the resulting argument is logically valid, as this proof shows:

1 $[p \supset (q \supset r)]$
2 $\sim r$
3 q
___
4 $(q \mathbin{\&} \sim r)$ 3, 2, Conj
5 $\sim\sim(q \mathbin{\&} \sim r)$ 4, DN
6 $\sim(q \supset r)$ 5, Def ⊃
7 $\sim p$ 1, 6, MT

2. The argument can be translated:

[(~ Jim smokes less than a pack of cigarettes a day v ~ Anne smokes less than a pack of cigarettes a day) ⊃ Jim and Anne spend a lot of money on cigarettes] ~(Jim smokes less than a pack of cigarettes a day & Anne smokes less than a pack of cigarettes a day) So [Jim and Anne spend a lot of money on cigarettes & (Jim has higher probability than average of contracting lung cancer v Anne has a higher probability than average of contracting lung cancer)]

This translation is not valid, but the following sentences are true and well known (they should be):

(~ Jim smokes less than a pack of cigarettes a day ⊃ Jim has a higher probability than average of contracting lung cancer) (~ Anne smokes less than a pack of cigarettes a day ⊃ Anne has a higher probability than average of contracting lung cancer)

If we add these two premisses, the resulting argument is logically valid:

1 $[(\sim p \mathbin{v} \sim q) \supset r]$
2 $\sim(p \mathbin{\&} q)$
3 $(\sim p \supset s_1)$
4 $(\sim q \supset s_2)$
___
5 $(\sim p \mathbin{v} \sim q)$ 2, De M

$$
\begin{array}{lll}
6 & r & 1, 5, \text{MP} \\
7 & \sim p & \\
8 & s_1 & 3, 7, \text{MP} \\
9 & (s_1 \text{ v } s_2) & 8, \text{Add} \\
10 & \sim q & \\
11 & s_2 & 4, 10, \text{MP} \\
12 & (s_1 \text{ v } s_2) & 11, \text{Add} \\
13 & (s_1 \text{ v } s_2) & 5, 7 - 9, 10 - 12, \text{vE} \\
14 & [r \, \& \, (s_1 \text{ v } s_2)] & 6, 13, \text{Conj}
\end{array}
$$

3. The argument can be translated:

> (Victor has steak more often than hot dogs $\supset$ $\sim$ Hot dogs are cheaper than steak) ($\sim$ Victor has steak more often than hot dogs $\supset$ $\sim$ Victor prefers steak to hot dogs) So (Victor prefers steak to hot dogs $\supset$ Victor prefers hot dogs to steak)

If we add this true, well-known sentence to the premisses:

> Hot dogs are cheaper than steak.

the resulting argument can be shown to be valid.

4. The argument can be translated:

> [Janet is in Rochester v (Janet is in Detroit & Janet will be gone for the Fourth of July)] (Janet will be gone for the Fourth of July $\supset$ $\sim$ Janet is in Rochester) So (Janet will be gone for the Fourth of July $\supset$ Janet is in Detroit)

This translation is already logically valid.

5. The sentences can be translated as follows:

> [Tom drinks more whiskey than coffee $\supset$ (Tom is sometimes drunk v Tom drinks no coffee at all)] $\sim$(Tom drinks no coffee at all & Whiskey contains alcohol) [Whiskey contains alcohol $\supset$ (Tom drinks more whiskey than coffee & $\sim$ Tom is sometimes drunk)]

These sentences are not logically incompatible. But it is a well-known truth that whiskey contains alcohol. If we add 'Whiskey contains alcohol' to the sentences above, the resulting sentences are logically incompatible.

6. The sentences can be translated:

> [(Jim plays tennis every Tuesday & Jim plays tennis every Thursday) v ($\sim$ Jim plays tennis every Tuesday & Jim runs ten miles every Tuesday)] (Jim runs ten miles every Tuesday $\equiv$ Jim plays tennis every Thursday) (Jim runs ten miles every Tuesday $\supset$ The moon is made of green cheese)

These sentences are not logically incompatible. If we add the well-known true sentence '$\sim$ The Moon is made of green cheese,' we can easily show the resulting sentences to be incompatible.

7. The sentences can be translated this way:

> [(Tom is Anne's oldest child v Rachel is Anne's oldest child) & $\sim$(Tom is Anne's oldest child & Rachel is Anne's oldest child)] (Anne's oldest child is a

boy ⊃ Tom is Anne's oldest child) (Anne's oldest child has dark hair ⊃ Rachel is Anne's oldest child) ∼(∼ Anne's oldest child is a boy v ∼ Anne's oldest child has dark hair)

These sentences are already logically incompatible.

8. The sentences can be translated:

Most people who are in prison deserve to be there. Most people who deserve to be in prison aren't there. (Most people who are in prison don't deserve to be there ⊃ The judicial system is unjust) (∼ The judicial system is unjust & The judicial system is ineffective) [There are many people who are guilty of crimes ⊃ (The judicial system is ineffective ⊃ The judicial system is unjust)]

These sentences are not logically incompatible, but it is a well-known truth that there are many people who are guilty of crimes. If we add the sentence 'There are many people who are guilty of crimes' to the sentences above, the resulting sentences can be proved to be incompatible:

$$1 \quad p$$
$$2 \quad q$$
$$3 \quad (r \supset s)$$
$$4 \quad (\sim s \, \& \, p_1)$$
$$5 \quad [p_2 \supset (p_1 \supset s)]$$

6 $(p_1 \, \& \sim s)$	4, Comm
7 $\sim\sim(p_1 \, \& \sim s)$	6, DN
8 $\sim(p_1 \supset s)$	7, Def ⊃
9 $\sim p_2$	5, 8, MT

CHAPTER TWELVE

Section 1
1. This is true; it says that 2 is an even number, but 1 isn't.
2. False
3. This is true. It says that 0 is less than 1 (which is true) or that 0 is less than 2 (which is also true).
4. True. The antecedent is false and the consequent is true.
5. True. Both antecedent and consequent are false.
6. This is true; 0 times 0 *is* 0.
7. True. Both antecedent and consequent are false.
8. False. The antecedent is true but the consequent is false.
9. False
10. False

Section 2
1. False
2. True
3. False
4. True
5. True
6. True

7. True
8. False
9. True
10. True

Section 3
1. The formula is true (has the value truth) for this assignment.
2. False
3. True
4. False
5. True

Section 4
1. This says that for everything, if it is a dog, then it isn't a cat. I.e., everything which is a dog isn't a cat. This is true.
2. This is false. The antecedent is true—there is a dog—but the consequent is false. The consequent says that everything is a cat.
3. This is true. It says that anything which is both a dog and a cat isn't an animal. Since every individual will make the antecedent false, every individual will make the whole sentence true.
4. This is true. It says that anything which is either a dog or a cat is an animal.
5. This is true; both the antecedent and consequent are false.
6. This is true.
7. $f(x) \supset (\exists x)f(x, x)$
8. $F(a) \supset [G(x, a) \lor G(a, x)]$
9. $(\forall x)[F(x) \supset [p \lor F(y)]]$
10. $[f(x) \& (\exists x)g(x)] \lor (\forall y)[f(y) \equiv g(x)]$
11. $(\forall x)(\exists y)[x = y]$
12. $(\forall x)[F(x) \lor (\exists x)G(x)]$

Section 5
1. This is false. It says that if one individual is the husband of the second, then the second is the husband of the first.
2. This is true. If x is y's husband, then x is married to y.
3. This is true. It says that if a female is married to an individual, then that individual is male.
4. This is true. It says that if a male is married to an individual, then the individual is female.
5. This is true. It says that for every individual x, there is a y such that if x is female and y is male, then x isn't married to y. This just means that for every female, we can find some male that she isn't married to.
6. This is false. It says that every male is husband to some female.
7. This is true. It says that there is a male, and everyone (if anyone) to whom he is husband is female.
8. This is true. It says that there is an individual x such that if x is male, then every-

thing is female. This is made true by every individual x that isn't male—when the antecedent is false, the whole formula is true.

Section 6
1. True
2. This is false. It says that no odd number in the domain is less than or equal to a number in the domain.
3. This is true. It says that every number in the domain is less than or equal to a number in the domain. But every number is less than or equal to itself.
4. This is true. It says that there are numbers in the domain such that they have no sum in the domain.
5. This is false. It says that for every number in the domain there is a different number which is greater than or equal to it. But this is false for the number 10.
6. This is true. It says that for every number in the domain, there is a number in the domain such that if the two numbers are different, then the first is less than or equal to the second. But for every number x, we can choose y as that same number. Then the antecedent will be false, so the whole horseshoe formula will be true.
7. This is true. It says that if $z + y = x$, then z is less than or equal to x.
8. This is false. It says that for any two even numbers in the domain, their sum is an even number in the domain. But 8 and 10, for example, have no sum in the domain.

Section 7
1. We can symbolize the sentence: $[f(x) \equiv \sim f(y)]$
2. We can use this formula: $[g(y, z) \lor g(z, x)] \supset h(z)$
3. $(\forall x)(\exists y)[g(x, y) \lor f(x, y)]$
4. $(\forall z)(\forall x)[[f(x) \, \& \, h(z)] \supset \sim(z = x)]$
5. $(\forall x)[h(x) \supset f(x)], h(y) \, / f(y)$
6. $(\forall y) \sim g(y), \sim(\exists x)h(x) \, / \, (\forall x)[g(x) \equiv h(x)]$
7. $(\forall x)[f(x) \supset g(x)], (\exists z)[h(z) \, \& \, f(z)] \, / \, (\exists z)[h(z) \, \& \, g(z)]$
8. $\{f(z) \lor [g(z) \lor h(z)]\} \, [f_1(y) \, \& \sim f(z)] \, / \, [h(z) \supset g(z)]$

CHAPTER THIRTEEN

Section 1
1.
1   $(\forall z)(\forall y)[f(z, z, y) \equiv g(y, z)]$
2   $(\exists y)(\exists z)[p \lor f(z, z, y)]$
_____
3   $(\exists y)(\exists z)[p \lor g(y, z)]$ 1, 2, Repl

2. The rule Replacement *cannot* be used to prove this theorem. One proof is as follows:

1   $\sim[f(x, y) \lor g(x)] \equiv [\sim f(x, y) \, \& \sim g(x)]$
_____
2     $\sim[f(x, y) \lor g(x)] \supset [\sim f(x, y) \, \& \sim g(x)]$ 1, $\equiv$E
3 | $\sim[\sim f(x, y) \, \& \sim g(x)]$
4 | | $\sim[f(x, y) \lor g(x)]$
5 | | $\sim f(x, y) \, \& \sim g(x)$ 2, 4, MP
6 | $[\sim f(x, y) \, \& \sim g(x)] \, \& \sim[\sim f(x, y) \, \& \sim g(x)]$ 5, 3, Conj

7	$f(x, y) \vee g(x)$	$4 - 6, \sim$E
8	$\sim[\sim f(x, y) \mathbin{\&} \sim g(x)] \supset [f(x, y) \vee g(x)]$	$3 - 7, \supset$I

3.
1	$(\exists x)[g(x) \vee h(x)] \equiv (\forall z)\sim f(z)$	
2	$p \supset (\forall z)\sim f(z)$	
3	$p \supset (\exists x)[g(x) \vee h(x)]$	1, 2, Repl

Section 2

1.
1	$[F(a) \supset \sim F(a)] \supset F(a)$	
2	$\sim F(a)$	
3	$F(a)$	
4	$\sim F(a)$	2, Rep
5	$F(a) \supset \sim F(a)$	$3 - 4, \supset$I
6	$F(a)$	1, 5, MP
7	$F(a) \mathbin{\&} \sim F(a)$	6, 2, Conj
8	$F(a)$	$2 - 7, \sim$E

2.
1	$p \mathbin{\&} [(\forall x)f(x) \vee (\forall x)g(x)]$	
2	p	1,Simp
3	$(\forall x)f(x) \vee (\forall x)g(x)$	1,Simp
4	$(\forall x)f(x)$	
5	$p \mathbin{\&} (\forall x)f(x)$	2, 4, Conj
6	$[p \mathbin{\&} (\forall x)f(x)] \vee (p \mathbin{\&} (\forall x)g(x)]$	5, Add
7	$(\forall x)g(x)$	
8	$p \mathbin{\&} (\forall x)g(x)$	2, 7, Conj
9	$[p \mathbin{\&} (\forall x)f(x)] \vee [p \mathbin{\&} (\forall x)g(x)]$	8, Add
10	$[p \mathbin{\&} (\forall x)f(x)] \vee [p \mathbin{\&} (\forall x)g(x)]$	$3, 4 - 6, 7 - 9,$ vE

3.
1	$(\forall x)[M(x) \equiv (\exists z)M(x, z)]$	
2	$(\exists x)[B(x) \mathbin{\&} (\exists z)M(x, z)] \supset \sim(\exists y)E(y)$	
3	$(\exists y)E(y)$	
4	$\sim(\exists x)[B(x) \mathbin{\&} (\exists z)M(x, z)]$	2, 3 MT
5	$\sim(\exists x)[B(x) \mathbin{\&} M(x)]$	1, 4, Repl

Section 3

1. $[f(x, y) \supset (q \supset p)] \supset \{ [f(x, y) \supset q] \supset [f(x, y) \supset p]\}$
2. $(\forall z)f(z) \supset f(y)$
3. $(\forall z)G(x) \supset G(y)$

4. $(\exists x)\{f(x) \supset [q \supset (\exists y)g(y)]\} \supset \{(\forall x)f(x) \supset [q \supset (\exists y)g(y)]\}$

5. $(\forall x)(\forall y)(\exists x)f(x, y, x) \supset (\exists x)f(a, y, x)$

6. $S^{q\,r}_{p\,p}(1)|$

7. $S^{f^3}_{h^3}(4)|$

8. $S^{f^1\;y}_{F^1\,a}(2)|$

9. $S^{\;\;\;p}_{(\exists x)f(x)}(3)|$

10. $S^{p\,q\,r}_{r\,p\,q}(1)|$

Section 4

1. $(\forall z)[f(x) \supset h(z)] \supset [f(x) \supset (\forall z)h(z)]$

2. $h(a, b, c) \supset (\exists y)(\exists z)h(a, y, z)$

3. When one substitution notation is applied to another, the inner (rightmost) substitution is performed first. For $\dot{S}^{y\;z}_{b\,c}(1)|$ is the formula:

$$(\forall z)[f(b) \supset h(z)] \supset [f(b) \supset (\forall z)h(z)]$$

So $S^{f^1}_{h^1}\,\dot{S}^{y\;z}_{b\,c}(1)|$ is the same as $S^{f^1}_{h}\{(\forall z)[f(b) \supset h(z)] \supset [f(b) \supset (\forall z)h(z)]\}|$

This is:

$$(\forall z)[h(b) \supset h(z)] \supset [h(b) \supset (\forall z)h(z)]$$

4. $[h(b) \vee (\forall y)h(y)] \supset [h(b) \vee h(b)]$

5. $h(x, x, z) \supset (\exists x)(\exists z)h(x, x, z)$

6. $[h(y) \vee (\forall y)h(y)] \supset [h(y) \vee h(y)]$

7. $\dot{S}^{y\,z}_{x\,x}(2)|$

8. $S^{\;\;\;q}_{(\forall x)f(x)}(3)|$

9. $S^{f^1}_{h^1}\,\dot{S}^{y}_{c}(1)|$

10. $S^{x\,y\,z}_{z\,x\,y}(2)|$

Section 5

1.
1 $(\forall y)[(\exists x)g(x) \vee f(y)]$
———————————————————
2 $(\forall x)[(\exists x)g(x) \vee f(x)]$ 1, CBV

2.
1 $(\forall x)(\forall y)[f(x, y) \equiv g(x, x, y)]$
———————————————————
2 $p \supset (\exists y)(\exists z)f(y, z)$
———————————————————
3 $(\forall x)(\forall z)[f(x, z) \equiv g(x, x, z)]$ 1, CBV
4 $(\forall y)(\forall z)[f(y, z) \equiv g(y, y, z)]$ 3, CBV
5 $p \supset (\exists y)(\exists z)g(y, y, z)$ 4, 2, Repl

3. 1 $[H(a) \supset (\exists z)M(a, z)]$

    2   $(\exists x)M(a, x) \supset (\exists x)W(x, a)$

    3   $H(a)$

    4   $(\exists z)M(a, z)$ 1, 3, MP

    5   $(\exists x)M(a, x)$ 4, CBV

    6   $(\exists x)W(x, a)$ 2, 5, MP

    7   $(\exists y)W(y, a)$ 6, CBV

    8   $[H(a) \supset (\exists y)W(y, a)]$ 3 − 7, $\supset$I

Section 6

1. 1 $(\forall x)[B(x) \supset C(x)]$

    2   $B(c)$

    3   $B(c) \supset C(c)$ 1, $\forall$E

    4   $C(c)$ 3, 2, MP

2. 1 $(\forall x)f(x)$

    2   $[f(x) \lor g(x)] \supset p$

    3   $f(x)$ 1, $\forall$E

    4   $f(x) \lor g(x)$ 3, Add

    5   p 2, 4, MP

3. 1 $(\forall x)[N(x) \supset (\exists y)L(x, y)]$

    2   $N(b)$

    3   $N(b) \supset (\exists y)L(b, y)$ 1, $\forall$E

    4   $(\exists y)L(b, y)$ 3, 2, MP

    5   $(\exists x)L(b, x)$ 4, CBV

Section 7

1. 1 $(\forall z)[f(z) \supset g(z)]$

    2   $(\forall y)f(y)$

    3   $f(y)$ 2, $\forall$E

    4   $f(y) \supset g(y)$ 1, $\forall$E

    5   $g(y)$ 4, 3, MP

    6   $(\forall y)g(y)$ 5, $\forall$I

    7   $(\forall y)f(y) \supset (\forall y)g(y)$ 2 − 6, $\supset$I

2. 1 $[p \lor (\forall x)f(x)]$

    2   p

3	$p \vee f(x)$	2, Add
4	$(\forall x)[p \vee f(x)]$	3, $\forall$I
5	$(\forall x)f(x)$	
6	$f(x)$	5, $\forall$E
7	$p \vee f(x)$	6, Add
8	$(\forall x)[p \vee f(x)]$	7, $\forall$I
9	$(\forall x)[p \vee f(x)]$	$1, 2 - 4, 5 - 8$, vE

3.

1	$(\forall x)[A(x) \supset B(x)]$	
2	$(\forall x)[B(x) \supset C(x)]$	
3	$A(x) \supset B(x)$	1, $\forall$E
4	$B(x) \supset C(x)$	2, $\forall$E
5	$A(x) \supset C(x)$	3, 4, HS
6	$(\forall x)[A(x) \supset C(x)]$	5, $\forall$I

4. It is a *mistake* to prove this problem as follows:

1	$(\forall y)[f(x) \supset g(y)]$	
2	$f(x)$	
3	$f(x) \supset g(x)$	1, $\forall$E
4	$g(x)$	3, 2, MP
5	$(\forall x)g(x)$	4, $\forall$I
6	$f(x) \supset (\forall x)g(x)$	$2 - 5$, $\supset$I

The rule $\forall$I is not allowed to derive step 5, for this move generalizes the variable 'x,' which occurs free in the hypothesis of the subproof. A correct proof is as follows:

1	$(\forall y)[f(x) \supset g(y)]$	
2	$f(x)$	
3	$f(x) \supset g(y)$	1, $\forall$E
4	$g(y)$	3, 2, MP
5	$(\forall y)g(y)$	4, $\forall$I
6	$(\forall x)g(x)$	5, CBV
7	$f(x) \supset (\forall x)g(x)$	$2 - 6$, $\supset$I

Section 8

1.

1	$(\forall x)g(x)$	
2	$g(x)$	1, $\forall$E
3	$(\exists x)g(x)$	2, $\exists$I
4	$(\forall x)g(x) \supset (\exists x)g(x)$	$1 - 3$, $\supset$I

2.

1	$\sim[h(y) \vee \sim h(y)]$	
2	$h(y)$	
3	$[h(y) \vee \sim h(y)]$	2, Add
4	$[h(y) \vee \sim h(y)] \ \& \sim[h(y) \vee \sim h(y)]$	3, 1, Conj
5	$\sim h(y)$	$2 - 4, \sim$ I
6	$[h(y) \vee \sim h(y)]$	5, Add
7	$[h(y) \vee \sim h(y)] \ \& \sim[h(y) \vee \sim h(y)]$	6, 1, Conj
8	$[h(y) \vee \sim h(y)]$	$1 - 7, \sim$ E
9	$(\exists y)[h(y) \vee \sim h(y)]$	8, $\exists$I

3.

1	$(\forall z)[(\exists y)f(y) \supset g(z)]$	
2	$f(a)$	
3	$(\exists y)f(y)$	2, $\exists$I
4	$(\exists y)f(y) \supset g(z)$	1, $\forall$E
5	$g(z)$	4, 3, MP
6	$(\forall z)g(z)$	5, $\forall$I
7	$[f(a) \supset (\forall z)g(z)]$	$2 - 6, \supset$I

4.

1	$(\forall x)(\forall y)[f(x, y) \supset p]$	
2	$(\forall y)[f(x, y) \supset p]$	1, $\forall$E
3	$[f(x, y) \supset p]$	2, $\forall$E
4	$(\exists y)[f(x, y) \supset p]$	3, $\exists$I
5	$(\forall x)(\exists y)[f(x, y) \supset p]$	4, $\forall$I

Section 9

1.

1	$(\exists x)[f(x) \ \& \sim f(x)]$	
2	$f(a) \ \& \sim f(a)$	
3	$\sim p$	
4	$f(a) \ \& \sim f(a)$	2, Rep
5	p	$3 - 4, \sim$E
6	p	$1, 2 - 5, \exists$E

2.

1	$(\forall x)[H(x) \supset M(x)]$	
2	$(\exists x)[G(x) \ \& \ H(x)]$	
3	$G(a) \ \& \ H(a)$	
4	$G(a)$	3, Simp

5	$H(a)$	3, Simp
6	$H(a) \supset M(a)$	1, $\forall$E
7	$M(a)$	6, 5, MP
8	$G(a)$ & $M(a)$	4, 7, Conj
9	$(\exists x)[G(x)$ & $M(x)]$	8, $\exists$I
10	$(\exists x)[G(x)$ & $M(x)]$	2, 3 − 9, $\exists$E

3.
1	$(\exists x)[f(x)$ & $g(x)]$	
2	$f(a)$ & $g(a)$	
3	$f(a)$	2, Simp
4	$(\exists x)f(x)$	3, $\exists$I
5	$g(a)$	2, Simp
6	$(\exists x)g(x)$	5, $\exists$I
7	$(\exists x)f(x)$ & $(\exists x)g(x)$	4, 6, Conj
8	$(\exists x)f(x)$ & $(\exists x)g(x)$	1, 2 − 7, $\exists$E

4.
1	$(\forall x)[f(x) \supset {\sim}g(x)]$	
2	$(\exists x)g(x)$	
3	$g(a)$	
4	$f(a) \supset {\sim}g(a)$	1, $\forall$E
5	${\sim}f(a)$	4, 3, MT
6	$g(a)$ & ${\sim}f(a)$	3, 5, Conj
7	$(\exists x)[g(x)$ & ${\sim}f(x)]$	6, $\exists$I
8	$(\exists x)[g(x)$ & ${\sim}f(x)]$	2, 3 − 7, $\exists$E

Section 10

1.
1	$f(x)$	
2	${\sim}f(y)$	
3	$x = y$	
4	$f(y)$	3, 1, IdR
5	$f(y)$ & ${\sim}f(y)$	4, 2, Conj
6	${\sim}(x = y)$	3 − 5, ${\sim}$I
7	${\sim}f(y) \supset {\sim}(x = y)$	2 − 6, $\supset$I
8	$f(x) \supset [{\sim}f(y) \supset {\sim}(x = y)]$	1 − 7, $\supset$I

2. 1 $x = y$

   2 $y = z$

   ——————————

   3 $x = z$ 1, 2, IdR

3. 1 $(\forall z)\{f(z) \supset [(z = x) \lor (z = y)]\}$

   2 $\sim f(x)$

   3 $(\exists x)f(x)$

   ——————————

   4 | $f(a)$

   5 | $f(a) \supset [(a = x) \lor (a = y)]$ 1, $\forall$E

   6 | $(a = x) \lor (a = y)$ 5, 4, MP

   7 | | $a = x$

   8 | | $f(x)$ 7, 4, IdR

   9 | | $f(x) \,\&\, \sim f(x)$ 8, 2, Conj

  10 | $\sim(a = x)$ $7 - 9$, I

  11 | $a = y$ 6, 10 DS

  12 | $f(y)$ 11, 4, IdR

  13 $f(y)$ $3, 4 - 12$, $\exists$E

Section II: Exercise A

1. 1 $(\forall x)f(x)$

   2 $(\forall x)g(x)$

   ——————————

   3 $f(x)$ 1, $\forall$E

   4 $g(x)$ 2, $\forall$E

   5 $f(x) \,\&\, g(x)$ 3, 4, Conj

   6 $(\forall x)[f(x) \,\&\, g(x)]$ 5, $\forall$I

2. 1 | $(\forall y)\,[f(y) \,\&\, g(y)]$

   2 | $[f(y) \,\&\, g(y)]$ 1, $\forall$E

   3 | $[f(y) \,\&\, g(y)] \lor [f(y) \,\&\, \sim g(y)]$ 2, Add

   4 | $[f(y) \equiv g(y)]$ 3, Def $\equiv$

   5 | $(\forall y)\,[f(y) \equiv g(y)]$ 4, $\forall$I

   6 $(\forall y)\,[f(y) \,\&\, g(y)] \supset (\forall y)\,[f(y) \equiv g(y)]$ $1 - 5$, $\supset$I

3. 1 $[f(x) \lor g(x)] \equiv \sim[\sim f(x) \,\&\, \sim g(x)]$ Def $\lor$

   2 $(\forall x)\{[f(x) \lor g(x)] \equiv \sim[\sim f(x) \,\&\, \sim g(x)]\}$ 1, $\forall$I

Since this proof begins with a theorem, it is a proof with no hypotheses. Its last step is a theorem.

4. 1 $p \supset [f(x) \vee g(x)]$

   2 $p \supset [\sim f(x) \& \sim g(x)]$

   3 | p

   4 | $f(x) \vee g(x)$ 1, 3, MP

   5 | $\sim[\sim f(x) \& \sim g(x)]$ 4, Def $\vee$

   6 | $\sim p$ 2, 5, MT

   7 | $p \& \sim p$ 3, 6, Conj

   8 $\sim p$ 3 – 7, $\sim$ I

Section II: Exercise C

1. 1 $(\forall y)h(y) \vee \sim(\forall y)h(y)$ LEM

   2   $(\forall y)h(y) \vee (\exists y)\sim h(y)$ 1, QEq

   3   $(\forall y)h(y) \vee (\exists z)\sim h(z)$ 2, CBV

2. 1 | $(\forall z)[g(z) \supset \sim f(z)]$

   2 | $(\forall z)\sim[g(z) \& \sim\sim f(z)]$ 1, Def $\supset$

   3 | $(\forall z)\sim[g(z) \& f(z)]$ 2, DN

   4 | $(\forall z)\sim[f(z) \& g(z)]$ 3, Comm

   5 $(\forall z)[g(z) \supset \sim f(z)] \supset (\forall z)\sim[f(z) \& g(z)]$ 1 – 4, $\supset$I

3. 1 $\sim(\exists x)g(x)$

   2 $(\forall x)[f(x) \supset g(x)]$

   3 | $f(x)$

   4 | $f(x) \supset g(x)$ 2, VE

   5 | $g(x)$ 4, 3, MP

   6 | $(\exists x)g(x)$ 5, $\exists$I

   7 | $(\exists x)g(x) \& \sim(\exists x)g(x)$ 6, 1, Conj

   8 $\sim f(x)$ 3 – 7, $\sim$I

   9 $(\forall x)\sim f(x)$ 8, $\forall$I

  10 $\sim(\exists x)f(x)$ 9, QEq

4. 1 $(\forall x)[f(x) \supset (x = a)]$

   2 | $f(x) \& f(y)$

   3 | $f(x)$ 2, Simp

   4 | $f(y)$ 2, Simp

   5 | $f(x) \supset (x = a)$ 1, $\forall$E

6	$x = a$	5, 3, MP
7	$f(y) \supset (y = a)$	1, ($\forall$E
8	$y = a$	7, 4, MP
9	$x = y$	6, 8, Id R
10	$[f(x) \& f(y)] \supset (x = y)$	$2 - 9, \supset$I
11	$(\forall y)[\,[f(x) \& f(y)] \supset (x = y)]$	10, $\forall$I
12	$(\forall x)(\forall y)[\,[f(x) \& f(y)] \supset (x = y)]$	11, $\forall$I

Section 12

1. We need to keep these values:

$$\begin{array}{cccccc} \sim[f(x, y, z) & \supset f(y, x)], & \sim f(x, y, z) & / f(y , x) \\ \text{t} & \text{t} \quad \text{f} & \text{f} & \text{t f} & \text{f} \end{array}$$

But this is impossible. We can prove the sequence to be a theorem like this:

1	$\sim[f(x, y, z) \supset f(y, x)]$	
2	$\sim f(x, y, z)$	
3	$\quad \sim f(y,x)$	
4	$\quad \sim f(x, y, z) \vee f(y, x)$	2, Add
5	$\quad f(x, y, z) \supset f(y, x)$	4,Def $\supset$
6	$\quad [f(x, y, z) \supset f(y,x)] \& \sim [f(x, y, z) \supset f(y, x)]$	5, 1, Conj
7	$f(y,x)$	$3 - 6, \sim$ E

2. We can invalidate this sequence if we can keep these values:

$$\begin{array}{cccccccc} \sim[f(y, x) & \& & g(z, x)], & \sim g(z, x) & / & \sim f(y, z) \\ \text{t} & \text{t} & \text{f} & \text{f} & \text{t} \quad \text{f} & \text{f} & \text{t} \end{array}$$

We can keep the values above if we make these assignments:

> Assign to 'f^2' the pairs of positive integers $< m, n >$ such that m is less than n. Assign to 'g^2' the pairs of positive integers $<m, n>$ such that m is greater than n. Assign 1 to 'x,' 2 to 'y,' and 3 to 'z.'

3. We can falsify the formula if we assign the collection of pairs $<$ husband, wife $>$ to 'h^2,' and assign George Washington to 'x,' Abraham Lincoln to 'y,' and Theodore Roosevelt to 'z.'

4. This sequence cannot be refuted. It is a therorem:

1	$(\forall x) [x = y]$
2	$(\exists x) [f(x) \& \sim g(x)]$
3	$\quad f(a) \& \sim g(a)$

4	$\sim g(a)$	3, Simp
5	$a = y$	1, $\forall$I
6	$\sim g(y)$	4, 5, IdR
7	$\sim g(y)$	2, 3 – 6, $\exists$E

5. If we assign all people to 'f^1' and all women to 'g^1,' the first premiss is true. For '$(\forall y)[f(y) \supset g(y)]$' now "says" that whatever is a person is a woman—this is false. We can assign Queen Elizabeth I as value of 'x.' Now '$f(x)$' is true—she is a person. And '$g(x)$' is also true, making '$\sim g(x)$' false.

6. If we assign the collection of vampires to 'f^1' (the collection is empty) and all girls to 'g^1,' then if we assign the Empire State Building as value for (the free occurrences of) 'y,' the premiss is true and the conclusion false.

7. If we assign the collection of vampires to 'f^1' and assign all people to g^1,' this formula is falsified. For '$(\forall y)\sim g(y)$' now "says" that nothing is a person, which is false. And '$(\forall x)\sim f(x)$' "says" that nothing is a vampire, which is true. The formula '$(\forall x)[f(x) \supset (\exists y)g(y)]$' is true if every value of 'x' makes '$f(x) \supset (\exists y)g(y)$' true. But every value of 'x' makes the antecedent false (every value of 'x' is a nonvampire), so every value of 'x' does make the formula true.

8. If we restrict our attention to the domain of positive integers, we can assign to 'f^2' every pair $< m, n >$ such than $n = m + 1$. With this assignment, the formula "says" that for every pair of positive integers x, y, if $y = x + 1$, then there is an integer z between x and y. This is false.

9. This is a theorem. It can be proved:

1	$(\forall x)(\forall y)(\forall z)[\,[f(x, y)\,\&\,f(y, z)] \supset f(x, z)]$	
2	$(\forall x)(\forall y)[f(x, y) \supset f(y, x)]$	
3	$f(x, y)$	
4	$(\forall y)[f(x, y) \supset f(y, x)]$	2, $\forall$E
5	$f(x, y) \supset f(y, x)$	4, $\forall$E
6	$f(y, x)$	5, 3, MP
7	$(\forall y)(\forall z)[\,[f(x, y)\,\&\,f(y, z)] \supset f(x, z)]$	1, $\forall$E
8	$(\forall z)[\,[f(x, y)\,\&\,f(y, z)] \supset f(x, z)]$	7, $\forall$E
9	$[f(x, y)\,\&\,f(y, x)] \supset f(x, x)$	8, $\forall$E
10	$f(x, y)\,\&\,f(y, x)$	3, 6, Conj
11	$f(x, x)$	9, 10, MP
12	$f(x, y) \supset f(x, x)$	3 – 11, $\supset$I
13	$(\forall y)[f(x, y) \supset f(x, x)]$	12, $\forall$I
14	$(\forall x)(\forall y)\,[f(x, y) \supset f(x, x)]$	13, $\forall$I

Section 13

1. These formulas symbolize incompatible sentences. We can prove this as follows:

1	$(\forall x)[f(x) \supset {\sim} f(x)]$	
2	$(\exists x)f(x)$	
3	$f(a)$	
4	$f(a) \supset {\sim} f(a)$	1, ∀E
5	${\sim}(p \mathbin{\&} {\sim} p)$	
6	${\sim} f(a)$	4, 3, MP
7	$f(a) \mathbin{\&} {\sim} f(a)$	3, 6, Conj
8	$p \mathbin{\&} {\sim} p$	5 – 7, ~ E
9	$p \mathbin{\&} {\sim} p$	2, 3 – 8, ∃E
10	${\sim}(\exists x)f(x)$	2 – 9, ~ I

2. These formulas don't symbolize incompatible sentences. If we restrict the domain to the positive integers, then to 'g^2' we can assign all pairs $< m, n >$ such that m is less than or equal to n. Both formulas are true for this assignment.

3. These formulas symbolize incompatible sentences. We can prove this:

1	$(\forall x){\sim} f(x, x)$	
2	$(\forall x)(\forall y)[f(x, y) \supset (\exists z)[f(x, z) \mathbin{\&} f(z, y)]]$	
3	$(\forall x)[f(a, x) \supset (x = b)]$	
4	$f(a, b)$	
5	$f(a, b) \supset (a = b)$	3, ∀E
6	$a = b$	5, 4, MP
7	$f(a, a)$	4, 6, IdR
8	${\sim} f(a, a)$	1, ∀E
9	$f(a, a) \mathbin{\&} {\sim} f(a, a)$	7, 8, Conj
10	${\sim} f(a, b)$	4 – 9, ~I

CHAPTER FOURTEEN

Section 1

1. b

2. a

3. b

4. c. If $[A^* \supset B^*]$ is false, then A^* is true and B^* is false. In that case, A is true and B is false. So 'If A, then B' is false. If 'If A, then B' is true, then it can't be that $[A^* \supset B^*]$ is false. So 'If A, then B' entails $[A^* \supset B^*]$.

Section 2

1. We can use 'a' for Megan and 'b' for Michele. If '$T(x)$' means *x is playing tennis*, we can translate the first part of the sentence like this: $[T(a) \, \& \sim T(b)]$. But we cannot use 'T^1' to say that Michele will play tennis. In the First-Order language, a given predicate has a certain tense "built-in" to it. To talk about playing tennis in the future, we must have a new predicate. We can use '$P(x)$' to say that x will play tennis. Then the sentence can be given this equivalent translation:

$$[\,[T(a) \, \& \sim T(b)] \, \& \, P(b)].$$

It is a disadvantage of the First-Order language that we cannot show that different predicates represent different tenses of a common verb.

*2. Let 'a' name Plato and 'b' name Socrates. Let '$P(x)$' mean *x is a philosopher* and '$H(x)$' mean *x is a haberdasher*. Then we can provide this weaker translation:

$$[P(a) \supset H(b)].$$

3. Let 'a' translate 'Andrea,' 'c' translate 'Chuck,' and 'd' translate 'Dave.' And let '$I(x, y, z)$' mean *x introduced y to z*. The following then provides an equivalent translation:

$$I(c, d, a).$$

4. Let 'a' name Frank, 'b' name Ken, and 'c' name Dick. Let '$K(x, y)$' mean *x knows y*. Then an equivalent translation is:

$$\sim[K(a, b) \lor K(a, c)] \, \& \, K(c, b).$$

**5. Let 'a' replace 'Frank' and 'b' replace 'Isabelle.' Let '$M(x)$' mean *x will become a mechanical engineer* and '$E(x)$' means *x is a mechanical engineer*. We can translate the sentence as follows:

$$\sim[M(b) \lor E(a)].$$

6. If we use 'a' for 'Franklin Roosevelt,' 'b' for 'the president of the U.S. in 1936,' and 'c' for 'the president of the U.S. in 1946,' we can translate the sentence like this:

$$(a = b) \, \& \sim (a = c).$$

A less revealing but still equivalent translation can be provided if we let '$P(x)$' mean *x was the president of the U.S. in 1936* and '$Q(x)$' mean *x was the president of the U.S. in 1946*. Then we can translate the sentence:

$$[P(a) \, \& \sim Q(a)].$$

*7. One way to translate the sentence uses 'a' to translate 'Jimmy,' 'b' to translate 'this election,' 'c' to translate 'Idaho,' '$W(x, y)$' to mean *x will win y*, and '$G(x, y)$' to mean *x will be the governor of y*. Then we can translate the sentence as follows:

$$[W(a, b) \supset G(a, c)].$$

We cannot supply a date to translate 'the governor of Idaho' by a singular term, unless we supply next year's date (thinking of the sentence as being uttered right now.) But we might use '*d*' for 'the next governor of Idaho' and translate the sentence like this:

$$[W(a, b) \supset (a = d)].$$

*8. We can use '*a*' for Myra and '*b*' for Betsy. Let '*M(x, y)*' mean *x is y's mother* and '*D(x, y)*' mean *x is y's daughter*. With this vocabulary, our translation will be:

$$[M(a, b) \equiv D(b, a)].$$

We could also replace 'Betsy's mother' by '*c*' and give this translation:

$$[(a = c) \equiv D(b, a)].$$

This second translation is less revealing than the first.

9. We can use '*a*' for 'Jorge,' '*b*' for 'Jorge's tennis racquet,' and '*c*' for 'Dale.' Then let '*L(x, y, z)*' mean *x loaned y to z*. Our translation now appears as follows:

$$\sim L(a, b, c).$$

10. Let '*a*' translate 'Mark Twain,' '*b*' translate 'Samuel Clemens,' and '*c*' translate 'the author of Tom Sawyer.' A safe translation for the sentence is this:

$$(a = c) \lor (b = c).$$

But the use of 'the' in 'the author of Tom Sawyer' tells us that there is only one author. The use of two names in the sentence could naturally be taken to indicate that they name different people. With this understanding, the following provides an equivalent translation:

$$[(a = c) \lor (b = c)] \& \sim(a = b).$$

With this understanding, the sentence is false. If the sentence is regarded as a kind of trick statement, and true, then the original translation is equivalent.

11. This sentence is ambiguous, but it is most natural to take the two 'Springfield's to name different cities. In the First-Order language, we do not allow (in the same context) one individual constant to name different individuals. To translate the sentence, we can use this vocabulary:

a − Springfield, Ohio	b − Ohio
c − Springfield, Illinois	d − the capital of Illinois
$I(x, y)$ − x is in y	

Our translation is:

$$[I(a, b) \& (c = d)].$$

12. We can use '*d*' to translate 'David' and '*a*' to translate 'David's mother.' Let '*S(x, y)*' mean *x is y's son*. Our translation is:

$$S(d, a).$$

*13. Let '*a*' replace 'Frank,' '*b*' replace 'Fred,' '*c*' replace 'Frank's father,' and '*d*' replace 'Fred's father.' Let '*B(x, y)*' mean *x is y's brother*. The our translation becomes:

$$[B(b, a) \supset (d = c)].$$

*14. Let '*a*' translate '5,' '*b*' translate '7,' and '*c*' translate '35.' Let '*P*(*x*, *y*, *z*)' mean *x times y is z*, and let '*D*(*x*, *y*, *z*)' mean *x divided by y is z*. Then we can give this translation:

$$[P(a, b, c) \supset D(c, b, a)].$$

15. We can use '*a*' for 'Jim's current wife' and '*b*' for 'Jim's first wife' to get this translation:

$$\sim(a = b).$$

16. We can use '*c*' for Stacey, '*d*' for Dan, and '*R*(*x*, *y*)' to mean *x refuses to pay y the five dollars that x borrowed*. Then the sentence can be translated:

$$R(d, c).$$

In this case, we don't want to treat 'the five dollars that he borrowed' as a singular term. It doesn't really name a specific individual. It doesn't name either a certain five dollar bill or a certain collection of five one dollar bills.

Section 3

1. We can paraphrase the sentence:

> For everything, if it is a person, then it is not at the door.

If we use this vocabulary:

> *d* − the (relevant) door   *P*(*x*) − *x* is a person
> *A*(*x*, *y*) − *x* is at *y*

we can give this translation:

$$(\forall x)[P(x) \supset \sim A(x, d)].$$

We can also paraphrase the sentence:

> It isn't true that for something, it is a person and it is at the door.

This yields the following translation:

$$\sim(\exists x)[P(x) \,\&\, A(x, d)].$$

2. We can paraphrase the sentence:

> For everything, if it is a student who correctly answers the fourth question, then it will please Professor Lambros.

We can use this vocabulary:

> *a* − Professor Lambros   *S*(*x*) − *x* is a student
> *C*(*x*) − *x* will correctly answer the fourth question
> *P*(*x*, *y*) − *x* will please *y*

Then we get this translation:

$$(\forall x)[\,[S(x) \,\&\, C(x)] \supset P(x, a)].$$

*We can also let '*F*(*x*)' mean x is a student who will correctly answer the fourth question* − which gives us:

$$(\forall x)[F(x) \supset P(x, a)].$$

3. We can paraphrase the sentence:

For everything, if it is a car, then Kevin doesn't own it.

With this vocabulary:

a − Kevin $\qquad\qquad$ $C(x)$ − x is a car
$O(x, y)$ − x owns y

we have this translation:

$(\forall x)[C(x) \supset {\sim}O(a, x)]$.

We can also paraphrase the sentence:

It isn't true that for something, it is a car, and Kevin owns it.

With this paraphrase, we get the following translation:

${\sim}(\exists x)[C(x) \,\&\, O(a, x)]$.

4. We can paraphrase the sentence:

For everything, if it is a member of the Union, then it voted in favor of the new contract.

Using this vocabulary:

a − the Union $\qquad$ c − the new contract $\qquad$ $M(x, y)$ − x is a member of y
$V(x, y)$ − x voted in favor of y

we get this translation:

$(\forall x)[M(x, a) \supset V(x, c)]$.

Section 4

1. With this vocabulary:

$H(x)$ − x is a high school student
$M(x)$ − x is a millionaire

we get this translation:

$(\exists x)[H(x) \,\&\, M(x)]$

2. We can use this vocabulary:

a − Leonard $\qquad\qquad$ $C(x)$ − x is a Cadillac
$M(x)$ − x is a Mercedes Benz $\qquad$ $O(x, y)$ − x owns y

We can translate the sentence:

${\sim}(\exists x)\,[C(x) \,\&\, O(a, x)] \,\&\, (\exists x)\,[M(x) \,\&\, O(a, x)]$.

3. If we use this vocabulary:

a − Martha $\qquad$ $C(x)$ − is a copy of Tom's book
$B(x, y)$ − x bought y

we can translate the sentence like this:

$(\exists x)\,(\exists y)\,[[[C(x)\;\&\;C(y)]\;\&\;\sim(x = y)]\;\&\;[B(a,\,x)\;\&\;B(a,y)]]$

*4. We can use this vocabulary:

a − the (relevant) front door b − John
c − the back door $P(x)$ − is a policeman
$A(x,\,y)$ − x is at y $S(x,\,y)$ − x will sneak out y

This yields the following translation:

$(\exists x)[P(x)\;\&\;A(x,\,a)] \supset S(b,\,c).$

5. The students in question didn't each put on a play; it was a collection of students that put on a play. So we will use this vocabulary:

a − Kathy $C(x,\,y)$ − x is a collection of y's students
$P(x)$ − x put on a play after school

This gives the following:

$(\exists x)[C(x,\,a)\;\&\;P(x)].$

*6. We use this vocabulary:

$P(x,\,y,\,z)$ − x times y is z
$D(x,\,y,\,z)$ − x divided by y is z

We get this translation:

$P(7,\,5,\,35) \supset D(35,\,5,\,7).$

7. We use this vocabulary:

a − Mr. Smith b − Mrs. Smith
$D(x,\,y)$ − x is a daughter of y $S(x,\,y)$ − x is a son of y

We obtain the following translation:

$(\exists x)(\exists y)[\,[\,[\sim(x = y)\;\&\;[D(x,\,a)\;\&\;D(y,a)]\,]\;\&\;[D(x,\,b)\;\&\;D(y,\,b)]\,]\;\&$
$(\forall z)[\,[D(z,\,a)\;\&\;D\,(z,\,b)] \supset [(x = z)\;v\;(y = z)]\,]\,]\;\&$
$(\exists x)[\,[S(x,\,a)\;\&\;S(x,\,b)]\;\&\;(\forall y)[\,[S(y,\,a)\;\&\;S(y,\,b)] \supset (x = y)]\,]$

8. We use this vocabulary:

$C(x)$ − x is a candidate
$R(x)$ − x will run for vice president

We get the following translation:

$(\forall x)(\forall y)(\forall z)(\forall x_1)[\,[\,[\,[\,[\,[C(x)\;\&\;R(x)]\;\&\;[C(y)\;\&\;R(y)]\,]\;\&\;[C(z)\;\&\;R(z)]\,]\;\&$
$[\,[\sim(x = y)\;\&\;\sim(x = z)]\;\&\;\sim(y = z)]\,]\;\&\;[C(x_1)\;\&\;R(x_1)]\,] \supset$
$[\,[(x_1 = x)\;v\;(x_1 = y)]\;v\;(x_1 = z)]\,]$

The original sentence does not say three candidates *will* run for vice president. It says no more than three will run. This would be true even if one candidate ran for vice president − even if no candidate ran for vice president.

9. We cannot provide an acceptable translation in the First-Order language. The quantified phrase 'the majority of towns in Texas' cannot be translated.

10. We understand the sentence to mean that Dawn bought at least two books. We use this vocabulary:

d — Dawn $B(x)$ — x is a book $B(x, y)$ — x bought y

which gives:

$(\exists x)(\exists y)[[\sim(x = y) \,\&\, [B(x) \,\&\, B(y)]] \,\&\, [B(d, x) \,\&\, B(d, y)]]$.

11. We cannot provide a reasonably short translation of this sentence in the First-Order language. We do not translate such sentences.

Section 5

1. With this vocabulary:

$F(x)$ — x is a Ferrari $P(x)$ — x is a person
$D(x, y)$ — x drives y $H(x)$ — x is happy

we get the following translation:

$(\forall x)[[P(x) \,\&\, (\exists y)[F(y) \,\&\, D(x,y)]] \supset H(x)] \,\&\, (\exists x)[P(x) \,\&\, (\exists y)[F(y) \,\&\, D(x, y)]]$

2. We use this vocabulary:

$P(x)$ — x is a positive integer
$G(x, y)$ — x is greater than y

The sentence is translated:

$(\forall x)[P(x) \supset G(x, 0)]$.

3. We will use this vocabulary:

a — Kevin $K(x, y)$ — x knows y
$I(x,y)$ — x is a person in y's class

We translate the sentence like this:

$\sim(\forall x)[I(x, a) \supset K(x, a)] \,\&\, (\exists x)I(x, a)$.

4. We use this vocabulary:

a — Fran $L(x, y)$ — x likes y
$M(x, y)$ — x is a person who has met y

The translation is:

$(\forall x)[M(x, a) \supset L(x, a)] \,\&\, (\exists x)M(x, a)$.

5. With this vocabulary:

a — the (relevant) college $F(x)$ — x is a freshman
$S(x, y)$ — x is a student in y $K(x, y)$ — x knows y

we get this translation:

$(\forall x)[S(x, a) \supset (\exists y)[F(y) \,\&\, K(x, y)]] \,\&\, (\exists x)S(x , a)$.

6. With the same vocabulary as in 5, we get the following translation:

$(\exists x)[F(x) \,\&\, [(\forall y)[S(y, a) \supset K(x, y)] \,\&\, (\exists y)S(y, a)]]$

*7. With this vocabulary:

$O(x)$ − x is an oak tree $A(x)$ − x is an acorn
$D(x, y)$ − x developed, is developing, or will develop from y

we get this translation:

$(\forall x)[O(x) \supset (\exists y)[A(y) \,\&\, D(x, y)]]$.

8. This sentence about types cannot be reformulated in terms of instances of the types. We must use this vocabulary:

b − the bird d − the dinosaur $E(x, y)$ − x evolved from y

We then translate the sentence:

$E(b, d)$.

*9. With this vocabulary:

$P(x)$ − x is a person $T(x)$ − x is a 12 story building
$K(x)$ − x is sure to be killed $J(x, y)$ − x is jumping or will jump off y

we have this translation:

$(\forall x)[[P(x) \,\&\, (\exists y)[T(y) \,\&\, J(x, y)]] \supset K(x)]$.

10 or **10. We can use this vocabulary:

d − Dale $P(x)$ − x is a person
$A(x, y)$ − x asked y for help $R(x, y)$ − x received help from y

If the component has no modal force, we get this equivalent translation:

$\sim(\forall x)[[P(x) \,\&\, A(x, d)] \supset R(x, d)]$

If the component has modal force, we use the same translation, but it is a stronger translation.

11. With this vocabulary:

$P(x)$ − x is a person $T(x)$ − x is a tattletale
$L(x, y)$ − x likes y

we have this translation:

$(\forall x)[P(x) \supset (\forall y)[T(y) \supset \sim L(x, y)]] \,\&\, (\exists x)P(x)$.

12. This vocabulary:

a − Professor Hood $S(x, y)$ − x is a student of y's
$G(x, y)$ − x gave y a favorable rating

can be used to provide this translation:

$(\forall x)[S(x, a) \supset \sim G(x, a)] \,\&\, (\exists x)S(x, a)$.

13. We will use this vocabulary:

c − Chuck d − the (relevant) pantry
$T(x)$ − x is a can of tuna $F(x, y, z)$ − x found y in z

Our translation is:

$(\forall x)[T(x) \supset \sim F(c, x, d)]$.

14. This vocabulary:

$P(x)$ − x is a penguin $F(x)$ − x can fly

yields this translation:

$(\forall x)[P(x) \supset \sim F(x)] \ \& \ (\exists x)P(x)$.

15. With this vocabulary:

$B(x)$ − x is a bat $R(x)$ − x has rabies

we get this translation:

$\sim(\forall x)[B(x) \supset R(x)]$.

16. With this vocabulary:

$B(x)$ − x is a boy $G(x)$ − x is a girl
$P(x, y)$ − x has made, is making, or will make a pass at y
$S(x)$ − x wears glasses

we get this translation:

$\sim(\forall x)[B(x) \supset (\forall y)[[G(y) \ \& \ S(y)] \supset \sim P(x, y)]]$.

Section 6
1. If we use this vocabulary:

a − the freshman class
b − the President's reception $M(x, y)$ − x is a member of y
$I(x, y)$ − x is invited to y

we get this translation:

$[(\forall x)[M(x, a) \supset I(x, b)] \ \& \ (\forall x)[I(x, b) \supset M(x, a)]] \ \& \ (\exists x)M(x, a)$

We don't need an existence claim for those invited to the President's reception, because '$(\exists x)I(x, b)$' follows from the translation above. However, it isn't a mistake to include the extra existence claim.

2. We use this vocabulary:

$M(x)$ − x is Mexican $T(x)$ − x likes tequila

We translate the sentence:

$(\forall x)[T(x) \supset M(x)] \ \& \ (\exists x)T(x)$.

3. If we use this vocabulary:

a − David's company $N(x)$ − x is a nonsmoker
$B(x, y)$ − x can buy life insurance from y

we obtain this translation:

$(\forall x)[B(x, a) \supset N(x)]$ & $(\exists x)B(x, a)$.

In this case, we don't want to use a three-place predicate '$B(x, y, z)$' for x *can buy* y *from z*, because life insurance isn't an individaul that can be purchased.

4. The translation for 4 is the same as that for 3.

5. With this vocabulary:

a − Isabelle b − Bruce
d − the dinner in question $I(x, y, z)$ − x invited y to z

we can make this translation:

$I(a, b, d)$ & $(\forall x)[I(a, x, d) \supset (x = b)]$.

Section 7

1. We use this vocabulary:

b − Barbara $B(x)$ − x is a book
$P(x, y)$ − x purchased y

This gives the following:

$(\forall x)[B(x) \supset {\sim} P(b, x)]$.

*2. Using this vocabulary:

c − Clare d − the (relevant) party
$K(x, y)$ − x knows y $M(x, y, z)$ − x will meet y at z
$R(x)$ − x will feel relieved

we can provide either of these translations:

$(\exists x)[K(c, x)$ & $M(c, x, d)] \supset R(c)$
$(\forall x)[[K(c, x)$ & $M(c, x, d)] \supset R(c)]$

3. Using this vocabulary:

a − Jesse $A(x)$ − x is an art gallery
$V(x, y)$ − x has visited y $K(x)$ − x knows what he has missed

we can translate the sentence in either of the following ways:

${\sim}(\exists x)[A(x)$ & $V(a, x)] \supset {\sim} K(a)$
$(\forall x)[A(x) \supset {\sim} V(a, x)] \supset {\sim} K(a)$

4. This vocabulary:

a − Jack's soccer team $S(x)$ − x is a game of soccer
$W(x, y)$ − x won y

produces this translation:

$(\forall x)[S(x) \supset {\sim} W(a, x)]$.

Section 8

*1. We use this vocabulary:

b — Barbara $\quad c$ — the meeting
$C(x)$ — x is a car $\quad O(x, y)$ — x owns y $\quad R(x, y)$ — x will need a ride to y

This gives us:

$(\exists x)[C(x) \& O(b, x)] \supset \sim R(b, c)$.

In this case we don't want a predicate for rides (for saying that something is a ride), because it doesn't seem that rides are individuals.

*2. We use this vocabulary:

$P(x)$ — x is a person $\quad\quad C(x)$ — x is a car
$O(x, y)$ — x owns y $\quad\quad B(x, y)$ — x must buy a license for y

We get this translation:

$(\forall x)(\forall y)[\,[P(x) \& [C(y) \& O(x, y)]\,] \supset B(x, y)]$.

We don't want to introduce a predicate for saying that something is a license for something else, for when a person is required to buy a license, that doesn't mean that there exists a license which the person will buy (or should buy).

*3. We use this vocabulary:

c — Victor's cat $\quad\quad O(x)$ — x is an old lady
$B(x, y)$ — x bit y

We get this translation:

$(\exists x)[\,[O(x) \& B(a, x)] \& B(x, a)]$.

*4. We use this vocabulary:

$B(x)$ — x is a boy $\quad\quad S(x)$ — x has sense
$G(x)$ — x will get a good education

This gives us:

$(\forall x)[\,[B(x) \& S(x)] \supset G(x)]$.

*5. With this vocabulary:

a — Mary $\quad\quad\quad\quad\quad\quad C(x, y)$ — x is a classmate of y's
$P(x, y)$ — x will pass y $\quad\quad W(x)$ — x will be walking
$R(x, y)$ — x will give y a ride

we get:

$(\forall x)[\,[\,[C(x, a) \& P(a, x)] \& W(x)] \supset R(a, x)]$.

Section 9

1. The sentence is analytic. With the following vocabulary:

$I(x)$ — x is a positive integer $\quad\quad P(x)$ — x is prime

we get this equivalent translation:

$(\forall x)[I(x) \supset [P(x) \vee \sim P(x)]\,]$.

The following proof shows that the translation is logically true. This is sufficient to establish that the original is analytically true.

$$1 \quad | \; I(x)$$
$$2 \quad | \; P(x) \lor \sim P(x) \qquad\qquad \text{LEM}$$
$$3 \quad I(x) \supset [P(x) \lor \sim P(x)] \qquad 1 - 2, \supset I$$
$$4 \quad (\forall x)[I(x) \supset [P(x) \lor \sim P(x)]] \qquad 3, \forall I$$

2. We can use this vocabulary:

$W(x) - x$ is a whale $\qquad F(x) - x$ is a fish

to get this equivalent translation:

$$\sim[(\forall x)[W(x) \supset \sim F(x)] \;\&\; (\exists x)W(x)] \lor (\exists x)[F(x) \;\&\; \sim W(x)]$$

If we replace '$F(x)$' by '$V(x)$,' which means *x is a vampire*, the resulting sentence is false; this shows that the transaction isn't logically true. The First-Order translation is equivalent to the original sentence, but isn't logically true. This result doesn't tell us about the original sentence. But we can see that there is no relevant feature of the original that fails to show up in the logical form of the translation. The original sentence isn't analytically true.

3. If we use this vocabulary:

$a -$ the fruit on Molly's dish
$G(x) - x$ is a grapefruit $\qquad C(x) - x$ is a citrus fruit

we obtain the following:

$$[(\forall x)[G(x) \supset C(x)] \;\&\; G(a)] \supset C(a).$$

The translation of the antecedent is weaker than the original antecedent. The translation of the consequent is equivalent. This means that the translation of the whole sentence isn't weaker than the original. The translation doesn't appear to be stronger either. We can't use the First-Order language to evaluate the original sentence, even though the original is obviously analytic.

4. If we use this vocabulary:

$a -$ Newton $\qquad S(x) - x$ will order a steak

we get this stronger translation:

$$\sim[S(a) \equiv \sim S(a)].$$

(We don't want to use '$S(x)$' for *x is a steak* and '$O(x, y)$' for *x will order y* in making our translation. A person who orders a steak doesn't usually order a specific steak.) We can use a truth-table to determine that the translation is logically true. The original sentence is analytic.

Section 10

1. With this vocabulary:

$P(x) - x$ is a person $\qquad\qquad L(x) - x$ is a lawyer
$C(x) - x$ is a college graduate $\qquad K(x, y) - x$ knows y

we can provide these equivalent translations:

$(\forall x)[P(x) \supset (\exists y)[L(y)\ \&\ K(x, y)]]\ \&\ (\exists x)P(x);$
$(\forall x)[L(x) \supset C(x)]\ \&\ (\exists x)L(x);\ (\exists x)[P(x)\ \&\ (\forall y)[C(y) \supset\ \sim K(x, y)]]$

The following proof shows that these sentences are incompatible:

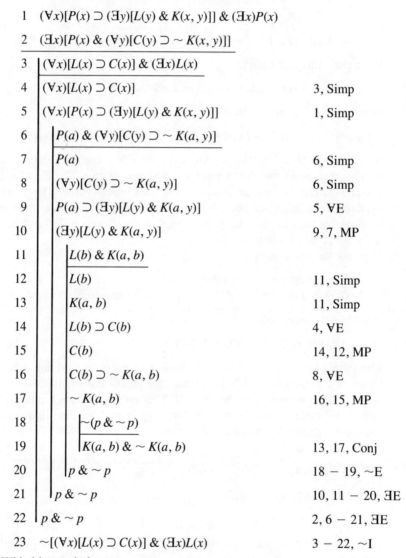

1	$(\forall x)[P(x) \supset (\exists y)[L(y)\ \&\ K(x, y)]]\ \&\ (\exists x)P(x)$	
2	$(\exists x)[P(x)\ \&\ (\forall y)[C(y) \supset\ \sim K(x, y)]]$	
3	$(\forall x)[L(x) \supset C(x)]\ \&\ (\exists x)L(x)$	
4	$(\forall x)[L(x) \supset C(x)]$	3, Simp
5	$(\forall x)[P(x) \supset (\exists y)[L(y)\ \&\ K(x, y)]]$	1, Simp
6	$P(a)\ \&\ (\forall y)[C(y) \supset\ \sim K(a, y)]$	
7	$P(a)$	6, Simp
8	$(\forall y)[C(y) \supset\ \sim K(a, y)]$	6, Simp
9	$P(a) \supset (\exists y)[L(y)\ \&\ K(a, y)]$	5, $\forall$E
10	$(\exists y)[L(y)\ \&\ K(a, y)]$	9, 7, MP
11	$L(b)\ \&\ K(a, b)$	
12	$L(b)$	11, Simp
13	$K(a, b)$	11, Simp
14	$L(b) \supset C(b)$	4, $\forall$E
15	$C(b)$	14, 12, MP
16	$C(b) \supset\ \sim K(a, b)$	8, $\forall$E
17	$\sim K(a, b)$	16, 15, MP
18	$\sim(p\ \&\ \sim p)$	
19	$K(a, b)\ \&\ \sim K(a, b)$	13, 17, Conj
20	$p\ \&\ \sim p$	$18 - 19$, $\sim$E
21	$p\ \&\ \sim p$	$10, 11 - 20$, $\exists$E
22	$p\ \&\ \sim p$	$2, 6 - 21$, $\exists$E
23	$\sim[(\forall x)[L(x) \supset C(x)]\ \&\ (\exists x)L(x)]$	$3 - 22$, $\sim$I

2. With this vocabulary:

$a\ -$ the final exam in question
$S(x)\ -\ x$ is a student in the relevant course
$E(x, y)\ -\ x$ will be excused from y
$A(x)\ -\ x$ has an A average in the relevant course

if the first sentence is not understood to have existential force, we get these translations:

$(\forall x)[[S(x)\ \&\ E(x, a)] \supset A(x)], (\forall x)[S(x) \supset \sim E(x, a)]$

If we assign the number 25 to '*a*,' let '*E(x, y)*' mean *x is a positive square root of y*, '*S(x)*' mean *x is even*, and '*A(x)*' mean *is divisible by three*, then both translations will be true. Therefore they aren't logically incompatible. But nothing of importance in the original sentences fails to show up in the logical forms of these translations. The original sentences are compatible. However, if the original sentence is understood to have existential force, the sentences are incompatible.

3. We can't use the First-Order language to evaluate these sentences, for the first sentence is the negation of an 'only if'-sentence. Our translation for 'only if' (the horseshoe) is weaker than the original; if we negate a weaker translation, we get a stronger one. But we cannot use a stronger translation to test for incompatibility.

Section 11

1. We will use this vocabulary:

$P(x)$ − *x* is a positive integer
$L(x, y)$ − *x* is less than *y* $G(x, y)$ − *x* is greater than *y*

Our translation is:

$(\exists x)[P(x)\ \&\ (\forall y)[P(y)\ \&\ \sim(x = y)] \supset L(x, y)]],$
$(\forall x)[[P(x)\ \&\ (\forall y)[P(y) \supset L(x, y)]] \supset (\forall y)[P(y) \supset G(x, y)]]$ /
$(\exists x)[P(x)\ \&\ (\forall y)[[P(y)\ \&\ \sim(x = y)] \supset G(x, y)]]$

This is invalid. The premisses are already true and the conclusion false. (But the second premiss is tricky. Be sure you understand what makes it true.) The translation of the second premiss is weaker than that premiss, but the second premiss is true. So the original argument is invalid, and has true premisses and a false conclusion.

2. With this vocabulary:

a − Ruth $A(x, y)$ − *x* ate *y*
$I(x, y)$ − *x* gave indigestion to *y* $S(x)$ − *x* was improperly stored
$C(x)$ − *x* was improperly cooked

we get this translation:

$(\exists x)[A(a, x)\ \&\ I(x, a)], (\forall x)[I(x, a) \supset [S(x) \lor C(x)]]$ /
$\sim(\exists x)[A(a, x)\ \&\ S(x)] \supset (\exists x)[A(a, x)\ \&\ C(x)]$

This translation is logically valid. It can be proved as follows:

1	$(\exists x)[A(a, x)\ \&\ I(x, a)]$	
2	$(\forall x)[I(x, a) \supset [S(x) \lor C(x)]]$	
3	$\sim(\exists x)[A(a, x)\ \&\ S(x)]$	
4	$A(a, b)\ \&\ I(b, a)$	
5	$A(a, b)$	4, Simp
6	$I(b, a)$	4, Simp
7	$I(b, a) \supset [S(b) \lor C(b)]$	2, $\forall$E

8	$S(b) \vee C(b)$	7, 6, MP
9	$S(b)$	
10	$A(a, b) \& S(b)$	5, 9, Conj
11	$(\exists x)[A(a, x) \& S(x)]$	10, ∃I
12	$(\exists x)[A(a, x) \& S(x)] \& \sim(\exists x)[A(a, x) \& S(x)]$	11, 3, Conj
13	$\sim S(b)$	9 − 12, ∼I
14	$C(b)$	8, 13, DS
15	$A(a, b) \& C(b)$	5, 14, Conj
16	$(\exists x)[A(a, x) \& C(x)]$	15, ∃I
17	$(\exists x)[A(a, x) \& C(x)]$	1, 4 − 16, ∃E
18	$\sim(\exists x)[A(a, x) \& S(x)] \supset (\exists x)[A(a, x) \& C(x)]$	3 − 17, ⊃I

3. If we use this vocabulary:

> a − William b − the AMA c − Neil
> $P(x)$ − x is a pediatrician $D(x)$ − x is a doctor
> $B(x, y)$ − x belongs to y $C(x, y)$ − x is more conservative than y

we get the following translation:

> $P(a) \& B(a, b), (\forall x)[[D(x) \& B(x, b)] \supset (\forall y)[[D(y) \& \sim B(y, b)] \supset C(x, y)]], D(c) \& \sim B(c, b) / C(a, c)$

This is not logically valid. If we reinterpret the vocabulary like this:

> a − 7 b − 2 c − 2 $P(x)$ − x is a prime number
> $B(x, y)$ − x is greater than y $D(x)$ − x is an even positive integer
> $C(x, y)$ − x is (exactly) divisible by y

The premises are true and the conclusion is false.

This is an inconclusive result. But if we consider the original argument, we can see that there is an important connection between being a pediatrician and being a doctor which does not show up in the logical form of our translation. Once we recognize this connection, we can tell that the original argument is valid.

4. We cannot use the First-Order language to evaluate this argument, for we can't provide a suitable translation for the conclusion.

Section 12

1. With this vocabulary:

> b − Barry c − the (relevant) beach
> d − the (relevant) Saturday $G(x, y, z)$ − x will go to y on z
> $N(x)$ − x is a nice day

we get this translation:

> $[N(d) \vee \sim N(d)] \supset G(b, c, d) / \sim[G(b, c, d) \equiv N(d)]$

This is not logically valid. In spite of this, the original appears to be valid.

2. If we use this vocabulary:

a − Judy	$T(x)$ − x is a tenant in the building
$F(x)$ − x lives on the first floor	$U(x)$ − x is unmarried
$L(x)$ − x is a lawyer	$D(x)$ − x is a doctor

we get the following translation:

$(\forall x)[[T(x) \,\&\, F(x)] \supset [U(x) \,\&\, [D(x) \lor L(x)]]] \,\&\, (\exists x)[T(x) \,\&\, F(x)]$,
$T(a) \,\&\, L(a) \,/\, U(a) \supset F(a)$

We can show that this is not logically valid by reinterpreting the vocabulary:

a − George Washington	$U(x)$ − x is a human being
$F(x)$ − x was alive in 1900	$T(x)$ − x is a man
$D(x)$ − x is a doctor	$L(x)$ − x is a nondoctor

Now the premisses are true and the conclusion is false. This is an inconclusive result. But it is clear that there is nothing about the original argument which is relevant to its validity and which fails to show up in the logical form of the translation.

3. With this vocabulary:

b − Tom c − Carol	$W(x, y)$ − x is a wife of y
$B(x)$ − x knows a lot about baseball	$R(x)$ − x reads *Sports Illustrated*
$F(x)$ − x knows a lot about football	

and using Russell's analysis of 'Tom's wife,' we get the following:

$W(c, b) \,\&\, (\forall x)[W(x, b) \supset (x = c)]$, $(\forall x)[W(x, b) \supset [B(x) \,\&\, F(x)]]$,
$(\forall x)[[B(x) \lor F(x)] \supset R(x)] \,/\, (\exists x)[[W(x, b) \,\&\, (\forall y)[W(y, b) \supset (y = x)]] \,\&\, R(x)]$

Strictly speaking, we used Russell's complete analysis only in translating the conclusion. If we used this for the first premiss, we would get the following redundant translation:

$(\exists x)[[W(x, b) \,\&\, (\forall y)[W(y, b) \supset (y = x)]] \,\&\, (c = x)]$

The translation is logically valid, as is shown:

1	$W(c, b) \,\&\, (\forall x)[W(x, b) \supset (x = c)]$	
2	$(\forall x)[W(x, b) \supset [B(x) \,\&\, F(x)]]$	
3	$(\forall x)[[B(x) \lor F(x)] \supset R(x)]$	
4	$W(c, b)$	1, Simp
5	$W(c, b) \supset [B(c) \,\&\, F(c)]$	2, $\forall$E
6	$B(c) \,\&\, F(c)$	5, 4, MP
7	$B(c)$	6, Simp
8	$B(c) \lor F(c)$	7, Add
9	$[B(c) \lor F(c)] \supset R(c)$	3, $\forall$E
10	$R(c)$	9, 8, MP

11	$W(c, b) \mathbin{\&} (\forall y)[W(y, b) \supset (y = c)]$	1, CBV
12	$[W(c, b) \mathbin{\&} (\forall y)[W(y, b) \supset (y = c)]] \mathbin{\&} R(c)$	11, 10, Conj
13	$(\exists x)[[W(x, b) \mathbin{\&} (\forall y)[W(y, b) \supset (y = x)]] \mathbin{\&} R(x)]$	12, ∃I

4. We will use this vocabulary:

d – Diane $B(x)$ – x is a bus driver
$T(x)$ – x is tall (for a woman) $S(x)$ – x is slender
$C(x)$ – x works for the City Transit Line $O(x)$ – x is overweight
$R(x)$ – x has bright red hair $J(x)$ – x has a job $F(x)$ – x is female

This gives the following translation:

$[T(d) \mathbin{\&} S(d)] \mathbin{\&} [F(d) \mathbin{\&} R(d)]$, $\{(\forall x)[[[F(x) \mathbin{\&} B(x)] \mathbin{\&} C(x)] \supset {\sim} S(x)] \mathbin{\&}$
$(\forall x)[[[F(x) \mathbin{\&} B(x)] \mathbin{\&} C(x)] \supset O(x)]\} \mathbin{\&} (\exists x)[[F(x) \mathbin{\&} B(x)] \mathbin{\&} C(x)]$,
$J(d) \supset C(d)$, $J(d) \mathbin{\&} B(d)$

Even though the first (original) sentence does not explicitly state that Diane is female, the pronoun 'she' gives the information. We need to include '$F(d)$' to capture this information. (It is not part of the meaning of a name like 'Diane' that Diane is female. Some cruel parent could give this name to a boy—consider the song "A boy Named 'Sue.'")

The translation is logically incompatible:

1	$[T(d) \mathbin{\&} S(d)] \mathbin{\&} [F(d) \mathbin{\&} R(d)]$	
2	$\{(\forall x)[[[F(x) \mathbin{\&} B(x)] \mathbin{\&} C(x)] \supset {\sim} S(x)] \mathbin{\&}$ $(\forall x)[[[F(x) \mathbin{\&} B(x)] \mathbin{\&} C(x)] \supset O(x)]\} \mathbin{\&} (\exists x)[[F(x) \mathbin{\&} B(x)] \mathbin{\&} C(x)]$	
3	$J(d) \supset C(d)$	
4	$(\forall x)[[[F(x) \mathbin{\&} B(x)] \mathbin{\&} C(x)] \supset {\sim} S(x)] \mathbin{\&}$ $(\forall x)[[[F(x) \mathbin{\&} B(x)] \mathbin{\&} C(x)] \supset O(x)]$	2, Simp
5	$(\forall x)[[[F(x) \mathbin{\&} B(x)] \mathbin{\&} C(x)] \supset {\sim} S(x)]$	4, Simp
6	$J(d) \mathbin{\&} B(d)$	
7	$J(d)$	6, Simp
8	$C(d)$	3, 7, MP
9	$F(d) \mathbin{\&} R(d)$	1, Simp
10	$F(d)$	9, Simp
11	$B(d)$	6, Simp
12	$F(d) \mathbin{\&} B(d)$	10, 11, Conj
13	$[F(d) \mathbin{\&} B(d)] \mathbin{\&} C(d)$	12, 8, Conj
14	$[[F(d) \mathbin{\&} B(d)] \mathbin{\&} C(d)] \supset {\sim} S(d)]$	5, ∀E
15	${\sim} S(d)$	14, 13, MP
16	$T(d) \mathbin{\&} S(d)$	1, Simp

17	$S(d)$	16, Simp
18	$S(d)$ & $\sim S(d)$	17, 15, Conj
19	$\sim[J(d)$ & $B(d)]$	6, $-$ 18, $\sim$ I

5. With this vocabulary:

> a $-$ Newton $P(x)$ $-$ x is a person
> $T(x, y, z)$ $-$ x will trespass on y's property at time z $H(x)$ $-$ x is a hunter
> $S(x)$ $-$ x is a time during the hunting season $A(x)$ $-$ x will be arrested

we obtain this translation:

> $(\forall x)[[[P(x)$ & $H(x)]$ & $(\exists y)[T(x, a, y)$ & $S(y)]] \supset A(x)]$,
> $(\forall x)[[P(x)$ & $(\exists y)[T(x, a, y)] \supset \sim A(x)]$

It is easy to find an interpretation which makes both translations true. And it is easy to see that the original sentences are compatible, for the first sentence does not say that some hunter will trespass.

6. If we use this vocabulary:

> c $-$ Nick $C(x)$ $-$ x is a car
> $M(x)$ $-$ x is a Mercedes $O(x, y)$ $-$ x owns y

we obtain these translations:

> $(\forall x)[[C(x)$ & $O(c, x)] \supset \sim M(x)]$, $(\exists x)[[[C(x)$ & $O(c, x)]$ &
> $(\forall y)[[C(y)$ & $O(c, y)] \supset (y = x)]]$ & $[\sim M(x) \supset \sim C(x)]]$

The following proof shows these to be incompatible:

1	$(\exists x)[[[C(x)$ & $O(c, x)]$ & $(\forall y)[[C(y)$ & $O(c, y)] \supset (y = x)]]$ & $[\sim M(x) \supset \sim C(x)]]$	
2	$(\forall x)[[C(x)$ & $O(c, x)] \supset \sim M(x)]$	
3	$[[C(a)$ & $O(c, a)]$ & $(\forall y)[[C(y)$ & $O(c, y)] \supset (y = a)]]$ & $[\sim M(a) \supset \sim C(a)]$	
4	$[C(a)$ & $O(c, a)]$ & $(\forall y)[[C(y)$ & $O(c, y)] \supset (y = a)]$	3, Simp
5	$\sim M(a) \supset \sim C(a)$	3, Simp
6	$C(a)$ & $O(c, a)$	4, Simp
7	$C(a)$	6, Simp
8	$M(a)$	5, 7, MT
9	$[C(a)$ & $O(c, a)] \supset \sim M(a)$	2, ($\forall$E
10	$\sim M(a)$	9, 6, MP
11	$\sim(p$ & $\sim p)$	
12	$M(a)$ & $M(a)$	8, 10, Conj
13	p & $\sim p$	11 $-$ 12, $\sim$ E

> 14 $|p \& \sim p$ 1, 3 − 13, ∃E
> 15 $\sim(\forall x)[[C(x) \& O(c, x)] \supset \sim M(x)]$ 2 − 14, ~I

So the original sentences are incompatible.

Section 13. Exercise A.

1. We will use this vocabulary:

> a − Anne $P(x)$ − x is a person
> $I(x, y)$ − x thinks y is intelligent $E(x)$ − x is a cousin of Ed's
> $R(x, y)$ − x is a relative of (related to) y
> $B(x, y)$ − x gave y at least a B $P(x, y)$ − x is a professor of y's

This gives us the following translation:

> $(\forall x)[P(x, a) \supset B(x, a)] \& (\exists x)P(x, a), (\forall x)[[P(x) \& B(x, a)] \supset I(x, a)],$
> $(\forall x)[R(x, a) \supset \sim I(x, a)] \& (\exists x)R(x, a), (\forall x)[E(x) \supset R(x, a)] /$
> $(\forall x)[P(x, a) \supset \sim E(x)] \& (\exists x)P(x, a)$

This translation is not logically valid, but it becomes so if we supply this analytic premiss:

> $(\forall x)[P(x, a) \supset P(x)]$

The proof is not given here; it is straightforward.

2. With this vocabulary:

> a − Martha $P(x)$ − x is a person
> $D(x, y)$ − x is a dish made by y $H(x, y)$ − x had a helping of y
> $S(x)$ − x is potato salad $C(x)$ − x is a good cook

we get this translation:

> $(\exists x)[[S(x) \& D(x, a)] \& (\forall y)[P(y) \supset \sim H(y, x)]] \& (\exists y)P(y),$
> $(\forall x)[[P(x) \& (\exists y)[D(y, x) \& \sim H(y, x)]] \supset \sim C(x)] / \sim C(a)$

This translation is not logically valid. We can fix this by adding the following analytic premiss: $P(a)$. The proof is omitted; it is straightforward.

3. With this vocabulary:

> a − Arlene b − Busch Gardens c − Tampa
> d − DisneyWorld $P(x)$ − x is a person $V(x, y)$ − x has visited y
> $B(x, y)$ − x has been to y $G(x, y)$ − x thinks y is vulgar
> $O(x, y)$ − x thinks y is overly commercial $L(x, y)$ − x likes y

we get the following translation:

> $(\forall x)[[P(x) \& V(x, c)] \supset [B(x, b) \lor B(x, d)]],$
> $[G(a, d) \& O(a, d)] \& \sim B(a, d), \sim L(a, b) / \sim V(a, c)$

There is no analytic premiss we can supply which will yield a logically valid translation. The original argument is not valid. Nothing says that Arlene hasn't been to Busch Gardens. (If the premises did say this, this argument would be valid.)

4. We can use this vocabulary:

a − Jose b − the Gracia's (house)
$T(x)$ − x is a time $A(x)$ − x is (a quantity of) an alcoholic beverage
$M(x, y, z)$ − x eats (i.e., has a meal) at y at time z
$D(x, y, z)$ − x drinks y at time z $E(x, y, z)$ − x eats y at time z
$W(x)$ − x is (a quantity of) wine $I(x)$ − x is invariably polite
$F(x)$ − x is (a quantity of) food $B(x)$ − x is (a quantity of) beverage

This yields the following (monstrous) translation:

$(\forall x)(\forall y)[[T(x) \,\&\, A(y)] \supset\, \sim D(a, y, x)]$,
$(\forall x)[[T(x) \,\&\, M(a, b, x)] \supset (\exists y)[W(y) \,\&\, S(a, y, x)]] \,\&\, (\exists x)[T(x) \,\&\, M(a, b, x)]$,
$I(a) \,\&\, (\forall x)(\forall y)[S(a, x, y) \supset [[F(x) \supset E(a, x, y)] \,\&\, [B(x) \,\&\, D(a, x, y)]]]$

This translation is not logically incompatible, but it will become so once we add these analytic sentences:

$(\forall x)[W(x) \supset A(x)]$, $(\forall x)[W(x) \supset B(x)]$.

The long proof to show incompatibility is omitted because it is straightforward.

5. We will use this vocabulary:

$R(x)$ − x is a U.S. Army Ranger
$S(x)$ − x is a soldier
$T(x)$ − x has been trained to kill people

One understanding of the original sentences gives this translation:

$(\forall x)[R(x) \supset S(x)] \,\&\, (\exists x)R(x)$, $(\forall x)[S(x) \supset T(x)]$,
$(\forall x)[R(x) \supset\, \sim T(x)] \,\&\, (\exists x)R(x)$

These sentences are logically incompatible; the proof is omitted. A second understanding gives this translation:

$(\forall x)[R(x) \supset S(x)] \,\&\, (\exists x)R(x)$, $(\forall x)[S(x) \supset T(x)]$,
$\sim[(\forall x)[R(x) \supset T(x)] \,\&\, (\exists x)R(x)]$

These sentences are also logically incompatible.

6. This is difficult to translate. We have decided not to translate large numerical statements. But if we use this vocabulary:

a − Ed Monnelly $L(x)$ − x got a letter this year
$P(x)$ − x is a person $T(x)$ − x ran in 12 meets and placed in the
$C(x)$ − x is on the cross   top ten each time
        country team $F(x)$ − x ran in 4 meets and placed in the
                top ten each time

we get the following:

$(\forall x)[[[P(x) \,\&\, C(x)] \,\&\, \sim(x = a)] \supset L(x)] \,\&\, [[P(a) \,\&\, C(a)] \,\&\, \sim L(a)]$,
$T(a)$, $(\forall x)[[P(x) \,\&\, F(x)] \supset L(x)]$

If we add this analytically true sentence:

$(\forall x)[T(x) \supset F(x)]$

the resulting sentences can easily be shown to be incompatible.

Section 13. Exercise D.

1. We can use this vocabulary:

> a − Jane $\quad$ $A(x, y)$ − x has reason to avoid y
> $F(x)$ − x is (an item of) food containing salt
> $H(x)$ − x is a person who has hypertension
> $C(x)$ − x contributes to high blood pressure

This gives the following translation:

> $(\forall x)[F(x) \supset C(x)] \& (\exists x)F(x), (\forall x)[H(x) \supset (\forall y)[C(y) \supset A(x, y)]] \&$
> $(\exists y)C(y) / (\forall x)[F(x) \supset A(a, x)] \vee \sim H(a)$

We can prove this argument to be valid in its present form:

1	$(\forall x)[F(x) \supset C(x)] \& (\exists x)F(x)$	
2	$(\forall x)[H(x) \supset (\forall y)[C(y) \supset A(x, y)]] \& (\exists y)C(y)$	
3	$(\forall x)[F(x) \supset C(x)]$	1, Simp
4	$(\forall x)[H(x) \supset (\forall y)[C(y) \supset A(x, y)]]$	2, Simp
5	$H(a) \vee \sim H(a)$	LEM
6	$H(a)$	
7	$H(a) \supset (\forall y)[C(y) \supset A(a, y)]$	4, ∀E
8	$(\forall y)[C(y) \supset A(a, y)]$	7, 6, MP
9	$F(x)$	
10	$F(x) \supset C(x)$	3, ∀E
11	$C(x)$	10, 9, MP
12	$C(x) \supset A(a, x)$	8, ∀E
13	$A(a, x)$	12, 11, MP
14	$F(x) \supset A(a, x)$	9 − 13, ⊃I
15	$(\forall x)[F(x) \supset A(a, x)]$	14, ∀I
16	$(\forall x)F(x) \supset A(a, x)] \vee \sim H(a)$	15, Add
17	$\sim H(a)$	
18	$(\forall x)[F(x) \supset A(a, x)] \vee \sim H(a)$	17, Add
19	$(\forall x)[F(x) \supset A(a, x)] \vee \sim H(a)$	5, 6 − 16, 17 − 18, ∨E

2. If we don't regard 'outstanding' as a relative adjective, we can use this vocabulary:

> a − *Huck Finn* $\qquad$ $W(x)$ − x is (or was) a writer
> b − Mark Twain $\qquad$ $B(x)$ − x is a book
> $G(x)$ − x is a great novel $\quad$ $W(x, y)$ − x wrote y
> $O(a)$ − x is outstanding $\quad$ $M(x)$ − x is mediocre

The argument can be translated:

$G(a)$, $(\forall x)(\forall y)[[G(x) \& W(y, x)] \supset [W(y) \& O(y)]]$,
$(\exists x)(\exists y)[[[\sim(x = y) \& [B(x) \& B(y)]] \& [W(b, x) \& W(b, y)]] \&$
$[M(x) \& M(y)]] / (\exists x)(\exists y)[[B(x) \& [W(y) \& O(y)]] \& [W(y, x) \& \sim O(x)]]$

This translation is not valid. But we can add two premises to change this. The following is true and well known: $W(b, a)$. The following is analytic, and obviously so: $(\forall x)[M(x) \supset \sim O(x)]$. Supplemented with these premises, the translation is logically valid. The proof is omitted here, but is straightforward.

3. We will use this vocabulary:

   b – Bradley c – Princeton
   $E(x)$ – x is an employee (of the relevant employer)
   $C(x)$ – x is a clerk who works on the first floor
   $D(x)$ – x has a college degree $L(x)$ – x is on lunch break now
   $M(x)$ – x is a management trainee $G(x, y)$ – x graduated from y

We get the following translation:

$(\forall x)[C(x) \supset \sim D(x)] \& (\exists x)C(x)$, $(\forall x)[[E(x) \& L(x)] \supset [C(x) \vee M(x)]] \&$
$(\exists x)[E(x) \& L(x)]$, $[E(b) \& G(b, c)] \& \sim M(b) / \sim L(b)$

This translation is not valid. But it is true and well known that Princeton is a university, so that anyone who graduated from Princeton has a college degree. We can add this premiss:

$(\forall x)[G(x, c) \supset D(x)]$.

The resulting argument is easily proved to be valid.

4. We will use this vocabulary:

   a – George b – Bermuda c – Fran
   $U(x)$ – x is in the U.S. $C(x)$ – x is in Canada $P(x)$ – x is a person
   $T(x, y)$ – x will travel to y $M(x, y)$ – x will marry y
   $H(x, y, z)$ – x will take y to z for their honeymoon.

This gives the following:

$(\forall x)[T(a, x) \supset [U(x) \vee C(x)]]$, $M(c, a) \supset H(a, c, b)$,
$(\forall x)[[P(x) \& \sim(x = a)] \supset \sim M(c, x)] \& (\exists x)M(c, x)$

These translations are not logically incompatible. But if we add these analytic sentences:

$(\forall x)[M(c, x) \supset P(x)]$, $(\forall x)[H(a, c, x) \supset T(a, x)]$

and this well-known true sentence:

$\sim U(b) \& \sim C(b)$

we can prove that the resulting sentences are incompatible. (The proof is omitted.)

5. With this vocabulary:

> a − Henri b − Montreal $C(x)$ − x is middle class
> $H(x)$ − x has heard of *Monopoly* $S(x)$ − x should have heard of *Monopoly*
> $O(x, y)$ − x owns y $A(x)$ − x is an adult American
> $L(x, y)$ − x has lived in y for his whole life $M(x)$ − x is a *Monopoly* set
> $P(x)$ − x has played *Monopoly* $T(x)$ − x is 27 years old

we get this translation:

> $(\forall x)[[C(x) \,\&\, A(x)] \supset P(x)] \,\&\, (\exists x)[C(x) \,\&\, A(x)],$
> $\sim(\exists x)[M(x) \,\&\, O(a, x)] \,\&\, C(a), \sim H(a) \,\&\, S(a), L(a, b) \,\&\, T(a)$

The translations are not incompatible. There are no suitable analytic sentences or well-known true sentences we can add to show incompatibility, for a native of Montreal is a Canadian. Although Canada is in North America, Canadians are not counted as Americans.

6. We use this vocabulary:

> $M(x)$ − x is a mathematically gifted person
> $A(x)$ − x is a person who really appreciates classical music
> $C(x)$ − x likes country music $L(x)$ − x lacks aesthetic sensibility
> $E(x)$ − x is an engineer

We get this translation:

> $(\forall x)[M(x) \supset A(x)] \,\&\, (\exists x)M(x), (\forall x)[A(x) \supset \sim C(x)] \,\&\, (\exists x)A(x),$
> $(\forall x)[L(x) \supset C(x)] \,\&\, (\exists x)L(x), (\forall x)[E(x) \supset L(x)] \,\&\, (\exists x)E(x)$

These sentences are not incompatible. But it is well known that some engineers are mathematically gifted. If we add this sentence:

> $(\exists x)[E(x) \,\&\, M(x)]$

we can show that the resulting sentences are incompatible.

Index